Contents

Legend for Club Stadium Plans

- Covered seating
- Covered standing
- Uncovered seating
- Uncovered standing
-  Disabled Facilities, wheelchairs access and viewing areas
- Main entrances
- Main exits

the complete package

Once again, I am delighted to introduce all football fans to this, the 2003/04 edition of Scottish football's most prestigious publication.

I am pleased to report that The Scottish Premier League have fully co-operated in the production of this, the 24th edition of this publication, hence the reason that the title has been slightly amended and is now referred to as "The Scottish Football Review". However, that is the only difference and I am sure that you will agree with me that the Review continues to be the most authoritative reference book on Scottish football.

It would be fair to say that the 2002/03 domestic football season proved not only to be extremely exciting and entertaining but, also one of the most dramatic to have been witnessed in recent times. Nearly all of the championship, promotion and relegation issues in the three divisions of the Bell's Scottish Football League were not decided until the final couple of weeks of the season and, as you will read elsewhere in this publication, to the very last kick of the ball...literally.

In the Bell's First Division, Falkirk, after gaining a reprieve from relegation to the Second Division the previous season, impressively won the title, although as has been well documented since, did not meet the Membership Criteria required by The Scottish Premier League. However, work is now well underway at their new stadium and all Bairns' fans will be hoping to emulate last season's success to enable them to reclaim their place amongst Scottish football's elite.

As the events in the Bell's Second Division reached its climax, there was complete uncertainty as to the outcome of all issues, with the majority of clubs finding themselves in the incredible position of either being able to be promoted...or, astonishingly enough, relegated! Congratulations to Raith Rovers for winning the championship and also to Brechin City for joining them, although it took an injury time goal to ensure that the Glebe Park club enjoyed promotion for the second season in succession, thereby narrowly edging out Airdrie United.

Events in the Bell's Third Division were no less dramatic with four clubs all having a realistic opportunity of promotion. Ultimately, a helicopter was required to transport the championship trophy down to Greenock and I would like to offer my congratulations to Morton for securing the title, particularly after the turbulent times experienced by the club recently. After a tension filled final day of the season, another injury time goal secured East Fife the second promotion spot, but congratulations should also be extended to both Peterhead and Albion Rovers for their sterling efforts during the season.

In The CIS Insurance Cup, Rangers won an action packed Final against old rivals Celtic that not only saw them claim the trophy for the second successive season but, also gave the Ibrox club the launchpad to go on and win the domestic treble. The Bell's Cup provided a new name on the trophy with Queen of the South defeating Brechin City 2-0 in the Final, resulting in the Doonhamers winning their second Bell's trophy within a six month period.

At the time of writing, Scotland still have an opportunity of reaching the Euro 2004 Play-Offs and on behalf of all Scottish football supporters, may I take this opportunity in wishing Berti Vogts and his players every success. Indeed, a number of young players are now beginning to emerge throughout all of the four divisions of the senior game in Scotland with some of these players now playing for both the full international and Under-21 teams on a regular basis and hopefully, more opportunities will arise during the course of the next few months to allow our youngsters the opportunity to showcase their talents at the highest level.

Finally, I do hope that you, the football fan, enjoys another exciting, memorable and dramatic football season.

JOHN SMITH
President, The Scottish Football League

drama and desire

The 2002/03 season proved to be an exciting, if at times turbulent, one. We had to resolve the well-documented differences between our member clubs. But on the field it was a pleasure to witness the drama that unfolded, both, in the final games in the SPL Championship race and also in Celtic's run to the UEFA Cup Final.

It is unlikely that any league in Europe could have matched the stunning finale to the league season. No one could have predicted the manner in which the pendulum swung back and forth as the goals rained in on the 25th of May. Both the fans, and our sponsors, the Bank of Scotland could not have asked for more. The fact that the BBC, for the first time in terrestrial TV history, decided to broadcast both games simultaneously proved how gripped the nation was to the climax of the SPL.

Rangers managed to achieve a record 50th League title along with winning the remaining domestic honours and it was a joy and a privilege to see Celtic and their support doing themselves and Scottish football proud on the road to Seville and at the UEFA Cup Final. The standing of the SPL both abroad and south of the border has been enhanced by these efforts. We now have a better platform for all the SPL clubs involved in Europe to enjoy further success and continue to build our reputation on the continent where our League is now ranked at 9th.

The current economic climate continues to be challenging. It is testament though to the youth structures put in place by the SPL that so many young players are beginning to have an impact at the top level. Our investment in, and commitment to, youth development will deliver more and more youngsters who can showcase their talent within the SPL. This will complement the hard work by all parties involved in Scottish football to continually push our national game forward. While the loss of Barry Ferguson, James McFadden and Neil McCann, who have decided to ply their trade in England, may sadden football fans north of the border, these transfers should be viewed as another opportunity to promote the successes of Scottish football. We shall expect good things from this exiled trio.

There remains a wealth of talent, however, in the SPL. Established stars such as Steven Pressley, Stevie Crawford and the evergreen Henrik Larsson will continue to excite as Stephen Pearson, Mikel Arteta and Garry O'Connor emerge to become integral players at their respective clubs.

Bearing all of this in mind we go into this season in good shape. With the memories of an enthralling finish to the season fresh in mind, there is justified optimism for the future.

I hope you enjoy this issue of The Scottish Football Review.

Lex Gold
Chairman, The Scottish Premier League

scottish football's annual report 2002/03

JULY

A consortium headed by Jim Ballantyne agrees to buy Clydebank, who had been in administration for some time, on condition that it could relocate to Airdrie, play its matches at the Excelsior Stadium and change the club's name to Airdrie United. The League Management Committee agree to this request.

Dundee appoint former captain and manager, Jim Duffy, as their new manager, replacing Italian Ivano Bonetti, who was dismissed.

John McClelland is appointed the new Chairman of Rangers as the Ibrox club's owner David Murray resigns the position after almost 14 years. Murray becomes Honorary Chairman and retains his controlling interest.

Ally Dawson is dismissed as manager of Hamilton Academical and replaced by Chris Hillcoat.

Hibernian sell Ecuador World Cup defender Ulises de la Cruz to Aston Villa for £2 million.

The Bank of Scotland Premierleague secure a two-year television deal with BBC Scotland, their plans for an in-house satellite channel having been vetoed by Rangers and Celtic.

Transfers this month: Scott Crabbe (Ayr United to Alloa Athletic).

AUGUST

Celtic make a double signing on the eve of the new season, capturing Swedish international goalkeeper Magnus Hedman from Coventry City for £1.5 million and Danish defender Ulrik Laursen from Hibs for £1 million.

The 10 SPL clubs outwith the Old Firm give formal notice of their intention to resign from the League in two years time as a result of the split over the failed television deal and disagreement over voting rights.

Former Argentinian international striker Sergio Berti is dismissed by Livingston without playing a competitive fixture for the West Lothian club when they find him guilty of spitting at a team-mate during a friendly match.

Dunfermline Athletic sign defender Scott Wilson on a free transfer from Rangers.

Hibs sign Finnish international striker Mixu Paatelainen on a free transfer from Strasbourg.

Former German international midfielder Rainer Bonhof is appointed coach of the Scotland Under-21 squad.

Scotland Under-21's draw 1-1 in a friendly with Denmark at East End Park, Kilmarnock's Peter Canero scoring the equaliser for the home side.

Jim Duffy

Scotland's dismal run under new manager Berti Vogts continues when they lose 1-0 to Denmark in a friendly at Hampden.

Celtic fail to reach the group stages of the Champions League when they lose to Swiss Champions Basel on away goals in the Third Qualifying Round, losing 2-0 in the second leg after a 3-1 victory at home.

Livingston win their first ever European tie, but only squeeze past Liechtenstein part-timers Vaduz on an away goal in their UEFA Cup Qualifying Round tie, drawing 1-1 in the first leg before a goalless draw at the City Stadium.

Aberdeen also reach the First Round proper of the UEFA Cup, following a 1-0 home win over Nistru Otaci with a goalless draw in the second leg in Moldova.

Hearts secure the signing of midfielder Phil Stamp from Middlesbrough on a free transfer.

Ukrainian winger Andrei Kanchelskis signs for Southampton after being released by Rangers.

Dundee's Spanish winger Javier Artero is forced to give up football when he is diagnosed with multiple sclerosis.

Hearts sell Finnish international goalkeeper Antti Niemi to Southampton for £2 million.

Norwegian striker Tore Andre Flo joins Sunderland in a £6.5 million move from Rangers, almost half the Scottish record fee of £12 million the Ibrox club paid Chelsea two seasons before.

SEPTEMBER

Tom Hendrie is relieved of his position as manager of St. Mirren. He later denies he resigned and insists he was dismissed by the Paisley club. His assistant John Coughlin becomes the new manager.

Celtic duo Shaun Maloney and John Kennedy score the goals as Scotland's Under-21 side defeat Israel 2-1 in a friendly at New Douglas Park.

Scotland's Under-21 side require an own goal to earn a 1-1 draw at home to Northern Ireland in a friendly at Love Street.

Old Firm captains Paul Lambert and Barry Ferguson spare Scotland from the worst result in their international history, scoring second half goals to salvage a 2-2 draw against the Faroe Islands in Toftir as the Euro 2004 qualifying campaign gets underway.

Australian defender Tony Vidmar signs for Middlesbrough after being released by Rangers.

David Weir, the Everton defender, announces his retirement from international football in the wake of comments directed towards him by Scotland manager Berti Vogts after the 2-2 draw against the Faroe Islands.

Transfers this month: Derek Scrimgour (St. Mirren to Dumbarton).

Barry Ferguson in action against the Faroes Islands

OCTOBER

Aberdeen are knocked out of the UEFA Cup in the First Round, losing 1-0 to Hertha Berlin in Germany after a goalless draw at Pittodrie in the first leg.

Livingston's 4-3 home win over Sturm Graz in the second leg of their UEFA Cup First Round tie is not enough to spare them from elimination, having been heavily beaten 5-2 in the first leg in Austria.

Rangers suffer an embarrassing First Round exit from the UEFA Cup, losing out on away goals to unheralded Czech side Viktoria Zizkov as the teams draw 3-3 on aggregate. Celtic are the only Scottish team to progress in the competition, easing into the Second Round with a 10-1 aggregate defeat of Lithuanian side Suduva.

Alex Smith is dismissed as manager of Dundee United by the club's new owner Eddie Thompson. Paul Hegarty is named caretaker manager when Thompson fails in his initial attempt to lure Ian McCall from Falkirk.

Goals from Kevin Kyle and Simon Lynch give Scotland's Under-21 side a 2-0 European Championship qualifying win over Iceland in Hafnarfjordur.

Scotland revive their Euro 2004 qualification campaign with a 2-0 win over Iceland in Reykjavik, Christian Dailly and Gary Naysmith scoring the goals.

Newcastle United duo Gary Caldwell and Brian Kerr score for Scotland's Under-21 side as they defeat Ghana 2-1 in a friendly at Palmerston Park.

Scotland defeat Canada 3-1 in a friendly international at Easter Road. Dunfermline Athletic striker Stephen

Transfers in August:

Gary Locke (Bradford City to Kilmarnock),
Gary Bowman (St. Mirren to Arbroath),
Paul Harvey (Stenhousemuir to Airdrie United),
Scott Livingstone (Stirling Albion to East Stirlingshire),
Ryan Meechan (Dundee United to Alloa Ath.),
Craig Stevenson (Ayr United to Albion Rovers),
Garry Brady (Portsmouth to Dundee),
Brendan Crozier (St. Johnstone to Queen's Park),
Nicolas Fabiano (Paris Saint-Germain to Aberdeen),
Tom Hutchinson (Fulham to Dundee),
Janos Matyus (Energie Cottbus to Hibs),
Kevin Steele (Arbroath to Elgin City),
Lee Sharp (Ayr United to Stranraer),
Michael Moore (Hamilton Academical to Stranraer),
Stephen Marshall (Queen's Park to Stranraer),
Alex Lurinsky (Hamilton Academical to Stranraer),
Michael Daly (Clyde to Alloa Athletic),
Ian Cumersky (Carlisle United to Gretna),
Gordon Burns (Queen of the South to Peterhead),
Martin Wood (Motherwell to Ross County),
Willie Wilson (East Fife to Airdrie United),
Marvyn Wilson (Ayr United to Airdrie United),
Jean-Louis Valois (Luton Town to Hearts),
Tommy Turner (St. Mirren to Gretna),
Anthony Smith (Hearts to Morton),
Colin Reilly (Dundee United to Morton),
Steven Nicholas (Motherwell to Stirling Albion),
Craig McEwan (Ayr United to Dumbarton),
Marc Millar (Raith Rovers to Brechin City),
David Mathieson (Queen of the South to Gretna),
Liam Keogh (St. Mirren to Inverness Cal. Thistle),
John Hore (Carlisle United to Gretna),
Martin Glancy (Stranraer to Airdrie United),
John Fallon (Motherwell to Stranraer),
Isaac English (Stenhousemuir to Hamilton Acccies),
Kenny Brannigan (Stirling Albion to Airdrie United),
Mark Anderson (Arbroath to Montrose),
Paddy Quinn (Preston North End to Livingston),
Colin McMenamin (Newcastle United to Livingston),
Jose Quitongo (St. Mirren to Kilmarnock),
Jamie Fullarton (Dundee United to Brentford),
Stuart Malcolm (St. Johnstone to Plymouth),
Justin Skinner (Dunfermline Athletic to Brechin City),
Allan Morrison (Carlisle United to Clyde),
Scott MacKenzie (St. Mirren to Falkirk),
Robbie Winters (Aberdeen to Brann Bergen),
Andy Roddie (Arbroath to Peterhead),
David Noble (St. Johnstone to St. Mirren),
Stewart McCarthy (Dundee United to Arbroath),
Michael Innes (Dundee to Arbroath),
Garry Duff (Dundee to Arbroath),
Scot Buist (Rangers to Stenhousemuir),
Yanick Zambernardi (Troyes to Hibs),
Marc Anthony (Berwick Rangers to Forfar Athletic),
David Hopkin (Crystal Palace to Morton),
Neil Murray (Falkirk to Ayr United),
Greig McDonald (Dunfermline Ath. to Brechin City),
Ross Cairns (Raith Rovers to East Fife),
David Grant (Hamilton Accies to East Stirlingshire),
Lee Duncan (Ayr United to Albion Rovers),
Kevin Slavin (Raith Rovers to Stenhousemuir),
Neil Scally (Ayr United to Dumbarton),
George Paterson (Raith Rovers to Morton),
Colin McKinnon (Albion Rovers to Stirling Albion),
John McCaig (Notts County to Albion Rovers),
Stephen McAuley (Clyde to Airdrie United),
Alex Hardie (Clyde to Stenhousemuir),
Steven Fallon (Arbroath to Queen's Park),
Craig Clark (Kilmarnock to Ayr United),
Ian Adams (East Stirlingshire to Stenhousemuir),
Paul McManus (East Fife to Raith Rovers),
Craig Stevenson (Ayr United to Albion Rovers).

Crawford scores twice with Steven Thompson of Dundee United also on target.

Queen of the South win their second trophy in six months by defeating Brechin City 2-0 in The Bell's Cup Final at Broadwood with John O'Neil and Derek Lyle scoring the vital goals for the Doonhamers.

Celtic defeat Blackburn Rovers 1-0 at Parkhead in the first leg of their UEFA Cup Second Round tie, Henrik Larsson claiming the late winner.

Transfers this month: Samuel Boutal (Troyes to Kilmarnock), Andrew Fleming (Morton to Queen's Park), Ryan Cusack (Albion Rovers to Queen's Park), Keith Brown (Falkirk to Berwick Rangers), Chris Lamb (Kilmarnock to Queen's Park).

NOVEMBER

Dundee United Chairman Eddie Thompson announces that Paul Hegarty will be manager of the club at least until the end of the season.

Neale Cooper resigns as manager of Ross County for personal reasons.

Morton dismiss Dave McPherson as manager, citing a disappointing start to the season as the reason.

Goals from Henrik Larsson and Chris Sutton give Celtic a fine 2-0 win over Blackburn Rovers at Ewood Park in the second leg of their UEFA Cup Second Round tie, completing a 3-0 aggregate victory.

John McCormack resigns as head coach of Queen's Park to become the new manager of Morton. Paul Martin takes temporary charge of the first team at Queen's Park.

Roger Mitchell resigns as chief executive of the SPL with the organisation still in disarray amid the threat of resignation from the 10 non-Old Firm clubs.

Gordon Dalziel steps down as manager of Ayr United, moving into a backroom position. He is replaced by Campbell Money who becomes Director of Football.

Scotland lose 2-0 to Portugal in a friendly international in Braga, both goals scored by Bordeaux striker Pauleta.

Alex Smith is appointed the new manager of Ross County.

Henrik Larsson is on target again as Celtic defeat Spanish side Celta Vigo 1-0 at Parkhead in the first leg of their UEFA Cup Third Round tie.

Transfers this month: Fan Zhiyi (Dundee to Cardiff City).

DECEMBER

Ebbe Skovdahl is relieved of his position as Aberdeen manager. The Dane is replaced by Steve Paterson who is recruited from Inverness Caledonian Thistle.

Celtic reach the Fourth Round of the UEFA Cup after securing an away goals win over Celta Vigo. John Hartson scores the precious goal as they lose the second leg in Spain 2-1.

The joint Scottish and Irish bid to host the 2008 European Championship Finals is soundly beaten at the vote in Geneva. Austria and Switzerland win the right to stage the tournament.

Stephen Hughes, Kevin Kyle and Robert Malcolm score for Scotland's Future team as they earn a 3-3 draw with Germany in Mainz.

Former Hearts and Scotland striker John Robertson leaves his position as first team coach at Livingston to become the new manager of Inverness Caledonian Thistle.

St. Mirren sign full-back Martin Baker on a free transfer from Kilmarnock.

Transfers this month: Andrew Bonner (Queen's Park to Stirling Albion), Steven Boyle (Dunfermline Athletic to Brechin City).

JANUARY

Rangers sign Scotland striker Steven Thompson from Dundee United in a deal which sees Billy Dodds return to Tannadice.

Celtic sell Scotland Under-21 striker Simon Lynch to Preston North End for £200,000. Scotland international goalkeeper Jonathan Gould also leaves Parkhead for Deepdale on a free transfer.

Rangers release Russell Latapy from his contract at the club.

Aberdeen sign midfielder Steve Tosh from Falkirk for £30,000.

Queen's Park name former player Kenny Brannigan as their new head coach.

Aberdeen sign striker Paul Sheerin from Inverness Caledonian Thistle for an undisclosed fee.

Martin O'Neill agrees a new 12-month rolling contract as manager of Celtic.

The 10 SPL clubs outwith Rangers and Celtic withdraw their

Steve Paterson

Tepi Moilanen

Transfers in January:

Keith Knox (Alloa Athletic to Gretna), Mike Galloway (Carlisle United to Gretna), Graham Fyfe (Celtic to Raith Rovers), Brian Fairbairn (Livingston to Gretna), Paul Browne (Raith Rovers to Nuneaton Borough), Mark Lukowiecki (Livingston to East Stirlingshire), Robbie Henderson (Kilmarnock to Morton), David Carr (Albion Rovers to Stenhousemuir), Duncan McLean (Dundee to Peterhead), Steven Renicks (Stranraer to Queen of the South), Gary McCutcheon (Kilmarnock to Dumbarton), Daniele Chiarini (Partick Thistle to Dundee United), Ray McKinnon (Montrose to Raith Rovers), Jonathan Crawford (Queen of the South to Stranraer), Dene Shields (Sunderland to Raith Rovers), Craig Russell (St. Johnstone to Carlisle United), Kenny Munro (Cowdenbeath to Montrose), Tassos Venetis (Dundee United to Ross County), Ally Mitchell (Kilmarnock to St. Mirren), Murray McDowell (Arbroath to Berwick Rangers), Craig Duncan (Cowdenbeath to East Fife), Graham Dale (Rangers to Morton), John Gallagher (Queen's Park to Elgin City), Chris Webster (Montrose to Cowdenbeath), Andy Smith (Armagh City to Stirling Albion), Paul Riley (Brechin City to Montrose), David Ormiston (Livingston to Gretna), Steven Miller (Raith Rovers to Livingston), Andy McConnell (Gretna to Albion Rovers), Barry Donachie (Brechin City to Montrose), Mark Dempsie (Hibs to St. Mirren), David Carr (Albion Rovers to Stenhousemuir), Michael Hart (Livingston to Aberdeen), Ramiro Gonzalez (Real Avila to Raith Rovers), Paul Deas (Ross County to Brechin City), David Rowson (Stoke City to Partick Thistle), Ian Ross (St. Mirren to Partick Thistle), Kevin McGowne (Dundee United to Partick Thistle), Alan Main (St. Johnstone to Livingston), Steven Craig (Falkirk to Motherwell), Mark Yardley (St. Mirren to Albion Rovers), Scott McLean (Partick Thistle to St. Mirren), Jordan Tait (Arbroath to Ross County), Derek Scrimgour (Dumbarton to Queen's Park), Iain Russell (Motherwell to Dumbarton), Mark Perry (Ross County to Peterhead), Craig Penman (Everton to East Stirlingshire), Fernando Pasquinelli (Temperley to Livingston), Emiliano Olcese (Racing Club to Livingston), Anton Nugent (Doncaster Rovers to Stirling Albion), Paco Luna (Hibs to Almeria), Simon Miotto (Raith Rovers to St. Johnstone), Chris Miller (Inverness Cal. Thistle to East Fife), Junior Mendes (St. Mirren to Mansfield), Calum McHattie (Aberdeen to Ross County), David McCallum (Partick Thistle to Queen's Park), Julian Maidana (Racing Club to Livingston), Steve Kerrigan (Halifax Town to Stirling Albion), Steven Hislop (Ross County to Inverness Cal. Thistle), Leigh Hinds (Clyde to Aberdeen), Mark Gardiner (Carlisle United to Ross County), Tom English (Newcastle United to Livingston), David Dunn (Clyde to Airdrie United), Barry Donald (Queen of the South to Dumbarton), Mark Crilly (Dumbarton to Stirling Albion), Mathias Coelho (Racing Club to Livingston), Mark Cairns (Brechin City to Queen's Park), Tony Caig (Hibs to Newcastle United), John Adam (Rangers to Morton).

notice of resignation from the organisation after a compromise agreement is reached between the rival parties.

Celtic sign Spanish goalkeeper Javier Sanchez Broto from Livingston for £50,000.

Rangers sign French full-back Jerome Bonnissel and Norwegian central defender Dan Eggen on free transfers until the end of the season.

Hearts sign Finnish international goalkeeper Tepi Moilanen on loan for the rest of the season from Preston North End.

Livingston sign former Spanish international midfielder Guillermo Amor from Villarreal on a free transfer.

Dundee United sign full-back Gary Bollan from Livingston on a free transfer.

Paul Hegarty is dismissed as manager of Dundee United and replaced by Ian McCall who this time agrees to leave Falkirk. The Brockville club, who will seek compensation for McCall, place players John Hughes and Owen Coyle in joint charge of the first team until the end of the season.

Dundee sign Scotland international striker Mark Burchill on loan from Portsmouth until the end of the season.

FEBRUARY

Ronald de Boer is the scorer as Rangers defeat Hearts 1-0 at Hampden to reach the Final of The CIS Insurance Cup.

Leeds United defender Dominic Matteo announces his retirement from international football, claiming he can no longer commit himself to Scotland because of injury problems.

Bobo Balde scores twice with Henrik Larsson also on target as Celtic defeat Dundee United 3-0 at Hampden in the second Semi-Final of The CIS Insurance Cup.

Bobo Balde

Celtic sign Slovakian central defender Stanislav Varga on a free transfer from Sunderland.

Shaun Maloney and Simon Lynch score the goals as Scotland's Under-21 side defeat the Republic of Ireland 2-0 in a friendly at Rugby Park.

Scotland slump to another depressing defeat when they lose 2-0 to the Republic of Ireland at Hampden. Kevin Kilbane and Clinton Morrison score the goals for the visitors.

Neil Cooper resigns as manager of Forfar Athletic to become the Under-21 coach at Aberdeen.

Dundee United sign midfielder Russell Latapy on a free transfer.

Former Scotland international Ray Stewart is named as the new manager of Forfar Athletic.

Hibs sign Swedish goalkeeper Daniel Andersson on a free transfer.

Partick Thistle announce that Gerry Collins will replace John Lambie as manager at the end of the season.

Bradford City striker Andy Gray scores for Scotland's Future team as they earn a 1-1 draw with Turkey in Antalya.

Alex Caldwell is dismissed as manager of Elgin City.

Celtic reach the Quarter Finals of the UEFA Cup, securing a dramatic 5-4 aggregate win over VfB Stuttgart. A 3-1 home win is followed up by a 3-2 defeat in the second leg in Germany.

Other transfers this month: Paul Shields (Celtic to Clyde).

MARCH

Former Rangers defender David Robertson is named as the new manager of Elgin City.

Danny Diver resigns as manager of East Stirlingshire who are firmly rooted to the bottom of the Bell's Third Division.

Aberdeen manager Steve Paterson admits to an alcohol problem after missing a match at home to Dundee. The Pittodrie club announce they will stand by Paterson and assist in his recovery.

Goals from Claudio Caniggia and Peter Lovenkrands earn Rangers a dramatic 2-1 win over Celtic in The CIS Insurance Cup Final at Hampden. Henrik Larsson scores for Celtic with John Hartson missing a last minute penalty kick. Celtic finish the match with 10 men after Neil Lennon is sent off.

Celtic reach the Semi-Finals of the UEFA Cup with an outstanding 2-0 win over Liverpool at Anfield in the second leg of their Quarter Final tie. Alan Thompson and John Hartson score the goals, completing a 3-1 aggregate victory after the first leg at Parkhead had finished 1-1.

David Winnie is dismissed as manager of Dumbarton.

Inverness Caledonian Thistle cause another Scottish Cup upset against Celtic, Dennis Wyness scoring the only goal of the Quarter Final tie for the First Division club at Caledonian Stadium.

Brian Fairley is appointed the new manager of Dumbarton.

Shaun Maloney is on target for Scotland's Under-21 side as they defeat Iceland 1-0 in a European Championship qualifier at Broadwood.

Scotland claim three crucial Euro 2004 qualifying points when goals from Wolves striker Kenny Miller and Dundee defender Lee Wilkie see them edge past Iceland 2-1 at Hampden.

Claudio Caniggia

The Scottish Premier League defer a decision until the end of the season on whether Falkirk will be allowed promotion on the basis of a groundshare with Airdrie United.

Transfers this month: Myles Hogarth (Alloa Athletic to Stirling Albion), Mohammed Camara (Arlesey Town to Peterhead), Ivan Petkov (CSKA Sofia to Peterhead), Dino Vita (Hearts to Stenhousemuir), David Hannah (AEL Limassol to Ross County), Valdes Lias (Atletico Madrid to Raith Rovers), Alan McDermott (Manchester United to Hamilton Academical).

Kevin Kyle

APRIL

Kevin Kyle's goal is not enough to spare Scotland's Under-21 side from defeat against Lithuania in Vilnius as the home team come from behind to win the European Championship qualifier 2-1.

Scotland's Euro 2004 qualifying hopes suffer a blow when they lose 1-0 to Lithuania in Kaunas. Tomas Razanaukas scores the only goal with a controversially awarded penalty kick.

Stevie Morrison is named as the new manager of East Stirlingshire and will be assisted by former Dundee United, Rangers and Everton defender Alex Cleland.

Rangers come from behind to defeat Motherwell 4-3 in a dramatic Scottish Cup Semi-Final at Hampden.

Falkirk clinch the Bell's First Division Championship with three matches to spare, their 4-1 home win over Arbroath also confirming the Gayfield club's relegation to the Second Division.

Georgi Nemsadze is the scorer as Dundee defeat Inverness Caledonian Thistle 1-0 at Hampden to reach the Scottish Cup Final for the first time since 1964.

Celtic become the first Scottish club for 16 years to reach a European Final when they defeat Boavista 2-1 on aggregate in the UEFA Cup Semi-Final. Henrik Larsson scores the only goal of the second leg in Portugal after a 1-1 draw at Parkhead.

Cowdenbeath are relegated to the Bell's Third Division after a 2-0 defeat against Hamilton Academical.

Rangers captain Barry Ferguson is named Player of the Year by the Scottish Professional Footballers' Association. Motherwell striker James McFadden lifts the Young Player of the Year award while the divisional honours go to Dennis Wyness of Inverness Caledonian

Chris Templeman

Thistle (First Division), Brechin City striker Chris Templeman (Second Division) and Alex Williams of Morton (Third Division).

Simon Lynch is on target as Scotland's Under-21 side defeat Austria 1-0 in a friendly at Dens Park.

Scotland slump to another friendly defeat at Hampden, goals from Roland Kirchler and Mario Haas giving Austria a comfortable 2-0 win.

MAY

Raith Rovers clinch the Bell's Second Division title and promotion to the First Division with a 1-0 win over Berwick Rangers at Stark's Park in their penultimate fixture of the season.

Martin O'Neill signs the one year rolling contract as manager of Celtic, which had previously been announced he had agreed in January.

Despite a 4-0 win over St. Mirren on the final day of the season, Alloa Athletic are relegated to the Bell's Second Division on goal difference as Ross County defeat Ayr United 4-1 at Victoria Park.

An injury time goal from Chris Templeman earns Brechin City a 2-2 draw at Hamilton and gives Dick Campbell's side promotion to the Bell's First Division at the expense of Airdrie United whose celebrations after a 2-1 win at Stranraer are cut short. Stranraer's defeat sees them relegated to the Bell's Third Division.

In an incredible finale to the Bell's Third Division season, Morton clinch the championship and promotion with a 1-0 win over Peterhead at Cappielow. East Fife claim the second promotion place with a last minute Kenny Deuchar goal to defeat Queen's Park at New Bayview. Albion Rovers, despite a 3-1 win over East Stirlingshire, narrowly miss out along with Peterhead.

Barry Ferguson completes an awards double when he is named Player of the Year by the Scottish Football Writers' Association.

Billy McLaren resigns as manager of Stranraer in the wake of their relegation to the Bell's Third Division.

Don Hutchison and Kevin Kyle score for Scotland's Future team as they defeat Northern Ireland 2-1 at Firhill.

Celtic narrowly fail in their bid to win the UEFA Cup, losing 3-2 in extra-time to Porto in a memorable Final in Seville. Henrik Larsson twice equalises for the Scottish club, who have Bobo Balde sent off, only for Brazilian striker Derlei to score the winner for the Portuguese Champions.

Martin O'Neill

Don Hutchison

Chris Hillcoat is dismissed as manager of Hamilton Academical after the club's takeover by former Clyde Chief Executive Ronnie MacDonald. Allan Maitland, the former Clyde manager, is named new boss at New Douglas Park and will be assisted by Derek Ferguson.

The Scottish Premier League clubs vote 7-5 against Falkirk being allowed promotion on the basis of a groundsharing agreement with Airdrie United, claiming they are not satisfied the First Division Champions have first option rights on use of the Excelsior Stadium. Falkirk announce they will appeal to the SFA against the decision.

A remarkable final day of the SPL season sees Rangers clinch their 50th Scottish Championship by a single goal. Their 6-1 home win over Dunfermline Athletic is just enough to edge out reigning title holders Celtic, who miss a penalty in their 4-0 victory over Kilmarnock at Rugby Park.

Hearts secure third place in the SPL and a UEFA Cup place with a 1-0 home win over Dundee.

Scotland draw 1-1 with New Zealand in a friendly international at Tynecastle. Stephen Crawford opens the scoring for the Scots who are pegged back by Ryan Nelsen's header.

Rangers complete the domestic "treble" when Lorenzo Amoruso

scores the only goal of the Tennent's Scottish Cup Final against Dundee at Hampden.

Transfers this month: Billy Mehmet (West Ham United to Dunfermline Athletic), Michael Bird (Bolton Wanderers to Aberdeen), Barry Robson (Inverness Caledonian Thistle to Dundee United), Andy Ross (Chelsea to Partick Thistle), Alex Bone (Peterhead to Elgin City), James White (Queen's Park to Elgin City), Brian McLaughlin (Queen of the South to St. Johnstone), Sandy Hodge (Stranraer to Queen of the South).

JUNE

Neil Watt is named as the new manager of Stranraer.

Livingston name Brazilian coach Marcio Maximo Barcellos as their new manager. David Hay moves into the general manager role which is vacated by Jim Leishman who becomes Chief Executive of the club.

Aberdeen sign defender Jamie McQuilken from Falkirk for £60,000.

Motherwell sign goalkeeper Gordon Marshall from Kilmarnock under freedom of contract. The Fir Park club also sign defender Stephen Craigan and striker Alex Burns, both also out of contract, from Partick Thistle.

Transfers in June:

Stuart Taylor (Falkirk to Partick Thistle),
Todd Lumsden (Albion Rovers to Hamilton Accies),
Paul Reid (Rangers to Northampton Town),
Alan Archibald (Partick Thistle to Dundee United),
Emmanuel Panther (St. Johnstone to Partick Thistle),
Craig Tully (Elgin City to Stenhousemuir),
Willie Martin (Queen's Park to Elgin City),
Chris Boyle (Kilmarnock to Dumbarton),
Stephane Bonnes (Celtic to Partick Thistle),
David Bingham (Livingston to Inverness Cal. Thistle),
Derek Townsley (Hibernian to Oxford United),
Paul Walker (Partick Thistle to Morton),
Robert Dunn (Stirling Albion to St. Mirren),
Craig Valentine (Berwick Rangers to Alloa Athletic),
Andy Seaton (Falkirk to Alloa Athletic),
Mark Cowan (Alloa Athletic to Berwick Rangers),
Gary McGlynn (Montrose to Alloa Athletic),
Stewart Greacen (Forfar Athletic to Morton),
Ross Beattie (Kilmarnock to Queen of the South),
Craig Nelson (Ayr United to St. Johnstone),
Martin Maher (St. Johnstone to Forfar Athletic),
John Gemmell (Queen's Park to Partick Thistle),
Hugh Davidson (Dundee United to Forfar Athletic),
Steve Convery (Clyde to Hamilton Academical),
Steven Rennie (Falkirk to Arbroath),
Paul Kaczan (Hearts to Partick Thistle).

Scotland come from behind to draw 1-1 with Germany in a Euro 2004 qualifier at Hampden. Kenny Miller scores for the Scots after Fredi Bobic had headed the visitors in front.

Falkirk lose their appeal to the SFA against the SPL's decision not to allow them promotion from the First Division. It means Motherwell, who finished bottom of the SPL, avoid relegation.

Rangers sign Portuguese international winger Nuno Capucho from Porto for £800,000.

Hearts and Hibs announce their intention to relocate to a new shared stadium at Straiton on the outskirts of Edinburgh by 2010.

Stephen Halliday
(The Scotsman)

Nuno Capucho

Kenny Miller scores against Germany

treble top

Breathtaking is the only way to describe the remarkable climax to the Bank of Scotland Premierleague Championship as Rangers clinched their 50th title. Howard and Angela may claim to "Giving You Extra" but there is little doubt that the Old Firm delivered the most exciting flag race for years.

Sunday, 25th May, 2003 will live long in the memory for every Rangers fan as the major prize was reclaimed but the whole campaign will be remembered for years to come as Alex McLeish and his players delivered a clean sweep of all of the domestic honours, giving Rangers the Treble for the seventh time.

It was sheer theatre on an incredible final day as Celtic took on Kilmarnock at Rugby Park and Rangers faced Dunfermline Athletic at Ibrox with the two sides level on points, level on goal difference but with Rangers ahead by virtue of scoring one more goal.

The goals rained in at each venue. There was a moment when Celtic went three up and the title was back in their hands. However, Rangers motored on to destroy Dunfermline 6-1 with Mikel Arteta's late penalty making absolutely certain of the world record 50th title.

Both sides had won 31 games, drawn four and lost three. It was also the first time since season 1994/95 that the side which came off worse in the Old Firm derbies managed to win the championship.

Little wonder the events are still indelibly marked in McLeish's mind. He said: "It was as good as it gets on the final day of last season – there is no question about that.

"To finish as Champions after a League race which went down to the last few minutes of the final game is just a phenomenal feeling.

"It was very nerve-wracking. As you would imagine, I kicked every ball with the players.

"I tried not to get agitated but I'm afraid I didn't hide my feelings very well during the match.

"Celtic pushed us all the way and I think we pipped a very good side. I think beating the UEFA Cup finalists to the title speaks volumes for my players.

"We set realistic targets but when you are at Rangers, the championship really matters and rightly so. I felt at the start of the season we had the players to push Celtic and we did just that.

"It was a fantastic season because we not only won our 50th title but we went on to seal the Treble with our Tennent's Scottish Cup Final win over Dundee.

"That said, I suppose I have just made things a little bit harder for myself.

Rangers win the Scottish Premier League 2002/03

"You simply don't stop at this club. You can't stand still. Of course, everyone has been entitled to celebrate what we achieved but now we have to be completely focused on what lies ahead."

The irony was that aspersions were cast about McLeish's title credentials on Day One when Rangers were held 1-1 at Kilmarnock.

However, McLeish's men then put together eight wins in succession to show everyone that they meant business. The fifth victory of the sequence against Hearts on 11th September 2002 put McLeish top of the table for the first time as Rangers boss.

The first Old Firm clash was epic as the old rivals fought out a 3-3 draw then McLeish claimed his first League victory over Celtic on 7th December to the utter joy of the Ibrox fans.

Defeat at Motherwell on Boxing Day soured the festivities. However, Rangers then racked up nine wins in a row including an absolutely crucial win at Easter Road on a cold night on 29th January. The star men of the season, Ronald de Boer and Barry Ferguson, combined with the Dutchman setting up the marauding skipper for a fantastic goal and then Claudio Caniggia sealed three vital points. It was a key moment in the campaign.

Defeat at Parkhead on 8th March gave Celtic hope and then when Martin O'Neill's side won 2-1 at Ibrox on 27th April, it was game on again with just four League matches left.

The nerves among the Rangers fans jangled again the following week as the Light Blues had to dig out a 2-2 draw at Dens Park, missing two penalties in the process.

Ronald de Boer recalled that crucial spell in the season. He said: "We knew we had to win and win well on our next game and we managed to do that, beating Kilmarnock 4-0.

"Then we were faced with a very difficult game against Hearts and the pressure was on us, not just to win but to score at least two goals.

"I was delighted to head the first goal and then Peter Lovenkrands got the second one and that meant that we went into the final fixture knowing that if we could score one more goal than Celtic we would be Champions.

"Of course we all know what happened and it is a day that I will never forget.

"I think the crucial thing was we made a good start to the season. Yes, we drew the first game at Kilmarnock but after that we displayed a high level of consistency.

"From my own point of view, I felt in really good physical shape and when I have that level of fitness and my mental strength is right then I can trust my ability."

Rangers as a team had to show considerable mental strength to retain The CIS Insurance Cup on 16th March as the Final against Celtic came just eight days after suffering SPL defeat at Parkhead.

Clockwise top left: Claudio Caniggia scores in the CIS Insurance Cup Final, Mikel Arteta scores the vital penalty against Dunfermline Athletic, Lorenzo Amoruso scores in the Tennent's Scottish Cup Final, Alex McLeish holding the CIS Insurance Cup

They had made their way to Hampden by virtue of defeating Hibernian 3-2 at Easter Road, edging Dunfermline at East End Park thanks to a late Claudio Caniggia goal and then beating Hearts in the Semi-Final at Hampden 1-0 with de Boer heading the all important goal.

De Boer recalled: "We had to show what we were made of after losing to Celtic in the League and winning The CIS Insurance Cup against them was a huge result for us because it gave us the confidence we needed for the rest of the season."

It was another epic contest as Rangers raced to a two-goal lead thanks to Caniggia and that perennial scorer against Celtic, Peter Lovenkrands.

Henrik Larsson pulled one back and then John Hartson had a goal disallowed but the drama was not over. In the final moments, the Welshman missed a penalty and the trophy belonged to Rangers.

The Tennent's Scottish Cup campaign proved to be equally profitable but the Ibrox men had to work extremely hard to get to the Hampden showdown on 31st May.

A 3-0 win at Gayfield in the Third Round was comfortable enough but Ayr United proved to be difficult opponents down at Somerset Park and it was de Boer who settled the Fourth Round tie, heading home Stevie Thompson's cross.

Playing away from home again in the Quarter Final, Rangers were held 1-1 by Dunfermline but won the replay 3-0 and that set up a Semi-Final with Motherwell.

They came from 2-1 down to win the match 4-3, with Thompson a major influence again, and that set up a Tennent's Scottish Cup Final meeting with Dundee.

History was on Rangers' side. They had beaten the Dark Blues in the 1964 Scottish Cup Final to claim the Treble and they desperately wanted to do it again to complete a memorable season.

Many of the players were nearly out on their feet at the end of it all and it just had to be Lorenzo Amoruso who decided the match. The popular Italian rose to power Neil McCann's free kick into the roof of the net on what was his final appearance for the club and signal Treble time.

For Scotland's Player of the Year, Barry Ferguson, it was a remarkable campaign. He led from the front and he also produced 20 goals which were hugely influential in the remarkable success.

He said: "It really took weeks to fully sink in. To win the Treble is a great achievement and something I have always dreamed of.

"I had a dream of winning all three trophies as captain and now I have done that. It's a fantastic feeling.

"I think we had tremendous performances from a number of players throughout the whole campaign and I could not have asked for a more memorable season.

Lindsay Herron
(Editor In Chief, Rangers Media)

Rangers win the Tennent's Scottish Cup 2002/03

near to perfection

Celtic's run to the UEFA Cup Final was the result of a series of firsts for Martin O'Neill's side. How inappropriate, therefore, that it should end with a second prize in Seville.

However, even before they set foot inside the magnificent Stadio Olimpico in the Andalucian capital, Celtic had re-written major chunks of the club's history. They had remained in Europe beyond Christmas for the first time in 22 years. To achieve this, they had overcome Spanish opposition for the first time in 41 years of competing against the Continent's best and, they followed this up by scoring on German soil for the first time in seven attempts. To spice things up even further, they got the better of Liverpool for the first time in three attempts, one of two Battle of Britains on this near-glory run which had a massive nationwide television audience salivating.

To then taste the bitter disappointment of conceding an extra-time goal in the baking heat of Seville – a goal which was as undeserved as it was avoidable – was hard to stomach for players, management and fans, 80,000 of whom had made the journey to Spain to celebrate the football fiesta. However, as O'Neill, Henrik Larsson and everyone else involved in the UEFA Cup run reflects on the amazing nine-month journey which culminated in Seville, they can do so with pride. The puffed-out-chest sort of pride which comes the way of Scottish clubs all too seldom.

Little wonder O'Neill insists: "There's no doubt it was a totally unforgettable experience.

"Great, great managers, great judges of the game, will tell you that you need to have this sort of European experience before you take it on a further step. You need to be steeped in it.

"We've now had a taste of the Champions League and gone this distance in the UEFA Cup. It has been very hard work, very rewarding and it's where I aspire to be."

O'Neill can take some consolation from the fact his team has helped put the Scottish game back on the map of Europe, and the all-important co-efficient points garnered en route to the UEFA Cup Final have done much to enhance the standing of our clubs.

Celtic's achievement in going all the way to the Final was all the more remarkable when it is remembered this was a European journey which appeared to have ended before it had even began. The club were only participating in the UEFA Cup as a result of falling to the unseeded Basel in the single qualifying round they had to play to gain entry to the Champions League proper. A 3-1 home leg victory – earned after conceding an early goal

Celtic fans at the UEFA Cup Final

– was considered good enough to secure safe passage, even though Larsson's penalty miss took a little of the sheen off the scoreline.

This optimism was as false as it was short-lived. O'Neill's warning that the Swiss Champions were a decent side echoed eerily around the modern Basel stadium as Celtic crashed 2-0 to go out on away goals.

Plan B had to be hatched and that meant going all the way back to the beginning in the UEFA Cup. You would struggle to fall much lower than a First Round tie against FK Suduva, a minnow even in their native Lithuania. To their credit, Celtic took the job in hand seriously, routing the visitors 8-1 – a Larsson hat-trick the feature – to make the return game a formality assigned to the fringe players. They ignored the ramshackle, dilapidated surroundings of the all-concrete Darius and Girona Stadium – and the typically Baltic conditions – to win 2-0 and move on to the Second Round.

There, much bigger fish waited to be fried, and when Celtic landed Blackburn Rovers, many believed O'Neill's men had had their chips. Well, many south of the border, that is.

It was another Battle of Britain – Rab Douglas referred to it as episode 49 – but, it was so much more. Celtic had played many English clubs in the past, but this time there was the Souness factor to fire up the fans. The former boss of Rangers milked his return to the city where he had cut his teeth in management, mostly by sinking them into Celtic.

The procession he led through Glasgow's Central Station when his squad hit town was pure theatre. The press conference he hosted 24 hours before the game was pure Vaudeville. And, his delayed appearance in the dug out after the game had started – he claimed he had been forced to answer a call of nature – was pure pantomime.

Most importantly, however, the lesson his players handed Celtic was pure class. They out passed the men in hoops, and retained possession with consummate ease. What they could not do, however, was convert their dominance into even a single goal. Larsson was the only man to achieve that feat to give Celtic a 1-0 lead to take to Ewood Park. There, Souness promised his players, it would be men against boys, a post-match remark indiscreetly relayed to the world at large by captain Gary Flitcroft.

What Souness failed to recognise, however, was that it would be his men against O'Neill's Bhoys, and they were Bhoys on a mission. Mission impossible, sceptics repeatedly told them. But, O'Neill had other ideas, one of which was to field John Hartson up front alongside Larsson and utilise Chris Sutton between the midfield and attack. A goal in each half for a 2-0 win was a turning point for everyone connected with re-energised Celtic, and one which put them on course for a fabulous run all the way to the Final.

Suddenly, listening to the unmistakable overtures of the Champions League was not quite so painful. Europe was still the place to be, even if it was in the second competition. The opposition might not be as grand as that in the Champions League, but there were still clubs you would have hoped to have avoided. Celta Vigo was certainly one, but that is who next

Clockwise from top left: Celtic v Blackburn, Celtic v Boavista, Celtic v Stuttgart, Celtic v Porto

stood in Celtic's path.

The omens were poor. Celtic had never defeated a Spanish club, this failing playing a major part in their double decade record of not managing to maintain an interest in Europe beyond the turn of the year. This time, it was to be different. Very different. Another 1-0 home leg win – another Larsson goal – set up a classic in Vigo, a fishing-dependant city ravaged by the oil-slick which had recently blighted the Galician coastline.

Star striker Benny McCarthy appeared to have not a care in the world, however, as he shared a soft drink or two with Celtic fans a few hours before the game. Celta's pre-match hotel base had been infiltrated by Hoops fans, and with sleep out of the question, McCarthy had decided to join the party. Just as well, because he had little to celebrate a few hours later after Celtic had gone down 2-1, but booked their place in the Fourth Round courtesy of the away goal scored by Hartson.

The wait for the next round, and the visit of Bundesliga challengers VfB Stuttgart, seemed like an eternity. Finally, Felix Magath's men hit town, the lucky sequence of home draws first continuing for Celtic. Unfortunately, luck had deserted Larsson who was out of both legs after sustaining a broken jaw against Livingston. With Hartson suspended, it was left to 20 year-old Shaun Maloney to fill the void, which he did magnificently, scoring one of the goals in Celtic's 3-1 win.

Hartson was back for the return, and was inspired as he heard fellow Welsh star Bonny Tyler belting out Looking Out for A Hero in the pre-match show. It was a slightly more appropriate song than the one which boomed out from the Press coach as it drew up at the stadium, the driver failing to understand why Rangers' adopted anthem, "Simply The Best", might be the rallying call for a lynch mob. Still, the scribes survived and were able to report on another great night for Celtic as they blasted into an early 2-0 lead which secured their place in the next round even though Stuttgart fought back to grab a consolation 3-2 win.

One more cup favourite removed, it was time to take on the next, Liverpool. Larsson and Emile Heskey defied medical science to recover from injuries and take their places in the first leg at Parkhead, both being rewarded for their bravery by getting on the scoresheet.

So the return in Liverpool was on a knife edge. But, it was to be Celtic who showed the better cutting edge, running out 2-0 winners and stunning Gerard Houllier and his all-star line up. On the night, Neil Lennon was imperious, but, he refuses to accept that he and his team-mates were driven by a desire to prove they were good enough to compete against a top Premiership side.

He explained: "I've always said we don't feel we have anything to prove to anyone.

"We just have to keep justifying ourselves to the Scottish press. I think a few of them were ready to write the epitaphs for our players that night.

"We've got a bit of a siege mentality among the lads. It's kind of us against them, and we have got a steely determination.

"But it didn't give us an extra edge against Liverpool as we didn't need one. We were one game away from the Semi-Finals of a European competition."

It was time to believe, truly believe, this could be Celtic's year and when the Semi-Final draw kindly paired Porto with Lazio, leaving Celtic to take on Boavista, you got the impression Lady Luck had a few bob on the Bhoys as well.

With thousands of Hoops fans having already acquired tickets for the Final, things started to get a bit sticky, however, as the Portuguese underdogs held out for a 1-1 draw at Celtic Park.

Surely this was not where it was all to end, at a building-site of a stadium in Porto against a team who could barely win a League game?

The answer appeared to be yes, until Larsson popped up again 12 minutes from time to knock in yet another vital goal.

O'Neill was ecstatic, and just a tad embarrassed when he entered the post-match press conference to a standing ovation.

He was to receive a similar tribute at the end of the Final itself, even though on that occasion he was required to give his thoughts on a night of glorious failure rather then success.

A see-saw match had swung one way then the other, with goals from Derlei and Alenitchev being cancelled out almost instantly by headers from Larsson.

So it was that the tension packed night extended into extra-time, with a penalty shoot-out appearing to be the most likely conclusion until Bobo Balde was sent off after picking up his second caution of the game with 10 minutes remaining.

The opportunity for UEFA's Silver Goal to decide the outcome had come and gone as the first half of extra-time passed goalless, punctuated only by the continued time-wasting tactics of Porto.

But, with one long stretch of a leg, Balde's time was up. Reduced to 10 men, the strength-sapping conditions finally took their toll, and Celtic conceded a third goal from Derlei which sparked outrageous scenes of celebration, delaying the restart for an agonising five minutes. Celtic could not hit back. Time and luck finally ran out on them in their 13th UEFA Cup tie of an amazing season.

To this day, O'Neill believes his side had done enough to add the trophy to the European Cup won in 1967.

He insisted: "In extra-time, we were beginning to look the stronger side, physically and mentally, but of course it all changed when we were reduced to 10 men.

"The ordering off to Bobo changed the direction of the game.

"But, it was a fantastic effort by the players and supporters. It was incredible, they were immense.

"They have been immense in victory at times, and they were immense in defeat." **Ronnie Cully**
(Evening Times)

photofinish

Peter Donald carrying the Bell's Third Division trophy to Greenock

What a ride last season was! And the journey ended with a helicopter landing in Greenock to present Morton with the Bell's Scottish Football League Third Division Championship. Almost 9,000 Morton fans brought the house down as they clinched the title in a winner take all against Peterhead.

However, the emotions weren't just pouring out at Cappielow. The final day of The Scottish Football League produced more drama than anyone had ever seen. Who could forget Dick Campbell's new £2,000 teeth and the beaming smile he gave as Brechin City clinched promotion thanks to a 92nd minute equaliser. What about the sheer elation of Kenny Deuchar's last minute winner against Queen's Park at a packed New Bayview to send East Fife up to the Second Division.

Then there was the other side of the coin. Poor Airdrie United thought they were promoted after their 2-1 win over Stranraer after the hapless tannoy announcer at Stair Park announced that Brechin had been beaten and they were up. Minutes later the reality sank in when it was announced the result was a mistake. Oh the pain!

If that was bad then what about Albion Rovers. The Coatbridge club were only 20 seconds away from going up only to be told East Fife had scored late on. The game can be cruel and for Rovers, it was the second season in a row they lost out in the dying seconds.

The First Division may have been clear cut with Falkirk winning the Championship but the relegation issue went down to the wire also. Alloa Athletic and Ross County were fighting to avoid the drop and in the end, veteran Alex Smith breathed a sigh of relief. Although Alloa defeated St. Mirren 4-0 at Recreation Park in the final day of the season, County comfortably beat Ayr United 4-1 to stay up.

To add the icing to the tension, SFL Secretary Peter Donald – accompanied by The Scottish Sun – was on stand-by with the Third Division trophy. Donald must have been the calmest man on the planet as the drama unfolded almost every second minute.

One minute the chopper was set to head to Cliftonhill, Cappielow and the possibility of Methil. With Morton 1-0 up, the chopper headed to the west coast as East Fife were still drawing 0-0 with Queen's Park. However, news of Deuchar's last minute winner meant that if Peterhead scored, the trophy would head to Fife. To add to the fingerbiting occasion, the mobile phones on the chopper went down for several minutes.

For all we know, anything could have happened......and nothing would have surprised anyone. But Morton withheld late Peterhead pressure and following touchdown at Langbank and a quick police escort to Cappielow, the trophy was presented to John McCormack and skipper Derek Collins.

Rewind to the start of the season and no-one could have predicted what the outcome would have been. Ian McCall was creating a real buzz of anticipation at Falkirk with his signings........most of them having worked with him at Airdrieonians the season before.

St. Johnstone were still the bookies' favourites though and went their opening six League games without conceding a goal. Youngster Kevin Cuthbert was in goal deputising for injured Alan Main and showed his potential.

But not even that record could match the rampant Bairns who won their opening five games, scoring 13 goals. Andy Lawrie was their main man in flying form but his season was ended in October through injury. Falkirk's only blip had come in The Bell's Cup Third Round when they lost to Brechin City on penalties. However, by the end of September, Falkirk were already seven points ahead of the Saints.

Kevin James struck near the death in a crunch game at Brockville between the leaders to gain a bigger advantage over their rivals. However, in their next match their bubble burst when Arbroath well and truly beat the Bairns 2-0 at Gayfield.

Raith Rovers – under the guidance of Spaniard Antonio Calderon – had already edged in front of the Second Division race whilst in the Third Division, at least six clubs were in striking distance of the top during the early part of the season.

Although Falkirk stuttered with draws against St. Mirren and Queen of the South, Lee Miller proved that blondes do have more fun when the peroxide striker grabbed a hat-trick at Love Street to start making his mark. However, it was veteran striker Owen Coyle who was banging the goals in for the Bairns on a regular basis and still showing that the wily golden oldie was at his best.

Stranraer meanwhile, briefly took over top spot from Raith in the Second Division although only six points separated the top seven in October. The same scenario was developing in the Third Division with Morton, Peterhead, East Fife, Stirling Albion and Albion Rovers all involved.

Bell's Cup winners – Queen of the South

First Division champions – Falkirk

The month of October provided the first trophy winners with Queen of the South crowned Bell's Cup winners. Brechin had reached the Final beating St. Johnstone and Falkirk on the way while the Dumfries club disposed of the likes of Peterhead, Morton and St. Mirren. In fact the two Semi-Finals provided an exciting 15 goals between them with Queen of the South beating St. Mirren 5-3 at Love Street while Brechin City defeated Queen's Park 4-3 in a thriller at Hampden.

A tremendous crowd of 6,438 turned out for the Final at Broadwood and watched John O'Neil and Derek Lyle score to give Queens a 2-0 victory to add to the Second Division trophy won the previous season.

Back to League business and by November, the Bairns had been knocked off top spot by Inverness Caledonian Thistle. Meanwhile, Steve Paterson's side hit a rich vein of form and stormed ahead by winning six matches on the bounce. Raith reclaimed top spot from Stranraer whilst East Fife had a small cushion in the Third Division. Alex Williams was the man making a name for himself for Morton with his blistering scoring rate and numerous Young Player of the Month Awards.

Caley's spell at the top of the table lasted just two weeks though

Second Division champions – Raith Rovers

Third Division champions – Morton

after several draws. Falkirk had the bottle when it mattered and again they did enough to beat St. Johnstone through a Kevin James winner at McDiarmid Park. But again Caley came back and held top spot going into the New Year.

January was a sensational month. Collin Samuel emerged on the scene for Falkirk with his hat-trick against Hearts in the Scottish Cup. John Hughes even urged Celtic to sign the Trinidad & Tobago striker after his devastating display.

But it was Bairns boss Ian McCall and Steve Paterson who stole the headlines with both leaving their clubs to manage in the SPL. Paterson took over at Aberdeen while the more controversial switch was McCall's move to Dundee United. McCall had already sworn his loyalty in public to Falkirk earlier in the season but money eventually talked and combined with Falkirk's stadium problems, he decided to head to Tannadice.

The Falkirk board reacted decisively and appointed players Owen Coyle and John Hughes co-managers. Their first match couldn't be tougher as they drew 1-1 with St. Johnstone at Brockville.

The next game proved the turning point of the season however, when Falkirk went to Inverness and won 4-3. Coyle was the inspiration with a stunning hat-trick and completed it with the winner in the dying seconds with a volley. It couldn't have been scripted better giving Falkirk a seven point cushion.

By this point, Raith looked certainties for the Second Division title with a strong lead while East Fife had a slight gap in the Third Division.

But by the start of March, St. Johnstone started to put an impressive run of results together and put in a challenge. By April, the Perth club had racked up eight straight wins before facing a do or die affair with the Bairns.

The gap was six points with five games to go and a win at McDiarmid Park was a must if Billy Stark's men wanted to keep in the hunt. But again, the Saints were unable to overcome their rivals with new signing Stuart Taylor grabbing the only goal of the game to all but secure the title for Falkirk.

Raith seemed to have a problem clinching the Second Division title as they stuttered to the winning line, including three successive 1-0 defeats in a row, while East Fife had a four point lead by the end of March with all other issues in the melting pot. But what a fitting way for the Bairns to clinch the title with a 4-1 drubbing of Arbroath at a packed Brockville with, who else, Owen Coyle grabbing a hat-trick.

The main focus of attention turned elsewhere in the final two weeks with Arbroath and Cowdenbeath's relegation from the First and Second Divisions respectively, the only other certainties.

Raith finally won the Second Division with an Andy Smith goal on the penultimate Saturday of the season clinching a 1-0 win over Berwick Rangers at Stark's Park to send boss Calderon into floods of tears.

So many permutations arose from the final day with League Secretary Peter Donald armed with every scenario. They say football lasts a season but it was those final minutes which won it and lost it and created the ecstasy and agony.

One thing is for sure, if we have a season half as good as last season then we are in for a treat!

Ronnie MacKay
(The Scottish Sun)

Rainer Bonhof's reflections on a year as the guiding influence of the nation's most talented young footballers requires the help of a pack of Marlboro and a steady supply of caffeine to the bloodstream. Old habits die hard. Success is a craving he has been unable to kick during his celebrated career.

When accepting the thankless task of restoring the country's football fortunes during the worst drought in memory, Berti Vogts enlisted the help of his closest friend to restructure the developmental roots of Scottish football. He lights up his first nicotine stick and ponders the progress thus far.

"When I took over, I soon discovered that nothing had been done for eight or nine months. The last Under-21 game was in October, 2001 and the time in between was wasted," he recalled, with a tone of astonishment undiminished with time.

"To be honest, the progress has been better than I expected because we have had to do a lot of work in a short space of time."

From a staple diet of tournament qualifiers, with only the very occasional friendly match, Bonhof has managed to squeeze roughly one friendly a month into an already claustrophobic Scottish calendar. Practice is a fundamental ingredient which has been largely ignored and the week-long get-together in Portugal at the start of 2003 is something he is keen to repeat, despite budgetary and time constraints and the scrapping of the winter break by the SPL, another bone of contention.

Practice was what turned the gifted young boy from a background of poverty into a wealthy World Cup winner and it is this simple principle upon which his coaching philosophy is founded.

"There was nothing to do back then but play football," he recalled of his formative years in Emmerich. "There were no computers, mobile phones or anything like that but, having come from a poor background, there was not even the possibility of playing golf and even tennis was far too expensive.

"There was no access to any other sport and I remember being told to work on my weak foot by hitting balls against the wall until it was as strong as the other. At first you wonder if you are wasting time but when you played in a match and took the ball inside with your left foot and scored a goal, you knew it was worthwhile."

Rainer Bonhof

RAINER BONHOF

The elements for success

Practice makes perfect, so the proverb goes. Bonhof the realist refutes the fanciful notion and so, while his current crop have been taught to strive to attain the highest standards, they do so with realistic ambition.

"I was not a player like Gunter Netzer, I was a fighter and worked hard for the team," he said, rather modestly for one remembered as much for his grace as his guile. "There is no point in looking back to the old Scotland players like Jimmy Johnstone or Jim Baxter and trying to emulate them because now the game is so different and there are so many different pursuits available.

"What I will say, though, is that if you like football, you always find a way."

While championing the cause for greater facilities, indoor and out, to improve the development, he has been heartened to discover that, despite the vegetative technological attractions, football remains at the hub of Scottish society.

"I like to take a walk around Kelvingrove Park," said Bonhof, a resident of Glasgow's West End, "and sometimes I sit at the sloping pitch at the bottom and watch young players kick the ball about. There are green and blue strips but there are also kids wearing Barcelona and Real Madrid and Bayern Munich strips and watching and supporting those kind of teams can only have a positive influence."

Of those under his influence, Bonhof predicts fulfilling futures for all who strive for constant improvement. James McFadden has recently graduated to the full Scotland side, Michael Stewart, Gary Caldwell and Brian Kerr are all approaching career crossroads, while the fiercely protected Darren Fletcher has emerged as the great Scottish hope and, indeed, the heir apparent to the departed David Beckham at Manchester United.

"I only hope he will be given the chance to demonstrate what he can do at Manchester United because the competition there can be overwhelming," said Bonhof.

"It must give him huge confidence to be told by Sir Alex Ferguson that he can take David Beckham's position but in Scotland there is the tendency to put too much expectation on players too soon. You only have to look at McFadden.

"From my experience of Darren, I can see he has the ability to make things happen. He can score, he can provide the final pass and that is so valuable to a team in the modern game. He is not David Beckham, though, he is Darren Fletcher and must be allowed to progress in his own style."

Darren Fletcher

James McFadden

Bonhof has enlisted the help of a variety of sources to scour both north and south of the border for emerging talent. Life in age-group football requires a perennial overhaul of personnel. Archie Gemmill heads the English scouting system, recently recommending Nick Montgomery from Sheffield United and Paul Gallagher at Blackburn Rovers, and Bonhof has clocked up tens of thousands of miles assessing at first hand players recommended to him throughout the Scottish and English divisions.

It is all a far cry from his previous post of employment, as coach of Sporting Club in Kuwait, but even as a player Bonhof was motivated by new adventures. The career paths of the men recruited to restore Scotland's respectability are entwined, the friendship forged in Monchengladbach reinforced in coaching from the Middle East to Mount Florida. It was not always thus.

"In the beginning, we hated each other," he remembers of their early encounters, when a scrawny 17-year-old Bonhof was treated suspiciously by the senior clique headed by Vogts.

"It was a club which reared its own players but there was an intensity which was intimidating. The experienced players like Berti and Gunter Netzer never said much, but I do remember them coming up and saying 'These are the rules, and if you abide by them, you will be fine. If not, you will be out.'."

Acceptance was quickly forthcoming. A debutant at 17 in the 1971 championship-winning season, he earned his first of 53 caps a year later and became a World Cup winner before his 21st birthday. From the mid to late 70's, Monchengladbach became the

Michael Stewart

foremost team in the Bundesliga, winning three successive titles as well as the UEFA Cup, while Bonhof was a losing finalist in the 1976 European Championship Final against Dr Jozef Venglos' Czechoslovakia.

The increasingly popular trend of playing abroad held a certain appeal for Bonhof and, having been voted the most valuable player at the European Championships, Valencia offered him the opportunity of a fresh challenge and some Spanish sunshine. The adventure was not without its teething troubles.

Boasting other famous foreign players such as Mario Kempes, Valencia had kept their financial difficulties a secret. "For the first three months my wages were delayed, and then from January to May we did not get our salaries or bonuses," he recalled. "The foreign players were not so desperate because we had some money saved, but that was not the case for a lot of the Spanish players, and so we decided that one day a week we would invite all the players and their families over and make paella for them."

With a Spanish Cup and European Cup Winners' Cup added to his collection, Bonhof had brief spells with Cologne and Hertha Berlin but was forced to retire at 31 after finally succumbing to a persistent hip injury.

"I had been taking painkilling injections every day and ended up getting the medication from the doctor and doing it myself to save time," he recalls.

"I had to give up after playing on a very cold day in Berlin. I tried to make a pass from the centre circle but there was too much chalk, which had frozen, and when I kicked it, my hip went again. I did not want to go through seven months of recovery again, so I gave up."

He subsequently underwent a hip replacement operation and, upon recovery, took to selling sports goods to keep him occupied. While Vogts had started on the DFB ladder, Bonhof gained his own coaching certificates and started with lowly Bayer Uerdingen, who had a certain talented teenager by the name of Brian Laudrup in their ranks. In 1990, after their World Cup win, Vogts was elevated to national coach, and there was only one choice as his assistant. In eight years they secured a win at Euro '96 but paid the price for a poor World Cup in France two years later.

After a brief spell as DFB's youth director, Bonhof became a member of Borussia Monchengladbach's executive board and, with the team struggling to recapture past glories, he was plunged into management to appease the fans.

Berti Vogts lifts the World Cup with Rainer Bonhof (far right) looking on.

"They forced me to do it, told me I had to, and I went along with it because I wanted to help the club. In the end we couldn't score, lost the most goals in the league, and were relegated. By that time, I was also general manager, coach, and youth team manager because there was no money."

With Vogts accepting the offer to become the coach of Kuwait's national team, Bonhof was recommended to take charge of the country's premier club, Sporting.

"Sometimes we would be training in 50-degree heat. You couldn't even swim because the water was boiling. Also, being an Islamic country, training was stopped every day for prayer, which could last up to half-an-hour. They wanted me to stay for another year but I was not interested."

Constant sunshine and no pressure? Defeats the purpose of nicotine and caffeine. Bonhof is in his element in Scotland and the next generation are already reaping the benefits.

Darryl Broadfoot
(The Herald)

dedicated to the cause

Victoria Park

John McVeigh

The dressing room door banged opened and there stood the gaffer. "Right, everybody out on the track!"

"Sure thing, just give us ten minutes to get showered and changed."

"NOW!"

And so there they were, 20 part-timers just back off a knackering pre-season blitz, half of them wearing only towels, marched down the corridor and down the tunnel.

They got outside and didn't know what they were meant to be looking at. Then the gaffer pointed to the far end of the stand, where a little gaggle of eight middle-aged blokes in overalls and sweatshirts were scrubbing the seats and brushing the steps.

"Know who they are," he barked.

Blank looks.

"They're the Directors. That's how much this club means to them. And if it doesn't mean as much to you lot, you're welcome to leave right now."

The ground was Ochilview, the players Stenhousemuir's, the gaffer John McVeigh. But the truth is it could have been any venue, any dressing room, any manager in the three divisions of the Bell's Scottish Football League.

The guys who pick the teams, who score the goals, who save the sudden-death penalties – they're the ones who get all the headlines. Yet they'd all be out of a job if it wasn't for an invisible army of men and women most fans have never even heard of.

Groundsmen, kitmen, sponge men, tea ladies, laundry ladies, programme sellers, turnstile operators, treasurers, secretaries. Without them, the grassroots would wither and die.

Everywhere I go, there's an unsung hero. From Dingwall, where Donnie MacBean has worked night and day for Ross County since Victoria Park was a Highland League public park, all the way down to Stranraer, where Stuart Marshall has driven the team bus since it was pulled by horses.

You never walk into Glebe Park, Brechin and see those famous hedges looking anything but immaculate. That wouldn't be the case if Alex Laing didn't put in endless hours keeping the place spick and span.

You sit in The Scottish Sun office and see match reports drop in from around the country and year after year you see the same names – John Simpson in Alloa, Bert Houston in Dumfries, Mike Wilson at Ayr, Bert Bell scooting from Cappielow to Dumbarton to Love Street and back,

Cappielow

all the while wishing he could write one more match report on his beloved Third Lanark.

Even managers, that most disposable of football souvenir, surprise you sometimes by becoming part of the furniture. On a frosty December day last season, I ended up at Berwick and Paul Smith let slip that he was, as of that weekend, the longest-serving boss in the Scottish game.

That's not so much unsung heroism as downright masochism.

Then you've got the supporters. Last season, Queen's Park diehard Keith McAllister was voted Bell's Fan of the Year and he and each of the monthly award winners have incredible tales of devotion to tell. Yet the fact is that the sponsors couldn't afford all the trinkets it would take to recognise the dedication of the punters who help keep the country's community clubs going.

When Craig Levein went back to Cowdenbeath to begin his managerial career, 15 years after he'd left to make it as a player with Hearts, he told me: "I walked out the tunnel for my first home game, looked around and saw the same guys standing in the same spots where they'd stood for my last game as a player. It was like they'd never left.

"When you've got a hardcore of

Campbell Money

maybe 300, that 300 will be there rain or shine, win, lose or draw. At your big clubs, huge numbers of fans can disappear like snow off a dyke when things go wrong. Not at clubs like these."

Luckily, the same goes for those behind the scenes. John McVeigh thinks back to that night he gave his new squad a short sharp lesson in dedication and said: "There is no club outside the SPL who could exist without the help of volunteers and dyed-in-the-wool Directors. That's a fact.

"You couldn't possibly afford to pay the amount of people who help around Ochilview. I can honestly say I've never known as hands-on a board as the one I work with here. They're not afraid to get their hands dirty – in fact, they're the first to volunteer when there are dirty jobs to be done.

"The same goes all over the country. The game runs on goodwill and you simply can't put a price on that."

Ayr boss Campbell Money echoes that. He says: "We've got a husband and wife here called David and Dorothy Harkness and they hold the place together.

"David's the groundsman, but does a whole load of other jobs around Somerset Park – and Dotty makes the tea, washes the strips for the first team, reserves and youths, gets the boardroom ship-shape for matchdays and so much more. They're in here every single day of the week.

"At a club in the SPL, there would probably be a dozen people on the staff to cope with the workload these two smashing folk put in.

"It was the same when I was at Stranraer. Stuart Marshall drove the team bus year after year after year even though he and most of the players are based in the Glasgow area, which makes every home game an AWAY game.

"And just as Ayr have Dottie, Stair Park has Sandra Clanaghan and Jeanette Sprott, always there, always helpful, always making people welcome."

You could go to dozens of clubs and come away with exactly the same

Keith McAllister (right), Bell's Fan of the Year – Queen's Park

Tommy Cumming

quotes. Only the names change. The contribution – it stays constant no matter what direction you look. And the great thing is that sometimes, just sometimes, the unsung heroes get their reward. Alex Laing and Brechin got a day at The Bell's Cup Final last season. Stranraer won it when Money was in charge. That's the beauty of a hugely under-publicised trophy.

When the once-in-a-lifetime moment comes, though, headlines and fame don't matter. All that counts is savouring every second. An hour or so before Inverness Caledonian Thistle played Dundee in last season's Tennent's Scottish Cup Semi-Final, I looked down to the Hampden pitch and saw a familiar face – and shape. The blazer open, the white shirt tail hanging out, the tie pulled down from the neck. Tommy Cumming, kitman and fount of all knowledge about all things Invernessian.

When I see guys like him having their day in the sun like that, I know the game is still good. Just as it was good the night Celtic pipped Boavista in Porto to reach the UEFA Cup Final. When it was all over and the tension burst like a dam, Martin O'Neill didn't run first to Larsson or Hartson or Lambert. He turned in the dugout and hugged John Clark, the barrel-chested kitman, a Lisbon Lion and a former assistant manager of the club, who still beavers away behind the scenes, making sure no superstar wants for as much as a tie-up.

He might not have scored the crucial goal that night, nor would he kick a ball in Seville the following month. But he's as part of any success his club have as any £30,000-a-week swaggerer.

They all are, all the unsung heroes. And I know there were 100 more I could have mentioned here. The good thing is, those who know football know who they are and best of all, deep inside, they themselves know their own worth.

At a rough estimate, it's more than all the money Roman Abramovich can count.

Bill Leckie
(The Scottish Sun)

Celtic manager Martin O'Neill with his kitman, John Clark

"Gaun then, hen, explain the offside rule". As a female wanting to be taken seriously in a football world dominated by men, it has long-since been the sneering, unofficial initiation test. But the sexists should be careful what questions they ask these days, because rather than a glorious strike, they are likely to score an own goal.

Scotland's first female Class One Official, Morag Pirie, could quote them any one of the game's 17 Laws, not just Law 11, and leave them looking pretty silly in the process.

"Morag is the first to progress this far through the ranks but she's not the first female to come into refereeing," said The Scottish Football Association's Head of Referee Department, Donald McVicar.

"There were some raised eyebrows initially, but I think with an increasing number of females getting involved in all areas of football, and with all the publicity surrounding Morag, it's not surprising that more and more are coming along to the coaching courses and expressing an interest."

Julie Fleeting

Indeed, the influence of the fairer sex on our national sport is growing at a rapid rate. The fact a recent survey showed that 25% of all fans are now female and there are well over 4,000 registered players in Scotland suggests there is more depth to it than that. For some, football is just a job but for others, the driving force is not necessarily the wage but their enthusiasm for a sport they too have grown up immersed in. Like it or lump it, the passion for many is instinctive and an understanding of the game ingrained.

"I just love it and anyone who knows me knows that. I grew up playing with boys in the street," says former Scotland cap Pauline Hamill. She was one of the first female professional players and is now setting a new trend with Rangers FC, as one of the few female community coaches in Scotland.

"Because of the rules then, girls weren't allowed to play competitively with boys, so it was only friendlies, but I think all the better players are the ones who grew up playing football with the boys from an early age. Girls who grew up with football as part of their lives definitely understand it as much as men and people who know me respect me. I've earned that respect because I'm good at what I do. I'm there on merit - it just so happens I'm female."

Maureen McGonigle, the Executive Administrator of Scottish Women's Football, has seen rapid growth in the women's game during the past decade.

"Things have improved tremendously since I started with Scottish Women's Football in 1991," says Maureen. "We are now an Affiliated National Association, with a seat on the SFA Council. The best part so far is the growing awareness of women and girls football, and the acceptance in many quarters.

"Young girls of school age now request football as their leisure activity, and it is a common sight on a Saturday morning to see over fifty Under-12 girls playing organised football at Glasgow

Pauline Hamill

Green, and enjoying every minute of it – a situation which is replicated throughout Scotland.

"Many male clubs throughout the SPL, SFL and Juniors now have a womens section, and assist in the promotion and the development of the club."

However, the big turnaround came in 1998 when the SFA finally agreed to finance the women's national team, which is now ranked 30th in the world by FIFA, compared to the men's team which is 60th. A full-time coach and a more professional approach to the women's game has reaped dividends with national coach Vera Pauw taking them into the European top flight.

In the same year, the senior teams in the Scottish Women's Football Association formed an official Scottish Women's Football League, which consisted of 30 teams. It now numbers 43, including the best 11 who broke away last season to form their own SPL. Julie Fleeting, this country's most successful goalscorer (male or female) on the international stage, who now plays professionally for San Diego Spirit, was also voted into the All-Star team in the highly-successful WUSA League, which is the female equivalent of the Premiership or La Liga, giving even greater credibility to women players from these shores.

"Things are definitely much better. Attitudes have changed for the better and it's quite normal to see girls playing football and opportunities are greater now than ever before for girls who want to play or women who want to get involved in the game," says Sheila Begbie, an Assistant Technical Director at the SFA and a former international. "There are more role models and it's no longer strange to see women in all sectors of the sport. Unfortunately, there will probably be a section of society who will always consider football a man's game but the likes of Pauline and Morag both came through the system as players before moving on to coaching and refereeing so they know the game as well as any man."

Knowing their business is the key. Even the women who couldn't recite the offside rule have a valuable part to play.

"I don't need to know about offside, the important thing is that I know how to treat the injuries and get the players rehabilitated and back playing as soon as possible," says Emily Goodlad, who has been the club physio at Inverness Caledonian Thistle for over three years.

"I do get the kind of shouts you would expect from the fans, things like 'hey love, I've got a groin strain as well, do you want to give me a rub?' but that's just the away fans. Everyone at the club has accepted me and, most importantly, the players have never treated me any differently because I'm a woman."

Emily actually finds it astonishing that she is such a minority in football, considering the fact that women vastly outnumber men in her chosen profession.

"If players were being treated on the NHS, then there is every chance they would be seen by a female and they wouldn't complain, so why not have a female physio at a football club," says Emily. "As long as they are a qualified professional who understands sports specific injuries then it shouldn't matter what sex the physio is. It's irrelevant."

It is a view taken by the game's administrators and a growing number of football clubs. Boardrooms are no longer a no-go area for women, with the club's purse strings being controlled by a woman, the PR handled by women and the day-to-day running of several clubs the responsibility of women. Business is business, whether it be a football club or a hosiery factory.

"I don't like stereotypes but I think, on the whole, women are better at juggling a few things at once," says SFL employee Maureen Cooper, "which makes them useful employees, whether that's in football or any other walk of life."

Having started as a secretary over 40 years ago, she has been responsible for the appointment of match officials for over 25 years to SFL matches, a job which requires a working knowledge of the history of certain clashes and an individual referee's ability to deal with high pressure matches or controversy.

"To be honest, the biggest problem I've had over the years has not been with men but with women. Because there were so few women involved in football, even up to a few years ago, the referee's wives were always very suspicious when you phoned their home."

Different women and different roles to play but the consensus is the same. The main thing to remember is that the women involved in our game now are not female players, female fans, female journalists or female referees. They are football players, football fans, football journalists and football referees.

Moira Gordon
(Scotland on Sunday)

Hibernian – Scottish Women's Football Cup Winners 2002/03

a national treasure

John Hampden was a man who relished a scrap. The man recorded in English history simply as 'The Patriot' paid the ultimate price for his passionate beliefs when he was killed at the Battle of Chalgrove Field during the English Civil War in 1643.

If that appears an incongruous introduction to an article in this publication, allow me to explain. Scottish football's most famous institution, Hampden Park, owes its name to the aforementioned English politician and soldier. Strange, but true. Our National Stadium, however, has never dealt in the ordinary or straightforward.

Since opening its turnstiles for the first time on its current Mount Florida site on 31st October, 1903, the world's most remarkable and storied football ground has played host to a diversity of famous names and dramatic events no other venue can match.

As Hampden celebrates a centenary at its current location this season, its future looks bright. Financial viability has been achieved and its UEFA five star status – European football's governing body say it would be their first six star stadium if such a rating existed – ensures a series of major occasions will continue to come its way.

But let's not get ahead of ourselves. Hampden is all about tradition and when landmarks such as 100 years are reached, it's well worth looking back as well as forward. Queen's Park, Scotland's oldest football club, called their first ground in the area Hampden after Hampden Terrace, a nearby row of houses which had been named by the property developer concerned in honour of that man John Hampden.

Oliver Cromwell's cousin, born in London and whose opposition in Parliament to King Charles I sparked the Cavaliers v Roundheads conflict, could hardly have imagined his moniker would one day be most recognised worldwide as a football stadium.

The first Hampden proved too small for the hugely successful Queen's Park and in 1884 they relocated to second Hampden. It would later be renamed Cathkin Park, home to the now defunct Third Lanark, and can still be visited as a haunting, overgrown memorial to financial failure in football.

Queen's Park decided they needed another move at the turn of the century, to a ground they could call their own after renting the first two incarnations of Hampden. Thirty Three acres of land were purchased on the opposite side of Prospecthill Road in 1900 and three years later it was completed at a cost of £30,000. Initial estimates of the new stadium's capacity were as much as 140,000 and it was acclaimed as a wonder of modern engineering and construction.

On Hallowe'en 1903, the third Hampden Park was opened for the first time. Appropriately enough, Queen's Park made a winning start, defeating Celtic 1-0 in a Scottish League match. The Amateurs would eventually slip away from the elite of Scottish football, but the stadium they still own to this day would survive, through good and bad times, to flourish.

Diego Maradona

Zinedine Zidane

Joe Jordan

Almost every legendary footballer of the past 100 years has graced its turf. Pele, Diego Maradona, George Best, perhaps regarded as the three greatest players of all time, have played at Hampden and relished the experience. Lev Yashin, arguably the finest goalkeeper the game has produced, kept a clean sheet at the ground when the USSR defeated Scotland 2-0 in a friendly in 1967.

Hampden has provided both players and spectators alike with cherished memories. There are few among the football fraternity who do not have a favourite Hampden moment logged in the back of their head.

For many, the 1960 European Cup Final between Real Madrid and Eintracht Frankfurt stands out above any other. Over 130,000 packed into Hampden for what is still regarded as the greatest football match of all time. Alfredo di Stefano, who along with fellow genius Ferenc Puskas, inspired Real to a dazzling 7-3 win over the outstanding West German champions, was visibly moved when he returned to Hampden in 2002 for the Champions League Final.

"It makes me feel old but it makes me feel special," said di Stefano as he watched Real Madrid defeat Bayer Leverkusen 2-1 to become champions of Europe for the ninth time. "The game in 1960 was the greatest moment of my career and the best thing about it was the ambience of Hampden Park."

It was a glowing testimony to the special atmosphere generated by a ground which, on that evening when Zinedine Zidane's wonderful winner created a million memories for a new generation of supporters, proved it can still host a big occasion in peerless style.

It is for Scotland internationals, of course, that Hampden is most synonymous. For many reading this article, a September evening in 1973 will stand out as the finest hour the national team enjoyed in Mount Florida. In front of 100,000 fervent fans, Willie Ormond's gifted side defeated Czechoslovakia 2-1 to clinch qualification for the World Cup Finals after a 16-year absence.

After Manchester United defender Jim Holton cancelled out Zdenek Nehoda's opener for a terrific Czech team, Ormond made a 63rd minute substitution which would transform the career of a young Joe Jordan. The Leeds United striker replaced Kenny Dalglish to win his fourth senior cap and, 12 minutes after coming on, headed a winner which is indelibly printed in Scottish football's collective consciousness.

Jordan, who remarkably would go on to score at three separate World Cup Final tournaments for Scotland, recalls: "It was my first goal for my country and it was certainly the most significant. The expectation among the crowd that night was huge and the noise when I scored was unbelievable.

"For me, that was what Hampden was all about. The noise the crowd generated made you believe anything was possible, you could beat any team there. I had been at Hampden as a supporter, in a crowd of 130,000, so to go on to play there for Scotland really was a dream come true.

"I was lucky enough to enjoy a few great occasions at Hampden as a player and if you ask any footballer in England or around the world, they will tell you that it was the most intimidating place to go and play."

Terry Butcher

Scotland v England 1985

Terry Butcher, the former England captain who now lives in Scotland, backs up Jordan's view, although he initially wondered if the famous Hampden Roar was simply a myth.

"As a kid in England, you grew up hearing stories about Hampden almost as much as Wembley," says the former Ipswich Town and Rangers defender. "My first visit was in 1982, just before both Scotland and England were going to Spain for the World Cup Finals. I had heard all about the Hampden roar and guys like Peter Shilton and Kevin Keegan were warning me I would never have experienced anything like it.

"However, we scored the only goal of the game after just 13 minutes through Paul Mariner, played really well, and there was hardly a sound from the Scotland fans. I wondered what all the fuss was about, but I found out when I came back with England in 1985. We lost that Rous Cup match 1-0 to a Richard Gough goal and I heard the Hampden roar alright.

"I was lucky enough to play at Hampden several times and won my first trophy as a Rangers player there in 1986 when we beat Celtic 2-1 in the Skol Cup Final. For me, it's a fantastic ground with a really unique atmosphere. It has changed a lot now, of course, and I was so impressed by it when I went back last season as manager of Motherwell for the Scottish Cup Semi-Final against Rangers. The dressing rooms alone are fantastic, far better than anything I've seen in England."

Hampden's £72 million redevelopment, of course, was not without its critics and there are those who still question whether Scotland needed such investment in a National Stadium.

David Kells, the stadium's Managing Director, feels Hampden has more than vindicated the decision to give it such a dramatic face-lift.

"The stadium attracts criticism from certain quarters, for whatever motives, but the facts are that it hasn't been the massive financial

Hampden Park in the 1930s

drain people predicted. We have been in the black for the last two years and the future is good.

"We are so much more than a football venue now. Our conference and hospitality facilities are outstanding and the stadium is used seven days a week. A lot of people don't realise what we have here and when you take them on a tour of the place, they are blown away by what they see."

A must on any visit to Hampden is the Scottish Football Museum where curator Ged O'Brien has created an endlessly fascinating record of a place he has clearly developed a deep and genuine affection for.

"The history of this ground is unrivalled in its depth and diversity," says O'Brien. "It is the spiritual home of world football and, in my opinion, the most famous and important building in Scotland. It's the people's building."

Indeed, Hampden is now the headquarters of Scottish football, hosting as it does the offices of The Scottish Football Association, The Scottish Football League, The Scottish Premier League and all the minor associations, which includes The Scottish Junior F.A., The Scottish Amateur F.A., The Scottish Schools F.A. and The Scottish Women's F.A.

Hampden now also boasts a state of the art Sports Medicine Centre which opened in March, 2002 and has already been acclaimed as the finest of its kind in Scotland.

"There is no other facility quite like this in Scotland," says Dr. John MacLean, the former Clyde and SFA doctor, who is the Medical Director of the Centre. "It is a centre of excellence for sports medicine and sports science and there is no doubt that there is an added attraction because it is based at Hampden."

Major names in the music world continue to include Hampden on their tour schedules, with American rapper Eminem, as well as the Live & Loud concert, recently joining a cast list which includes Tina Turner, Rod Stewart, Bon Jovi, The Eagles and Robbie Williams.

The ground also plays host to the home fixtures of the Scottish Claymores team and NFL Europe's World Bowl was staged at Hampden in 2003 with a crowd of nearly 30,000 attending the showpiece Final between Frankfurt Galaxy and Rhein Fire.

Characters as diverse as preacher Billy Graham and former world heavyweight champion Mike Tyson have taken centre stage at the ground, which has also hosted speedway, Rugby League, Rugby Union and hockey, and even the famous Hollywood actor, Edward G. Robinson, appeared on the pitch during a baseball match played by American servicemen during the Second World War.

All in all, an extraordinary stadium with a million and one extraordinary stories to tell. Here's to the next 100 years of history at the jewel in Scottish football's crown.

Stephen Halliday
(The Scotsman)

aberdeen

Pittodrie Stadium, Pittodrie Street, Aberdeen, AB24 5QH
CHAIRMAN Stewart Milne
VICE-CHAIRMAN Ian R. Donald
DIRECTORS
Gordon A. Buchan, Martin J. Gilbert, Hugh Little, Christopher Gavin & Keith Wyness
CHIEF EXECUTIVE Keith Wyness
GENERAL MANAGER David Johnston
SECRETARY
Duncan Fraser (01224 650424)
MANAGER Steve Paterson
ASSISTANT MANAGER Duncan Shearer
FIRST TEAM COACH Oshor Williams
GOALKEEPING COACH Jim Leighton
U-21/19 COACH Neil Cooper
DIRECTOR OF YOUTH DEVELOPMENT
Chic McLelland
SENIOR COMMUNITY COACH
Neil Simpson
COMMUNITY CO-ORDINATOR
Sandy Finnie
COMMUNITY COACHES
Jim Crawford, Stuart Glennie & Scott Anderson
CHIEF SCOUT John Kelman
FOOTBALL SAFETY OFFICERS' ASSOCIATION REPRESENTATIVE/ STADIUM MANAGER
John Morgan (01224) 650405
SALES & MARKETING MANAGER
Ian Riddoch (01224) 650443
HOSPITALITY MANAGER
Paul Quick (01224) 650430
CORPORATE SALES MANAGER
Harvey Smith (01224) 650426
CUSTOMER SERVICES MANAGER
Peter Roy (01224) 650428
CLUB DOCTORS
Dr. Derek Gray & Dr. Stephen Wedderburn
PHYSIOTHERAPISTS
David Wylie & John Sharp
GROUNDSMAN Paul Fiske
KIT MANAGER Jim Warrender
MEDIA LIAISON PERSON/ MATCHDAY PROGRAMME EDITOR
Dave Macdermid
TELEPHONES
Ground/General Enquiries (01224) 650400
Football Dept (01224) 650479
Commercial Dept (01224) 650426
Marketing & PR Dept (01224) 650406
Community Dept (01224) 650432
Ticket Enquiries (01224) 631903
Fax (01224) 644173
Operations Dept (01224) 650405
E-MAIL & INTERNET ADDRESS
davidj@afc.co.uk & feedback@afc.co.uk
www.afc.co.uk
CLUB SHOPS
AFC Direct, 19 Bridge Street, Aberdeen, Tel (01224) 212797, Fax (01224) 592250
Pittodrie Superstore, Pittodrie Stadium, Aberdeen
Tel (01224) 642800
Buy on-line at www.afc.co.uk/shop
OFFICIAL SUPPORTERS CLUB
Association Secretary: Mrs. Susan Scott, 'Aldon', Wellington Road, Aberdeen, AB12 4BJ
Tel (01224) 898260/450378
susan.scott1@virgin.net
TEAM CAPTAIN Russell Anderson
SHIRT SPONSOR A-FAB
KIT SUPPLIER Le Coq Sportif

LIST OF PLAYERS 2003/04

SQUAD NO.	SURNAME	FIRST NAME	MIDDLE NAME	DATE OF BIRTH	PLACE OF BIRTH	DATE OF SIGNING	HEIGHT FT INS	WEIGHT ST LBS	POS. ON PITCH	PREVIOUS CLUB
5	Anderson	Russell		25/10/78	Aberdeen	19/07/96	6 0	11st 10lb	Def	Dyce Juniors
20	Bird	Michael		07/11/83	Chester	26/05/03	6 2	12st 13lb	Fwd	Bolton Wanderers
–	Blanchard	James	Findlay	03/07/86	Banff	16/07/02	5 10	11st 7lb	Gk	Deveronvale
9	Booth	Scott		16/12/71	Aberdeen	14/07/03	5 9	11st 10lb	Fwd	Twente Enschede
–	Buckley	Richard		25/01/85	Rutherglen	10/07/03	5 11	11st 2lb	Mid	Aberdeen Youths
14	Clark	Christopher		15/09/80	Aberdeen	16/08/97	5 8	10st 8lb	Fwd	Hermes
–	Considine	Andrew		01/04/87	Torphins	28/08/03	6 0.5	11st 2lb	Def	Aberdeen Youths
4	Deloumeaux	Eric		12/05/73	Montbeliard	16/07/02	5 8	12st 0lb	Def	Motherwell
27	Diamond	Alexander		12/03/85	Alexandria	12/07/02	6 1	11st 0lb	Def	Aberdeen 'S' Form
–	D'Jaffo	Laurent		05/11/70	Aquitane	16/07/02	5 11.5	13st 3lb	Fwd	Sheffield United
23	Esson	Ryan		19/03/80	Aberdeen	23/10/96	6 1	12st 7lb	Gk	Rotherham United
18	Foster	Richard	Martyn	31/07/85	Aberdeen	02/09/98	5 9	11st 7lb	Mid	Aberdeen Youths
–	Fraser	Grant	Callum	22/03/86	Aberdeen	09/07/03	5 11.5	11st 2lb	Def	Aberdeen 'S' Form
2	Hart	Michael		10/02/80	Bellshill	24/01/03	5 10	11st 11lb	Def	Livingston
29	Heikkinen	Markus		13/10/78	Katrineholm	04/08/03	6 0	12st 9lb	Mid	Portsmouth
–	Higgins	Craig		24/07/85	Paisley	28/08/02	6 2	12st 6lb	Def	Renfrew Victoria
7	Hinds	Leigh	Michael	17/08/78	Beckenham	31/01/03	5 10	12st 0lb	Fwd	Clyde
43	Hutton	David		18/05/85	Glasgow	09/08/01	5 9	10st 0lb	Gk	Airdrieonians
25	Jones	Duncan		18/07/84	Fort William	12/07/00	5 9	11st 5lb	Def	Colony Park
–	Lombardi	Michele		02/07/86	Irvine	08/09/99	5 10	11st 7lb	Fwd	Aberdeen 'S' Form
11	Mackie	Darren	Graham	05/01/82	Inverurie	13/07/98	5 9	10st 4lb	Fwd	Aberdeen 'S' Form
30	McCulloch	Murray	John	09/03/84	Aberdeen	21/05/98	5 6	10st 6lb	Def	Middlefield B.C.
–	McDonald	Jason	Norman	15/01/87	Aberdeen	13/01/03	5 5	10st 0lb	Mid	Aberdeen 'S' Form
6	McGuire	Philip		04/03/80	Glasgow	19/09/97	5 11.5	11st 4lb	Def	Dyce Juniors
–	McInnes	Ashley		22/04/87	Aberdeen	09/07/03	5 7	9st 8lb	Fwd	Aberdeen Youths
17	McNaughton	Kevin	Paul	28/08/82	Dundee	20/07/99	5 10	10st 6lb	Def	Aberdeen 'S' Form
3	McQuilken	James	Charles	03/10/74	Glasgow	05/06/03	5 9	11st 2lb	Def	Falkirk
–	Michie	Scott		22/08/83	Aberdeen	20/07/99	5 10	11st 1lb	Fwd	Aberdeen 'S' Form
24	Morrison	Scott	Alexander	23/05/84	Aberdeen	26/05/99	5 8	11st 2lb	Def	Colony Park
22	Muirhead	Scott		08/05/84	Paisley	27/09/01	6 0	11st 0lb	Mid	Neilston Thistle
–	O'Leary	Ryan		24/08/87	Glasgow	09/07/03	6 0	11st 11lb	Def	Aberdeen Youths
21	Payne	Stephen		23/12/83	Glasgow	10/05/02	5 9	11st 1lb	Def	Aberdeen Youths
1	Preece	David	Douglas	26/08/76	Darlington	30/07/99	6 2	12st 10lb	Gk	Darlington
15	Rutkiewicz	Kevin		10/05/80	Glasgow	25/03/98	6 0.5	12st 6lb	Def	Larkhall Thistle
10	Sheerin	Paul	George	28/08/74	Edinburgh	10/01/03	5 10	13st 4lb	Mid	Ayr United
26	Souter	Kevin		07/01/84	Aberdeen	22/05/98	5 9	11st 3lb	Mid	Westhill B.C.
–	Stewart	John		08/03/85	Bellshill	13/01/03	5 11	9st 5lb	Fwd	Airdrie United
28	Tarditi	Stephen		23/02/85	Airdrie	27/09/01	6 3	13st 2lb	Fwd	Airdrie B.C.
–	Thomson	Robert		24/05/87	Bellshill	09/07/03	5 8.5	10st 2lb	Def	Aberdeen Youths
16	Tiernan	Fergus		03/01/82	Helensburgh	13/07/98	5 10	11st 1lb	Mid	Aberdeen 'S' Form
8	Tosh	Steven	William	27/04/73	Kirkcaldy	08/01/03	5 11	11st 12lb	Mid	Falkirk
19	Zdrilic	David	Allen	13/04/74	Sydney	05/08/03	6 1	12st 6lb	Fwd	Walsall

milestones

YEAR OF FORMATION: 1903
MOST CAPPED PLAYER: Alex McLeish
NO. OF CAPS: 77
MOST LEAGUE POINTS IN A SEASON: 64 (Premier Division – Season 1992/93) (44 games)(2 Points for a Win)
MOST LEAGUE GOALS SCORED BY A PLAYER IN A SEASON: Benny Yorston (Season 1929/30)
NO. OF GOALS SCORED: 38
RECORD ATTENDANCE: 45,061 (-v- Heart of Midlothian – 13.3.1954)
RECORD VICTORY: 13-0 (-v- Peterhead – Scottish Cup, 9.2.1923)
RECORD DEFEAT: 0-8 (-v- Celtic - Division 1, 30.1.65)

ticket information

SEASON TICKET INFORMATION

	ADULT	CONC	U12	1 ADULT /2CONC	2 ADULT 2 CONC	1 ADULT 2 U12	2 ADULT 2 U12
MAIN STAND	325	168	110	577	820	435	750
RDS CENTRE							
PADDED	350	175	90	612	875	440	790
RDSTAND	260	135	85	462	655	345	605
SOUTH STAND	235	120	60	415	590	295	530
MERKLAND	215	95	45	357	525	260	475

MATCH TICKET INFORMATION

	ADULTS			SENIOR CITIZENS		
GAME GRADE	A	B	C	A	B	C
MAIN STAND	28	25	22	20	18	15
SOUTH STAND	20	18	15	15	10	7
RICHARD DONALD STAND	23	20	17	18	15	12
MERKLAND FAMILY STAND	18	15	12	10	8	5
	U18			U12		
GAME GRADE	A	B	C	A	B	C
MAIN STAND	20	18	15	12	10	8
SOUTH STAND	15	10	7	8	6	4
RICHARD DONALD STAND	18	15	12	11	9	7
MERKLAND FAMILY STAND	10	8	5	8	5	2

leading goalscorers 1993-2003

Season	Div	No. of Goals	Player
1993-94	P	17	D. Shearer
1994-95	P	15	W. Dodds
1995-96	P	9	S. Booth, J. Miller
1996-97	P	15	W. Dodds
1997-98	P	10	W.Dodds
1998-99	P	14	E. Jess
1999-00	P	9	A. Stavrum
2000-01	P	17	A. Stavrum
2001-02	P	13	R. Winters
2002-03	P	8	P. Sheerin

the dons' club factfile 2002/03

Date	Venue	Opponents	Att.	Res	Kjaer P.	McGuire P.	McNaughton K.	Anderson R.	McAllister J.	Young Dn.	Bisconti R.	Deloumeaux E.	Thornley B.	Young Dk.	Mackie D.	Mike L.	Clark C.	Tiernan F.	D'Jaffo L.	Fabiano N.	Michie S.	O'Donoghue R.	Billio P.	Preece D.	Rutkiewicz K.	Muirhead S.	Payne S.	Tosh S.	Sheerin P.	Hinds L.	Hart M.	Morrison S.	Foster R.	Diamond A.	Soutar K.
Aug 3	A	Hibernian	13,340	2-1	1	2	3	4	5	6	7	8	9	10	11^{1}	12	13^{1}	14																	
10	H	Celtic	17,314	0-4	1	2	3	4	5	6	7	8			11	9	10	13	12																
18	H	Hearts	12,825	1-1	1	2	3	4	12	6	7	5		10	11	14	9	13	8^{1}																
25	A	Rangers	49,219	0-2	1	2	3	4	5	6		7		10	11	12	13	8	9																
Sep 1	H	Partick Thistle	12,591	0-1	1	2		4	5	6		3	9			8	11		7	10	12	13													
11	H	Dundee United	10,724	1-2	1	2	3	4	5	6		7	13	10	11^{1}	9	14				12		8												
14	A	Kilmarnock	6,538	2-2		2	3	4	5	12^{1}	7	6	13		11				9^{1}	10	14		8	1											
22	A	Livingston	5,852	2-1	1	2	3^{1}	4^{1}	5	6		7		10	11	9				13	12	14	8												
28	H	Dunfermline Athletic	11,678	3-1	1	2		4	5	6	7	3		10^{1}	11	12			9^{1}	14			8^{1}		13										
Oct 5	A	Motherwell	6,014	2-1	1	2		4	5	6	8	7^{1}		10^{1}	11	9				13	12		14		3										
19	H	Dundee	14,003	0-0	1	2		4	5	6	8	7		10		11	13			9	12				3										
27	H	Hibernian	12,321	0-1	1	2		4	5	6	8	7		10		11				9	12		13		3										
Nov 3	A	Celtic	57,797	0-7		2		4	5	6	8	7		10		13		12		9	11		14	1	3										
9	A	Hearts	11,920	0-0	1	2			5	6	8	4	12			10		7		9	11				3										
16	H	Rangers	14,915	2-2		2		4	5	6	8	7		10	11^{1}	9^{1}		12			13			1	3										
23	A	Partick Thistle	6,182	1-2	1	2				6		4	13	10	11	9^{1}		5		8	12		7		3										
30	A	Dundee United	8,261	1-1		2^{1}		4		6		5		10	11	14		7	8		9		13	1	3	12									
Dec 3	H	Kilmarnock	8,816	0-1		2		4	5	6		7			11	12		8	10		9		14	1	3	13									
7	H	Motherwell	9,569	1-1		2	12	4	5	6		7		10^{1}	11	13		8	9					1	3										
15	A	Dunfermline Athletic	4,835	0-3		2	3	4	5	6		7		10	11	12	13	8	9		14			1											
21	H	Livingston	11,253	0-0		2	8	4	5	6		7		10	13		11	14	9		12			1	3										
26	A	Dundee	8,574	†2-1		2^{1}	8	4	5			7		10		14	11	6	9		12			1	3										
29	A	Hibernian	11,604	0-2		2	8	4	5			7		10	13		11	6	9		12			1	3										
Jan 2	H	Celtic	16,331	1-1		2	6	4^{1}	5			7		10	11		8		9		13			1	3		12								
28	H	Hearts	9,322	0-1		2		4	5					13	11	9	8				12			1	3		6	7	10						
Feb 1	A	Rangers	49,667	1-2		2	6	4	5					13	11	9	8							1	3			7^{1}	10	12					
8	H	Partick Thistle	11,332	0-1		2	6	4	5					14	11	9	8					12		1	3			7	10	13					
16	H	Dundee United	9,146	3-0		2^{1}		4				3		13	14		8		11	12		5		1			6	7	10^{2}	9					
Mar 1	A	Kilmarnock	5,769	0-2	1			4	5			2		10	13		8		9	6					12			7	11		3				
8	A	Motherwell	5,636	1-0	1	2		4	5	6				10	13		8		9									7	11^{1}	12	3				
15	H	Dundee	12,119	3-3	1	2^{1}			5	6				10		12	8								3		13	7	11^{2}	9	4				
Apr 5	A	Livingston	4,994	2-1	1	2	13	4		6		3		10^{1}		12	8											7	11^{1}	9	5				
12	H	Dunfermline Athletic	10,030	1-0	1	2	12	4				3		10			8	6									13	7	11^{1}	9	5				
26	H	Livingston	8,912	1-0	1	2	14	4				3		10			8	6	12		13							7	11	9^{1}	5				
May 3	A	Hibernian	7,904	1-3	1	2	5	4				3			12		8	6^{1}			10						13	7	11	9					
10	H	Partick Thistle	9,960	2-1	1	2^{1}	5	4				3			10			6									12	7	11	9^{1}		8	13		
17	A	Motherwell	4,731	3-2	1		5		12			3^{1}			10		8	6				13					2	7	11^{1}	9^{1}	4				
24	A	Dundee United	8,516	2-0	1	2	3								10^{1}		8	6										7^{1}	11	9	4	5	13	12	14
TOTAL FULL APPEARANCES					23	36	18	33	27	23	11	32	2	25	22	13	20	15	16	8	5	1	5	15	18		3	14	14	9	8	2			
TOTAL SUB APPEARANCES							4		2	1			4	4	6	12	5	6	2	4	16	4	5		2	2	5			3			2	1	1
TOTAL GOALS SCORED						5	1	2		1		2		4	4	2	1	1	3				1					2	8	3					

Small bold figures denote goalscorers. † denotes opponent's own goal.

pittodrie stadium

PITTODRIE STREET

MAIN STAND

MERKLAND STAND

RICHARD DONALD STAND

GOLF ROAD

SOUTH STAND

CAPACITY: 21,662 (All Seated)

PITCH DIMENSIONS: 110 yds x 72 yds

FACILITIES FOR DISABLED SUPPORTERS:
There are 26 wheelchair spaces in front of the Merkland Stand and in the front row of the Richard Donald Stand. It is essential to book in advance. Please telephone (01244) 650444.

team playing kits

how to get there

You can reach Pittodrie Stadium by these routes:

BUSES: The following buses all depart from the city centre to within a hundred yards of the ground: Nos. 1, 2, and 11.

TRAINS: The main Aberdeen station is in the centre of the city and the above buses will then take fans to the ground.

CARS: Motor vehicles coming from the city centre should travel along Union Street, then turn into King Street and the park will be on your right, about half a mile further on.

Parking on Beach Boulevard and Beach Esplanade.

celtic

Celtic Park, 95 Kerrydale Street, Glasgow, G40 3RE

CHAIRMAN
Brian Quinn, C.B.E.

CELTIC PLC DIRECTORS
Brian Quinn, C.B.E., Dermot F. Desmond, Eric J. Riley, Kevin Sweeney, Tom Allison & Eric Hagman, C.B.E.

CELTIC F.C. DIRECTORS
John S. Keane, Michael A. McDonald & James P. Hone

COMPANY SECRETARY
Robert M. Howat

FOOTBALL MANAGER
Martin O'Neill

FOOTBALL ASSISTANT MANAGER
John Robertson

FIRST TEAM COACH
Steve Walford

UNDER 21 COACH
Kenny McDowall

DIRECTOR OF YOUTH DEVELOPMENT
Tommy Burns

YOUTH DEVELOPMENT MANAGER
John Stephenson

HEAD YOUTH COACH
Willie McStay

CLUB DOCTOR
Roddy McDonald

PHYSIOTHERAPIST
Tim Wilkinson

FOOTBALL SAFETY OFFICERS' ASSOCIATION REPRESENTATIVE
Ronnie Hawthorn (0141) 551 4256

COMMERCIAL MANAGER
David McNally (0141) 551 4246

LOTTERY MANAGER
John Maguire (0141) 551 4006

GROUNDSMAN
John Hayes

KIT CONTROLLER
John Clark

PUBLIC RELATIONS MANAGER
Iain Jamieson (0141) 551 4235

CORPORATE SERVICES MANAGER
Frank McNally (0141) 551 4278

MATCHDAY PROGRAMME EDITOR
Paul Cuddihy

TELEPHONES
Ground (0141) 556 2611
Ticket Hotline (0141) 551 8653/4
Celtic Hotline (09066) 555562
Celtic View (0141) 551 4218
Stadium (Matchday) Catering (0141) 551 2931
Mail Order Hotline (0141) 550 1888
Museum (0141) 551 4308
Ticket Hotline Fax (0141) 551 4223
Fax (0141) 551 8106

CELTIC INTERNET ADDRESS
www.celticfc.net

CLUB SHOPS
Superstore, Celtic Park, Glasgow, G40 3RE
Tel (0141) 551 4231
(9.00 a.m. to 6.00 p.m. Mon-Sat, 10.00a.m. to 5.00p.m. Sunday)
40 Dundas Street, Glasgow G1 2AQ
Tel (0141) 332 2727
(9.00 a.m. to 5.00 p.m. Mon-Sat) and
21 High Street, Glasgow, G1 1LX
Tel (0141) 552 7630
(9.30 a.m. to 5.30 p.m. Mon-Sat, 11.30 a.m. to 4.30 p.m. Sunday)

OFFICIAL SUPPORTERS CLUB
Celtic Supporters Association, 1524 London Road, Glasgow G40 3RJ
Tel (0141) 556 1882/554 6250/554 6342

TEAM CAPTAIN
Paul Lambert

SHIRT SPONSOR
Carling

KIT SUPPLIER
Umbro

LIST OF PLAYERS 2003/04

SQUAD NO.	SURNAME	FIRST NAME	MIDDLE NAME	DATE OF BIRTH	PLACE OF BIRTH	DATE OF SIGNING	HEIGHT FT INS	WEIGHT ST LBS	POS. ON PITCH	PREVIOUS CLUB
17	Agathe	Didier		16/08/75	St. Pierre La Reunion	01/09/00	5 11	12st 0lb	Fwd	Hibernian
6	Balde	Dianbobo		05/10/75	Marseille	25/07/01	6 3	13st 6lb	Def	Toulouse
37	Beattie	Craig		16/01/84	Glasgow	04/07/03	6 1	11st 10lb	Fwd	Celtic Youths
40	Crainey	Stephen	Danial	22/06/81	Glasgow	03/07/97	5 9	9st 11lb	Def	Celtic B.C.
20	Douglas	Robert	James	24/04/72	Lanark	18/10/00	6 3	14st 12lb	Gk	Dundee
2	Gray	Michael		03/08/74	Sunderland	31/08/03	5 7	10st 7lb	Def	Sunderland
30	Guppy	Steve		29/03/69	Winchester	02/08/01	5 11	12st 0lb	Fwd	Leicester City
10	Hartson	John		05/04/75	Swansea	02/08/01	6 1	14st 6lb	Fwd	Coventry City
21	Hedman	Magnus	Carl	19/03/73	Stockholm	01/08/02	6 4	14st 10lb	Gk	Coventry City
–	Jack	Steven		09/08/83	Bellshill	20/08/99	5 9	11st 2lb	Def	Celtic 'S' Form
31	Kennedy	John		18/08/83	Bellshill	20/08/99	6 1	12st 6lb	Def	Celtic 'S' Form
14	Lambert	Paul		07/08/69	Paisley	07/11/97	5 11	11st 6lb	Mid	BV09 Borussia Dortmund
7	Larsson	Henrik		20/09/71	Helsingborg	29/07/97	5 10	11st 11lb	Fwd	Feyenoord
16	Laursen	Ulrik	Rosenloev	28/02/76	Odense	01/08/02	6 3	13st 0lb	Def	Hibernian
18	Lennon	Neil		25/06/71	Lurgan	08/12/00	5 9	13st 2lb	Mid	Leicester City
29	Maloney	Shaun	Richard	24/01/83	Malaya	07/07/99	5 6	10st 12lb	Fwd	Celtic Youth Initiative
22	Marshall	David	James	05/03/85	Glasgow	06/07/01	6 2	14st 3lb	Gk	Celtic Youths
–	McBride	Kevin		14/06/81	Bellshill	10/07/98	5 6	9st 3lb	Mid	Celtic B.C.
–	McManus	Stephen		10/09/82	Lanark	09/07/03	6 0	9st 6lb	Mid	Celtic 'S' Form
4	McNamara	Jackie		24/10/73	Glasgow	04/10/95	5 8	9st 7lb	Mid	Dunfermline Athletic
25	McParland	Anthony	Patrick	20/09/82	Rutherglen	20/07/99	5 7	10st 4lb	Mid	Celtic 'S' Form
43	Miller	Liam	William Peter	13/02/81	Cork	20/05/02	5 9	11st 2lb	Mid	Ballincollig AFC
35	Mjallby	Johan		09/02/71	Sweden	19/11/98	6 1	13st 4lb	Def	AIK Stockholm
19	Petrov	Stilian		05/07/79	Bulgaria	06/08/99	5 9	12st 1lb	Mid	CSKA Sofia
15	Petta	Bobby	Alfred Manuel	06/08/74	Rotterdam	14/07/99	5 7	11st 3lb	Mid	Ipswich Town
32	Prunty	Bryan		12/01/83	Coatbridge	15/01/99	5 8	10st 7lb	Fwd	Celtic B.C.
39	Smith	James		20/11/80	Alexandria	28/12/96	5 6.5	11st 0lb	Mid/Fwd	Celtic B.C.
9	Sutton	Christopher	Roy	10/03/73	Nottingham	11/07/00	6 3	13st 8lb	Fwd	Chelsea
3	Sylla	Mohammed		13/03/77	Conakry	02/08/01	6 0	11st 9lb	Mid	St. Johnstone
8	Thompson	Alan		22/12/73	Newcastle	01/09/00	6 0	12st 8lb	Mid	Aston Villa
5	Valgaeren	Joos		03/03/76	Louvain	28/07/00	6 1	14st 2lb	Def	Roda J.C.
23	Varga	Stanislav		08/10/72	Slovakia	16/07/03	6 2	13st 2lb	Def	Sunderland
33	Wallace	Ross		23/05/85	Dundee	13/07/01	5 8	10st 2lb	Fwd	Celtic 'S' Form

milestones

YEAR OF FORMATION: 1888
MOST CAPPED PLAYER: Paul McStay
NO. OF CAPS: 76
MOST LEAGUE POINTS IN A SEASON: 72 (Premier Division – Season 1987/88) (2 Points for a Win)
103 (SPL – Season 2001/02) (3 Points for a Win)
MOST LEAGUE GOALS SCORED BY A PLAYER IN A SEASON: Jimmy McGrory (Season 1935/36)
NO. OF GOALS SCORED: 50
RECORD ATTENDANCE: 92,000 (-v- Rangers – 1.1.1938)
RECORD VICTORY: 11-0 (-v- Dundee – Division 1, 26.10.1895)
RECORD DEFEAT: 0-8 (-v- Motherwell - Division 1, 30.4.1937)

ticket information

SEASON TICKET INFORMATION

SOUTH STAND REAR	ADULT 510 CONC 295
SOUTH STAND FRONT	ADULT 455
WEST CORNER STAND	JUV 190 PAR&JUV 475
NORTH STAND UPPER	ADULT 490/415/380
NORTH STAND LOWER	ADULT 510/465/415/380 CONC 295/260/190
JOCK STEIN STAND UPPER	ADULT 490/415/380
JOCK STEIN STAND LOWER	ADULT 605/415/380
EAST STAND UPPER	ADULT 490/415/420/350/380
EAST STAND LOWER	ADULT 490/415/380 PAR&JUV 400 ADULT 390 JUV 145

LEAGUE ADMISSION PRICES

SOUTH STAND REAR	ADULT 24 CONC 14
SOUTH STAND FRONT	ADULT 24
WEST CORNER STAND	JUV 14 PAR&JUV 38
NORTH STAND UPPER	ADULT 24 RESTRICTED VIEW 21
NORTH STAND LOWER	ADULT 24 CONC 14
JOCK STEIN STAND UPPER	ADULT 24
JOCK STEIN STAND LOWER	ADULT 24
EAST STAND UPPER	ADULT 24
EAST STAND LOWER	ADULT 24 PAR&JUV 38 JUV 14

leading goalscorers 1993-2003

Season	Div	No. of Goals	Player
1993-94	P	10	P. McGinlay
1994-95	P	8	J. Collins
1995-96	P	26	P. Van Hooijdonk
1996-97	P	25	J. Cadete
1997-98	P	16	H. Larsson
1998-99	P	29	H. Larsson
1999-2000	P	25	M. Viduka
2000-01	P	35	H. Larsson
2001-02	P	29	H. Larsson
2002-03	P	28	H. Larsson

the bhoys' club factfile 2002/03

Date	Venue	Opponents	Att.	Res	Douglas R.	Mjallby J.	Valgaeren J.	Balde D.	Lennon N.	Petrov S.	Sylla M.	Lambert P.	Petta B.	Larsson H.	Sutton C.	Fernandez D.	Crainey S.	Maloney S.	Hedman M.	Laursen U.	McNamara J.	Guppy S.	Hartson J.	Agathe D.	Thompson A.	Gould J.	Lynch S.	Smith J.	Healy C.	Broto J.	Varga S.
Aug 3	H	Dunfermline Athletic	56,438	2-1	1	2	3	4	5	6	7	8	9	10[2]	11	12	13														
10	A	Aberdeen	17,314	4-0	1	2[1]	3	4	5	6	7[1]	8[1]	9	10	11[1]	12	14	13													
17	H	Dundee United	56,247	5-0		2	3		8	6[1]	7			10[1]	11[1]	13	14		1	4	5[1]	9	12[1]								
24	A	Partick Thistle	8,053	1-0	1		3	4	6			8		10[1]	11		13			2	5	9	12	7							
Sep 1	H	Livingston	55,334	2-0			3	4[1]		6				10[1]	11	9		13	1	2	5	8	12	7	14						
10	A	Motherwell	8,448	1-2	1		3	4		6		8		10	11			13		2		9	12[1]	7	5						
14	H	Hibernian	56,462	1-0			3	4	8		7			10				12		2	6	9	11[1]		5	1					
22	A	Dundee	9,483	1-0	1		3	4	5	6	7	8		10[1]	11		13			2		9	12								
28	H	Kilmarnock	57,070	5-0	1		3	4	5	6	7	8		10[3]	11[2]			14		2		9	12	13							
Oct 6	H	Rangers	58,939	3-3	1		3	4	9	6	7	8		10[2]	11[1]			14		2			13	12	5						
20	A	Hearts	13,911	4-1	1		3	4	5	6[1]		8		10[2]	11[1]		13			2		9	14	7	12						
27	A	Dunfermline Athletic	9,139	4-1			3	4	9	6[1]	13	8		10[1]	11[1]			14		2			12	7	5[1]	1					
Nov 3	H	Aberdeen	57,797	7-0	1		3	4[1]		6	7			10[1]	8	12	13	14[1]		2		9	11[4]		5						
10	A	Dundee United	10,664	2-0	1		3	4	6		7	13		10	8[1]					2		9	11[1]	12	5						
17	H	Partick Thistle	57,231	4-0	1		3	4	9	6[2]		8		10[1]	11[1]	12	14	13			5			7	2						
24	A	Livingston	8,320	2-0	1		3	4	9	6	7	8		10[2]	11					2	12				5						
Dec 1	H	Motherwell	56,610	†3-1	1		3[1]	4			13	8		10[1]		9	2	12			14	6	11	7	5						
4	A	Hibernian	12,042	1-0	1		3	4	9	6[1]	7	8				10		13		2	14	12	11		5						
7	A	Rangers	49,874	2-3	1		3	4	5	6				10	9[1]					2		8	11[1]	7	12						
15	A	Kilmarnock	9,225	1-1	1		3[1]	4		6		8		10	9						5	12	11	7	2						
21	H	Dundee	56,162	2-0	1		3	4		6		8		10[1]	9					2			11[1]	7	5		12				
26	H	Hearts	58,480	4-2			3	4		6		8		10[1]	9				1	2			11[3]	7	5						
29	H	Dunfermline Athletic	58,387	1-0		2	3	4		6		8		10[1]	9				1		13	12	11	7	5						
Jan 2	A	Aberdeen	16,331	1-1		2	3	4		6		8		10[1]	9	12		14	1		7		11		5			13			
29	H	Dundee United	54,912	2-0		2	3	4		6		8		10[1]	9		13		1		12		11[1]	7				5			
Feb 2	A	Partick Thistle	7,119	2-0			3	4	8	6				10	11[2]				1	2	7			9				5	12		
9	H	Livingston	56,982	2-1			3	4	8	6	7[1]			10	11[1]			12	1	2	9							5			
Mar 2	H	Hibernian	57,096	3-2		2[1]	3		7	6	13	8					4	10				12	11[2]	9	5					†	
8	H	Rangers	58,336	1-0	1	2	3	4	6	7	12	8			10						13		11[1]	9	5						
Apr 6	A	Dundee	9,013	1-1		2		4	6	7	9	8		10			3						11		5[1]			12		1	
13	H	Kilmarnock	56,736	2-0	1	2	3	4	6	7[1]		8		10[1]				13					11	9	5			12			
19	A	Hearts	15,855	1-2	1	2	3	4	6	7		8		10[1]				12					11	9	5			13			
27	A	Rangers	49,740	2-1	1		3	4	6	13				10	9					2	7		11[1]	8	5[1]					15	
May 3	A	Dunfermline Athletic	8,923	4-1			3	4	8	7[2]		12		10[1]		13		11		2	6			9	5[1]			14		1	
7	A	Motherwell	12,037	4-0				4	6	7[2]	13	8[2]		10			14	11		2	3			9	5			12		1	
10	H	Hearts	58,906	1-0		2	3	4	6	7		8		10	11						13			9	5[1]			12		1	
14	H	Dundee	59,500	6-2		2[1]	3	4	6	7		8		10[1]				11[2]						9	5[2]			12		1	
25	A	Kilmarnock	16,722	4-0		2		4	6	7[1]		12		10	11[2]			9						8	5[1]			13		1	3
TOTAL FULL APPEARANCES					21	14	35	36	28	33	13	27	2	35	28	3	3	5	8	22	12	12	18	24	26	2		3		7	1
TOTAL SUB APPEARANCES										1	5	3				7	10	15			7	4	9	3	3		1	9	1	1	
TOTAL GOALS SCORED						3	2	2		12	2	3		28	15			3			1		18		8						

Small bold figures denote goalscorers. † denotes opponent's own goal.

celtic park

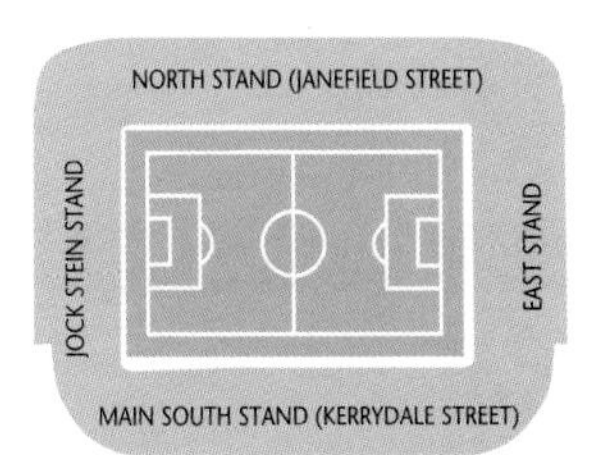

CAPACITY: 60,355 (All Seated)

PITCH DIMENSIONS: 115 yds x 74 yds

FACILITIES FOR DISABLED SUPPORTERS:
There is provision for 142 wheelchair positions for disabled supporters and their helpers. These are split into 87 in the North Stand, at the front of the lower terracing, 10 in the East Stand, lower terracing and 37 in the South Stand, lower terracing. Celtic fans should contact the club for availability. There is also a provision for 6 away positions in the lower East Stand.

team playing kits

how to get there

The following routes may be used to reach Celtic Park:

BUSES: The following buses all leave from the city centre and pass within 50 yards of the ground. Nos. 43, 62, and 64.

TRAINS: There is a frequent train service from Glasgow Central Low Level station to Bridgeton Cross Station and this is only a ten minute walk from the ground. There is also a train from Queen Street Station (lower level) to Bellgrove Rail Station, approximately 20 minutes walk from the ground.

CARS: From the city centre, motor vehicles should travel along London Road and this will take you to the ground. Parking spaces are available in various areas close to the ground. On matchdays all car parking is strictly limited and is only available to those in possession of a valid car park pass.

dundee

Dens Park Stadium,
Sandeman Street, Dundee, DD3 7JY

CHAIRMAN
James M. Marr

DIRECTORS
James H. C. Connor, Peter Marr
& Giovanni Di Stefano

OFFICE ADMINISTRATOR
Laura Hayes

ASSOCIATE DIRECTORS
Dave Forbes, Bob Hynd & James L. Thomson

CHIEF EXECUTIVE
Peter Marr

COMPANY SECRETARY
A. Ritchie Robertson

OFFICE ADMINISTRATOR
Laura Hayes

MANAGER
Jim Duffy

UNDER 21 COACH
Ray Farningham

GOALKEEPING COACH
Paul Mathers

YOUTH CO/ORDINATOR
Kenny Cameron

COMMUNITY COACH
Kevin Lee

YOUTH DEVELOPMENT COACH
Stevie Campbell

CLUB DOCTORS
Dr. Phyllis Windsor, M.D., FRCR. &
Dr. John Vernon

PHYSIOTHERAPIST
Jim Law

MASSEUR
Jack Cashley

FOOTBALL SAFETY OFFICERS' ASSOCIATION REPRESENTATIVE
John Malone

OPERATIONS MANAGER
Jim Thomson (01382) 815250

TICKET OFFICE MANAGER
Neil Cosgrove

GROUNDSMAN
Brian Robertson

KIT MANAGER
Brian Duncan

COMMERCIAL DIRECTOR
Jim Connor Tel (01382) 884450
Fax (01382) 858963

COMMERCIAL MANAGER
Tommy Dickson (01382) 884450

COMMERCIAL SECRETARY
Kirsty Cameron

FINANCIAL MANAGER
Ian W. Coyle

MEDIA LIAISON OFFICER
Niall Scott

MATCHDAY PROGRAMME EDITOR
Peter Rundo

TELEPHONES
Football/Manager (01382) 826104
Administration/Accounts/
Youth Development (01382) 889966
Commercial/ Marketing
(01382) 884450
Ticket Office (01382) 889966
Operations Manager (01382) 815250
Fax (01382) 832284
Commercial Fax (01382) 858963

E-MAIL & INTERNET ADDRESS
laura@dundeefc.co.uk
www.dundeefc.co.uk

CLUB SHOP
DFC XARA Shop, situated between
Main Stand and Bobby Cox Stand

OFFICIAL SUPPORTERS CLUB
Contact: Norrie Price (01224) 639967

TEAM CAPTAIN
Barry Smith

SHIRT SPONSOR
Magners Original

KIT SUPPLIER
XARA

LIST OF PLAYERS 2003/04

SQUAD NO.	SURNAME	FIRST NAME	MIDDLE NAME	DATE OF BIRTH	PLACE OF BIRTH	DATE OF SIGNING	HEIGHT FT INS	WEIGHT ST LBS	POS. ON PITCH	PREVIOUS CLUB
–	Allison	Mark		22/02/87	Perth	29/08/03	6 0	11st 13lb	Def	Dundee Youths
14	Beith	Gavin		07/10/81	Dundee	25/05/99	5 10	9st 2lb	Mid	Dundee 'S' Form
–	Blackwood	John		13/08/85	Dundee	31/08/01	5 9	11st 3lb	Def	Dundee 'S' Form
–	Boylan	Colin	Hugh	19/07/83	Glasgow	25/08/99	5 4	10st 8lb	Fwd	Dundee 'S' Form
–	Bradley	John		15/09/84	Paisley	01/06/01	5 6	9st 11lb	Mid	Dundee 'S' Form
26	Brady	Garry		07/09/76	Glasgow	30/08/02	5 8	10st 10lb	Mid	Portsmouth
28	Brash	Kristofer		01/03/83	Dundee	08/09/00	5 8	10st 7lb	Mid	Dundee 'S' Form
32	Burley	Craig		24/09/71	Ayr	12/09/03	5 11.5	13st 1lb	Mid	Derby County
7	Caballero	Fabian	Orlando	31/01/78	Missions	31/07/01	5 10	13st 7lb	Fwd	Sol Del America
–	Cameron	Douglas		08/02/83	Dundee	08/09/00	5 10	12st 0lb	Mid	Dundee 'S' Form
5	Carranza	Luis Alberto (Beto)		15/06/72	Quilmes	10/09/00	5 8	10st 4lb	Mid	Universitario De Deportes
–	Clark	Neil		12/04/84	Dundee	13/07/02	5 11	11st 10lb	Mid	Dundee 'S' Form
–	Cook	Steven	Derek	13/06/85	Dundee	13/07/02	5 9	10st 1lb	Def	Dundee 'S' Form
23	Cowan	Thomas		28/08/70	Bellshill	07/08/03	5 8	10st 8lb	Def	York City
–	Cumming	Kevin	Neil	04/04/86	Dundee	20/01/03	6 0.5	11st 8lb	Fwd	Dundee Youths
–	Dixon	Paul	Andrew	22/11/86	Aberdeen	10/07/03	5 9	11st 3lb	Def	Dundee Youths
–	Engele	Matthew	William	22/04/84	Australia	20/01/03	6 0.5	11st 7lb	Fwd	Northern Spirit
20	Forbes	Barry		08/09/81	Dundee	25/05/99	6 0	11st 5lb	Mid	Dundee 'S' Form
30	Fotheringham	Mark	McKay	22/10/83	Dundee	28/08/03	5 11	12st 10lb	Mid	Celtic
–	Hay	Graham		11/06/87	Dundee	10/07/03	6 0	11st 12lb	Def	Dundee 'S' Form
–	Hegarty	Christopher		24/07/84	Dundee	05/10/01	5 8	10st 6lb	Mid	Dundee Youths
–	Hendry	Robert	David	19/01/87	Dundee	10/07/03	5 9	11st 2lb	Mid	Dundee Youths
16	Hernandez Santos	Jonay	Miguel	15/02/79	Venezuela	26/07/02	5 11	12st 1lb	Def/Mid	Real Madrid
4	Hutchinson	Thomas	Peter	23/02/82	Kingston	30/08/02	6 0	12st 6lb	Def	Fulham
24	Jablonski	Neil		09/03/83	Kirkcaldy	08/09/00	5 9	11st 0lb	Mid	Dundee 'S' Form
–	Jellye	Paul		27/03/86	Perth	13/07/02	5 8	10st 1lb	Def	Dundee Youths
12	Langfield	James		22/12/79	Paisley	26/12/96	6 4	13st 0lb	Gk	Dundee Youths
–	Linn	Robert		10/10/85	Dundee	01/02/02	5 7	9st 8lb	Fwd	Dundee 'S' Form
25	Lovell	Steve		06/12/80	Amersham	23/08/02	6 0	12st 11lb	Fwd	Portsmouth
27	Macdonald	Callum		31/05/83	Perth	08/09/00	6 1	11st 7lb	Def	Dundee 'S' Form
3	Mackay	David		02/05/81	Rutherglen	28/08/99	5 5	11st 0lb	Def	Banbury Thistle
19	Mair	Lee		09/12/80	Aberdeen	07/06/99	6 0	11st 3lb	Def	Formartine United A
–	McCafferty	John		21/03/85	Dundee	13/07/02	5 10	13st 1lb	Gk	Dundee Youths
–	McDonald	Andrew	James	06/02/87	Dundee	10/07/03	5 8	9st 4lb	Mid	Dundee Youths
–	McLaughlin	Garry		08/02/86	Dundee	13/07/02	5 6	9st 1lb	Mid	Dundee Youths
–	McLean	Duncan		07/08/83	Dundee	08/09/00	5 10	10st 8lb	Fwd	Dundee 'S' Form
–	McNally	Stephen		15/03/84	Dundee	29/03/02	5 8.5	11st 10lb	Def	Downfield Juniors
15	Milne	Steven		05/05/80	Dundee	16/10/97	5 7	10st 0lb	Fwd	Downfield Juniors
–	Muckersie	Garry		09/03/87	Dundee	29/08/03	5 6	10st 2lb	Fwd	Dundee Youths
10	Nemsadze	George		10/05/72	Tblisi	19/07/00	5 11	12st 11lb	Mid	Locomotiv Tblisi
17	Novo	Ignacio	Javier Gomez	26/03/79	Ferrol	09/07/02	5 7.5	11st 7lb	Fwd	Raith Rovers
8	Rae	Gavin		28/11/77	Aberdeen	19/09/95	5 11	11st 4lb	Mid	Hermes Juniors
11	Ravanelli	Fabrizio		12/11/68	Perugia	22/09/03	6 2	13st 4lb	Fwd	Derby County
	Reilly	Andrew		25/05/86	Dundee	13/07/02	5 7	10st 8lb	Mid	Dundee 'S' Form
21	Robb	Steven		08/03/82	Perth	25/08/99	5 6	9st 4lb	Mid	Dundee 'S' Form
–	Robertson	Euan		25/01/87	Dundee	31/01/03	5 10	11st 7lb	Mid	Dundee 'S' Form
11	Robertson	Mark	William	06/04/77	Sydney	02/03/01	5 9	12st 2lb	Mid	Burnley
–	Robertson	Scott		07/04/85	Dundee	13/07/02	6 0	11st 4lb	Mid	Dundee 'S' Form
18	Sancho	Brent		13/03/77	Trinidad & Tobago	31/07/03	5 11	12st 2lb	Def	Portland Timbers
9	Sara	Juan	Manuel	13/10/76	Argentina	24/07/01	6 2	12st 7lb	Fwd	Cerra Portina
2	Smith	Barry	Martin	19/02/74	Paisley	08/12/95	5 10	12st 0lb	Def	Celtic
22	Soutar	Derek	Robert James	04/06/81	Dundee	25/05/99	6 1.5	12st 0lb	Gk	Dundee 'S' Form
1	Speroni	Julian		18/05/79	Buenos Aires	16/07/02	6 1	14st 3lb	Gk	Athletico Platense
–	Stewart	Steven		04/12/84	Dundee	17/10/01	5 9	11st 0lb	Mid	Dundee 'S' Form
–	Voigt	Jon	Werner	06/10/86	Arbroath	20/01/03	5 11	10st 10lb	Fwd	Aberdeen
–	Walker	Jason		21/03/84	Barrow-in-Furness	08/09/00	5 8.5	11st 3lb	Fwd	Dundee Youths
6	Wilkie	Lee		20/04/80	Dundee	08/09/98	6 4	13st 0lb	Def	Dundee Youths
–	Youngson	Allan		29/09/84	Aberdeen	31/08/01	5 10	11st 1lb	Def	Dundee Youths

milestones

YEAR OF FORMATION: 1893
MOST CAPPED PLAYER: Alex Hamilton
NO. OF CAPS: 24
MOST LEAGUE POINTS IN A SEASON: 58 (First Division – Season 1991/92) (2 Points for a Win)
70 (First Division – Season 1997/98) (3 Points for a Win)
MOST LEAGUE GOALS SCORED BY A PLAYER IN A SEASON: Alan Gilzean (Season 1963/64)
NO. OF GOALS SCORED: 32
RECORD ATTENDANCE: 43,024 (-v- Rangers – 1953)
RECORD VICTORY: 10-0 (-v- Fraserburgh, 1931; -v- Alloa, 1947; -v- Dunfermline Athletic, 1947; -v- Queen of the South, 1962)
RECORD DEFEAT: 0-11 (-v- Celtic – Division 1, 26.10.1895)

ticket information

SEASON TICKET INFORMATION		SEASON	GATE PRICES CAT A	CAT B
CENTRE STAND	ADULT	280	20	17
	JUV/SEN (Over 60)	130	12	10
BOBBY COX FAMILY STAND	ADULT	190	14	12
	SENIOR (Over 60)	110	10	8
	U18	70	10	8
	U12	50	8	4
WING STAND FAMILY SECTION	ADULT	190	14	12
	SENIOR (Over 60)	110	10	8
	U18	70	10	8
	U12	50	8	4
SOUTH ENCLOSURE	ADULT	210	16	14

leading goalscorers 1993-2003

Season	Div	No. of Goals	Player
1993-94	P	6	D. Ristic
1994-95	F	16	G. Shaw
1995-96	F	14	J. Hamilton
1996-97	F	10	J. O'Driscoll
1997-98	F	15	J. Grady
1998-99	P	9	E. Annand
1999-00	P	13	W. Falconer
2000-01	P	14	J. Sara
2001-02	P	11	J. Sara
2002-03	P	13	S. Lovell

the dark blues' club factfile 2002/03

Date	Venue	Opponents	Att.	Res	Speroni J.	Mackay D.	Hernandez J.	Mair L.	Wilkie L.	Smith B.	Nemsadze G.	Rae G.	Novo I.	Caballero F.	Sara J.	Milne S.	Robb S.	Forbes B.	Beith G.	Jablonski N.	Lovell S.	Hutchinson T.	Brady G.	Khizanishvili Z.	Robertson M.	Burchill M.	Carranza B.
3 Aug	H	Hearts	7,705	1-1	1	2	3	4	5	6	7	8	9	10^{1}	11												
10	A	Rangers	46,774	0-3	1	2	3	4	5	6	7	8	9	13	11	10	12										
17	A	Dunfermline Athletic	5,852	2-4	1	2	3	4	5	6	7	8	9^{2}	10	11	13		12									
24	H	Hibernian	6,411	2-1	1	2	3		5	6	7	8		10^{1}	11	13		9	4	12	14^{1}						
31	A	Dundee United	12,402	0-0	1	2	3	13	5	6	7	8	9	10	12						11	4					
11 Sep	H	Livingston	5,391	2-1	1	2	3	13	5	6	7	8^{1}	9^{1}	10	12						11	4	14				
14	A	Partick Thistle	4,552	1-1	1	2	3		5	6		8^{1}	9	10	12						11	4	7				
22	H	Celtic	9,483	0-1	1	2	3		5	6	7	8	9	10	11						12	4					
28	A	Motherwell	4,025	1-1	1	2	3	7	5	6		8	12	10	11						9^{1}	4					
5 Oct	H	Kilmarnock	5,567	2-1	1	2	3		5	4	7	8^{1}	9	10^{1}	11	12	13						6				
19	A	Aberdeen	14,003	0-0	1	2	3		5	6	7	8	9	10	13	11						4		12			
26	A	Hearts	10,169	2-1	1	2	3		5	6		8	9	10							11^{2}	4	7				
2 Nov	H	Rangers	10,124	0-3	1	2	3	12	5	6	7	8	11	10	13								9	4	14		
12	H	Dunfermline Athletic	5,475	†2-3	1	2	3	12	5	6		8	9	10	13						11^{1}	4	7				
16	A	Hibernian	8,870	1-2	1	2	3			6	7	8	12^{1}	10	11		13				9	4		5			
23	H	Dundee United	11,593	3-2	1	2	3^{1}		5	6	7	8	9	10^{1}	13	14					11^{1}	4		12			
30	A	Livingston	4,151	1-1	1	2	3		5	6	7	8	9^{1}	10	12	14					11	4	13				
4 Dec	H	Partick Thistle	5,363	4-1	1	2	3	4	5	6		12	9	10	11^{1}	13		14			8^{2}		7^{1}				
7	A	Kilmarnock	4,806	0-2	1	2	3	4	5	6		8	9	10	12						11		7				
14	H	Motherwell	5,527	1-1	1	2	3	4	5	6		12	9	10	11^{1}	13	8						7				
21	A	Celtic	56,162	0-2	1	2	3	4	5	6		8	9	10		13	14				11		12	7			
26	H	Aberdeen	8,574	1-2	1		3	4	5	6		8	9	10		12^{1}	14				11		7	2	13		
29	H	Hearts	7,340	1-2	1	2		3		6		8	9	10		7^{1}	13				11		5	4	12		
2 Jan	A	Rangers	49,112	1-3	1	2	3	4		6		8	12	10		9					11^{1}		7	5	13		
28	A	Dunfermline Athletic	4,237	†1-0	1	2		4	5	6	7	8	13	10		11							9	3	12		
9 Feb	A	Dundee United	10,547	1-1	1	2		4	5	6	7	8	11^{1}	10							12		9	3		13	
25	H	Hibernian	8,414	†3-0	1	2		4	5	6	7	8^{1}	9	10		13^{1}					12		14	3		11	
1 Mar	A	Partick Thistle	4,599	3-1	1	2^{1}		4	5	6	7	8	13^{1}	12		9^{1}					11		14	3		10	
5	H	Livingston	7,554	0-0	1	2		3	5	6	7	8	9	10		14					11		12	4		13	
8	H	Kilmarnock	6,531	2-2	1	2	13	3	5^{1}		7	8	12	10		9^{1}					11		6	4			
15	A	Aberdeen	12,119	3-3	1	2		3	5^{1}	6		8	12	10^{1}		9	13				11^{1}		7	4			
6 Apr	H	Celtic	9,013	1-1	1	2	4	3	5	6	7	8	12	10		13					11		14			9^{1}	
12	A	Motherwell	4,693	2-1	1		4	3	5	6	7	8	12	10		11^{1}	13						2	14		9^{1}	
27	H	Kilmarnock	5,964	0-1	1	2	4	3	5	6		8	9	10		13					12		7			11	14
4 May	H	Rangers	9,204	2-2	1	2	3	14	5	6	7	8		10^{2}		12					11			4		13	9
10	H	Dunfermline Athletic	9,195	2-2	1	2	3	12	5	6	7		13			9					10^{2}		8	4		11	14
14	A	Celtic	59,500	2-6	1	2	3	7^{1}	5	6^{1}		8	9			10		12					14	4		11	13
25	A	Hearts	12,205	0-1	1		3	2	4	6	7	8	9	10						12	11		5			13	14
TOTAL FULL APPEARANCES					38	35	30	23	35	37	24	35	26	34	10	11	1	1	1		23	11	19	16		7	1
TOTAL SUB APPEARANCES							1	6				2	10	2	9	14	8	3		2	5		8	3	5	4	4
TOTAL GOALS SCORED						1	1	1	2	1		4	7	7	2	7					12		1			2	

Small bold figures denote goalscorers. † denotes opponent's own goal.

dens park stadium

SANDEMAN STREET
TANNADICE STREET
MAIN STAND
BOBBY COX STAND
BOB SHANKLY STAND
PROVOST ROAD
SOUTH ENCLOSURE
DENS ROAD

CAPACITY: 11,506 (All Seated)

PITCH DIMENSIONS: 113 yds x 74 yds

FACILITIES FOR DISABLED SUPPORTERS:
There is provision for disabled supporters in both the East and West Stands.

team playing kits

how to get there

The following routes may be used to reach Dens Park:

BUSES: There is a frequent service of buses from the city centre. Nos. 1A and 1B leave from Albert Square and Nos. 18, 19 and 21 leave from Commercial Street.

TRAINS: Trains from all over the country pass through the mainline Dundee station and fans can then proceed to the ground by the above buses from stops situated close to the station.

CARS: Cars may be parked in the car park (Densfield Park) and local streets adjacent to the ground.

dundee united

Tannadice Park, Tannadice Street, Dundee, DD3 7JW

CHAIRMAN
Eddie H. Thompson
DIRECTORS
Gilbert S. Haggart, J.D. Scott Carnegie, John M. Bennett, Derek W. Robertson, Stephen E. Thompson & Lord Watson of Invergowrie
SECRETARY
Spence Anderson
MANAGER
Ian McCall
ASSISTANT MANAGER
Gordon Chisholm
PLAYER/COACH & U21 COACH
Owen Coyle
RESERVE COACH
Tony Docherty
GOALKEEPING COACH
Bobby Geddes
DIRECTORS OF YOUTH DEVELOPMENT
Tony Docherty & Graeme Liveston
YOUTH CO/ORDINATOR
Graeme Liveston
COMMUNITY COACH & SCHOOLS DEVELOPMENT COACH
Gavin Levey
YOUTH TEAM COACHES
U19/Tony Docherty
U17/Graeme Liveston
U16/David Bowman
U15/Mark Reilly
U14/Willie Pettigrew
U13/Dougie Robertson
CLUB DOCTOR
Dr. Derek J. McCormack
CHIEF SCOUT
Graeme Liveston
GROUNDSMAN
Albert Dawson
FOOTBALL SAFETY OFFICERS' ASSOCIATION REPRESENTATIVE/ OPERATIONS MANAGER
David Anderson (01382) 833166
STADIUM MANAGER
Ron West
GENERAL/COMMERCIAL MANAGER
Bill Campbell (01382) 832202
LOTTERY MANAGER
Kate Hay (01382) 833166
SALES MANAGER
Ronnie Dare
COMMERCIAL ASSISTANTS
Paul Reid, Bill Guthrie & Gordon Grady
MATCHDAY PROGRAMME EDITOR
Peter Rundo
TELEPHONES
Ground/Ticket Office (01382) 833166
Commercial Dept (01382) 832202
Fax (01382) 889398
E-MAIL & INTERNET ADDRESS
dundee.united.fc@blueyonder.co.uk
www.dundeeunitedfc.co.uk
CLUB SHOP
The United Shop, Unit 2, 5/15 Victoria Road, Dundee
Tel/Fax (01382) 204066 / Open 9.00 a.m. to 5.30 p.m. Mon/Fri, 9.00a.m. to 5.00 p.m. Sat.
Souvenir shops are also situated within the ground in the East and George Fox Stands and are open on home matchdays.
OFFICIAL SUPPORTERS CLUB
Chairman – Angus Falconer
E/Mail: federationdufc@hotmail.com
TEAM CAPTAIN
Derek McInnes
SHIRT SPONSOR
Morning Noon & Night
KIT SUPPLIER
TFG

LIST OF PLAYERS 2003/04

SQUAD NO.	SURNAME	FIRST NAME	MIDDLE NAME	DATE OF BIRTH	PLACE OF BIRTH	DATE OF SIGNING	HEIGHT FT INS	WEIGHT ST LBS	POS. ON PITCH	PREVIOUS CLUB
41	Abbot	Stuart		21/06/86	Dundee	07/07/03	5 7	10st 0lb	Def	Dundee United Youths
30	Anderson	Steven		19/12/85	Edinburgh	19/12/01	5 11	11st 4lb	Def	Dalkeith B.C.
35	Andrew	Joseph		02/01/86	Glasgow	28/06/02	5 8	11st 13lb	Fwd	Dundee United Youths
5	Archibald	Alan	Maxwell	13/12/77	Glasgow	04/06/03	6 0	11st 7lb	Def	Partick Thistle
31	Bell	Steven		24/02/85	Glasgow	31/07/01	6 0	10st 13lb	Def/Mid	Clyde
6	Bollan	Gary		24/03/73	Dundee	28/01/03	5 11	12st 12lb	Def	Livingston
17	Bullock	Anthony	Brian	18/02/73	Warrington	02/07/03	6 1	14st 10lb	Gk	Ross County
42	Callaghan	Barry		30/11/86	Glasgow	07/07/03	5 8	9st 7lb	Fwd	Dundee United Youths
32	Conway	Aaron		29/03/85	Dundee	13/03/01	5 11	11st 7lb	Fwd	Dundee United B.C.
16	Coyle	Owen	Columba	14/07/66	Paisley	08/08/03	5 11	10st 6lb	Fwd	Falkirk
36	Craig	Steven		03/08/85	Glasgow	28/06/02	5 7	10st 8lb	Mid	Dundee United B.C.
14	Dodds	William		05/02/69	New Cumnock	01/01/03	5 8	12st 2lb	Fwd	Rangers
15	Duff	Stuart		23/01/82	Aberdeen	05/07/99	5 11	10st 3lb	Mid	Dundee United B.C.
18	Easton	Craig		26/02/79	Bellshill	31/08/95	5 10	11st 3lb	Mid	Dundee United B.C.
43	Easton	William		17/07/86	Rutherglen	07/07/03	5 7	9st 5lb	Fwd	Dundee United Youths
1	Gallacher	Paul	James	16/08/79	Glasgow	02/09/97	6 0	11st 11lb	Gk	Lochee United Juniors
44	Gardiner	Ross	John	30/12/86	Bellshill	07/07/03	5 11	9st 10lb	Fwd	Aberdeen
2	Griffin	Daniel	Joseph	10/08/77	Belfast	23/06/03	5 10	10st 12lb	Def/Mid	St. Johnstone
27	Holmes	Graeme		26/03/84	Motherwell	02/07/01	5 9	10st 4lb	Mid	Dundee United Youths
33	Hunter	Andrew		21/06/85	Motherwell	28/06/02	5 9	10st 10lb	Def/Mid	Dundee United Youths
25	Innes	Christopher		13/07/76	Broxburn	29/08/03	6 1	13st 3lb	Def	Kilmarnock
24	Jarvie	Paul		14/06/82	Aberdeen	16/05/00	6 0	12st 3lb	Gk	Stoneywood B.C.
37	Jarvis	Kenneth		26/08/85	Glasgow	28/06/02	5 6	9st 2lb	Mid	Dundee United Youths
7	Kerr	Mark		02/03/82	Bellshill	02/07/03	5 11.5	10st 11lb	Mid	Falkirk
38	Lau	Michael		25/06/85	Paisley	11/10/01	5 7	9st 3lb	Mid	Dundee United Youths
47	McCann	Gavin	John	15/03/86	Bangour	19/08/03	5 11	11st 11lb	Gk	Falkirk
19	McCracken	David		16/10/81	Glasgow	30/06/98	6 2	11st 6lb	Def	Dundee United B.C.
39	McDonald	Nicky		22/01/86	Glasgow	28/06/02	5 5	8st 6lb	Mid	Dundee United Youths
28	McGowan	Stephen		24/09/84	Glasgow	28/11/00	5 6	9st 1lb	Fwd	Dundee United Youths
4	McInnes	Derek		05/07/71	Paisley	17/07/03	5 7	11st 5lb	Mid	West Bromwich Albion
10	McIntyre	James		24/05/72	Alexandria	06/07/01	5 11	11st 5lb	Fwd	Reading
22	McLaren	Andrew		05/06/73	Glasgow	28/08/03	5 10.5	11st 7lb	Fwd	Kilmarnock
8	Miller	Charles	David	18/03/76	Glasgow	03/11/00	5 8.5	10st 8lb	Mid	Watford
40	Molloy	Shaun		14/06/85	Glasgow	06/06/01	5 11	12st 0lb	Def	Dundee United Youths
26	O'Donnell	Stephen		10/07/83	Bellshill	04/07/00	5 11.5	11st 2lb	Mid	Dundee United Youths
29	Ogunmade	Daniel		26/08/83	Glasgow	04/07/00	5 10	11st 0lb	Mid	Dundee United Youths
3	Paterson	James	Lee	25/09/79	Bellshill	03/07/96	5 11	12st 13lb	Mid	Dundee United B.C.
12	Paterson	Scott	Thomas	13/05/72	Aberdeen	04/06/03	6 2	13st 0lb	Def	Partick Thistle
45	Robertson	David		23/09/86	Bangour	07/07/03	5 10	10st 0lb	Mid	Dundee United Youths
11	Robson	Barry		07/11/78	Aberdeen	03/06/03	5 11	12st 0lb	Mid/Fwd	Inverness Cal. Th.
9	Samuel	Collin		27/08/81	Manzinilla	25/07/03	5 9	12st 7lb	Mid	Falkirk
20	Scotland	Jason		18/02/79	Trinidad & Tobago	01/08/03	5 9	11st 10lb	Fwd	Defence Force
46	Smith	Edward		16/03/86	Dundee	07/07/03	5 10	11st 7lb	Mid	Arbroath
21	Wilson	Mark		05/06/84	Glasgow	02/06/00	5 11	11st 13lb	Mid	Dundee United 'S' Form

milestones

YEAR OF FORMATION: 1923 (1909 as Dundee Hibs)
MOST CAPPED PLAYER: Maurice Malpas
NO. OF CAPS: 55
MOST LEAGUE POINTS IN A SEASON: 60 (Premier Division – Season 1986/87) (2 Points for a Win)
67 (First Division – Season 1995/96) (3 Points for a Win)
MOST LEAGUE GOALS SCORED BY A PLAYER IN A SEASON: John Coyle (Season 1955/56)
NO. OF GOALS SCORED: 41
RECORD ATTENDANCE: 28,000 (-v- Barcelona – 16.11.1966)
RECORD VICTORY: 14-0 (-v- Nithsdale Wanderers – Scottish Cup, 17.1.1931)
RECORD DEFEAT: 1-12 (-v- Motherwell – Division 2, 23.1.1954)

ticket information

		SEASON TICKET INFORMATION	
GEORGE FOX STAND	TOP TIER	ADULT 280/305	JUV/OAP 130/180
	MIDDLE TIER	ADULT 330/355	JUV/OAP 140/195
	LOWER TIER	ADULT 220/270	JUV/OAP 120/165
EAST STAND	TOP TIER	ADULT 270/290	JUV/OAP 120/160
	LOWER TIER	ADULT 190/210	JUV/OAP 60/140
		LEAGUE ADMISSION PRICES	
GEORGE FOX STAND	TOP TIER	ADULT 20/18	JUV/OAP 12/11
	MIDDLE TIER	ADULT 22/20	JUV/OAP 12/11
	LOWER TIER	ADULT 20/18	JUV/OAP 10/9
EAST STAND	TOP TIER	ADULT 20/18	JUV/OAP 11/10
	LOWER TIER	ADULT 18/16	JUV/OAP 10/9
JERRY KERR STAND (AWAY SUPPORTERS)		ADULT 20/18	JUV/OAP 10/11
WEST STAND		ADULT 18/16	JUV/OAP 10/9

leading goalscorers 1993-2003

Season	Div	No. of Goals	Player
1993-94	P	16	C. Brewster
1994-95	P	7	C. Brewster
1995-96	F	17	C. Brewster, G. McSwegan
1996-97	P	12	K. Olofsson
1997-98	P	18	K. Olofsson
1998-99	P	17	W. Dodds
1999-00	P	9	W. Dodds
2000-01	P	6	D. Lilley
2001-02	P	6	D. Lilley, J. McIntyre, S. Thompson
2002-03	P	9	J. McIntyre

the terrors' club factfile 2002/03

Date	Venue	Opponents	Att.	Res	Gallacher P.	McGowne K.	Lauchlan J.	McCunnie J.	Griffin D.	Duff S.	Easton C.	Miller C.	Venetis A.	McIntyre J.	Thompson S.	Gunnlaugsson A.	Paterson J.	Lilley D.	Smart A.	Aljofree H.	Cummings W.	Winters D.	Wilson M.	O'Donnell S.	McCracken D.	Carson S.	Hamilton J.	Ogunmade D.	Dodds W.	Bollan G.	Chiarini D.	Tod A.	Combe A.	Latapy R.	McGowan S.	Conway A.
Aug 3	A	Partick Thistle	6,375	0-0	1	2	3	4	5	6	7	8	9	10	11	12	13	14																		
10	H	Kilmarnock	6,366	1-2	1	2	3	4	5	6	7	8		9	10^{1}	12	14	11	13																	
17	A	Celtic	56,247	0-5	1	2	3	4	5	6	7	8	13	11	10		14		12	9																
25	H	Motherwell	5,795	1-1	1	2	3	4	5	6	7	13		9^{1}	10	14		11	8		12															
31	H	Dundee	12,402	0-0	1	2	3		5	6	7	8		9	10	11	13		12		4	14														
Sep 11	A	Aberdeen	10,724	2-1	1	2	3		5	7	9	8			10^{2}		12	11			6		4													
14	H	Dunfermline Athletic	6,041	1-2	1	2	3		5	7	9	8		13	10		12	11^{1}			6		4	14												
21	A	Hearts	11,532	0-2	1	2	3		5	7	9	8		14	10		12	11	13		6		4													
28	H	Rangers	10,013	0-3	1		3		5	7	9	8			10	14	13	12			6		4	11	2											
Oct 5	A	Hibernian	9,175	1-2	1	3	12			7	8	13			10^{1}		5	11			6		4	9	2	14										
19	H	Livingston	5,572	2-3	1	2	3	13		5	6	8		9^{1}	10		14	11^{1}			4			7			12									
26	H	Partick Thistle	6,369	1-1	1	2		4		5	7	8		9	10^{1}			11						6	3		12									
Nov 2	A	Kilmarnock	5,411	2-1	1			2		5	7	8		6^{1}	10^{1}		13	11	12				4		3		9									
10	H	Celtic	10,664	0-2	1		3	2			7	8		9	10		6	11	12				4		5											
16	A	Motherwell	5,381	2-1	1		3	2		13	7	8		9		12	6	11					4		5		10^{2}									
23	A	Dundee	11,593	2-3	1		3	2			7	8		9^{1}	10		6	11	13				4		5		12^{1}									
30	H	Aberdeen	8,261	1-1	1		3				6	8		9	10		2	11					4		5		7^{1}									
Dec 4	A	Dunfermline Athletic	4,342	1-4	1		3			12	6	8		9^{1}	10		2	11	14				4		5	13	7									
7	H	Hibernian	5,673	1-1	1			2		6	7	8		9	13		3	11			12		4^{1}		5		10									
14	A	Rangers	47,639	0-3	1			2			7	8		9	10		3	11	12				4		5	13	6									
21	H	Hearts	6,025	0-3	1	4	3	2		6	7	8					5	11	14		12			13		9	10									
26	A	Livingston	3,969	0-3	1			2		5	7	8		9				11					4	13	3	6	10	12								
29	A	Partick Thistle	5,109	0-0	1		3			6	7	8			10		2	11			12		4	9	5											
Jan 2	H	Kilmarnock	7,183	2-2	1		3			6	7	8		12^{1}			2	11					4	9	5		13		10^{1}							
29	A	Celtic	54,912	0-2	1					7		8		9			2	11					4	13	5				10	3	6	12				
Feb 1	H	Motherwell	6,672	2-1	12					6	9	8^{1}		11				14	7				13		5				10	3	2	4^{1}	1			
9	H	Dundee	10,547	†1-1	1					6	7	8		9			2	13	14				4		5		11		10	3	12					
16	A	Aberdeen	9,146	0-3	1					6	8			9			7	11	13				2		5	12			10	3	14	4				
Mar 1	H	Dunfermline Athletic	6,004	3-0	1			2		6	8^{1}			10			7	11	14						5			13^{1}	12	3		4^{1}		9		
9	A	Hibernian	7,518	1-1	1			2		6	8			10^{1}			7	11							5	12			13	3		4		9		
15	H	Livingston	6,247	0-1	1			2	14	6	9	8		10			7	11							5			13	12	3		4				
Apr 5	A	Hearts	10,747	1-2	1			12	5^{1}	6	9	8		11			7		13						2			14		3		4		10		
13	H	Rangers	10,271	1-4	1		13		5	6	9	8		11			7		14				2						12^{1}	3		4		10		
26	H	Hibernian	6,758	1-2	1		13		5	6		8		10			7	11	14				2		3^{1}				12			4		9		
May 3	A	Motherwell	9,056	2-2			12		5	6	9	8^{1}		10^{1}			7	11					14		3				13	2		4	1			
10	A	Livingston	5,462	2-1			3		5	6	12	8^{1}		10^{1}			7	11					13						14	2		4	1	9		
17	A	Partick Thistle	6,357	1-0			3		5	6	9	8		10			7^{1}	11					13						14	2		4	1	12		
24	H	Aberdeen	8,516	0-2					5	6	9			11									7	13	3			8	10	2		4	1		12	14
TOTAL FULL APPEARANCES					33	12	20	16	16	32	35	32	1	30	19	1	23	29	2	1	7		22	6	25	2	9	1	6	13	2	12	5	6		
TOTAL SUB APPEARANCES					1		4	2	1	2	1	2	1	3	1	5	10	4	16		4	1	4	5		5	4	4	8		2	1		1	1	1
TOTAL GOALS SCORED									1		1	3		9	6		1	2					1		1		4	1	2			2				

Small bold figures denote goalscorers. † denotes opponent's own goal.

tannadice park

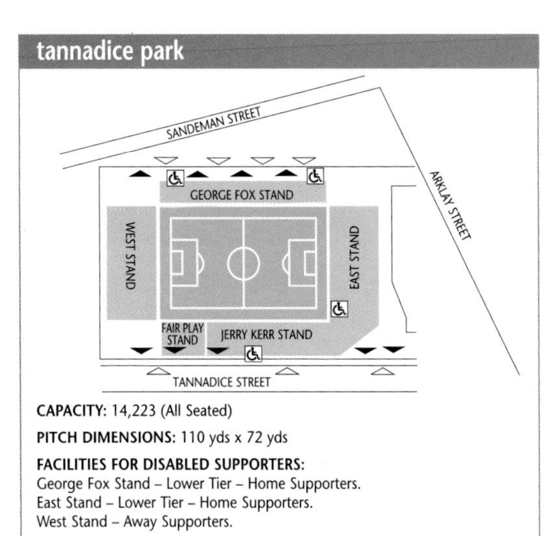

CAPACITY: 14,223 (All Seated)

PITCH DIMENSIONS: 110 yds x 72 yds

FACILITIES FOR DISABLED SUPPORTERS:
George Fox Stand – Lower Tier – Home Supporters.
East Stand – Lower Tier – Home Supporters.
West Stand – Away Supporters.

team playing kits

how to get there

Tannadice Park can be reached by the following routes:

BUSES: The following buses leave from the city centre at frequent intervals:/ Nos. 1a, 18, 19 and 21 from Meadowside and No. 22 from Littlewoods Store, High Street.

TRAINS: Trains from all over the country pass through the main Dundee station and fans can then proceed to the ground by the above bus services from stops situated within walking distance of the station.

CARS: There is parking in the streets adjacent to the ground.

dunfermline athletic

East End Park, Halbeath Road,
Dunfermline, Fife, KY12 7RB
CHAIRMAN John W. Yorkston
DIRECTORS
C. Roy Woodrow,
Gavin G. Masterton, C.B.E., F.I.B. (Scot),
Andrew T. Gillies, John Meiklem,
W. Brian Robertson, W.S.,
Graham A Thomson &
Francis M. McConnell, SSC.
CLUB SECRETARY Jim Leishman
MANAGER Jimmy Calderwood
ASSISTANT MANAGER Jimmy Nicholl
COACH Sandy Clark
COMMUNITY COACH
Hamish French
GOALKEEPING COACH
Scott Y. Thomson
YOUTH CO/ORDINATOR
John B. Ritchie
YOUTH COACHES
U/19 John B. Ritchie,
U/17 Andrew Hutton, U/16 Alex Rae, U/15 John Young, U/14 Kenny Black
CHIEF SCOUT Bobby Jenks
OFFICE ADMINISTRATOR
Claire Simpson (01383) 724295
FOOTBALL SAFETY OFFICERS' ASSOCIATION REPRESENTATIVE
David Dickson (01383) 724295
COMMERCIAL MANAGER
Karen McNeill, Stadia Advisory Services Ltd.
MEDIA LIAISON OFFICER
Stuart Arnott
CLUB DOCTOR Dr. Gerry D. Gillespie
PHYSIOTHERAPIST
Paul Atkinson (First Team)
STADIUM MANAGER
Brian Gallagher (01383) 724295
GROUNDSMAN John Wilson
KIT PERSON Andrew Hutton
CONFERENCE & BANQUETING
Graeme Pacitti
MARKETING & PR Tracey Martin
MATCHDAY PROGRAMME EDITOR
Duncan Simpson
CLUB SHOP
Manager: Kevin Gillespie
Club Shop situated at
Kingsgate Shopping Centre.
Ground only on matchdays.
Open 9.00 a.m. – 5.00 p.m.
Mon to Sat. Tel: (01383) 626737
TELEPHONES
Ground/Secretary (01383) 724295
Fax (01383) 723468
Ticket Office 0870 300 1201
Ticket Office Fax (01383) 626452
Conference & Banqueting
(01383) 741147
Conference & Banqueting Fax
(01383) 741411
Pars Superstore (01383) 626737
Pars Personal Health (01383) 623655
Sports Bar (01383) 745914
E/MAIL & INTERNET ADDRESS
pars@dafc.co.uk & www.dafc.co.uk
OFFICIAL SUPPORTERS CLUB
c/o Mrs. Joan Malcolm, Secretary,
Dunfermline Athletic Supporters Club,
13 South Knowe, Crossgates, KY4 8AW
Fod Arms Travel Club – Linda Cummings (01383) 729909
Lothian68 – John 07719 564920
Millers Bar (01383) 723695
TEAM CAPTAIN Scott M. Thomson
SHIRT SPONSOR
RAC Auto Windscreens
KIT SUPPLIER TFG

SPL
SCOTTISH PREMIER LEAGUE

LIST OF PLAYERS 2003/04

SQUAD NO.	SURNAME	FIRST NAME	MIDDLE NAME	DATE OF BIRTH	PLACE OF BIRTH	DATE OF SIGNING	HEIGHT FT INS	WEIGHT ST LBS	POS. ON PITCH	PREVIOUS CLUB
–	Atha	David	William	15/06/85	Glasgow	12/08/03	5 6	9st 9lb	Fwd	East Kilbride Thistle U/21
41	Bishop	Jamie		14/01/85	Dundee	28/08/00	6 1	12st 4lb	Def	Dunfermline Athletic Youths
10	Brewster	Craig		13/12/66	Dundee	04/07/02	6 1	12st 9lb	Fwd	Hibernian
2	Bullen	Lee		29/03/71	Edinburgh	03/05/00	6 2	12st 7lb	Mid	PAE Kalamata
18	Byrne	Richard		24/09/81	Dublin	30/08/03	6 1	12st 5lb	Def	Shamrock Rovers
42	Campbell	Iain		28/06/85	Kirkcaldy	14/08/02	5 9	10st 12lb	Def	Dunfermline Athletic Youths
43	Clark	Patrick		18/05/85	Edinburgh	23/06/03	5 11.5	9st 9lb	Fwd	Hibernian
9	Crawford	Stephen		09/01/74	Dunfermline	26/02/99	5 10.5	12st 0lb	Fwd	Hibernian
12	Dempsey	Gary		15/01/81	Wexford	19/06/02	5 9	11st 8lb	Mid	Waterford United
48	Frew	Michael		11/01/86	Dunfermline	12/08/03	5 5	8st 13lb	Fwd	Dunfermline Athletic Youths
44	Greenhill	Gary		16/06/85	Kirkcaldy	13/07/02	5 10	10st 12lb	Mid	Dunfermline Athletic Youths
22	Grondin	David		08/05/80	Paris	06/02/03	5 9.5	11st 5lb	Def	Arsenal
14	Hunt	Noel		26/12/82	Waterford	28/01/03	5 8	11st 5lb	Fwd	Shamrock Rovers
45	Innes	Paul		02/02/86	Glasgow	14/08/02	5 7	10st 2lb	Def	Dunfermline Athletic Youths
17	Kilgannon	Sean		08/03/81	Stirling	22/03/02	5 11	11st 8lb	Mid	Middlesbrough
28	Labonte	Aaron		27/11/83	Middlesbrough	14/07/03	5 10.5	10st 10lb	Def	Newcastle United
27	MacNicol	Scott		25/02/83	Brisbane	18/07/03	5 10	11st 6lb	Def/Mid	Rochdale Rovers
8	Mason	Gary		15/10/79	Edinburgh	22/12/00	5 8.5	10st 12lb	Mid	Manchester City
26	McGarty	Mark		03/08/82	Fauldhouse	10/07/03	5 10	10st 0lb	Mid	Dunfermline Athletic Youths
16	McGroarty	Christopher	Martin	06/02/81	Bellshill	22/10/98	5 10	10st 5lb	Mid	Dunfermline Athletic Youths
–	McGuire	Kieran		29/03/86	Kirkcaldy	06/08/03	5 10	11st 8lb	Fwd	Dunfermline Athletic Youths
–	McKeown	Craig	Allan	16/03/85	Aberdeen	06/08/03	6 0	12st 12lb	Def	Fortmartine United
31	Mehmet	Billy		03/01/84	London	10/07/03	6 1	12st 13lb	Fwd	West Ham United
–	Murdoch	Sean		31/07/86	Edinburgh	12/08/03	6 2	11st 10lb	Gk	Hearts Youths
7	Nicholson	Barry		24/08/78	Dumfries	04/08/00	5 7.5	10st 12lb	Mid	Rangers
–	Rossi	Youssef		28/06/73	Casablanca	11/09/00	5 11	11st 8lb	Def	Stade Rennes
1	Ruitenbeek	Marco		12/05/68	Amsterdam	06/07/00	6 3	16st 2lb	Gk	Go Ahead Eagles
5	Skerla	Andrius		29/04/77	Lithuania	28/07/00	6 1	12st 9lb	Def	Dundee United
–	Smith	Daniel		11/09/86	Glasgow	06/08/03	5 5	9st 5lb	Mid/Fwd	Bosco Juniors
20	Stillie	Derek		03/12/73	Irvine	04/07/02	6 0	12st 6lb	Gk	Wigan Athletic
29	Storey	Anthony		16/11/83	Bishop Auckland	10/07/03	5 10	12st 5lb	Mid	Middlesbrough
46	Tawse	Kenneth		21/10/85	Aberdeen	30/08/02	5 11	11st 8lb	Def	Keith
30	Thomson	Scott	Yuill	08/11/66	Edinburgh	23/07/03	6 0.5	12st 0lb	Gk	Airdrieonians
6	Thomson	Scott Munro		29/01/72	Aberdeen	06/07/98	5 10	11st 4lb	Def/Mid	Raith Rovers
15	Tod	Andrew		04/11/71	Dunfermline	08/08/03	6 3	12st 6lb	Def	Bradford City
–	Vaughan	Kris		05/08/86	Dunfermline	12/08/03	6 1	13st 4lb	Def	Dunfermline Athletic Youths
–	Wilson	Craig		28/05/86	Dunfermline	06/08/03	5 8	10st 2lb	Fwd	Dunfermline Athletic Youths
3	Wilson	Scott		19/03/77	Edinburgh	09/08/02	6 2	12st 8lb	Def	Rangers
4	Young	Darren		13/10/78	Glasgow	10/07/03	5 9	11st 11lb	Mid	Aberdeen
11	Young	Derek		27/05/80	Glasgow	10/07/03	5 8.5	10st 10lb	Mid	Aberdeen

milestones

YEAR OF FORMATION: 1885
MOST CAPPED PLAYER: Istvan Kozma
NO. OF CAPS: Hungary 29 (13 whilst with Dunfermline Athletic)
MOST LEAGUE POINTS IN A SEASON: 65 (First Division – Season 1993/94) (2 Points for a Win)
71 (First Division – Seasons 1995/96 and 1999/2000) (3 Points for a Win)
MOST LEAGUE GOALS SCORED BY A PLAYER IN A SEASON: Bobby Skinner (Season 1925/26)
NO. OF GOALS SCORED: 53
RECORD ATTENDANCE: 27,816 (-v- Celtic – 30.4.1968)
RECORD VICTORY: 11-2 (-v- Stenhousemuir – Division 2, 27.9.1930)
RECORD DEFEAT: 0-10 (-v- Dundee – Division 2, 22.3.1947)

ticket information

SEASON TICKET INFORMATION

MAIN STAND	ADULT	CONCS		U18		U12
	290	155		75		50
ALL OTHER AREAS	ADULT	CONCS		U18		U12
	240	120		60		35
FAMILY TICKET	ADULT	1 CHILD	2 CHILD	3 CHILD	4 CHILD	SENIOR
(ALL AREAS EXCEPT MAIN STAND)	230	30	25	20	FREE	115

MATCH TICKET INFORMATION

CATEGORY A – RANGERS & CELTIC

MAIN STAND	ADULT	OAP/U18	U12
	18	13	10
ALL OTHER AREAS	ADULT	OAP/U18	U12
	16	11	8

CATEGORY B – ALL OTHER SPL CLUBS

MAIN STAND	ADULT	OAP/U18	U12
	15	11	8
ALL OTHER AREAS	ADULT	OAP/U18	U12
	12	10	6

leading goalscorers 1993-2003

Season	Div	No. of Goals	Player
1993-94	F	17	G. O'Boyle
1994-95	F	14	S. Petrie
1995-96	F	13	S. Petrie
1996-97	P	13	G. Britton
1997-98	P	16	A. Smith
1998-99	P	8	A. Smith
1999-00	F	16	S. Crawford
2000-01	P	9	S. Crawford
2001-02	P	7	B. Nicholson
2002-03	P	19	S. Crawford

the pars' club factfile 2002/03

Date	Venue	Opponents	Att.	Res	Ruitenbeek M.	Bullen L.	Thomson S.M.	Skerla A.	Dair J.	Mason G.	Nicholson B.	Kilgannon S.	Hampshire S.	Crawford S.	Brewster C.	Walker S.	Dempsey G.	McGroarty C.	Petrie S.	Wilson S.	MacPherson A.	Nicholls D.	Karnebeek A.	Stillie D.	McLeish K.	McCarty M.	Hunt N.	Brannan G.	Grondin D.	Hamilton J.	McNicol S.
Aug 3	A	Celtic	56,438	1-2	1	2	3	4	5	6	7	8	9	10	11	12	13[1]														
10	H	Livingston	4,751	2-1	1	2	3	4	5		7	8	9	10[1]	11[1]	12	6	13	14												
17	H	Dundee	5,852	4-2	1	2	3	4	5		7	8	9	10[3]	11[1]		6	13		12											
24	A	Hearts	11,367	0-2	1	5	3	4	9	8	7	13	14	10	11		6	12			2										
Sep 1	H	Rangers	8,950	0-6	1	5	3	4	12	6	7	8	9	10	11		13	14		2											
11	A	Hibernian	9,837	4-1	1	6	3	4	14	8	7	12	13	10[1]	11[2]	2[1]	9			5											
14	A	Dundee United	6,041	2-1	1	6	3	4	14	8	7	13	12	10[1]	11	2	9[1]			5											
21	H	Motherwell	4,987	1-0	1	5[1]	3	4	12	6	7	8		10	11	14	9	13		2											
28	A	Aberdeen	11,678	1-3	1	6[1]	3	4		9	7	8	12	10	11	2	13	14		5											
Oct 5	H	Partick Thistle	5,522	4-1	1	5	3[1]	4	12	8	7[1]	11		10[2]			9	13	14		2	6									
19	A	Kilmarnock	5,515	2-2	1	6[1]		4	13	8	7			10	11[1]		9	3		5	2	12									
27	H	Celtic	9,139	1-4	1	6	3	4			7		13	10	11[1]	2	9	12		5			8								
Nov 2	A	Livingston	5,578	1-1	1	6	3	4		12	7			10	11[1]		9			5	2	8									
12	A	Dundee	5,475	3-2	1	2	3	4	6[1]	8	7	12		10[1]	11[1]	13	9			5											
17	H	Hearts	5,683	3-1		6[1]	3	4	8	12	7[1]	9		10[1]	11	14	13	2		5				1							
23	A	Rangers	48,431	0-3		6	3	4	8		7	12	14	10	11		9	13		5	2			1							
30	H	Hibernian	7,506	1-1		6	3	4	8		7		12	10[1]	11	2	9			5				1	13						
Dec 4	H	Dundee United	4,342	4-1		6	3	4	8		7[1]	9	14	10	11[2]	2[1]	13	12		5				1							
7	A	Partick Thistle	4,110	0-4		5	3	4	8	6	7	9	13	10	11	2	14	12						1							
15	H	Aberdeen	4,835	†3-0		2	3	4	8	6	7		9	10[1]	11[1]		12			5				1		13					
26	H	Kilmarnock	5,847	0-2		6	3	4	8	9	7	12	13	10	11		14	2		5				1							
29	A	Celtic	58,387	0-1		6	3	4	13	9	7		14	10	11	8	12	2		5				1							
Jan 2	H	Livingston	5,218	2-0		6	3	4	8	12	7	14		10[2]	11	13	9	2		5				1							
28	H	Dundee	4,237	0-1		3		4	6		7	12	9	10	11		8			5	2			1		14	13				
Feb 1	A	Hearts	11,281	0-3		3		4	6		7	13	9	10	11	2	14			5				1			12	8			
8	H	Rangers	8,754	1-3		3		4	6		7	14	12	10	11[1]						2		13	1			9	8	5		
15	A	Hibernian	9,175	3-1		3		4	12	9	7[1]			10[2]	11					5	2			1			13	8	6		
19	A	Motherwell	3,741	1-2				4	8	9	7		12	10[1]	11		3			5	2			1		14	13		6		
Mar 1	A	Dundee United	6,004	0-3				4	8	9	7	13		10	11					5	2			1			12	6	3		
9	H	Partick Thistle	4,746	0-0				4	13		7	14		10	11		12			5	2			1		6	9	8	3		
16	A	Kilmarnock	4,021	†1-1		6					7	9		10	11	4	13	12		5	2			1			14	8	3		
Apr 5	H	Motherwell	4,086	3-0		4				6	7[1]	9	10[1]		11			14		5	2			1			12[1]	8	3	13	
12	A	Aberdeen	10,030	0-1		6		4		9	7			10	11			5			2			1		13	12	8	3	14	
26	H	Hearts	6,968	0-1	1	2		4	6	8	7	13	9	10	11	14										5	12		3		
May 3	H	Celtic	8,923	1-4	1	2			5	8	7	9		10	11	4	6				13						12		3		14[1]
10	A	Dundee	9,195	2-2	1	6[1]			12	8	7	9		10[1]	11	4				5	2								3		13
17	H	Kilmarnock	6,896	2-2		3			6	8[1]	7	9		10[1]	11		12	4		5	2			1		13			14		
25	A	Rangers	49,731	1-6		6			9[1]	8	7			10	11	13	12	4		5	2			1		14			3		
TOTAL FULL APPEARANCES					17	35	22	32	22	24	38	15	9	37	37	12	17	8		28	17	2	1	21		2	2	8	12		
TOTAL SUB APPEARANCES									10	3		13	13			8	14	13	2	1	1	1	1		1	6	10		1	2	2
TOTAL GOALS SCORED						5	1		2	1	5		1	18	12	2	2										1				1

Small bold figures denote goalscorers. † denotes opponent's own goal.

east end park

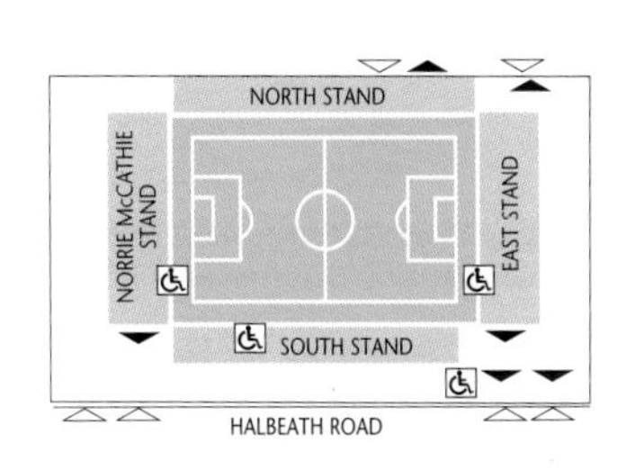

CAPACITY: 11,998 (All Seated)

PITCH DIMENSIONS: 115 yds x 70 yds

FACILITIES FOR DISABLED SUPPORTERS:
12 spaces in East Stand for Away Supporters. 12 spaces in the Norrie McCathie Stand for Home Supporters. 24 seats for helpers.

team playing kits

how to get there

East End Park may be reached by the following routes:

TRAINS: There is a regular train service from Edinburgh to either Dunfermline Town or Dunfermline Queen Margaret Stations. The ground is a 15 minute walk from either station.

BUSES: Buses destined for Kelty, Perth, St. Andrews and Kirkcaldy all pass close to East End Park.

CARS: Car Parking is available in a large car park adjoining the East End of the ground and there are also facilities in various side streets. Multi/storey car parking approximately 10 minutes walk from the ground.

hearts

LIST OF PLAYERS 2003/04

SQUAD NO.	SURNAME	FIRST NAME	MIDDLE NAME	DATE OF BIRTH	PLACE OF BIRTH	DATE OF SIGNING	HEIGHT FT INS	WEIGHT ST LBS	POS. ON PITCH	PREVIOUS CLUB
47	Armstrong	David	Trevor Maradona	23/01/87	Lisburn	04/07/03	5 11	11st 2lb	Fwd	Lisburn Youths
35	Berra	Christophe		31/01/85	Edinburgh	26/04/02	6 1	12st 10lb	Def	Heart of Midlothian Youths
12	Boyack	Steven		04/09/76	Edinburgh	12/01/01	5 10	10st 7lb	Mid	Ayr United
9	De Vries	Mark		24/08/75	Surinam	08/07/02	6 3	12st 1lb	Fwd	Dordrecht 90
50	Driver	Andrew	David	12/11/87	Oldham	04/07/03	5 8.5	10st 10lb	Mid	Heart of Midlothian Youths
27	Dunn	David		01/03/84	Edinburgh	30/11/01	6 2	11st 10lb	Def	Heart of Midlothian 'S' Form
30	Fox	Liam		02/02/84	Edinburgh	21/07/00	5 10	11st 12lb	Mid	Heart of Midlothian Youths
40	Gardiner	Christopher		05/01/86	Bellshill	20/07/01	6 0	11st 10lb	Fwd	Heart of Midlothian Youths
46	Gay	Ryan		03/07/86	Edinburgh	01/07/02	5 10	10st 9lb	Mid	Leith Athletic
13	Gordon	Craig	Sinclair	31/12/82	Edinburgh	26/10/99	6 4	12st 2lb	Gk	Heart of Midlothian Youths
26	Hamill	Joseph	Patrick	25/02/84	Bellshill	22/08/00	5 9	10str 10lb	Mid	Heart of Midlothian Youths
18	Hartley	Paul	James	19/10/76	Glasgow	03/06/03	5 8	10st 7lb	Fwd	St. Johnstone
22	Janczyk	Neil		07/04/83	Edinburgh	16/07/99	5 10	11st 0lb	Def	Heart of Midlothian Youths
45	Kennedy	Ryan		22/05/86	Bellshill	07/01/02	5 10	10st 7lb	Mid	Rangers Youths
32	King	Mathu		26/03/84	Edinburgh	03/12/01	5 11	10st 8lb	Fwd	Heart of Midlothian Youths
10	Kirk	Andrew		29/05/79	Belfast	18/02/99	5 10	11st 0lb	Fwd	Glentoran
20	Kisnorbo	Patrick		24/03/81	Melbourne	03/07/03	6 0	12st 0lb	Def	South Melbourne
31	Knox	John	David	17/02/84	Kirkcaldy	21/07/00	5 9	11st 7lb	Def	Heart of Midlothian Youths
46	MacDonald	Jamie		17/04/86	Broxburn	15/08/03	6 1	11st 2lb	Gk	Musselburgh Athletic Juniors
14	Macfarlane	Neil		10/10/77	Dunoon	08/07/02	6 1	13st 1lb	Mid	Airdrieonians
36	MacLeod	Ross		12/04/85	Glasgow	04/08/01	6 2	11st 12lb	Mid	Heart of,Midlothian Youths
2	Maybury	Alan	Paul	08/08/78	Dublin	12/10/01	5 10	11st 10lb	Def	Leeds United
3	McCann	Henry	Austin	21/01/80	Clydebank	05/02/01	5 9.5	11st 13lb	Mid	Airdrieonians
29	McGeown	David	Peter M	06/01/84	Glasgow	21/07/00	6 0	11st 4lb	Mid	Heart of Midlothian Youths
5	McKenna	Kevin		20/01/80	Calgary	17/07/01	6 2	12st 6lb	Def	Energie Cottbus
28	McMullan	Paul		13/03/84	Bellshill	27/06/01	5 9	11st 12lb	Def	Heart of Midlothian Youths
1	Moilanen	Teuvo		12/12/73	Oulu	18/07/03	6 4	13st 7lb	Gk	Preston North End
37	Murtagh	Conall	Francis	29/06/85	Belfast	10/07/03	6 0	11st 12lb	Mid	Crusaders
49	Neill	John		17/08/87	Bellshill	06/08/03	5 11	11st 4lb	Mid	Hibernian
16	Neilson	Robbie		19/06/80	Paisley	25/10/96	5 8	11st 0lb	Mid	Rangers B.C.
44	Pelosi	Marco	Giancarlo	22/04/86	Edinburgh	30/08/02	5 10	11st 12lb	Def	Heart of Midlothian Youths
4	Pressley	Steven	John	11/10/73	Elgin	10/07/98	6 0	12st 6lb	Def	Dundee United
7	Severin	Scott	Derek	15/02/79	Stirling	22/05/97	5 11	12st 7lb	Mid	Musselburgh Athletic Juniors
19	Simmons	Stephen	Christopher	27/02/82	Glasgow	10/09/97	6 0.5	11st 10lb	Mid	Celtic B.C.
42	Sives	Craig	Stuart	09/04/86	Edinburgh	01/07/02	6 3	12st 2lb	Def	Heart of Midlothian Youths
23	Sloan	Robert		14/07/83	Paisley	14/07/99	5 8	9st 12lb	Mid	Heart of Midlothian Youths
8	Stamp	Philip		12/12/75	Middlesbrough	29/08/02	5 11	12st 12lb	Mid	Middlesbrough
39	Strickland	Colin	Thomas	03/12/85	Broxburn	10/07/03	5 7	9st 11lb	Mid	St. Johnstone
48	Thomson	Jason		26/07/87	Edinburgh	10/07/03	5 11	11st 7lb	Def	Heart of Midlothian Youths
41	Tierney	Garry		19/03/86	Bellshill	04/07/03	5 11	11st 5lb	Def	Heart of Midlothian Youths
11	Valois	Jean-Louis		15/10/73	Lyon	01/08/02	5 11	12st 0lb	Mid	Luton Town
15	Wales	Gary		04/01/79	East Calder	28/07/99	5 10	11st 2lb	Fwd	Hamilton Academical
6	Webster	Andrew	Neil	23/04/82	Dundee	30/03/01	6 0	12st 0lb	Def	Arbroath
21	Weir	Graham		10/07/84	Harthill	22/08/00	5 7	10st 9lb	Fwd	Heart of Midlothian Youths
38	Windrum	Lee		14/08/85	Belfast	17/07/01	6 0	11st 4lb	Gk	Lisburn Youths
17	Wyness	Dennis		22/03/77	Aberdeen	03/06/03	5 10.5	12st 7lb	Fwd	Inverness Cal. Th.

Tynecastle Stadium, Gorgie Road, Edinburgh, EH11 2NL

CHAIRMAN
Douglas A. Smith

DIRECTORS
Christopher P. Robinson, Stewart Fraser, Brian J. Duffin & David Archer

CHIEF EXECUTIVE
Christopher P. Robinson

P.A. to CHIEF EXECUTIVE
Irene McPhee (0131) 200 7245

FINANCE DIRECTOR/ COMPANY SECRETARY
Stewart Fraser (0131) 200 7270

HEAD COACH
Craig Levein

ASSISTANT HEAD COACH
Peter Houston

FITNESS COACH
Tom Ritchie

U21/19 COACH
John McGlynn

ASSISTANT RESERVE COACH
Gary Kirk

DIRECTOR OF YOUTH DEVELOPMENT
John Murray

CLUB DOCTOR
Dr. Dewar Melvin

PHYSIOTHERAPIST
Alan Rae

KIT PERSON
Gordon Paterson

RETAIL MANAGER
Clare Sargent (0131) 200 7206

CORPORATE HOSPITALITY/ BANQUETING
Craig Haddow (0131) 200 7240

SALES & MARKETING MANAGER & COMMERCIAL MANAGER
Kenny Wittmann (0131) 200 7205

FOOTBALL SAFETY OFFICERS' ASSOCIATION REPRESENTATIVE
Tom Purdie (0131) 200 7254

STADIUM MANAGER
John Boag (0131) 200 7258

TICKET MANAGER
Neil Hunter (0131) 200 7201

MEDIA LIAISON OFFICER/ MATCHDAY PROGRAMME EDITOR
Nadine Urquhart (0131) 200 7260

TELEPHONES
Ground (0131) 200 7200
Fax (0131) 200 7222
Ticket Office (0131) 200 7201
Sales & Marketing (0131) 200 7205
Credit Card Bookings (0131) 200 7209
Superstore (0131) 200 7211

E-MAIL & INTERNET ADDRESS
hearts@homplc.co.uk
www.heartsfc.co.uk

CLUB SHOP
Heart of Midlothian Superstore, Tynecastle Stadium, Gorgie Road, Edinburgh. Tel (0131) 200 7211
Open 9.30 a.m. – 5.30 p.m.
Mon. to Sat. and matchdays.

OFFICIAL SUPPORTERS CLUB
Heart of Midlothian Federation, John N. Borthwick, 21/9 Festival Gardens, Edinburgh, EH11 1RB

TEAM CAPTAIN
Steven Pressley

SHIRT SPONSOR
all:sports

KIT SUPPLIER
Reebok

milestones

YEAR OF FORMATION: 1874
MOST CAPPED PLAYER: Bobby Walker
NO. OF CAPS: 29
MOST LEAGUE POINTS IN A SEASON: 63 (Premier Division – Season 1991/92) (2 Points for a Win)
67 (Premier Division – Season 1997/98) (3 Points for a Win)
MOST LEAGUE GOALS SCORED BY A PLAYER IN A SEASON: Barney Battles (Season 1930/31)
NO. OF GOALS SCORED: 44
RECORD ATTENDANCE: 53,396 (-v- Rangers – 13.2.1932)
RECORD VICTORY: 21-0 (-v- Anchor – EFA Cup, 1880)
RECORD DEFEAT: 1-8 (-v- Vale of Leven – Scottish Cup, 1883)

ticket information

SEASON TICKET INFORMATION

MAIN STAND		
ALL SECTIONS	ADULT	305 or 250
T&N UPPER & LOWER	ADULT	200
WHEATFIELD STAND		
UPPER	ADULT	355 or 300
LOWER	ADULT	325 or 270
GORGIE STAND		
ADULT & 1 JUV		325/125 or 275/110
ADULT & 2 JUV		325/250 or 275/220
ADULT & 3 JUV		325/375 or 275/330
JUVS/SENIOR		175 or 150
DISABLED/CARER		75 or 100

LEAGUE TICKET INFORMATION

HOME SUPPORT	
CATEGORY A	20 & 18
CATEGORY B	18 & 16
CAT A&B JUV	10
AWAY SUPPORT – ROSEBURN STAND	
CATEGORY A	20 & 21
CATEGORY B	18
CAT A&B JUV	10

CATEGORY A INCLUDES RANGERS, CELTIC, HIBERNIAN & ABERDEEN

leading goalscorers 1993-2003

Season	Div	No. of Goals	Player
1993-94	P	10	J. Robertson
1994-95	P	10	J. Robertson
1995-96	P	11	J. Robertson
1996-97	P	14	J. Robertson
1997-98	P	14	J. Hamilton
1998-99	P	10	S. Adam
1999-00	P	13	G. McSwegan
2000-01	P	12	C. Cameron
2001-02	P	9	K. McKenna
2002-03	P	15	M. De Vries

the jam tarts' club factfile 2002/03

Date	Venue	Opponents	Att.	Res	Niemi A.	Pressley S.	McCann A.	Maybury A.	McKenna K.	Valois J.	Severin S.	Boyack S.	Simmons S.	Kirk A.	Wales G.	De Vries M.	Twaddle K.	McMullen P.	Mahe S.	Weir G.	Janczyk N.	McKenzie R.	Stamp P.	Gordon C.	McGeown D.	Webster A.	Sloan R.	Macfarlane N.	Oueifio W.	Dunn D.	Knox J.	Hamill J.	Moilanen T.	Neilson R.
Aug 3	A	Dundee	7,705	1-1	1	2	3	4	5	6	7	8	9	10	11[1]	12	13	14																
11	H	Hibernian	15,245	5-1	1	2		4	5	6	7	8	9	10[1]	14	11[4]	12	13	3															
18	A	Aberdeen	12,825	1-1	1	2		4	5	6	7	8	9		10	11[1]		3		12	13													
24	H	Dunfermline Athletic	11,367	2-0		2		4	5	6	7	8	9			11[1]	12	3		10[1]		1												
31	H	Kilmarnock	11,912	1-1		2		4	5	6	7	8		12		11	13	3[1]		10		1	9											
Sep 11	A	Rangers	48,581	0-2		2		4	5	6	7	8		10	12	11	13	3				1	9											
15	H	Motherwell	8,759	4-2		2		4	5	6	7	8[1]		10[2]	12	11[1]		3				1	9											
21	H	Dundee United	11,532	2-0		2		4	5	6[1]	7	8		10	12	11[1]		3				1	9											
28	A	Partick Thistle	6,111	2-2		2		4	5	6[1]	7[1]	8	12		13	11		3		10		1	9											
Oct 6	A	Livingston	6,492	1-1		2		4	5	6	7	8	13	10	12	11		3		14			9[1]	1										
20	H	Celtic	13,911	1-4		2		4	5	6	7		13	10	14[1]	11		3				1	9		8	12								
26	H	Dundee	10,169	1-2		2		4	5[1]	6	7		9	14	10	11	12	3			13	1	8											
Nov 3	A	Hibernian	15,560	2-1		2		4	5[1]	8	7		10	11			13	6		12	14	1	9[1]			3								
9	H	Aberdeen	11,920	0-0		2		4	5	8	7		10		14		9	6		11	12	1				3	13							
17	A	Dunfermline Athletic	5,683	1-3		2		4	5	8	7[1]			10	11	12		6		14	13	1	9			3								
23	A	Kilmarnock	6,511	1-0		2	3	4	5	6	7		13	10		11[1]		14				1				12		8	9					
Dec 1	H	Rangers	12,156	0-4			3	4	5	6	7		12	13	14	11						1	8			2		10	9					
4	A	Motherwell	4,114	1-6			3		5	6[1]	7		8	10		11			13	14		1				2			9	4	12			
7	H	Livingston	8,074	2-1			3	4	5	6	7			10[2]	9	11				14	12	1				2		8				13		
14	H	Partick Thistle	9,734	1-0				4[1]	5	6	7	12	3	10	9	11			2		1						8							
21	A	Dundee United	6,025	3-0		2	3	4	5	6	7	8	14	10[2]		11[1]						1	12					9				13		
26	A	Celtic	58,480	2-4		2	3	4	5	6		8	12			11[2]			14	10		1	7					9				13		
29	A	Dundee	7,340	2-1		2		4	5	6	7	8	13	10[1]		11			3	12[1]		1						9						
Jan 2	H	Hibernian	17,732	4-4		2[1]		4	5	6	7	8	13	10		11[1]			3	14[2]		1	12					9						
28	A	Aberdeen	9,322	1-0		2	12	4	13	6	7	8			14[1]	11			3	10						5		9					1	
Feb 1	H	Dunfermline Athletic	11,281	3-0		2	12	4	5[1]	8	7[1]				11[1]				3				9			6		10					1	
8	H	Kilmarnock	10,426	3-0		2	3	4[1]	13[1]	6	7	14	12		10	11[1]							8			5		9					1	
15	A	Rangers	49,459	0-1		2		4	12	6	7	8	13	14	10	11			3							5		9					1	
Mar 1	H	Motherwell	11,704	2-1		2		4	5[1]	8	7	14	12[1]	13	11				3				9			6		10					1	
8	A	Livingston	6,448	1-1		2	3	4	5	8	7	12		13	11	14							9[1]			6		10					1	
Apr 5	H	Dundee United	10,747	2-1			3		5	8	7	12		13[1]	11	10					6		9			2[1]							1	4
12	A	Partick Thistle	5,288	1-1		2[1]	3		13	6	7	8		11	14	10							9			5		12					1	4
19	H	Celtic	15,855	2-1		2	3[1]	4		6	7	12		14	13	10				11			8[1]			5		9					1	
26	A	Dunfermline Athletic	6,968	1-0		2[1]	3	4	12	6	7			13		10				11			8			5		9					1	
May 3	A	Kilmarnock	9,091	0-1		2	3	4	5	8	7	13		12	14					11			9			6		10					1	
10	A	Celtic	58,906	0-1		2		4	5	6	7	8	13	14						11	12		9					10					1	3
18	H	Rangers	15,632	0-2		2		4	12	6	7	8	13	14		10				11						5		9					1	3
25	H	Dundee	12,205	1-0		2	3	4		13	7				12	10[1]			14	11						5		9				8	1	6
TOTAL FULL APPEARANCES					3	33	15	35	30	37	37	19	9	17	12	29	1	13	8	12	1	20	22	1	1	19		20	3	1		1	14	5
TOTAL SUB APPEARANCES							2		6	1		7	14	12	14	3	7	3	3	8	7		2			2	1	1			1	3		
TOTAL GOALS SCORED						3	1	2	5	3	3	1	1	9	4	15		1		4			4			1								

Small bold figures denote goalscorers. † denotes opponent's own goal.

tynecastle stadium

WHEATFIELD ROAD
WHEATFIELD STAND
GORGIE ROAD
GORGIE STAND
ROSEBURN STAND
MAIN STAND
McLEOD STREET
RUSSELL ROAD

CAPACITY: 17,700 (All Seated)

PITCH DIMENSIONS: 107 yds x 74 yds

FACILITIES FOR DISABLED SUPPORTERS:
There are 15 spaces for visiting fans at the Roseburn Stand. Regarding facilities for home supporters, fans should contact the club in advance for availability.

team playing kits

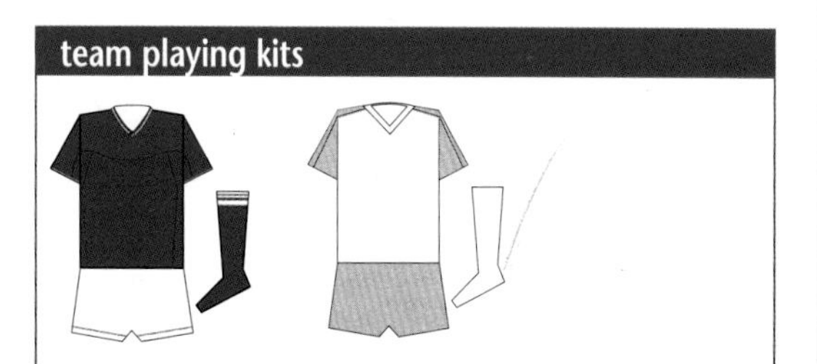

how to get there

Tynecastle Stadium can be reached by the following routes:

BUSES: A frequent service of buses leaves from the city centre, Nos. 1, 2, 3, 4, 33, 34, 35 and 44 all pass the ground.

TRAINS: Haymarket Station is about half a mile from the ground.

CARS: Car Parking facilities exist in the adjacent side streets in Robertson Avenue and also the Westfield area.

hibernian

Easter Road Stadium,
12 Albion Place,
Edinburgh, EH7 5QG

CHAIRMAN
Kenneth Lewandowski

MANAGING DIRECTOR
Rod M. Petrie

DIRECTORS
Stephen W. Dunn (Non Executive),
Scott Lindsay (Executive)
& Tim Gardiner (Financial)

SECRETARY & STADIUM MANAGER
Garry O'Hagan (0131) 656 7077

MANAGER
Bobby Williamson

ASSISTANT MANAGERS
Gerry McCabe & Jim Clark

FITNESS COACH
Dougie Fowler

GOALKEEPING COACH
Ian Westwater

ACADEMY DIRECTOR
John Park

FOOTBALL SAFETY OFFICERS' ASSOCIATION REPRESENTATIVE
John Couper
(0131) 656 7081

COMMERCIAL DEPARTMENT
Contact (0131) 656 7095
Fax (0131) 652 2202

CLUB DOCTOR
Dr. Tom Schofield

PHYSIOTHERAPIST
Malcolm Colquhoun

GROUNDSMAN
Tam McCourt

KIT PERSON
Jim McCafferty

CATERING MANAGER
Billie Wilson/Lindley Catering
(0131) 661 8066

CONFERENCE & BANQUETING
Nadia Christie
(0131) 656 7075

CORPORATE HOSPITALITY MANAGER
Amanda Vitesse
(0131) 656 7073

MEDIA LIAISON OFFICER
David Forsyth/Benchmark Media
Tel (0131) 473 2347
Fax (0131) 473 2348

MATCHDAY PROGRAMME EDITOR
Jim Jeffrey

TELEPHONES
Ground (0131) 661 2159
Fax (0131) 659 6488
Fax Commercial (0131) 652 2202
Ticket Office (0131) 661 1875
24 Hour Ticket Hotline
(0870) 840 1875

E-MAIL & INTERNET ADDRESS
club@hibernianfc.co.uk
www.hibernianfc.co.uk

CLUB SHOP
12 Albion Place, Edinburgh
Open Mon.-Sat.: 9.00a.m. – 5.00p.m.,
Home matchdays:
9.30a.m. – 3.00p.m (& after match).
Away First Team matchdays:
9.00a.m. – 3.00p.m.
Tel (0131) 656 7078
e-mail: shop@hibernianfc.co.uk

OFFICIAL SUPPORTERS CLUB
11 Sunnyside Lane, Off Easter Road,
Edinburgh, EH7

TEAM CAPTAIN
Ian Murray

SHIRT SPONSOR
Carlsberg

KIT SUPPLIER
Le Coq Sportif

LIST OF PLAYERS 2003/04

SQUAD NO.	SURNAME	FIRST NAME	MIDDLE NAME	DATE OF BIRTH	PLACE OF BIRTH	DATE OF SIGNING	HEIGHT FT INS	WEIGHT ST LBS	POS. ON PITCH	PREVIOUS CLUB
13	Andersson	Daniel		18/12/72	Sweden	06/02/03	6 2	13st 11lb	Gk	AIK
–	Baillie	Jonathan		02/09/85	Irvine	25/07/02	6 2	12st 9lb	Def	Hibernian Youths
8	Brebner	Grant	Ian	06/12/77	Edinburgh	19/08/99	5 10	11st 13lb	Mid	Reading
18	Brown	Alistair	Hugh	12/12/85	Irvine	03/07/02	6 1	12st 4lb	Gk	Hibernian Youths
–	Brown	Scott		25/06/85	Dunfermline	25/07/02	5 9	11st 4lb	Fwd	Hibernian 'S' Form
–	Colgan	Nick		19/09/73	Drogheda	29/07/99	6 1	13st 4lb	Gk	AFC Bournemouth
–	Crooks	Gary	Alistair	15/02/87	Falkirk	11/09/03	5 8	11st 0lb	Mid	St. Johnstone
–	Cruickshank	Andrew		27/03/85	Aberdeen	30/08/02	6 2	12st 9lb	Def	Hibernian Youths
17	Dobbie	Stephen		05/12/82	Glasgow	04/07/03	5 8.5	10st 4lb	Fwd	Rangers
3	Edge	Roland		25/11/78	Gillingham	11/08/03	5 11	12st 7lb	Def	Gillingham
25	Fenwick	Paul	Joseph	25/08/69	London	02/06/00	6 2	12st 7lb	Def	Raith Rovers
–	Fletcher	Steven		26/03/87	Shrewsbury	04/07/03	6 1	12st 0lb	Fwd	Hibernian Youths
11	Glass	Stephen		23/05/76	Dundee	10/07/03	5 9.5	10st 13lb	Mid/Fwd	Watford
1	Hyldgaard	Morten		26/01/78	Herning	17/07/03	6 6	13st 7lb	Gk	Coventry City
14	Kouo/Doumbe	Mathias		28/10/79	Paris	26/10/01	6 1	12st 5lb	Def	Paris St. Germain
–	Mackison	Scott		24/07/86	Stirling	04/07/03	5 11	11st 0lb	Def	Rangers
–	McDonald	Kevin	Alan	26/06/85	Newcastle	25/07/01	5 10	10st 9lb	Mid	Sunderland
–	McKenzie	Jamie		08/05/86	Kirkcaldy	04/07/03	6 1	12st 10lb	Def	Hibernian Youths
7	McManus	Thomas	Kelly	28/02/81	Glasgow	10/07/97	5 10	10st 2lb	Fwd	Hibernian 'S' Form
5	Murdock	Colin	James	02/07/75	Ballymena	17/07/03	6 3	13st 7lb	Def	Preston North End
6	Murray	Ian	William	20/03/81	Edinburgh	13/07/99	6 0	11st 5lb	Mid	Dundee United
12	Nicol	Kevin		19/01/82	Kirkcaldy	17/01/02	5 10	11st 7lb	Mid	Raith Rovers
–	Noble	Steven	John	21/08/86	Edinburgh	19/08/03	5 9	10st 6lb	Mid	Rangers
–	Notman	Steven		29/09/86	Edinburgh	04/07/03	5 11	10st 11lb	Mid	Hibernian Youths
9	O'Connor	Garry	Lawrence	07/05/83	Edinburgh	14/05/99	6 1	12st 7lb	Fwd	Salvesen B.C.
–	O'Neill	Kevin		16/05/86	Edinburgh	09/07/02	6 2	12st 6lb	Def	Hibernian Youths
23	Orman	Alen		31/05/78	Bugojno	28/06/01	6 0	12st 12lb	Def/Mid	Royal Antwerp
–	Pow	Ryan		30/06/87	Edinburgh	04/07/03	5 8	10st 2lb	Mid	Airdrieonians
22	Reid	Alan		21/10/80	Paisley	06/07/98	5 8	10st 8lb	Mid/Fwd	Renfrew Victoria
10	Riordan	Derek	George	16/01/83	Edinburgh	14/05/99	5 11	10st 8lb	Fwd	Hutchison Vale B.C.
–	Shields	Jay		06/01/85	Edinburgh	05/07/01	5 7	11st 4lb	Mid	Hibernian Youths
–	Smith	Darren	James	06/12/86	Edinburgh	04/07/03	5 10	11st 6lb	Mid	Hibernian Youths
2	Smith	Gary		25/03/71	Glasgow	13/07/00	6 0	12st 3lb	Def	Aberdeen
19	Thomson	Kevin		14/10/84	Edinburgh	10/08/01	5 11	11st 4lb	Mid	Hibernian Youths
–	Weightman	Nicholas	John	06/04/87	Lanark	04/07/03	5 10	10st 11lb	Mid	Hibernian Youths
15	Whittaker	Steven	Gordon	16/06/84	Edinburgh	01/08/00	6 1	13st 9lb	Mid	Star A B.C.
16	Wiss	Jarkko		17/04/72	Finland	22/01/02	6 0	12st 8lb	Mid	Stockport County
4	Zambernardi	Yannick		03/09/77	Ajaccio	23/08/02	6 2	12st 4lb	Def	ES Troyes

milestones

YEAR OF FORMATION: 1875
MOST CAPPED PLAYER: Lawrie Reilly
NO. OF CAPS: 38
MOST LEAGUE POINTS IN A SEASON: 57 (First Division – Season 1980/81) (2 Points for a Win)
89 (First Division – Season 1998/99) (3 Points for a Win)
MOST LEAGUE GOALS SCORED BY A PLAYER IN A SEASON: Joe Baker (Season 1959/60)
NO. OF GOALS SCORED: 42
RECORD ATTENDANCE: 65,840 (-v- Heart of Midlothian – 2.1.1950)
RECORD VICTORY: 22-1 (-v- 42nd Highlanders 3.9.1881)
RECORD DEFEAT: 0-10 (-v- Rangers – 24.12.1898)

ticket information

SEASON TICKET INFORMATION

	ADULT	18-US	STUDENT	SENIOR
WEST STAND – LOWER	248-425	41-175	135-150	72-275
WEST STAND – UPPER	248-680	41-175	135-175	72-175

LEAGUE ADMISSION PRICES

STAND	CAT A ADULT	CAT A CHILD/SENIOR	CAT B ADULT	CAT B CHILD/SENIOR
WEST UPPER	22-25	10	19-22	10
LOUNGE ACCESS	47		40	
WEST LOWER	22-25	10	19-22	10
LOUNGE ACCESS	47		40	
FAMOUS FIVE UPPER	24	10	20	10
LOUNGE ACCESS	47		40	
FAMOUS FIVE LOWER	22	10	19	10
EAST	20	10	17	10
SOUTH UPPER	24		20	10
SOUTH LOWER	24		20	10

leading goalscorers 1993-2003

Season	Div	No. of Goals	Player
1993-94	P	16	K. Wright
1994-95	P	10	D. Jackson, M. O'Neill, K. Wright
1995-96	P	9	D. Jackson, K. Wright
1996-97	P	11	D. Jackson
1997-98	P	9	S. Crawford
1998-99	F	14	S. Crawford
1999-00	P	11	K. Miller
2000-01	P	11	M. Paatelainen
2001-02	P	10	G. O'Connor
2002-03	P	12	T. McManus

the hibees' club factfile 2002/03

Date	Venue	Opponents	Att.	Res	Caig T.	Orman A.	Smith G.	Dempsie M.	Townsley D.	Murray I.	Arpinon F.	Brebner G.	O'Neil J.	O'Connor G.	Luna P.	Wiss J.	McManus T.	Whittaker S.	Jack M.	Paatelainen M.	Colgan N.	Fenwick P.	Doumbe M.	Daquin F.	Zambernardi Y.	Dempsie A.	Janos M.	James C.	Reid A.	Riordan D.	Anderson D.	Brown S.	Thomson D.	Nicol K.
Aug 3	H	Aberdeen	13,340	1-2	1	2	3	4	5	6	7	8	9	10	11¹	12	13	14																
11	A	Hearts	15,245	1-5	1	2	3	4	8	6¹	7	12	9	10	11		14		5	13														
18	H	Rangers	11,633	2-4			3		12¹	6	7	8		13¹	11		10		5	14	1	2	4	9										
24	A	Dundee	6,411	1-2			3		7	6		8		11¹		13	9		5	10	1	2		12	4									
31	A	Motherwell	5,888	2-0					7²	6				11			12	8	5	10	1	2			4	9	3							
Sep 11	H	Dunfermline Athletic	9,837	1-4	1				7	6		13			11		14	8	5	10¹		2			4	9	3	12						
14	A	Celtic	56,462	0-1	1	9	3			6		8		12	11	7	10			13		2			4		5							
21	H	Kilmarnock	8,680	2-0		9	3		13	6¹		8		12	11	7	10¹				1	2			4		5							
28	H	Livingston	9,451	1-0		9	3			6¹		8		10	11	7	13				1	2			4	12	5							
Oct 5	H	Dundee United	9,175	2-1		3			9	6¹		8		10¹	11	7	12				1	2			4		5							
19	A	Partick Thistle	5,946	3-0		3	12		9	6		8		11²		7	13			10¹	1	2			4			5						
27	A	Aberdeen	12,321	1-0		3	12		9	6		8¹		11	14	7	13			10	1	2			4			5						
Nov 3	H	Hearts	15,560	1-2		9	3			6		8		11	12	7	13			10¹	1	2			4			5						
10	A	Rangers	49,032	1-2		6	3					8	13	11	12	7	9¹			10	1	2			4			5						
16	H	Dundee	8,870	2-1		8	3			6			9		11	7			13	10²	1	2	12		4			5						
23	H	Motherwell	8,859	3-1		8	3		13	6		14	9¹		11	7	12¹			10¹	1	2			4			5						
30	A	Dunfermline Athletic	7,506	1-1		8	3		12	6			9			7	11¹			10	1	2			4			5	13					
Dec 4	H	Celtic	12,042	0-1		10	3		8	6		12	9			7	11		13		1	2			4			5	14					
7	A	Dundee United	5,673	1-1		8	3		13	6¹			9			7	11			10	1	2			4			5	12					
14	A	Livingston	5,501	2-1		8	3			6¹			9			7	11			10	1	2			4			5¹						
21	A	Kilmarnock	5,814	1-2		8	3		12	6		14	9		13¹	7	11			10	1	2			4			5						
26	H	Partick Thistle	10,317	1-1		8	3			6			9¹		11	7				10	1	2			4			5						
29	H	Aberdeen	11,604	2-0	1	2	3		6	14		12	9		11	7	13¹			10¹			8		4			5						
Jan 2	A	Hearts	17,732	4-4		8	3		9¹	6		12¹			13	7	11¹			10	1	2			4			5¹						
29	H	Rangers	13,686	0-2		5	3		9	6		8	12	10		7	11				1	2			4									
Feb 8	A	Motherwell	4,999	1-2		3			7	6	13	8	9	11¹					5	10	1	2			4			12	14					
15	H	Dunfermline Athletic	9,175	1-3		3			7	6	13	8	9	11			12¹			10	1	2			4			5		14				
25	A	Dundee	8,414	0-3		2	3		13	6	14	8	9	12			11		4	10	1		7					5						
Mar 2	A	Celtic	57,096	2-3			3		9	6	13	8	12	10			11²		4			2	7					5		14	1			
9	H	Dundee United	7,518	1-1			3			6		8	13	12			11¹		7	10	1		9		4		2	5						
15	A	Partick Thistle	4,551	1-0			3			6		8	9	12			11¹		2	10	1		7				4	5		13				
Apr 5	A	Kilmarnock	5,558	2-6			3			6¹	13	8	9	14			11		2¹		1	12	7				4	5		10				
12	H	Livingston	8,150	2-2		5¹			12	6		8	9	10			11		3		1	2	7		4				14	13¹				
26	A	Dundee United	6,758	2-1			3			6¹		8		10			11¹		7		1	2	9		4		5			12				
May 3	H	Aberdeen	7,904	3-1			3		14	6		8		10			11		7¹		1	2	9		4		5			12²		13		
10	H	Motherwell	7,809	1-0			3			6		8¹				12		4	7			2	9				5		13	10	1	11		
17	A	Livingston	5,243	2-1			3					8				6	12	4	7			2					5			10	1	11²	9	
24	H	Partick Thistle	8,986	2-3			3			6		8				7	12	4	2¹		1						5			10		11¹	9	13
TOTAL FULL APPEARANCES					5	25	30	2	15	35	3	25	17	17	12	21	20	5	17	21	30	30	11	1	28	2	14	20		4	3	3	2	
TOTAL SUB APPEARANCES							2		9	1	5	7	4	7	5	3	14	1	2	3		1	1	1		1		2	6	6		1		1
TOTAL GOALS SCORED						1			4	8		3	2	6	2		12		3	7								2		3		3		

Small bold figures denote goalscorers. † denotes opponent's own goal.

easter road stadium

CAPACITY: 17,458 (All Seated)
PITCH DIMENSIONS: 115 yds x 70 yds
FACILITIES FOR DISABLED SUPPORTERS:
Home Supporters:
Famous Five (North) Stand / Wheelchair Disabled and Hearing Impaired.
West Stand / Wheelchair and Ambulant Disabled and Visually Impaired
Away Supporters:
South Stand / Wheelchair and Ambulant Disabled and Hearing and Visually Impaired.

team playing kits

how to get there

Easter Road Stadium can be reached by the following routes:

BUSES: The following Lothian Regional Transport buses depart Princes Street every few minutes and stop in London Road at Easter Road (Nos. 1, 4, 15, 26 and 44). The No. 1 bus travels down Easter Road and stops near the Stadium. The following First Bus Service stop on London Road, at the top of Easter Road (66, 106, 113, 124, 129, X5).

TRAINS: Edinburgh Waverley is served by trains from all over the country and adjoins Princes Street. The Stadium is about a 20/25 minute walk from Princes Street. There is a taxi rank situated within the Station.

CARS: Supporters travelling by car should note that there are no special parking arrangements for cars in the immediate vicinity of the Stadium. Parking is controlled by a Temporary Traffic Regulation Order (coned areas). A tow/away scheme is in operation for illegally parked vehicles. Persons with disabilities displaying Orange Badges on their vehicles will be permitted to park on the south side of St. Clair Street under the direction of Parking Attendants/Police.

kilmarnock

Rugby Park, Rugby Road, Kilmarnock, KA1 2DP
CHAIRMAN
Sir John Orr, O.B.E.
VICE CHAIRMAN
James H. Moffat
DIRECTORS
James H. Clark, Robert Wyper, & Michael Johnston
GENERAL MANAGER
David MacKinnon
SECRETARY, OFFICE ADMINISTRATOR & MEDIA LIAISON OFFICER
Mrs Angela Burnett
MANAGER
Jim Jefferies
ASSISTANT MANAGER
Billy Brown
FIRST TEAM COACH
Ian Durrant
RESERVE COACH
Alan Robertson
FITNESS COACH & PHYSIOTHERAPIST
Alex MacQueen
GOALKEEPING COACH
Jim Stewart
CHIEF SCOUT
Walter Kidd
YOUTH DEVELOPMENT COACH
Alan Robertson
YOUTH COACHES
Paul Clarke & Stuart McLean
CLUB DOCTOR
Mr Ivan Brenkel
GROUNDSMAN
Mark Gallacher
KIT PERSON
Manson Fowler
LOTTERY MANAGER & MEDIA LIAISON OFFICER
David MacKinnon
COMMERCIAL ASSISTANT/ MATCHDAY HOSPITALITY
Anne Clark & Ray Montgomerie
(01563) 543312
PARK HOTEL
On site hotel situated at ground
(01563) 545999
FOOTBALL SAFETY OFFICERS' ASSOCIATION REPRESENTATIVE
Bob Pitt
MATCHDAY PROGRAMME EDITOR
Richard Cairns
TELEPHONES
Ground & Matchday/Ticket Information (01563) 545300
Sec Bus (01563) 545302
Fax (01563) 545303
E/MAIL & INTERNET ADDRESS
aburnett@kilmarnockfc.co.uk
www.kilmarnockfc.co.uk
CLUB SHOP
Situated in the Commercial Centre at the ground. Tel (01563) 545310.
Open Mon to Fri
9.00 a.m.–5.00 p.m.
Saturday home matchdays
10.00 a.m.–5.30 p.m.
Saturday away matchdays
10.00 a.m.–2.00 p.m.
OFFICIAL SUPPORTERS CLUB
c/o Rugby Park, Kilmarnock, KA1 2DP
TEAM CAPTAIN
Stevie Fulton
SHIRT SPONSOR
Seriously Strong
KIT SUPPLIER
TFG

LIST OF PLAYERS 2003/04

SQUAD NO.	SURNAME	FIRST NAME	MIDDLE NAME	DATE OF BIRTH	PLACE OF BIRTH	DATE OF SIGNING	HEIGHT FT INS	WEIGHT ST LBS	POS. ON PITCH	PREVIOUS CLUB
32	Bell	Cameron		18/09/86	Dumfries	30/08/02	5 11	12st 4lb	Gk	Queen of the South
12	Boyd	Kris		18/08/83	Irvine	25/08/99	6 0	12st 12lb	Fwd	Kilmarnock 'S' Form
33	Boyle	John Paul		27/08/85	Glasgow	28/01/01	5 5	9st 9lb	Fwd	Kilmarnock Youths
34	Campbell	Robert	Lindsay	22/07/86	Glasgow	15/01/03	6 2	12st 8lb	Fwd	Kilmarnock Youths
11	Canero	Peter		18/01/81	Glasgow	25/06/98	5 9.5	12st 0lb	Def/Mid	Kilmarnock Youths
23	Canning	Mark		12/09/83	Bellshill	27/10/99	5 11	12st 2lb	Def/Mid	Kilmarnock Youths
35	Cochrane	Robbie		20/05/86	Irvine	22/05/02	6 2	11st 3lb	Def	Kilmarnock Youths
10	Dargo	Craig		03/01/78	Edinburgh	06/06/00	5 6	10st 1lb	Fwd	Raith Rovers
20	Di Giacomo	Paul		30/06/82	Glasgow	08/07/98	5 11	11st 12lb	Fwd	Kilmarnock Youths
17	Dillon	Shaun		24/08/84	Greenock	18/09/00	5 9.5	11st 1lb	Def	Kilmarnock Youths
6	Dindeleux	Frederic		16/01/74	Lille	24/07/99	5 11	11st 10lb	Def	Lille Olympic Sporting Club
29	Dodds	Rhian		10/03/79	Irvine	29/08/03	5 9	11st 3lb	Mid	Robert Morris Unv.
28	Dubourdeau	Francois		12/04/80	Angouleme	20/08/03	6 3	13st 5lb	Gk	Motherwell
–	Durrant	Ian		29/10/66	Glasgow	16/07/02	5 8	11st 4lb	Mid	Rangers
7	Fowler	James		26/10/80	Stirling	18/10/97	5 9	10st 11lb	Def/Mid	Gairdoch B.C.
8	Fulton	Stephen		10/08/70	Greenock	28/06/02	5 10	11st 0lb	Mid	Heart of Midlothian
30	Gilroy	Greig	James	26/01/85	Irvine	16/02/01	5 10	11st 9lb	Mid	Kilmarnock Youths
5	Greer	Gordon		14/12/80	Glasgow	31/08/03	6 2	12st 5lb	Def	Blackburn Rovers
37	Hamill	Jamie		29/07/86	Irvine	16/01/03	5 8	11st 2lb	Def	Kilmarnock 'S' Form
16	Hardie	Martin		22/04/76	Alexandria	22/07/03	6 0	11st 0lb	Mid/Fwd	Partick Thistle
24	Hay	Garry		07/09/77	Irvine	18/08/95	5 7.5	10st 4lb	Def/Mid	Kilmarnock B.C.
15	Hessey	Sean		19/09/78	Liverpool	31/08/99	6 0	12st 7lb	Def	Huddersfield Town
27	Invincibile	Daniele	Anthony	31/03/79	Brisbane	30/07/03	5 11	12st 3lb	Mid	Swindon Town
38	Johnstone	Scott		13/01/85	Paisley	23/05/02	5 8	10st 3lb	Mid	Kilmarnock Youths
4	Locke	Gary		16/06/75	Edinburgh	06/08/02	5 10	11st 8lb	Mid	Bradford City
25	Logan	Fraser	Ian	13/09/84	Irvine	15/08/00	5 10	11st 4lb	Fwd	Kilmarnock Youths
14	Mahood	Alan	Scott	26/03/73	Kilwinning	09/07/98	5 8	11st 5lb	Mid	Morton
39	Masterton	Steven	Allan	02/01/85	Irvine	22/05/02	6 0	12st 12lb	Def	Rangers
18	McDonald	Gary	Matthew	10/04/82	Irvine	04/06/99	6 0	11st 6lb	Fwd	Kilmarnock Youths
31	McGregor	Neil		17/07/85	Irvine	26/07/01	5 11	11st 9lb	Def	Kilmarnock 'S' Form
22	McGuinness	Liam		19/07/84	Irvine	26/07/01	5 10	11st 4lb	Fwd	Kilmarnock 'S' Form
3	McLaughlin	Barry	John	19/04/73	Paisley	30/05/02	6 1	13st 1lb	Def	St. Mirren
9	McSwegan	Gary	John	24/09/70	Glasgow	05/07/02	5 7.5	12st 8lb	Fwd	Heart of Midlothian
1	Meldrum	Colin	George	26/11/75	Kilmarnock	03/09/93	5 10.5	14st 3lb	Gk	Kilwinning Rangers
19	Murray	Stephen		18/04/83	Bellshill	20/12/00	5 3.5	9st 12lb	Mid/Fwd	Kilmarnock 'S' Form
42	Naismith	Steven	John	14/09/86	Irvine	30/08/02	5 9	10st 3lb	Fwd	Kilmarnock Youths
21	Nish	Colin	John	07/03/81	Edinburgh	08/07/03	6 3	11st 3lb	Mid	Dunfermline Athletic
26	Samson	Craig	Ian	03/04/84	Irvine	08/07/00	6 2	12st 7lb	Gk	Kilmarnock Youths
40	Sangster	Stuart	Douglas	05/08/85	Paisley	23/05/02	5 10	10st 13lb	Def	Kilmarnock Youths
2	Shields	Greg		21/08/76	Falkirk	05/06/02	5 9	10st 10lb	Def	Charlton Athletic
41	Sloan	Lewis		22/06/87	Dumfries	01/07/03	5 7	9st 11lb	Mid	Kilmarnock Youths
13	Smith	Graeme		03/10/82	Bellshill	09/06/99	6 2	12st 8lb	Gk	Kilmarnock Youths

milestones

YEAR OF FORMATION: 1869
MOST CAPPED PLAYER: Joe Nibloe
NO. OF CAPS: 11
MOST LEAGUE POINTS IN A SEASON: 58 (Division 2 – Season 1973/74)
MOST LEAGUE GOALS SCORED BY A PLAYER IN A SEASON: Harry "Peerie" Cunningham (Season 1927/28) and Andy Kerr (Season 1960/61)
NO. OF GOALS SCORED: 34
RECORD ATTENDANCE: 34,246 (-v- Rangers – August, 1963)
RECORD VICTORY: 13-2 (-v- Saltcoats – Scottish Cup, 12.9.1896)
RECORD DEFEAT: 0-8 (-v- Rangers and Hibernian – Division 1)

ticket information

SEASON TICKET INFORMATION
THERE IS A SEASON TICKET INITIATIVE – PLEASE CONTACT CLUB FOR DETAILS

CATEGORY	EAST & WEST STAND	MOFFAT STAND
ADULT	270	250
STUDENT	175	155
SENIOR CITIZEN	135	115
YOUTH 16/17	110	90
CHILD 13-15	75	55
U13	55	35
ADULT & U13	N/A	270

LEAGUE ADMISSION INFORMATION

STANDS		CAT A	CAT B
WEST/EAST/	ADULT	22	18
MOFFAT & NORTH	OAP/U16	22	12

CATEGORY A – RANGERS & CELTIC
CATEGORY B – ALL OTHER SPL CLUBS

leading goalscorers 1993-2003

Season	Div	No. of Goals	Player
1993-94	P	7	R. Williamson
1994-95	P	6	C. McKee
1995-96	P	13	P. Wright
1996-97	P	15	P. Wright
1997-98	P	10	P. Wright
1998-99	P	7	A. McCoist
1999-00	P	8	C. Cocard
2000-01	P	8	P. Wright
2001-02	P	7	T. Johnson
2002-03	P	12	K. Boyd

killie's club factfile 2002/03

Date	Venue	Opponents	Att.	Res	Marshall G.	Shields G.	Dindeleux F.	Hessey S.	Hay G.	Fulton S.	Mahood A.	Mitchell A.	Sanjuan J.	Dargo C.	McSwegan G.	McLaren A.	Boyd K.	McLaughlin B.	Locke G.	Canero P.	Fowler J.	Quitongo J.	Di Giacomo P.	Murray S.	Innes C.	Boutal S.	McDonald G.	Dillon S.	Meldrum C.	Canning M.	Stewart C.
Aug 3	H	Rangers	13,972	1-1	1	2	3	4	5	6	7	8	9	10	11	12[1]	13	14													
10	A	Dundee United	6,366	2-1	1	2	3	4	5	6	7		9	12[1]	11	10	13[1]	14	8												
17	H	Motherwell	6,164	0-3	1	2	3	4	5	6	7		9	13	11	10	14		8	12											
25	A	Livingston	5,852	1-0	1	2	3	4		6	7	9		10			11[1]	5		8	12	13									
31	A	Hearts	11,912	1-1	1	2	3	4		6	7			10	13	9	11[1]	5	8	12											
Sep 11	H	Partick Thistle	6,848	1-0	1	2	3			6	7				11	9	10	5	8	4[1]	12	13	14								
14	H	Aberdeen	6,538	2-2	1	2	3			6	7[1]				11		10	5[1]	8	4	12	9	14	13							
21	A	Hibernian	8,680	0-2	1	2	3		14	6	7	13			11		10	5	8	4	12	9									
28	A	Celtic	57,070	0-5	1	2			13	6	7	12	11				14	5		4	8	10	9		3						
Oct 5	A	Dundee	5,567	1-2	1	2	3		4	6	7	14	12				10	5	8		9		13			11[1]					
19	H	Dunfermline Athletic	5,515	2-2	1	2[1]	3		5	7					10		14[1]	6	8			13		12	4	11	9				
27	A	Rangers	48,368	1-6	1	2	3			7[1]			6		14		10	5	8	4	13	9			12	11					
Nov 2	H	Dundee United	5,411	1-2	1	2	3			8[1]	7				12		10			4		13	11	9	5			6			
9	A	Motherwell	4,439	1-0	1	2			14	8	7		13		12		10[1]			4	6		11	9	5			3			
16	H	Livingston	5,270	2-0	1	2	3		14	8	7				12[1]		10		13	4	6		11[1]	9				5			
23	H	Hearts	6,511	0-1	1	2	3			8	7			12	13		10		14	4	6		11	9				5			
30	A	Partick Thistle	5,055	0-3	1	2	3			8	7			10	11	9	12			4	6		13					5			
Dec 3	A	Aberdeen	8,816	1-0	1	2			3	8	7			10	11[1]	9	14		6	4	12		13					5			
7	H	Dundee	4,806	2-0	1	2				8[1]	7			10	11	9	12[1]		6	4	14			13	3			5			
15	H	Celtic	9,225	1-1	1	2				8	7	9	12	14	11	10[1]	13			4	6				3			5			
21	H	Hibernian	5,814	2-1	1	2			14	8[1]	7	12		10	11[1]	9	13			4	6				3			5			
26	A	Dunfermline Athletic	5,847	2-0	1	2			14	8	7	12		10	11[1]	9	13[1]			4	6				3			5			
29	H	Rangers	13,396	0-1	1	2				8	7	9		12	11	10	13			4	6				3			5			
Jan 2	A	Dundee United	7,183	2-2	1	2				8	7	12		11		9[1]	10			4[1]	6				3			5			
29	H	Motherwell	4,457	1-0		2	3		5	8	7			11			10[1]	4			6		12				9		1		
Feb 1	A	Livingston	4,144	4-0		2	3		14	8	7					11[2]	10[1]	5	13	4[1]	6		12				9		1		
8	A	Hearts	10,426	0-3		2				8					13	11	10	5	7	4	6		12		3		9		1	14	
23	H	Partick Thistle	8,651	1-0			3			8	7				11	10	13	5	12	4[1]	6		14		2		9		1		
Mar 1	H	Aberdeen	5,769	2-0		2	3		8		7				11[1]	10	12			4[1]	6		13		5		9		1		
8	A	Dundee	6,531	2-2		2	3		9	8	7				11[1]	10	12		13	4[1]	6				5				1		
16	H	Dunfermline Athletic	4,021	1-1		2	3		9	8	7				11	10	12[1]			4	6			13	5				1		
Apr 5	H	Hibernian	5,558	6-2		2	3			8	7				11[4]	10	12[1]		13	4	6			14	5		9[1]				1
13	A	Celtic	56,736	0-2	1	2				8	7				11	10	13	12	6	4	5				3		9				
27	A	Dundee	5,964	1-0	1		3		9		7				11	10	12	6	8	4	5		14		2[1]			13			
May 3	H	Hearts	9,091	1-0	1		3		6	8	7				11[1]	10	13			4	5		12		2		9				
11	A	Rangers	49,036	0-4	1	2	3			8	7				11	9	13	6	12	4	5		10				14				
17	A	Dunfermline Athletic	6,896	2-2	1	2	3		12	8	7				11	14	10[1]	6		4	5		13				9[1]				
25	H	Celtic	16,722	0-4	1		3		14	8	7				11		10	6	9	4	5		13				12	2			
TOTAL FULL APPEARANCES					30	34	27	5	12	36	35	4	5	10	25	23	17	17	15	31	25	4	6	4	19	3	10	13	7		1
TOTAL SUB APPEARANCES									9			6	3	5	7	2	21	3	7	2	7	4	14	5	1		2	1		1	
TOTAL GOALS SCORED						1				4	1			1	11	5	12	1		6			1		1	1	2				

Small bold figures denote goalscorers. † denotes opponent's own goal.

rugby park

East Stand
Moffat Stand
Chadwick Stand
West Stand
Car Park
DUNDONALD RD
RUGBY ROAD
SOUTH HAMILTON STREET

CAPACITY: 18,128 (All Seated)

PITCH DIMENSIONS: 112 yds x 74 yds

FACILITIES FOR DISABLED SUPPORTERS:
Contact: Grace Jamieson, Secretary, Persons with a Disability Association
Tel: (01563) 555933

team playing kits

how to get there

Rugby Park can be reached by the following routes:

BUSES: The main bus station, which is served by buses from all over the country, is ten minutes walk from the ground, but there are three local services which run from here to within a two minute walk of the park. These are the Kilmarnock/Saltcoats, Kilmarnock/Ardrossan and Kilmarnock/Largs.

TRAINS: Kilmarnock Station is well served by trains from Glasgow and the West Coast, and the station is only 15 minutes walk from the ground.

CARS: Car parking is available in the club car park by permit only. Entry **ONLY** from Dundonald Road. Visiting supporters enter **ONLY** from Rugby Road Entrance.

livingston

The City Stadium,
Alderstone Road, Livingston,
West Lothian, EH54 7DN

CHAIRMAN
Dominic W. Keane

VICE-CHAIRMAN
John McGuinness

DIRECTORS
Anthony K. Kinder & Derek J. Milne

HON VICE-PRESIDENTS
William L. Mill &
John L. Bain, B.E.M.

SECRETARY
James R.S. Renton

ASSISTANT SECRETARY
Duncan Bennett

PA TO CHAIRMAN
Dianne Blair

HEAD COACH
Marcio Maximo Barcellos

FIRST TEAM COACH
Allan Preston

UNDER 21 COACH
Billy Kirkwood

GENERAL MANAGER OF FOOTBALL
David Hay

FITNESS COACH
George McNeil

GOALKEEPING COACH
Roy Baines

DIRECTOR OF YOUTH DEVELOPMENT
Tony Fitzpatrick

YOUTH DEVELOPMENT MANAGER
John McLaughlan

CHIEF SCOUT
James McArthur

CLUB DOCTOR
Dr. Gerard Canning

PART/TIME PHYSIOTHERAPIST
Arthur Duncan

COMMERCIAL MANAGER
Charles Burnett (01506) 417000

LOTTERY MANAGER
Ray Ballantyne

CATERING MANAGER
Allison Ross

GROUNDSMAN
Colin Fraser

KIT PERSON
Danny Cunning

FOOTBALL SAFETY OFFICERS' ASSOCIATION REPRESENTATIVE
John O'Lone (01506) 432142

OPERATIONS DIRECTOR
Alistair Hood

MEDIA LIAISON OFFICER
Archie Reid (01506) 417000

SALES & MARKETING MANAGER
Penny Dunn

MATCHDAY PROGRAMME EDITOR
David Stoker

TELEPHONES
Ground (01506) 417000
Fax (01506) 418888

E-MAIL & INTERNET ADDRESS
dianne.blair@blueyonder.co.uk (General)
jirenton@pkc.gov.uk (Football)
www.livingstonfc.co.uk

CLUB SHOP
Contact Stadium (01506) 417000

SUPPORTERS LIAISON
Kay Robertson (01506) 403431

TEAM CAPTAIN
Stuart Lovell

SHIRT SPONSOR
Intelligent Finance

KIT SUPPLIER
Jerzees

LIST OF PLAYERS 2003/04

SQUAD NO.	SURNAME	FIRST NAME	MIDDLE NAME	DATE OF BIRTH	PLACE OF BIRTH	DATE OF SIGNING	HEIGHT FT INS	WEIGHT ST LBS	POS. ON PITCH	PREVIOUS CLUB
–	Adam	Stephen		10/11/86	Paisley	09/07/03	5 10	11st 6lb	Mid	Livingston Youths
5	Andrews	Marvin		22/12/75	Trinidad & Tobago	05/10/00	6 3	14st 0lb	Def	Raith Rovers
–	Arthur	Robbie		12/08/86	Edinburgh	09/07/03	5 6	10st 9lb	Mid	Livingston Youths
–	Boyd	Scott		04/06/86	Bangour	21/10/02	6 1.5	11st 11lb	Def	Livingston Youths
25	Brittain	Richard		24/09/83	Bangour	03/08/00	5 9	10st 7lb	Mid	Livingston 'S' Form
8	Camacho Barnola	Juan Jose		02/08/80	Spain	18/07/02	5 10.5	11st 7lb	Mid	Real Zaragoza
20	Capin Martino	Salvador		10/09/75	Gijon	11/09/03	5 9	11st 0lb	Mid	Universidad Las Palmas
–	Caulfield	Ruairidh	Alexander	25/11/86	Glasgow	09/07/03	5 6	10st 10lb	Def	Livingston Youths
38	Creer	Allan	William	12/11/86	Rutherglen	03/01/03	6 1	13st 5lb	Gk	Livingston Youths
6	Dorado-Rodriguez	Emmanuel		28/03/73	France	27/06/02	6 2	13st 0lb	Def	Malaga
–	Dorrans	Graham		05/05/87	Glasgow	08/07/03	5 9	10st 0lb	Mid	Livingston Youths
24	English	Tommy		25/12/83	Easington	31/01/03	5 10	11st 13lb	Mid	Newcastle United
7	Fernandez	Davide		20/01/76	Corvina	31/05/02	5 9	11st 2lb	Mid	Celtic
33	Findlay	Scott		16/10/83	Perth	21/07/01	6 2	12st 6lb	Gk	St. Johnstone
–	Fleming	Greg	William Edward	27/09/86	Dunfermline	09/07/03	6 2	10st 7lb	Gk	Livingston Youths
50	Fullerton	Eamon	John	19/03/85	Falkirk	07/07/01	5 10.5	11st 8lb	Def	Livingston Youths
–	Geggan	Andrew		08/05/87	Glasgow	21/08/03	5 8	9st 4lb	Def	St. Johnstone
12	Guinovart	Francisco	Cabrera	05/03/71	Malaga	04/07/02	5 9	12st 0lb	Mid	Deportivo Badajoz
–	Hamilton	Christopher		21/11/87	Germany	13/08/03	5 7.5	9st 2lb	Mid	Queen's Park
30	Harding	Ryan		27/04/84	Edinburgh	01/08/03	6 1	13st 0lb	Def	Hibernian
–	Howe	Kevin		28/01/87	Glasgow	16/01/03	5 10	9st 11lb	Def	Celtic
27	Ipoua	Guy		14/01/76	Douala	07/08/03	5 10	13st 5lb	Mid	Gillingham
–	Jordan	Ryan		24/03/85	Glasgow	21/01/02	6 2	12st 6lb	Def	Pollok United
21	Kerr	Brian		12/10/81	Bellshill	08/08/03	5 10.5	11st 5lb	Mid	Newcastle United
25	Lauchlan	James	Harley	02/02/77	Glasgow	11/09/03	6 1	12st 1lb	Def	Dundee United
16	Lilley	Derek		09/02/74	Paisley	07/07/03	5 10.5	12st 7lb	Fwd	Dundee United
17	Lovell	Stuart		09/01/72	Sydney	06/07/01	5 10	11st 10lb	Mid	Hibernian
1	Main	Alan	David	05/12/67	Elgin	28/01/03	5 11.5	12st 13lb	Gk	St. Johnstone
14	Makel	Lee	Robert	11/01/73	Sunderland	12/06/03	5 10	11st 4lb	Mid	Heart of Midlothian
3	McAllister	James	Reynolds	26/04/78	Glasgow	02/07/03	5 10	11st 0lb	Def	Aberdeen
19	McEwan	David		26/02/82	Lanark	28/07/98	6 2	14st 3lb	Gk	Shotts Bon Accord
11	McGovern	Jon Paul		03/10/80	Glasgow	28/07/03	5 7	9st 6lb	Fwd	Celtic
18	McKenzie	Roderick		08/08/75	Bellshill	04/08/03	6 0	12st 0lb	Gk	Heart of Midlothian
32	McLaughlin	Paul		20/02/84	Glasgow	18/06/01	6 1	14st 0lb	Mid	Livingston Youths
22	McLaughlin	Scott		20/01/84	Glasgow	23/07/02	5 9	10st 7lb	Mid	Hamilton Academical
–	McMenamin	Colin		12/02/81	Glasgow	02/08/02	5 10	11st 0lb	Fwd	Newcastle United
2	McNamee	David		10/10/80	Glasgow	31/08/02	5 11	10st 7lb	Def	Blackburn Rovers
31	McPake	James		24/06/84	Bellshill	01/08/00	6 2.5	12st 4lb	Fwd	Livingston Youths
–	Miller	Gary		15/04/87	Glasgow	29/08/03	5 11.5	10st 9lb	Fwd	St. Mirren
49	Miller	Steven		21/04/84	Paisley	20/01/03	5 9	10st 7lb	Mid	Raith Rovers
39	Montgomery	Kevin		03/01/86	Glasgow	31/08/02	5 10	11st 6lb	Gk	Rangers
15	O'Brien	Burton		10/06/81	South Africa	31/08/02	5 11	10st 7lb	Mid	Blackburn Rovers
–	Parker	Martin		17/04/86	Kilmarnock	04/08/03	5 7.5	10st 10lb	Fwd	Kilmarnock
9	Pasquinelli	Fernando	Adrian	13/03/80	Buenos Aires	31/01/03	5 11	13st 4lb	Fwd	Talleres
4	Ramos (Rubio)	Oscar		17/05/76	Portugal	23/07/02	6 0	12st 5lb	Def	Farense
–	Scott	Martin		15/02/86	Livingston	12/02/00	5 11	11st 0lb	Mid	Livingston Youths
–	Snodgrass	Robert		07/09/87	Glasgow	09/07/03	5 11.5	12st 2lb	Mid	Livingston 'S' Form
23	Snowdon	William	Robert	07/01/83	Colchester	09/08/02	5 11.5	11st 10lb	Def	Livingston Youths
19	Toure Maman	Cherif		13/01/81	Togo	02/11/01	6 0	12st 12lb	Mid	Al Nasar
–	Walker	Allan		03/01/86	Edinburgh	26/07/02	5 10	10st 12lb	Mid	Hibernian
10	Whitmore	Theodore	Eccleston	05/08/72	Montego Bay	04/08/03	5 11	13st 2lb	Mid	Seba United

milestones

YEAR OF FORMATION: 1974 (From Seasons 1974/75 to 1994/95 known as Meadowbank Thistle F.C.)
MOST LEAGUE POINTS IN A SEASON: 55 (Second Division – Season 1986/87) (2 Points for a Win)
77 (Third Division – Season 1998/99) (3 Points for a Win)
MOST LEAGUE GOALS SCORED BY A PLAYER IN A SEASON: John McGachie (Season 1986/87)
NO. OF GOALS SCORED: 21
RECORD ATTENDANCE: 2,818 (-v- Albion Rovers, 10.8.1974 at Meadowbank Stadium)
10,024 (-v- Celtic, 18.8.2001 at West Lothian Courier Stadium)
RECORD VICTORY: 6-0 (-v- Raith Rovers – Second Division, 9.11.1985; -v- Alloa Athletic – First Division, 26.8.2000)
RECORD DEFEAT: 0-8 (-v- Hamilton Academical – Division 2, 14.12.1974)

ticket information

SEASON TICKET INFORMATION

ADULT	175/275
PARENT & JUVENILE	185/310
PARENT & 2 JUVENILES	195/335
2 PARENTS & 1 JUVENILE	360/575
2 PARENTS & 2 JUVENILES	370/600
OAP & JUVENILE	75

LEAGUE ADMISSION PRICES

	CAT A	CAT B
ADULT	20	15
CONCESSIONS	10	10

CATEGORY A – CELTIC, HEARTS, HIBERNIAN & RANGERS
(PLEASE NOTE CONCESSIONS NOT ALWAYS APPLICABLE)

CATEGORY B – ALL OTHER MATCHES

leading goalscorers 1993-2003

Season	Div	No. of Goals	Player
1993-94	S	12	I. Little
1994-95	S	6	L. Bailey
1995-96	T	18	J. Young
1996-97	S	15	G. Harvey
1997-98	S	15	G. Harvey
1998-99	S	12	J. Robertson
1999-00	F	15	D. Bingham
2000-01	F	14	D. Bingham
2001-02	P	9	B. Wilson
2002-03	P	9	R. Zarate

SPL
SCOTTISH PREMIER LEAGUE

livi lions' club factfile 2002/03

Date	Venue	Opponents	Att.	Res	Broto J.	Brinquin P.	Bollan G.	Rubio O.	Andrews M.	Quino F.	Lovell S.	Makel L.	Dadi E.	Camacho J.	Zarate R.	Bingham D.	Toure-Maman C.	Xausa D.	Wilson B.	Bahoken G.	Dorado E.	Hart M.	O'Brien B.	McNamee D.	McMenamin C.	McEwan D.	Amor G.	Main A.	Maidana J.	Pasquinelli F.	Brittain R.	McLaughlin S.
Aug 3	H	Motherwell	5,567	3-2	1	2	3	4^{1}	5	6	7	8	9	10	11^{2}	12	13	14														
10	A	Dunfermline Athletic	4,751	1-2	1	2	3	4	5	6		8	9	10	11	13	7	12^{1}	14													
17	A	Partick Thistle	4,255	2-2	1	2	3	4^{2}		6	7		13	12	10	11	9	14	8	5												
25	H	Kilmarnock	5,852	0-1	1	2	3	4	5	6	7	14	9	12	10	11	8	13														
Sep 1	A	Celtic	55,334	0-2	1	2	14	4	5	6	7	8	10		13	11	12			3	9											
11	A	Dundee	5,391	†1-2	1			4	5	6		8	9		14	11		10		3	7	2	12	13								
14	H	Rangers	8,787	0-2	1		3	4	5	6	7		14	10	11	12	9		8				13	2								
22	H	Aberdeen	5,852	1-2	1	2	3	4	5	6			9	13	10	11		12^{1}	8				7		14							
28	A	Hibernian	9,451	0-1	1		12	4	5	6				13		11		10	8	3		7	9	2	14							
Oct 6	H	Hearts	6,492	1-1	1		3	4	5	6				14	10	11	13	12	8^{1}			7	9	2								
19	A	Dundee United	5,572	3-2	1	2	3^{1}	4	5	6		14	12^{1}		13	11		10	8^{1}			7	9									
26	A	Motherwell	4,342	5-1	1	2	3	4	5	6		7^{1}	10			11^{1}	112	14^{1}	8			13	9									
Nov 2	H	Dunfermline Athletic	5,578	1-1	1	2	3	4	5	6		7	10		12	11	14^{1}	13	8				9									
9	H	Partick Thistle	5,426	3-0	1		3	4	5^{1}	6		7	10^{1}		13	11^{1}	8	14	12				9	2								
16	A	Kilmarnock	5,270	0-2	1	2	3		5	6		7	9	11		13	8	10	12	4			14									
24	H	Celtic	8,320	0-2	1	2	3	4	5	6		9	12		13	11	8		10	7												
30	H	Dundee	4,151	1-1	1	2	3	4	5	12		7	9	10^{1}	13	11	8	14					6									
Dec 4	A	Rangers	45,992	3-4	1	2	3	4	5	14		7	9	10	13^{2}	11	8		12^{1}				6									
7	A	Hearts	8,074	1-2	1			4	5	6		7		14	10^{1}	11	13	12	9	3		2	8									
14	H	Hibernian	5,501	1-2	1	2^{1}	3		5	6		7			10	11	12	13	9			4	8									
21	A	Aberdeen	11,253	0-0	1	2	3	14	5	6		7	9		10	11		13	8			4			12							
26	H	Dundee United	3,969	3-0	1	2	3		5^{1}	6		7		9^{1}	10	11^{1}	14	12	8			4			13							
29	H	Motherwell	5,558	1-0	1	2	3	12	5	6		7		9	10^{1}	11		8				4	13		14							
Jan 2	A	Dunfermline Athletic	5,218	0-2	1		3	4	5	6		7		9	10	11	13	8				2			14	15						
28	A	Partick Thistle	3,541	3-1		2		4	5^{1}	6		7			10^{1}	11		9		3			8		13^{1}	1	12					
Feb 1	H	Kilmarnock	4,144	0-4		2		4	5			7			10	11	12	9	13	3			8		14	1	6					
9	A	Celtic	56,982	1-2		2		4	5	6	9		11		10^{1}	14			12	3			8				13	1	7			
Mar 2	H	Rangers	8,439	1-2		2			5	6	9	7	12^{1}		10		14	13	11	3			8					1	4			
5	A	Dundee	7,554	0-0		2			5	12	9	7	11	14	10		6	13	12	3			8					1	4			
8	H	Hearts	6,448	1-1		2		13^{1}	5	6	9	7	11		10		8	12		3					14			1	4			
15	A	Dundee United	6,247	1-0		2		4	5^{1}	13	9	7		14	12			11		3			8		10			1	6			
Apr 5	H	Aberdeen	4,994	1-2		2				12	9^{1}	7		6	13	14		11		3			8	5	10			1	4			
12	A	Hibernian	8,150	2-2		2			5	14	9	7	13	6				11	12^{1}				8^{1}	3				1	4	10		
26	A	Aberdeen	8,912	0-1					3	12	9	7	14	5	10	13			8				6	2				1	4	11		
May 3	H	Partick Thistle	4,438	3-1		2			5	12	9			6^{1}	10^{1}	14		8^{1}					7	3	13			1	4	11		
10	H	Dundee United	5,462	1-2		2					9	7		5	10	13^{1}		8					6	3	14			1	4	11	12	
17	H	Hibernian	5,243	1-2		2				6		7		5	14	11	8		9				12	3				1	4	10^{1}	13	
24	A	Motherwell	4,790	2-6		2						7^{1}		5		13			9				12	3	10^{1}			1	4	11	8	6
TOTAL FULL APPEARANCES					24	30	20	23	33	27	15	29	16	16	22	23	12	13	17	15	2	10	22	11	3	2	1	12	12	6	1	1
TOTAL SUB APPEARANCES							2	3		8		2	7	8	11	10	11	17	8			1	6	1	11	1	2				2	
TOTAL GOALS SCORED						1	1	4	4		1	2	3	3	9	4	3	4	4				1		2					1		

Small bold figures denote goalscorers. † denotes opponent's own goal.

the city stadium

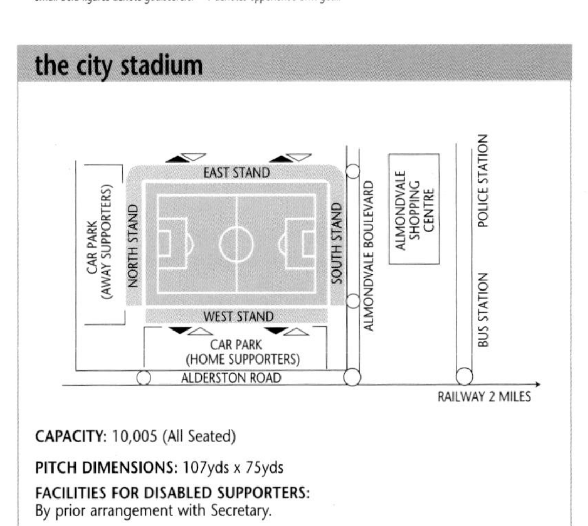

CAPACITY: 10,005 (All Seated)

PITCH DIMENSIONS: 107yds x 75yds

FACILITIES FOR DISABLED SUPPORTERS:
By prior arrangement with Secretary.

team playing kits

how to get there

The City Stadium can be reached by the following routes:

BUSES: By bus to terminus at Almondvale Shopping Centre. Follow direction signs for St. John's Hospital or the City Stadium and it is a short 5 minute walk.

TRAINS: To either Livingston North or South Stations, and by taxi to stadium. Approximate cost is £2.00.

CARS: Leave M8 at Livingston Junction (East). Follow signs for St. John's Hospital or the City Stadium.

motherwell

Fir Park, Firpark Street, Motherwell, ML1 2QN
HON. LIFE PRESIDENT
James C. Chapman, O.B.E.
CHAIRMAN
John Boyle
DIRECTORS
William H. Dickie, R.I.B.A., A.R.I.A.S, Alisdair F. Barron, Mrs. Fiona Boyle, Andrew Lapping, John Swinburne, James McMahon & Ian Stillie
SECRETARY
Stewart Robertson
OFFICE ADMINISTRATOR
Betty Pryde
MANAGER & FIRST TEAM COACH
Terry Butcher
ASSISTANT MANAGER, FIRST TEAM COACH & U21 COACH
Maurice Malpas
YOUTH DEVELOPMENT MANAGER & U19 YOUTH TEAM COACH
Chris McCart
COMMUNITY COACH
Graham Diamond
YOUTH TEAM COACHES
Gordon Young & Brian Reynolds (U17)
Bobby Barr & Willie Falconer (U16)
Graham Ogg & Andy Brown (U15)
Ricky Reid & Graeme Mathie (U14)
Willie Devine & Bill Raeside (U13)
Robert Clark & Tommy McAteer(U12)
CLUB DOCTOR
Dr. Robert Liddle
PHYSIOTHERAPISTS
John Porteous & Peter Salila
FOOTBALL SAFETY OFFICERS' ASSOCIATION REPRESENTATIVE
Kenneth Davies
07762 871049 (Mobile)
GROUNDSMAN
Gus Hollas
KIT PERSON
Alan MacDonald
STADIUM MANAGER
Bill McGill
HOSPITALITY CO-ORDINATOR
Wendy McFarlane (01698) 338008/9
MATCHDAY PROGRAMME EDITOR
Graham Barnstaple
TELEPHONES
Ground (01698) 333333
Ticket Information (01698) 333033
Fax (01698) 338001
Hospitality Hotline (01698) 338008/9
E-MAIL & INTERNET ADDRESS
mfc@motherwellfc.co.uk
www.motherwellfc.co.uk
CLUB SHOP
Provan Sports, The Well Shop, Fir Park, Motherwell. Tel (01698) 338025
Open Tues, Thurs, Fri from 9.30a.m. to 4.00p.m. and home matchdays 10.00a.m. to 3.00p.m. and away matchdays 10.00a.m. to 1.00p.m.
OFFICIAL SUPPORTERS CLUB
c/o Fir Park, Firpark Street, Motherwell, ML1 2QN.
TEAM CAPTAIN
Scott Leitch
SHIRT SPONSOR
Untouchables
KIT SUPPLIER
XARA

LIST OF PLAYERS 2003/04

SQUAD NO.	SURNAME	FIRST NAME	MIDDLE NAME	DATE OF BIRTH	PLACE OF BIRTH	DATE OF SIGNING	HEIGHT FT INS	WEIGHT ST LBS	POS. ON PITCH	PREVIOUS CLUB
7	Adams	Derek	Watt	25/06/75	Glasgow	15/09/98	5 10	11st 8lb	Fwd	Ross County
24	Ballantyne	Ross		27/01/84	Glasgow	07/02/03	5 8	11st 0lb	Mid	Celtic
27	Barkey	Kevin		05/02/85	Glasgow	05/06/01	5 7.5	10st 1lb	Mid	Motherwell Youths
11	Burns	Alexander		04/08/73	Bellshill	06/06/03	5 7	12st 4lb	Mid/Fwd	Partick Thistle
47	Calder	Douglas		01/02/86	Glasgow	22/08/03	5 11.5	11st 11lb	Gk	Hamilton Academical
37	Cameron	Mark		07/02/87	Rutherglen	21/01/03	5 7.5	9st 6lb	Def	Motherwell 'S' Form
18	Clarkson	David		10/09/85	Bellshill	02/06/01	5 10.5	10st 2lb	Fwd	Motherwell Youths
39	Connolly	Kenneth		08/04/87	Glasgow	09/06/03	5 10	10st 7lb	Mid	Motherwell Youths
15	Corr	Barry John		13/01/81	Glasgow	05/08/03	6 2	13st 2lb	Gk	Celtic
2	Corrigan	Martyn	Alexander	14/08/77	Glasgow	21/01/00	5 11	12st 0lb	Def	Falkirk
16	Cowan	David	Robert	05/03/82	Whitehaven	20/06/03	5 11.5	11st 2lb	Def/Mid	Newcastle United
17	Craig	Steven		05/02/81	Blackburn	29/01/03	5 11	12st 2lb	Fwd	Falkirk
5	Craigan	Stephen	James	29/10/76	Newtonards	09/06/03	6 1	13st 1lb	Def	Partick Thistle
9	Dair	Jason		15/06/74	Dunfermline	04/09/03	5 11	12st 2lb	Mid	Dunfermline Athletic
38	Donnelly	Robert	Stevenson	19/01/87	Glasgow	21/01/03	6 1	13st 0lb	Mid	Motherwell Youths
25	Ewings	Jamie		04/08/84	Bellshill	30/07/00	5 11.5	11st 6lb	Gk	Hibernian
21	Fagan	Shaun	Michael	22/03/84	Bellshill	14/06/00	5 10	10st 7lb	Mid	Motherwell Youths
35	Fitzpatrick	Marc		11/05/86	Lanark	30/08/02	5 10.5	10st 9lb	Def	Motherwell Youths
33	Grant	Ryan		05/01/85	Bellshill	02/06/01	5 5.5	9st 5lb	Mid	Motherwell Youths
3	Hammell	Steven		18/02/82	Rutherglen	31/08/99	5 9.5	11st 11lb	Def	Motherwell 'X' Form
31	Higgins	Christopher	James	04/07/85	Broxburn	02/06/01	5 11	10st 11lb	Def	Motherwell Youths
44	Keogh	David	John	29/08/86	Edinburgh	09/06/03	6 1.5	12st 5lb	Def	Motherwell Youths
22	Kinniburgh	William	Daniel	08/09/84	Glasgow	14/06/00	6 1.5	11st 7lb	Def	Motherwell Youths
4	Lasley	Keith	William Robert	21/09/79	Glasgow	20/03/99	5 8.5	11st 0lb	Mid	Gleniffer Thistle
8	Leitch	Donald Scott		06/10/69	Motherwell	25/06/03	5 10	11st 10lb	Mid	Swindon Town
20	MacDonald	Kevin	Graham	05/02/83	Glasgow	29/06/00	5 10.5	10st 12lb	Mid	Gleniffer Thistle
40	Maguire	Stephen		14/02/87	Bellshill	09/06/03	5 7	9st 8lb	Def/Mid	Motherwell Youths
1	Marshall	Gordon	George Banks	19/04/64	Edinburgh	04/07/03	6 3	14st 1lb	Gk	Kilmarnock
23	Mathie	Graeme	Ross	17/10/82	Lanark	26/08/02	6 0.5	11st 12lb	Def	AFC Bournemouth
32	McAndie	Brian	James	04/05/85	Glasgow	02/06/01	5 9	10st 8lb	Mid	Motherwell Youths
36	McColl	Bobby		21/04/86	Glasgow	30/08/02	5 9	9st 5lb	Def	Aberdeen
42	McStay	John		10/07/87	Bellshill	09/06/03	5 7.5	9st 0lb	Def	Celtic Youths
29	Neville	Barry	Robert	18/04/85	Rutherglen	02/06/01	5 10	10st 10lb	Def	Motherwell Youths
14	Partridge	David	William	26/11/78	London	22/07/02	6 1	14st 0lb	Def	Dundee United
6	Pearson	Stephen	Paul	02/10/82	Lanark	31/07/00	6 1	11st 6lb	Mid	Motherwell B.C.
41	Quinn	Mark	James	13/05/87	Glasgow	09/06/03	5 10.5	10st 11lb	Def	Motherwell Youths
19	Quinn	Paul	Charles	21/07/85	Lanark	28/08/00	6 1	11st 4lb	Def	Motherwell Youths
30	Reid	Andrew		06/03/85	Aberdeen	09/06/03	6 1	14st 0lb	Gk	Nottingham Forest
43	Reid	Philip		03/04/87	Aberdeen	09/06/03	5 11	10st 12lb	Fwd	Celtic Youths
34	Reilly	James	Alfred	07/02/86	Glasgow	25/08/00	5 9.5	10st 10lb	Fwd	Motherwell Youths
46	Russell	Ryan		09/04/87	Dunfermline	09/06/03	5 8.5	10st 12lb	Fwd	Motherwell Youths
28	Scott	Robert (Andy)	Andrew	30/01/85	Glasgow	25/08/00	5 9.5	10st 5lb	Fwd	Motherwell Youths
26	Wright	Kenneth	Thomas	01/08/85	Bellshill	05/06/01	5 10.5	11st 5lb	Fwd	Motherwell Youths

milestones

YEAR OF FORMATION: 1886
MOST CAPPED PLAYER: Tommy Coyne (Republic of Ireland)
NO. OF CAPS: 13
MOST LEAGUE POINTS IN A SEASON: 66 (Division 1 – Season 1931/32)
MOST LEAGUE GOALS SCORED BY A PLAYER IN A SEASON: William McFadyen (Season 1931/32)
NO. OF GOALS SCORED: 52
RECORD ATTENDANCE: 35,632 (-v- Rangers – Scottish Cup, 12.3.1952)
RECORD VICTORY: 12-1 (-v- Dundee United – Division 2, 23.1.1954)
RECORD DEFEAT: 0-8 (-v- Aberdeen – Premier Division, 26.3.1979)

ticket information

SEASON TICKET INFORMATION – SEATED

EAST STAND

ADULT	JUV	OAP/STU
180	55	100

DAVID COOPER STAND

ADULT	PAR&JUV	ADDIT JUV	JUV	OAP/STU	COOPER	PARKING
210	240	30	70	125	BOX 458.50	50

MAIN STAND

ADULT	JUV	OAP/STU	CENTENARY	MILLENNIUM	PARKING
260	90	150	458.25	940	50

SOUTH STAND

MOTOROLA BOX	PARKING
1,880	50

LEAGUE ADMISSION INFORMATION – SEATED

EAST STAND	ADULT – 13	JUV – 4	OAP/STU – 8
DAVID COOPER STAND	ADULT – 15	JUV – 5	OAP/STU – 9
MAIN STAND	ADULT – 17	JUV – 6	OAP/STU – 10
SOUTH STAND (VISITING FANS ONLY)	ADULT – 17	JUV – 6	OAP/STU – 10

leading goalscorers 1993-2003

Season	Div	No. of Goals	Player
1993-94	P	12	T. Coyne
1994-95	P	16	T. Coyne
1995-96	P	5	W. Falconer
1996-97	P	11	T. Coyne
1997-98	P	15	T. Coyne
1998-99	P	7	O. Coyle, J. Spencer
1999-00	P	11	J. Spencer
2000-01	P	10	S. Elliott
2001-02	P	10	S. Elliott, J. McFadden
2002-03	P	13	J. McFadden

the well's club factfile 2002/03

Date	Venue	Opponents	Att.	Res	Woods S.	Corrigan M.	Partridge D.	Hammell S.	Ramsay D.	Lasley K.	Pearson S.	Leitch S.	MacDonald K.	McFadden J.	Lehmann D.	Clarke D.	Kinniburgh W.	Adams D.	Fagan S.	Ferguson S.	Sengewald D.	Russell I.	Cowan D.	Jack D.	Kemas K.	Dubourdeau F.	Dempsie B.	Quinn P.	Clarkson D.	Craig S.	Vaughan A.	Offiong R.	Ballantyne R.	Wright I.	Scott A.
Aug 3	A	Livingston	5,567	2-3	1	2	3	4	5	6	7	8[1]	9	10	11[1]	12																			
10	H	Partick Thistle	5,788	1-1	1	2	3	4	5	6	7[1]	8	9	10	11		12																		
17	A	Kilmarnock	6,164	3-0	1	2	3	4	5[1]	6	7[1]	8		10[1]	11		12	9	13																
25	A	Dundee United	5,795	1-1	1	2	3	4	5	6	7[1]	8	14	10	11		13	9		12															
31	H	Hibernian	5,888	0-2	1	2	3	4	5	6	7	8		10	11			9	13	12															
Sep 10	H	Celtic	8,448	2-1	1	2	3	4	12	6	7	8		10[1]	11			9	13[1]	14	5														
15	A	Hearts	8,759	2-4	1	2	3	4	5	6			12	10[1]	11[1]			9	8	13	7	14													
21	A	Dunfermline Athletic	4,987	0-1	1	2	3	4	12	6	7	8		10	11			9	13	14	5														
28	H	Dundee	4,025	1-1	1	2	3	4	5	6	7			10[1]	11			9		8															
Oct 5	H	Aberdeen	6,014	1-2	1	2	3	4	5	6		8		10[1]	11			9		7	12	13													
19	A	Rangers	49,376	0-3	1	2	3	4	5	6	7				11			10		9		12	8	13											
26	H	Livingston	4,342	1-5	1	2		4	3	6	7	8			11			10		12			5	13	9[1]										
Nov 2	A	Partick Thistle	5,405	0-2	1	2		4		13	7	8		10	12		3	11		14	5		6		9										
9	H	Kilmarnock	4,439	0-1		2	3	4	5		7		8		11			10		12		13	6		9	1									
16	H	Dundee United	5,381	1-2		2	3	4	5		7				11[1]			10	12	8		13	6		9	1									
23	A	Hibernian	8,859	1-3		2	3	4			7			12	11			10	8	9[1]	5		6			1									
Dec 1	A	Celtic	56,610	1-3		2		4				8	14	10	11[1]		3	9	6	7					12	1	5	13							
4	H	Hearts	4,114	6-1		2[1]	3	4			7[1]	8		10[2]	11		5	9[1]		12[1]	6					1									
7	A	Aberdeen	9,569	1-1		2		4				8	12	10	11		3[1]	9	6	7						1		5	13						
14	A	Dundee	5,527	1-1		2		4				8		10	11[1]		3	9	6	7						1		5	12						
26	H	Rangers	11,234	1-0		2	3	4			7	8		10[1]	11		5	9					6			1									
29	A	Livingston	5,558	0-1		2	3	4			7	8		10	11		5	9		12			6			1			13						
Jan 2	H	Partick Thistle	6,262	2-2		2	3[1]	4	14		7	8		10	11		5	9	12	13						1			6[1]						
29	A	Kilmarnock	4,457	0-1	13	2	3			6	7	8					5	9	12				4			1			10	11					
Feb 1	A	Dundee United	6,672	1-2	1	2	3	4		14	7	8					6	9[1]	13										10	11	5	12			
8	H	Hibernian	4,999	2-1		2	3	4			7	8						9	12[1]				6		13	1			10[1]	11	5				
19	H	Dunfermline Athletic	3,741	2-1		2	3	4	12	13	7[1]							9	8				6			1			10	11[1]	5				
Mar 1	A	Hearts	11,704	1-2		2	3	4	6	9[1]	7			10	13				8							1			11		5	12			
8	H	Aberdeen	5,636	0-1		2	3	4	6	8	7			10	12				9							1			11	14	5	13			
19	A	Rangers	49,420	0-2		2	3	4	6	7				10	9				8				12			1			11	14	5	13			
Apr 5	A	Dunfermline Athletic	4,086	0-3		2	3	4		6		8		10	11			9	14				7			1			12	13	5				
12	H	Dundee	4,693	1-2		2	3	4		6		7		10[1]	11			9					5			1			12	8		13			
26	A	Partick Thistle	4,870	0-3		2	3	4						10	11			9					6			1			7	8	5	12			
May 3	H	Dundee United	9,056	2-2	1	2	3	4			7[1]	8		10	13			9											11	6	5[1]	12			
7	H	Celtic	12,037	0-4	1	2	3	4			7	8		10	14		12	9					6						11		5	13			
10	A	Hibernian	7,809	0-1		2	3	4	6	7	9	8		10	11											1			12	13	5				
17	H	Aberdeen	4,731	2-3		2	3	4		6	7	8		10[1]				9								1			11[1]	12	5	13			
24	H	Livingston	4,790	6-2		2		4		6[2]	7		9	10[3]			3									1		5	11	8[1]			12	13	14
TOTAL FULL APPEARANCES					16	38	32	37	16	21	29	26	4	29	27		11	31	9	8	6		15		4	22	1	3	13	8	12				
TOTAL SUB APPEARANCES					1				4	3			4	1	5	1	4		10	11	1	5	1	2	2			1	6	5		9	1	1	1
TOTAL GOALS SCORED						1	1		1	3	6	1		13	5		1	2	2	2					1				3	2	1				

Small bold figures denote goalscorers. † denotes opponent's own goal.

fir park

DALZELL DRIVE
EAST STAND
KNOWETOP AVENUE
DAVIE COOPER STAND
MOTOROLA STAND
MAIN STAND
Chapman Building
FIRPARK STREET

CAPACITY: 13,757 (All Seated)

PITCH DIMENSIONS: 110 yds x 75 yds

FACILITIES FOR DISABLED SUPPORTERS:
Area between Main Stand and South Stand. Prior arrangement must be made with the Secretary and a ticket obtained.

team playing kits

how to get there

The following routes can be used to reach Fir Park:

BUSES: Fir Park is less than a quarter of a mile from the main thoroughfare through the town and numerous buses serving Lanarkshire and Glasgow all pass along this road. De-bus at the Civic Centre.

TRAINS: Motherwell Station is a twenty minute walk from Fir Park, while the station at Airbles Road is only ten minutes away. East Coast access is via Motherwell Central Station on the Glasgow/London East Coast line. Travel from West Coast and Glasgow areas is via the low level Glasgow Central line to Airbles and Motherwell Central. This is a regular service on a 30 minute basis (8 mins & 38 mins past).

CARS: Controlled supervised car parking is available in the immediate area of Fir Park. Car park season tickets are available for closest proximity car parks. Away fan car parking is extensive in the grounds of Motherwell College on a day rate basis of £5.00.

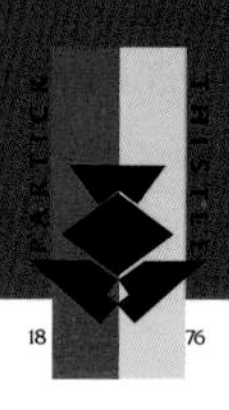

partick thistle

Firhill Stadium, 80 Firhill Road, Glasgow, G20 7AL
CHAIRMAN
Thomas Hughes
VICE-CHAIRMAN
Allan Cowan
DIRECTORS
James Oliver, T. Brown McMaster, Edward Prentice, Norman Springford Gordon D. Peden & Ronald S. Gilfillan
HON. VICE-PRESIDENT
Robert W. Reid
ASSOCIATE DIRECTORS
Robert W. Reid, Les Hope & John Lambie
CHIEF EXECUTIVE/SECRETARY
Alan C. Dick
MANAGER
Gerry Collins
ASSISTANT MANAGER & U21 COACH
Bobby McCulley
GOALKEEPING COACH
Alan Rough
PLAYER/FIRST TEAM COACH
Gerry Britton
RESERVE COACH
Chic Charnley
FITNESS COACH
Greg McEwan
YOUTH TEAM COACHES
Chic Charnley & John Wales (U19), Willie Davies (U17), Scott Shaw (U16), Rikki Roughan (U15) & John Hamilton (U14)
YOUTH CO-ORDINATOR
George Wilson
CHIEF SCOUT
Martin Boyle
CLUB DOCTOR
Dr Alan W. Robertson
PHYSIOTHERAPIST
George Hannah
STADIUM MANAGER & CHIEF OF SECURITY
Alan C. Dick
GROUNDSMAN
George Furze
KIT PERSON
Rikki Roughan
CHIEF STEWARD
Brian McKigen
FOOTBALL SAFETY OFFICERS' ASSOCIATION REPRESENTATIVE
Alan C. Dick (0141) 579 1971
COMMERCIAL MANAGER
Amanda Barrie (0141) 579 1971
LOTTERY MANAGER
Bobby Briggs
MEDIA LIAISON OFFICER
Alan C. Dick
MATCHDAY PROGRAMME EDITOR
Tom Hosie
SHOP MANAGERESS
Liz Gordon
TELEPHONES
Ground/Ticket Office/Commercial (0141) 579 1971
Fax (0141) 945 1525
Jagsline (09068) 666474
E-MAIL AND INTERNET ADDRESS
mail@ptfc.co.uk
www.ptfc.co.uk
CLUB SHOP
80 Firhill Road, Glasgow, G20 7AL Tel (0141) 579 1971.
Open each matchday and every Tuesday from 12.30p.m. - 4.30p.m. Upstairs office shop open daily from 9.00 a.m. - 4.30 p.m.
OFFICIAL SUPPORTERS CLUB
c/o Firhill Stadium, 80 Firhill Road, Glasgow, G20 7AL
TEAM CAPTAIN
Derek Whyte
SHIRT SPONSOR
D.H. Morris
KIT SUPPLIER
TFG

LIST OF PLAYERS 2003/04

SQUAD NO.	SURNAME	FIRST NAME	MIDDLE NAME	DATE OF BIRTH	PLACE OF BIRTH	DATE OF SIGNING	HEIGHT FT INS	WEIGHT ST LBS	POS. ON PITCH	PREVIOUS CLUB
28	Anis	Jean-Yves		30/11/80	Oume	04/08/03	5 11	10st 12lb	Def	Chelsea
12	Arthur	Kenneth		07/12/78	Bellshill	01/06/97	6 3	13st 8lb	Gk	Possilpark YMCA
8	Bonnes	Stephane		26/02/78	France	18/06/03	5 6	10st 0lb	Mid	Celtic
31	Boyle	Joseph		16/05/83	Glasgow	03/07/02	6 0.5	11st 8lb	Mid	Falkirk
9	Britton	Gerard	Joseph	20/10/70	Glasgow	03/07/01	6 0	11st 11lb	Fwd	Livingston
29	Budinauckas	Kevin		16/09/74	Bellshill	08/03/02	5 11	13st 4lb	Gk	Clyde
38	Cassidy	Paul	John	18/11/86	Glasgow	02/07/03	5 11	10st 7lb	Mid	Partick Thistle B.C.
18	Fleming	Derek	Adam	05/12/73	Falkirk	21/06/01	5 8	10st 5lb	Mid	Livingston
15	Forrest	Edward	Alexander	17/12/78	Edinburgh	10/07/03	6 0	12st 0lb	Def	Arbroath
19	Gemmell	John	O'Neill	06/09/84	Glasgow	03/06/03	6 2	12st 7lb	Fwd	Queen's Park
21	Gibson	Andrew	Stewart	02/03/82	Glasgow	03/07/00	5 10	10st 9lb	Mid	Partick Thistle B.C.
16	Grady	James		14/03/71	Paisley	03/06/03	5 7	10st 4lb	Fwd	Ayr United
24	Howie	William		09/07/82	Rutherglen	21/05/99	5 9	10st 1lb	Mid	Partick Thistle B.C.
13	Kaczan	Paul		03/02/83	Bellshill	30/06/03	5 11	10st 0lb	Def	Heart of Midlothian
2	Lilley	David	William	31/10/77	Bellshill	02/07/02	6 1	11st 4lb	Def	Aberdeen
14	McBride	John Paul		28/11/78	Hamilton	18/06/03	5 10	10st 2lb	Mid	Derry City
37	McBride	Martin	Anthony	21/05/86	Glasgow	27/05/03	5 10	10st 5lb	Fwd	Giffnock North B.C.
1	Mikkelsen	Jakup		14/08/70	Torshavn	28/07/03	5 11	12st 6lb	Gk	Molde FK
30	Miller	Colin		01/11/83	Glasgow	18/05/02	6 0	11st 0lb	Fwd	Cowdenbeath
6	Milne	Kenneth		26/08/79	Stirling	17/06/02	6 2.5	12st 8lb	Fwd	Heart of Midlothian
7	Mitchell	James	McGilvray	06/01/76	Glasgow	18/05/02	5 7	10st 0lb	Mid	Clyde
5	Murray	Grant	Robert	29/08/75	Edinburgh	23/06/03	5 10	12st 0lb	Def	St. Johnstone
20	Panther	Emmanuel	Ugochukwu Ezenwa	11/05/84	Glasgow	18/06/03	5 11	13st 1lb	Mid	St. Johnstone
17	Ross	Andrew	Cameron	18/09/82	Irvine	02/07/03	5 10	10st 7lb	Mid	Chelsea
3	Ross	Ian		27/08/74	Broxburn	21/01/03	5 10	11st 10lb	Mid	St. Mirren
10	Rowson	David	Andrew	14/09/76	Aberdeen	02/07/03	5 10.5	12st 2lb	Mid	Stoke City
25	Rushford	Gavin		05/05/86	Glasgow	30/08/02	5 11	10st 7lb	Def	Partick Thistle 'S' Form
26	Shields	Matthew	John	17/02/86	Glasgow	30/08/02	5 9	10st 2lb	Fwd	Partick Thistle 'S' Form
11	Taylor	Stuart		26/11/74	Glasgow	03/06/03	6 1	11st 10lb	Mid	Falkirk
27	Thomson	Andrew		01/04/71	Motherwell	16/07/03	5 10	10st 10lb	Fwd	Queens Park Rangers
23	Waddell	Richard		04/02/81	Falkirk	24/06/02	5 9	11st 7lb	Fwd	Falkirk
4	Whyte	Derek		31/08/68	Glasgow	03/07/02	5 11.5	13st 2lb	Def	Aberdeen
39	Wilson	David		22/01/86	Glasgow	02/07/03	5 11	12st 3lb	Def	Rangers

milestones

YEAR OF FORMATION: 1876
MOST CAPPED PLAYER: Alan Rough
NO. OF CAPS: 53
MOST LEAGUE POINTS IN A SEASON: 57 (First Division – Season 1991/92) (2 Points for a Win)
75 (Second Division – Season 2000/01) (3 Points for a Win)
MOST LEAGUE GOALS SCORED BY A PLAYER IN A SEASON: Alex Hair (Season 1926/27)
NO. OF GOALS SCORED: 41
RECORD ATTENDANCE: 49,838 (-v- Rangers – 18.2.1922)
RECORD VICTORY: 16-0 (-v- Royal Albert – Scottish Cup, 17.1.1931)
RECORD DEFEAT: 0-10 (-v- Queen's Park – Scottish Cup, 3.12.1881)

ticket information

SEASON TICKET INFORMATION
SEATED

ADULT	OAP/U16/STUDENT	U12
260	135	70

LEAGUE ADMISSION INFORMATION
SEATED

ADULT	OAP/U16/STUDENT
16	9

STANDING (overspill only)

ADULT	OAP/U16/STUDENT
16	9

leading goalscorers 1993-2003

Season	Div	No. of Goals	Player
1993-94	P	14	A. Craig
1994-95	P	7	W. Foster
1995-96	P	5	A. Lyons, R. McDonald
1996-97	F	11	D. Moss
1997-98	F	6	J. Stirling
1998-99	S	10	R. Dunn
1999-00	S	5	R. Dunn
2000-01	S	16	S. McLean
2001-02	F	12	G. Britton
2002-03	P	16	A. Burns

the jags' club factfile 2002/03

Date	Venue	Opponents	Att.	Res	Budinauckas K.	Paterson S.	Archibald A.	Craigan S.	Whyte D.	McKinstry J.	Mitchell J.	Buchan M.J.	Hardie M.	McLean S.	Burns A.	Walker P.	Lennon D.	Britton G.	Gibson A.	Arthur K.	Lilley D.	Waddell R.	Milne K.	Charnley J.	Morris I.	Chiarini D.	McGowne K.	Rowson D.	Ross I.	Fleming D.	Elliot B.	Rushford G.	Shields M.
Aug 3	H	Dundee United	6,375	0-0	1	2	3	4	5	6	7	8	9	10	11	12	13																
10	A	Motherwell	5,788	1-1	1	2	3	4	5	6	7	8	9	10	11^{1}			12	13														
17	H	Livingston	4,255	2-2		2	3	4	5		7^{2}	8	9		11	13	12	10	14	1	6												
24	H	Celtic	8,053	0-1		2	3	4	5		7	8	9		11	12	13		10	1	6	14											
Sep 1	A	Aberdeen	12,591	1-0		2	3	4	5		7	8	9		11		13	14	12	1	6^{1}	10											
11	A	Kilmarnock	6,848	0-1		2	3	4	5			8	9	12	11			10		1	6	7	13										
14	H	Dundee	4,552	1-1		2	3	4	5		7^{1}	8	9		11	13	12			1	6	10		14									
21	A	Rangers	48,696	0-3		2	3	4	5		7	8	9		11		12	13		1	6	10	14										
28	H	Hearts	6,111	2-2		2	3^{2}	4	5		7	8	9	10	11			12		1	6												
Oct 5	A	Dunfermline Athletic	5,522	1-4		2	3	4	5		7^{1}	8	10		11	9		12		1	6	13			14								
19	H	Hibernian	5,946	0-3		2	3	4	5	6	7	8	9	10	11	12				1		13											
26	A	Dundee United	6,369	1-1		2	3	4	5		7	8	9		11	12		10	13	1		14^{1}				6							
Nov 2	H	Motherwell	5,405	2-0		2	3	4	5			13	8^{1}	9	11^{1}			10	14	1	6	12				7							
9	A	Livingston	5,426	0-3		2		4	3	14		8	9		11			10	13	1	6	12	5			7							
17	A	Celtic	57,231	0-4		2	3	4	5	13	7		9		11	12		10	14	1	6					8							
23	H	Aberdeen	6,182	2-1		2	3	4	5		12	13	8^{1}	9	11			10		1	6^{1}					7							
30	H	Kilmarnock	5,055	3-0		2	3	4	5		7		9		11^{3}	12		10		1	6					8							
Dec 4	A	Dundee	5,363	1-4		2	3	4	5		7	12	9	13	11			10^{1}	14	1	6					8							
7	H	Dunfermline Athletic	4,110	4-0		2	3	4			7		9	12^{1}	11^{2}			10^{1}		1	6	13	8			5							
14	A	Hearts	9,734	0-1		2	3	4			7		9		11			10		1	6		8			5							
22	H	Rangers	8,022	1-2		2	3	4			7		9	12	11^{1}		13	10		1	6		8			5							
26	A	Hibernian	10,317	1-1		2	3	4			7		9	12	11^{1}		13	10		1	6		8			5							
29	H	Dundee United	5,109	0-0		2	3	4			7	8	9		11		12	10		1	6					5							
Jan 2	A	Motherwell	6,262	2-2		2	3	4		14	7	8	9		11^{2}	12	5	10		1	6	13											
28	H	Livingston	3,541	1-3		2	3	4					9	13	11^{1}			10		1	6	12					5	7	8				
Feb 2	H	Celtic	7,119	0-2		2	3	4				13	9		11	12		10	14	1	6		8				5	7					
8	A	Aberdeen	11,332	1-0		2	3	4			13	8	9		11^{1}			10		1	6						5	7		12			
23	A	Kilmarnock	8,651	0-1		2	3	4			12	8	9		11					1	6						5	7		13	10		
Mar 1	H	Dundee	4,599	1-3		2	3				6	8^{1}	9		11	12		10		1	4						5	7					
9	A	Dunfermline Athletic	4,746	0-0		2	3	4				8	9		11			10	13	1	6							7		5	12		
15	H	Hibernian	4,551	0-1		2	3	4				8	9		11			10		1	6							7		5	12		
Apr 5	A	Rangers	49,472	0-2		2	3	4	12		9	8			11	14		10		1	6	13						7		5			
12	H	Hearts	5,288	1-1			3	4	2		9^{1}	8	12		11			10		1	6							7	5				
26	H	Motherwell	4,870	3-0			3	4	2		8	12	9		11^{1}			10^{2}		1	6		14					7	5			13	
May 3	A	Livingston	4,438	1-3			3	4	2		8		9^{1}		11			10	13	1	6		12					7	5				
10	A	Aberdeen	9,960	1-2			3	4	2		9	8	12		11^{1}			10		1	6	14						7	5	13			
17	H	Dundee United	6,357	0-1	1		3	4	14		12		9		11		7	10			6		8				2			5			13
24	A	Hibernian	8,986	3-2					13		8		9		11^{1}			10^{1}		1	6	3	5	14			2	7^{1}	4	12			
TOTAL FULL APPEARANCES					3	32	36	36	22	3	27	23	35	6	38	1	2	28	1	35	34	5	8			12	7	13	6	4	1		
TOTAL SUB APPEARANCES									3	3	4	5	2	6		12	9	5	11			11	4	2	1					4	2	1	1
TOTAL GOALS SCORED							2				5	1	3	1	16			5			2	1						1					

Small bold figures denote goalscorers. † denotes opponent's own goal.

firhill stadium

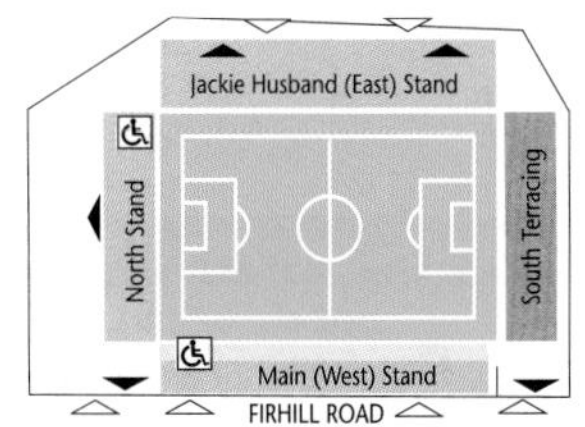

CAPACITY: 13,141; Seated 10,921; Standing 2,220

PITCH DIMENSIONS: 110 yds x 75 yds

FACILITIES FOR DISABLED SUPPORTERS:
Covered places are available for 17 supporters in front of the Main Stand (North area). A total of 14 spaces are available in front of the North Stand for visiting disabled fans. Prior arrangement must be made with the Secretary and a ticket obtained.

team playing kits

how to get there

The following routes may be used to reach Firhill Stadium:
TRAINS: The nearest railway stations are Glasgow Queen Street and Glasgow Central and buses from the centre of the city pass within 100 yards of the ground.
BUSES: The following buses from the city centre all pass near the ground: No's. 40, 61, 109 and 119 and the frequency of the buses is just under 10 minutes from Hope Street.
CARS: Street parking in the vicinity of the ground is somewhat limited. Supporters Buses can park in Panmure Street under Police direction.
UNDERGROUND: The nearest Strathclyde PTE Underground station is St.George's Cross and supporters walking from here should pass through Cromwell Street into Maryhill Road and then walk up this road as far as Firhill Street. The ground is then on the right. The Kelvinbridge Underground Station is also not far from the ground and supporters from here should walk along Great Western Road as far as Napiershill Street and then follow this into Maryhill Road.

rangers

LIST OF PLAYERS 2003/04

SQUAD NO.	SURNAME	FIRST NAME	MIDDLE NAME	DATE OF BIRTH	PLACE OF BIRTH	DATE OF SIGNING	HEIGHT FT INS	WEIGHT ST LBS	POS. ON PITCH	PREVIOUS CLUB
23	Arteta Amatriain	Mikel		26/03/82	San Sebastian	01/07/02	5 9	10st 13lb	Mid	Barcelona
7	Arveladze	Shota		22/02/73	Tblisi	11/09/01	5 11	11st 7lb	Fwd	Ajax
18	Ball	Michael		02/10/79	Liverpool	20/08/01	5 10	12st 2lb	Def	Everton
25	Berg	Henning		01/09/69	Eidsvel	06/08/03	6 0	12st 7lb	Def	Blackburn Rovers
30	Burke	Christopher		02/12/83	Glasgow	05/07/00	5 6	10st 1lb	Fwd	Rangers Youths
29	Christiansen	Jesper		24/04/78	Roskilde	06/08/03	6 2	13st 5lb	Gk	VfB Wolsburg
4	Costa	Emerson	Moises	12/04/72	Rio De Janeiro	29/08/03	6 1	12st 13lb	Mid	Atletico Madrid
14	De Boer	Ronald		15/05/70	Hoorn	01/09/00	5 11	12st 2lb	Mid	Barcelona
34	Dowie	Andrew	John	25/03/83	Bellshill	12/07/99	6 1	11st 6lb	Def	Rangers 'S' Form
33	Gibson	William		01/08/81	Bellshill	25/08/97	5 10.5	11st 13lb	Mid	Rangers 'S' Form
20	Capucho	Nuno Fernando		21/02/72	Portugal	01/07/03	5 11	12st 4lb	Fwd	Porto
27	Hughes	Stephen		14/11/82	Motherwell	12/07/99	5 11	10st 6lb	Mid	Rangers 'S' Form
32	Hutton	Alan		30/11/84	Glasgow	04/09/00	6 1	11st 4lb	Mid	Rangers Youths
15	Khizanishvili	Zurab		06/10/81	Tblisi	23/07/03	6 1	12st 8lb	Def	Dundee
1	Klos	Stefan		16/08/71	Dortmund	23/12/98	5 10.5	13st 5lb	Gk	BV09 Borussia Dortmund
26	Lovenkrands	Peter		29/01/80	Horsholm	14/06/00	5 11	11st 1lb	Fwd	AB Copenhagen
12	Malcolm	Robert		12/11/80	Glasgow	01/07/97	5 11.5	12st 2lb	Def	Rangers 'S' Form
22	McGregor	Allan		31/01/82	Edinburgh	14/07/98	6 0.5	11st 12lb	Gk	Rangers Youths
24	McLean	Steven		23/08/82	Edinburgh	17/09/98	5 11.5	11st 13lb	Fwd	Rangers Youths
10	Mols	Michael		17/12/70	Amsterdam	13/07/99	5 10.5	12st 4lb	Fwd	FC Utrecht
3	Moore	Craig	Andrew	12/12/75	Canterbury, Australia	31/03/99	5 11.5	12st 4lb	Def	Crystal Palace
8	Nerlinger	Christian		21/03/73	Dortmund	26/06/01	6 0	11st 8lb	Mid	BV09 Borussia Dortmund
9	Ostenstad	Egil		02/01/72	Haugensund	31/08/03	6 0	12st 6lb	Fwd	Blackburn Rovers
2	Ricksen	Fernando		27/07/76	Heerlen	05/07/00	5 8	11st 1lb	Def	AZ Aalkmar
21	Ross	Maurice		03/02/81	Dundee	01/07/97	6 0	11st 1lb	Def	Rangers S.A.B.C.
31	Smith	Graeme		08/06/83	Edinburgh	13/07/99	6 1.5	12st 4lb	Gk	Rangers 'S' Form
42	Smith	Steven		30/08/85	Bellshill	18/07/00	5 10	11st 7lb	Def	Rangers Youths
19	Thompson	Steven		14/10/78	Paisley	01/01/03	6 2	12st 10lb	Fwd	Dundee United
16	Vanoli	Paolo		12/08/72	Italy	05/08/03	6 0.5	12st 6lb	Def	Bologna

Ibrox Stadium,150 Edmiston Drive, Glasgow, G51 2XD
CHAIRMAN
John McClelland
DIRECTORS
David E. Murray (Honorary Chairman), R. Campbell Ogilvie, Daniel P. Levy, Donald Wilson, David C. King, Martin Bain, David Jolliffe & Nick Peel
ASSOCIATE DIRECTOR
Ian Russell
GENERAL SECRETARY
R. Campbell Ogilvie
DIRECTOR OF FOOTBALL BUSINESS
Martin Bain (0141) 580 8569
MANAGER
Alex McLeish
ASSISTANT MANAGER
Andy Watson
FIRST TEAM COACH
Jan Wouters
GOALKEEPING COACH
Billy Thomson
U21 COACH
John Brown
HEAD OF YOUTH DEVELOPMENT
George Adams
YOUTH DEVELOPMENT COACH
Tommy McLean
CHIEF SCOUT
Ewan Chester
CLUB DOCTOR
Dr. Ian McGuinness
PHYSIOTHERAPIST
David Henderson
PUBLIC RELATIONS EXECUTIVE
Carol Patton
OPERATIONS EXECUTIVE/ FOOTBALL SAFETY OFFICERS' ASSOCIATION REPRESENTATIVE
Laurence MacIntyre M.B.E. (0141) 580 8630
GROUNDSMAN
David Roxburgh
KIT PERSON
Jim Bell
STADIUM MANAGER
Ross MacAskill
MATCHDAY PROGRAMME EDITOR
Lindsay Herron
FINANCIAL CONTROLLER
Andrew Dickson
RETAIL DIRECTOR
Nick Peel
TELEPHONES
Main Switchboard (0141) 580 8500
Football Administration (0141) 580 8609
Fax-Football Administration (0141) 580 8947
Ticket Centre 0870 600 1993
Fax (0141) 580 8504
Customer Services 0870 600 1972
Hospitality 0870 600 1964
Commercial 0870 600 1899
Retail/Mail Order 0870 599 1997
Fax Enquiries 0870 600 1978
E-MAIL & INTERNET ADDRESS
dorahowie@rangers.co.uk
www.rangers.co.uk
CLUB SHOPS
1873 Superstore, Ibrox Stadium, Glasgow G51. Open until 10.00p.m. on Matchdays and 9.30a.m.-5.30p.m. Mon to Sat Sunday 11.00a.m. to 5.00p.m.
The Rangers Shop, 84-92 Sauchiehall Street, Glasgow, G2. Open 9.00a.m.-5.30p.m. Mon to Sat and Sun Noon-4.00p.m.
Additional Shops,
St. Enoch Centre, Glasgow. Open 9.00a.m.-6.00p.m. Mon, Tue, Wed, Fri and Sat., 9.00a.m.-8.00p.m. Thurs and Sun, 11.00a.m.-5.00p.m.
East Kilbride, Unit 23, Princes Square
Clydebank, 66 Sylvania Way, Clydebank Shopping Centre
OFFICIAL SUPPORTERS CLUB
Rangers F.C. Supporters' Association, 250 Edmiston Drive, Glasgow, G51 1YU
TEAM CAPTAIN
Craig Moore
SHIRT SPONSOR
Carling
KIT SUPPLIER
Diadora

milestones

YEAR OF FORMATION: 1873
MOST CAPPED PLAYER: Alistair McCoist
NO. OF CAPS: 58
MOST LEAGUE POINTS IN A SEASON: 76 (Division 1 - Season 1920/21) (2 Points for a Win)
97 (Scottish Premier League - Season 1999/2000) (3 Points for a Win)
MOST LEAGUE GOALS SCORED BY A PLAYER IN A SEASON: Sam English (Season 1931/32)
NO. OF GOALS SCORED: 44
RECORD ATTENDANCE: 118,567 (-v- Celtic – 2.1.1939)
RECORD VICTORY: 14-2 (-v- Blairgowrie – Scottish Cup, 20.1.1934)
RECORD DEFEAT: 2-10 (-v- Airdrieonians – 1886)

ticket information

SEASON TICKET INFORMATION – SEATED

	Block	Adult/Conc./Juv.
MAIN STAND (Front)	F/G/O/P	380/270/180
	H	540/380/210
	J/K/M/N	515/360/210
	L (Section MLF)	570/320/–
MAIN STAND (Rear)	E	485/340/210
	C/D/Q/R	395/280/180
	A/B/S/T	365/250/180
MEMBERS CLUB	Hospitality area only	
GOVAN (Rear)	3/4/5	530/370/210
	2/6	485/340/210
	1/7	445/315/210
GOVAN (Front)	2/3/4/5/6	400/280/180
	1/7/East	360/–/–
ENCLOSURE	SE 1/2/3 SW 3/4/5	–/270/180
	SE 4/5 SW1/2	390/–/–
COPLAND (Rear)		380/275/180
COPLAND (Front)		370/260/180
LEAGUE ADMISSION PRICES	ADULT	22/19
	CONCS/JUV	11

leading goalscorers 1993-2003

Season	Div	No. of Goals	Player
1993-94	P	22	M. Hateley
1994-95	P	13	M. Hateley
1995-96	P	17	G. Durie
1996-97	P	16	B. Laudrup
1997-98	P	32	M. Negri
1998-99	P	18	R. Wallace
1999-00	P	17	J. Albertz
2000-01	P	11	T. A. Flo
2001-02	P	17	T. A. Flo
2002-03	P	16	R. de Boer, B. Ferguson

the gers' club factfile 2002/03

Date	Venue	Opponents	Att.	Res	Klos S.	Ricksen F.	Moore C.	Amoruso L.	Numan A.	Arteta M.	Ferguson B.	McCann N.	de Boer R.	Arveladze S.	Lovenkrands P.	Latapy R.	Konterman B.	Flo T/A.	Muscat K.	Malcolm R.	Ross M.	Caniggia C.	Hughes S.	Dodds W.	Mols M.	Nerlinger C.	Hutton A.	McLean S.	Thompson S.	Bonnissel J.
Aug 3	A	Kilmarnock	13,972	1-1	1	2	3	4	5	6	7	8	9	10^{1}	11	12	13	14												
10	H	Dundee	46,774	3-0	1	2	3	4	5	8	7		9^{1}	10^{1}	12^{1}			11	6											
18	A	Hibernian	11,633	4-2	1	2	3	4	5	8	7^{1}		9^{1}	10	11^{2}			12	6											
25	H	Aberdeen	49,219	2-0	1	2	3		5	8	7^{1}		9^{1}	10	11	14		12	6	4	13									
Sep 1	A	Dunfermline Athletic	8,950	6-0	1	2^{1}	3		5	8^{1}	7^{1}		9	10			14		6	4		11^{3}	12	13						
11	H	Hearts	48,581	2-0	1	2	3		5	8	7		9	10^{1}			14		6	4	13	11^{1}		12						
14	A	Livingston	8,787	2-0	1	2	3			8	7^{1}			10	12	13			6	4	5^{1}	11		9						
21	H	Partick Thistle	48,696	3-0	1	2	3	4		8	7		9^{2}	10	11^{1}	14	12		6		5				13					
28	A	Dundee United	10,013	3-0	1	2	3	4^{1}		8	7^{1}		9	10^{1}	11		13		6		5	12								
Oct 6	A	Celtic	58,939	3-3	1	2	3	4	5	8^{1}	7	13	9^{1}	10^{1}	11		12				6	14								
19	H	Motherwell	49,376	3-0	1	2	3	4^{1}	5	8	7		9^{1}		11^{1}		14				6	10	13		12					
27	H	Kilmarnock	48,368	6-1	1	2	3^{1}		5		7^{2}		9^{1}		11		14		12	4	6		8	13	10^{2}					
Nov 2	A	Dundee	10,124	3-0	1	2	3^{1}		5	8	7		9		11^{1}		13		6	4^{1}			12		10					
10	H	Hibernian	49,032	2-1	1	2		4	5	8	7			10^{1}		14	12			3	6	9	13		11^{1}					
16	A	Aberdeen	14,915	2-2	1	2			5^{1}		7^{1}	12	9	10		8	3			4	6				11					
23	H	Dunfermline Athletic	48,431	3-0	1	2	3		5	8	7	9^{1}		10^{1}					6	4		12		13	11^{1}					
Dec 1	A	Hearts	12,156	4-0	1	12	3	4	5	8	7^{1}	11	9	10					6	14			12^{1}		13					
4	H	Livingston	45,992	4-3	1	2	3	4	5		7^{1}	8	9	10^{3}	12				6		14				11	13				
7	H	Celtic	49,874	3-2	1	2	3^{1}	4	5		7	8	9^{1}	10						12	6	14	13		11^{1}					
14	H	Dundee United	47,639	3-0	1	2	3	4			7^{3}		9	10	11				6	12			5		8	13				
22	A	Partick Thistle	8,022	2-1	1		3	4			7		9^{1}		11	8			6	13		12	5		10^{1}		2	14		
26	A	Motherwell	11,234	0-1	1	2	3	4			7		9		11				6	5		8		12	10					
29	A	Kilmarnock	13,396	1-0	1		3	4			7		9	10	11^{1}				6	5	2	12			8					
Jan 2	H	Dundee	49,112	3-1	1		3	4			7^{1}		9^{1}		11				6	5	2	8			10	14		13	12^{1}	
29	A	Hibernian	13,686	2-0	1	2	3		5		7^{1}	8	9	10						4	6	12^{1}			11					
Feb 1	H	Aberdeen	49,667	2-1	1	2	3		5	8	7	11	9							4	6	12			10^{2}			14		13
8	A	Dunfermline Athletic	8,754	3-1	1	2	3	4^{1}	5	8	7	11^{1}	9	10						12	6	13^{1}			14					
15	H	Hearts	49,459	†1-0	1	2		4	5	8	7		9	13	12				6	3		11			10					
Mar 2	A	Livingston	8,439	2-1	1	2	3	4^{1}		8	7	9		10^{1}					6			12			11				13	5
8	A	Celtic	58,336	0-1	1	2	3	4		8	7	9		10	11		14				6	13							12	5
19	H	Motherwell	49,420	2-0	1	2	3				7^{1}	14	9	13	11^{1}		12		6	4	5				10				8	
Apr 5	H	Partick Thistle	49,472	2-0	1	2	3			8		12	9	14	11		5			4	6	13	7		10^{2}					
13	A	Dundee United	10,271	4-1	1	2	3		5	8		14	9^{2}	10^{2}	11		6		7	4		12							13	
27	H	Celtic	49,740	1-2	1	2	3	4	5	12	7	13	9^{1}		11		6					8			10				14	
May 4	A	Dundee	9,204	†2-2	1	2	3		5	8^{1}	7		9	12	11				6	4		13	14		10					
11	H	Kilmarnock	49,036	4-0	1	2	3	4	5	8	7	14	9	12^{1}	11							13^{1}	6		10^{2}					
18	A	Hearts	15,632	2-0	1	2	3	4	5	8	7		9^{1}	11	12^{1}								6		10				13	
25	H	Dunfermline Athletic	49,731	6-1	1	2	3	4	5	6^{1}	7	12	9^{1}	11^{1}								8^{1}			10^{1}				13^{1}	
TOTAL FULL APPEARANCES					38	35	35	24	26	26	36	10	33	25	21	2	4	1	22	19	17	10	6	1	23		1		1	2
TOTAL SUB APPEARANCES										1		8		5	5	5	12	3	1	5	3	15	7	5	4	3		3	7	1
TOTAL GOALS SCORED						3	3	4	1	4	16	2	16	15	9					1	1	8	1		13				2	

Small bold figures denote goalscorers. † denotes opponent's own goal.

ibrox stadium

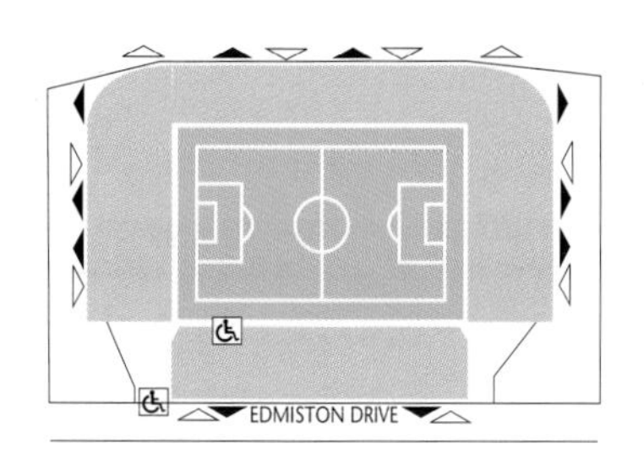

CAPACITY: 50,444 (All Seated)

PITCH DIMENSIONS: 115yds x 75yds

FACILITIES FOR DISABLED SUPPORTERS:
Special area within stadium and also special toilet facilities provided. The club also have a Rangers Disabled Supporters' Club. Contact: David Milne, Secretary, Disabled Supporters' Club, c/o Ibrox Stadium, Glasgow, G51 2XD.
This is free of charge.

team playing kits

how to get there

You can reach Ibrox Stadium by these routes:

BUSES: The following buses all pass within 300 yards of the Stadium and can be boarded from Glasgow city centre:- Nos. 4, 9A, 23, 23A, 52, 53, 53A, 54A, 54B, 65, 89 and 91.

UNDERGROUND: GGPTE Underground station is Ibrox, which is two minutes walk from the Stadium.

CARS: Motor Vehicles can head for the Stadium from the city centre by joining the M8 Motorway from Waterloo Street. Take the B768 turn-off for Govan. This will then take you to the ground. A limited number of parking spaces will be available in the Albion Car Park.

ayr united

Somerset Park, Tryfield Place,
Ayr, KA8 9NB

HONORARY PRESIDENT
William J. Barr, O.B.E., C. Eng., F.I.C.E., F.C.I.O.B., F.I.Mgt

CHAIRMAN
John L. Duncan Q.P.M.,D.L.

VICE-CHAIRMAN
Donald R. Cameron B.Sc.

DIRECTORS
John E. Eyley, B.A., ACMA, Roy G. Kennedy, M.R.I.C.S., David J. Quayle, CA, Hugh L. Cameron & John B. Dalton

COMPANY SECRETARY
John E. Eyley, B.A., ACMA

ADMINISTRATOR
Brian Caldwell
Mobile (07977) 900972

DIRECTOR OF FOOTBALL & YOUTH CO-ORDINATOR
I. Campbell Money

YOUTH COACHES
Sammy Conn (U17), Peter Leonard (U16), Lawrie Dinwoodie (U15), Kenny Cairns (U14)

WOMEN'S DEVELOPMENT COACH
Hugh Flynn

CLUB DOCTOR
Dr. John A.M. Hannah, B.Sc (Hons), M.B.Ch.B., M.R.C.G.P., D.R.C.O.G.

PHYSIOTHERAPIST
John Kerr, L.V.M.C. Inst. of H.T.

FOOTBALL SAFETY OFFICERS' ASSOCIATION REPRESENTATIVES
Roy Kennedy

GROUNDSMAN
David Harkness

KIT MANAGER & ASSISTANT PHYSIOTHERAPIST
Bobby McIntyre

COMMERCIAL MANAGER
Louis Jardine (08712) 221910

LOTTERY MANAGER
Andrew Downie

HOSPITALITY/CATERING MANAGER
Lynne Martin

MEDIA LIAISON OFFICER & MATCHDAY PROGRAMME EDITOR
Brian Caldwell

TELEPHONES
Ground/Ticket Office
(08712) 221910
Fax (01292) 281314

E-MAIL & INTERNET ADDRESS
info@aufc.co.uk
www.aufc.co.uk

CLUB SHOP
Open at Ground
8.30am - 5.30p.m. (weekdays) and home matches 11.00a.m. - 3.00p.m.

OFFICIAL SUPPORTERS CLUB
c/o Ayr United F.C., Somerset Park, Ayr, KA8 9NB

TEAM CAPTAIN
Steven Ferguson

SHIRT SPONSOR
First Choice Playing Kit: Kerr & Smith
Second Choice Playing Kit: Iveco Daily

KIT SUPPLIER
TFG

LIST OF PLAYERS 2003/2004

SURNAME	FIRST NAME	MIDDLE NAME	DATE OF BIRTH	PLACE OF BIRTH	DATE OF SIGNING	HEIGHT FT INS	WEIGHT ST LBS	POS. ON PITCH	PREVIOUS CLUB
Adams	Jamie	Stewart	26/08/87	Stranraer	21/08/03	5 11.0	10 8	Mid	Ayr United Form D U15
Black	Aaron		19/12/83	Larne	06/09/00	6 1.0	12 2	Mid	Larne Youth
Boyd	Ryan		04/05/87	Paisley	21/08/03	5 9.0	11 4	Def	Ayr United Form D U16
Burgess	Robert	George	11/03/85	Irvine	09/07/02	6 0.0	11 4	Def	Ayr United Form S
Campbell	Mark	Thomas	04/02/78	Irvine	26/02/99	6 2.0	14 5	Def	Stranraer
Chaplain	Scott		09/10/83	Bellshill	27/07/00	5 9.0	11 7	Mid	Rangers
Conway	Craig	Ian	02/05/85	Irvine	02/08/03	5 9.0	10 7	Fwd	Ayr United Form D U16
Craig	David	William	11/06/69	Glasgow	01/07/02	6 2.0	13 0	Def	Hamilton Academical
Denim	Gary Findlay	James	19/01/87	Irvine	21/08/03	6 2.0	12 5	Mid	Ayr United Form S
Dunlop	Michael		05/11/82	Glasgow	07/07/03	6 1.0	11 12	Def	Renfrew Juniors
Edmond	Stephen		22/01/87	Glasgow	21/08/03	5 8.0	10 5	Mid	Rangers
Ferguson	Andrew	David	24/03/85	Glasgow	23/01/02	6 0.0	11 13	Fwd	Ayr United Form S
Ferguson	Steven		18/05/77	Edinburgh	17/07/03	5 9.0	12 1	Mid	Ross County
Hillcoat	John	George	16/12/70	Paisley	23/05/03	6 0.0	12 6	Gk	Stranraer
Johnson	Darren		08/03/86	Irvine	31/08/03	5 11.0	11 12	Gk	Ardrossan Winton Rovers Jrs
Kean	Stewart		04/03/83	Irvine	15/01/00	5 9.0	11 8	Fwd	Craigmark Burntonians Jnrs.
Kerr	Christopher		06/09/78	Paisley	25/07/03	6 0.0	11 10	Def	St. Mirren
Latta	James William Boyd		31/01/85	Kilwinning	15/09/01	5 7.0	9 10	Mid	Ayr United Form S
Lawrie	Martin		04/06/87	Irvine	21/08/03	5 7.0	10 5	Def	Ayr United Form D U16
Lyle	William		14/04/84	Irvine	27/07/00	5 10.0	10 7	Def	Ayr United Form S
McCluskey	Steven		06/05/87	Irvine	21/08/03	6 2.0	12 4	Def	Girvan B.C.
McColl	Mark	James	26/12/84	Greenock	27/06/01	5 8.0	10 5	Fwd	Morton
McGrady	Stuart	Ian	08/04/85	Irvine	08/08/03	5 10.0	10 2	Def/Mid	Ayr United Form S
McKnight	Christopher		23/06/87	Irvine	21/08/03	5 9.0	9 10	Mid	Ayr United Form D U16
McNeill	Gary		10/01/87	Larne	21/08/03	5 9.0	10 2	Def	Ayr United Form D U16
Money	Israel	Campbell	31/08/60	Maybole	31/08/02	5 11.0	15 5	Gk	Stranraer
Moyles	Muir	Henry	05/02/87	Irvine	27/08/03	5 8.0	9 8	Mid	Annbank United Juniors
Mullen	Boyd		02/01/86	Irvine	18/01/02	5 9.0	9 7	Mid	Ayr United Form S
Ramsay	Douglas		26/04/79	Irvine	21/08/03	5 11.0	12 9	Mid	Motherwell
Roy	Ludovic		18/08/77	Tours	07/07/03	6 1.0	13 0	Gk	St. Mirren
Smyth	Marc		27/12/82	Edinburgh	14/09/01	6 0.0	11 7	Def	Glenafton Athletic Juniors
Whalen	Stephen		02/05/82	Irvine	15/01/03	5 10.0	12 3	Fwd	Livingston

milestones

YEAR OF FORMATION: 1910
MOST CAPPED PLAYER: Jim Nisbett
NO. OF CAPS: 3
MOST LEAGUE POINTS IN A SEASON: 61 (Second Division – Season 1987/88) (2 Points for a Win)
77 (Second Division – Season 1996/97) (3 Points for a Win)
MOST LEAGUE GOALS SCORED BY A PLAYER IN A SEASON: Jimmy Smith (Season 1927/28)
NO. OF GOALS SCORED: 66
RECORD ATTENDANCE: 25,225 (-v- Rangers – 13.9.1969)
RECORD VICTORY: 11-1 (-v- Dumbarton – League Cup, 13.8.1952)
RECORD DEFEAT: 0-9 (-v- Rangers, Heart of Midlothian, Third Lanark – Division 1)

ticket information

SEASON TICKET PRICES

SEATED
CENTRE STAND
Adult £210; OAP £110
WING STAND
Adult £185
Juvenile/OAP £95
FAMILY STAND
Adult/Juvenile £185;
Additional Juvenile £50

STANDING
GROUND/ENCLOSURE
Adult £145
Juvenile/OAP £60
Adult & Juvenile £185

LEAGUE ADMISSION PRICES

SEATED
MAIN STAND (CENTRE)
Adult £13
MAIN STAND (WING)
Adult £12; Concession £7
FAMILY STAND
Adult/Juvenile £12
(Plus £5.00 For Each Additional Juvenile)

STANDING
ENCLOSURE Adult £10.50
GROUND Adult £10
Juvenile/OAP £5

leading goalscorers 1993-2003

Season	Div	No. of Goals	Player
1993-94	F	12	S. McGivern
1994-95	F	4	J. Jackson
1995-96	S	5	B. Bilsland, I. English
1996-97	S	14	S. Kerrigan
1997-98	F	10	L. D'Jaffo
1998-99	F	18	G. Hurst
1999-00	F	14	G. Hurst
2000-01	F	18	E. Annand
2001-02	F	14	E. Annand
2002-03	F	7	S. Kean

the honest men's club factfile 2002/03

Date	Venue	Opponents	Att.	Res	Nelson C.	Bossy F.	Lovering P.	McManus A.	Campbell M.	Craig D.	Chaplain S.	Nicolson I.	Annand E.	Grady J.	Sheerin P.	Kean S.	Lyle W.	Black A.	Smyth M.	McDermott A.	Dunlop M.	Murray N.	Dodds J.	McColl M.	Mullen B.	Ferguson A.	Whalen S.	Latta J.	McVeigh A.	Burgess R.	McGrady S.	Conway C.	Ferry M.
Aug 3	H	Falkirk	3,030	1-3	1	2	3	4	5	6	7	8	9	10	11	12^1	14	16															
10	A	Clyde	1,123	0-1	1	4	3	5		6	8	7	9	10	11	12	2																
17	H	Ross County	1,692	†2-1	1		3		5	6	8	7	9	10^1	11	12	2		4	15	16												
24	A	Queen of the South	2,803	2-1	1				5^1		7	3	9	10^1	11	12	2		4	6	14	8											
31	H	Arbroath	1,732	1-0	1			6	5	12	7	3	9	10	11^1	14	2		4		16	8											
Sep 14	H	St. Johnstone	2,320	0-0	1				5	6	7	3	9	10	11	14	2	15	4		16	8											
21	A	Alloa Athletic	619	1-0	1		3		5	6	7^1	12	9	10	11	14	2		4		16	8											
28	H	St. Mirren	2,489	1-1	1				5		7	6	9	10^1	11	12	2		4		3	8											
Oct 5	A	Inverness Cal Th	1,803	0-2	1		3	15	5	6	7	12	9	10	11	14	2		4			8											
19	A	Falkirk	3,441	0-3	1		3	6	5	12		7	9	10	11	15	2		4			8											
26	H	Clyde	1,989	1-1	1		3		5	6	7	2	9^1	10	11		14	16	4			8											
Nov 5	A	Arbroath	381	1-1	1		3	5		6	7	8	9^1	10	11		2	15	4		14												
9	H	Queen of the South	2,234	0-1	1		3	4	5	6	7	8	9	10		12	2	15			14	11											
16	A	St. Johnstone	1,943	2-0			3	4	5	6^2	7	2	9	10	11	16			8		15		1										
23	H	Alloa Athletic	1,632	†3-1			3	5		6	7^1	4	9	10	11^1	16	2	14	8				1	15									
30	A	St. Mirren	2,426	0-1			3	4	5	6	7	2	9	10	11	16	12		8				1	15									
Dec 7	H	Inverness Cal Th	1,663	3-3			3^1	4	5	6	7^1	2	9^1	10	11	16	12					8	1										
14	A	Ross County	2,352	0-1			3	4	5	6	7		9		11	10	2		8				1	15									
28	H	Arbroath	1,664	4-0	1			4	5^1	6	7	3			11	9^1	2		8			12		10^1	15	16^1							
Jan 1	A	Queen of the South	2,921	1-1	1			4	5	6	7	3	15		11	9^1	2	14	8			12		10									
18	A	Inverness Cal Th	2,021	1-0	1		3	4	5	6	7			10		9^1	2	14	8		12	11					15						
Feb 1	H	St. Mirren	2,738	0-0	1			4	5	6	7			10		9	2	11	8		3	14					16						
8	H	Ross County	1,486	1-1	1			4	5	6	7			16		9	2		8		3	11					10^1	15					
25	H	Falkirk	1,783	1-0	1		3	4	5	6	7^1			10		16	2		8		12	11					9						
Mar 1	A	Arbroath	505	2-1	1			4	5	6	7	14		10		16^2	2	12	8		3	11					9						
4	H	St. Johnstone	1,690	0-1	1			4	5	6	7	3		10		16	2	14	8		12						9	11					
8	H	Queen of the South	1,730	0-1	1			4	5	6	7			16		10	2	14	8		3						9	11	15				
15	H	Alloa Athletic	1,363	0-1	1		3	4	5	6	7			10		16	2	8	15		14			11		9							
22	A	Clyde	1,015	0-3	1		3	4		6	7			10		9	2	8	5		14	11		15									
25	A	Alloa Athletic	454	3-2	1		3		5		7	2		10		16		11	4		8	6					9^3						
Apr 5	A	St. Johnstone	2,123	0-1	1		6		5		7	2		10			12	14	4		3	11					9	8		16			
12	A	St. Mirren	2,248	1-1	1		6		5		7^1	15		10		9	2		4		3	8		11					16		14		
26	A	Falkirk	4,042	0-3	1			4	5	6	7	11				16	2	15	8		3			10			9						
29	H	Inverness Cal Th	1,114	1-0	1			4		6	12			10		9^1	2	11	5		3	8			7		16					15	
May 3	H	Clyde	1,795	0-3	1		15	4		6	12			10		16	2	11	5			8			7		9				3		
10	A	Ross County	3,449	1-4	1					6	7					9	2		4		3	8		11	15		10^1	14					5
TOTAL FULL APPEARANCES					31	2	21	25	29	29	33	21	18	29	19	11	29	6	31	1	11	21	5	6	2	1	10	3			1		1
TOTAL SUB APPEARANCES							1	1		2	2	4	1	2		22	5	13	1	1	13	3		4	2	1	3	2	2	1	1	1	
TOTAL GOALS SCORED							1		2	2	5		3	3	2	7								1		1	5						

Small bold figures denote goalscorers. † denotes opponent's own goal.

somerset park

A77 ►
HOME SUPPORTERS
SOMERSET ROAD
VISITING SUPPORTERS
TRYFIELD PLACE
HOME SUPPORTERS

CAPACITY: 10,185; Seated 1,597, Standing 8,588

PITCH DIMENSIONS: 110 yds x 72 yds

FACILITIES FOR DISABLED SUPPORTERS:
Enclosure and toilet facilities for wheelchairs. Match commentary available for blind persons at all first team matches.

team playing kits

how to get there

Somerset Park can be reached by the following routes:

TRAINS: There is a half hourly train service from Glasgow to either Ayr or Newton-on-Ayr. The ground is a ten minute walk from both stations.

BUSES: There are several buses from the town centre with a frequency approximately every five minutes. Fans should board buses bound for Dalmilling, Whitletts or any bus passing Ayr Racecourse. The ground is only a ten minute walk from the town centre.

CARS: A77 to Ayr and at Whitletts Roundabout, take third exit (A719) and follow until after Ayr Racecourse. Take first right at traffic lights then left and right into Somerset Road. Car parking facilities are available at Craigie Road, Ayr Racecourse and also at Somerset Road car parks.

brechin city

Glebe Park, Trinity Road,
Brechin, Angus, DD9 6BJ

CHAIRMAN
David H. Birse

VICE-CHAIRMAN
Hugh A. Campbell Adamson

DIRECTORS
Martin G. Smith (Treasurer), Calum I. McK. Brown, Kenneth W. Ferguson, Stephen D. Mitchell, Henry G. Stewart & Angus A. Fairlie

HON. LIFE PRESIDENT
David H. Will C.B.E

HON. LIFE MEMBERS
David K. Lindsay & George C. Johnston

SECRETARY
Kenneth W. Ferguson

MANAGER
Richard M. Campbell

ASSISTANT MANAGER
Ian Campbell

FIRST TEAM COACH
Bert Paton

KIT PERSON
Alan Grieve

YOUTH DEVELOPMENT COACH & TEAM COACH (U19)
Paul Martin

CLUB DOCTOR
Dr. Alan Dawson

PHYSIOTHERAPIST
Tom Gilmartin

BACKROOM STAFF
Norman Ross

FOOTBALL SAFETY OFFICERS' ASSOCIATION REPRESENTATIVE
Calum Brown (01307) 461222

GROUNDSMAN
Alex Laing

COMMERCIAL MANAGER/ MEDIA LIAISON OFFICER/ MATCHDAY PROGRAMME EDITOR
Steve Mitchell (01356) 626336

LOTTERY MANAGER
Angus Fairlie

TELEPHONES
Ground (Matchdays Only) (01356) 622856
Sec. Bus. (01356) 625285
Sec. Mobile 07803 089060
Sec. Home Fax (01356) 625667
Sec. Bus. Fax (01356) 625524

E-MAIL/INTERNET ADDRESS
bcfc@glebepk.demon.co.uk
www.brechincity.co.uk

CLUB SHOP
Glebe Park, Brechin, Angus, DD9 6BJ
Open during home match days.

OFFICIAL SUPPORTERS CLUB
c/o Glebe Park, Brechin, Angus, DD9 6BJ

TEAM CAPTAIN
Paul Deas

SHIRT SPONSOR
Delson Contracts

KIT SUPPLIER
Paulas Benara

LIST OF PLAYERS 2003/2004

SURNAME	FIRST NAME	MIDDLE NAME	DATE OF BIRTH	PLACE OF BIRTH	DATE OF SIGNING	HEIGHT FT INS	WEIGHT ST LBS	POS. ON PITCH	PREVIOUS CLUB
Anderson	David		21/04/86	Dundee	21/08/03	6 0.0	11 10	Def	Brechin City Form D U16
Bennett	Paul	Mark	22/04/86	Dundee	21/08/03	5 10.0	13 11	Def	Brechin City Form S
Brownhill	Myles	Gordon	03/08/86	Aberdeen	21/08/03	5 9.0	10 4	Fwd	Keith
Clark	Derek	Grant	24/08/76	Stirling	23/01/02	5 8.0	11 0	Mid	Alloa Athletic
Davidson	Iain	Scott	14/01/84	Kirkcaldy	22/07/03	6 1.0	10 5	Def	Sunderland
Deas	Paul	Andrew	22/02/72	Perth	24/01/03	5 11.0	12 1	Def	Ross County
Farquharson	John Robertson		24/08/86	Dundee	21/08/03	5 11.0	10 7	Fwd	Tayview Thistle
Forsyth	Ross		10/10/86	Dundee	21/08/03	5 11.0	10 4	Def	Carnoustie Panmure Juniors
Fotheringham	Kevin George		13/08/75	Dunfermline	15/02/01	5 10.0	12 4	Def/Mid	Arbroath
Gibson	Graham		19/07/80	Kirkcaldy	12/03/02	6 3.0	11 6	Fwd	Lochore Welfare Juniors
Hampshire	Steven	Gary	17/10/79	Edinburgh	30/08/03	5 11.0	11 7	Mid	Dunfermline Athletic
Hay	David	Alexander	02/01/80	Edinburgh	19/07/02	6 4.0	14 0	Gk	East Stirlingshire
Jablonski	Neil		09/03/83	Kirkcaldy	22/08/03	5 9.5	11 0	Mid	Dundee
Jackson	Christopher	Robert	29/10/73	Edinburgh	05/06/02	5 9.5	11 8	Mid	Stenhousemuir
Johnson	Ian	Grant	24/03/72	Dundee	22/07/03	5 11.0	11 3	Mid	Montrose
King	Charles	Alexander	15/11/79	Edinburgh	18/07/01	5 7.0	10 2	Fwd	Livingston
McCulloch	Marc	Raymond	14/03/80	Edinburgh	22/07/03	5 9.0	12 8	Mid	St. Johnstone
McCulloch	Scott Anderson	James	29/11/75	Cumnock	03/07/03	6 0.0	14 10	Def	Forfar Athletic
McLeish	Kevin	Michael	03/12/80	Edinburgh	31/08/03	5 10.0	12 0	Mid	Dunfermline Athletic
Miller	Greg	Allan	01/04/76	Glasgow	12/01/01	5 8.0	10 10	Mid	Vasteras
Mitchell	Alistair	Robert	03/12/68	Kirkcaldy	03/07/03	5 7.0	11 8	Fwd	St. Mirren
Robertson	Gary		08/03/86	Dundee	21/08/03	5 10.0	12 0	Def	Brechin City Form S
Skinner	Justin		30/01/69	London	19/08/02	6 1.0	13 2	Mid	Dunfermline Athletic
Smith	James		11/07/78	Glasgow	21/09/01	6 3.0	13 0	Def	Partick Thistle
Stein	Jay		13/01/79	Dunfermline	22/07/03	5 8.0	10 7	Mid	Stenhousemuir
Templeman	Christopher		12/01/80	Kirkcaldy	18/07/01	6 5.0	15 2	Fwd	Stirling Albion
Thomson	Andrew	William	19/09/86	Dundee	21/08/03	5 10.0	12 0	Mid	Tayview Thistle
Traynor	Gavin	Brian	06/08/86	Dundee	21/08/03	5 10.0	10 3	Mid	Brechin City Form D U16
White	David	William	09/08/79	Edinburgh	03/07/03	6 1.5	11 0	Def	Cowdenbeath
Wyllie	Walter	Kerr	03/03/85	Irvine	21/08/03	6 0.0	11 0	Fwd	Dundee
Yarwood	Ross		22/12/85	Dundee	25/08/03	5 10.0	11 0	Fwd	Dundee

milestones

YEAR OF FORMATION: 1906
MOST LEAGUE POINTS IN A SEASON: 55 (Second Division – Season 1982/83) (2 Points for a Win)
73 (Third Division – Season 2001/02) (3 Points for a Win)
MOST LEAGUE GOALS SCORED BY A PLAYER IN A SEASON: Ronald McIntosh (Season 1959/60)
NO. OF GOALS SCORED: 26
RECORD ATTENDANCE: 8,122 (-v- Aberdeen – 3.2.1973)
RECORD VICTORY: 12-1 (-v- Thornhill – Scottish Cup, 28.1.1926)
RECORD DEFEAT: 0-10 (-v- Airdrieonians, Albion Rovers and Cowdenbeath – Division 2, 1937/38)

ticket information

SEASON TICKET INFORMATION

SEATED	ADULT	£150
	PARENT & JUVENILE (UNDER 12)	£165
	OAP	£85
	JUVENILE	£45

LEAGUE ADMISSION PRICES

SEATED	ADULT	£10
	JUVENILE/OAP	£5
ENCLOSURE	ADULT	£10
	JUVENILE/OAP	£5
STANDING	ADULT	£10
	JUVENILE/OAP	£5
	PARENT & JUVENILE	£12

leading goalscorers 1993-2003

Season	Div	No. of Goals	Player
1993-94	F	10	M. Millar
1994-95	S	6	G. Price, R. Smith
1995-96	T	8	A. Ross
1996-97	S	7	S. Kerrigan
1997-98	S	7	C. Feroz
1998-99	T	15	J. Dickson
1999-00	T	11	B. Honeyman
2000-01	T	22	R. Grant
2001-02	T	15	C. Templeman
2002-03	S	21	C. Templeman

the city's club factfile 2002/03

Date	Venue	Opponents	Att.	Res	Cairns M.	Miller G.	Black R.	Smith J.	Cairney H.	Fotheringham K.	King Charles	Millar M.	Gibson G.	Templeman C.	Jackson C.	Smith D.	Campbell P.	Riley P.	McCulloch G.	Grant R.	Hay D.	Skinner J.	McKechnie G.	Clark D.	Donachie B.	McDonald G.	King Christopher	Boyle S.	Fotheringham M.	Deas P.	Thomson S.Y.	Coulston D.
Aug 3	H	Berwick Rangers	501	2-4	1	2	3	4	5	6	7	8	9^2	10	11	17	14	12														
10	A	Dumbarton	735	0-1	1	3	12	4	5	6	7	10	11	9	8		15		2	16												
17	H	Hamilton Academical	498	1-0		2	3	4	5	6^1		10	12	7	11					9	1	8										
24	H	Forfar Athletic	761	1-0		2	3	4	5	6	14	11	12	10	8			15		9^1	1	7										
31	A	Stranraer	348	1-3		14		4	5	6^1	7	11	16	10	3		15	8		9	1	2										
Sep 14	H	Cowdenbeath	453	0-0		14	3	4	5	6	7	8	12		2	16				9	1	10	11									
21	A	Airdrie United	1,373	4-2		12	3	4	5		7		16	10^1	8				2	9^3	1	6		11	15							
28	A	Raith Rovers	2,007	1-3			3	4^1	5	6		7	14	11	10		16		2	9	1	8		12								
Oct 5	H	Stenhousemuir	489	1-0			3	4	5	6	11^1	14	12	15	10			8	2	9	1			7								
26	A	Berwick Rangers	410	3-0	1	7	12	4	5	6	14			11^2	10			15	2	9^1		8		3								
29	H	Dumbarton	377	1-1	1	7	3	4	5	6	14		16	11^1	10				2	9		8				15						
Nov 2	H	Stranraer	426	3-1	1	7	3	4	5	6	15^1		14	11	10			12		9^1		8		2^1								
9	A	Forfar Athletic	868	1-2	1	7	3	4	5	6	2		16	11^1	10	12				9		8		15								
16	A	Cowdenbeath	267	1-0	1	10	12	4	5	6^1	2		14	8	11					9				3	7							
23	H	Airdrie United	557	1-5	1	10			5	6	7^1		12	8	11		16			9				3	4	2	17					
30	A	Stenhousemuir	331	1-1	1	7	3	4	5		2^1		11	8	10					9		6										
Dec 14	H	Raith Rovers	746	1-2		14	12	4	5	6	7^1		10	9	11	2					1	8		3			15					
28	A	Hamilton Academical	1,418	2-1		10	16	4		6	7		9	8	11	2^1		14			1	5		3^1								
Jan 1	H	Forfar Athletic	743	3-4	1	2	16^1	4		6	7		10	9^2	11	8		12				5		3				15				
18	H	Cowdenbeath	452	5-7		16	3	12^1	5	6^1	7		15	9^2	8						1	4		10^1				11	2			
25	H	Berwick Rangers	402	2-2	1	2	11		5^1	6	7			8^1	10					9		4		12				14		3		
Feb 1	A	Airdrie United	1,275	0-3		2	12	4		8	7			9	10	16				15	1	5						3	11	6		
8	A	Raith Rovers	1,776	2-1		12	3		5	10	7		16	11^1	8	2				9^1		4								6	1	
25	A	Stranraer	371	3-2		7	3			6	11^1		12	10^2	8				2	9		4		14						5	1	
Mar 1	H	Hamilton Academical	441	4-1		7	3			6^1			10^2	9^1	8				2			4		12				11	14	5	1	16
8	A	Forfar Athletic	774	†5-1		8	3^1	4		6^2	7^1		9	10	11				2					14				17	12	5	1	
11	A	Dumbarton	513	3-1		8	3	4	5	6	7		11	9^3	10				2					12				14	16		1	
15	H	Stranraer	488	3-1		10	3^1	4		6^1	7^1		11	9	8				2					15					12	5	1	
22	H	Airdrie United	672	0-1		11	3	2	4	6	7		10	9	8					12								15	14	5	1	
29	H	Stenhousemuir	435	2-1		8	3	11	4	6	7		10	9^2					2	16										5	1	
Apr 5	A	Cowdenbeath	274	0-1		2	3	4	5	6	7		10	9					8	12									15	11	1	
12	A	Stenhousemuir	510	2-2		11		8	5	6	7		14	10					2	9^1				3					16	4	1	15^1
19	H	Raith Rovers	1,819	1-0		2		4	5		7		16	11^1	8				12	9								15	10	6	1	3
26	A	Berwick Rangers	442	0-2		2		4	5		7		12	10	11	15				9								14	8	6	1	3
May 5	H	Dumbarton	895	1-1		2		4	5		7^1		12	10	11				15	9								14	8	6	1	3
10	A	Hamilton Academical	1,644	2-2		2		4	5	6^1	7		12	10^1					14	9								16	8	3	1	11
TOTAL FULL APPEARANCES					**11**	**28**	**22**	**30**	**29**	**31**	**29**	**7**	**13**	**34**	**32**	**4**		**2**	**14**	**22**	**11**	**20**	**1**	**11**	**2**	**1**		**3**	**6**	**15**	**14**	**4**
TOTAL SUB APPEARANCES						**6**	**7**	**1**			**4**	**1**	**20**	**1**		**5**	**5**	**6**	**3**	**5**				**8**	**1**	**1**	**2**	**9**	**7**			**2**
TOTAL GOALS SCORED							**3**	**2**	**1**	**9**	**9**		**4**	**21**		**1**				**8**				**3**								**1**

Small bold figures denote goalscorers. † denotes opponent's own goal.

glebe park

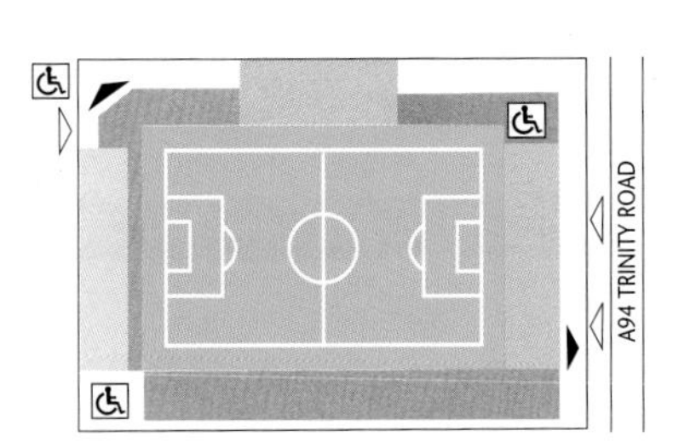

CAPACITY: 3,060; Seated 1,518, Standing 1,542

PITCH DIMENSIONS: 110 yds x 67 yds

FACILITIES FOR DISABLED SUPPORTERS:
Section of Terracing designated for disabled supporters. Disabled access from both ends of the Ground.

team playing kits

how to get there

The following routes may be used to reach Glebe Park:

TRAINS: The nearest railway station is Montrose, which is eight miles away. There is a regular Inter-City service from all parts of the country and fans alighting at Montrose can then catch a connecting bus service to Brechin.

BUSES: Brechin bus station is only a few hundred yards from the ground and buses on the Aberdeen-Dundee and Montrose-Edzell routes stop here.

CARS: Car parking is available in the Brechin City car park, which is capable of holding 50 vehicles. There are also a number of side streets which may be used for this purpose.

clyde

Broadwood Stadium,
Cumbernauld, G68 9NE

CHAIRMAN
William B. Carmichael

DIRECTORS
Gerard W. Dunn, M.A.,
Harry McCall, B.A., C.Eng., M.I.C.E.,
John D. Taylor, A.C.I.B. &
David D. Fleming

SECRETARY
John D. Taylor, A.C.I.B.
Bus. (01236) 451511
(H) (0141) 633 1013

OFFICE ADMINISTRATOR
Mrs. Lynn Calder

PLAYER/MANAGER
Alan Kernaghan

ASSISTANT MANAGER
Billy Reid

PLAYER/FIRST TEAM COACH
Andy Millen

YOUTH COACHES
Billy Reid & Andy Millen (U19),
Chris Hillcoat (U17)

CLUB DOCTORS
Dr. Michael McGavigan,
Dr. Michael McLaughlin &
Dr. Frank Dunn

PHYSIOTHERAPIST
Iain McKinlay

STADIUM MANAGER
Peter Eadie

KIT PERSON
Bill Munro

MATCHDAY PROGRAMME EDITOR
John D. Taylor

TELEPHONES
Ground (01236) 451511
Fax (01236) 733490

E-MAIL & INTERNET ADDRESS
info@clydefc.co.uk
www.clydefc.co.uk

CLUB SHOP
Situated at Ground
Open on Home Matchdays 1 hour
before and for 1 hour after match.

TEAM CAPTAIN
Jack Ross

SHIRT SPONSOR

KIT SUPPLIER
TFG

LIST OF PLAYERS 2003/2004

SURNAME	FIRST NAME	MIDDLE NAME	DATE OF BIRTH	PLACE OF BIRTH	DATE OF SIGNING	HEIGHT FT INS	WEIGHT ST LBS	POS. ON PITCH	PREVIOUS CLUB
Baird	John	David	22/08/85	Rutherglen	05/06/02	5 7.0	9 2	Mid	Motherwell
Bradley	Kevin		18/06/86	Glasgow	29/05/03	5 6.0	8 7	Fwd	Clyde Youth Team
Bryson	Craig	James	06/11/86	Rutherglen	29/05/03	5 7.0	9 7	Mid	Motherwell Form D U 15
Chisholm	Grant		16/05/86	Glasgow	05/06/02	5 10.0	10 7	Def	Clyde Youth Team
Clark	Charles		20/03/86	Stirling	05/06/02	5 10.0	9 7	Gk	Carse Thistle
Doyle	Paul		26/09/84	Bellshill	05/06/02	5 10.5	11 6	Def	Larkhall Thistle Juniors
Fraser	John		17/01/78	Dunfermline	09/11/01	5 10.0	11 4	Mid	Ross County
Gibson	James	Robert	19/02/80	Bellshill	21/08/03	5 7.0	11 3	Mid	Rangers
Gilhaney	Mark		04/11/84	Lanark	05/06/02	5 7.0	10 5	Fwd	Cambuslang Rangers Juniors
Greenhill	David		08/07/85	Edinburgh	01/07/03	5 7.0	9 7	Mid	St. Johnstone
Hagen	David		05/05/73	Edinburgh	08/09/01	5 11.0	13 5	Fwd	Livingston
Halliday	Robert	Lynch	14/01/86	Glasgow	05/06/02	5 8.0	8 7	Def	Clyde Youth Team
Halliwell	Bryn	Steven	01/10/80	Epsom	12/06/00	6 1.0	12 10	Gk	Wimbledon
Harty	Ian	McGuinness	08/04/78	Bellshill	21/05/03	5 9.0	12 6	Fwd	Stranraer
Keogh	Patrick	Sebastian	07/05/76	Redlands	04/08/98	6 2.0	12 10	Fwd	Maryhill Juniors
Kernaghan	Alan	Nigel	25/04/67	Otley	10/09/01	6 2.0	14 0	Def	Brechin City
Marshall	Colin	Jenkins	25/10/84	Glasgow	29/08/03	5 8.0	11 4	Mid	Aston Villa
McBride	Christopher	Charles	03/05/84	Glasgow	26/02/03	5 8.0	12 1	Mid	Kilmarnock
McConalogue	Stephen		16/06/81	Glasgow	10/06/03	5 9.0	11 8	Fwd	Dundee United
McCracken	Graeme		23/07/86	Coatbridge	05/06/02	5 9.0	10 6	Mid	Clyde Youth Team
McGroarty	Christopher		06/12/81	Bellshill	28/08/03	5 10.0	10 5	Mid/Fwd	Dunfermline Athletic
McIlroy	Mark		23/01/86	Glasgow	05/06/02	5 11.0	11 3	Def	Clyde Youth Team
McIntyre	Steven	Peter	03/07/85	Paisley	01/07/03	5 11.0	11 2	Def	St. Johnstone
McLaughlin	Mark		02/12/75	Greenock	28/07/99	6 2.0	13 5	Def	Arthurlie Juniors
Mensing	Simon	Ross	27/06/82	Wolfenbuttll	26/10/01	6 0.0	13 3	Def	Wimbledon
Millen	Andrew	Frank	10/06/65	Glasgow	13/01/01	5 11.0	11 4	Def	Morton
Morrison	Allan	James	31/03/82	Irvine	23/08/02	6 1.0	13 6	Gk	Carlisle United
Potter	John	Paul	15/12/79	Dunfermline	27/03/02	6 1.0	13 2	Def	Dunfermline Athletic
Reid	William	Thomas	11/01/86	Glasgow	05/06/02	5 7.0	9 2	Mid	Clyde Youth Team
Ross	John	James	05/06/76	Falkirk	02/07/99	6 1.0	11 5	Mid	Camelon Juniors
Sloman	Christopher		12/05/85	Glasgow	05/06/02	5 9.0	11 2	Def	Clyde Youth Team
Smith	Andrew	Mark	27/11/68	Aberdeen	07/08/03	6 1.0	13 8	Fwd	Raith Rovers
Zok	Christopher		21/06/86	Glasgow	12/08/02	5 8.0	9 4	Fwd	Syngenta Juveniles

milestones

YEAR OF FORMATION: 1877
MOST CAPPED PLAYER: Tommy Ring
NO. OF CAPS: 12
MOST LEAGUE POINTS IN A SEASON: 64 (Division 2 – Season 1956/57) (2 Points for a Win)
72 (First Division – Season 2002/03) (3 Points for a Win)
MOST LEAGUE GOALS SCORED BY A PLAYER IN A SEASON: Bill Boyd (Season 1932/33)
NO. OF GOALS SCORED: 32
RECORD ATTENDANCE: 52,000 (-v- Rangers – 21.11.1908 – at Shawfield Stadium)
7,382 (-v- Celtic – 14.8.1996 (Coca-Cola Cup) – at Broadwood Stadium)
RECORD VICTORY: 11-1 (-v- Cowdenbeath – Division 2, 6.10.1951)
RECORD DEFEAT: 0-11 (-v- Dumbarton and Rangers, Scottish Cup)

ticket information

SEASON TICKET INFORMATION

SEATED	ADULT	£200
	OAP/STUDENTS	£100
	JUVENILE (U18)	£50
	JUVENILE (U12)	£20

LEAGUE ADMISSION PRICES

SEATED	ADULT	£13
	OAP/ JUVENILE/STUDENT	£6
	PARENT & CHILD	£16

leading goalscorers 1993-2003

Season	Div	No. of Goals	Player
1993-94	F	5	I. McConnell
			G. Parks
1994-95	S	10	J. Dickson
1995-96	S	21	E. Annand
1996-97	S	21	E. Annand
1997-98	S	8	P. Brownlie
1998-99	S	12	S. Convery
1999-00	S	18	B. Carrigan
2000-01	F	7	A. Kane
2001-02	F	11	P. Keogh
2002-03	F	12	P. Keogh

the bully wee's club factfile 2002/03

Date	Venue	Opponents	Att.	Res	McEwan D.	Mensing S.	Potter J.	Smith B.	Kane P.	Ross J.	Millen A.	Fraser J.	Keogh P.	Falconer W.	Dunn D.	Kane A.	Convery S.	Hinds L.	Halliwell B.	McClay A.	Hagan D.	Cosgrove S.	Bossy F.	McConalogue S.	Nish C.	McLaughlin M.	Kernaghan A.S	hields P.	Morrison A.	Gilhaney M.	Reid W.	Baird J.	Doyle P.
Aug 3	A	Queen of the South	3,206	1-2	1	2	3	4	5	6	7^{1}	8	9	10	11	14	12	15															
10	H	Ayr United	1,123	1-0		2	3	4		6	5	7	12	9			14	10^{1}	1	8	11												
17	A	Arbroath	744	1-1		2	3	4		6	5	8^{1}			11	12	9	10	1	7		15											
24	H	St. Mirren	1,874	2-3		2	3	4		6	5	8	12^{2}		11		16	9	1			14	7	10									
31	A	Ross County	2,059	1-1		2	3	4		6^{1}	5	8	9				12		1	14		16	7	11	10								
Sep 14	H	Alloa Athletic	973	0-0		2	3			6	5	8	7				12	9	1	14	11	16	4		10								
21	A	Falkirk	3,595	1-2		2	4		5^{1}	6	7	14	8				12	10	1		11		16		9	3							
28	H	Inverness Cal Th	936	3-0		3			5	6	8	15	10				12^{1}	11	1		7		2		9^{2}		4						
Oct 5	A	St. Johnstone	2,037	1-0		3	2		5	6	8	16	10				14	11^{1}	1		7				9		4						
12	H	Queen of the South	1,026	2-1		3	2		5	6	8	15	10^{1}				12	11	1		7				9		4^{1}						
26	A	Ayr United	1,989	1-1		3	2		5	6		8	10^{1}				12	11	1		7			15	9		4						
Nov 2	H	Ross County	1,047	2-1		3	2		5	6^{1}		8	10^{1}				12	11	1		7	15			9		4						
9	A	St. Mirren	2,703	4-1		3	2		5	6^{1}	10^{1}	8					12	11	1		7				9^{2}		4						
16	A	Alloa Athletic	736	4-1		3^{1}	2^{1}		5	6	10	8^{1}		14			12	11	1		7	15	4		9^{1}								
23	H	Falkirk	3,415	2-0		3	2			6	8	5	10				12	11^{2}	1		7		16		9		4						
30	A	Inverness Cal Th	2,829	0-1		3	2			6		5	10				12	11	1		7		8		9		4						
Dec 7	H	St. Johnstone	1,367	1-2		3				6	8	5	10	15				11^{1}	1		7	14	2		9		4						
14	H	Arbroath	861	3-0		3^{1}	2			6	8	5	10^{1}	9			12	11^{1}	1		7			16			4						
28	A	Ross County	2,534	1-1		3	2			6		5	10	9			12	11	1		7	8^{1}	14		15		4						
Jan 1	H	St. Mirren	1,553	3-2		3				6	8	5	10^{1}	9^{2}				11	1		7		2		14		4						
18	A	St. Johnstone	2,455	2-1		3^{1}	2			6	8	5^{1}		9			12	11	1		7		10	15			4						
Feb 8	A	Arbroath	686	2-1		3	2		5	6	8			9^{1}			12		1		7^{1}	10		11			4	16					
25	A	Queen of the South	1,375	1-1		2	14		5	6	8	16		9			12				7^{1}	10				3	4	11	1				
Mar 1	H	Ross County	980	1-0			2		5	6	8	10					9^{1}		1		7	14		16		3	4	11					
4	A	Falkirk	3,706	0-3		6	2		5		8	10		15			9		1		7	12				3	4	11					
8	A	St. Mirren	2,683	2-1		3	2		14		8	5	15	9					1		7	10	6				4^{1}	11		16^{1}			
11	H	Alloa Athletic	665	2-2		3	2		5		8	12	14^{1}	9					1		7	10	6				4	11		15^{1}			
15	H	Falkirk	3,002	0-0		3	2			6	8	5	9	15					1		7	10		16			4	11		12			
18	H	Inverness Cal Th	703	4-1		3	2			6	8^{1}	5	9	15					1		7	16		10^{1}			4	14^{1}		11^{1}			
22	H	Ayr United	1,015	3-0		3	2			6	8^{2}		9	14^{1}					1		7	5		10			4	15		11	16		
Apr 5	A	Alloa Athletic	687	2-1		3	2			6		5	9^{1}						1			8		10^{1}			4	7		11			
12	A	Inverness Cal Th	1,682	2-1		3^{1}	2			6		5	9	14					1		15	8		10^{1}			4	7		11			
19	H	St. Johnstone	1,143	2-1		3	2^{1}			6	8^{1}	5	9	16					1		7			10		11	4	15		14			
26	H	Queen of the South	960	2-2		3	2			6	8	5	9^{1}						1		7	15		10			4	14		11^{1}			
May 3	A	Ayr United	1,795	3-0		3	2			6	8	5	9						1		7^{1}		16	10^{2}		4				11		15	
10	H	Arbroath	1,002	4-2		3	2			6	8^{1}	5	9^{2}				12		1		7^{1}			10		4				11	15		14
TOTAL FULL APPEARANCES					1	35	32	5	14	33	30	28	24	10	3		3	19	34	2	30	9	11	11	13	7	26	8	1	7			
TOTAL SUB APPEARANCES							1		1			6	4	8		2	21	1		2	1	11	4	5	2			5		4	2	1	1
TOTAL GOALS SCORED						4	2		1	3	7	3	12	4			2	6			4	1		5	5		2	1		4			

Small bold figures denote goalscorers. † denotes opponent's own goal.

broadwood stadium

CAR PARK
CAR PARK
WEST STAND
SOUTH STAND
OKI STAND
CAR PARK
CAR PARK
CAR PARK
To A80 & A73

CAPACITY: 8,006 (All Seated)

PITCH DIMENSIONS: 112 yds x 76 yds

FACILITIES FOR DISABLED SUPPORTERS:
Facilities available in OKI, West and South Stands.

team playing kits

how to get there

The following routes may be used to reach Broadwood Stadium:

BUSES: From Buchanan Street Bus Station in Glasgow, fans should board Bus No. 36A (Glasgow to Westfield).

TRAINS: There are regular trains from Queen Street Station, Glasgow to Croy Station. The Stadium is a 15 minute walk from here.

CARS: From Glasgow City Centre, fans should take the Stepps By-Pass joining the A80 towards Stirling. Take Broadwood turn-off to Stadium.

FALKIRK

Ochilview Park, Gladstone Road, Stenhousemuir, FK5 4QL

ALL CORRESPONDENCE SHOULD BE ADDRESSED TO:
Falkirk F.C., Grangemouth Enterprise Centre, Falkirk Road, Grangemouth, FK3 8XS

CHAIRMAN
Campbell Christie, C.B.E.

VICE-CHAIRMAN
Colin Liddell

DIRECTORS
W. Martin Ritchie O.B.E., Ann M. Joyce, Colin McLachlan, Graham Crawford & Douglas Paterson

SECRETARY
Alexander Blackwood

GENERAL MANAGER
Crawford B. Baptie

MANAGER
John Hughes

FIRST TEAM COACH
Brian Rice

DIRECTOR OF FOOTBALL
Alexander Totten

COMMUNITY COACH
Tom Elliott

YOUTH DEVELOPMENT COACH
Ian McIntyre

YOUTH CO-ORDINATORS
Ian McIntyre & Fraser Cooper

YOUTH TEAM COACHES
Ian McIntyre & Eddie May (U19), Bryan Purdie, Andy Dunleavie & Kevin Holland (U17), Richard Fox & David Henry (U16), Scott Miller & Billy Wilson (U15), John Darian & Jim Easton (U14), Pat Dunne (U13)

CLUB DOCTOR
Dr. R. Gillies Sinclair

PHYSIOTHERAPIST
Stuart Yule

COMMERCIAL MANAGER
Sarah Scott

FOOTBALL SAFETY OFFICERS' ASSOCIATION REPRESENTATIVES
Crawford Baptie & Tom McGunnigle (01324) 666808

CHIEF SCOUT
Bill Parker

GROUNDSMAN
James Dawson

MEDIA LIAISON OFFICER
Crawford Baptie (01324) 666808

MATCHDAY PROGRAMME EDITOR
Gordon McFarlane (07801) 798916

TELEPHONES
Ground/Commercial/ Ticket Office/Information Service (01324) 666808
Fax (01324) 664539

E-MAIL & INTERNET ADDRESS
post@falkirkfc.co.uk
www.falkirkfc.co.uk

CLUB SHOP
47 Glebe Street, Falkirk, FK1 1HX
Tel (01324) 639366
Open Mon. – Sat. 9.30 a.m. – 12 Noon and 1.00 p.m. – 5.00 p.m.
Closed on Wednesday

OFFICIAL SUPPORTERS CLUB
Association of Falkirk F.C. Supporters Clubs–Chairman: Gordon McFarlane
Tel (01324) 638104

TEAM CAPTAINS
Kevin James & Scott MacKenzie

SHIRT SPONSOR
Budweiser Budvar

KIT SUPPLIER
TFG

falkirk

LIST OF PLAYERS 2003/2004

SURNAME	FIRST NAME	MIDDLE NAME	DATE OF BIRTH	PLACE OF BIRTH	DATE OF SIGNING	HEIGHT FT INS	WEIGHT ST LBS	POS. ON PITCH	PREVIOUS CLUB
Alexiou	Peter		07/07/87	Broxburn	01/09/03	5 11 0	12 10	Gk	Falkirk Form D U 16
Barr	Darren		17/03/85	Glasgow	12/07/02	5 10.0	10 4	Mid	Falkirk Form D U 16
Bissett	Callum	Rutherford	21/05/85	Edinburgh	12/07/02	6 1.0	10 4	Def	Raith Rovers Form D U 16
Buchanan	Jack		06/12/86	Glasgow	22/08/03	5 8.0	11 0	Mid	Falkirk Form D U 16
Burns	Paul	Graham	25/07/85	Stirling	12/07/02	6 0.0	9 5	Fwd	Livingston Form D U 16
Christie	Kevin		01/04/76	Aberdeen	31/07/03	6 1.0	13 0	Mid	Motherwell
Churchill	Graeme		20/07/87	Glasgow	01/09/03	5 11.0	10 8	Fwd	Falkirk Form D U 16
Colquhoun	Derek		23/03/85	Edinburgh	31/07/02	6 1.0	12 0	Mid	Falkirk Form D U 16
Cosgrove	Nicholas		15/07/85	Glasgow	12/07/02	5 11.0	10 2	Mid	Falkirk Form D U 16
Creaney	Philip		12/02/83	Bellshill	09/06/00	5 11.5	11 5	Mid	Falkirk Form S
Davidson	Alan	Martin	10/01/85	Falkirk	22/08/03	6 2.0	12 4	Def	Raith Rovers
Devine	Craig	Thomas	01/04/85	Falkirk	22/01/03	6 1.0	11 2	Mid	Livingston Youth
Ferguson	Allan	Thomas	21/03/69	Lanark	04/07/02	5 11.0	13 0	Gk	Airdrieonians
Freeman	William		30/04/86	Ghana	02/09/03	5 9.0	10 0	Gk	Charlton Athletic
Harvey	David		25/01/85	Bellshill	12/07/02	5 10.0	9 1	Def	Falkirk Form D U 16
Hayman	Ross		07/08/86	Glasgow	07/08/03	5 9.0	10 3	Def	Falkirk Form S
Henry	John		31/12/71	Vale of Leven	10/07/02	5 10.0	10 5	Mid	Airdrieonians
Hill	Darren		03/12/81	Falkirk	07/07/98	6 1.5	12 3	Gk	Falkirk B.C.
Hill	Douglas		16/01/85	Edinburgh	18/07/02	6 0.0	11 2	Def	Falkirk Form D U 16
Hughes	John		09/09/64	Edinburgh	18/07/03	6 0.0	13 10	Def	Ayr United
Hutchison	John	Charles	14/05/85	Bellshill	29/07/03	6 2.0	12 9	Gk	Hibernian
James	Kevin	Francis	03/12/75	Edinburgh	06/06/02	6 7.0	14 7	Def	Airdrieonians
Latapy	Russell	Nigel	02/08/68	Trinidad & Tobago	18/07/03	5 7.0	11 4	Mid	Dundee United
Lawrie	Andrew		24/11/78	Galashiels	18/06/96	6 0.0	12 6	Def	Falkirk Form D U 16
Leckie	Craig		10/01/87	Edinburgh	01/09/03	6 0.0	11 1	Def	Falkirk Form D U 16
Leckie	Paul		10/01/87	Edinburgh	01/09/03	6 0.0	11 0	Def	Falkirk Form D U 16
Lee	Jason		09/05/71	London	01/08/03	6 0.0	15 0	Fwd	Peterborough United
Lynch	Sean		26/10/85	Stirling	07/08/03	5 11.0	12 0	Mid	Livingston
MacAloney	Paul		31/01/86	Bellshill	08/08/03	5 11.0	11 2	Mid	Livingston
MacKenzie	Scott		07/07/70	Glasgow	23/08/02	5 9.0	11 2	Mid	St. Mirren
MacSween	Ian		07/06/84	Edinburgh	10/07/01	5 11.5	11 0	Fwd	Falkirk Form D U 16
Maley	David		27/02/87	Falkirk	01/09/03	5 8.0	10 6	Mid	Falkirk Form D U 16
Manson	Stephen		25/02/86	Edinburgh	07/08/03	5 9.0	10 2	Fwd	Hibernian
May	Edward	Skillion	30/08/67	Edinburgh	28/07/03	5 10.0	11 7	Mid	Berwick Rangers
McAnespie	Kieran		11/09/79	Gosport	22/07/03	5 8.0	11 2	Mid	Plymouth Argyle
McMenamin	Colin		12/02/81	Glasgow	22/07/03	5 10.0	11 0	Fwd	Livingston
McPherson	Craig		27/03/71	Greenock	04/07/02	5 10.0	11 6	Mid	Airdrieonians
McStay	Ryan Michael		04/12/85	Bellshill	12/07/02	6 1.0	10 0	Mid	Falkirk Form D U 16
Morgan	Garry		28/03/87	Falkirk	01/09/03	6 1.0	11 2	Def	Falkirk Form D U 16
Moss	Steven		07/05/87	Falkirk	01/09/03	5 10.0	10 0	Mid	Falkirk Form D U 16
Nicholls	David		05/04/72	Bellshill	09/08/03	5 10.0	12 7	Mid	Dunfermline Athletic
O'Neil	John	Thomas	06/07/71	Bellshill	29/08/03	5 8.0	12 0	Mid	Hibernian
Rahim	Brent		08/08/78	Trinidad & Tobago	08/08/03	5 10.0	12 0	Mid	Levski Sofia
Ramsay	Mark		24/01/86	Dunfermline	07/08/03	5 7.0	10 0	Mid	Falkirk Form D U 16
Rodgers	Andrew		18/10/83	Falkirk	07/07/00	5 10.5	10 1	Fwd	Falkirk Form S
Scally	Neil		14/08/78	Paisley	08/07/03	5 11.0	12 7	Mid	Dumbarton
Sharp	James		02/01/76	Reading	18/07/03	6 1.0	14 4	Mid	Hartlepool United
Twaddle	Marc	Ian	27/08/86	Glasgow	22/08/03	6 1.0	12 0	Mid	Rangers
Xausa	Davide	Antonio	10/03/76	Vancouver	29/08/03	6 0.0	12 11	Fwd	Livingston

milestones

YEAR OF FORMATION: 1876
MOST CAPPED PLAYER: Alex H. Parker
NO. OF CAPS: 14
MOST LEAGUE POINTS IN A SEASON: 66 (First Division – Season 1993/94) (2 Points for a Win) and 81 (First Division – Season 2002/03) (3 Points for a Win)
MOST LEAGUE GOALS SCORED BY A PLAYER IN A SEASON: Evelyn Morrison (Season 1928/29)
NO. OF GOALS SCORED: 43
RECORD ATTENDANCE: 23,100 (-v- Celtic – 21.2.1953)
RECORD VICTORY: 12-1 (-v- Laurieston – Scottish Cup, 23.3.1893)
RECORD DEFEAT: 1-11 (-v- Airdrieonians – Division 1, 28.4.1951)

ticket information

SEASON TICKET PRICES

SEATED	
MAIN STAND	
ADULT	£255
CONCESSION	£200
TEMPORARY STAND	
ADULT	£210
CONCESSION	£105
STANDING	
TERRACING	
ADULT	£180
CONCESSION	£90
PRIMARY SCHOOL	£30

LEAGUE ADMISSION PRICES

SEATED	
MAIN STAND	
ADULT	£17
CONCESSION	£13.50
TEMPORARY STAND	
ADULT	£14
CONCESSION	£7
STANDING	
TERRACING	
ADULT	£12
CONCESSION	£6

leading goalscorers 1993-2003

Season	Div	No. of Goals	Player
1993-94	F	18	R. Cadette
1994-95	P	9	C. McDonald
1995-96	P	6	P. McGrillen
1996-97	F	8	M. McGraw
1997-98	F	12	D. Moss
1998-99	F	17	M. Keith
1999-00	F	14	S. Crabbe
2000-01	F	11	G. Hutchison
2001-02	F	11	L. Miller
2002-03	F	20	O. Coyle

the bairns' club factfile 2002/03

Date	Venue	Opponents	Att.	Res	Ferguson A.	Lawrie A.	McQuilken J.	Rennie S.	Hughes J.	James K.	Kerr M.	Miller L.	Coyle O.	McPherson C.	Tosh S.	Henry J.	Rodgers A.	Samuel C.	MacSween I.	May E.	MacKenzie S.	Cringean S.	Hill Darren	Craig S.	Nicholls D.	Taylor S.	Reid B.	Christie K.	Creaney P.
Aug 3	A	Ayr United	3,030	3-1	1	2	3[1]	4	5	6[1]	7	8	9[1]	10	11	12	14												
10	H	St. Mirren	4,360	2-0	1	2[1]	3	4	5	6	7	8	9[1]		11	10		14	15										
17	A	Inverness Cal Th	2,267	2-1	1	2	3	4	5	6	14	8[1]	9	10	11[1]	7		12		15									
24	A	Alloa Athletic	2,613	6-1	1	2[2]	3		5	6	15	8	9[1]	10[1]	11	7		12[2]			4							14	
31	H	Queen of the South	4,091	†3-0	1	2[1]	3		5	6	14	8	9	10	11	7		12[1]			4	16							
Sep 14	A	Ross County	2,729	1-1	1	2	3	15	5	6	7	8	9[1]	10	11	14		12			4								
21	H	Clyde	3,595	2-1	1	2	3[1]	6	5		15	8	9[1]	10	11	7		12			4	14							
29	H	St. Johnstone	5,872	1-0	1		3	5		6[1]	7	8	9	10	11	12	15	2			4								
Oct 5	A	Arbroath	1,730	0-2	1		3	5		6	7	8	9	10	11	12	15	2	16		4								
19	H	Ayr United	3,441	3-0	1		3	6	5		7	8[1]	9[2]	10	11		15	2			4	14		16					
26	A	St. Mirren	3,661	4-4	1		3	2	5	6	7[1]	8[3]	9	10	11	16		14			4								
Nov 2	A	Queen of the South	3,017	1-1			3		5	6	7	8	9	10	2	11[1]		12			4		1						
9	H	Alloa Athletic	3,390	3-0	1		3	14	5	6[1]	7	8	9[1]	10	11	2[1]		12			4			15					
16	H	Ross County	3,255	2-0	1		3	12	5	6	7	8[2]	9	10	11	2		14	15		4								
23	A	Clyde	3,415	0-2	1		3	6	5		7	8	9	10	11	2		12			4	14		15					
30	A	St. Johnstone	3,696	1-0	1		3	15	5	6[1]	7		9	10	11	2		8			4	12							
Dec 7	H	Arbroath	2,673	2-1	1		3		5		7		9[1]	10		2		8[1]	11		4	6		14					
14	H	Inverness Cal Th	4,671	1-1	1		3	6	5[1]		7	8	9	10		2		11			4								
28	H	Queen of the South	3,858	5-0			3	6	5		7	8[1]	9[1]	10		2[1]	16	11[2]	14		4	12	1						
Jan 18	A	Arbroath	1,950	4-1	1		3	12	5		7	8	9[1]	10		2		11[3]	14		4				6				
Feb 1	H	St. Johnstone	4,694	1-1	1		3		5		7	8	9	10		2[1]		11			4				6				
8	A	Inverness Cal Th	3,322	4-3	1		3		5		7	8	9[3]	10		2	16	11[1]			4				6	12			
15	H	St. Mirren	4,094	3-1			3		5		7	8	9[1]	10		2[1]	14	11[1]			4		1		6	12			
25	A	Ayr United	1,783	0-1	1		3		5		7	8	9	10		2	14	11			4				6	12			
Mar 1	H	Queen of the South	2,555	1-2	1		3		5		7	8[1]	9	10		2		11			4				6		15		
4	H	Clyde	3,706	3-0	1		3		5		7	8[1]	9	10		2	14	11	16		4				6	12			
8	H	Alloa Athletic	3,320	3-1	1		3		5		7	8[1]	9	10		2	14[1]	11	16		4				6	12[1]			
11	A	Ross County	2,161	1-0	1		3		5		7	8[1]	9	10		2	14	11			4				6	12	15		
15	A	Clyde	3,002	0-0	1				5		7	8	9	10		2	14	11			4				6	12	3		
29	A	Alloa Athletic	1,686	3-1	1		3		5		7	8[1]	9[1]	10		2	14		16		4				6	11[1]			
Apr 5	H	Ross County	3,523	3-0	1		3		5		7	8[2]	9[1]	10		2		15			4				6	11	12	16	
12	A	St. Johnstone	6,579	1-0	1		3		5		7	8	9	10		2[1]		16			4				6	11	12		
19	H	Arbroath	4,950	4-1	1		3		5		7[1]	8	9[3]	10		15	14	15			4				6	11	2		
26	H	Ayr United	4,042	3-0			3	5			7	8[1]	9	10			16	14			4[1]		1		6	11[1]	2		
May 3	A	St. Mirren	3,062	2-1	1		3	5			7	8[1]	9	10			12	15			4				6	11[1]	2		16
10	H	Inverness Cal Th	7,300	2-3	1		3	5			7	8	9	10		2		14				16			6	11[2]		4	
TOTAL FULL APPEARANCES					32	7	35	14	31	13	32	34	36	35	16	27		17	1		32	1	4		17	7	4	1	
TOTAL SUB APPEARANCES								5			4					6	16	17	8	1		7		4		7	4	2	1
TOTAL GOALS SCORED						4	2		1	4	2	17	20	1	1	6	1	11			1					6			

Small bold figures denote goalscorers. † denotes opponent's own goal.

ochilview park

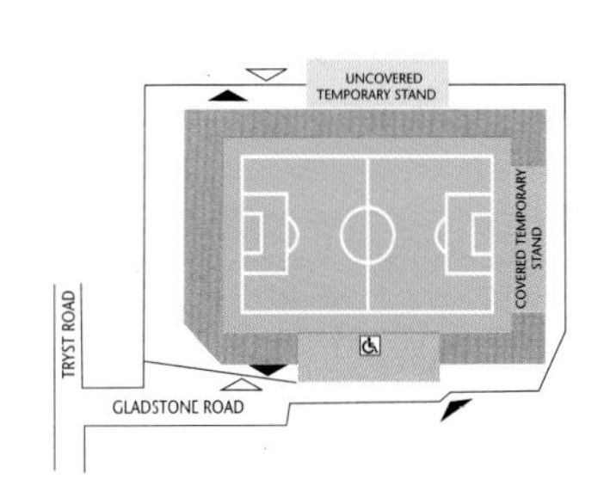

CAPACITY: 5,267; Seated 2,117 Standing 3,150

PITCH DIMENSIONS: 110 yds x 72 yds

FACILITIES FOR DISABLED SUPPORTERS:
Accommodation for disabled in new Stand. Toilet facilities also provided.

team playing kits

how to get there

Ochilview Park can be reached by the following routes:

TRAINS: The nearest station is Larbert, which is about 1 mile from the ground.

BUSES: There are regular bus services from Falkirk.

CARS: There is a large car park on the north side of the ground.

inverness caledonian thistle

Caledonian Stadium, East Longman, Inverness, IV1 1FF
CHAIRMAN
Kenneth Mackie
VICE-CHAIRMAN
Graeme Bennett
DIRECTORS
Ian MacDonald, Alexander Catto & Kenneth Cameron
HON. PRESIDENT
John S. McDonald O.B.E.
HON. VICE-PRESIDENT
Norman H. Miller
SECRETARY
James Falconer
MANAGER
John Robertson
ASSISTANT MANAGER
Donald Park
DIRECTOR OF FOOTBALL
Graeme Bennett
RESERVE COACH
John Docherty
YOUTH CO-ORDINATOR
John Beaton
YOUTH DEVELOPMENT COACH & LOTTERY MANAGER
Charlie Christie
YOUTH COACHES
Gary Davidson & Matthew McInnes (U17), Graeme MacDonald & George Mann (U16), Joe MacMillan & Rae Sinclair (U14), George Gibb & Brian MacDonald (U13)
COMMUNITY DEVELOPMENT MANAGER
Danny MacDonald
ASSISTANT COMMUNITY DEVELOPMENT MANAGER
Fiona McWilliams
CLUB DOCTORS
Dr. Ian Smith & Dr. Derek MacLeod
PHYSIOTHERAPIST
Emily Goodlad
COMMERCIAL MANAGER
Debbie Ross
CLUB CHAPLAIN
Rev. Arthur Fraser
FOOTBALL SAFETY OFFICERS' ASSOCIATION REPRESENTATIVE
John Sutherland M.B.E.
GROUNDSMAN/KIT PERSON
Tommy Cumming
MATCHDAY PROGRAMME EDITOR
Bryan Munro (01463) 230721
E-MAIL: bryan.munro@lineone.net
TELEPHONES
Ground (01463) 222880
Fax (01463) 715816
Sec. Home (01463) 792358
Sec. Bus. (01463) 720603
Sec. Mobile (07881) 770207
INTERNET ADDRESS
accounts@caleythistleonline.com
CLUB SHOP
Shop available at Inverness Courier, New Century House, Stadium Road, Inverness & Courier Office, Bank Lane, Inverness. Stadium Shop open on Home Match days.
On-line at www.inverness.courier.co.uk
OFFICIAL SUPPORTERS CLUB
Secretary, Caledonian Stadium, East Longman, Inverness, IV1 1FF
TEAM CAPTAIN
Bobby Mann
SHIRT SPONSOR
Inverness Medical
KIT SUPPLIER
ERREA

S·F·L ©

LIST OF PLAYERS 2003/2004

SURNAME	FIRST NAME	MIDDLE NAME	DATE OF BIRTH	PLACE OF BIRTH	DATE OF SIGNING	HEIGHT FT INS	WEIGHT ST LBS	POS. ON PITCH	PREVIOUS CLUB
Begg	Donald	Andrew	30/07/86	Inverness	07/08/03	6 1.0	11 10	Mid	Inverness Cal.Th. Form D U'16
Bingham	David	Thomas	03/09/70	Dunfermline	11/06/03	5 10.0	11 7	Fwd	Livingston
Brown	Mark		28/02/81	Motherwell	02/08/02	6 1.5	13 2	Gk	Motherwell
Chisholm	Gavin	Matson	10/02/85	Nairn	11/07/03	6 0.0	11 6	Mid	Brora Rangers
Christie	Arron	Ian	29/06/86	Kirkcaldy	11/06/03	5 8.0	9 10	Mid/Fwd	Inverness Cal.Th. Form D U'16
Christie	Charles		30/03/66	Inverness	05/08/94	5 8.5	11 4	Mid/Fwd	Caledonian
Duncan	Russell	Allan	15/09/80	Aberdeen	03/08/01	5 10.0	10 10	Def/Mid	Forfar Athletic
Finnigan	Christopher	James	05/04/86	Glasgow	11/06/03	5 10.0	11 0	Mid/Fwd	Inverness Cal.Th. Form D U'16
Fraser	Michael	Alan	08/10/83	Inverness	09/01/03	6 3.0	12 7	Gk	Brora Rangers
Golabek	Stuart	William	05/11/74	Inverness	27/05/99	5 10.0	11 0	Def	Ross County
Hart	Richard		30/03/78	Inverness	01/08/02	5 10.0	12 5	Def/Mid	Brora Rangers
Hislop	Steven	James	14/06/78	Edinburgh	31/01/03	6 2.0	12 0	Fwd	Ross County
Keogh	Liam	Michael	06/09/81	Aberdeen	02/08/02	5 9.0	12 3	Fwd	St. Mirren
Low	Anthony	Kevin	18/08/83	Glasgow	28/08/03	5 8.0	10 7	Mid/Fwd	Brora Rangers
MacKinnon	Lewis	Craig	21/03/85	Inverness	11/07/03	6 0.0	11.7	Fwd	Dufftown Juniors
MacLaren	Paul	Alan	14/04/86	Inverness	11/06/03	5 10.0	10 6	Mid	Inverness Cal.Th. Form D U'16
MacMillan	Craig	Alexander	25/06/84	Inverness	21/05/03	6 0.0	11 0	Fwd	Clachnacuddin
MacRae	David	Alexander	25/10/84	Drumnadrochit	21/05/03	5 11.0	11 6	Mid	Clachnacuddin
Mann	Robert	Alexander	11/01/74	Dundee	05/02/99	6 3.0	14 7	Def	Forfar Athletic
McBain	Roy	Adam	07/11/74	Aberdeen	04/08/00	5 11.0	11 5	Def/Mid	Ross County
McCaffrey	Stuart	Muir	30/05/79	Glasgow	01/12/00	5 11.5	12 0	Def	Aberdeen
Munro	Grant	John	15/09/80	Inverness	21/02/00	6 0.0	12 7	Def	Inverness Cal. Th. Form S
Proctor	David	William	04/05/84	Bellshill	07/07/03	6 0.0	11 2	Mid	Hibernian
Ridgers	Alexander	Trevor	30/06/82	Inverness	31/08/03	6 2.0	12 8	Gk	Clachnacuddin
Ritchie	Paul	Michael	25/01/69	St. Andrews	02/08/01	6 1.0	12 12	Fwd	Happy Valley A.A.
Smith	Mark	Charles	15/10/85	Inverness	11/07/03	5 11.0	12 7	Def	Brora Rangers
Sutherland	James	John Murray	01/12/86	Inverness	29/01/03	5 10.0	10 7	Mid	Inverness Cal.Th. Form D U'16
Thomson	Darran	Hunter	31/01/84	Edinburgh	09/07/03	5 10.0	10 7	Mid	Hibernian
Tokely	Ross	Norman	08/03/79	Aberdeen	03/06/96	6 3.0	13 6	Def/Mid	Huntly
Wilson	Barry	John	16/02/72	Kirkcaldy	31/08/03	5 11.0	13 0	Mid/Fwd	Livingston

milestones

YEAR OF FORMATION: 1994
MOST LEAGUE POINTS IN A SEASON: 76 (Third Division – Season 1996/97) (3 Points for a Win)
MOST LEAGUE GOALS SCORED BY A PLAYER IN A SEASON: Iain Stewart (Season 1996/97)
NO. OF GOALS SCORED: 27
RECORD ATTENDANCE: 4,931 (-v- Ross County – 23.1.1996 - at Telford Street Park)
6,290 (-v- Aberdeen – 20.2.2000 (Scottish Cup) at Caledonian Stadium)
RECORD VICTORY: 8-1 (-v- Annan Athletic – Scottish Cup, 24.1.1998)
RECORD DEFEAT: 1-5 (-v- Morton – First Division, 12.11.1999)
(-v- Airdrieonians – First Division, 15.4.2000)

ticket information

SEASON TICKET INFORMATION

SEATED	ADULT	£180
	JUVENILE/OAP	£90
STANDING	ADULT	£120
	JUVENILE/OAP	£36

LEAGUE ADMISSION PRICES

SEATED	ADULT	£11
	JUVENILE/OAP	£6
STANDING	ADULT	£9
	JUVENILE/OAP	£3

leading goalscorers 1993-2003

Season 1994-95 was the Club's first season in membership of SFL

Season	Div	No. of Goals	Player
1994-95	T	6	C. Christie, A. Hercher
1995-96	T	23	I. Stewart
1996-97	T	27	I. Stewart
1997-98	S	16	I. Stewart
1998-99	S	20	S. McLean
1999-00	F	13	B. Wilson
2000-01	F	24	D. Wyness
2001-02	F	18	D. Wyness
2002-03	F	19	D. Wyness

caley thistle's club factfile 2002/03

Date	Venue	Opponents	Att.	Res	Brown M.	Tokely R.	Golabek S.	Mann R.	McCaffrey S.	Munro G.	Duncan R.	Wyness D.	Ritchie P.	Christie C.	Robson B.	Keogh L.	Hart R.	McBain R.	Low A.	Gilfillan B.	Miller C.	Stewart G.	Bagan D.	Hislop S.
Aug 3	H	Alloa Athletic	1,623	0-0	1	2	3	4	5	6	7	8	9	10	11	12	14	15						
10	A	St. Johnstone	3,770	0-1	1	2	3	4	5	6	7	8	12	10	11	9								
17	H	Falkirk	2,267	1-2	1	2^{1}	3	4	5	6	7	8	12	10	11	9		14	16					
24	H	Ross County	3,699	2-0	1	2	3	4	5		7	8^{2}	12	10	11		9	6	15	16				
31	A	St. Mirren	2,485	4-0	1	2	3	4		5	7	8	12	10^{1}	11^{2}		9^{1}	6	14		16			
Sep 14	A	Queen of the South	1,611	3-1	1	2	3	4^{1}		5	7	8^{2}	9		11	12	10	6	15					
21	H	Arbroath	1,686	5-0	1	2^{2}	3	4		5	7	8^{1}	9^{1}		11		10^{1}	6	12	15		14		
28	A	Clyde	936	0-3	1		3	4		5	7	8	9		11		10	6	2			15		
Oct 5	H	Ayr United	1,803	2-0	1		3	4		5	7	8^{1}	9^{1}		11		10	6	2					
19	A	Alloa Athletic	531	6-0	1	2	3	4		5	7	8^{3}	9^{3}	12	11	16	10	6	15					
26	H	St. Johnstone	2,541	2-1	1	2	3	4		5	7	8^{1}	9	12	11	16	10^{1}	6						
Nov 2	H	St. Mirren	2,023	4-1	1	2	3	4		5	7	8^{2}	9	12	11^{1}	16	10^{1}	6	15					
9	A	Ross County	5,449	†2-0	1	2	3	4		5	7	8	9	12	11^{1}	18	10	6	15					
16	H	Queen of the South	1,855	5-3	1	2	3	4		5	7	8	9^{3}	12	11^{2}	16	10	6	15					
23	A	Arbroath	653	2-1	1	2	3	4		5	7	8^{1}	9		11	18	10^{1}	6						
30	H	Clyde	2,829	1-0	1	2	3	4		5	7	8	9	12	11^{1}	16	10	6						
Dec 7	A	Ayr United	1,663	3-3	1	2	3	4^{1}		5	7	8^{1}	9^{1}		11		10	6						
14	A	Falkirk	4,671	†1-1	1	2	3	4	14	5		8	9	7	11	16	10	6	15					
21	H	Alloa Athletic	1,639	1-1	1	2	3	4^{1}		5		8	9	7	11	14	10	6					15	
28	A	St. Mirren	3,054	4-1	1	2^{1}	3	4	5			8^{1}	9^{1}	10	11	12		6	16			7^{1}	14	
Jan 18	H	Ayr United	2,021	0-1	1	2	3	4	5		12	8	9	10	11	16	14	6				7		
Feb 8	H	Falkirk	3,322	3-4	1	2	3	4	5		7	8^{1}	9^{1}	14	11^{1}		10	6						16
15	A	St. Johnstone	2,631	0-2	1	2	3	4	6	5	7	8	9	10		16		11					12	15
25	H	Ross County	3,443	1-5	1	2	3	4	5	12	7	8^{1}	9	10	11			6					15	14
Mar 1	H	St. Mirren	1,973	3-1	1	2	3		5	4		8	9^{3}		11	15	7	6				12	10	14
4	H	Arbroath	1,396	2-0	1	2	3		5	4		8	9^{1}		11	15	7	6	16^{1}				10	14
8	A	Ross County	4,621	2-0	1	2	3		5	4		8	9	10	11^{1}		7^{1}	6				12	14	15
11	A	Queen of the South	1,405	0-0	1	2	3		5	4		8	9		11	16	7	6					10	15
15	A	Arbroath	550	3-1	1	7	3	4	2	5		8^{2}	15		11	16	10	6				12		9^{1}
18	A	Clyde	703	1-4	1	7	3	4	2	5		8	15		11^{1}	16	10	6				12		9
Apr 5	H	Queen of the South	1,656	1-0	1	7^{1}	3	4	2	5	12	8	9	14		16	10	6						11
12	H	Clyde	1,682	1-2	1	2		4	5	3	6	15		10	11	8	7						12	9^{1}
26	A	Alloa Athletic	485	5-1	1	2	3^{1}	4^{1}	5	6	7	8	9^{3}		11			10	16				15	14
29	A	Ayr United	1,114	0-1	1	2	3		4	5	6	8	12		11		14	10				7	15	9
May 3	H	St. Johnstone	1,814	1-2	1	2	3	4	5	12	6	8	9		11	16	7^{1}	10					14	
10	A	Falkirk	7,300	†3-2	1	2		4^{1}	5	3	6	8	9	14^{1}	11		7	10					15	12
TOTAL FULL APPEARANCES					**36**	**34**	**34**	**31**	**21**	**30**	**25**	**35**	**28**	**13**	**34**	**3**	**27**	**32**	**2**			**3**	**3**	**5**
TOTAL SUB APPEARANCES									**1**	**2**	**2**	**1**	**7**	**9**		**21**	**3**	**2**	**13**	**2**	**1**	**6**	**10**	**9**
TOTAL GOALS SCORED						**5**	**1**	**5**				**19**	**18**	**2**	**10**		**7**		**1**			**1**		**2**

Small bold figures denote goalscorers. † denotes opponent's own goal.

caledonian stadium

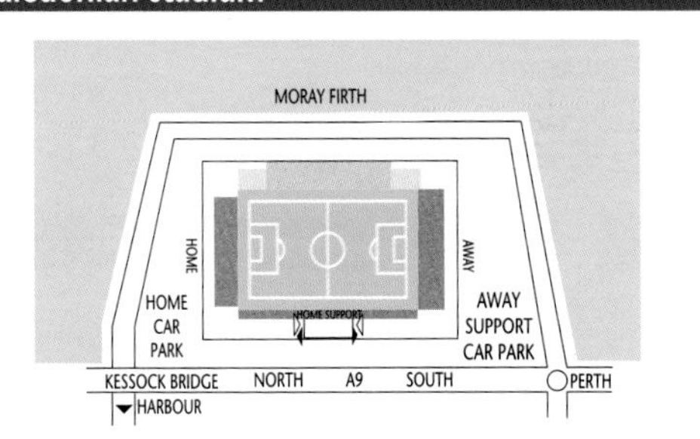

CAPACITY: 6,280; Seated 2,280, Standing 4,000

PITCH DIMENSIONS: 115 yds x 74 yds

FACILITIES FOR DISABLED SUPPORTERS:
By prior arrangement with the Secretary

team playing kits

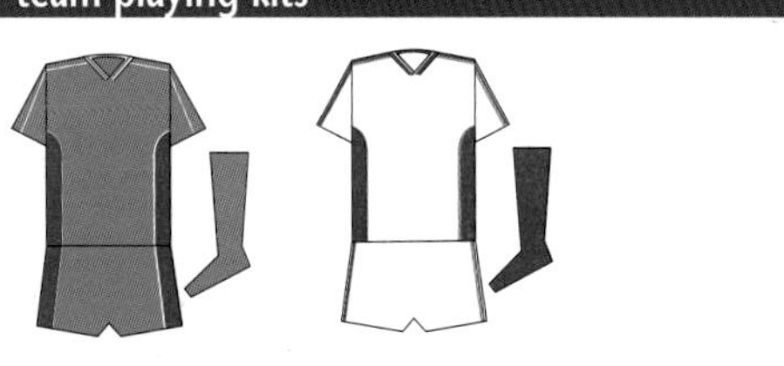

how to get there

The following routes can be used to reach Caledonian Stadium:

TRAINS: Nearest Railway Station is Inverness which is approximately one mile from the ground.

BUSES: Local services from Farraline Park Bus Station.

CARS: The Ground is located on the North side of the A9 Perth/Inverness trunk road and fans should access off the roundabout (first after Perth) before Kessock Bridge. Parking available at stadium.

queen of the south

Palmerston Park, Terregles Street, Dumfries, DG2 9BA

CHAIRMAN

VICE-CHAIRMAN
Thomas G. Harkness

DIRECTORS
Keith M. Houliston, Craig Paterson & David Rae

SECRETARY
Richard Shaw, M.B.E.

OFFICER ADMINISTRATOR
Margaret Bell

MANAGER
John Connolly

ASSISTANT MANAGER
Ian Scott

FIRST TEAM COACH
Warren Pearson

RESERVE COACHES
Gordon Hyslop & Fred Smith

GOALKEEPING COACH
Gordon Doig

YOUTH TEAM COACHES
U17 – Ian Pagan, Sandy Whitelaw & Neil Graham
U15 – George Paterson, Tim Leighfield & Mark Turner
U14 – Neil Muirhead, Keith Middlemiss & Alan Goodwin
U13 – Alan Murray & David McCann

CLUB DOCTORS
Dr. Andrew Downie & Dr. Bill Balfour

PHYSIOTHERAPIST
Kenneth Crichton

FOOTBALL SAFETY OFFICERS' ASSOCIATION REPRESENTATIVE
George Galbraith (01387) 254853

CHIEF SCOUT
Iain McChesney

GROUNDSMAN
Kevin McCormick

COMMERCIAL MANAGER
Margaret Heuchan (H) (01556) 504569
(B) (01387) 254853

LOTTERY MANAGER
Ian Heuchan

MEDIA LIAISON OFFICER
Bill Goldie (01387) 265569
(M) 07733 203171

MATCHDAY PROGRAMME EDITOR
Bruce Wright
(B)(01387) 262960 (H)(01387) 252400

TELEPHONES
Ground/Ticket Office/Information Service (01387) 254853
Football Office Only (01387) 251666
Restaurant (01387) 252241
Fax (01387) 254853

E-MAIL & INTERNET ADDRESS
mail@qosfc.co.uk
www.qosfc.co.uk

CLUB SHOP
Contact: John Paterson
Palmerston Park, Terregles Street, Dumfries, DG2 9BA (01387) 254853
Open 9.00am – 4.00pm Mon. to Fri. and 1.30pm – 5.00pm on home match days.

OFFICIAL SUPPORTERS CLUB
c/o Palmerston Park, Terregles Street, Dumfries, DG2 9BA

TEAM CAPTAIN
Jim Thomson

SHIRT SPONSOR
G.R. Blount Pharmacy

KIT SUPPLIER
Nike

LIST OF PLAYERS 2003/2004

SURNAME	FIRST NAME	MIDDLE NAME	DATE OF BIRTH	PLACE OF BIRTH	DATE OF SIGNING	HEIGHT FT INS	WEIGHT ST LBS	POS. ON PITCH	PREVIOUS CLUB
Aitken	Andrew	Robert	02/02/78	Dumfries	10/07/96	6 0.0	12 7	Def	Annan Athletic
Allan	Derek		24/12/74	Irvine	14/06/01	6 0.0	12 8	Def	Kingstonians
Allison	Steven		02/08/87	Irvine	16/07/03	5 7.0	9 8	Mid	Troon Kay Park
Atkinson	Patrick		22/05/70	Singapore	31/07/00	5 10.0	11 10	Def	Blyth Spartans
Bagan	David		26/04/77	Irvine	16/07/03	5 6.0	10 7	Mid	Inverness Cal. Th.
Beattie	Ross		17/07/86	Dumfries	20/06/03	5 7.0	9 0	Mid	Kilmarnock
Bowey	Steven		10/07/74	Durham	14/02/02	5 9.0	11 2	Mid	Gateshead
Burke	Alexander		11/11/77	Glasgow	30/06/03	5 9.0	10 12	Fwd	Berwick Rangers
Burns	Paul		18/05/84	Irvine	17/06/02	5 9.0	9 7	Mid	Queen of the South Form S
Carnochan	Colin	George	05/11/87	Dumfries	16/07/03	5 9.0	9 9	Fwd	Queen of the South Form D U'15
Cluckie	Stuart		10/04/86	Dumfries	19/06/03	6 1.0	11 8	Mid	Queen of the South Form S
Coates	Craig		26/10/82	Durham	24/07/03	5 7.0	11 0	Fwd	Jarrow Roofing
Dodds	John George William		16/12/81	Edinburgh	04/06/03	6 3.0	14 0	Gk	Ayr United
Ferguson	Jamie		12/12/87	Irvine	16/07/03	5 10.0	10 3	Def	Auchinleck Talbot Juniors
Ferrie	Shaun	Murray	02/07/84	Glasgow	17/06/02	5 8.0	11 0	Fwd	Queen of the South Form S
Gibson	Calum		02/03/87	Irvine	11/08/03	6 0.0	11 2	Mid	Galston B.C.
Gibson	William		06/08/84	Dumfries	27/09/00	5 10.0	10 0	Mid	Maxwelltown Thistle
Greenhorn	Fraser	William	02/06/86	Irvine	30/06/03	6 0.0	11 6	Fwd	Queen of the South Form D U'16
Hayes	Scott		16/02/87	Irvine	16/07/03	5 7.0	10 0	Mid	Troon Kay Park
Jaconelli	Emilio		05/06/83	Lanark	09/07/03	5 8.0	12 5	Fwd	Kilmarnock
Leishman	Andrew		04/12/87	Irvine	16/07/03	6 3.0	12 0	Gk	Auchinleck Talbot Juniors
Lennox	Thomas		02/02/84	Lanark	26/07/01	5 9.0	9 5	Def	Queen of the South Form D U'16
Lyle	Derek		13/02/81	Glasgow	01/07/02	5 9.0	11 2	Fwd	Partick Thistle
MacBeth	John		13/01/85	Dumfries	17/06/02	5 11.0	10 0	Def	Maxwelltown Thistle
Mackay	Steven		04/01/84	Irvine	13/09/01	5 11.0	9 8	Def	Valspar B.C.
McAlpine	Joseph	Charles	12/09/81	Glasgow	02/09/01	5 9.5	11 9	Mid	Airdrieonians
McColligan	Brian		31/10/80	Glasgow	06/06/02	5 9.0	10 10	Mid	Clydebank
O'Connor	Sean		07/07/81	Wolverhampton	14/03/02	6 3.0	13 0	Fwd	Dundee United
Parris	Kenneth		20/05/87	Irvine	16/07/03	6 0.0	11 4	Mid	Afton B.C.
Paton	Eric	John	01/08/78	Glasgow	06/06/02	5 10.0	12 0	Mid	Clydebank
Reid	Brian	Robertson	15/06/70	Paisley	11/08/03	6 3.0	14 2	Def	Falkirk
Richardson	Matthew		23/04/87	Irvine	16/07/03	5 7.0	9 9	Def	Crosshouse
Robertson	Scott		26/11/87	Irvine	16/07/03	5 11.0	10 0	Mid	Troon Kay Park
Robertson	Stuart	Eric	27/12/84	Irvine	31/07/03	6 0.0	12 0	Gk	Queen of the South Form S
Scott	Colin	George	19/05/70	Glasgow	03/11/00	6 2.0	14 0	Gk	Clydebank
Shankland	Steven		18/10/87	Irvine	16/07/03	5 8.0	9 9	Fwd	Afton B.C.
Sloan	Steven	George	21/03/84	Dumfries	26/07/01	5 8.0	8 11	Mid	Queen of the South Form S
Talbot	Paul		11/08/79	Newcastle	16/07/03	5 10.0	12 0	Mid	Burton Albion
Thomson	James		15/05/71	Stirling	23/05/01	6 4.0	14 0	Def	Arbroath
Whorlow	Mark		03/07/86	Dumfries	19/06/03	5 10.0	11 0	Mid	Queen of the South Form D U'16
Wood	Garry Pringle Gillan		18/09/76	Edinburgh	05/08/03	5 11.0	12 2	Fwd	Berwick Rangers

milestones

YEAR OF FORMATION: 1919
MOST CAPPED PLAYER: William Houliston
NO. OF CAPS: 3
MOST LEAGUE POINTS IN A SEASON: 55 (Division 2 – Season 1985/86) (2 Points for a Win)
67 (Second Division – Season 2001/02) (3 Points for a Win)
MOST LEAGUE GOALS SCORED BY A PLAYER IN A SEASON: Jimmy Gray (Season 1927/28)
NO. OF GOALS SCORED: 37
RECORD ATTENDANCE: 26,552 (-v- Hearts – Scottish Cup, 23.2.1952)
RECORD VICTORY: 11-1 (-v- Stranraer – Scottish Cup, 16.1.1932)
RECORD DEFEAT: 2-10 (-v- Dundee – Division 1, 1.12.1962)

ticket information

SEASON TICKET INFORMATION

MAIN STAND	ADULT/UNDER 16 & OAP	£180/£100
EAST STAND	ADULT/UNDER 16 & OAP	£160/£90
GROUND	ADULT/UNDER 16 & OAP	£160/£90
EAST STAND	JUNIOR BLUES	£30

LEAGUE ADMISSION PRICES

MAIN STAND	(NO CONCESSIONS)	£12
EAST STAND	ADULT/JUVENILE & OAP	£10/£6
STANDING	ADULT	£10
	JUVENILE, OAP & UNEMPLOYED (WITH UB40) /FAMILY SUPPLEMENT	£6

leading goalscorers 1993-2003

Season	Div	No. of Goals	Player
1993-94	S	29	A. Thomson
1994-95	S	9	D. Campbell, S. Mallan
1995-96	S	12	S. Mallan
1996-97	S	13	S. Mallan
1997-98	S	11	T. Bryce
1998-99	S	15	S. Mallan
1999-00	S	13	S. Mallan
2000-01	S	16	P. Weatherson
2001-02	S	19	J. O'Neil
2002-03	F	9	J. O'Neil

the doonhamers' club factfile 2002/03

Date	Venue	Opponents	Att.	Res	Goram A.	Atkinson P.	Anderson D.	Allan D.	Aitken A.	Paton E.	Gray A.	Bowey S.	O'Connor S.	Weatherson P.	McAlpine J.	Lyle D.	McLaughlin B.	O'Neil J.	McColligan B.	Shields P.	Neilson R.	Crawford J.	Henderson R.	Scott C.	Thomson J.	Renicks S.	Dawson B.	Burns P.	Gibson W.	Campbell J.
Aug 3	H	Clyde	3,206	2-1	1	2	3	4	5	6^{1}	7	8	9^{1}	10	11	12	16													
10	A	Ross County	2,894	0-2	1	2	3	4	5	6	7	8	10	12	11	9	16	14												
17	H	St. Johnstone	3,137	0-0	1		3	4	5	7	2	8		10	14	9	11	12	6											
24	H	Ayr United	2,803	1-2	1	2	3	4	5	7		8^{1}		12	15	9	11	16	6	10										
31	A	Falkirk	4,091	0-3	1		3	4	5			8		6	11	9	15	7		10	2	14								
Sep 14	H	Inverness Cal Th	1,611	1-3	1		3		5	11	2	8		9^{1}	16		14	7		10		4	6	13						
21	A	St. Mirren	2,492	1-2					5	16		8		4	11	9	12	7		10^{1}	2	6	3	1	14					
28	H	Arbroath	1,733	2-2	1		3		5			8		4	11	10^{2}	14	7		9	2				6					
Oct 5	A	Alloa Athletic	658	1-0	1		3		5	15		8		4	11	10	14	7^{1}	16	9	2				6					
12	A	Clyde	1,026	1-2	1		3		5		15	8		4	11	10	14	7		9	2				6^{1}					
26	H	Ross County	1,533	2-0	1		3		5			8	12	9	11	10^{2}	15	7	4		2				6					
Nov 2	H	Falkirk	3,017	1-1	1		3		5			8	12	9		10	11	7	4^{1}		2				6					
9	A	Ayr United	2,234	1-0	1		3		5			8	9	11		10	7^{1}	12	4	16	2				6					
16	A	Inverness Cal Th	1,855	3-5	1	11	3		5			8	9^{2}	4		10	13	12^{1}	7	14	2				6					
23	H	St. Mirren	2,663	3-0	1		3		5	4^{1}	16	8	9^{1}		15	12	11	7^{1}		10	2				6					
30	A	Arbroath	630	2-1	1				5	7		8^{1}	9	4		10^{1}	11	14	15		2	3			6					
Dec 7	H	Alloa Athletic	2,111	1-1	1		3		5	7		8	9	4		10	11	12	14^{1}	16	2				6					
14	A	St. Johnstone	1,948	2-2	1				5	7^{1}		8^{1}	9	10		14	11	12	4		2	3			6					
28	A	Falkirk	3,858	0-5	1	14			5	4	15			9	11	10	8	7	2	16		3			6					
Jan 1	H	Ayr United	2,921	1-1	1		3		5	14	2	8		7^{1}		10	11	15	4	9					6					
18	A	Alloa Athletic	561	3-3			3		5	9		8		10^{2}			11	7^{1}	4					1	6	2				
Feb 8	H	St. Johnstone	1,862	1-2			3		5	10		8	9	14	16		11^{1}	7	4					1	6	2				
22	A	St. Mirren	1,888	2-2				4	5	10	12	8^{1}		9	15	14	11	7^{1}	3					1	6	2				
25	H	Clyde	1,375	1-1			3	4	5	16		8		9	11^{1}	10		7	2					1	6					
Mar 1	H	Falkirk	2,555	2-1			3	4	5			8		9^{1}	11	10	12	7^{1}	2					1	6					
8	A	Ayr United	1,730	1-0			3	4	5			8	12	9	11	10	7		2					1	6^{1}	16				
11	H	Inverness Cal Th	1,405	0-0			3	4	5			8	12	9	11	10		7	2					1	6					
15	H	St. Mirren	1,911	0-2			3	4	5	12	16	8	9		11	10	7	15	2					1	6					
18	H	Arbroath	1,108	3-0		3			5	10		8	9^{1}		16	14	11	7^{2}						1	6	2	4	15		
22	A	Ross County	1,976	†3-0		3		4	5	12		8	14^{1}	9	11	10		7^{1}	2					1	6					
Apr 5	A	Inverness Cal Th	1,656	0-1		3		4	5	14		8	7	9	11	10	15		2					1	6					
12	A	Arbroath	502	0-0				3	5	10		8	9	12	3	14	11	7	2					1	6			16		
19	H	Alloa Athletic	1,873	0-1				4	5			8	7	9	3	10	11	14	2					1	6			16	15	
26	A	Clyde	960	2-2				4	5			8	7	9^{1}	3	10	11	12						1	6^{1}		2			
May 3	H	Ross County	1,810	1-0					5	4		8	7^{1}	9	3	10	11		14					1	6		2		16	
10	A	St. Johnstone	1,796	1-0				14	5	4			7	9	3	10^{1}	15		2						6			8	11	1
TOTAL FULL APPEARANCES					19	7	23	16	36	17	5	34	17	29	21	27	20	19	22	9	13	5	2	16	29	4	3	1	1	1
TOTAL SUB APPEARANCES						1		1		7	5		5	4	7	6	13	12	4	4		1		1	1	1		3	2	
TOTAL GOALS SCORED										3		4	7	6	1	6	2	9	2	1					3					

Small bold figures denote goalscorers. † denotes opponent's own goal.

palmerston park

PORTLAND DRIVE
EAST STAND
NORTH ENCLOSURE
WEST STAND
TERREGLES STREET

CAPACITY: 6,412; Seated 3,509, Standing 2,903

PITCH DIMENSIONS: 112 yds x 73 yds

FACILITIES FOR DISABLED SUPPORTERS:
Situated in East Stand including toilets.

team playing kits

how to get there

Palmerston Park can be reached by the following routes:

TRAINS: There is a reasonable service to Dumfries Station from Glasgow on Saturdays, but the service is more limited in midweek. The station is about $\frac{3}{4}$ mile from the ground.

BUSES: Buses from Glasgow, Edinburgh, Ayr and Stranraer all pass within a short distance of the park.

CARS: The car park may be reached from Portland Drive or King Street and has a capacity for approximately 174 cars. Please note that the car park is closed 30 minutes prior to kick-off.

RAITH ROVERS
FOOTBALL CLUB

raith rovers

Stark's Park, Pratt Street,
Kirkcaldy, Fife, KY1 1SA

CHAIRMAN
Daniel Smith

DIRECTORS
Eric W. Drysdale, Mario Caira
& William H. Gray

HONORARY PRESIDENT
John Urquhart

COMPANY SECRETARY
Eric W. Drysdale

OFFICE ADMINISTRATOR
Bob Mullen

PLAYER/MANAGER
Antonio Calderon

ASSISTANT MANAGER
Francisco Ortiz Rivas

RESERVE COACH
Shaun Dennis

YOUTH TEAM COACHES
George Gemmell (U17)

COMMERCIAL/LOTTERY MANAGER
Keith Pitkin (M) 07766 331872

CLUB DOCTOR
Dr. Robert Robertson

PHYSIOTHERAPIST
Angel Escontrela

FOOTBALL SAFETY OFFICERS' ASSOCIATION REPRESENTATIVE
Bill Brown (01592) 263514

GROUNDSMAN
John Murray

MATCHDAY PROGRAMME EDITOR
Tom Bell

CLUB PHOTOGRAPHER
Tony Fimister (01592) 201645

HOSPITALITY MANAGER
Tom Smith

WEBSITE NEWS EDITOR
Mike Melville

TELEPHONES
Ground (01592) 263514
Fax (01592) 642833

E-MAIL & INTERNET ADDRESS
raithrovers@starkspark.fsnet.co.uk
www.raithroversfc.com

CLUB SHOP
South Stand Shop situated within stand. Open during Office hours 9.00 a.m. to 5.00 p.m. and on home match days 2.00 p.m. to 5.00 p.m.

OFFICIAL SUPPORTERS CLUB
c/o Fraser Hamilton, 22 Tower Terrace, Kirkcaldy, Fife

TEAM CAPTAIN
Darren Brady

SHIRT SPONSOR
Bar Itza

KIT SUPPLIER
XARA

LIST OF PLAYERS 2003/2004

SURNAME	FIRST NAME	MIDDLE NAME	DATE OF BIRTH	PLACE OF BIRTH	DATE OF SIGNING	HEIGHT FT INS	WEIGHT ST LBS	POS. ON PITCH	PREVIOUS CLUB
Blackadder	Ryan	Robert	11/10/83	Kirkcaldy	10/07/00	5 9.0	11 2	Mid	Raith Rovers Form D Under 16
Boyle	John		22/10/86	Bellshill	24/07/03	5 9.0	10 0	Mid	Raith Rovers Form D Under 16
Brady	Darren		04/11/81	Glasgow	08/07/03	5 11.0	11 0	Mid	Livingston
Brittain	Richard		24/09/83	Bangour	22/07/03	5 9.0	10 7	Fwd	Livingston
Brown	Ian		16/03/84	Kirkcaldy	10/07/00	6 2.0	11 7	Def	Greig Park Rangers
Calderon	Antonio		02/06/67	Cadiz	05/07/02	6 0.0	11 7	Mid	Airdrieonians
Carroll	Richard		15/08/83	Dundee	26/08/03	6 3.0	13 10	Gk	Elmwood Juniors
Dennis	Shaun		22/12/69	Kirkcaldy	23/02/01	6 1.0	14 8	Def	Hibernian
Devlin	William	John	16/01/86	Glasgow	09/07/03	5 11.0	11 7	Def	Raith Rovers Form S
Evans	David	Charles	07/12/81	Dundee	22/08/03	5 8.0	10 4	Fwd	Tayport Juniors
Fox	Mark		31/05/87	Bellshill	26/08/03	5 6.0	10 0	Mid	Raith Rovers Form D Under 16
Gonzalez	Ramiro	Daniel	23/07/80	Junin	24/01/03	6 1.0	12 8	Gk	Real Avila
Haddow	Mark	Lyle	14/01/86	Lanark	09/07/03	6 1.0	11 0	Mid	Raith Rovers Form D Under 16
Hawley	Karl	Leon	06/12/81	Wallsall	29/08/03	5 10.0	11 7	Fwd	Walsall
Henry	James		07/07/75	Dundee	26/08/03	5 10.0	13 0	Mid	Carnoustie Panmure Juniors
Howitt	Kyle		16/06/87	Dundee	26/08/03	5 7.0	10 7	Fwd	Linlithgow B.C.
Ireland	Lee		12/04/87	Bangour	26/08/03	6 0.0	10 9	Def	Whitburn B.C.
Leiper	Colin		05/12/87	Kirkcaldy	26/08/03	6 1.0	11 0	Mid	Raith Rovers Form D Under 16
Main	Ross		05/06/87	Glasgow	26/08/03	5 7.0	10 9	Def	Rangers East
Malcolm	Craig		30/12/86	Bellshill	24/07/03	5 10.0	10 0	Mid/Fwd	Raith Rovers Form D Under 16
Martin	John		04/05/85	Kirkcaldy	09/07/03	5 11.0	11 7	Fwd	East Fife
McCann	Liam		28/02/86	Glasgow	09/07/03	5 11.0	13 2	Mid	Pollok United
McCann	William		11/05/87	Rutherglen	01/09/03	5 6.0	10 2	Mid	Dundee United
McKeown	Frank		18/08/86	Glasgow	16/07/03	6 1.0	12 1	Def	St. Mirren Form D Under 16
O'Hara	Shane		11/11/87	Bangour	26/08/03	5 7.0	10.7	Def	Broxburn Colts
O'Neil	Steven		18/05/87	Bangour	26/08/03	5 11.0	11 0	Mid	Raith Rovers Form D Under 16
Patino	Cristian	Fabian	07/03/80	Sante Fe	20/09/02	6 0.0	12 10	Def	Jorge Newbury
Peers	Mark		14/05/84	Liverpool	22/07/03	5 9.0	11 0	Fwd	Liverpool
Prest	Martin	Hugo	30/11/78	Mar Del Plata	04/07/02	6 1.0	11 7	Fwd	Ross County
Raffell	Bruce	John	19/03/86	Aberdeen	18/07/03	5 10.0	9 7	Mid	Dundee United
Richardson	Gary	Steven	13/05/86	Lanark	18/05/03	5 10.0	10 3	Mid	Heart of Midlothian
Ritchie	Kieran	Owen	14/07/87	Dundee	18/07/03	5 9.0	8 7	Fwd	Dundee
Rivas	Francisco	Ortiz	12/08/69	Granada	04/07/02	5 10.0	12 0	Mid	U.D. Las Palmas
Robb	Steven		08/03/82	Perth	29/08/03	5 6.0	9 4	Mid	Dundee
Semple	Gary		18/02/87	Bellshill	27/08/03	5 10	11 0	Fwd	Hibernian
Stanic	Goran		08/09/72	Skopje	22/08/03	5 9.0	11 0	Def	Rad Belgrade
Stanley	Craig		03/03/83	Nuneaton	29/07/03	6 0.0	11 8	Mid	Wallsall
Sutton	John William Michael		26/12/83	Norwich	22/07/03	6 2.0	13 4	Fwd	Leicester City
Sweeney	Jamie		01/08/85	Edinburgh	09/07/01	5 11.0	10 10	Gk	Raith Rovers Form S
Talio	Vincent		07/03/87	Saint Nazaire	07/08/03	6 1.0	11 0	Def	F.C. Lugon

milestones

YEAR OF FORMATION: 1883
MOST CAPPED PLAYER: David Morris
NO. OF CAPS: 6
MOST LEAGUE POINTS IN A SEASON: 65 (First Division - Season 1992/93) (2 Points for a Win)
69 (First Division - Season 1994/95) (3 Points for a Win)
MOST LEAGUE GOALS SCORED BY A PLAYER IN A SEASON: Norman Heywood (Season 1937/38)
NO. OF GOALS SCORED: 42
RECORD ATTENDANCE: 31,306 (-v- Hearts – Scottish Cup, 7.2.1953)
RECORD VICTORY: 10-1 (-v- Coldstream – Scottish Cup, 13.2.1954)
RECORD DEFEAT: 2-11 (-v- Morton – Division 2, 18.3.1936)

ticket information

SEASON TICKET PRICES
SEATED

MAIN STAND/	ADULT	£200
RAILWAY STAND/	JUVENILE/OAP	£100
SOUTH STAND	PARENT & JUVENILE	£275

LEAGUE ADMISSION PRICES
SEATED

MAIN STAND/ RAILWAY STAND/	ADULT	£12
SOUTH STAND/NORTH STAND	JUVENILE/OAP	£6

leading goalscorers 1993-2003

Season	Div	No. of Goals	Player
1993-94	P	8	G. Dalziel
1994-95	F	15	G. Dalziel
1995-96	P	9	C. Cameron
1996-97	P	5	P. Duffield, D. Lennon
1997-98	F	10	P. Hartley, K. Wright
1998-99	F	8	C. Dargo
1999-00	F	12	C. Dargo
2000-01	F	9	P. Tosh
2001-02	F	19	I. Novo
2002-03	S	7	K. Hawley

the rovers' club factfile 2002/03

Date	Venue	Opponents	Att.	Res	Ojeda R.	Ross D.	Parkin P.	Brady D.	Browne P.	Nanou W.	Carrigan B.	Rivas F.	Smith A.	Hampshire P.	Prest M.	Paliczka S.	Blackadder R.	Moffat A.	Matheson R.	Boylan C.	Brown I.	Dennis S.	Calderon A.	Hawley K.	Ellis L.	Miller S.	McManus P.	Patino C.	Monin S.	Fyfe G.	McKinnon R.	Shields D.	Sweeney J.	El Khebir K.	Gonzalez R.	Valdes Lias D.A.	Davidson A.
Aug 3	H	Stranraer	1,790	1-1	1	2	3	4	5	6	7¹	8	9	10	11	15	14																				
10	A	Berwick Rangers	804	1-1	1	2	3	4	5		14	8	9	10			15	6	7	11¹																	
17	H	Dumbarton	1,866	1-0	1		3	6				8	9	10	16			4	7	11	2	5	14	15¹													
24	A	Cowdenbeath	1,678	1-3	1			4		14		8	9	10	16		15	6		7¹	2	5		11	3												
31	H	Stenhousemuir	1,661	1-0	1			15		4		8	9¹	3	11		14			7		5	6	10	2	16											
Sep 14	H	Airdrie United	1,962	0-0	1			4		6	15	8	9		11		14			16	2	5	10	7	3												
21	A	Hamilton Academical	1,961	4-0	1			4		6¹	7²	8		12			10			11¹	2	5	14	9	3		16										
28	H	Brechin City	2,007	3-1	1			4		6	7	8					10			11¹	2	5	14	9²	3		16										
Oct 5	A	Forfar Athletic	1,054	2-1	1			4¹		6	7	8		14			10¹			11		5		9	3		16	2									
19	H	Berwick Rangers	1,906	1-2	1		3	4		6	7	8	15				10			11			14	9¹	2		16	5									
26	A	Stranraer	608	2-2	1			4		6	7¹	8¹		10	14		11			16			3	9	2			5									
Nov 2	A	Stenhousemuir	1,066	1-0	1			4		6¹		8	15	11	14		7			16		5	10	9	3			2									
9	H	Cowdenbeath	2,428	4-1	1			4		6		8¹	9	11			10²			15		5		7¹	3		16	2									
16	A	Airdrie United	1,717	0-0	1		3	2		6		8	9	7	14		10			15		5		11	4		16										
23	H	Hamilton Academical	1,897	1-1	1		3	4				8	9	10	15		6			7¹		5		11	2		16		19								
30	H	Forfar Athletic	1,779	5-1			3	12		6	14	8¹	9	4			7¹					5¹	10	16	2		11²		1								
Dec 14	A	Brechin City	746	2-1	1			4		6		8	9	14	15		7					5	10		3		11²	2									
28	A	Hamilton Academical	1,300	3-0	1			4		6	16	8	9²	15	14		7					5	10	11¹	3			2									
Jan 1	A	Cowdenbeath	1,875	1-1	1			4		6	16	8	9	14	15		7					5		11¹	3			2		10							
18	H	Airdrie United	2,247	1-0	1			4		6	7	8	9¹	10			14					5	3	11			16	2		15							
Feb 1	A	Hamilton Academical	1,292	0-0	1		12	4		6	15	8	9				7					5			3		11	2			10	16					
8	H	Brechin City	1,776	1-2	1			4				8	9		15		7					5	3				16	2		10	6¹	11					
22	A	Berwick Rangers	820	1-1	1					6	12	8	9				7					5	14		3			2		10	4	11¹					
Mar 1	H	Dumbarton	1,790	2-1	1			4		7	15	8			9¹							5¹	14		3		16	2		10	6	11					
4	H	Stranraer	1,448	3-0	1			4		7¹	15	8		12	9¹							5			3		16	2		10¹	6	11					
8	H	Cowdenbeath	1,900	2-1	1			4		7	15	8		6	11							5			3		9¹	2¹		10	14	16					
11	A	Forfar Athletic	688	2-4				4		7	15	8		6	11²							5			3		9	2		10	14	16	1				
15	A	Stenhousemuir	929	3-1	1			6		14	9	8¹			11		7					5	3					4			10	16¹		2			
22	H	Hamilton Academical	1,762	1-1	1			6			7	8			9		11					5	3					4¹		15	10	16		2			
26	H	Stenhousemuir	1,627	0-1	1			6		2	7	8			9		14					5			3		16	4		15	10	11					
Apr 5	A	Airdrie United	1,788	1-1				4		14	15	8	9¹	6	11		7				5		10		3			2							1		
12	H	Forfar Athletic	2,036	0-1			3	6		14		8	9		11		7						10		5			2		15	4	16			1		
19	A	Brechin City	1,819	0-1				4		14		8	9	3	11		15					5	10					2			6	16			1	7	
26	A	Stranraer	617	0-1				4		7		8	9	6	15				14			5	10		3		16	2				11			1		
May 3	H	Berwick Rangers	2,746	1-0				4		6		8	9¹	14	11							5	10		3		7	2				16			1		
10	A	Dumbarton	1,501	1-4		4	3						9			16	10¹	6	8						5		7			11		15			1	2	12
TOTAL FULL APPEARANCES					28	3	9	32	2	25	10	35	23	17	14		21	4	3	9	6	29	16	15	28		7	24	1	8	10	6	1	2	6	2	
TOTAL SUB APPEARANCES							1	2		5	12		2	7	11	2	8		1	5			6	2		1	13		1	4	2	9					1
TOTAL GOALS SCORED								1		3	4	4	6		4		5			5		2		7			5	2		1	2	2					

Small bold figures denote goalscorers. † denotes opponent's own goal.

stark's park

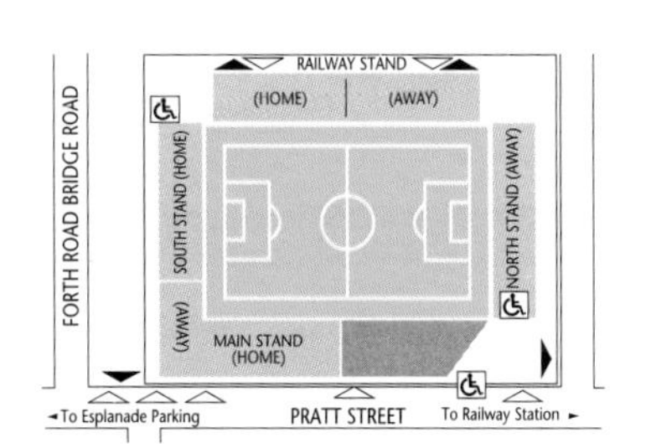

CAPACITY: 10,104 (All Seated)

PITCH DIMENSIONS: 113 yds x 70 yds

FACILITIES FOR DISABLED SUPPORTERS:
By prior arrangement with the Office Administrator.
North Stand – Away Supporters. South Stand – Home Supporters.
Limited disabled parking immediately adjacent to North Stand.

team playing kits

how to get there

The following routes may be used to reach Stark's Park:

TRAINS: Kirkcaldy railway station is served by trains from Dundee, Edinburgh and Glasgow (via Edinburgh) and the ground is within 10-15 minutes walking distance of the station.

BUSES: The main bus station in Kirkcaldy is also within 15 minutes walking distance of the ground, but the Edinburgh, Dunfermline and Leven services pass close by the park.

CARS: Car parking is available in the Esplanade, which is on the south side of the ground and in Beveridge Park, which is on the north side of the ground.

ross county

Victoria Park Stadium, Jubilee Road, Dingwall, Ross-shire, IV15 9QZ

CHAIRMAN
Roy J. MacGregor

VICE-CHAIRMAN
Gordon M. R. MacRae

DIRECTORS
Thomas A. Mackenzie, Andrew R. Duncan & Alexander Matheson

MANAGEMENT COMMITTEE
Donald MacBean, David R. Patience & Calum Grant

CHIEF EXECUTIVE
Alastair Kennedy

SECRETARY
Donald MacBean

OFFICE ADMINISTRATOR
Marie Ewan

MANAGER
Alexander N. Smith

FIRST TEAM COACHES
Jimmy Bone & Brian Irvine

FIRST TEAM ASSISTANT COACH
Ronnie Duncan

GOALKEEPING COACH
Les Fridge

DIRECTOR OF YOUTH DEVELOPMENT
Calum Grant

YOUTH CO-ORDINATOR
Michael Fridge

SFA FOOTBALL DEVELOPMENT OFFICER COMMUNITY COACH
Neil Mackintosh

YOUTH COACHES
Ronnie Duncan & Michael Fridge (U19)
Peter Budge & Rob Watson (U16),
Martin Rae & Alan Gair (U15)
Rod Houston & Muir Morton (U14)

CLUB DOCTOR
Dr. Colin Fettes

PHYSIOTHERAPIST
Dougie Sim

FOOTBALL SAFETY OFFICERS' ASSOCIATION REPRESENTATIVE
David R. Patience (01463) 222893

STADIUM MANAGER
David Fraser

COMMERCIAL MANAGER
Morven Reid

MEDIA LIAISON OFFICER
Alastair Kennedy (01349) 860860

MATCHDAY PROGRAMME EDITOR
Bryan Munro (01463) 230721
E-MAIL: bryan.munro@lineone.net

TELEPHONES
Ground/Ticket Office (01349) 860860
Fax (01349) 866277
Youth Department (01349) 860862

E-MAIL & INTERNET ADDRESS
donnie@rosscountyfootballclub.co.uk
www.rosscountyfootballclub.co.uk

CLUB SHOP
Official Ross County F.C. merchandising available from MacLean Sport, 33 High Street, Dingwall, as well as a shop being situated at Ground (Matchdays only) and other Sports shops in local area

OFFICIAL SUPPORTERS CLUB
George Shiels, 4 Tulloch Place, Dingwall (01349) 865135

TEAM CAPTAIN
David Hannah

SHIRT SPONSOR
Aberdeen Asset Management

KIT SUPPLIER
XARA

LIST OF PLAYERS 2003-2004

SURNAME	FIRST NAME	MIDDLE NAME	DATE OF BIRTH	PLACE OF BIRTH	DATE OF SIGNING	HEIGHT FT INS	WEIGHT ST LBS	POS. ON PITCH	PREVIOUS CLUB
Bayne	Graham		22/08/79	Kirkcaldy	29/07/02	6 1.0	12 9	Fwd	Arbroath
Buzzeo	Stephen		07/06/86	Newcastle	30/08/03	5 11.0	11 2	Mid	Montague North Fenham
Canning	Martin		03/12/81	Glasgow	28/07/99	6 2.5	12 10	Def	Clydebank
Cowie	Don		15/02/83	Inverness	23/08/00	5 5.0	8 5	Mid	Ross County Form S
Dodds	Kerr		05/05/85	Edinburgh	29/07/02	5 9.0	10 8	Def	Heart of Midlothian
Dunnett	Michael	Thomson	13/03/86	Inverness	27/05/03	5 10.0	10 6	Mid	Ross County Form D U 16
Farrimond	Karl	David	19/01/85	Rochdale	29/07/02	5 7.0	9 6	Fwd	Deveronvale
Fridge	Leslie	Francis	27/08/68	Inverness	26/03/02	5 11.0	13 0	Gk	Inverness Caledonian Thistle
Gardiner	Mark	John	10/03/85	Irvine	29/01/03	5 8.0	10 8	Mid	Carlisle United
Gethins	Conor		01/11/83	Lifford	04/09/00	5 7.0	9 0	Fwd	Lifford Celtic
Gilbert	Kenneth	Robert	08/03/75	Aberdeen	29/07/02	5 7.0	11 7	Mid	Hull City
Gray	Christopher	Michael	27/06/85	Edinburgh	29/07/02	6 0.0	11 0	Def	Heart of Midlothian
Hamilton	James		09/02/76	Aberdeen	01/08/03	6 0.0	12 12	Fwd	Dunfermline Athletic
Hannah	David		04/08/73	Coatbridge	28/03/03	5 11.5	11 10	Mid	AEL Limasol
Higgins	Sean		29/10/84	Glasgow	07/08/02	5 8.5	10 1	Fwd	St. Johnstone
Irvine	Brian	Alexander	24/05/65	Bellshill	27/07/99	6 2.5	14 2	Def	Dundee
Kane	Callum	William	02/03/85	Edinburgh	29/07/02	5 10.0	10 0	Mid	Leith Athletic
Kerr	Shaun	Steven	23/04/86	Birkenhead	27/05/03	5 11.0	11 5	Fwd	Ross County Form D U 16
Lawrie	Blair	John	02/07/86	Inverness	27/05/03	5 6.0	8 7	Mid	Ross County Form D U 16
Logan	Scott		13/03/85	Broxburn	29/07/02	5 9.0	9 11	Mid	Heart of Midlothian
MacAskill	John	Roderick	22/03/85	Dingwall	29/07/02	5 10.0	12 0	Mid	Ross County Form D U 16
MacDonald	Neil	MacLeod	15/06/87	Dunfermline	22/08/03	5 10.0	11 7	Def	Dunfermline Athletic
Mackay	Steven		26/06/81	Invergordon	29/07/02	5 11.0	12 3	Def/Mid	Nairn County
Malcolm	Stuart	Ross	20/08/79	Edinburgh	26/07/03	6 3.0	13 0	Def	Plymouth Argyle
McCulloch	Mark	Ross	19/05/75	Inverness	29/07/02	5 11.0	13 7	Mid	Partick Thistle
McCunnie	Jamie		15/04/83	Bellshill	18/07/03	5 10.0	11 0	Def	Dundee United
McConald	John	William	24/09/85	Irvine	30/08/03	6 1.0	11 7	Fwd	Rangers
McGarry	Steven	Thomas	28/09/79	Paisley	29/07/02	5 9.0	10 0	Fwd	St. Mirren
Miller	Kevin		05/04/85	Edinburgh	13/08/02	6 0.0	11 2	Gk	Heart of Midlothian
Moffat	Adam		15/05/86	Glasgow	30/08/03	5 11.0	11 9	Def	Rangers
O'Donnell	Stephen		10/07/83	Bellshill	30/07/03	5 11.5	11 2	Mid	Dundee United
Rankin	John		27/06/83	Bellshill	10/07/03	5 8.0	10 8	Mid	Manchester United
Robertson	Hugh	Scott	19/03/75	Aberdeen	02/02/01	5 9.0	14 0	Def	Dundee
Stewart	Colin		10/01/80	Middlesbrough	18/07/03	6 3.0	12 12	Gk	Kilmarnock
Tait	Jordan	Alexander	27/09/79	Berwick Upon Tweed	30/01/03	5 10.0	12 0	Def	Arbroath
Townsley	Christopher	James	04/03/85	Edinburgh	29/07/02	6 1.0	11 8	Def	Heart of Midlothian
Webb	Sean	Michael	04/01/83	Dungannon	26/09/00	6 2.0	12 5	Def	Dungannon Swifts
Wilson	David	Gavin	28/02/84	Bellshill	31/05/01	6 1.0	11 7	Fwd	Heart of Midlothian
Winters	David		07/03/82	Paisley	09/07/03	5 11.0	11 10	Fwd	Dundee United
Young	Bryan		02/09/86	Paisley	21/08/03	5 7.0	10 0	Mid	Kilmarnock

milestones

YEAR OF FORMATION: 1929
MOST LEAGUE POINTS IN A SEASON: 77 (Third Division – Season 1998/99) (3 Points for a Win)
MOST LEAGUE GOALS SCORED BY A PLAYER IN A SEASON: Derek Adams (Season 1996/97)
NO. OF GOALS SCORED: 22
RECORD ATTENDANCE: 8,000 (-v- Rangers – Scottish Cup, 28.2.66)
RECORD VICTORY: 13-2 (-v- Fraserburgh – Highland League, 1965)
RECORD DEFEAT: 1-10 (-v- Inverness Thistle – Highland League)

ticket information

SEASON TICKET PRICES

SEATED	
ADULT	£180
JUVENILE (U-18)/OAP	£100
JUVENILE (U-12)	£90
FAMILY SECTION	
ADULT/OAP	£160/£90
JUVENILE (U-18)	£50
JUVENILE (U-12)	£30
STANDING	
ADULT/OAP	£150/£75
JUVENILE (U-18)	£40
JUVENILE (U-12)	£25

LEAGUE ADMISSION PRICES

SEATED	
ADULT	£13
JUVENILE/OAP	£7
STANDING	
ADULT	£11
JUVENILE/OAP	£6

leading goalscorers 1993-2003

Season 1994-95 was the Club's first season in membership of SFL

Season	Div	No. of Goals	Player
1994-95	T	12	B. Grant
1995-96	T	15	C. Milne
1996-97	T	22	D. Adams
1997-98	T	16	D. Adams
1998-99	T	17	S. Ferguson/N. Tarrant
1999-00	S	13	G. Shaw
2000-01	F	14	A. Bone
2001-02	F	14	S. Hislop
2002-03	F	6	G. Bayne, S. Ferguson

the county's club factfile 2002/03

Date	Venue	Opponents	Att.	Res	Bullock A.	McCulloch M.	Deas P.	Perry M.	Irvine B.	Gilbert K.	McCarry S.	Ferguson S.	Bone A.	Cowie D.	Mackay S.	Bayne G.	Wood M.	Webb S.	Gethins C.	Canning M.	Robertson H.	Campbell C.	Hislop S.	Higgins S.	Davidson G.	Lynch P.	McLeish K.	Winters D.	Venetis A.	Tait J.	Hannah D.	Bolochoweckyj M.
Aug 3	A	Arbroath	761	3-0	1	2	3	4	5	6	7	8[1]	9[1]	10[1]	11	13	16															
10	H	Queen of the South	2,894	2-0	1	2	14	4	5	6	7	8[1]	15	10	11		16[1]	3	9													
17	A	Ayr United	1,692	1-2	1	2	3	4	5	6	7	8	15	10	13		9		16[1]	11												
24	A	Inverness Cal Th	3,699	0-2	1	2		4		6	16	8		14	7	9	13	3	10	5	11											
31	H	Clyde	2,059	1-1	1	6		4	5		7		9	10	3	13	8		15	2[1]	11											
Sep 14	H	Falkirk	2,729	1-1	1	8		4	5	6[1]	11		9			7	10		16	2	3											
21	A	St. Johnstone	2,434	1-1	1	8		4	5	6	11	14	9		13	7[1]	10		16	2	3											
28	H	Alloa Athletic	1,921	0-1	1	8		4	5	6	14		9	10		7	11		15	2	3	16										
Oct 5	A	St. Mirren	3,737	1-1	1	8	13	4	5[1]	6	7			10	3				16	2	11		9									
19	H	Arbroath	2,065	4-0	1	8	15	4	5	6	9				3[1]	7			13	2	11[1]		10[2]	14								
26	A	Queen of the South	1,533	0-2	1	8	4		5	6	7			11	13					2	3		10	9	15	16						
Nov 2	A	Clyde	1,047	1-2	1	6	5	4			15	8		11		7	9			2[1]	3		10		13							
9	H	Inverness Cal Th	5,449	0-2	1	6	5	4			15	8		10	11		7			2	3		9									
16	A	Falkirk	3,255	0-2	1	6	3	4	5		7	8	14	10	11	13				2	15		9									
23	H	St. Johnstone	2,614	0-0	1	6		4	5		7	8	9	10	3	13				2	11		15									
30	A	Alloa Athletic	445	1-1	1	6		4	5[1]		7	8		10	3	9				2	11		15									
Dec 7	H	St. Mirren	2,429	4-0	1	8	3	6	5	4	7		10	14	15[1]	9[3]				2	11		16									
14	A	Ayr United	2,352	1-0	1	8	3		5	4	7		10[1]	14		9		6		2	11		16									
21	A	Arbroath	580	1-2	1	8	3	6	5	4	7	14	10	16	15	9				2	11		15[1]									
28	H	Clyde	2,534	1-1	1		3	8	5	4	15			7	11[1]	9		6		2			10									
Jan 11	A	St. Johnstone	2,400	0-2	1		3	8	5	4				15	11	9		6		2	12		10				7	13				
18	A	St. Mirren	2,366	0-1	1	8		14	5	4				15		9		6		2	3		10				11	13	7			
Feb 1	H	Alloa Athletic	2,096	1-2	1	8			5[1]	4	9			16	15					6	3			13			7	11	10	2		
8	A	Ayr United	1,486	1-1	1	4			5	2	7			10	15	9		6			3[1]						11	16	14	8		
25	A	Inverness Cal Th	3,443	5-1	1	4			5		14	8[1]		10	13	9		6	15[1]		3[1]						11[1]		7[1]	2		
Mar 1	A	Clyde	980	0-1	1	4			5	16		8		10	13	9		6	15		3						11		7	2		
8	H	Inverness Cal Th	4,621	0-2	1	4			5	2	7			10		9		6	15	14	3			16			11			8		
11	H	Falkirk	2,161	0-1	1	4			5	8				14	10	9		6	15	13	3						11	7		2		
15	H	St. Johnstone	2,689	2-3	1	4			5	7	14	8[1]		10	15	13[1]		6	9	2	3								11			
22	H	Queen of the South	1,976	0-3	1	4			5	7	10	8		14	11	9				6	3							16	15	2		
Apr 5	A	Falkirk	3,523	0-3	1	6			5			14		8		9		4			3	13					11	15	7	2	10	
14	A	Alloa Athletic	876	1-2	1	4			5		7	8[1]		10		9	16	2	14		3							15	11		6	
19	H	St. Mirren	1,967	2-0	1	4			5		15[1]	8[1]			3	16			10		11	2		9			14	7			6	
26	H	Arbroath	2,204	3-1	1	4						8			3	16[1]		5	10		11[1]	2		9			14	7[1]			6	13
May 3	A	Queen of the South	1,810	0-1	1	4			5			8			3	16		14			11	2		9			10	7		13	6	
10	H	Ayr United	3,449	4-1	1	4					10[2]	8		15	3[1]	16		5			11	13		9[1]				7		2	6	
TOTAL FULL APPEARANCES					**36**	**34**	**11**	**19**	**31**	**22**	**21**	**18**	**9**	**20**	**18**	**21**	**7**	**16**	**5**	**23**	**30**	**3**	**9**	**5**			**10**	**6**	**7**	**9**	**6**	
TOTAL SUB APPEARANCES							**3**	**1**		**1**	**8**	**3**	**3**	**10**	**10**	**9**	**4**	**1**	**12**	**2**	**2**	**3**	**5**	**3**	**2**	**1**	**2**	**6**	**2**	**1**		**1**
TOTAL GOALS SCORED									**3**	**1**	**3**	**6**	**2**	**1**	**4**	**6**	**1**		**2**	**2**	**4**		**3**	**1**			**1**	**1**	**1**			

Small bold figures denote goalscorers. † denotes opponent's own goal.

victoria park stadium

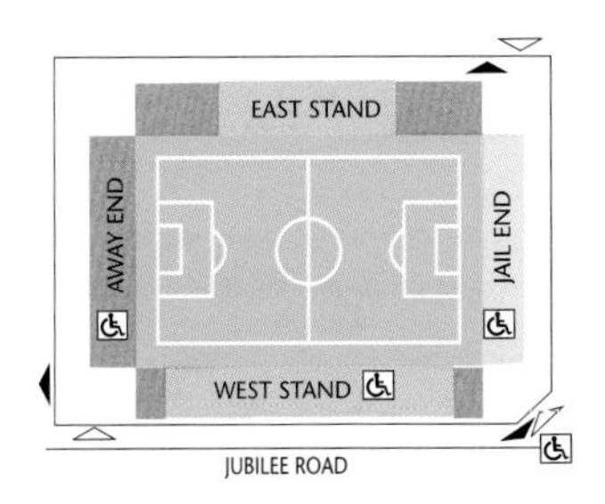

CAPACITY: 6,900, Seated 3,000, Standing 3,900

PITCH DIMENSIONS: 110 yds x 75 yds

FACILITIES FOR DISABLED SUPPORTERS:
Areas in Main Stand and Terracing. Toilet facilities are also available.

team playing kits

how to get there

The following routes may be used to reach Victoria Park Stadium:

TRAINS: The nearest mainline station is Inverness and fans travelling from the south should alight and board a train that takes them direct to Dingwall Station.

BUSES: Regular buses on a daily basis from Glasgow, Edinburgh and Perth.

CARS: The major trunk roads, A9 and A96, connect Dingwall with the North, the South and the East.

st. johnstone

McDiarmid Park, Crieff Road, Perth, PH1 2SJ

CHAIRMAN
Geoffrey S. Brown

VICE CHAIRMAN
Ian Dewar

DIRECTORS
Douglas B. McIntyre, Robert Reid, James Donnachie, Dr. Alistair McCracken & A. Stewart M. Duff

MANAGING DIRECTOR/ SECRETARY
A. Stewart M. Duff

MANAGER
William Stark

PLAYER/FIRST TEAM COACH
Mika-Matti Paatelainen

RESERVE COACH
Jim Weir

YOUTH FOOTBALL CO-ORDINATOR
Tommy Campbell

COMMUNITY COACH
Atholl Henderson

CLUB DOCTOR
Dr. Alistair McCracken

PHYSIOTHERAPIST
Nick Summersgill

STADIUM MANAGER
Jimmy Hogg

FOOTBALL SAFETY OFFICERS' ASSOCIATION REPRESENTATIVES
A. Stewart M. Duff & George Smith (01738) 459090

SALES & MARKETING EXECUTIVES
Susan Weir (Sales)
Paul Fraser (Marketing)

MEDIA LIAISON OFFICER
A. Stewart M. Duff

MATCHDAY PROGRAMME EDITORS
Alastair Blair & Helen Green

TELEPHONES
Ground (01738) 459090
Ticket Office (01738) 455000
Fax (01738) 625771
Clubcall (09068) 121559

E-MAIL & INTERNET ADDRESS
anyone@saints.sol.co.uk
www.stjohnstonefc.co.uk

CLUB SHOP
Open Mon-Fri at Main Reception at Ground. A shop is also open on matchdays and is situated at Ormond (South) Stand

OFFICIAL SUPPORTERS CLUB
157 Dunkeld Road, Perth
Tel: (01738) 442022

TEAM CAPTAIN
Jim Weir

SHIRT SPONSOR
Scottish Citylink

KIT SUPPLIER
XARA

LIST OF PLAYERS 2003/2004

SURNAME	FIRST NAME	MIDDLE NAME	DATE OF BIRTH	PLACE OF BIRTH	DATE OF SIGNING	HEIGHT FT INS	WEIGHT ST LBS	POS. ON PITCH	PREVIOUS CLUB
Band	Kenneth	John	22/10/86	Perth	11/08/03	5 10.0	10 3	Gk	St. Johnstone Form S
Baxter	Mark		16/04/85	Perth	04/07/01	5 7.0	9 4	Def	St. Johnstone Form S
Bernard	Paul Robert	James	30/12/72	Edinburgh	22/07/03	6 0.0	13 0	Mid	Plymouth Argyle
Connolly	Patrick	Martin	25/06/70	Glasgow	14/03/98	5 9.5	11 0	Fwd	Airdrieonians
Cuthbert	Kevin	Scott	08/09/82	Perth	21/09/98	5 11.0	10 6	Gk	St. Johnstone B.C.
Dods	Darren		07/06/75	Edinburgh	02/07/98	6 1.0	13 2	Def	Hibernian
Donnelly	Simon	Thomas	01/12/74	Glasgow	01/08/03	5 9.0	11 6	Mid/Fwd	Sheffield Wednesday
Ferry	Mark		19/01/84	Glasgow	04/07/00	5 11.0	11 13	Mid	St. Johnstone Form S
Forsyth	Ross David	James	20/11/82	Glasgow	09/07/99	5 10.0	11 7	Def	St. Johnstone Form S
Fotheringham	Martyn	Fraser	23/03/83	Perth	09/07/99	5 10.0	11 6	Mid	Forfar B.C.
Fraser	Stephen		01/03/85	Glasgow	02/07/03	5 11.0	10 0	Def	St. Johnstone Form D U 16
Gibson	Neil		14/05/86	Dunfermline	02/07/02	5 10.0	12 0	Def	St. Johnstone Form D U 16
Hay	Christopher	Drummond	28/08/74	Glasgow	29/08/02	5 11.0	12 6	Fwd	Huddersfield Town
Johnston	Craig		29/06/85	Perth	02/07/02	6 0.0	11 0	Mid	St. Johnstone Form D U 16
Lovering	Paul	James	25/11/75	Glasgow	04/06/03	5 10.0	12 0	Def	Ayr United
MacDonald	Peter	Ian Ronald	17/11/80	Glasgow	03/08/01	5 9.5	11 2	Fwd	Rangers
Malone	Edward	Joseph	06/04/85	Edinburgh	08/07/02	5 11.0	11 0	Def	St. Johnstone Form D U 16
Maxwell	Ian		02/05/75	Glasgow	16/05/02	6 3.0	12 5	Def	Ross County
McLaughlin	Brian		14/05/74	Bellshill	22/05/03	5 4.0	9 7	Mid	Queen of the South
McManus	Steven		24/04/87	Perth	02/07/03	5 8.0	10 7	Mid/Fwd	St. Johnstone Form S
Nelson	Craig	Robert	28/05/71	Coatbridge	04/06/03	6 1.0	13 4	Gk	Ayr United
Paatelainen	Mika-Matti	Petteri	03/02/67	Helsinki	02/07/03	6 0.0	14 0	Fwd	Hibernian
Parker	Keigan		08/06/82	Livingston	06/07/98	5 7.0	10 5	Fwd	St. Johnstone B.C.
Reilly	Mark	Francis	30/03/69	Bellshill	07/06/02	5 8.0	11 8	Mid	Kilmarnock
Robertson	John	Alexander	28/03/76	Irvine	03/06/02	6 0.0	12 4	Def	Ayr United
Robertson	Mark		06/04/77	Sydney	29/08/03	5 9.0	12 2	Mid	Dundee
Stevenson	Ryan	Cairns	24/08/84	Irvine	28/03/02	5 11.0	13 7	Mid	Chelsea
Weir	James	McIntosh	15/06/69	Motherwell	18/11/94	6 1.0	12 5	Def	Heart of Midlothian

milestones

YEAR OF FORMATION: 1884
MOST CAPPED PLAYER: Nick Dasovic (Canada)
NO. OF CAPS: 26
MOST LEAGUE POINTS IN A SEASON: 59 (Second Division – Season 1987/88) (2 Points for a Win)
80 (First Division – Season 1996/97) (3 Points for a Win)
MOST LEAGUE GOALS SCORED BY A PLAYER IN A SEASON: Jimmy Benson (Season 1931/32)
NO. OF GOALS SCORED: 38
RECORD ATTENDANCE: 29,972 (-v- Dundee 10.2.1951 at Muirton Park)
10,545 (-v- Dundee – SPL, 23.05.1999 at McDiarmid Park)
RECORD VICTORY: 8-1 (-v- Partick Thistle – League Cup, 16.8.1969)
RECORD DEFEAT: 1-10 (-v- Third Lanark – Scottish Cup, 24.1.1903)

ticket information

SEASON TICKET PRICES

WEST STAND	
Executive	£295
Adult	£250
OAP/Juvenile	£175
EAST STAND	
Adult	£230
OAP/Juvenile	£80/£40
Parent & Juvenile	£200

LEAGUE ADMISSION PRICES

WEST STAND	
Adult	£17
OAP/Juvenile	£10
EAST STAND	
Adult	£15
OAP	£5
Juvenile	£4

leading goalscorers 1993-2003

Season	Div	No. of Goals	Player
1993-94	P	7	P. Wright
1994-95	F	19	G. O'Boyle
1995-96	F	21	G. O'Boyle
1996-97	F	19	R. Grant
1997-98	P	10	G. O'Boyle
1998-99	P	4	G. Bollan, R. Grant, M. Simao
1999-00	P	10	N. Lowndes
2000-01	P	9	K. Parker
2001-02	P	5	P. Hartley
2002-03	F	9	C. Hay

the saints' club factfile 2002/03

Date	Venue	Opponents	Att.	Res	Cuthbert K.	Robertson J.	McCulloch M.	McCluskey S.	Murray G.	Maxwell I.	McCann R.	Reilly M.	Hartley P.	Connolly P.	Parker K.	Dods D.	Russell C.	Stevenson R.	MacDonald P.	Lovenkrands T.	Hay C.	Main A.	Ferry M.	McClune D.	Weir J.	Baxter M.	Panther E.	Forsyth R.	Robertson M.	Noble S.	Malone E.	Maher M.
Aug 3	A	St. Mirren	3,376	2-0	1	2	3	4	5	6	7	8	9^{1}	10	11^{1}	12	16	17														
10	H	Inverness Cal Th	3,770	†1-0	1	2	3	4	5	6	7	8	9	10	11		14	17	16													
17	A	Queen of the South	3,137	0-0	1	2		4	5	6	7	8	9	10	11		16	17	14	3												
24	A	Arbroath	1,467	1-0	1	2		4	5	6	7	8	9^{1}	10	11		16	17	14	3												
31	H	Alloa Athletic	2,274	2-0	1	2		4	5	6	7^{1}	8	9	10^{1}	16		14	17	11	3												
Sep 14	A	Ayr United	2,320	0-0	1	2	14	4	5	6	7	8	9	10	16		11	17		3												
21	H	Ross County	2,434	1-1	1	2	3	4	5	6	7^{1}	8	9	10	14		11	17			16											
28	A	Falkirk	5,872	0-1	1	2	3	4	5	6	7	8	9	10	16		14	17			11											
Oct 5	H	Clyde	2,037	0-1		2	3	4	5	6	7	8	9	10	14			17			11	1	16									
19	H	St. Mirren	2,457	2-0		2	3	4	5	6		8	9^{1}	14	11			7			10^{1}	1	17									
26	A	Inverness Cal Th	2,541	1-2		2	3	4	7	6	16	8	9	12	11	5		10			14^{1}	1										
Nov 2	A	Alloa Athletic	952	3-1		2			3	6	4	8	9	10^{1}	11	5		16			7^{2}	1	14									
9	H	Arbroath	1,994	2-0		2			3	6	4	8	9^{1}	10	14	5				16	7^{1}	1	11	17								
16	H	Ayr United	1,943	0-2				5	3	6	4	8	9		11			16		14	7	1	10	2								
23	A	Ross County	2,614	0-0					3	6		8		14	9	4				11	7	1	10	2	5							
30	H	Falkirk	3,696	0-1					3		4	8		14	9	6		17		11	7	1			5	2	10	16				
Dec 7	A	Clyde	1,367	2-1					5	6	12	8	9	14		4				11^{1}	7^{1}	1				2	10	3				
14	H	Queen of the South	1,948	2-2		2			4	6	12^{1}	8^{1}	9	14	16	5				11	7	1					10	3				
28	H	Alloa Athletic	2,090	†3-0		2	4		5	6	16	8	9	14	10					11^{1}	7	1				17		3^{1}				
Jan 1	A	Arbroath	1,252	3-2		2	4		5	6^{1}		8	9	14^{1}	10					11^{1}	7	1						3				
11	H	Ross County	2,400	2-0		2	4		5	6		8	9	7	10	12				11	14^{1}	1				17		3^{1}				
18	H	Clyde	2,455	1-2		2	4		5	6		8	9	7^{1}	10					11	14	1				17	16	3				
Feb 1	A	Falkirk	4,694	1-1	1	2			3	6		8	9^{1}	10	16	5				11						7			4	17		
8	A	Queen of the South	1,862	2-1	1	3	14		5	6		8	9	10	16					11	7					2			4^{1}	17^{1}		
15	H	Inverness Cal Th	2,631	2-0	1	3			8	6			9	10	14	5				11	12^{2}					2			4	7		
Mar 1	A	Alloa Athletic	884	2-1	1		3		4	6			9	10^{1}		5^{1}			16	11				7		2			8			
4	A	Ayr United	1,690	1-0	1		3		4	6			9	10	11	5^{1}			7					12		2			8	17		
8	H	Arbroath	1,938	2-1	1		3		4^{1}	6			9	10	16	5			7^{1}		14					2		17	8	11		
15	A	Ross County	2,689	3-2	1				3	6		8	9^{1}	10		5			7		14			12		2			4	11^{2}		
22	A	St. Mirren	2,369	3-1	1		16		3	6^{1}		8	9	10		5^{1}			7^{1}	17	14					2			4	11		
Apr 5	H	Ayr United	2,123	1-0	1				3	6		8	9	10	16	5			7^{1}		14					2			4	11		
12	H	Falkirk	6,579	0-1	1	11	16		3	6		8	9	10		5			7		14					2			4	12		
19	A	Clyde	1,143	1-2	1	3			4	6		8	9	10	17	5			7^{1}		14					2		16		11		
26	H	St. Mirren	1,819	1-1	1	2		4		6		8		10	16	5			9				11			7		3		12^{1}	17	
May 3	A	Inverness Cal Th	1,814	2-1	1	2		4		6^{1}		8^{1}	9	10	7	5												12		11	3	16
10	H	Queen of the South	1,796	0-1	1	6		4				8	9	10	7	5							16			2		14		11	3	17
TOTAL FULL APPEARANCES					22	26	14	15	33	34	13	32	33	27	17	20	2	2	9	16	13	14	4	3	2	15	3	7	10	8	2	
TOTAL SUB APPEARANCES							4				4			8	14	2	6	12	4	3	11		4	3		3	1	5		5	1	2
TOTAL GOALS SCORED									1	3	3	2	6	5	1	3			4	3	9							2	1	4		

Small bold figures denote goalscorers. † denotes opponent's own goal.

mcdiarmid park

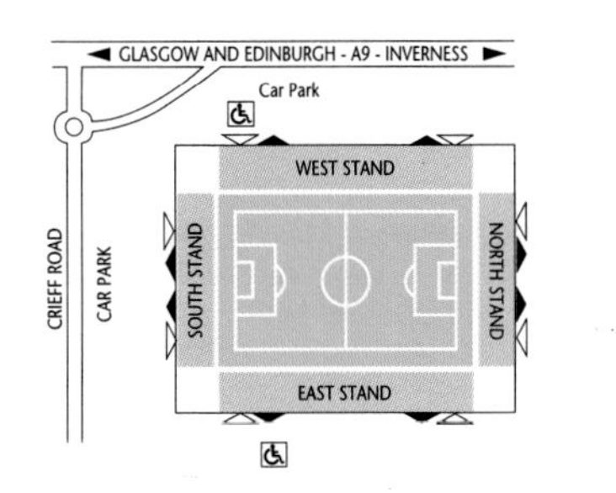

CAPACITY: 10,723 (All Seated)

PITCH DIMENSIONS: 115 yds x 74 yds

FACILITIES FOR DISABLED SUPPORTERS:
Entrance via south end of West Stand and south end of East Stand. Visiting disabled fans should contact the club in advance. Headphones available in West and North Stands for blind and partially sighted supporters.

team playing kits

how to get there

The following routes can be used to reach McDiarmid Park:
TRAINS: Perth Station is well served by trains from all parts of the country. The station is about 40 minutes walk from the park.
BUSES: Local services nos. 1 and 2 pass near the ground. Both leave from Mill Street in the town centre.
CARS: The car park at the park holds 1,500 cars and 100 coaches. Vehicles should follow signs A9 to Inverness on Perth City by-pass, then follow "Football Stadium" signs at Inveralmond Roundabout South onto slip road adjacent to McDiarmid Park. Vehicle charges are £2.00 for cars and no charge for coaches.

st. mirren

LIST OF PLAYERS 2003/2004

SURNAME	FIRST NAME	MIDDLE NAME	DATE OF BIRTH	PLACE OF BIRTH	DATE OF SIGNING	HEIGHT FT INS	WEIGHT ST LBS	POS. ON PITCH	PREVIOUS CLUB
Annand	Edward		24/03/73	Glasgow	21/07/03	5 11.0	12 0	Fwd	Ayr United
Broadfoot	Kirk		08/08/84	Irvine	01/07/02	6 2.0	14 1	Def	Hibernian
Crilly	Mark	Patrick	23/05/80	Glasgow	28/05/03	5 11.0	11 7	Mid	Stirling Albion
Cuddihy	John		06/11/85	Glasgow	01/08/03	5 10.0	11 3	Def	Pollok United B.C.
Dempsie	Mark	William	19/10/80	Bellshill	22/01/03	6 0.0	12 10	Def	Hibernian
Dunn	Robert		28/06/79	Glasgow	13/06/03	5 10.0	10 10	Fwd	Stirling Albion
Ellis	Laurence		07/11/79	Edinburgh	02/06/03	5 11.0	10 7	Def	Raith Rovers
Ferguson	Jeffrey	Stuart	24/01/86	Glasgow	31/08/02	5 7.0	9 7	Fwd	St. Mirren Form D U 16
Gemmill	Scott		09/06/87	Rutherglen	17/07/03	5 10.0	10 0	Fwd	St. Mirren Form D U 16
Gillespie	Gary		10/04/87	Paisley	17/07/03	5 10.0	11 4	Mid	St. Mirren Form D U 16
Gillies	Richard	Charles	24/08/76	Glasgow	23/06/00	5 10.0	12 2	Fwd	Aberdeen
Gordon	Brian Andrew Peter		29/01/86	Glasgow	31/08/02	6 1.0	11 8	Def	St. Mirren B.C.
Hinchcliffe	Craig	Peter	05/05/72	Glasgow	26/06/03	5 11.0	12 6	Gk	Arbroath
Jack	David		30/01/84	Glasgow	31/08/02	5 7.0	10 5	Mid	Albion Rovers B.C.
Lappin	Simon		25/01/83	Glasgow	07/10/99	5 11.0	10 0	Mid	St. Mirren B.C.
Lavety	Barry		21/08/74	Paisley	29/07/03	6 0.0	14 10	Fwd	Team Bath
MacPherson	Angus	Ian	11/10/68	Glasgow	10/07/03	5 10.0	11 6	Def	Dunfermline Athletic
Martin	David		02/02/87	Paisley	18/07/03	5 9.0	10 7	Def	Rangers
McCay	Ryan	John James	04/05/86	Paisley	31/08/02	5 8.0	10 8	Mid	St. Mirren Form S
McGinty	Brian		10/12/76	East Kilbride	31/10/01	6 1.0	12 7	Fwd	Cumnock Juniors
McGowne	Kevin		16/12/69	Kilmarnock	10/07/03	6 1.0	13 0	Def	Partick Thistle
McHard	Thomas		15/11/86	Glasgow	01/08/03	5 7.0	11 0	Fwd	Livingston
McKay	Stephen		23/12/86	Johnstone	31/03/03	5 7.0	11 0	Def	St. Mirren Form S
McKenna	David		19/09/86	Paisley	31/03/03	5 8.0	11 4	Fwd	St. Mirren Form D U 16
McKnight	Paul	Ronald	08/02/77	Belfast	11/07/03	5 8.0	11 0	Fwd	Linfield
McWilliam	Graham		07/02/86	Paisley	31/08/02	6 2.0	13 3	Def	St. Mirren Form D U 16
Molloy	Craig		26/04/86	Greenock	31/08/02	5 7.0	10 3	Mid	St. Mirren Form D U 16
Muir	Alan		05/11/86	Paisley	31/03/03	5 8.0	9 9	Mid	St. Mirren Form D U 16
Murray	Hugh		08/01/79	Bellshill	23/08/02	5 10.0	11 9	Mid	Mansfield Town
O'Neil	John	Joseph	03/01/74	Glasgow	28/05/03	5 11.0	12 0	Mid	Queen of the South
Russell	Allan	John	13/12/80	Glasgow	08/08/03	6 0.0	12 1	Mid	Hamilton Academical
Taggart	Bryan	Duncan	17/09/85	Irvine	31/08/02	5 10.0	11 5	Fwd	Kilwinning Eglington B.C.
Taylor	John	Paul	05/09/86	Glasgow	31/03/03	5 7.0	10 0	Fwd	St. Mirren Form D U 16
Twaddle	Kevin		31/10/71	Edinburgh	22/07/03	6 3.0	13 7	Mid	Heart of Midlothian
Van Zanten	David		08/05/82	Dublin	28/07/03	5 10.0	11 0	Def	Celtic
Woods	Stephen	Gerard	23/02/70	Glasgow	02/07/03	6 2.0	13 5	Gk	Motherwell

St. Mirren Park, Love Street, Paisley, PA3 2EJ
CHAIRMAN
Stewart G. Gilmour
VICE-CHAIRMAN
George P. Campbell
DIRECTORS
Bryan A. McAusland, Dr. Roger W. Lucas, Kenneth D. McGeoch, James Purves & Allan W. Marshall LL.B.,
HON. PRESIDENT
William Todd, M.B.E., J.P.
SECRETARY
Allan W. Marshall, LL.B.
MANAGER
John Coughlin
PLAYER/ASSISTANT MANAGER
Angus MacPherson
DIRECTOR OF YOUTH DEVELOPMENT
Bryan McAusland
YOUTH CO-ORDINATOR & CHIEF SCOUT
Arthur Bell
YOUTH COACHES
Gus MacPherson (U19)
John MacDonald (U17)
Gordon Wylde (U16)
Stewart Ferguson (U15)
David Longwell (U14)
COMMUNITY COACH
David Longwell
FITNESS COACH
David Murray
CLUB DOCTOR
Stewart McCormick, M.B., Ch.B.
PHYSIOTHERAPIST
Karen Stark, M.Sc, M.S.C.P.
GROUNDSMAN
Tommy Docherty
KIT PERSON
Jim Munro
COMMERCIAL MANAGER
Campbell Kennedy
Bus. (0141) 840 1337
Mobile (07768) 816078
LOTTERY MANAGER
Jim Crawford
SPORTS COMPLEX MANAGER
Jack Copland
FOOTBALL SAFETY OFFICERS' ASSOCIATION REPRESENTATIVE/ STADIUM MANAGER
Robert Money
Home (0141) 889 1096
Mobile (07855) 098921
MATCHDAY PROGRAMME EDITOR & MEDIA LIAISON OFFICER
Alastair MacLachlan
TELEPHONES
Ground/Administration
(0141) 889 2558
Enquiries (0141) 849 0611
Sec. Bus. (01563) 820216
Commercial/Marketing
(0141) 840 1337
Sports Leisure Complex
(0141) 849 0609
Fax (0141) 848 6444
E-MAIL & INTERNET ADDRESS
commercial@saintmirren.net
www.saintmirren.net
CLUB SHOP
Situated in Provan Sports, 23 Causeyside Street, Paisley
Tel (0141) 889 1629
OFFICIAL SUPPORTERS CLUB
St. Mirren Supporters' Club, 11 Knox Street, Paisley
TEAM CAPTAIN
Kevin McGowne
SHIRT SPONSOR
First Choice: Phoenix Kia
Second Choice: Phoenix Suzuki
KIT SUPPLIER
XARA

milestones

YEAR OF FORMATION: 1877
MOST CAPPED PLAYERS: Iain Munro & Billy Thomson
NO. OF CAPS: 7
MOST LEAGUE POINTS IN A SEASON: 62 (Division 2 – Season 1967/68) (2 Points for a Win)
76 (First Division – Season 1999/2000) (3 Points for a Win)
MOST LEAGUE GOALS SCORED BY A PLAYER IN A SEASON: Dunky Walker (Season 1921/22)
NO. OF GOALS SCORED: 45
RECORD ATTENDANCE: 47,438 (-v- Celtic 7.3.1925)
RECORD VICTORY: 15-0 (-v- Glasgow University – Scottish Cup, 30.1.1960)
RECORD DEFEAT: 0-9 (-v- Rangers – Division 1, 4.12.1897)

ticket information

SEASON TICKET PRICES

MAIN STAND/ LOWER ENCLOSURE	
Adult	£220
Juvenile/OAP	£130
NORTH STAND/PAISLEY DAILY EXPRESS STAND	
Adult	£200
OAP	£120
Juvenile	£70

LEAGUE ADMISSION PRICES

MAIN STAND	
Adult	£13
Juvenile/OAP	£7
LOWER ENCLOSURE	
Adult	£13
Juvenile/OAP	£7
NORTH STAND	
Adult	£12
Juvenile/OAP	£7
1 Parent & 1 Juvenile	£16
PAISLEY DAILY EXPRESS STAND	
Adult	£12
Juvenile/OAP	£7
1 Parent & 1 juvenile	£16

leading goalscorers 1993-2003

Season	Div	No. of Goals	Player
1993-94	F	10	B. Lavety
1994-95	F	7	B. Lavety
1995-96	F	11	B. Lavety
1996-97	F	15	M. Yardley
1997-98	F	9	J. Mendes
1998-99	F	11	M. Yardley
1999-00	F	19	M. Yardley
2000-01	P	10	R. Gillies
2001-02	F	6	R. Gillies, B. McGinty
2002-03	F	12	M. Cameron

the buddies' club factfile 2002/03

Date	Venue	Opponents	Att.	Res	Roy L.	Rudden P.	Kerr C.	McGowan J.	Robb R.	Dow A.	Gillies R.	MacKenzie S.	McGinty B.	Cameron M.	Ross I.	Lappin S.	Guy G.	Yardley M.	Baltacha S.	Mendes J.	Fellner G.	Lowing D.	Robertson K.	Dietrich K.	Murray H.	Dunbar J.	Broadfoot K.	Jack D.	Baker M.	Denham G.	Dempsie M.	Mitchell A.	McHale P.	McLean S.	Roberts M.	Ferguson J.	Muir A.	McKenna D.	Bald W.	McWilliam G.
Aug 3	H	St. Johntone	3,376	0-2	1	2	3	4	5	6	7	8	9	10	11	14	12	16																						
10	A	Falkirk	4,360	0-2	1		12	4	5	3	7		9	10	6	11	8	15	2	16																				
17	H	Alloa Athletic	3,104	3-1	1		3	5		6	7^1	14^1	9	10^1	11	15	4		2	8																				
24	A	Clyde	1,874	3-2	1	14	3		7	6			9	10	11			12	2	8^3	5	16			4															
31	H	Inverness Cal Th	2,485	0-4			3		15		4		9	10	11		7	12	2	8		16	1	5	6															
Sep 14	A	Arbroath	1,008	2-2	1		6		5		8^1		9	10^1	11	3	2	12	4	14					7															
21	H	Queen of the South	2,492	†2-1	1	4	6		5		8			9^1	10	3	2	11				16			7	15														
28	A	Ayr United	2,489	1-1	1	5	15		4		8		14	9^1	10	3	16	11				6			7	2														
Oct 5	H	Ross County	3,737	1-1	1	4					7		11	9	8	3	15	12		10^1		6				2	5													
19	A	St. Johntone	2,457	0-2	1	4	15		5		7		11	9	8	3				10		6			12	2	14													
26	H	Falkirk	3,661	4-4	1	4	16		5^1	15	7		11	9^3	8	3	12			10		6				2														
Nov 2	A	Inverness Cal Th	2,023	1-4		4	14		5	12	7^1		11	9	8	3	2			10		6	1			15														
9	H	Clyde	2,703	1-4	1		14		5^1	12	7		11	9	8	3	2			10		6				15	4													
16	H	Arbroath	3,021	2-0	1	16			4^1		7		11	9	8	3	2			10^1		6				15	5													
23	A	Queen of the South	2,663	0-3			6			10	7		11	9	8	3	2					5	1			12	4	15												
30	H	Ayr United	2,426	1-0					4		7			9	6	14	2	11		10^1		3	1		8	16	5													
Dec 7	A	Ross County	2,429	0-4		15	12		4		7				6	9	2	11		10		3	1		8		5													
14	A	Alloa Athletic	783	3-2			16	4		14	7^1			9^2	6	15	2	11		10		3	1		8		5													
28	H	Inverness Cal Th	3,054	1-4	1		15	4	2		7			9^1	6	11	8			10						16	14		3	5										
Jan 1	A	Clyde	1,553	2-3	1	2				12	7^1			9	11	6	8	16		10		15					4^1		3	5										
18	H	Ross County	2,366	1-0	1		15				7			9^1		11	2			10					8	16			3	5	4	6								
Feb 1	A	Ayr United	2,738	0-0	1				2				9			11									8				3	5	4	6	7	10	12					
8	H	Alloa Athletic	2,105	1-1	1				2		7		11			15						16			8				3	5	4	6	12	9	10^1					
15	A	Falkirk	4,094	1-3		3					7		12			11						15	1			14	6			5^1	4	2	8	9	10					
22	H	Queen of the South	1,888	2-2		2					7^1		11			3						14	1			15	6			5	4		8	9^1	10					
Mar 1	A	Inverness Cal Th	1,973	1-3				15			7		11			14						3	1			16	6			5	4	2	8^1	9	10					
8	H	Clyde	2,683	1-2				2			7		9			11							1			12	4		3	5		6	8		10^1					
15	A	Queen of the South	1,911	2-0	1			2			7^1		11	9		15										16	4		3	5^1		6	8	14	10					
22	H	St. Johntone	2,369	1-3	1			2			7^1			9		11	16								12	15	4		2	5		6	8		10					
29	A	Arbroath	509	1-1	1			2			7					11						14			6	9	4		3	5			8		10	16				
Apr 5	H	Arbroath	2,122	1-0	1		3	2			7			9^1		11	12								6	14	4			5		15	8		10					
12	H	Ayr United	2,248	1-1		14	3				7		6	9		11							1			10	4			5	2		8				16	15^1		
19	A	Ross County	1,967	0-2		16	14	2					7	9		11							1				4			5	3	6	8	10	12					
26	A	St. Johntone	1,819	1-1				2			7^1		6	9		11						12	1				4		3		5	14	8		10			15		
May 3	H	Falkirk	3,062	1-2				5	2		7		8^1	9		11						3	1			16	4					6			10		15	14		
10	A	Alloa Athletic	1,084	0-4		2			5		7			9		11						3				8	4								10	14	6	12	1	15
TOTAL FULL APPEARANCES					21	11	9	13	18	5	33	1	23	28	20	27	15	5	5	15	1	14	14	1	13	7	21		10	15	9	10	12	6	12		1		1	
TOTAL SUB APPEARANCES						5	11	1	1	5		1	2			7	6	7		2		9			2	16	2	1				2	1	1	2	2	2	4		1
TOTAL GOALS SCORED									3		9	1	1	12						6							1			2			1	1	3			1		

Small bold figures denote goalscorers. † denotes opponent's own goal.

st. mirren park

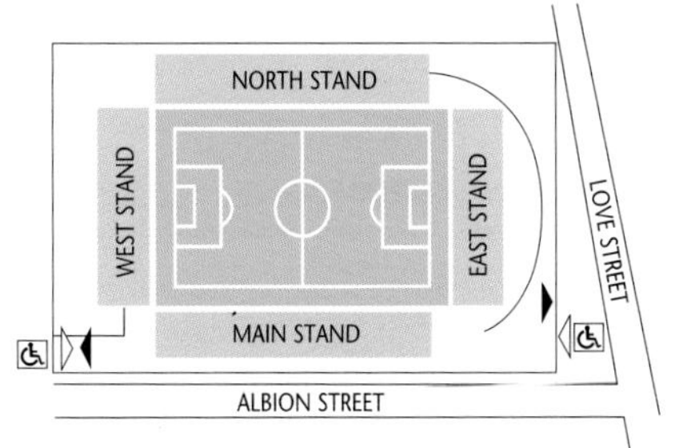

CAPACITY: 10,622; (All Seated)

PITCH DIMENSIONS: 112 yds x 74 yds

FACILITIES FOR DISABLED SUPPORTERS:
Full wheelchair facilities available for visiting supporters in the Caledonia Stand.

team playing kits

how to get there

St. Mirren Park can be reached by the following routes:

TRAINS: There is a frequent train service from Glasgow Central Station and all coastal routes pass through Gilmour Street. The ground is about half a mile from the station.

BUSES: All SMT coastal services, plus buses to Johnstone and Kilbarchan, pass within 300 yards of the ground.

CARS: The only facilities for car parking are in the streets surrounding the ground.

airdrie united

Excelsior Stadium,
Broomfield Park,
Airdrie, ML6 8QZ

ALL CORRESPONDENCE SHOULD BE ADDRESSED TO:
Secretary, Airdrie United F.C.
60 St. Enoch Square,
Glasgow, G1 4AG

CHAIRMAN
James W. Ballantyne

DIRECTORS
Ann Marie Ballantyne,
Gavin W. Speirs,
Mrs. Rose Mary Ballantyne,
John Ballantyne &
W. Gardner Speirs

HONORARY PRESIDENT
Ian McMillan

SECRETARY
Ms. Ann Marie Ballantyne

PLAYER/MANAGER
Sandy Stewart

PLAYER/ASSISTANT MANAGER
Kenny Black

YOUTH CO-ORDINATOR
Jimmy Boyle

YOUTH TEAM COACHES
Jimmy Boyle (U19)
Ian Black (U17)

COMMERCIAL/LOTTERY MANAGER
Les Jones
Mobile 07949 976116

STADIUM MANAGER
Alistair Cameron,
Tel (01236) 622000

CLUB DOCTOR
Dr. Brian Dunn, M.B., CLB, M.R.C.P.(UK)

PHYSIOTHERAPIST
Ian Constable

GROUNDSMAN
John McGuire

KIT PERSON
John Donnelly

COMMERCIAL DIRECTOR & MEDIA LIAISON OFFICER
James W. Ballantyne

MATCHDAY PROGRAMME EDITOR
John O'Brien

SEASON TICKET ADMINISTRATOR
Scott Gilkison

TELEPHONES
Ground (Match Days Only)
(01236) 622000
Fax (0141) 221 1497
Sec. Bus. (07710) 230775

E-MAIL & INTERNET ADDRESS
www.airdrieunitedfc.com
jim@airdrieunitedfc.com
annmarie@airdrieunitedfc.com

CLUB SHOP
Situated at Ground
Open on Home Match Days Only

FANS REPRESENTATIVE
Veronica McGregor

TEAM CAPTAIN
Stephen Docherty

SHIRT SPONSOR
Pertemps

KIT SUPPLIER
Global Sports

LIST OF PLAYERS 2003/04

SURNAME	FIRST NAME	MIDDLE NAME	DATE OF BIRTH	PLACE OF BIRTH	DATE OF SIGNING	HEIGHT FT INS	WEIGHT ST LBS	POS. ON PITCH	PREVIOUS CLUB
Arundel	David		05/04/87	Falkirk	21/08/03	6 0.0	10 10	Fwd	East Stirlingshire
Baxter	Gordon		05/01/86	Falkirk	29/08/03	6 1.0	11 5	Def	Stenhousemuir
Black	Kenneth	George	29/11/63	Stenhousemuir	01/08/03	5 9.0	12 12	Mid	Edinburgh University
Black	Scott		23/05/87	Bellshill	21/08/03	5 10.0	10 12	Fwd	East Stirlingshire
Brock	Ross		17/05/86	Perth	19/07/01	6 0.0	11 2	Def	Stenhousemuir
Cherrie	Peter		01/10/83	Bellshill	30/08/02	6 2.0	12 7	Gk	Airdrie B.C.
Cochrane	John		26/12/87	Bellshill	21/08/03	5 11.0	11 1	Def	East Stirlingshire
Craig	Thomas		28/05/87	Bellshill	21/08/03	5 8.0	10 5	Mid	East Stirlingshire
Cullen	Paul	Francis	15/04/88	Lanark	21/08/03	5 10.0	10 2	Def	Hamilton Acad. Form D U16
Docherty	Stephen		18/02/76	Glasgow	26/07/02	5 10.0	12 0	Def/Mid	Airdrieonians
Dunn	David	Hugh	01/11/81	Bellshill	31/01/03	5 11.0	12 1	Mid	Clyde
Flannigan	Andrew		03/07/87	Bellshill	21/08/03	6 2.0	12 0	Def	East Stirlingshire
Frater	Gary	James	24/01/87	Falkirk	21/08/03	5 6.0	10 0	Mid	East Stirlingshire
Gardner	Robert	Lee	11/07/70	Ayr	26/07/02	5 8.0	10 6	Mid	Airdrieonians
Gemmell	Michael		01/07/86	Edinburgh	29/07/03	5 8.0	10 10	Mid	Gairdoch United
Glancy	Martin	Paul	24/03/76	Glasgow	02/08/02	5 8.0	11 0	Fwd	Stranraer
Gow	Alan		09/10/82	Glasgow	30/08/02	6 0.0	12 0	Mid	Clydebank
Grant	Barry		08/09/87	Bellshill	11/08/03	5 6.0	9 0	Mid	Motherwell
Hoey	Thomas		14/04/86	Glasgow	21/08/03	6 0.0	10 6	Mid	Arsenal B.C.
Hollis	Lee	James Mcl.	12/03/86	Glasgow	11/08/03	6 0.0	11 0	Gk	Hillwood B.C.
Hunter	Grant		24/01/87	Rutherglen	21/08/03	5 9.0	10 6	Mid	Queen of the South B.C.
Jones	Gordon	Francis	03/10/85	Paisley	29/08/03	5 11.0	11 7	Def	Morton
Kerr	Daniel	Frew	19/03/85	Irvine	21/08/03	5 6.0	10 4	Fwd	Ayr United
Lawrie	Christopher		29/03/87	Aberdeen	21/08/03	6 0.0	10.9	Def	East Stirlingshire
Masterson	Patrick		30/04/85	Rutherglen	29/07/03	5 10.0	10 0	Fwd	Stenhousemuir
Matthews	James		27/11/87	Bellshill	21/08/03	5 7.0	10 2	Def	Stonehouse B.C.
McDougall	Steven	David	17/06/86	Paisley	11/08/03	5 11.0	10 6	Fwd	Rangers
McGeown	Mark		10/05/70	Paisley	26/07/02	5 10.5	12 0	Gk	Stranraer
McGowan	Neil	William	15/04/77	Glasgow	29/08/02	5 10.0	11 4	Def	KA Iceland
McKenna	Stephen		25/11/85	Glasgow	01/08/03	6 1.0	12 4	Mid	Rangers
McKeown	Stephen	James	17/07/81	Rutherglen	29/08/02	5 10.0	12 10	Fwd	Airdrieonians
McLaren	William		06/11/84	Glasgow	21/08/03	5 10.0	10 0	Mid	Benburb Juniors
McManus	Allan	William	17/11/74	Paisley	06/06/03	6 1.0	13 4	Def	Ayr United
Miller	Darren		25/05/83	Bellshill	01/08/03	6 0.0	11 6	Mid	Hamilton Academical
Moyes	Mark		29/05/87	Bellshill	21/08/03	6 0.0	11 0	Mid	East Stirlingshire Form D U16
Roberts	Mark	Kingsley	29/10/75	Irvine	16/07/03	5 11.0	11 10	Fwd	St. Mirren
Ronald	Paul		19/07/71	Glasgow	02/08/02	6 2.0	12 10	Fwd	Airdrieonians
Rutherford	Greig		25/03/87	Falkirk	21/08/03	5 8.0	10 3	Mid	Rosebank B.C.
Stewart	Alexander		14/10/65	Bellshill	26/07/02	5 7.0	11 10	Def	Airdrieonians
Turner	Kevin		10/07/87	Glasgow	22/08/03	5 9.0	10 6	Mid	Rangers
Vareille	Jerome		01/06/74	Vernoux	20/09/02	6 1.0	12 13	Fwd	Airdrieonians
Watson	Jamie		07/07/86	Glasgow	21/08/03	5 11.0	10 5	Mid	Stenhousemuir Form D U16
Watson	Paul		18/12/85	Bellshill	29/07/03	6 0.0	11 7	Def	Calderbraes B.C.
Wilson	Mark	James	15/02/86	Glasgow	29/08/03	6 0.0	11 5	Gk	Hamilton Academical Form D
Wilson	Marvyn		01/12/73	Bellshill	01/08/03	5 8.0	11 8	Mid	Ayr United
Wilson	Scott	William	20/04/82	Bellshill	16/08/02	6 3.0	11 7	Def	Motherwell
Wilson	William	Stewart	19/08/72	Glasgow	02/08/02	5 8.0	10 2	Def	East Fife
Wright	Scott		14/10/87	Falkirk	21/08/03	5 11.0	10 7	Def	Unattached

milestones

YEAR OF FORMATION: 1965 (From seasons 1965/66 to 2001/02 known as Clydebank F.C.)
MOST LEAGUE POINTS IN A SEASON: 58 (Division 1 – Season 1976/77)(2 Points for a Win)
60 (Second Division – Season 1997/98)(3 Points for a Win)
MOST LEAGUE GOALS SCORED BY A PLAYER IN A SEASON: Ken Eadie (Season 1990/91)
NO. OF GOALS SCORED: 29
RECORD ATTENDANCE: 14,900 (-v- Hibernian – 10.2.1965 at Kilbowie Park)
2,285 (-v- Forfar Athletic – 3.8.2002 at Excelsior Stadium)
RECORD VICTORY: 8-1 (-v- Arbroath – Division 1, 3.1.1977)
RECORD DEFEAT: 1-9 (-v- Gala Fairydean – Scottish Cup, 15.9.1965)

ticket information

SEASON TICKET PRICES

SEATED	ADULT	£225 RESERVED SEAT
	ADULT	£200 UNRESERVED SEAT
	OAP/UNEMPLOYED	£85
	JUVENILE (12-16)	£70
	CHILD UNDER 12	FREE with Parent & Child Ticket
	DISABLED	£50

LEAGUE ADMISSION PRICES

SEATED	ADULT	£12
	JUVENILE/OAP/ UNEMPLOYED (WITH UB40)	£5

leading goalscorers 1993-2003

Season	Div	No. of Goals	Player
1993-94	F	11	K. Eadie
			C. Flannigan
1994-95	F	9	K. Eadie
1995-96	F	11	J. Grady
1996-97	F	8	J. Grady
1997-98	S	13	C. McDonald
1998-99	F	9	C. McDonald
1999-00	F	5	I. Cameron
2000-01	S	8	A. Burke
2001-02	S	9	A. Burke
2002-03	S	18	J. Vareille

S·F·L

the diamonds' football club's factfile 2002/03

Date	Venue	Opponents	Att.	Res	McGeown M.	Boyle J.	McVey W.	Stewart A.	Brannigan K.	Vella S.	Gardner R. L.	Wilson M.	Ronald P.	Docherty S.	Glancy M.	Armstrong P.	McGuire D.	Harvey P.	Wilson W.	Miller D.	McGowan N.	Gow A.	Vareille J.	Cherrie P.	Wilson S.	McKeown S.	Risser O.	McAuley S.	Dunn D.	Black K.
Aug 3	H	Forfar Athletic	2,285	1-0	1	2	3	4	5	6	7	8	9	10[1]	11	12	16													
10	A	Hamilton Academical	2,366	0-1	1	2	3	4	5	6	7	8	14	10	11	12	8	15												
17	H	Stranraer	1,518	2-1	1	2	3	4	5	6	16		9[1]	10	11	7[1]		8	12	14										
24	A	Dumbarton	1,417	1-3	1	12	3	4	5	6	7	8	9	10	11	2[1]	14		16											
31	H	Cowdenbeath	1,486	0-0	1			4	5	6	7	8	9	10	11	2	14	15			3	16								
Sep 14	A	Raith Rovers	1,962	0-0	1	12	3	4	5		7			10	16	2	11	8			6	9								
21	H	Brechin City	1,373	2-4	1			4	5		7			10	14[1]	2	16	8	3		6	9[1]	11	17						
28	A	Stenhousemuir	842	3-4		7		4	5		14			10	8	2		15			3	9	11[1]	1	6	16[2]				
Oct 5	H	Berwick Rangers	1,349	2-1	1	3			5		7	8	9	4	10	2	14[1]	15			6		11[1]			12				
19	H	Hamilton Academical	1,593	0-0	1	2						8	11	4	7	3	16	6	14		5	10	9			15				
26	A	Forfar Athletic	666	1-5	1	2						8	9	4[1]	10	3	7	6	12		5	14	11			15				
Nov 2	A	Cowdenbeath	603	1-0	1			4	5	6			9	10		8	7		2		3	15	11[1]			16				
9	H	Dumbarton	1,323	0-1	1		12		5	6			9	4	14	8	7		2		3	10	11			15				
16	H	Raith Rovers	1,717	0-0	1			4	5	6			12			3	7	10	2				9			11	8			
23	A	Brechin City	557	5-1	1			4	5	6		10[1]	14	8		3	7	12	2			15	11[1]			9[3]				
30	A	Berwick Rangers	647	2-2	1			4	5	6		8		10		3	7	15	2			14	11[1]			9[1]				
Dec 14	H	Stenhousemuir	1,228	2-0	1			4	5	6	14	8	16			10	7		2		3	15[1]	11[1]			9				
28	A	Stranraer	695	0-2	1			4		5	12	8	14			3		10	2		6	7	11			9				
Jan 1	A	Dumbarton	1,024	1-2	1			4	5	6	7	8			15	12			2		3	11	9[1]			10				
18	A	Raith Rovers	2,247	0-1	1		3	4			14	8	10	5		2	15				6	11	9			7		16		
Feb 1	H	Brechin City	1,275	3-0	1		3	4			14	8	9[2]	5		2	11				6		7[1]			10			15	
8	A	Stenhousemuir	954	3-3	1		3					8	9	4		2[1]					6		7		5	10[1]			11[1]	
11	H	Cowdenbeath	1,070	1-1	1		3				14	8	9	5	15	2					6	10	7			4		16[1]	11	
25	H	Forfar Athletic	921	0-0	1					5	7	8	14	4		2	11		12		6	15	10			9			3	
Mar 1	H	Stranraer	1,187	3-3	1		3			6		8	15	4		5			2			16	7[2]		12	9[1]			11	10
8	H	Dumbarton	1,136	2-1	1		16	4				8		10		2					6	11[1]	7		5	9			3[1]	
11	A	Hamilton Academical	1,620	1-2	1		3[1]	4				8		10		2	16				6		7		5	9			11	
15	A	Cowdenbeath	585	2-1	1		3[1]	4			14	8	12	10		5			2	15		11	7		6[1]	9				
22	A	Brechin City	672	1-0	1		3	4			14	8	15	10		5			2		12	11	7		6	9[1]				
28	H	Berwick Rangers	1,276	2-0	1		3	4			10	8	14	6	15[1]	5			2			11	7[1]			9			12	
Apr 5	H	Raith Rovers	1,788	1-1	1		3	4			8		12	10	14	6			2			11[1]	7		5	9			15	
12	A	Berwick Rangers	631	3-0	1						10	8	12	4	14	2			3		6	11	7[3]		5	9			15	
19	H	Stenhousemuir	1,468	1-0	1			4			10	8	12	2	14				3		6	11	7[1]		5	9			15	
26	A	Forfar Athletic	884	1-1	1						10	8	11	4		2			3		6	9	7[1]		5			15	12	
May 3	H	Hamilton Academical	1,960	2-2	1						10	8	12	4	8	2			3		6	11	7[2]		5	15			14	
10	A	Stranraer	1,343	2-1	1			4			10	8	11	5	15	2			3		6	14[1]	7			9[1]				
TOTAL FULL APPEARANCES					35	7	15	25	16	15	16	28	15	32	10	32	11	7	19		24	18	30	1	11	21	1		6	1
TOTAL SUB APPEARANCES						2	2				9		14		10	3	8	6	5	2	1	9		1	1	7		3	7	
TOTAL GOALS SCORED							2					1	3	2	2	3	1					5	18		1	10		1	2	

Small bold figures denote goalscorers. † denotes opponent's own goal.

excelsior stadium

CAPACITY: 10,170 (All Seated)

PITCH DIMENSIONS: 115 yds x 74 yds

FACILITIES FOR DISABLED SUPPORTERS:
Disabled facilities are provided in the North, East & South Stands.

team playing kits

how to get there

Excelsior Stadium can be reached by the following routes:

TRAINS: From Glasgow Queen Street to Airdrie there is a train every 15 minutes. From the station beyond Airdrie, Drumgelloch, there is a train every 30 minutes, then a 10 minute walk to the stadium.

BUSES: Nos 260 or 15 from Airdrie Town Centre.

CARS: From Glasgow or Edinburgh leave the M8 at Newhouse junction (A73) and the stadium is $2^{1}/_{2}$ miles north of Newhouse. From Cumbernauld, the stadium is 6 miles south on the A73.

alloa athletic

Recreation Park, Clackmannan Road, Alloa, FK10 1RR

CHAIRMAN
David Murray

VICE-CHAIRMAN
Ian Henderson

DIRECTORS
Ewen G. Cameron, William J. McKie, Robert F. Hopkins & Patrick Lawlor

HONORARY PRESIDENT
George Ormiston

HONORARY DIRECTOR
Ronald J. Todd

SECRETARY
Ewen G. Cameron

OFFICE ADMINISTRATOR
Susan Gillon

MANAGER
Terry Christie

FIRST TEAM COACH
Gareth Evans

HEAD OF YOUTH DEVELOPMENT
Hugh McCann

YOUTH CO-ORDINATOR
Robert Wilson

YOUTH TEAM COACHES
Hugh McCann (U19)
Derek Brown (U16)
Robert Hutton (U14)

CLUB DOCTOR
Dr. Clarke Mullen

PHYSIOTHERAPIST
Vanessa Smith

FOOTBALL SAFETY OFFICERS' ASSOCIATION REPRESENTATIVE
Ian Love (01259) 722695

KIT PERSON
Nicol Campbell

COMMERCIAL MANAGER & MEDIA LIAISON OFFICER
William McKie
Bus. (01259) 722695
Home (01259) 730572
Mobile (07979) 754979

MATCHDAY PROGRAMME EDITOR
John Glencross
Bus. (01324) 622061
Home (01786) 817362

TELEPHONES
Ground (01259) 722695
Fax (01259) 210886
Sec. Bus. (01324) 619708
Sec. Home (01259) 722696

E-MAIL & INTERNET ADDRESS
fcadmin@alloaathletic.co.uk
www.alloaathletic.co.uk

CLUB SHOP
Situated adjacent to Refreshment Kiosk

CLUB SHOP MANAGER
Susan Gillon Tel: (01259) 722696

OFFICIAL SUPPORTERS CLUB
c/o Recreation Park, Clackmannan Road, Alloa, FK10 1RY
Contact: Charlotte Glass
Tel: (01259) 216758

TEAM CAPTAIN
Craig Valentine

SHIRT SPONSOR
Alloa Advertiser

KIT SUPPLIER
Pendle

LIST OF PLAYERS 2003/04

SURNAME	FIRST NAME	MIDDLE NAME	DATE OF BIRTH	PLACE OF BIRTH	DATE OF SIGNING	HEIGHT FT INS	WEIGHT ST LBS	POS. ON PITCH	PREVIOUS CLUB
Barclay	Craig		24/08/86	Edinburgh	19/07/03	5 9.0	10 7	Def	Alloa Athletic Form D U16
Bruce	Harry		15/03/86	Stirling	19/07/03	5 9.0	10 7	Def	Alloa Athletic Form D U16
Callaghan	Stuart		20/07/76	Calderbank	03/06/03	5 9.0	11 7	Mid	Hamilton Academical
Chalmers	Adam		25/04/86	Stirling	19/07/03	6 0.0	10 12	Mid	Alloa Athletic Form D U16
Cole	Stephen		21/01/85	Stirling	19/07/03	5 8.0	11 2	Mid	East Stirlingshire
Crabbe	Scott		12/08/68	Edinburgh	27/07/02	5 8.0	11 7	Fwd	Ayr United
Elliott	Graeme		12/08/85	Glasgow	19/07/03	6 2.0	12 7	Def	Alloa Athletic Form D U16
Evans	Barry		03/07/86	Stirling	19/07/03	5 8.0	9 7	Mid	Alloa Athletic Form D U16
Evans	Gareth	John	14/01/67	Coventry	13/06/03	5 7.5	11 7	Fwd	Airdrieonians
Evans	James		27/01/82	Glasgow	25/06/03	6 0.0	11 7	Gk	Bolton Wanderers
Ferguson	Alexander	Brown	04/06/81	Falkirk	16/07/02	5 10.0	11 8	Mid	East Stirlingshire
Fraser	Mark	Stewart	27/02/86	Stirling	19/07/03	5 8.0	10 8	Fwd	Alloa Athletic Form D U16
Gillan	Graeme		02/08/84	Edinburgh	10/06/03	5 10.0	11 0	Mid	Preston Athletic
Hamilton	Ross		17/06/80	Falkirk	31/07/00	5 10.0	11 0	Fwd	Stenhousemuir
Haney	George		05/08/86	Stirling	19/07/03	5 7.0	10 0	Fwd	Alloa Athletic Form D U16
Janczyk	Neil		07/04/83	Edinburgh	22/08/03	5 10.0	11 0	Mid	Heart of Midlothian
Kelbie	Kevin		21/12/84	Stirling	17/06/03	5 11.0	11 7	Fwd	Rangers Form D U16
Knox	Gary		11/01/86	Edinburgh	19/07/03	5 11.0	11 7	Fwd	Salvesen B.C.
Learmonth	Steven	James	25/05/86	Falkirk	22/08/03	5 10.0	10 0	Def	B.P. Under 19's
Little	Ian	James	10/12/73	Edinburgh	09/07/03	5 8.0	10 7	Mid	Livingston
McGlynn	Gary	Dominic	24/11/77	Falkirk	18/06/03	5 11.0	12 0	Gk	Montrose
McGowan	Jamie		05/12/70	Morecambe	19/07/03	6 0.0	11 5	Def	St. Mirren
McLaughlin	Paul		20/02/84	Glasgow	01/08/03	6 0.0	12 7	Def	Heart of Midlothian
Nicolson	Iain		13/10/76	Glasgow	30/06/03	5 10.0	11 11	Def	Ayr United
O'Raw	Michael		15/04/86	Edinburgh	26/08/03	6 0.0	11 7	Mid	Alloa Athletic Form D U16
Reilly	Christopher		27/04/85	Glasgow	19/07/03	6 4.0	12 7	Def	Queen's Park Form D U16
Seaton	Andrew	Murray	16/09/77	Edinburgh	17/06/03	5 10.0	12 2	Def	Falkirk
Stanton	John		05/03/86	Edinburgh	19/07/03	6 0.0	12 0	Fwd	Alloa Athletic Form D U16
Tiropoulos	Robert		01/02/86	Alexandria	21/08/03	6 0.0	11 7	Gk	Falkirk
Valentine	Craig		16/07/70	Edinburgh	17/06/03	5 8.0	12 0	Def	Berwick Rangers
Walker	Richard	Alan	08/07/82	Edinburgh	13/06/01	5 11.0	11 0	Fwd	Whitehill Welfare Colts
Watson	Murray	James	25/01/84	Bellshill	29/08/03	5 7.0	10 0	Fwd	Aberdeen
Westwater	Kevin		25/07/86	Falkirk	22/08/03	6 1.0	12 0	Def	B.P. Under 16's
Wood	Ryan		06/04/86	Stirling	19/07/03	5 9.0	10 7	Fwd	Alloa Athletic Form D U16

milestones

YEAR OF FORMATION: 1883
MOST CAPPED PLAYER: Jock Hepburn
NO. OF CAPS: 1
MOST LEAGUE POINTS IN A SEASON: 60 (Division 2 – Season 1921/22)(2 Points for a Win)
76 (Third Division – Season 1997/98)(3 Points for a Win)
MOST LEAGUE GOALS SCORED BY A PLAYER IN A SEASON: William Crilley (Season 1921/22)
NO. OF GOALS SCORED: 49
RECORD ATTENDANCE: 13,000 (-v- Dunfermline Athletic – 26.2.1939)
RECORD VICTORY: 9-2 (-v- Forfar Athletic – Division 2, 18.3.1933)
RECORD DEFEAT: 0-10 (-v- Dundee – Division 2 and Third Lanark – League Cup)

ticket information

	SEASON TICKET PRICES	
SEATED	ADULT	£150
	JUVENILE/OAP	£80
STANDING	ADULT	£140
	JUVENILE/OAP	£70
	LEAGUE ADMISSION PRICES	
SEATED	ADULT	£10
	JUVENILE/OAP	£6
STANDING	ADULT	£9
	JUVENILE/OAP	£5

leading goalscorers 1993-2003

Season	Div	No. of Goals	Player
1993-94	S	7	W. Newbigging
1994-95	T	13	B. Moffat
1995-96	T	5	B. Moffat, S. Rixon
1996-97	T	12	W. Irvine
1997-98	T	18	W. Irvine
1998-99	S	15	M. Cameron, W. Irvine
1999-00	S	15	M. Cameron
2000-01	F	9	R. Hamilton
2001-02	S	14	G. Hutchison
2002-03	F	8	R. Sloan

S·F·L ©

the wasps' club factfile 2002/03

Date	Venue	Opponents	Att.	Res	Hogarth M.	Valentine C.	Watson G.	Ferguson D.	Thomson S.	Christie M.	Hamilton R.	Macdonald W.	Crabbe S.	Hutchison G.	Little I.	Evans G.	Cowan M.	Ferguson A. B.	Fisher J.	Seaton A.	Knox K.	Walker R.	Evans J.	Gillan G.	Elliot R.	Stevenson J.	Sloan R.	Davidson R.	Soutar D.
Aug 3	A	Inverness Cal Th	1,623	0-0	1	2	3	4	5	6	7	8	9	10	11	16													
10	H	Arbroath	518	0-3	1	2		4	5	6	7		9	10		15	3	8	11	12									
17	A	St. Mirren	3,104	1-3		2			5		7	6	9[1]	10		15		8	11	3	4	12	1						
24	H	Falkirk	2,613	1-6	1	2		16	5		7	6	9	10	11		4	8[1]	12	3									
31	A	St. Johnstone	2,274	0-2		2	4	10	5		7		9	15	11			8	12	3			1	6	16				
Sep 14	A	Clyde	973	0-0		2	4		5	6	7	8		10	9	14	3		11		12		1						
21	H	Ayr United	619	0-1		2	4	16	5		7		9	10	11	14	6		8	3	15		1						
28	A	Ross County	1,921	1-0		2	4	8	5	6	7		9	10	11	14[1]			12	3			1						
Oct 5	H	Queen of the South	658	0-1		2	4	8	5	6	7	16		10	11	9			12	3		15	1						
19	H	Inverness Cal Th	531	0-6		2	4	8	5	6	9	7		10						3	12	14	1	15		11			
26	A	Arbroath	687	1-0		2		8	5	6	9[1]			10		14			11	3	4	7	1						
Nov 2	H	St. Johnstone	952	1-3		2	8		5	6	9	12		10		14			11	3[1]	4	7	1						
9	A	Falkirk	3,390	0-3		2	4		5		9			10		8	6		11	3	12	7	1	14	15				
16	H	Clyde	736	1-4		2			5	8	9			10			6[1]		11	3	4	7	1	14	16				
23	A	Ayr United	1,632	1-3	1				5		7		8	10	11	15	4[1]		6	3		2			16	9			
30	H	Ross County	445	1-1	1	2		4	5	6	8		12	10	9[1]				11	3	15	7							
Dec 7	A	Queen of the South	2,111	1-1		4	12	8	5	6	7		9	10[1]	11	16				3		2	1	15					
14	H	St. Mirren	783	2-3		4		8	5[1]	6	7		9[1]	10	11					3		2	1						
21	A	Inverness Cal Th	1,639	1-1	1	4	12	8	5		7		9	10[1]	11	15			6	3		2							
28	A	St. Johnstone	2,090	0-3	1	4		8	5	6	7		9	10	11	15			12	3		2							
Jan 18	H	Queen of the South	561	3-3	1	4			5[1]	6	7		14	10	11					3[2]		2					8	9	
Feb 1	A	Ross County	2,096	2-1		2	4	8	5	6	10		9	14						3		7					11[2]	15	1
8	A	St. Mirren	2,105	1-1		4		8	5	6	7[1]		9	12	10					3		2					11	14	1
25	H	Arbroath	340	3-2		4	5[1]	8		14	7		9	12[1]	11[1]		15			3		2					6	10	1
Mar 1	H	St. Johnstone	884	1-2		2	4	8	5	6			12	14	11					3		7		16			10[1]	9	1
8	A	Falkirk	3,320	†1-3		4			5	6	7		9	10	11					3		2					8	12	1
11	A	Clyde	665	†2-2		2	4	8	5	6	9		15	14	11					3		7					10[1]	12	1
15	A	Ayr United	1,363	1-0		2	4	8	5		9		15[1]	6	11					3		7					10	12	1
25	H	Ayr United	454	2-3			2		5	6	8		9	4	11[1]					3		7	1		14		10	12[1]	
29	H	Falkirk	1,686	1-3		2	4	8	5	6	7[1]		12	14	11					3			1				10	9	
Apr 5	H	Clyde	687	1-2		2	4	8	5	6	9[1]			14	11		16			3		7					10	12	1
12	H	Ross County	876	2-1		2	4	8	5	6	9[1]		15	14	11					3		7					10[1]		1
19	A	Queen of the South	1,873	1-0		2	4	8	5[1]	6	9		15	14	11					3		7	1				10		
26	H	Inverness Cal Th	485	1-5		2	4	8	5	6	9		15	14	11					3		7					10[1]	12	1
May 3	A	Arbroath	405	1-0		2	3	4	5	6	9		15	8	11			14[1]				7					10		1
10	H	St. Mirren	1,084	4-0		2	6	4	5		9		10	14[1]	15			8		3[1]		7					11[2]	12	1
TOTAL FULL APPEARANCES					8	34	22	25	35	26	35	5	18	24	27	2	7	5	11	32	4	25	16	1		2	16	4	12
TOTAL SUB APPEARANCES							2	2		1		2	10	12	1	12	2	1	5	1	5	3		5	5			9	
TOTAL GOALS SCORED							1		3		5		3	4	3	1	2	2		4							8	1	

Small bold figures denote goalscorers. † denotes opponent's own goal.

recreation park

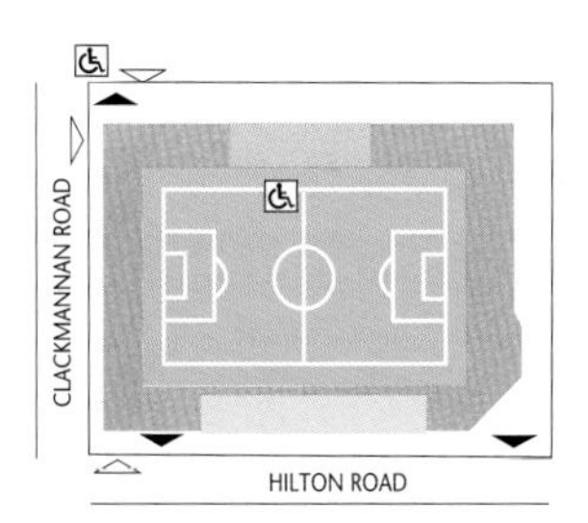

CAPACITY: 3,100; Seated 400, Standing 2,700

PITCH DIMENSIONS: 110 yds x 75 yds

FACILITIES FOR DISABLED SUPPORTERS:
Accommodation for wheelchairs and invalid carriages in front of Stand. Disabled toilets are also available.

team playing kits

how to get there

Recreation Park can be reached by the following routes:

TRAINS: The nearest railway station is Stirling, which is seven miles away. Fans would have to connect with an inter-linking bus service to reach the ground from here.

BUSES: There are three main services which stop outside the ground. These are the Dunfermline-Stirling, Stirling-Clackmannan and Falkirk-Alloa buses.

CARS: Car Parking is available in the car park adjacent to the ground and this can hold 175 vehicles.

arbroath

Gayfield Park,
Arbroath, Angus, DD11 1QB

PRESIDENT
John D. Christison

COMMITTEE
R. Alan Ripley (Treasurer), Michael Caird, Malcolm L. Fairweather, Dr. Gary J. Callon, Mark R. Davies, Ian J. Angus & Charles W. Kinnear

HONORARY PRESIDENTS
I. Stirling, G. Johnson, B. Pearson, J. King J. Leslie, D. Ferguson, J. Milne, & W. Smith

HONORARY PATRONS
Earl of Airlie, Lord Inchcape & Lord Fraser

SECRETARY
Dr. Gary J. Callon

OFFICE ADMINISTRATOR
Mike Cargill

MANAGER
John Brownlie

ASSISTANT MANAGER
Stephen Kirk

FIRST TEAM COACH/RESERVE COACH
Jake Ferrier

YOUTH CO-ORDINATOR/YOUTH DEVELOPMENT COACH
Gordon Wallace

GOALKEEPING COACH
Dave Gorman

U-19 YOUTH TEAM COACH
Gordon Wallace

U-17 YOUTH TEAM COACH
Mike Cargill

CLUB DOCTOR
Dr. Dick Spiers

PHYSIOTHERAPIST
Jim Crosbie

CHIROPODIST
Alexander McKinnon

FOOTBALL SAFETY OFFICERS' ASSOCIATION REPRESENTATIVE
William Scorgie (Bus)(01241) 878778

COMMERCIAL MANAGER
Malcolm Fairweather
Bus. (01241) 434765

STADIUM MANAGER
Michael Caird

GROUNDSMAN
James Gauld

MATCHDAY PROGRAMME EDITOR
George Cant (Herald Press)
Bus. (01241) 872000

TELEPHONES
Ground/Ticket Office/Club Shop (01241) 872157
Fax (01241) 431125
Sec. Home (01241) 872394
Sec. Bus. (01382) 348616

E-MAIL & INTERNET ADDRESS
afc@gayfield.fsnet.co.uk
www.arbroathfc.co.uk

CLUB SHOP
Contact: Karen Fleming
Gayfield Park, Arbroath, DD11 1QB.
Open on home matchdays.

TEAM CAPTAIN
Andy Dow

SHIRT SPONSOR

KIT SUPPLIER
ERREA

LIST OF PLAYERS 2003/04

SURNAME	FIRST NAME	MIDDLE NAME	DATE OF BIRTH	PLACE OF BIRTH	DATE OF SIGNING	HEIGHT FT INS	WEIGHT ST LBS	POS. ON PITCH	PREVIOUS CLUB
Bannon	Michael	David	06/10/86	Dundee	17/07/03	5 10.0	10 6	Mid	Maryfield United B.C.
Bell	Michael		11/12/85	Dundee	14/07/03	5 8.0	10 0	Fwd	Forfar West End Juniors
Brown	Mark		26/01/86	Kirkcaldy	19/07/03	6 1.0	12 0	Def	Newport Boys U' 18's
Browne	Paul	Gerard	17/02/75	Glasgow	15/08/03	6 2.0	13 0	Def	Nuneaton Borough
Cairney	John	Alexander	22/01/85	Dundee	14/07/03	6 1.0	12 12	Def	Celtic B.C.
Cargill	Andrew		02/09/75	Dundee	30/05/01	5 6.5	10 8	Mid	Dundee
Cargill	Christopher	James	30/05/86	Dundee	01/08/03	6 1.0	13 6	Gk	Abroath Form D Under 16
Cusick	John	James	16/01/75	Kirkcaldy	14/06/00	5 8.0	12 8	Def/Mid	East Fife
Denham	Greig	Paterson	05/10/76	Glasgow	14/07/03	6 2.0	13 3	Def	St. Mirren
Dow	Andrew	James	07/02/73	Dundee	30/01/03	5 9.0	11 7	Mid	St. Mirren
Duff	Garry		05/08/85	Arbroath	19/07/03	5 9.0	11 10	Mid	Dundee
Durno	Paul		19/06/84	Arbroath	13/06/03	5 10.0	10 12	Mid	Arbroath Form S
Farquharson	Paul		16/10/84	Dundee	13/06/03	5 9.0	10 12	Mid	Celtic B.C.
Glennie	Chris		20/02/86	Dundee	14/07/03	5 10.0	10 12	Mid	Maryfield United
Graham	Ewan	Douglas	11/01/83	Arbroath	13/06/03	6 1.0	12 6	Def	Arbroath Sporting Club Jnrs.
Graham	James	Ross	03/06/71	Baillieston	31/05/03	6 2.0	14 0	Fwd	East Fife
Henslee	Greig		13/01/83	Dundee	20/02/01	5 10.0	11 10	Mid	Arbroath Form S
Herkes	James		28/02/78	Kirkcaldy	31/05/03	5 11.0	11 7	Fwd	East Fife
Innes	Michael	Anthony	10/11/85	Dundee	17/07/03	6 1.0	13 1	Mid	Dundee
Johnston	Matthew	Richard	16/01/86	Arbroath	17/07/03	6 1.5	12 2	Def	Arbroath Lads Club
Kelly	Kevin		06/05/85	Dundee	29/08/03	5 9.0	11 2	Mid	Celtic B.C.
Kerrigan	Steven		09/10/72	Bellshill	24/07/03	6 0.0	12 10	Fwd	Stirling Albion
King	David	William	13/07/79	Falkirk	26/06/03	6 0.0	12 0	Mid	Bo'ness United Juniors
Kirk	Greg	David	18/08/86	Dundee	22/08/03	6 0.0	11 5	Mid/Fwd	Maryfield United
Martin	Jamie	Andrew	10/01/86	Dundee	18/08/03	6 1.0	12 2	Def	Dundee United
McAulay	John		28/04/72	Glasgow	04/07/95	5 9.0	12 6	Mid	Clyde
McCarthy	Stewart		13/10/85	Dundee	19/07/03	6 2.0	11 11	Def	Dundee United
McGlashan	John		03/06/67	Dundee	15/08/00	6 1.0	12 0	Mid	Ross County
McMullan	Kevin	Andrew	15/06/83	Kirkcaldy	13/06/03	5 10.0	11 0	Def	Newburgh Juniors
Mitchell	Anthony	Martin	10/01/79	Glasgow	14/08/03	6 1.0	13 8	Gk	Queen's Park
Newall	Christopher		12/03/80	Glasgow	31/08/03	6 2.0	12 0	Def	Wishaw Juniors
O'Leary	Marc	Blair	11/02/86	Dundee	14/07/03	5 10.0	11 2	Mid	Maryfield United U' 16's
Peat	Mark		13/03/82	Bellshill	23/06/03	6 1.0	12 0	Gk	Aberdeen
Rennie	Steven		03/08/81	Stirling	30/06/03	6 2.0	12 7	Def	Falkirk
Smith	Greg		01/09/85	Dundee	01/08/03	6 1.0	12 10	Def	Montrose Form S
Swankie	Gavin		22/11/83	Arbroath	20/02/01	5 10.0	10 12	Fwd	Arbroath Form S
Warren	Garry		01/07/86	Dundee	17/07/03	5 10.0	10 13	Fwd	Arbroath Form S
Watson	Paul		22/11/85	Dundee	29/08/03	6 2.0	11 10	Def/Mid	Dundee
Woodcock	Timothy	Martin	04/02/84	Dundee	30/05/03	6 0.0	12 1	Gk	Arbroath Form S

milestones

YEAR OF FORMATION: 1878
MOST CAPPED PLAYER: Ned Doig
NO. OF CAPS: 2
MOST LEAGUE POINTS IN A SEASON: 57 (Division 2 – Season 1966/67) (2 Points for a Win)
68 (Third Division – Season 1997/98) (3 Points for a Win)
MOST LEAGUE GOALS SCORED BY A PLAYER IN A SEASON: David Easson (Season 1958/59)
NO. OF GOALS SCORED: 45
RECORD ATTENDANCE: 13,510 (-v- Rangers – Scottish Cup, 23.2.1952)
RECORD VICTORY: 36-0 (-v- Bon Accord – Scottish Cup, 12.9.1885)
RECORD DEFEAT: 1-9 (-v- Celtic – League Cup, 25.8.1993)

ticket information

SEASON TICKET PRICES

SEATED	ADULT	£160
	JUVENILE/OAP	£75
STANDING	ADULT	£160
	JUVENILE/OAP	£75
	JUVENILE UNDER 12 YEARS	£30

LEAGUE ADMISSION PRICES

SEATED	ADULT	£10
	JUVENILE/OAP	£6
STANDING	ADULT	£9
	JUVENILE/OAP/ UNEMPLOYED WITH UB40	£5
	PARENT & CHILD	£12

leading goalscorers 1993-2003

Season	Div	No. of Goals	Player
1993-94	S	10	D. Diver
1994-95	T	11	S. Tosh
1995-96	T	8	S. McCormick, D. Pew
1996-97	T	5	B. Grant
1997-98	T	16	W. Spence
1998-99	S	12	C. McGlashan
1999-00	S	16	C. McGlashan
2000-01	S	10	S. Mallan
2001-02	F	6	G. Bayne, J. McGlashan S. Mallan
2002-03	F	4	J. Cusick M. McDowell

the red lichties' club factfile 2002/03

Date	Venue	Opponents	Att.	Res	Hinchcliffe C.	Tait J.	McInally D.	Currie R.	Ritchie I.	Cusick J.	Heenan K.	Cargill A.	McDowell M.	McGlashan J.	Swankie G.	Feroz C.	Brownlie P.	Spink D.	Florence S.	McCaig J.	McAulay J.	Henslee G.	Graham E.	Browne P.	Bowman G.	Durno P.	McMullan K.	Dow A.	Forrest E.	McDermott A.	McMillan K.	Farquharson P.
Aug 3	H	Ross County	761	0-3	1	2	3	4	5	6	7	8	9	10	11	12	14	15														
10	A	Alloa Athletic	518	3-0	1	2			5[1]	6	14		9[1]		16	11	7	15[1]	3	4	8	10										
17	H	Clyde	744	1-1	1	2		15	5	6			9[1]		12	11	7	8		4	10	3	16									
24	H	St. Johnstone	1,467	0-1	1			2	4		14	8	9	10	12	11	7	15		5	6	3										
31	A	Ayr United	1,732	0-1	1			2	5		16	8	9	10	15	11	14				7	3		4	6							
Sep 14	H	St. Mirren	1,008	2-2	1		15	10	4	6[1]	8	7	9	12	16	11[1]						2		5	3							
21	A	Inverness Cal Th	1,686	0-5	1		15	10	4	6	7		9	8		11		16			12	2		5	3							
28	A	Queen of the South	1,733	2-2	1	2	10	8[1]	4	6	12	7[1]	14		9	11			3			16		5								
Oct 5	H	Falkirk	1,730	2-0	1	2	14		5	6[1]	16	7	9	10		11[1]			3		12			4	8							
19	A	Ross County	2,065	0-4	1	2	11		5	6	7	8		10	14	9			3		12	16		4								
26	H	Alloa Athletic	687	0-1	1	2		6	5		7		8	10	14	9			3		12	16		4	11							
Nov 5	H	Ayr United	381	1-1	1	2					7	8	12[1]	10		9		4	3		6	14		5	11	16						
9	A	St. Johnstone	1,994	0-2	1	2	14				12	8	9	10	7	15		4	3		6			5	11							
16	A	St. Mirren	3,021	0-2	1	2		14	5			11		10	7	9	12	8	3		6			4	15							
23	H	Inverness Cal Th	653	1-2	1	2[1]		8	5	6		11	9	10		12	7	15	3			16		4								
30	H	Queen of the South	630	1-2	1	2		8	5	6	7		9[1]		12		10		3		14	16		4	11							
Dec 7	A	Falkirk	2,673	1-2	1	2		8	5		12		9		14		10	6[1]	3		15	7		4	11							
14	A	Clyde	861	0-3	1	2		10	5	6	12		9		7		11	8	3		14		16	4								
21	H	Ross County	580	2-1	1	2		6	5			8	12		10[2]	9	11	14	3		16	7		4								
28	A	Ayr United	1,664	0-4	1	2		6	5			8	12		10	9	11	14	3			7		4	15							
Jan 1	H	St. Johnstone	1,252	2-3	1			2	5		7	8	14	10[1]	15	9	11[1]		3		12	4	6									
18	H	Falkirk	1,950	1-4	1	2		6	5			7		10[1]	15	9	11	16	3		12	8	4									
Feb 8	H	Clyde	686	1-2	1			6	5		7			10	8	9	11	16			14	12					2	3[1]	4			
25	A	Alloa Athletic	340	2-3	1			8	5	4[1]	7				16	9	11					10[1]				14	2	2	6			
Mar 1	H	Ayr United	505	1-2	1		14	2	5	4	7				9		11				16	8	3			15		10	6[1]			
4	A	Inverness Cal Th	1,396	0-2	1			8	5	4	7						11		3			8	14			12	2	10	6			
8	A	St. Johnstone	1,938	1-2	1		15	8	5		11				9[1]		4	16	3		14	7					2	10	6			
15	H	Inverness Cal Th	550	1-3	1			8	5		10[1]				9		11	15	3		12	7			16		2	6		4		
18	A	Queen of the South	1,108	0-3	1			6	5						10	9	8	2	3			7	16			14		11		4	15	
29	H	St. Mirren	509	1-1	1			6	5		8	12			9		14	16	3			7			10		2	11[1]	4			
Apr 5	A	St. Mirren	2,122	0-1	1			6	5	4	14	8			12		9		3			7			10		2	11				16
12	H	Queen of the South	502	0-0	1			6	5	4	9	8		15	10				3			7	16				2	11				12
19	A	Falkirk	4,950	1-4	1			4	5	8[1]	15	10			11	9	14				12	7					2	3	6			
26	A	Ross County	2,204	1-3	1			16		4	14	8					11[1]		3		15	7	6			9	2	10	5			
May 3	H	Alloa Athletic	405	0-1	1			4	5		7	8			9		11	16	3		2	14				12		10	6			
10	A	Clyde	1,002	2-4	1		11[1]	6	5		15	8					7		3		2	9[1]	12			10	14		4			
TOTAL FULL APPEARANCES					36	17	4	28	33	18	17	21	14	14	16	20	22	7	26	3	9	23	4	16	11	2	10	13	10	2		
TOTAL SUB APPEARANCES							6	3			12	1	5	2	13	3	5	13			16	8	6		3	6	1				1	2
TOTAL GOALS SCORED						1	1	1	1	4	1	1	4	2	3	2	2	2				2						2	1			

Small bold figures denote goalscorers. † denotes opponent's own goal.

gayfield park

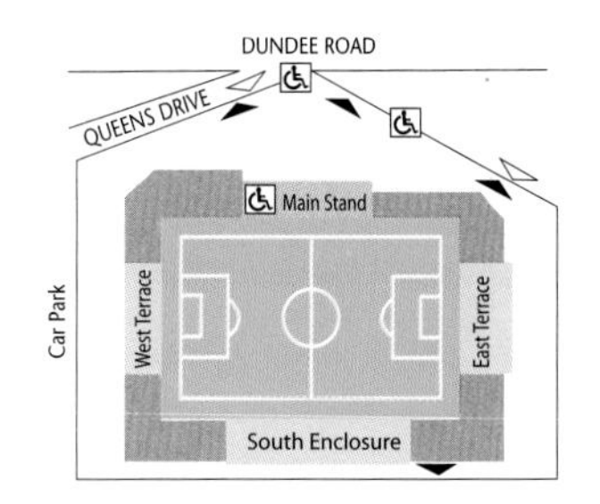

CAPACITY: 5,025; Seated 860, Standing 4,165

PITCH DIMENSIONS: 115 yds x 71 yds

FACILITIES FOR DISABLED SUPPORTERS:
Enclosure at east and west ends of Stand with wide steps to take a wheelchair. Toilet facilities are also available.

team playing kits

how to get there

The following routes may be used to reach Gayfield Park:
BUSES: Arbroath is on the main route from both Glasgow and Edinburgh to Aberdeen. Buses from these three cities, plus Stirling, Dundee and Perth all stop at Arbroath Bus Station at hourly intervals. There is also a local service between Dundee-Arbroath and Montrose and this service is half hourly until 7.00 p.m. Between 7.00 p.m. and 10.45 p.m. the service is hourly. The bus station is 10 minutes walk from the ground.
TRAINS: Abroath is on the Inter-City 125 route from London to Aberdeen and there are frequent local services between Arbroath, Dundee and Edinburgh. Trains also travel north from Glasgow, Stirling and Perth. The station is a 15 minute walk from the ground.
CARS: There is free parking for 500 cars just next to the ground in Queen's Drive.

berwick rangers

Shielfield Park,
Shielfield Terrace, Tweedmouth,,
Berwick-Upon-Tweed, TD15 2EF

CHAIRMAN
Robert L. Wilson

VICE-CHAIRMAN
W. Moray McLaren

DIRECTORS
John H. Hush, Peter McAskill, John G. Robertson, Ian R. Smith, John Bell, Robert J. Darling & Craig Forsyth

HONORARY PRESIDENT
Rt. Hon. Alan Beith M.P.

CLUB SECRETARY
Dennis J. McCleary

TREASURER & OFFICE ADMINISTRATOR
J. Neil Simpson

MANAGER
Paul Smith

ASSISTANT MANAGER/ FIRST TEAM COACH
Greg Shaw

DIRECTOR OF FOOTBALL & YOUTH DEVELOPMENT DIRECTOR/COACH
Ian R. Smith

YOUTH COACH
Andy Raeburn (U19)

STADIUM MANAGER & KIT PERSON
Ian Oliver

HONORARY PARAMEDIC
Paul Ross BAEMT-P, IHCD, SRP

PHYSIO STAFF
Rev. Glyn Jones
& Ian Smith

TRAINEE PHYSIO
Jamie Dougal

FOOTBALL SAFETY OFFICERS ASSOCIATION REPRESENTATIVE
John G. Robertson

GROUNDSMEN
Ian Oliver & Ross Aitchison

COMMERCIAL MANAGER
Conrad Turner (01289) 307969

MEDIA LIAISON OFFICER
Paul Smith (0131) 449 6834

MATCHDAY PROGRAMME EDITOR
Dennis McCleary (01289) 307623

TELEPHONES
Ground/Ticket Office (01289) 307424
Fax (01289) 309424
Club Sec. Home (01289) 307623
Club Sec. Mobile: (07713) 101372
Manager Bus: (0131) 449 6834
24 Hour Hotline (09068) 800697

E-MAIL
dennis@mccleary133.fsnet.co.uk

CLUB SHOP
Supporters Shop situated within the ground. Open during first team home matchdays.

OFFICIAL SUPPORTERS CLUB
c/o Shielfield Park, Tweedmouth, Berwick-Upon-Tweed, TD15 2EF
(01289) 307424

TEAM CAPTAIN
Alan Neill

SHIRT SPONSOR
Haggerston Castle Holiday Park

KIT SUPPLIER
Pro Star

LIST OF PLAYERS 2003/04

SURNAME	FIRST NAME	MIDDLE NAME	DATE OF BIRTH	PLACE OF BIRTH	DATE OF SIGNING	HEIGHT FT INS	WEIGHT ST LBS	POS. ON PITCH	PREVIOUS CLUB
Bain	Christopher		24/01/86	Edinburgh	11/07/03	6 2.0	11 12	Mid	Tynecastle Hearts
Bennett	John	Neil	22/08/71	Falkirk	01/08/01	5 9.0	11 2	Mid	Stirling Albion
Benzie	Dean		29/03/86	Edinburgh	11/07/03	6 1.0	10 1	Fwd	St. Bernards
Birrell	Jamie		07/04/86	Edinburgh	11/07/03	5 11.0	10 13	Mid	Tynecastle Hearts
Blackley	Douglas	Michael	30/09/83	Edinburgh	28/08/02	5 8.0	10 2	Mid	Ross County
Bower	Robert		02/07/85	Kirkcaldy	08/08/03	5 8.0	10 12	Fwd	Kirkcaldy Y.M.
Bracks	Kevin		01/10/86	Edinburgh	08/08/03	5 11.0	10 2	Def	Hibernian
Connell	Graham		31/10/74	Glasgow	21/06/02	5 10.0	11 7	Mid	Queen of the South
Connelly	Gordon		01/11/76	Glasgow	04/07/02	6 0.0	12 7	Mid	Queen of the South
Cowan	Mark		16/01/71	Edinburgh	17/06/03	6 0.0	13 0	Def	Alloa Athletic
Devlin	Daryl	Brian	23/11/86	Edinburgh	28/08/03	5 9.0	9 8	Mid	Redpath Albion
Forrest	Gordon	Iain	14/01/77	Dunfermline	12/06/00	5 9.0	10 10	Def	East Fife
Gibson	Scott	Matthew	07/01/86	Edinburgh	11/07/03	6 0.0	10 10	Def	Tynecastle Hearts
Godfrey	Ross		21/01/77	Edinburgh	25/05/02	6 0.0	13 0	Gk	East Fife
Grieve	Gary	Alexander	25/11/86	Edinburgh	08/08/03	5 11.0	10 2	Def	Leith Athletic B.C.
Hampshire	Paul	Christopher	20/09/81	Edinburgh	24/06/03	5 11.0	11 0	Mid	Raith Rovers
Hilland	Paul		28/07/83	Glasgow	27/08/03	6 1.0	12 7	Def	Hibernian
Hutchison	Gareth	William McK.	04/06/72	Edinburgh	05/06/03	5 11.0	11 10	Fwd	Alloa Athletic
Inglis	Neil	David	10/09/74	Glasgow	26/07/02	6 1.0	12 2	Gk	Ards
Lord	Kevin	James	15/08/86	Edinburgh	18/07/03	5 11.0	9 12	Def	Livingston
Lucas	Scott		28/05/86	Edinburgh	11/07/03	6 0.0	11 2	Mid	Tynecastle Hearts
MacDonald	Steven	Swan	16/03/85	Edinburgh	29/08/03	5 8.0	11 0	Mid	St. Johnstone
McAllister	John		09/07/81	Kirkcaldy	24/06/03	5 11.0	10 7	Fwd	Hutchison Vale U'21's
McConnel	Craig	Russell	23/05/86	Edinburgh	11/07/03	5 11.0	10 2	Fwd	Leith Athletic
McCormick	Mark	Thomas	11/07/79	Bellshill	29/07/02	5 9.0	11 0	Fwd	Ross County
McCutcheon	Gary	Kyle	08/10/78	Dumfries	16/08/03	5 6.0	11 5	Fwd	Dumbarton
McNicoll	Grant		07/09/77	Edinburgh	30/07/97	5 11.0	11 1	Def	Heart of Midlothian
McQuade	Daniel		10/06/86	Edinburgh	11/07/03	6 1.0	11 4	Def	Redpath Albion
Murie	David		02/08/76	Edinburgh	14/06/01	5 9.0	11 0	Def	Morton
Neil	Martin		16/04/70	Ashington	17/11/94	5 8.0	11 4	Mid	Bolton Wanderers
Neill	Alan	John	13/12/70	Baillieston	25/06/98	6 1.0	12 7	Def	East Stirlingshire
Newby	Peter		21/03/86	Edinburgh	11/07/03	5 9.0	10 8	Mid	Cowdenbeath Form D U16
Noon	Daniel	Hendry	04/10/85	Edinburgh	11/08/03	6 2.0	11 10	Fwd	St. Johnstone
Robb	Leon		31/03/86	Edinburgh	11/07/03	5 9.0	10 2	Mid	Salvesen B.C.
Scott	William	James	03/02/85	Edinburgh	11/07/03	6 2.0	12 2	Gk	Lothian Thistle
Smith	Darren		04/06/80	Edinburgh	16/10/98	5 7.0	10 2	Mid	Berwick Rangers Colts
Waldie	Colin		06/02/81	Lanark	15/08/03	5 9.0	11 0	Mid	Stenhousemuir

milestones

YEAR OF FORMATION: 1881
MOST LEAGUE POINTS IN A SEASON: 54 (Second Division – Season 1978/79)(2 Points for a Win)
66 (Third Division – Season 1999/2000)(3 Points for a Win)
MOST LEAGUE GOALS SCORED BY A PLAYER IN A SEASON: Ken Bowron (Season 1963/64)
NO. OF GOALS SCORED: 38
RECORD ATTENDANCE: 13,365 (-v- Rangers – 28.1.1967)
RECORD VICTORY: 8-1 (-v- Forfar Athletic (H) – Division 2, 25.12.1965)
8-1 (-v- Vale of Leithen – Scottish Cup at Innerleithen, 17.12.1966)
RECORD DEFEAT: 1-9 (-v- Hamilton Academical – First Division, 9.8.1980)

ticket information

SEASON TICKET PRICES
Tickets for seated or standing valid for all Bell's Second Division games & pre-season friendlies

SEATED &	ADULT	£140
STANDING	CONCESSIONS	£60

(Includes Juvenile/OAP/Unemployed with UB40/Registered Disabled)

LEAGUE ADMISSION PRICES

SEATED &	ADULT	£9
STANDING	CONCESSIONS	£4
	CHILDREN UNDER 13	£1 with paying adult

N.B. All fans for Stand enter via either Ground 'A' or 'B' and transfer to Stand(s).

leading goalscorers 1993-2003

Season	Div	No. of Goals	Player
1993-94	S	15	W. Irvine
1994-95	S	16	W. Hawke
1995-96	S	13	W. Irvine
1996-97	S	6	P. Forrester
1997-98	T	10	P. Forrester
1998-99	T	12	M. Leask
1999-00	T	9	M. Anthony
2000-01	S	14	G. Wood
2001-02	S	9	G. Wood
2002-03	S	12	A. Burke G. Wood

the borderers' club factfile 2002/03

Date	Venue	Opponents	Att.	Res	Godfrey R.	Murie D.	Smith A.	Forrest E.	Neill A.	Bennett J.N.	Connelly G.	Connell G.	Wood G.	Burke A.	Smith D.	Gray D.	Bradley M.	Ferguson I.	Inglis N.	Neil M.	Forrest G.	McCormick M.	McNicoll G.	Smith H.	Brown J.K.	Blackley D.	McDowell M.	Robertson J.
Aug 3	A	Brechin City	501	†4-2	1	2	3	4	5	6	7	8	9[3]	10	11	14	13	15										
10	H	Raith Rovers	804	1-1				4	5	3	7	8	9[1]	10	11	2	6	14	1									
17	A	Stenhousemuir	379	0-2				4	5	3	7	6	9	10	11	2	13		1	8	14	15						
24	A	Hamilton Academical	1,486	†2-1		2		5	3	11	7	8	9[1]	10	15		6		1		13	14	4					
31	H	Dumbarton	509	1-2	1	2			5	3	7	8	9	10[1]	11		6			14	13		4					
Sep 14	H	Stranraer	388	3-4		2	3		12		7		9[1]	10	11[2]	5				8	6		4	1				
21	A	Forfar Athletic	483	2-0	1	2	3		5	12	7		9	10	11[1]	4				8[1]	6	14						
28	H	Cowdenbeath	458	2-1	1	2	3		5	12	7	13	9	10	11[1]	4				8	6[1]	14						
Oct 5	A	Airdrie United	1,349	1-2	1	2	3		5	12	7		9	10	11	4				8	6[1]							
19	A	Raith Rovers	1,906	2-1	1	2	3	4			7		9[1]	10	11[1]		13	14		8	6				5			
26	H	Brechin City	410	0-3	1	2	3	4	12		7		9	10	11			14		8	6				5	15		
Nov 2	A	Dumbarton	763	2-1	16	2	3	4			7		9[1]	10[1]	11				1	8	6				5			
9	A	Hamilton Academical	461	2-1	1	2	3	4		13	7		9	10[2]	11					8	6				5			
16	A	Stranraer	412	0-1	1	2	3	4	12		7		9	10	11		15	14		8	6				5			
23	H	Forfar Athletic	387	2-1	1	2	3	4			7		9	10[1]	11		15			8	6[1]				5			
30	H	Airdrie United	647	2-2	1	2	3	4			7		9[2]	10	11			14		8	6				5			
Dec 14	A	Cowdenbeath	306	2-1	1		3		5		12			10[1]	11[1]	2	7	9		8	6		4					
28	H	Stenhousemuir	543	2-2	1		3		5[1]		7	12		10[1]	11	2	6	9		8			4					
Jan 11	H	Dumbarton	580	0-1	1	2	3		5		7	15	9	10	11		8	13	16		6		4					
18	H	Stranraer	422	1-0		2	3		5		7		9	10	11[1]		8		1		6		4		14			
25	A	Brechin City	402	2-2		2	3				7		9	10[1]	11		6		1		5		4[1]				8	15
Feb 8	H	Cowdenbeath	530	1-2		2	3				7	13	9	10	11[1]	12	6		1		5		4				8	14
22	H	Raith Rovers	820	1-1		2					7	8		10[1]	11	3			1		6		4		5		9	
25	A	Hamilton Academical	626	0-3		2			15		7	8		10	11	3	12		1		6		4		5		9	14
Mar 1	A	Stenhousemuir	684	0-1	1		15		5		7	8		10	14	2					6		4		3		9	11
4	A	Forfar Athletic	420	2-2	1	3				13	7	8		10[1]	11	2	6						5		4[1]	12	9	
8	H	Hamilton Academical	406	1-0	1	3					7	14	9	10[1]	11	2	6				8		4		5			13
15	A	Dumbarton	916	†2-2	1		3				7	8		10[1]	13	2	6						4		5	12	9	11
22	H	Forfar Athletic	389	0-0	1		3				7			10	11	2	6				8		4		5	12	9	
28	A	Airdrie United	1,276	0-2	1		3				7		15	10	11	2	6				8		4		5		9	13
Apr 5	A	Stranraer	354	0-0	1	2			3		7		9	10	11		6				8		4		5		13	15
12	H	Airdrie United	631	0-3	1	2			3	8	7			10	11		13				6		4		5		9	
19	A	Cowdenbeath	256	1-0	1	2	3		5	11	7	13	9	10			8				6[1]		4		12		14	
26	H	Brechin City	442	2-0	1	2			5	3	7	13	9[2]	10	11		8				6		4				15	
May 3	A	Raith Rovers	2,746	0-1	1	2			5	3	7	13	9	10	11		8				6		4				15	14
10	H	Stenhousemuir	579	0-0		2			5	3		8	9	10			13		1			15	4			6	7	11
TOTAL FULL APPEARANCES					25	28	22	11	19	10	34	11	26	36	31	16	18	2	10	14	27		23	1	17	1	11	3
TOTAL SUB APPEARANCES					1	1	1		4	5	1	8	1		3	2	8	7	1	1	3	5			2	4	4	7
TOTAL GOALS SCORED									1				12	12	8					1	4		1		1			

Small bold figures denote goalscorers. † denotes opponent's own goal.

shielfield park

To Berwick by-pass (North and South)
Boardroom, Dressing Rooms & Sponsors Suite
Offices
Turnstiles B
(ALSO ACCESS TO STANDS)
SHIELFIELD TERRACE
Turnstiles A
Town Centre and Edinburgh North

CAPACITY: 4,131; Seated 1,366, Standing 2,765

PITCH DIMENSIONS: 110 yds x 70 yds

FACILITIES FOR DISABLED SUPPORTERS:
Supporters should enter via gate adjacent to ground turnstiles (see ground plan above) or via official entrance.

team playing kits

how to get there

Shielfield Park can be reached by the following routes:
The ground is approximately 1½ miles south of Berwick town centre and is situated in Shielfield Terrace, Tweedmouth (signposted).

TRAINS: The railway station is Berwick, which is situated on the East Coast line and a frequent service operates at various stages during the day. The ground is 1½ miles (approx.) from the station and a taxi service operates from there or alternatively, fans can take the local bus service as detailed.

BUSES: The local bus route from the town centre is the Prior Park service and the nearest stop is Shielfield Terrace, only yards from the ground.

CARS: There is a large car park at the rear of the ground. (Nominal charge).

dumbarton

Strathclyde Homes Stadium, Dumbarton Castle, Castle Road, Dumbarton, G82 1JJ

CHAIRMAN
John G. MacFarlane

MANAGING DIRECTOR
Neil Rankine

DIRECTORS
Colin J. Hosie, John Benn, Callum L. Hosie, Donald McK. MacIntyre, Sidney S. Collumbine & Jack Gammie

ASSOCIATE DIRECTORS
Alan T. Jardine, Andrew Gemmell & James Todd

HON. PRESIDENTS
Ian A. Bell, J.P., R. Campbell Ward, C.A. & Douglas S. Dalgleish

CLUB SECRETARY
J. David Prophet

COMPANY SECRETARY
John Benn M.Sc.

OFFICE ADMINISTRATOR
Freida McMahon

DIRECTOR OF FOOTBALL
Sidney S. Collumbine
Bus. (01324) 611777
Mob. (07710) 079459
Fax (01324) 635590

MANAGER
Brian Fairley

ASSISTANT MANAGER
Allan McGonigal

FIRST TEAM COACH/ GOALKEEPING COACH
Alan Banner

COACH
Alan Fraser

CLUB DOCTOR
Neil MacKay, MBC, HB

SPORTS THERAPIST
Linda McIlwraith, Diploma Sports Therapy

CHIEF SCOUT
Willie Hughes

GROUND MAINTENANCE
Barr Facility

KIT PERSON
Steven Hunter

COMMERCIAL MANAGER
John Sharp (01389) 762569

FOOTBALL SAFETY OFFICER'S ASSOCIATION REPRESENTATIVE
Martin Love
Home (01389) 602866
Bus. (07713) 151023

MEDIA LIAISON OFFICERS
Colin J. Hosie & John Benn

MATCHDAY PROGRAMME EDITOR
Graeme Robertson (0131) 441 5451

TELEPHONES
Ground (01389) 762569
Sec. Home (01389) 602567
Sec. Bus (01389) 723510
Sec. Mobile (07796) 881002
Fax (01389) 762629

E-MAIL & INTERNET ADDRESS
www.dumbartonfootballclub.com
dumbarton.footballclub@btopenworld.com
david_prophet58@hotmail.com

CLUB SHOP
Situated in ground. Open on home matchdays and 10.00 a.m. – 4.00 p.m. Mon-Fri

OFFICIAL SUPPORTERS CLUB
c/o Dumbarton FC, Strathclyde Homes Stadium, Castle Road, Dumbarton, G82 1JJ

TEAM CAPTAIN
Neil Duffy

SHIRT SPONSOR
Teachers

KIT SUPPLIER
Vandanel

LIST OF PLAYERS 2003/04

SURNAME	FIRST NAME	MIDDLE NAME	DATE OF BIRTH	PLACE OF BIRTH	DATE OF SIGNING	HEIGHT FT INS	WEIGHT ST LBS	POS. ON PITCH	PREVIOUS CLUB
Bonar	Steven	Andrew	20/05/79	Glasgow	30/03/00	5 9.5	10 6	Mid	Albion Rovers
Boyle	Christopher	Thomas	10/06/82	Irvine	11/06/03	5 7.0	10 7	Mid	Kilmarnock
Bradley	Mark		10/08/76	Glasgow	06/06/03	5 8.0	10 7	Mid	Berwick Rangers
Brittain	Craig		10/01/74	Glasgow	14/06/97	5 5.0	10 0	Def	Ashfield Juniors
Christie	Thomas	Kerr	27/08/84	Aberdeen	31/08/03	5 10.0	11 5	Mid	Benburb Juniors
Collins	Neill	William	02/09/83	Irvine	27/07/02	6 3.0	12 7	Def	Queen's Park
Dillon	John	Peter	16/12/78	Vale of Leven	30/07/99	5 7.0	10 5	Mid	Clyde
Dobbins	Ian	Alexander	24/08/83	Bellshill	29/08/03	6 2.0	12 7	Def	Hamilton Academical
Donald	Barry		24/12/78	Glasgow	31/01/03	6 1.0	12 0	Mid	Queen of the South
Duffy	Cornelius		05/06/67	Glasgow	16/07/02	6 1.0	13 7	Def	Ayr United
English	Isaac		12/11/71	Paisley	19/07/03	5 9.5	11 10	Fwd	Bo'ness United Juniors
Flannery	Patrick	Martin Francis	23/07/76	Glasgow	27/12/97	6 1.0	11 9	Fwd	Morton
Grindlay	Stephen	John	13/03/82	Vale of Leven	02/08/02	6 2.0	13 12	Gk	Dumbarton Academy
Herd	Gordon	Robert Walker	28/06/81	Falkirk	07/07/03	5 10.0	12 7	Fwd	Bo'ness United Juniors
Martin	Gary	James	20/11/84	Glasgow	27/05/03	6 0.0	12 0	Def	Rangers
McEwan	Craig	George	03/10/77	Glasgow	15/08/03	5 8.5	11 4	Def	Ayr United
McKinstry	James	Anthony	03/07/79	Glasgow	07/07/03	5 10.0	12 1	Def	Partick Thistle
Obidile	Emeka	Aboy	27/08/77	Onitha	29/08/03	5 10.0	11 2	Mid	Panseraikos
Renicks	Steven	John	28/11/75	Bellshill	06/06/03	5 8.5	11 0	Def	Queen of the South
Russell	Iain	Thomas	14/11/82	Dumfries	31/01/03	5 10.0	11 0	Fwd	Motherwell
Smith	Daniel	Gerard	30/05/77	Falkirk	07/07/03	5 11.0	11 6	Mid	Linlithgow Rose Juniors
Wight	John	Campbell	11/12/73	Alexandria	04/08/00	6 0.0	13 0	Gk	Beith Juniors

milestones

YEAR OF FORMATION: 1872
MOST CAPPED PLAYERS: J. Lindsay and J.McAulay
NO. OF CAPS: 8 each
MOST LEAGUE POINTS IN A SEASON: 53 (First Division – Season 1986/87) (2 Points for a Win)
61 (Third Division – Season 2001/02) (3 Points for a Win)
MOST LEAGUE GOALS SCORED BY A PLAYER IN A SEASON: Kenneth Wilson (Season 1971/72)
NO. OF GOALS SCORED: 38
RECORD ATTENDANCE: 18,001 (-v- Raith Rovers – 2.3.1957 at Boghead Park)
1,959 (-v- Queen's Park – 27.4.2002 at Strathclyde Homes Stadium)
RECORD VICTORY: 13-2 (-v- Kirkintilloch – Scottish Cup)
RECORD DEFEAT: 1-11 (-v- Ayr United/Albion Rovers)

ticket information

SEASON TICKET PRICES

SEATED		
BUSINESS CLUB	ADULT	£1,000
STAND	ADULT	£135
	JUVENILE/OAP	£70
	PARENT & JUVENILE	£180
	FAMILY OF FOUR	£280
	DISABLED	£70
	PRESIDENT'S CLUB	£200
	PREMIER SEAT	£150

LEAGUE ADMISSION PRICES

SEATED	ADULT	£10
	JUVENILE/OAP/DISABLED	£5

leading goalscorers 1993-2003

Season	Div	No. of Goals	Player
1993-94	F	13	C. Gibson
1994-95	S	17	M. Mooney
1995-96	F	5	M. Mooney
1996-97	S	7	H. Ward
1997-98	T	10	C. McKinnon
1998-99	T	17	P. Flannery
1999-00	T	14	P. Flannery
2000-01	T	17	P. Flannery
2001-02	T	18	P. Flannery
2002-03	S	8	P. Flannery G. McCutcheon

the sons' club factfile 2002/03

Date	Venue	Opponents	Att.	Res	Wight J.	McEwan C.	Stewart D.	Dillon J.	Duffy C.	Collins N.	McCann K.	Bonar S.	Brown T.	Brown A.	Robertson J.	Flannery P.	Lynes C.	McKeown J.	Grindlay S.	McKelvie D.	Dickie M.	Crilly M.	McCutcheon G.	Scally N.	Brittain C.	Obidile E.	Donald B.	Russell I.
Aug 3	A	Stenhousemuir	437	2-2	1	2	3	4	5	6	7	8[1]	9	10	11	16[1]	15	12										
10	H	Brechin City	735	1-0		2	3	11	5	6[1]	7		4	10		9	8		1	15	16	12						
17	A	Raith Rovers	1,866	0-1			3	11	5	6	14	8	4	10		9	16		1		2	7						
24	H	Airdrie United	1,417	3-1		2	3	11[1]	5	6[1]	14	8	4	10[1]	15			12	1			7	9					
31	A	Berwick Rangers	509	2-1		2	3	11		6		8	4	10			15	5	1			7	9[2]	12				
Sep 14	H	Forfar Athletic	827	1-2		2	3	11	5	6		8	4	10		15	16		1			7	9[1]	14				
21	A	Stranraer	455	0-1	17	2	3	11	5	6		8		10	16	14			1			7	9	4				
28	H	Hamilton Academical	1,202	1-1	1		3	11	5	6		8	4	10[1]	14	15		12			2	7	9					
Oct 5	A	Cowdenbeath	363	1-3	1		3	11	5	6	15	8	4	10	16	12					2	7	9[1]					
26	H	Stenhousemuir	815	0-0			6	11	5			8	4	10	15			12	1		2	7	9	16	3			
29	A	Brechin City	377	1-1			6	11	5			8	4[1]	10	16	15	14		1		2	7	9		3			
Nov 2	H	Berwick Rangers	763	1-2			6	11	5			14	4		15	10	8[1]		1		2	7	9		3			
9	A	Airdrie United	1,323	1-0				11	5	6		14		15	4	9[1]	8		1		2	7	10	12	3			
16	A	Forfar Athletic	556	0-2				11	5	6		8		12	7	9	16		1		2	15	10	4	3			
23	H	Stranraer	772	3-0		8		11	5	6		16[1]		10	15	9[1]			1		2	7	12[1]	4	3			
30	H	Cowdenbeath	754	1-1		8		11	5	6		12		10	7	9			1	16	2		14[1]	4	3			
Dec14	A	Hamilton Academical	1,062	0-1		8	7	11	5	6		14		9		16	15		1		2		10	4	3			
28	H	Raith Rovers	1,300	0-3		15		11		6		8	7		16	14		5	1	10	2		9	4	3			
Jan 1	H	Airdrie United	1,024	2-1		8	12	10[1]		6		16	7			9		5	1	15	2			4	3	11[1]		
11	A	Berwick Rangers	580	1-0		8		10[1]		6		14	7	12				5	1		2		9	4	3	11		
18	H	Forfar Athletic	867	1-2				10[1]		6		14	7	8				5	1		2		9	4	3	11		
25	A	Stenhousemuir	460	1-2			12	10[1]		6		16	4	8			15	5	1		2		9	7	3	11		
Feb 1	A	Stranraer	408	2-1			12	10		6		11	7	16		9		5	1		2		8[1]	4[1]	3	14		
8	H	Hamilton Academical	1,108	3-1				11		6[1]		8	7	15		9		5	1		2		10[1]	4[1]	3	14		16
Mar 1	A	Raith Rovers	1,790	1-2		16		10		6		8	7	12				5	1		2		9	4[1]	3	11	14	
8	A	Airdrie United	1,136	1-2		2	12	11		6		8	7			9[1]		5	1				10	4	3		14	15
11	H	Brechin City	513	1-3		2	5			6		8	7			9[1]	11		1				14	4	3			10
15	H	Berwick Rangers	916	2-2		2		11		6		8[1]	7	10[1]				5	1				9	4	3		12	15
18	A	Cowdenbeath	184	0-2		2		11		6		8	7	10		14	15	5	1				9	4	3		12	
Apr 1	H	Stranraer	596	1-1		2	6	12	5	4		7		9			15		1				10		3	14	8[1]	11
5	A	Forfar Athletic	485	1-0		2		11	5	4		7				9			1		16		12	6[1]	3	14	8	10
12	H	Cowdenbeath	1,203	3-1		2		11[1]	5	4		7				9[1]			1		16		12	6	3	14[1]	8	10
19	A	Hamilton Academical	1,270	2-2				11	5	4		8	15	16[1]		9[1]			1		2		12	6	3	7		10
26	H	Stenhousemuir	906	3-1		2		11	5	4		8	15	16		9[1]			1				12	6[1]	3	7		10[1]
May 3	A	Brechin City	895	1-1		2	3	11	5	4		8	14	12		9			1					6		7[1]		10
10	H	Raith Rovers	1,501	4-1		2		11[1]	5	4		8	15	14		9			1				16	6	3	7		10[3]
TOTAL FULL APPEARANCES					**3**	**21**	**16**	**34**	**23**	**33**	**2**	**26**	**23**	**19**	**4**	**18**	**4**	**12**	**33**	**1**	**20**	**12**	**23**	**23**	**26**	**9**	**3**	**8**
TOTAL SUB APPEARANCES					**1**	**2**	**4**	**1**			**3**	**9**	**4**	**10**	**9**	**9**	**10**	**4**		**3**	**3**	**2**	**8**	**4**		**5**	**4**	**3**
TOTAL GOALS SCORED								**7**		**3**		**3**	**1**	**4**		**8**	**1**						**8**	**5**		**3**	**1**	**4**

Small bold figures denote goalscorers. † denotes opponent's own goal.

strathclyde homes stadium

CAR PARK

CAR PARK

COACH PARK

CAR PARK

CASTLE ROAD

CAPACITY: 2,020 (All Seated)

PITCH DIMENSIONS: 114 yds x 75 yds

FACILITIES FOR DISABLED SUPPORTERS:
20 Wheelchair spaces are accommodated at the front of the stand. Contact the Club Secretary in advance regarding availability.

team playing kits

how to get there

Strathclyde Homes Stadium can be reached by the following routes:

TRAINS: The train service from Glasgow Queen Street and Glasgow Central Low Level both pass through Dumbarton East Station (fans best choice) situated just under a ten minute walk from the ground.

BUSES: There are two main services which pass close to the ground. These are bound for Helensburgh and Balloch from Glasgow.

CARS: Follow A82 then A814 Helensburgh/Dumbarton sign post. Follow road for about 1 mile. Pass under Dumbarton East Railway Bridge and take second right – Victoria Street (also signposted Dumbarton Castle). The car park at the stadium holds 400 cars and 6 coaches.

east fife

Bayview Park Stadium, Harbour View, Methil, Leven, Fife, KY8 3RW

CHAIRMAN
J. Derrick Brown

DIRECTORS
David Hamilton, David McK. Stevenson, James M. Stevenson, John Barclay, Ian Johnson, Kenneth R. Mackay & W. Bruce Black

ASSOCIATE DIRECTORS
Douglas Briggs & James Stewart

CHIEF EXECUTIVE/ SECRETARY & MEDIA LIAISON
J. Derrick Brown

HONORARY VICE-PRESIDENT
John Fleming

OFFICE ADMINSTRATOR
Leona Guidi

MANAGER
James Moffat

ASSISTANT MANAGER/ FIRST TEAM COACH/RESERVE COACH
Craig Robertson

RESERVE COACH
Robert Morris

GOALKEEPING COACH
Kevin McKeown

DIRECTOR OF YOUTH DEVELOPMENT & WOMEN'S DEVELOPMENT COACH
David Hamilton

U19 YOUTH TEAM COACHES
Robert Morris & Alex Hamill

LOTTERY MANAGERS
John Band & Wallace Wright

CLUB DOCTOR
Dr. Michael Ward

SURGEON
Ivan Brenkell, M.B., Ch.B., F.R.C.S.

PHYSIOTHERAPISTS
Gordon McEwan & Brian Murray

FOOTBALL SAFETY OFFICERS' ASSOCIATION REPRESENTATIVE
James Dick (01333) 426323/424094

COMMERCIAL DIRECTOR
David Hamilton (01333) 425750

DIRECTOR (MATCHDAY)
Kenneth R. Mackay

DIRECTOR (CATERING)
John Barclay

STADIUM DIRECTOR
James Stevenson

GROUNDS PERSONS
Adam Porteous & Leanne Hamilton

KIT PERSONS
David Wight & Steven Mair

MATCHDAY PROGRAMME EDITOR
Jim Stewart

TELEPHONES
Ground/Commercial (01333) 426323
Sec. Home (01333) 422770
Sec. Bus (01592) 413135 ext 3135
Sec. Mobile (07766) 558410
Fax (01333) 426376

E-MAIL & INTERNET ADDRESS
secretary@eastfife.org
www.eastfife.org

CLUB SHOP
A Club Shop is situated within the Ground. Goods available via post and the Internet

OFFICIAL SUPPORTERS CLUB
c/o Bayview Stadium, Harbour View Methil, Leven, Fife, KY8 3RW

TEAM CAPTAIN
Gordon Russell

SHIRT SPONSOR
First Choice: Glenrothes College
Second Choice: Leslie Bike Shop

KIT SUPPLIER
Paulas Benara

LIST OF PLAYERS 2003/04

SURNAME	FIRST NAME	MIDDLE NAME	DATE OF BIRTH	PLACE OF BIRTH	DATE OF SIGNING	HEIGHT FT INS	WEIGHT ST LBS	POS. ON PITCH	PREVIOUS CLUB
Anderson	Gary	William	10/09/85	Kirkcaldy	03/07/03	5 7.0	10 7	Fwd	East Fife Form S
Barr	Stuart		05/07/85	Kirkcaldy	03/07/03	6 2.0	11 6	Def	Leslie Hearts U' 18's
Bennett	Thomas		06/05/85	Kirkcaldy	03/07/03	6 2.0	11 11	Fwd	Burntisland Shipyard
Bissett	Callum	James	01/04/86	Kirkcaldy	03/07/03	6 0.0	11 5	Mid	Blue Brazil B.C. U' 16's
Blackwood	David	Andrew	12/11/85	Kirkcaldy	03/07/03	5 9.0	9 0	Mid	Glenrothes Strollers
Blair	Brian		10/03/83	Rutherglen	07/07/03	6 2.0	12 0	Mid	Dunfermline Athletic
Byle	Leslie		29/08/82	Glasgow	01/08/03	5 10.0	11 7	Mid	Hibernian
Colgan	Steven	James	16/06/84	Dundee	03/07/03	6 4.0	13 0	Gk	Forfar Athletic
Condie	Craig	John	27/06/86	Kirkcaldy	03/07/03	5 10.0	10 10	Def	Lomond Colts
Crawford	Robert	Edward W.	26/01/87	Dunfermline	07/07/03	5 10.0	11 0	Def	Dunfermline Athletic
Curran	Jason	Cameron	02/07/85	Kirkcaldy	03/07/03	5 11.0	11 7	Gk	Burntisland Shipyard
Deuchar	Kenneth	Robert John	06/07/80	Stirling	09/07/02	6 3.0	13 0	Fwd	Falkirk
Dickson	Martin	Joseph	19/04/86	Kirkcaldy	21/07/03	5 9.0	11 0	Def	Cowdenbeath Form D U16
Donaldson	Euan	Gordon	20/08/75	Falkirk	17/05/02	5 10.0	11 0	Def	Forfar Athletic
Duncan	Craig		10/04/85	Kirkcaldy	13/01/03	5 8.0	9 8	Mid	Cowdenbeath
Fairbairn	Brian		07/04/83	Broxburn	21/07/03	5 10.0	11 0	Fwd	Gretna
Ferguson	John	Neil	12/03/86	Glasgow	07/07/03	5 8.0	10 10	Fwd	Dunfermline Athletic
Gardiner	Ross	Murray	29/09/86	Kirkcaldy	03/07/03	6 1.0	11 4	Gk	Lomond Colts
Geissler	Michael	Lawrie	18/04/85	Kirkcaldy	03/07/03	5 11.0	11 3	Mid	East Fife Form D Under 16
Gilbert	Gordon		10/12/82	Witbank	30/03/02	6 1.0	13 5	Mid	Bo'ness United Juniors
Graham	Marc	John	15/07/77	Kirkcaldy	08/08/03	6 3.0	13 8	Gk	Cowdenbeath
Hall	Michael		11/12/74	Edinburgh	16/05/02	6 2.0	12 6	Def	East Stirlingshire
Hodge	Robert		31/03/87	Kirkcaldy	03/07/03	5 9.0	10 5	Mid	Thornton Y.F.C. U' 15's
Kelly	Patrick		26/04/78	Kirkcaldy	01/08/03	6 1.0	12 0	Def	Partick Thistle
Linton	Samuel	Peter	10/05/86	Kirkcaldy	29/07/03	6 2.0	12 0	Def	Hibernian
Love	Gordon		17/03/83	Coatbridge	31/07/02	5 9.0	11 0	Mid	Nottingham Forest
Lumsden	Craig	McDonald	26/04/84	Kirkcaldy	11/07/02	6 1.0	11 4	Def	Dunfermline Athletic
Lynes	Craig		07/02/81	Edinburgh	03/07/03	6 4.0	12 0	Mid	Dumbarton
McDonald	Greig	James	12/05/82	Dunfermline	06/03/03	6 1.0	12 0	Def	Dunfermline Athletic
McDonald	Ian		07/03/78	N'castle U Tyne	03/07/03	6 1.0	13 10	Def	Cowdenbeath
McKay	Grant	John	24/05/86	Kirkcaldy	07/07/03	5 10.0	11 8	Def	Dunfermline Athletic
McKeown	Kevin		12/10/67	Glasgow	03/07/03	6 1.0	14 0	Gk	Linlithgow Rose Juniors
McLaughlin	William	Scott	16/08/86	Kirkcaldy	03/07/03	6 0.0	11 5	Mid	Kinghorn Royals
McMillan	Craig		04/12/81	Dunfermline	16/05/02	6 0.0	12 0	Mid	Cowdenbeath
Miller	Christopher	Thomas	19/11/82	Paisley	31/01/03	5 8.0	12 0	Def	Inverness Cal. Thistle
Mitchell	Jonathan	Andrew	22/06/81	Dundee	03/07/03	5 10.0	11 0	Mid	Tayport Juniors
Morris	Craig		26/02/85	Kirkcaldy	03/07/03	6 1.0	9 12	Def	Benarty Youths
Morrison	Shaun		03/04/86	Kirkcaldy	03/07/03	5 8.0	11 4	Fwd	Blue Brazil B.C. U' 16's
Mortimer	Paul		14/02/80	Falkirk	03/08/00	6 2.0	12 5	Mid	Stirling Albion
O'Connor	Gary		07/04/74	Newtongrange	03/07/03	6 3.0	14 0	Gk	Cowdenbeath
Ogilvie	Fraser	MacLeod	12/04/84	Edinburgh	27/07/03	5 11.0	11 0	Fwd	Hibernian
Russell	Gordon	Alan	03/03/68	Falkirk	03/07/03	5 10.0	11 7	Def	East Stirlingshire
Stewart	William	Paul	16/04/77	Glasgow	03/07/03	5 10.0	12 0	Fwd	Forfar Athletic

milestones

YEAR OF FORMATION: 1903
MOST CAPPED PLAYER: George Aitken
NO. OF CAPS: 5
MOST LEAGUE POINTS IN A SEASON: 57 (Division 2 – Season 1929/30)(2 Points for a Win)
71 (Third Division – Season 2002/03)(3 Points for a Win)
MOST LEAGUE GOALS SCORED BY A PLAYER IN A SEASON: Henry Morris (Season 1947/48)
NO. OF GOALS SCORED: 41
RECORD ATTENDANCE: 22,515 (-v- Raith Rovers – 2.1.1950 at Bayview Park – old Stadium)
1,996 (-v- Queen's Park – 10.5.2003 at Bayview Stadium – new Stadium)
RECORD VICTORY: 13-2 (-v- Edinburgh City – Division 2, 11.12.1937)
RECORD DEFEAT: 0-9 (-v- Heart of Midlothian – Division 1, 5.10.1957)

ticket information

SEASON TICKET PRICES

SEATED	ADULT	£162
	JUVENILE/OAP	£81
	PARENT & JUVENILE	£200

LEAGUE ADMISSION PRICES

SEATED	ADULT	£10
	JUVENILE/OAP	£5

leading goalscorers 1993-2003

Season	Div	No. of Goals	Player
1993-94	S	10	R. Scott
1994-95	S	14	R. Scott
1995-96	S	11	R. Scott
1996-97	F	4	M. Dyer, P. Ronald
1997-98	S	11	M. Dyer
1998-99	S	13	B. Moffat
1999-00	T	11	B. Moffat
2000-01	T	8	S. Kerrigan
2001-02	T	11	P. McManus
2002-03	T	20	K. Deuchar

Date	Venue	Opponents	Att.	Res	Butter J.	Allison J.	Ovenstone J.	Farnan C.	Hall M.	Graham J. R.	Russell G.	Mortimer P.	McMillan C.	Deuchar K.	Donaldson E.	Gilbert G.	Cunningham G.	Nairn J.	Love G.	Kerr B.	Herkes J.	Walker D.	Lumsden C.	Rollo A.	McLean B.	Miller C.	McDonald G.
Aug 3	A	Peterhead	510	2-0	1	2	3	4	5	6[2]	7	8	9	10	11	15	12	14									
10	H	East Stirlingshire	494	4-1	1	2	3[2]	8	5	9	4	6	12	16	11	10[1]			7[1]	15							
17	A	Queen's Park	537	0-0	1	2	3	4	5	9	6	8	12	14	11	10	15		7								
24	H	Montrose	578	2-0	1	2	5		3	9	4	6	12	10[2]	8	11		15	7		16						
31	A	Albion Rovers	451	5-1	1		3	4	5		7	6		10	2[1]	11[1]		8[1]	14[1]		9[1]	16					
Sep 14	A	Elgin City	599	1-1	1	15		4	5	8	2	6		10	3	9[1]		7	14		11						
21	H	Stirling Albion	588	1-1	1		3	2	5	9	4	6		8[1]	11	16			10		7						
28	A	Morton	1,821	1-2	1	14		8	5	9[1]	4	6	2	10	11	3			12		7						
Oct 5	H	Gretna	462	3-2	1	6	16	8	5	10[3]	4		12	9	3	11	15		7				2				
19	A	East Stirlingshire	315	4-1	1			4	5[1]		2	6	7	9[2]	3	11[1]	8		16		10	14		15			
26	H	Peterhead	847	3-3	1	8[1]	14	6	5	9	2	4	3		11	10[1]		12	16		7[1]						
Nov 2	H	Albion Rovers	575	0-4	1	10	11	8	5		6	4	2		3		15		7		9	16					
9	A	Montrose	373	5-0	1	8		6[1]	5	9	2	4	12	10[1]	3		11[1]	14	15		7[2]						
16	H	Elgin City	525	4-0	1	8	14		5		2	4		9[2]	3		11	6	7		10[2]						
23	A	Stirling Albion	808	0-0	1	8	3	14	5		2	4		9		16	11	6	7		10						
30	A	Gretna	352	3-2	1	8	3[1]	6	5	16	2	4[1]		9[1]		11		15	7		10						
Dec 14	H	Morton	1,005	1-4	1	8	3	6	5	10	2	4		9[1]		11			16		7						
21	A	Peterhead	717	2-2	1	8		6	3[1]	16	4	5	11	9[1]	2	10			15		7						
28	H	Queen's Park	808	1-1	1	8		10	5	16	4	6	11	9[1]	3	14			2		7		12				
Jan 1	H	Montrose	519	2-0	1	6		14	5	8	3	4	7[1]	9[1]	2	11	15		16		10						
18	A	Elgin City	435	1-0	1	8		14	5	6	2	4	11[1]	9	3	15			7		10				16		
25	A	Albion Rovers	475	0-0	1	6			5	8	2	4	7	9	3	15	11		16		10						
Feb 8	A	Morton	2,953	1-1	1	7			6	11	4	5	2	9	3	16					10			12	14[1]	8	
11	H	Stirling Albion	602	2-1	1	6		12	5	9[1]	2		10		11	16					7[1]		4	8	15	3	
22	H	East Stirlingshire	525	3-0	1	6		12[1]	5	10[1]	4		7	9	11[1]	15							2	8	14	3	
Mar 1	A	Queen's Park	697	2-1	1			6	5	10[1]	2		11	9	3	16					7		4		15	8[1]	
4	H	Gretna	503	2-1	1			6	5[1]	8	4		7	9[1]	11	16					10		2		15	3	
8	A	Montrose	455	2-0	1			4	5	8	2		7	9	3[1]				12		11[1]			15	10	6	
15	H	Albion Rovers	780	1-1	1			6	5	8	2	4		9	11	15			14[1]		10				7	3	
22	A	Stirling Albion	866	2-1	1	12		6[1]	5	8	2	4	7	9	11				15		10				14[1]	3	
Apr 5	H	Elgin City	514	5-0	1	8		6	5		2	4	11	9[4]		16			15		10			14	7[1]	3	
12	A	Gretna	409	3-3	1	8		6	5	10[2]	2	4	11			16			15		7[1]				9	3	
19	H	Morton	1,991	0-1	1	12		6	5	8	2	4		9	11	16			15		7				10	3	
26	H	Peterhead	1,071	0-2	1			6	5	8	2	4		9	11	16			15		7				10	3	
May 3	A	East Stirlingshire	511	4-0	1	8		6[1]	5[1]		2	4		9[1]	15	11			16		10[1]				7	3	14
10	H	Queen's Park	1,996	1-0	1			6	5	8	2	4	12	9[1]	15	11			16		10				7	3	
TOTAL FULL APPEARANCES					36	23	10	27	36	26	36	30	19	30	29	15	5	4	11		30		5	2	8	14	
TOTAL SUB APPEARANCES						4	3	5		3			6	2	2	16	5	5	19	1	1	3	1	4	7		1
TOTAL GOALS SCORED						1	3	4	4	11		1	2	20	3	5	1	1	3		10				3	1	

Small bold figures denote goalscorers. † denotes opponent's own goal.

bayview park stadium

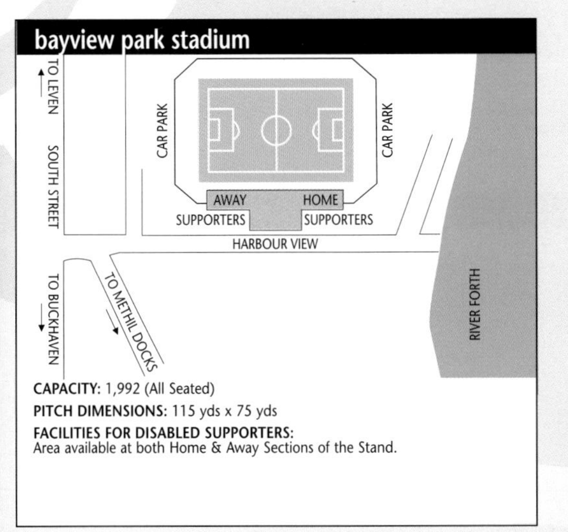

CAPACITY: 1,992 (All Seated)

PITCH DIMENSIONS: 115 yds x 75 yds

FACILITIES FOR DISABLED SUPPORTERS:
Area available at both Home & Away Sections of the Stand.

team playing kits

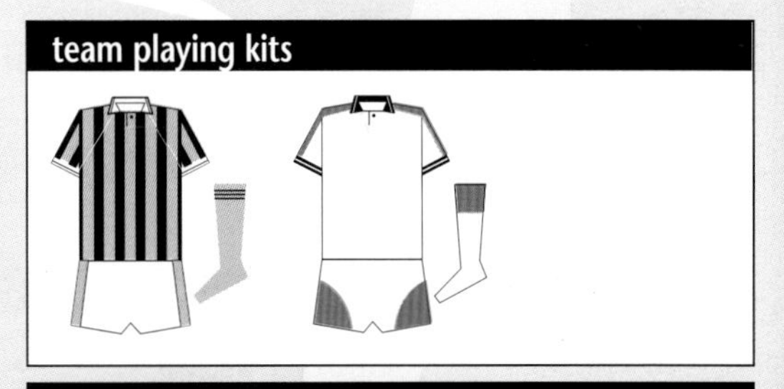

how to get there

Bayview Park can be reached by the following routes:

TRAINS: The nearest railway station is Kirkcaldy (8 miles away), and fans will have to catch an inter-linking bus service from just outside the station to the ground.

BUSES: A regular service from Kirkcaldy to Leven passes close to the ground, as does the Leven to Dunfermline service. The Leven bus terminus is approximately $^{2}/_{3}$ mile from the ground (5 minutes walk).

CARS: There are Car Parking facilities available for both Home and Away fans at the ground.

email: info@scottishfootballleague.com • website: www.scottishfootballleague.com

forfar athletic

Station Park, Carseview Road, Forfar, DD8 3BT

CHAIRMAN
David McGregor

VICE-CHAIRMAN
Neill McK. Wilson

DIRECTORS
Alastair S. Nicoll, Michael S. McEwan, Gordon Menmuir (Treasurer) & Ronald Blair

HONORARY PATRON
Rt. Hon. Lord Lyell of Kinnordy

SECRETARY
David McGregor

COMPANY SECRETARIES
McLean & Lowson

MANAGER
Raymond Stewart

FIRST TEAM COACH
Ian Miller

GOALKEEPING COACH
George Browning

YOUTH CO-ORDINATOR
Peter Castle

YOUTH TEAM COACHES
Peter Castle & Derek Mitchell (U19)

CLUB DOCTORS
Dr. Peter Dick & Dr. Susan Woodruffe

PHYSIOTHERAPIST
Brian McNeill

ASSISTANT PHYSIOTHERAPIST
Donald Ritchie

GROUNDSMAN/KIT SUPERVISOR
Martin Gray

MEDIA LIAISON OFFICER
David McGregor
Tel: Home (01307) 464924
Tel: Bus (01307) 475519

MATCHDAY PROGRAMME EDITOR
Alan Ducat (01307) 464899

TELEPHONES
Ground (01307) 463576/462259
Sec. Home (01307) 464924
Sec. Bus. (01307) 475519
Sec. Bus. Fax (01307) 466956

E-MAIL & INTERNET ADDRESS
pat@ramsayladders.co.uk
www.forfarathletic.co.uk

OFFICIAL SUPPORTERS CLUB
c/o Mrs. Yvonne Nicoll,
7 Fyfe Jamieson, Forfar
Tel: Home (01307) 467255

TEAM CAPTAIN
Alan Rattray

SHIRT SPONSOR
Universal Telecom

KIT SUPPLIER
Paulas Benara

LIST OF PLAYERS 2003/04

SURNAME	FIRST NAME	MIDDLE NAME	DATE OF BIRTH	PLACE OF BIRTH	DATE OF SIGNING	HEIGHT FT INS	WEIGHT ST LBS	POS. ON PITCH	PREVIOUS CLUB
Bannon	Mark	Steven	22/08/83	Dundee	30/08/02	5 11.0	11 0	Def	Broughty Ferry
Berry	Philip	Andrew	25/09/85	Dundee	23/07/03	6 0.0	11 2	Fwd	Forfar Athletic Form D U16
Bremner	Kit		07/06/84	High Wycombe	06/08/03	5 11.0	11 0	Fwd	Broughty Athletic Juniors
Brown	Michael		07/11/79	Stranraer	06/06/01	6 1.0	12 8	Gk	Partick Thistle
Bruce	Ryan	John	07/11/85	Dundee	26/08/03	6 0.0	12 1	Def	Forfar Athletic Form D U16
Byers	Kevin		23/08/79	Kirkcaldy	31/07/01	5 10.0	10 10	Mid	Inverness Cal Th
Cathro	Ian	Francis	11/07/86	Dundee	23/08/03	5 8.0	10 5	Mid	Carnoustie Panmure U16s
Davidson	Hugh	Norman	03/08/80	Dundee	06/06/03	5 11.5	12 6	Mid	Dundee United
Dow	Lewis	Roy	04/01/85	Dundee	26/08/03	5 11.0	11 9	Mid	Arbroath Sporting Club
Duncan	George		26/08/83	Dundee	30/08/02	5 11.0	10 8	Def/Mid	Downfield Juniors
Farquhar	John		22/12/86	Dundee	29/07/03	5 10.0	10 5	Def	Maryfield B.C.
Ferrie	James		23/09/83	Dundee	26/08/02	5 8.0	10 0	Def	Dundee Violet Juniors
Ferrie	Neal		23/11/81	Dundee	07/06/00	6 0.0	11 4	Gk	Dundee United
Florence	Steven		28/10/71	Dundee	18/07/03	5 6.0	11 0	Def	Arbroath
Gibb	Liam	Robert	07/03/85	Dundee	23/08/03	5 8.0	10 7	Fwd	Brechin City Form S
Henderson	Darren	Ronald	12/10/66	Kilmarnock	12/06/02	5 11.0	12 7	Mid	Raith Rovers
Hodge	Colin	Bateman	24/12/84	Kirkcaldy	26/01/01	6 0.0	10 10	Fwd	Forfar Athletic Form S
Horn	Robert	David	03/08/77	Edinburgh	28/06/00	5 9.0	11 0	Def	Heart of Midlothian
Lowing	David		04/09/83	Paisley	02/07/03	6 0.0	10 0	Def	St. Mirren
Luke	David	Andrew	15/01/85	N'castle U Tyne	23/07/03	5 11.0	13 7	Gk	Dundee United Social Club
Lunan	Paul	James	20/09/82	Dundee	04/08/01	5 10.0	10 0	Mid	Dundee Violet Juniors
Maher	Martin	Neil	05/11/83	Perth	04/06/03	5 10.5	11 6	Mid	St. Johnstone
Mann	Paul		23/04/85	Dundee	26/08/03	5 8.0	9 0	Mid	Dundee Celtic B.C.
McClune	David	James	08/02/83	Glasgow	03/07/03	5 7.0	10 0	Def	St. Johnstone
McKenzie	Daryl		24/06/85	Dundee	29/07/03	6 0.0	11 0	Def	Forfar Athletic Form D
Melville	Kevin	Richard	28/01/85	Dundee	26/08/03	5 10.0	9 12	Def	Forfar B.C.
Menzies	Ryan	Kenneth	07/05/85	Perth	29/07/03	5 11.0	10 2	Mid	F.C. Guildtown
Ogunmade	Daniel		26/08/83	Glasgow	29/08/03	5 10.0	11 0	Fwd	Dundee United
Rattray	Alan	Raymond	08/06/79	Dundee	16/11/96	5 10.0	11 0	Def	Dundee Violet Juniors
Scott	Darren	Kevin	20/01/85	Dundee	23/08/03	6 1.0	9 9	Fwd	Forfar Athletic Form D U16
Sellars	Barry	Michael	06/12/75	Arbroath	02/11/00	6 1.0	12 10	Mid	Clyde
Shields	Paul	Martin	15/08/81	Dunfermline	24/07/03	6 0.0	12 0	Fwd	Clyde
Stark	Bruce		01/03/85	Dundee	29/07/03	6 0.0	13 5	Mid	Dundee United B.C.
Stewart	David		14/08/78	Irvine	02/07/03	6 1.0	12 0	Def	Dumbarton
Taylor	Scott	Andrew	23/01/77	Forfar	31/01/03	5 9.0	11 0	Fwd	Forfar West End Juniors
Tosh	Paul	James	18/10/73	Arbroath	28/06/01	6 1.0	13 4	Fwd	Raith Rovers
Vella	Simon		19/09/79	London	03/07/03	6 2.0	13 0	Def	Airdrie United
Watson	Allan	Lindsay	20/04/85	Forfar	23/08/03	5 8.0	9 8	Fwd	Forfar Athletic Form D U16
Williams	David		29/09/81	Glasgow	03/07/01	5 10.0	11 0	Fwd	Kilmarnock

milestones

YEAR OF FORMATION: 1885
MOST LEAGUE POINTS IN A SEASON: 63 (Second Division – Season 1983/84) (2 Points for a Win)
80 (Third Division – Season 1994/95) (3 Points for a Win)
MOST LEAGUE GOALS SCORED BY A PLAYER IN A SEASON: Dave Kilgour (Season 1929/30)
NO. OF GOALS SCORED: 45
RECORD ATTENDANCE: 10,800 (-v- Rangers – 7.2.1970)
RECORD VICTORY: 14-1 (-v- Lindertis – Scottish Cup, 1.9.1888)
RECORD DEFEAT: 2-12 (-v- King's Park – Division 2, 2.1.1930)

ticket information

	SEASON TICKET PRICES	
SEATED	ADULT	£130
	JUVENILE/OAP	£65
	JUVENILE (U-12)	£40
STANDING	ADULT	£120
	JUVENILE/OAP	£60
	JUVENILE (U-12)	£40
	LEAGUE ADMISSION PRICES	
SEATED	ADULT	£9.50
	JUVENILE/OAP	£4.50
STANDING	ADULT	£9
	JUVENILE/OAP	£4.50

leading goalscorers 1993-2003

Season	Div	No. of Goals	Player
1993-94	S	13	D. Bingham
1994-95	T	22	D. Bingham
1995-96	S	12	G. Higgins
1996-97	T	17	B. Honeyman
1997-98	S	14	M. McLauchlan
1998-99	S	10	R. Brand
1999-00	T	16	S. Milne
2000-01	S	9	W. Stewart
2001-02	S	19	P. Tosh
2002-03	S	15	M. Bavidge

S·F·L ©

the loons' club factfile 2002/03

Date	Venue	Opponents	Att.	Res	Brown M.	Rattray A.	McCulloch S.	McCloy B.	Good I.	Byers K.	Shaw G.	Sellars B.	Tosh P.	Bavidge M.	Henderson D.	Milne K.	Stewart W.	Lunan P.	Horn R.	Anthony M.	Williams D.	Ferrie N.	Greacen S.	Hodge C.	Cocozza M.	Taylor S.	Bannon M.
Aug 3	A	Airdrie United	2,285	0-1	1	2	3	4	5	6	7	8	9	10	11	16	14										
10	H	Stenhousemuir	492	1-0	1	2	15	4	5	6	7	3^1	9	10	11		14	8									
17	A	Cowdenbeath	347	1-1	1	2	3	4	5	8	7	6	9	10	11^1		14	15									
24	A	Brechin City	761	0-1	1		3		5	2		8	9	10	11		14	6	4	7							
31	H	Hamilton Academical	486	1-1	1		3		5	8		2	9	10^1	11	14		6	4	7							
Sep 14	A	Dumbarton	827	2-1	1	2	3		5	7^1	12		9	10^1	11	15	14	6	4	8							
21	H	Berwick Rangers	483	0-2	1	2	15	4	5	8	7		9	10	3	14	11	6		12							
28	A	Stranraer	385	0-2	1		3		5	6	7		9	10	11		2	12	4	8							
Oct 5	H	Raith Rovers	1,054	1-2	1		3	15	5	7^1	12	6	9	10		11	2	14	4	8							
19	A	Stenhousemuir	295	1-2	1	2	3		5	7^1		8		10		11	9	6	4	12	15						
26	H	Airdrie United	666	5-1	1	2	3		5	7		8^1	9^2	10^1		11	12	6^1	4	14							
Nov 2	A	Hamilton Academical	960	2-1	1	2	3		5	7		8^1	9^1	10	12	11		6	4								
9	H	Brechin City	868	2-1	1	2	3		5	7		8	9	10^2		11		6	4								
16	H	Dumbarton	556	2-0	1	2	3		5	7		8	9	10^2		11	14	6	4								
23	A	Berwick Rangers	387	1-2	1	2	3		5	7		8	9^1	10		11		6	4	15		18					
30	A	Raith Rovers	1,779	1-5		2	3		5	7^1		8	9	10		11	14	6	4	15		1					
Dec 28	H	Cowdenbeath	596	2-1		2	3		5	6^2		8	9	10		11	7	12	4	16		1					
Jan 1	A	Brechin City	743	4-3		2	3		5	7		8^1	9^2	10^1	16		12	6	4	11		1					
18	A	Dumbarton	867	2-1		2^1	3		5	8^1			9	10	11	14	7	6	4	12		1					
Feb 8	A	Stranraer	362	2-3		2	3		5	8^1	9			10	11	7^1		6		12	14	1	4				
22	H	Stenhousemuir	449	3-3	1	2	5	15		6	14	8	9^3	10	11	3		7		12			4	16			
25	A	Airdrie United	921	0-0	1	2	3	4		6		7	9	10	11					8	12		5				
Mar 1	A	Cowdenbeath	323	2-2	1	2	3	4		6	14	7	9^1	10						8	11		5	12^1			
4	H	Berwick Rangers	420	2-2	1		3	4		6		7	9	10^1			12			8	11^1		5	16	2		
8	H	Brechin City	774	1-5	1	2		4		6	14	7	9^1	10			11	8					5	15	3		
11	H	Raith Rovers	688	4-2	1	2	3	4		6		7	9	10^2			15^1	8		11^1			5				
15	A	Hamilton Academical	934	0-2	1		3	4		6		7	9	10	2	12	14	8		11			5	15			
22	A	Berwick Rangers	389	0-0	1	2	3	4		6		7		10	14	12	15	8		11			5			9	
25	H	Hamilton Academical	453	0-1	1	2	3	4	6	8			9	10	11		15	7		12			5				
30	H	Stranraer	394	†2-1	1	2	3		6	8		4	9^1	10	11		14	7			15		5			16	
Apr 5	H	Dumbarton	485	0-1	1		3		5	8		2	9	10	11		7	6		16	14		4			15	
12	A	Raith Rovers	2,036	1-0	1		3		5	6		2		9^1	10		7	8		15	11		4			12	
19	H	Stranraer	391	4-0	1	5	3^1			6		2^1		9^1	10		7	8		14	11		4^1			12	16
26	H	Airdrie United	884	1-1	1	5	3		12	6		2	7	9^1	10		16	8			11		4				
May 3	A	Stenhousemuir	497	4-1	1	5	3			6^1	14	2^1	7	9^1	10		15^1	8		12			4			11	
10	H	Cowdenbeath	465	1-1	1	5	3			6	12		9^1	10	8		14	2		7			4	15		11	
TOTAL FULL APPEARANCES					**31**	**28**	**33**	**12**	**24**	**36**	**6**	**29**	**31**	**36**	**21**	**11**	**10**	**28**	**15**	**13**	**5**	**5**	**17**		**2**	**3**	
TOTAL SUB APPEARANCES							**2**	**2**	**1**		**7**				**3**	**7**	**18**	**4**		**14**	**5**	**1**		**6**		**4**	**1**
TOTAL GOALS SCORED						**1**	**1**			**9**		**6**	**13**	**15**	**1**	**1**	**2**	**1**		**1**	**1**		**1**	**1**			

Small bold figures denote goalscorers. † denotes opponent's own goal.

second division

station park

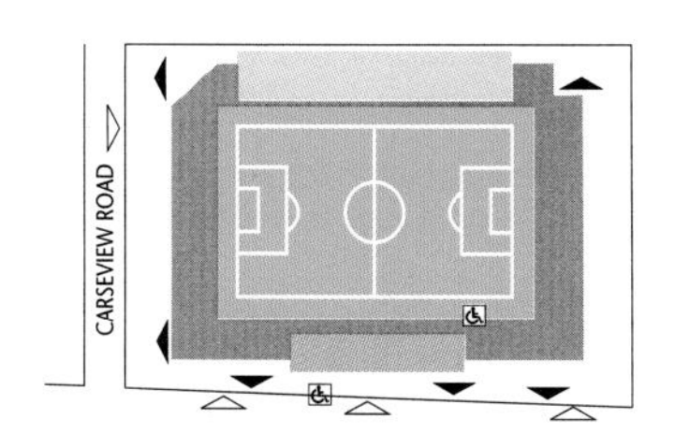

CAPACITY: 4,640; Seated 739, Standing 3,901

PITCH DIMENSIONS: 115 yds x 69 yds

FACILITIES FOR DISABLED SUPPORTERS:
Ramp entrance via Main Stand.

team playing kits

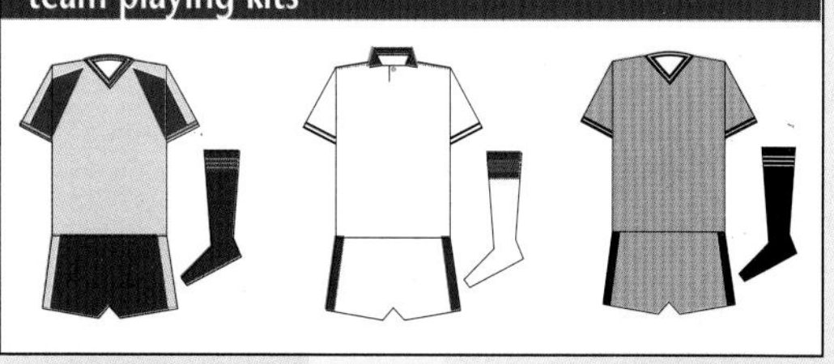

how to get there

Station Park can be reached by the following routes:

BUSES: There is a regular service of buses departing from Dundee City Centre into Forfar. The bus station in the town is about half a mile from the ground. There is also a local service.

TRAINS: The nearest railway station is Dundee (14 miles away) and fans who travel to here should then board a bus for Forfar from the city centre. Arbroath station is also about 14 miles away.

CARS: There are car parking facilities in adjacent streets to the ground and also in the Market Muir car park.

hamilton academical

New Douglas Park, Cadzow Avenue, Hamilton, ML3 0FT

CHAIRMAN
Ronnie MacDonald

DIRECTORS
George W. Fairley, Kenneth Blake, Brian Cairney, Denis Gowans, Leslie Gray & Arthur Lynch

HON. PRESIDENTS
Dr. Alexander A. Wilson & Dr. Jan W. Stepek

CHIEF EXECUTIVE
George W. Fairley

SECRETARY & YOUTH CO-ORDINATOR
Scott A. Struthers, B.A.(Hons)

MANAGER
Allan Maitland

ASSISTANT MANAGERS
Dennis McDaid & Jimmy McQuade

RESERVE COACHES
James Ward & John Bean

DIRECTOR OF YOUTH DEVELOPMENT
Leslie Gray

YOUTH DEVELOPMENT COACH
John Bean

YOUTH TEAM COACHES
James Ward (U19)
Gerry McGregor & Robert McMillan (U17)
John Joyce (U16 & U15)
David Stewart (U14)
Steve Harvey & Les Gray (U13)

COMMERCIAL MANAGER
Arthur Lynch (01698) 368652

STADIUM MANAGER
Denis Gowans (01698) 368657

CLUB DOCTOR
Dr. Sandy Wilson

PHYSIOTHERAPIST
Michael Valentine

FOOTBALL SAFETY OFFICERS' ASSOCIATION REPRESENTATIVES
Scott A. Struthers & Denis Gowans
Tel (01698) 368650

MEDIA LIAISON OFFICER & MATCHDAY PROGRAMME EDITOR
Scott A. Struthers, B.A. (Hons)
(01698) 368655

GROUNDSMAN
Willie Roberts

KIT CONTROLLER
Jim Kennedy

TELEPHONES
Ground (01698) 368650
Sec Bus. (01698) 368655
(Fax-Office) (01698) 285422

CLUB SHOP
"The Acciesshop",
Hamilton Academical F.C.,
New Douglas Park, Cadzow Avenue,
Hamilton, ML3 0FT

OFFICIAL SUPPORTERS CLUB
Jim Galloway, Secretary, HAFC Supporters Club, 3 Pitcairn Terrace, Burnbank, Hamilton

TEAM CAPTAIN
Steven W. Thomson

SHIRT SPONSOR
First Choice - Cullen Packaging
Second Choice - Hawkhead Carpets

KIT SUPPLIER
TFG

LIST OF PLAYERS 2003/04

SURNAME	FIRST NAME	MIDDLE NAME	DATE OF BIRTH	PLACE OF BIRTH	DATE OF SIGNING	HEIGHT FT INS	WEIGHT ST LBS	POS. ON PITCH	PREVIOUS CLUB
Aitken	Christopher	Ian	31/03/81	Glasgow	30/06/03	5 9.0	11 6	Mid	Neilston Juniors
Anderson	Derek		12/02/87	Bellshill	02/08/03	6 1.0	10 12	Fwd	Clyde
Arbuckle	Andrew	Paul	06/02/85	Munster	31/07/03	5 9.0	11 0	Def	Hamilton Acad. Form D U16
Bailey	John		02/07/84	Manchester	29/08/03	5 5.5	10 6	Mid	Preston North End
Buckley	Sean	Patrick	07/07/87	Vale of Leven	25/08/03	5 10.0	10 2	Fwd	Celtic
Carrigan	Brian	Eric	26/09/79	Glasgow	30/06/03	5 8.0	11 5	Fwd	Raith Rovers
Convery	Steven		27/10/72	Glasgow	30/06/03	5 11.0	12 1	Fwd	Clyde
Corcoran	Mark	Christian	30/11/80	Perth	03/07/03	5 10.0	11 3	Fwd	Linlithgow Rose Juniors
Donnelly	Ciaran	Anthony	30/04/86	East Kilbride	31/07/03	5 11.0	12 4	Mid	Hamilton Acad. Form D U16
Ferguson	Derek		31/07/67	Glasgow	03/07/03	5 8.5	11 12	Mid	Alloa Athletic
Fitter	John	Anthony	01/10/84	Birmingham	22/07/03	5 10.0	11 10	Def	Wolverhampton Wanderers
Forbes	Barry		08/09/81	Dundee	01/08/03	5 10.5	11 2	Mid	Dundee
Glackin	Ronald		06/04/87	Glasgow	23/08/03	5 9.5	11 11	Fwd	Clyde Form D Under 15
Gourlay	Mark		27/01/85	Glasgow	31/08/03	5 7.5	10 12	Def	Clyde
Gribben	Darren		27/03/86	Bellshill	28/01/03	5 11.0	10 3	Fwd	Hamilton Acad. Form D U16
Hodge	Sandy	George	04/10/80	Lanark	22/08/03	6 3.0	13 5	Mid	Queen of the South
Houston	Scott	John	04/05/85	Irvine	31/08/03	5 8.0	12 7	Def	Troon Juniors
Jellema	Raymond	James	27/09/85	Irvine	31/07/03	5 11.0	11 10	Gk	Prestayr B.C.
Lawley	James		23/10/87	Lanark	23/08/03	5 9.0	9 8	Mid	Hamilton Acad. Form D
Lumsden	Todd		06/02/78	Consett	30/06/03	6 2.0	12 5	Def	Albion Rovers
Lynch	David	Hugh	18/05/87	Glasgow	23/08/03	5 8.0	9 13	Def	Clyde Form S
Maxwell	Daniel	Ryan	14/06/83	Larne	28/07/03	5 9.0	10 7	Mid	Reading
McArthur	James		07/10/87	Glasgow	23/08/03	5 6.0	10 0	Fwd	Clyde Form D Under 15
McEwan	David		26/02/82	Lanark	30/07/03	6 0.0	12 7	Gk	Livingston
McGeachie	Ross		10/06/85	Lanark	31/07/03	6 0.0	11 4	Fwd	Hamilton Acad. Form D U16
McGeoghegan	Jamie		20/01/87	Glasgow	25/08/03	5 11.5	9 6	Fwd	Celtic
McGiff	Martin		10/09/86	Bellshill	31/07/03	5 7.5	10 0	Mid	Hamilton Acad. Form D U16
McGregor	Ryan	James	04/10/87	Glasgow	23/08/03	5 7.0	10 0	Mid	Clyde Form D Under 15
McLenaghan	Gary	Alexander	25/05/87	Bellshill	23/08/03	6 2.0	11 4	Gk	East Stirlingshire
McLeod	Paul		22/05/87	Bellshill	27/08/03	5 10.0	10 10	Fwd	Dundee United
McPhee	Brian		23/10/70	Glasgow	23/11/01	5 10.0	11 10	Fwd	Livingston
Murphy	Craig	Matthew	19/12/86	Glasgow	31/07/03	5 3.5	9 0	Def	Clyde Form D Under 16
Neil	Anthony		02/06/87	Glasgow	23/08/03	5 8.5	10 12	Mid	Clyde Form D Under 15
Nicoll	Kevin		16/06/86	Glasgow	02/08/03	6 1.5	11 0	Def	Clyde Form D Under 16
Orr	Ricky	Alexander	20/06/86	Bellshill	31/07/03	5 9.0	10 6	Mid	Hamilton Acad. Form D
Paterson	Nicholas	Stephen	19/01/85	Lanark	31/07/03	5 10.0	10 3	Mid	Motherwell Form D
Porte	Richard		02/03/87	Motherwell	23/08/03	5 11.0	9 4	Mid	Clyde Form D Under 15
Sherry	James	Cunningham	09/09/73	Glasgow	15/12/00	5 8.0	12 6	Mid	Portadown
Sim	Andrew		04/02/87	Lanark	23/08/03	5 4.0	8 0	Fwd	Hamilton Acad. Form D U16
Stewart	Iain		10/08/87	Bellshill	23/08/03	5 6.0	8 4	Fwd	Clyde Form D Under 15
Thomson	Steven	John	31/08/85	Bellshill	31/08/03	6 1.0	12 4	Def	Lanark United Juniors
Thomson	Steven	William	19/04/73	Glasgow	30/06/03	6 2.0	12 7	Def	Alloa Athletic
Tough	Graham	Robert	22/10/87	Bellshill	23/08/03	6 0.5	11 7	Def	Clyde Form D Under 15
Waddell	Alan		25/01/79	Glasgow	30/06/03	5 10.0	11 7	Fwd	Neilston Juniors
Walker	John		12/12/73	Glasgow	08/06/01	5 7.0	10 6	Mid	Clydebank
Walker	Robert		16/06/82	Glasgow	31/08/03	6 0.0	13 0	Def	Maryhill Juniors
Whiteford	Andrew		22/08/77	Bellshill	30/06/03	5 11.0	12 5	Def	Neilston Juniors
Wilson	James		04/05/87	Glasgow	07/08/03	5 9.0	10 0	Def	Clyde Form D Under 15

milestones

YEAR OF FORMATION: 1874
MOST CAPPED PLAYER: Colin Miller (Canada)
NO. OF CAPS: 29
MOST LEAGUE POINTS IN A SEASON: 57 (First Division – Season 1991/92) (2 Points for a Win)
76 (Third Division – Season 2000/01) (3 Points for a Win)
MOST LEAGUE GOALS SCORED BY A PLAYER IN A SEASON: David Wilson (Season 1936/37)
NO. OF GOALS SCORED: 35
RECORD ATTENDANCE: 28,690 (-v- Hearts – Scottish Cup 3.3.1937 at Douglas Park)
4,280 (-v- Sunderland – Opening of The Ballast Stadium 28.7.2001)
RECORD VICTORY: 10-2 (-v- Cowdenbeath – Division 1, 15.10.1932)
RECORD DEFEAT: 1-11 (-v- Hibernian – Division 1, 6.11.1965)

ticket information

SEASON TICKET PRICES

SEATED	ADULT	£150
	YOUTH/OAP	£75
	JUVENILE (U-14)	£40
	ADULT & JUVENILE (U-14)	£160

LEAGUE ADMISSION PRICES

WEST (MAIN) STAND

SEATED	ADULT	£10
	JUVENILE (U-16)/OAP	£5

NORTH STAND

SEATED	ADULT	£10
	JUVENILE (U-16)/OAP	£5

leading goalscorers 1993-2003

Season	Div	No. of Goals	Player
1993-94	F	19	P. Duffield
1994-95	F	20	P. Duffield
1995-96	F	11	P. Hartley
1996-97	S	31	P. Ritchie
1997-98	F	7	P. Ritchie
1998-99	F	11	G. Wales
1999-00	S	6	D. Henderson
			N. Henderson
2000-01	T	24	D. McFarlane
2001-02	S	12	M. Moore
2002-03	S	11	B. McPhee

the accies' club factfile 2002/03

Date	Venue	Opponents	Att.	Res	Macfarlane I.	Nelson M.	McDonald P.	Dobbins I.	Sweeney S.	Paterson N.	Bonnar M.	Walker J.	Armstrong G.	Graham Alastair S.	Graham Alisdair	Potter G.	Elfallah M.	McCreadie I.	Davidson S.	Callaghan S.	McPhee B.	Sherry J.	Smillie C.	Hillcoat C.	Keegans M.	Cunnington E.	Russell A.	Arbuckle A.	Thomson S.	Gribben D.	Kerr D.	Flynn P.	McDermott A.
Aug 3	A	Cowdenbeath	427	3-1	1	2	3	4	5	6	7	8	9^1	10^2	11	17	15	12															
10	H	Airdrie United	2,366	1-0	1	2	12	4	5	3	7	8	9^1	10	11		14	6	16														
17	A	Brechin City	498	0-1	1	2	3	4	5	12	7	8	9	10	11	17	15	6															
24	H	Berwick Rangers	1,486	1-2	1	2	15	4	5	3	7	8	9^1	10	6					11	16	14											
31	A	Forfar Athletic	486	1-1				4	5		7	8	9	16	2^1	1				11	10	3	6	15									
Sep 14	A	Stenhousemuir	463	2-1			3	4	5			8	9	7	2	1		16		11	10^2			6	14								
21	H	Raith Rovers	1,961	0-4			3	4	5			8	9	7	2	1	14			11	10	12	15	6									
28	A	Dumbarton	1,202	1-1				4^1	5		7		16	9	2	1	3			11	10	8	6										
Oct 5	H	Stranraer	1,175	1-5			12	4	5		7		9		2^1	1	3	15		11	10	8	6		16								
19	A	Airdrie United	1,593	0-0	1		3	4	5		7	8	9		2		6	12		11	10				15								
26	H	Cowdenbeath	1,052	1-0	1	15	3	4	5		7	8	9		2		6			11	10^1				12	14							
Nov 2	H	Forfar Athletic	960	1-2	1		3	4	5		7	8	9		2		6			11	10^1				15	12	16						
9	A	Berwick Rangers	461	1-2	1	2		4	5		7	14		9	6	17				11^1	10	8				3	15						
16	H	Stenhousemuir	1,226	2-3		2	12	4	5		7		16	9	6	1				11	10^2	8				3	15						
23	A	Raith Rovers	1,897	1-1		2		4	5					9	6	1	15			11	10^1	8			7	3	16						
30	A	Stranraer	397	2-1		2	7	4	5		16			12	6	1	15			11^1		8			10	3	9^1						
Dec 14	H	Dumbarton	1,062	1-0		2		4							6	1	16			11	10	8	5		9	3	7^1						
28	H	Brechin City	1,418	1-2		2		4			7			12	6	1				11	10^1		5		8	3	9	16					
Jan 18	A	Stenhousemuir	581	2-2		2			5		7^1	8		12	6	1	14			11	10					3	9		4	15^1			
Feb 1	H	Raith Rovers	1,292	0-0					5		7	8	2	14	6	1				11	10	16	4				9			15	3		
8	A	Dumbarton	1,108	1-3				4	5		7	8	2^1	14	6	1	16			11							9			10	3		
25	H	Berwick Rangers	626	3-0			3	12	5		7		9	10^2	2	1				11		8					14^1	16			4	6	
Mar 1	A	Brechin City	441	1-4			3	12	5		7		9	10	2	1				11		8					14^1				4	6	
4	A	Cowdenbeath	281	1-0			3		5		7		14^1	10	2	1				11		8					9				4	6	
8	A	Berwick Rangers	406	0-1			3	12	5		7		14	10		1				11		8					9	2			4	6	
11	H	Airdrie United	1,620	2-1			3	5			7		6^2	10	2	1				11	14	8					9				4		
15	H	Forfar Athletic	934	2-0			3	5			7		6^2	10	2	1				11	14	8					9				4	16	
18	H	Stranraer	743	1-2			3	5					6	10^1	2	1				11	7	8		14			9				4	16	
22	A	Raith Rovers	1,762	†1-1			3	5					6		2	1				11	10	8				12	9				4	16	7
25	A	Forfar Athletic	453	1-0			3	5			7		6	10	2	1				11	9^1	8		15		12	14				4		
Apr 5	H	Stenhousemuir	1,247	0-1			3	4			7		11	9	2	1				14	10	8		5		12	15						6
12	A	Stranraer	402	0-0	1		12	4			7				2		6			11	10	8				3	9				5		
19	H	Dumbarton	1,270	2-2	1		8	5^1			7			14	2		6			11^1	10			12	9	3					4		
26	H	Cowdenbeath	1,055	2-0	1		8	5	12		7^1			14	2		6			11	10^1				9	3				15	4		
May 3	A	Airdrie United	1,960	2-2	1			5	12		7				2		15			11	10	8				3	9^2	6			4		
10	H	Brechin City	1,644	2-2	1		7	5	3					14			2			11^1	10^1	8					9	6			4		
TOTAL FULL APPEARANCES					13	11	21	30	24	3	28	13	21	19	34	23	9	2		32	24	21	6	3	6	11	15	3	1	1	16	4	2
TOTAL SUB APPEARANCES						1	5	3	2	1	1	1	4	9		3	10	4	1	1	3	3	1	4	5	5	8	2		3		3	
TOTAL GOALS SCORED								2			2		9	5	2					4	11						6			1			

Small bold figures denote goalscorers. † denotes opponent's own goal.

second division

new douglas park

HAMILTON RACECOURSE
M74 Glasgow
M74 Town Centre & Motherwell
AUCHINRAITH ROAD
NEWPARK STREET
CAIRD STREET
CADZOW AVENUE
Car Parking
North Stand
Main (West) Stand
Car Parking
Path to Station

CAPACITY: 5,404 (All Seated)

PITCH DIMENSIONS: 115 yds x 75 yds

FACILITIES FOR DISABLED SUPPORTERS:
Available trackside and in front row of Main (West) Stand

team playing kits

how to get there

The following routes may be used to reach New Douglas Park:

TRAINS: Hamilton West Station is situated adjacent to the ground. Normally there are 2 trains per hour to Glasgow, Lanark (change at Motherwell) and Motherwell. A path connects the station to the ground.
BUSES: Buses from across Lanarkshire and Glasgow pass close to the ground. Buses from across Scotland and the UK call at Hamilton Bus Station 1mile away.
CARS: Exit M74 at Junction 5 (A725 Coatbridge – East Kilbride Road goes through this interchange as well). Follow signs for Hamilton Racecourse and Football Traffic.Turn right at lights at Racecourse and first right again into New Park Street. Stadium is on the left.

morton

Cappielow Park, Sinclair Street, Greenock, PA15 2TY

CHAIRMAN
Douglas D. F. Rae

DIRECTORS
Iain D. Brown, James McColl, W. Arthur M. Montford & Crawford McL. Rae

CHIEF EXECUTIVE
Gillian Donaldson

COMPANY SECRETARY
Mrs Mary Davidson

MANAGER
John McCormack

YOUTH MANAGER
Stephen Frail

YOUTH COACHES
Chris Norris, Ian McGeachy & Andrew Bowman (U16)

CLUB DOCTORS
Dr. R. Craig Speirs M.B., Ch.B & Dr. Fraser Gray

PHYSIOTHERAPIST
Paul Kelly

CHIEF SCOUT
Jack Jolly

GROUNDSMAN
Campbell Stevenson

STADIUM DIRECTOR
Crawford Rae

FOOTBALL SAFETY OFFICERS' ASSOCIATION REPRESENTATIVE
Peter Copland

KIT PERSON
Andy Bryan

COMMERCIAL MANAGER/ MATCHDAY PROGRAMME EDITOR
Chris Norris

LOTTERY MANAGER
Derek Collins

TELEPHONES
Ground/Ticket Office (01475) 723571
Fax (01475) 781084

E-MAIL & INTERNET ADDRESSES
info@gmfc.net
www.gmfc.net

CLUB SHOP
Morton F.C. Cappielow Park, Sinclair Street, Greenock PA15 2TY.
Opening Hours Mon - Fri 12 noon - 4pm.
Also open on Match days

OFFICIAL SUPPORTERS CLUB
Morton Supporters Club, Regent Street, Greenock

TEAM CAPTAIN
Derek Collins

SHIRT SPONSOR
Millions – The Tiny Tasty Chewy Sweets

KIT SUPPLIER
Vandanel

LIST OF PLAYERS 2003/04

SURNAME	FIRST NAME	MIDDLE NAME	DATE OF BIRTH	PLACE OF BIRTH	DATE OF SIGNING	HEIGHT FT INS	WEIGHT ST LBS	POS. ON PITCH	PREVIOUS CLUB
Adam	John		26/12/84	Falkirk	29/01/03	6 1.0	13 0	Mid	Rangers
Bannerman	Scott	John	21/03/79	Edinburgh	03/08/01	5 7.0	11 0	Def	Airdrieonians
Bottiglieri	Emilio	Hugh	13/04/79	Port Hardy	16/07/02	5 8.0	11 2	Def	East Fife
Cannie	Philip		12/11/77	Greenock	27/03/02	6 0.0	12 0	Fwd	Pollok Juniors
Collins	Derek	Joseph	15/04/69	Glasgow	10/09/01	5 8.0	11 0	Def	Sliema Wanderers
Coyle	Craig	Robert	06/09/80	Edinburgh	03/08/01	5 11.0	12 0	Gk	Raith Rovers
Dale	Graham	James	07/08/85	Paisley	20/01/03	6 2.0	11 12	Def	Rangers
Gaughan	Paul		27/09/80	Glasgow	16/07/02	6 2.0	14 7	Def	Hamilton Academical
Greacen	Stewart		31/03/82	Lanark	20/06/03	6 2.0	14 0	Def	Forfar Athletic
Hawke	Warren	Robert	20/09/70	Durham	23/11/01	5 10.5	11 4	Fwd	Queen of the South
Henderson	Robbie		11/10/82	Bellshill	07/01/03	6 1.0	13 2	Def	Kilmarnock
Keenan	Dean	Matthew	15/10/85	Glasgow	16/08/02	5 11.0	11 0	Mid	Pollok United
MacDonald	Stuart		15/05/81	Glasgow	02/08/02	5 10.0	11 5	Def/Mid	Airdrieonians
MacGregor	David	George	09/06/81	Greenock	03/08/01	5 11.0	11 10	Mid	Morton Form S
Maisano	John	Marcel	06/01/79	Melbourne	12/07/02	5 6.0	10 7	Mid	Marconi Stallions
Maisano	Marco	Miguel	15/02/81	Haedo	06/03/02	5 10.0	12 0	Mid	Marconi Stallions
McAlister	James	Duncan	02/11/85	Rothesay	27/12/02	5 10.0	11 0	Fwd	Linwood Rangers
McGlinchey	Paul		20/03/84	Glasgow	29/08/03	5 7.0	9 7	Mid	Kilmarnock
McGurn	David	Edward	14/09/80	Glasgow	29/11/02	6 1.0	13 3	Gk	Hillwood B.C.
Millar	Christopher	Alexander	30/03/83	Glasgow	18/02/03	5 9.0	10 3	Def	Celtic
Rankin	Neil	Alexander	11/01/86	Glasgow	23/06/03	5 10.0	11 0	Def/Mid	Morton Form D Under 16
Robertson	Lee		29/01/81	Adelaide	17/01/03	6 0.0	11 10	Def	Playford City
Stark	John	Paul	03/06/86	Glasgow	24/06/03	6 2.0	13 0	Gk	Queen's Park
Uotinen	Jani		17/05/78	Finland	25/06/02	5 7.0	10 5	Mid	Kuusankoski
Walker	Paul		20/08/77	Kilwinning	13/06/03	5 7.0	9 7	Forward	Partick Thistle
Weatherson	Peter	Joseph	29/05/80	North Shields	24/06/03	6 0.0	12 10	Forward	Queen of the South
Williams	Alexander	Boyd	15/01/83	Glasgow	17/05/02	5 10.5	11 0	Forward	Stirling Albion

milestones

YEAR OF FORMATION: 1874
MOST CAPPED PLAYER: Jimmy Cowan
NO. OF CAPS: 25
MOST LEAGUE POINTS IN A SEASON: 69 (Division 2 – Season 1966/67) (2 Points for a win)
72 (Third Division - Season 2002/03) (3 Points for a win)
MOST LEAGUE GOALS SCORED BY A PLAYER IN A SEASON: Allan McGraw (Season 1963/64)
NO. OF GOALS SCORED: 58
RECORD ATTENDANCE: 23,500 (-v- Celtic – 1922)
RECORD VICTORY: 11-0 (-v- Carfin Shamrock – Scottish Cup, 13.11.1886)
RECORD DEFEAT: 1-10 (-v- Port Glasgow Athletic, 5.5.1884)

ticket information

SEASON TICKET INFORMATION
SEATED

GRANDSTAND (Sections A & B)

ADULT	£160
CONCESSIONS	£85
PARENT & JUVENILE	£180

GRANDSTAND (Sections C & D – numbered seats)

ADULT	£180

STANDING

ADULT	£130
CONCESSIONS	£70
CHILD (15 & UNDER)	£35
PARENT & JUVENILE	£165

LEAGUE ADMISSION PRICES
SEATED

GRANDSTAND (Sections A,B,E & F)

ADULT	£11
CONCESSIONS	£6
PARENT & JUVENILE	£14

STANDING

ADULT	£9
CONCESSIONS	£5
CHILD (15 & UNDER)	£2
PARENT & JUVENILE	£11

leading goalscorers 1993-2003

Season	Div	No. of Goals	Player
1993-94	F	11	R. Alexander
1994-95	S	16	D. Lilley
1995-96	F	14	D. Lilley
1996-97	F	15	D. Lilley
1997-98	F	10	W. Hawke
1998-99	F	9	K. Thomas
1999-00	F	9	H. Curran
2000-01	F	9	R. Matheson
2001-02	S	8	S. Bannerman
2002-03	S	23	A. Williams

the tons' club factfile 2002/03

Date	Venue	Opponents	Att.	Res	Coyle C.	Collins D.	Bottiglieri E.	MacGregor D.	Gaughan P.	Maisano M.	Uotinen J.	Hawke W.	Williams A.	Maisano J.	Reilly C.	Cannie P.	MacDonald S.	Bannerman S.	Smith A.	Curran S.	Duncan L.	Hopkin D.	Struthers K.	McAlister J.	Henderson R.	Robertson L.	Millar C.	Annand E.	Adam J.	Dale G.
Aug 3	A	Gretna	1,566	1-1	1	2	3	4	5	6	7	8^{1}	9	10	11	12	14													
10	H	Stirling Albion	1,757	5-1	1	2	3	4	5^{1}	6	7^{1}	8^{1}	9^{2}	10		12	14	11	15											
17	A	Peterhead	729	2-4	1	2	3	4		6	7^{1}	8	9	10^{1}		12		11	5	16										
24	H	Queen's Park	2,001	3-0	1	2	3	4		5	7		9^{2}	10	14	12	15	8	6		11^{1}									
31	A	East Stirlingshire	748	1-1	1	2	3	4		6	7		9^{1}	10		12	15	11	5			8								
Sep 14	H	Albion Rovers	1,739	0-1	1	2	3	4	15		7	8	9	10		12	14	11	5			6								
21	A	Montrose	543	5-2	1	2	3	4	5	6^{1}	7^{2}	11^{1}		10		9	8^{1}	12												
28	H	East Fife	1,821	2-1	1	2	3	4	5	6	7^{1}	11	9^{1}	10			8	13												
Oct 5	A	Elgin City	895	1-0	1	2	3	4	6		7	14	9^{1}	10	15	11	5	12	8											
19	A	Stirling Albion	1,089	0-2	1	2	3	4	6	11		12	9	10	7	13		14	5			8								
26	H	Gretna	1,705	2-2	1	2	3	4	6		7	11	9^{1}			12		10	5			8^{1}								
Nov 2	H	East Stirlingshire	1,640	4-1	1	2	3	4	5	6	11		9^{3}	10		7^{1}	13	12				8								
9	A	Queen's Park	1,775	1-1	1	2	3	4^{1}	5	6	11	14	9	10		7	15	12				8								
16	A	Albion Rovers	843	1-2	1	2	3	4	5	6	8	10	9	7		11^{1}	12													
23	H	Montrose	1,748	†4-2	1	2	3	4	5	6	11	10^{1}	9^{2}	8	14		7			15										
30	H	Elgin City	1,658	4-0	1	2	3	4	5	6	11^{1}		9^{1}	8^{2}		10	7	12					16							
Dec 7	H	Queen's Park	1,669	1-1	1	2	3	4	5	6	11	10	9^{1}	8			7	12												
14	A	East Fife	1,005	4-1	1	2	3	4	5	6	11^{1}	10	9^{2}	8^{1}	14		12	7												
28	H	Peterhead	2,640	1-0	1	2	3	4	5	6	11	10	9^{1}	8			7							16						
Jan 18	H	Albion Rovers	2,405	2-1	1	2	3	4^{1}		6	11	10	9^{1}	8		14								16	5	7				
Feb 8	H	East Fife	2,953	1-1	1	2	3	4		6	11	14	9	8		10	7^{1}							15	5					
12	A	East Stirlingshire	627	1-0	1	2	3	4		6	11	14	9	8^{1}		10	7								5					
15	A	Elgin City	701	0-0	1	2	3	4		6	15	10		8		9	7	14						11	5					
25	A	Montrose	343	0-0	1	2	3	4	14	6		15	9	12			7	8						10	5		11			
Mar 1	A	Peterhead	1,086	1-3	1	2	3		4	6	14	12^{1}				9	7	8							5	15	11	10		
8	A	Queen's Park	1,361	1-0	1	2	3	4	5	6	12			8		9								16			7		10^{1}	11
11	H	Stirling Albion	1,617	2-2	1	2		4	5	6	15		9	8		12											7	11^{2}	10	3
15	H	East Stirlingshire	2,039	2-1	1	2		4	5	6	9			8		14		12^{1}						15			7	11^{1}	10	3
22	H	Montrose	2,047	1-0	1	2		4	5^{1}	6	12		9	16		10	15	8									7	11		3
29	A	Gretna	601	1-0	1	2		4	5	6	10	12	9	14				8									7	11^{1}	15	3
Apr 5	A	Albion Rovers	1,381	1-2	1	2		4^{1}	5		14		9	6		12		8									7	11	10	3
12	H	Elgin City	1,662	2-0	1	2	3		5	6	14	16^{1}	9	10		15		8^{1}							4		7	11		
19	A	East Fife	1,991	1-0	1	2	3		5	6		16^{1}	9	10		15	12	8							4		7	11		
26	H	Gretna	2,422	5-0	1	2	3^{1}		5	6	14	16	9^{2}	10^{1}		15		8							4		7	11^{1}		
May 3	A	Stirling Albion	2,039	3-0	1	2	3		5	6	14^{1}	16	9^{2}	10		15		8							4		7	11		
10	H	Peterhead	8,497	1-0	1	2	3		5	6	14	16	9	10			12	8^{1}							4		7	11		
TOTAL FULL APPEARANCES					36	36	31	30	27	32	23	14	31	31	2	12	12	17	7		1	6		2	11	1	13	11	4	6
TOTAL SUB APPEARANCES									2		10	13		3	4	16	12	10	1	2			1	5		1			1	
TOTAL GOALS SCORED							1	3	2	1	8	7	23	6		2	2	3			1	1						5	1	

Small bold figures denote goalscorers. † denotes opponent's own goal.

cappielow park

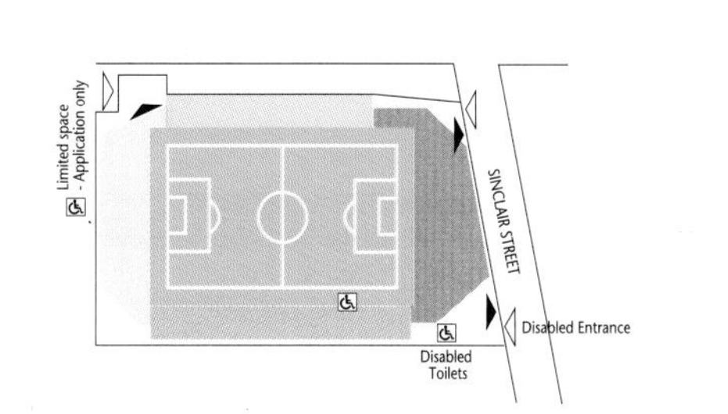

CAPACITY: 11,550; Seating 5,890, Standing 5,660

PITCH DIMENSIONS: 110 yds x 70 yds

FACILITIES FOR DISABLED SUPPORTERS:
Seating facilities below Grandstand. Disabled toilets located at Main Entrance. Disabled Access and facilities within Club Hospitality areas.

team playing kits

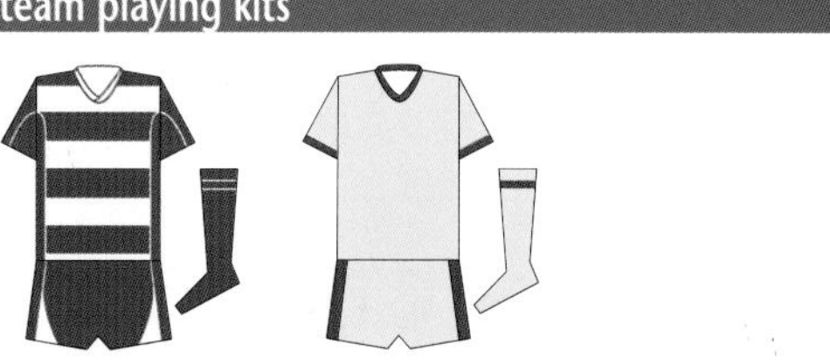

how to get there

Cappielow Park may be reached by the following routes:

BUSES: Services from Glasgow stop just outside the park. There are also services from Port Glasgow and Gourock.

TRAINS: The nearest local station is Cartsdyke and is a five minute walk from the ground. There are two to three trains every hour from Glasgow and from Gourock.

CARS: Car parking is available adjacent to the ground.

stenhousemuir

Ochilview Park, Gladstone Road, Stenhousemuir, FK5 4QL

CHAIRMAN
Michael R. Laing

VICE-CHAIRMAN
David O. Reid

DIRECTORS
John Rolland, James S. B. Gillespie, Martin I. McNairney, Gordon T. Cook, William Darroch, Alan J. McNeill & A. Terry Bulloch

SECRETARY
David O. Reid

OFFICE ADMINISTRATOR
Margaret Kilpatrick

MANAGER
John McVeigh

ASSISTANT MANAGER
Andrew Smith

DIRECTOR OF YOUTH DEVELOPMENT
Bill Darroch

YOUTH TEAM COACHES
Kevin Brown (U19), John Morrison (U17), Bill Higgins (U15) & David Halcrow (U14)

CLUB DOCTOR
Dr. Steven Brown

PHYSIOTHERAPIST
Alan Davidson

COMMERCIAL MANAGER
John Rolland (01324) 562992

GROUNDSMAN
James Cuthill

MEDIA LIAISON OFFICER
David O. Reid (0141) 566 8231

MATCHDAY PROGRAMME EDITOR
Margaret Kilpatrick (01324) 562992

TELEPHONES
Ground (01324) 562992
Fax (01324) 562980
Sec. Home (01324) 719898
Sec. Bus. (0141) 566 8231

E-MAIL & INTERNET ADDRESS
stenhousemuir.fc@talk21.com

CLUB SHOP
Ochilview Park, Gladstone Road, Stenhousemuir, FK5 4QL. (01324) 562992. Open during first team home match days between 2.00pm until 3.00pm & Mon to Fri 9.00am till 5.00pm. Contact Mrs M. Kilpatrick

OFFICIAL SUPPORTERS CLUB
Ochilview Park, Gladstone Road, Stenhousemuir, FK5 4QL

SUPPORTERS CLUB CHAIRMAN
Harry Larkin

WARRIORS ABROAD
Alan McNeill at the club's address

TEAM CAPTAIN
Craig Tully

SHIRT SPONSOR
3MCM Limited

KIT SUPPLIER
The Branded Group

S·F·L

LIST OF PLAYERS 2003/04

SURNAME	FIRST NAME	MIDDLE NAME	DATE OF BIRTH	PLACE OF BIRTH	DATE OF SIGNING	HEIGHT FT INS	WEIGHT ST LBS	POS. ON PITCH	PREVIOUS CLUB
Bodel	Craig		14/02/86	Bangour	27/08/03	5 8.0	11 9	Def	Stenhousemuir Form D U16
Bonar	Paul		28/12/76	Glasgow	07/07/03	6 0.0	11 8	Def	Albion Rovers
Booth	Mark		07/03/80	Coatbridge	06/06/02	5 10.0	12 0	Mid	Albion Rovers
Brown	Andrew	Stewart	11/10/76	Edinburgh	06/06/03	6 4.0	14 7	Fwd	Dumbarton
Buist	Scot	Campbell	05/03/85	Falkirk	22/08/02	6 0.0	11 0	Def	Rangers
Cairney	Christopher		05/12/85	Bellshill	14/05/02	5 7.0	10 9	Mid	Airdrie B.C.
Carr	David		23/09/83	Bellshill	08/01/03	5 7.0	11 0	Fwd	Albion Rovers
Craig	Jamie	William	23/07/86	Stirling	27/08/03	6 0.0	11 7	Mid	Stenhousemuir Form D U16
Crawford	Brian		27/07/78	Lanark	06/06/02	5 10.0	11 10	Fwd	Clyde
Cunningham	Craig		25/08/87	Glasgow	26/08/03	5 11.0	11 11	Gk	Stenhousemuir B.C.
Dolla	Mark		21/04/85	Glasgow	31/08/02	5 6.0	9 7	Mid	Northern Spirit
Donnelly	Kevin	Francis	05/07/83	Glasgow	11/07/02	6 1.0	12 7	Mid	Albion Rovers
Easton	Stewart		10/10/81	Coatbridge	06/06/02	5 9.0	11 2	Mid	Albion Rovers
Forrest	Fraser	Wilson	14/09/83	Galashiels	14/08/03	6 1.0	12 0	Def	Sauchie Juniors
Gaughan	Kevin		06/03/78	Glasgow	14/07/03	6 1.0	12 9	Def	Stranraer
Hamilton	Steven	James	19/03/75	Baillieston	06/06/02	5 9.0	12 5	Def/Mid	Albion Rovers
Harty	Martin	John	11/07/82	Bellshill	24/06/02	6 0.0	11 5	Fwd	Albion Rovers
Hill	Craig		01/08/87	Falkirk	02/09/03	6 4.0	13 6	Def	Stenhousemuir B.C.
Johnstone	Darren	Philip	25/10/78	Dumfries	28/05/03	6 2.0	12 7	Fwd	Crichton Amateurs
Jones	Dean	M.	05/04/87	Sydney	02/09/03	5 10.0	10 0	Mid	Stenhousemuir Form D U15
Lauchlan	Martin	Thomas	01/10/80	Rutherglen	14/07/03	5 10.0	11 8	Mid	St. Johnstone
Lee	Andrew		19/02/86	Bellshill	27/08/03	6 0.0	12 7	Fwd	Stenhousemuir Form D U16
Mallan	Stephen	Patrick	30/08/67	Glasgow	25/08/03	5 11.0	12 4	Fwd	Stirling Albion
May	Gareth		25/05/87	Glasgow	02/09/03	5 9.0	10 11	Fwd	Stenhousemuir B.C.
McCafferty	Michael		01/06/85	Falkirk	11/07/02	6 2.0	14 0	Def	Stenhousemuir B.C.
McCloy	Brian		06/08/79	Pontefract	06/06/03	6 0.0	13 0	Def	Forfar Athletic
McCulloch	Greig		18/04/76	Girvan	30/06/03	5 8.0	11 7	Def	Brechin City
McCulloch	William		02/04/73	Baillieston	04/06/03	6 1.0	13 7	Gk	Stranraer
McDowell	Murray	John Lauden	17/02/78	Dundee	07/07/03	6 0.0	11 7	Fwd	Berwick Rangers
McGowan	Michael	Valentine	22/08/85	Glasgow	29/08/02	5 7.0	10 7	Mid	Sheffield Wednesday
McHendrie	David		07/12/87	Glasgow	02/09/03	5 10.0	11 6	Def	Stenhousemuir B.C.
McKenna	Gerard		02/02/77	Bellshill	06/06/02	5 9.0	11 6	Mid	Albion Rovers
McKenzie	James		29/11/80	Bellshill	06/06/02	5 7.5	11 4	Mid	Albion Rovers
McKirdy	Martin		10/07/86	Oxford	27/08/03	6 2.0	11 0	Gk	Stenhousemuir Form D U16
McLeod	Colin		27/08/87	Glasgow	02/09/03	5 11.0	11 0	Mid	Stenhousemuir B.C.
McVittie	Mark	Joseph	24/06/85	Bellshill	11/07/02	5 11.0	11 7	Def	Stenhousemuir Form D U16
Menzies	Craig		10/07/86	Paisley	27/08/03	5 10.0	11.0	Mid	Stenhousemuir Form D U16
Miles	Craig		10/07/87	Glasgow	02/09/03	5 10.0	11 5	Fwd	Stenhousemuir B.C.
Morrison	Bryan		22/03/87	Glasgow	02/09/03	5 8.0	10 2	Def	Stenhousemuir B.C.
Morrison	David	James	02/01/86	Falkirk	09/07/03	6 1.0	10 7	Mid	Stenhousemuir Form D U16
Morrison	Lee		22/03/87	Glasgow	02/09/03	5 8.0	10 0	Mid	Stenhousemuir Form D U15
Morrison	Mark		15/08/86	Dunfermline	03/09/03	5 9.0	11 7	Def	Stenhousemuir Form D U16
Murphy	Paul	David	01/08/85	Peterhead	14/05/02	6 1.0	11 0	Mid	Celtic B.C.
Murphy	Stephen	Daniel	06/03/86	Glasgow	28/08/03	5 7.0	10 7	Fwd	Stenhousemuir Form D U16
Murray	Marc		24/10/85	Motherwell	25/08/03	6 0.0	12 0	Mid	St. Mirren
Nisbet	Sean		26/09/86	Glasgow	02/09/03	5 10.0	10 7	Mid	Campsie Blackwatch
O'Boyle	Jamie		20/11/87	Glasgow	02/09/03	5 11.0	10 4	Def	Stenhousemuir B.C.
Orr	David		25/08/87	Glasgow	25/08/03	6 0.0	10 4	Gk	Stenhousemuir Form D U15
Parry	Neil		08/11/85	Rutherglen	01/07/03	6 3.0	13 0	Gk	Petershill Juniors
Ramsay	Andrew		11/07/85	Falkirk	13/06/02	5 11.0	11 4	Def	Gairdoch United
Reilly	Stephen		01/06/86	Falkirk	27/08/03	5 4.0	9 11	Mid	Stenhousemuir Form D
Ruddick	Scott		06/11/85	Glasgow	11/07/02	5 8.0	10 9	Def	Stenhousemuir Form D U16
Savage	Joseph	Gerard	22/05/84	Bellshill	29/08/03	6 1.0	11 0	Fwd	Bo'ness United Juniors
Scott	Craig		15/08/87	Edinburgh	02/09/03	5 5.0	9 0	Fwd	Stenhousemuir Form D U15
Shanks	Paul		01/03/84	Dunfermline	14/08/03	6 1.0	11 0	Mid	Sauchie Juniors
Simpson	Andrew		13/08/87	Rutherglen	02/09/03	5 6.0	9 2	Mid	Stenhousemuir Form D U15
Sinclair	Thomas		22/05/87	Glasgow	08/08/03	5 8.0	12 2	Mid	Stenhousemuir B.C.
Smith	Anthony		28/10/73	Bellshill	04/06/03	5 8.0	11 7	Def/Mid	Berwick Rangers
Tully	Craig		07/01/76	Stirling	11/06/03	6 0.0	12 5	Def	Elgin City
Tully	Jon		04/06/86	Stirling	18/07/03	6 2.0	11 7	Def	Rangers
Vita	Dino		22/05/86	Edinburgh	09/07/03	5 4.0	9 10	Fwd	Heart of Midlothian
Weir	Philip		28/07/87	Glasgow	02/09/03	5 8.0	9 12	Mid	Stenhousemuir B.C.

milestones

YEAR OF FORMATION: 1884
MOST LEAGUE POINTS IN A SEASON: 50 (Division 2 – Season 1960/61) (2 Points for a Win)
64 (Second Division – Season 1998/99) (3 Points for a Win)
MOST LEAGUE GOALS SCORED BY A PLAYER IN A SEASON: Evelyn Morrison (Season 1927/28) and Robert Murray (Season 1936/37)
NO. OF GOALS SCORED: 31
RECORD ATTENDANCE: 12,500 (-v- East Fife – 11.3.1950)
RECORD VICTORY: 9-2 (-v- Dundee United – Division 2, 16.4.1937)
RECORD DEFEAT: 2-11 (-v- Dunfermline Athletic – Division 2, 27.9.1930)

ticket information

SEASON TICKET PRICES

SEATED	ADULT	£135
	JUVENILE/OAP/STUDENT	£70
	FAMILY FLEXI - ADD £60 FOR EACH ADDITIONAL ADULT & £30 FOR EACH ADDITIONAL OAP/JUVENILE (UP TO 4 PERSONS) TO FULL PRICE SEASON TICKET	

LEAGUE ADMISSION PRICES

SEATED	ADULT	£9
	JUVENILE/OAP	£5
STANDING	ADULT	£8
	JUVENILE/OAP	£4

leading goalscorers 1993-2003

Season	Div	No. of Goals	Player
1993-94	S	14	M. Mathieson
1994-95	S	10	G. Hutchison
1995-96	S	10	M. Mathieson
1996-97	S	14	I. Little
1997-98	S	15	I. Little
1998-99	T	11	R. Hamilton
1999-00	S	8	M. Mooney
2000-01	S	18	I. English
2001-02	S	7	W. Irvine
2002-03	S	9	M. Booth

the warriors' club factfile 2002/03

Date	Venue	Opponents	Att.	Res	Gillespie A.	Forrest F.	Easton S.	Hamilton S.	McKenzie J.	Booth M.	Waldie C.	Donnelly K.	McCormick S.	McFarlane D.	Stein J.	Harty M.	Graham D.	Smith G.	McMillan A.	McKenna G.	Wilson M.	Crawford B.	Sandison J.	Murphy J. S.	Stone M.	Coulter R.	Armstrong M.	Martin C.	Carlin A.	Carr D.	McGowan M. V.
Aug 3	H	Dumbarton	437	2-2	1	2	3	4	5	6^{2}	7	8	9	10	11	12	15														
10	A	Forfar Athletic	492	0-1			8	4	5	6		15	9	10	11	12		1	2	3	7	16									
17	H	Berwick Rangers	379	2-0			2	4	5	6	7		9	10^{1}	11			1		3		12	8^{1}	16							
24	H	Stranraer	295	2-0			8	4	5^{1}	6	7		9	10^{1}	11		16	1		3		14		14	2						
31	A	Raith Rovers	1,661	0-1			8	4	5	6	7		9	10	11		16	1		3		12		15	2						
Sep 14	H	Hamilton Academical	463	1-2			8	4	5	6	7		10^{1}	14	11			1		3	12	9			2	16					
21	A	Cowdenbeath	340	0-1			6	4	5		7		9	10	12	11	15	1		3	8			16	2						
28	H	Airdrie United	842	4-3			5	4	12		7^{1}	6^{1}	9	14	11		10^{1}	1		3	8			16^{1}		2					
Oct 5	A	Brechin City	489	0-1			6	4	5		7			10	11		9	1		3	8	12		15	16	2					
19	H	Forfar Athletic	295	2-1			2	4	5	6	7			10^{1}	11	15	14	1		3		9^{1}		8		12					
26	A	Dumbarton	815	0-0			2	4	5	6	7		16	10	11	15	14	1		3		9		8							
Nov 2	H	Raith Rovers	1,066	0-1			3		5	8	7		10		11	15	14	1		4		9		12		2	6				
9	A	Stranraer	411	1-2			5	4		6	7		10		11	12	8^{1}	1		3		9		14	16	2					
16	A	Hamilton Academical	1,226	3-2			5	4		6^{1}	7		10	14	11	15^{1}	8	1		3					9	2^{1}		16			
23	H	Cowdenbeath	377	4-1			5	4		6^{2}	7		9	10	11	12	8	1				14^{1}			3	2^{1}					
30	H	Brechin City	331	1-1			5	4		6		14		10	11	7	8	1		3		9		12^{1}		2					
Dec 14	A	Airdrie United	1,228	0-2			5	4	12	6	7		14	10	11		8	1		3		9		15		2					
28	A	Berwick Rangers	543	2-2			2	14	12	6^{1}	7		9	10	11	8				3	16^{1}			5				4	1		
Jan 1	H	Stranraer	356	1-0			5	4	14	6^{1}		16	9	10	11		8	1		3	7	15				2					
18	H	Hamilton Academical	581	2-2		2	3	4	5	6^{1}	7		9^{1}	10	11		12	1			8									15	
25	H	Dumbarton	460	2-1		2	3	4	5	6^{1}		8	9	10^{1}	11	16	12	1			7			15							
Feb 8	H	Airdrie United	954	3-3		2	3	4	5				9^{1}	10^{1}	11		12	1			8			6		16^{1}					7
22	A	Forfar Athletic	449	3-3		2		4	5	6	14^{1}		9	10^{1}	11		12	1		3	8^{1}			16							7
25	A	Cowdenbeath	258	3-3					5^{1}	6	7		9^{1}	10^{1}	11		12	1		3	8		4	14		2					
Mar 1	H	Berwick Rangers	684	1-0			5		12	6	7		9	10	11		8			3	4	15^{1}				2			1		
15	H	Raith Rovers	929	1-3			5	14		6	7		9	10^{1}	11		8			3	4	12				2			1	16	
22	H	Cowdenbeath	488	1-1			2			6	7	16^{1}	9		11	15	14	1		3	8	10	4	5							
26	A	Raith Rovers	1,627	1-0			2	5		6	7	8	9		11^{1}	14	15	1		3	12	10	4								
29	A	Brechin City	435	1-2			2	5			7	6	9		11	12	14	1		3	8	10^{1}	4			16					
Apr 5	A	Hamilton Academical	1,247	1-0			2	14	5		7		9	10	11	6		1		3	8	12^{1}	4			15					
8	A	Stranraer	321	1-0			2	14	5		7		9	12	11	6^{1}	16	1		3	8	10	4								
12	H	Brechin City	510	2-2			2	4		6	7		14	10	11	8^{1}	16	1		3	5	9^{1}									
19	A	Airdrie United	1,468	0-1			2		12	6	7		10		15	11	8	1		3	5	9						4		16	
26	A	Dumbarton	906	1-3			2	4	5	14		6	12		11	7		1		15		9^{1}				3		8		10	
May 3	H	Forfar Athletic	497	1-4			8	4	5	6	7	15	10		11		16^{1}	1		3		9				2					
10	A	Berwick Rangers	579	0-0			2	12	7	6	14	8	10		11		15	1		3		9	4	5							
TOTAL FULL APPEARANCES					1	5	34	26	21	28	28	7	29	23	34	8	11	32	1	30	18	16	8	6	6	14	1	3	3	1	2
TOTAL SUB APPEARANCES								5	6	1	2	5	4	4	2	12	19			1	3	10		13	2	5		1		3	
TOTAL GOALS SCORED									2	9	2	2	4	8	1	3	3				2	7	1	2		3					

Small bold figures denote goalscorers. † denotes opponent's own goal.

ochilview park

CAPACITY: 5,267; Seated 2,117, Standing 3,150

PITCH DIMENSIONS: 110 yds x 72 yds

FACILITIES FOR DISABLED SUPPORTERS:
Accommodation for disabled in new Stand. Toilet facilities also provided.

team playing kits

how to get there

Ochilview Park can be reached by the following routes:

TRAINS: The nearest station is Larbert, which is about 1 mile away from the ground.

BUSES: There are regular bus services from Falkirk.

CARS: There is a large car park on the north side of the ground.

albion rovers

Cliftonhill Stadium, Main Street, Coatbridge, ML5 3RB

CHAIRMAN
Andrew Dick, M.Sc., B.Sc., C.Eng.

VICE-CHAIRMAN
David T. Shanks, B.Sc.

DIRECTORS
Robert Watt, David Wright, Thomas Young & Gordon Dishington

GENERAL MANAGER/OFFICE ADMINISTRATOR
John Reynolds

SECRETARY
David T. Shanks, B.Sc.

MANAGER
Peter Hetherston

ASSISTANT MANAGER
Jock McStay

FIRST TEAM COACH
Kevin McAllister

DIRECTOR OF YOUTH DEVELOPMENT/ YOUTH CO-ORDINATOR
Jimmy Lindsay

U19 YOUTH TEAM COACH
Frank Connor & Andy Paterson

U17 YOUTH TEAM COACH
John Bell

RESERVE COACH
Dennis Newall

PHYSIOTHERAPIST
Alan Anderson

FOOTBALL SAFETY OFFICERS' ASSOCIATION REPRESENTATIVE
John Reynolds 07719 736287

GROUNDSMAN
Hugh McBride

KIT PERSON
Wilma McBride

COMMERCIAL MANAGERS
Chris Fahey & Gordon Dishington

MEDIA LIAISON OFFICER
Gordon Dishington

MATCHDAY PROGRAMME EDITOR
Maxwell Crichton (01236) 602552

CLUB STEWARD
Chic Young

TELEPHONES
Ground (01236) 606334/607041
Fax (01236) 606334
Sec. Home (01236) 421686
Sec. Bus. (01236) 762775

INTERNET ADDRESS
www.albionrovers.com

CLUB SHOP
Cliftonhill Stadium, Main Street, Coatbridge, ML5 3RB. Open one hour prior to kick-off at first team home matches.

OFFICIAL SUPPORTERS CLUB
John Smith, 45 Blair Road, Coatbridge (01236) 420417

TEAM CAPTAIN
Jim Mercer

SHIRT SPONSOR
Reigart

KIT SUPPLIER
Pro Star

LIST OF PLAYERS 2003-2004

SURNAME	FIRST NAME	MIDDLE NAME	DATE OF BIRTH	PLACE OF BIRTH	DATE OF SIGNING	HEIGHT FT INS	WEIGHT ST LBS	POS. ON PITCH	PREVIOUS CLUB
Black	Daniel		22/01/86	New Plymouth	08/07/03	6 0.0	12 5	Def	Heart of Midlothian Form D
Bradford	John		15/12/79	Irvine	11/07/02	5 11.0	12 4	Fwd	Ayr United
Calderwood	John		27/10/85	Lanark	25/07/02	5 7.0	9 0	Def	Albion Rovers Form D U16
Connelly	Paul		24/06/86	Motherwell	08/07/03	5 8.0	10 7	Def	Kilmarnock Form D
Connolly	Charles		18/07/85	Glasgow	30/01/03	6 0.0	10 4	Def	Cumbernauld United Juniors
Cormack	Peter	Robert	08/06/74	Liverpool	29/07/02	6 1.0	12 0	Def	Stenhousemuir
Crolla	Dario		04/01/86	Edinburgh	08/07/03	5 9.0	11 0	Mid	Heart of Midlothian Form D
Cross	Darren		26/03/86	Glasgow	09/07/03	5 7.0	10 0	Fwd	Kilmarnock
Diack	Iain	Gordon	17/02/81	Glasgow	21/10/98	6 1.0	11 6	Fwd	Celtic B.C.
Fahey	Christopher		28/06/78	Coatbridge	06/07/00	6 0.0	12 8	Gk	Larkhall Thistle Juniors
Farrell	David	John	29/10/69	Glasgow	10/07/03	5 9.0	12 0	Mid	Stranraer
Fleming	Garry		17/05/87	Vale of Leven	09/07/03	5 8.0	9 0	Fwd	Celtic Form D
Kerr	Steven		30/04/86	Glasgow	25/07/02	5 10.0	10 6	Def	Stenhousemuir
Lynch	Paul		28/06/86	Edinburgh	09/07/03	5 10.0	11 0	Fwd	Hibernian Form D
McAllister	Kevin		08/11/62	Falkirk	09/08/02	5 5.0	11 0	Fwd	Falkirk
McBride	Kevin	James	12/04/80	Glasgow	04/08/03	5 11.0	10 8	Def	Glenafton Athletic Juniors
McCaig	John	George	19/11/82	Ayr	30/08/02	6 2.0	13 1	Def	Notts County
McCaul	Graeme		05/10/84	Edinburgh	11/07/02	5 11.0	10 8	Mid	Heart of Midlothian
McKenzie	Marc		11/07/85	Glasgow	17/07/02	5 6.0	10 1	Fwd	Raith Rovers Form D U16
McLeish	Andrew		08/12/85	Glasgow	18/07/02	5 10.0	11 0	Def	Hibernian
McManus	Paul	John	26/12/82	Kirkcaldy	29/07/03	5 10.0	10 5	Fwd	Raith Rovers
Mercer	James		30/07/74	Glasgow	13/07/02	6 5.0	14 6	Mid	Arbroath
O'Hara	James		24/10/86	Glasgow	07/07/03	6 0.0	10 7	Mid	Pollok United
Paterson	Andrew		05/05/72	Glasgow	17/07/02	5 9.5	11 10	Def	Stranraer
Patrick	Ricky		14/03/86	Kirkcaldy	09/07/03	5 10.0	10 5	Mid	Hibernian Form D
Potter	Kerr	Alan	13/08/86	Edinburgh	09/07/03	6 0.0	10 0	Def	Heart of Midlothian Form D
Robertson	Gary	David	12/04/85	Irvine	18/07/02	5 11.0	11 2	Fwd	Kilmarnock
Selkirk	Andrew		12/09/86	Glasgow	17/07/02	5 10.0	10 6	Fwd	Albion Rovers Form D U15
Silvestro	Christopher		16/03/79	Bellshill	15/04/99	5 7.0	11 0	Mid	Glenboig
Skinner	Stephen	Karl	25/11/81	Whitehaven	30/08/03	5 11.0	13 2	Mid	Gretna
Smith	Jordan		02/02/82	Bellshill	29/07/99	6 2.0	13 0	Def	Albion Rovers Form S
Stirling	Jered		13/10/76	Stirling	19/07/02	6 0.0	13 2	Def	Stranraer
Stirling	John	Christopher	19/12/84	Glasgow	07/07/03	6 0.0	11 8	Def	East Stirlingshire
Swain	Kevin		10/09/85	Edinburgh	17/07/02	6 1.5	10 3	Gk	Raith Rovers Form D U16
Thompson	Lee		04/05/87	Irvine	03/09/03	6 1.0	10 5	Gk	Dundonald Amateurs
Valentine	James	McInnes	24/07/85	Broxburn	17/07/02	5 9.0	10 0	Mid	Raith Rovers Form D U16
Woods	Paul	Charles	18/09/86	Bellshill	07/07/03	5 7.0	10 0	Mid	Motherwell
Wynn	Bryan		11/09/87	Bellshill	09/07/03	6 1.0	11 0	Mid	Motherwell Form D
Yardley	Mark		14/09/69	Livingston	29/01/03	6 2.0	15 7	Fwd	St. Mirren

milestones

YEAR OF FORMATION: 1882
MOST CAPPED PLAYER: John White
NO. OF CAPS: 1
MOST LEAGUE POINTS IN A SEASON: 54 (Division 2 – Season 1929/30)(2 Points fo a win)
70 (Third Division – Season 2002/03)(3 Points fo a win)
MOST LEAGUE GOALS SCORED BY A PLAYER IN A SEASON: John Renwick (Season 1932/33)
NO. OF GOALS SCORED: 41
RECORD ATTENDANCE: 27,381 (-v- Rangers 8.2.1936)
RECORD VICTORY: 12-0 (-v- Airdriehill – Scottish Cup, 3.9.1887)
RECORD DEFEAT: 1-11 (-v- Partick Thistle – League Cup, 11.8.1993)

ticket information

	SEASON TICKET PRICES	
SEATED	ADULT	£90
	OAP/UNEMPLOYED	£50
	12-16 YEARS UNACCOMPANIED	FREE
	UNDER 12'S	FREE
	(WHEN ACCOMPANIED BY A PAYING ADULT)	
STANDING	ADULT	£90
	LEAGUE ADMISSION PRICES	
SEATED	ADULT	£8
	OAP/UNEMPLOYED	£4
STANDING	ADULT	£8
	OAP/UNEMPLOYED	£4

leading goalscorers 1993-2003

Season	No. of Div	Goals	Player
1993-94	S	17	M. Scott
1994-95	T	7	M. Scott
1995-96	T	12	G. Young
1996-97	T	11	W. Watters
1997-98	T	13	W. Watters
1998-99	T	10	D. Lorimer
1999-00	T	7	I. Diack
2000-01	T	6	M. Booth
2001-02	T	11	C. McLean
2002-03	T	10	J. Mercer

S·F·L

the wee rovers' club factfile 2002/03

Date	Venue	Opponents	Att.	Res	Shearer S.	Paterson A.	Stirling J.	Smith J.	Cormack P.	Lumsden T.	Dick J.	Silvestro C.	Bradford J.	Diack I.	Mercer J.	McKinnon C.	Coulter J.	McLean C.	McAllister K.	Carr D.	Duncan L.	McCaig J.	McCaul G.	Weir M.	Yardley M.	McKenzie M.
Aug 3	A	Stirling Albion	579	1-0	1	2	3	4	5	6	7[1]	8	9	10	11	15	14	12								
10	H	Peterhead	430	3-0	1	2	3	4	5[1]	6		8	9	10[1]	11	14		12	7	15[1]						
17	A	East Stirlingshire	321	3-0	1	2	3	4	5	6[1]	14	8	9[2]	10	11		16	12	7							
24	A	Gretna	443	0-2	1	2	3	4	5	6	8		9	10	11		14	12	7	15						
31	H	East Fife	451	1-5	1	2	3	4	5	6	8		9[1]		11		15	14	7		10	12				
Sep 14	A	Morton	1,739	1-0	1	2	3	4	5	6[1]			9	16			8	10	7	15		11				
21	H	Elgin City	303	1-1	1	2	3	4	5	6	14	12	9	15			8	10[1]	7			11				
28	A	Queen's Park	506	4-2	1	2	3[2]	4	5	6	8	11	9[1]	16[1]			14	10	7			12				
Oct 5	H	Montrose	380	1-1	1	2	3	4	5	6	8	11	9	10[1]	16				7		15					
19	A	Peterhead	543	0-2	1	2	3	4	5	6		8	9	10	11		15	14	7		16					
26	H	Stirling Albion	489	1-3	1	2	3	4	5	6		8	9		11		14	10[1]	7	16	15					
Nov 2	A	East Fife	575	4-0	1	2	3[1]	4		6		8	14	15	11[1]		16	10[1]	7		9	5[1]				
9	H	Gretna	332	2-1	1	2		4		6		8	14	12	11		3	10[1]	7		9[1]	5	16			
16	H	Morton	843	2-1	1	2		4[1]	5	6		8	14	15[1]			11	10	7		9	3				
23	H	Elgin City	253	1-1	1	2		4	5	6		8	15	14	11		12	10	7		9[1]	3				
30	A	Montrose	271	1-0	1			4	5	6	12		14	8	11		2	10[1]	7		9	3		15		
Dec 7	A	Gretna	289	2-1	1	2		4	5	6		8[1]	7	14	11[1]			10			9	3		16		
14	H	Queen's Park	442	0-2	1	2		4	5	6	12	8		14	11			10	7		9	3		16		
28	H	East Stirlingshire	326	6-0	1	2	3	4		6[1]	11	8	9[2]	10[3]	12			14	7			5		16		
Jan 18	A	Morton	2,405	1-2	1	2	3	4		6	15	8	9	10	11[1]			14	7			5		16		
25	H	East Fife	475	0-0	1	2	3	4	5	6		8	9	10	11			12	7							
Feb 8	A	Queen's Park	671	1-1	1	2	3	4	5	6	14[1]	8	7	10	11			16	15						9	
26	A	Stirling Albion	466	†4-3	1	14	3	4	5	6[1]	2	8	16	10[1]	11				7			12			9[1]	
Mar 1	A	East Stirlingshire	273	4-0	1	14	3	4	5	6	2	8	16	10	11[2]			15[1]	7						9[1]	
4	H	Montrose	224	3-0	1		3	4[1]	5	6	14	8[1]	15[1]	10	11			16	7			2			9	
8	H	Gretna	327	1-1	1		3	4	5	6[1]		8	10	16	11				7			2			9	
11	H	Peterhead	389	0-0	1		3	4	5	6	2	8	10	15	11			14	7						9	
15	A	East Fife	780	1-1	1		3	4	5		2	8	10	16	11[1]			15	7			6			9	
22	A	Elgin City	333	1-0	1	12	3	4	5		2	8	10	15	11			14	7			6			9[1]	
29	A	Elgin City	280	2-1	1		3	4	5	6	2	8	16	10	11			15[1]	7						9[1]	
Apr 5	H	Morton	1,381	2-1	1	12	3	4	5	6	2	8	10	15	11[1]				7			14			9[1]	
12	A	Montrose	282	1-1	1	2	3	4	5	6		8	10[1]	15	11			16	7						9	
19	H	Queen's Park	581	2-1	1	12	3	4	5	6	2	8	10	15	11			16[1]	7						9[1]	
26	H	Stirling Albion	533	2-1	1		3	4	5	6				8	11			10	7			2	14		9[2]	16
May 3	A	Peterhead	1,693	0-0	1	2	3		5	6	8		16	15	11			10	7			4	14		9	
10	H	East Stirlingshire	682	3-1	1	2	3	4	5	6	8		10	15	11[3]			16	7				14		9	
TOTAL FULL APPEARANCES					36	24	30	35	32	34	16	28	24	16	30		5	13	33		8	17			15	
TOTAL SUB APPEARANCES						5					7	1	10	18	2	2	9	19	1	4	3	4	4	5		1
TOTAL GOALS SCORED							3	2	1	5	2	2	8	8	10			8		1	2	1			8	

Small bold figures denote goalscorers. † denotes opponent's own goal.

cliftonhill stadium

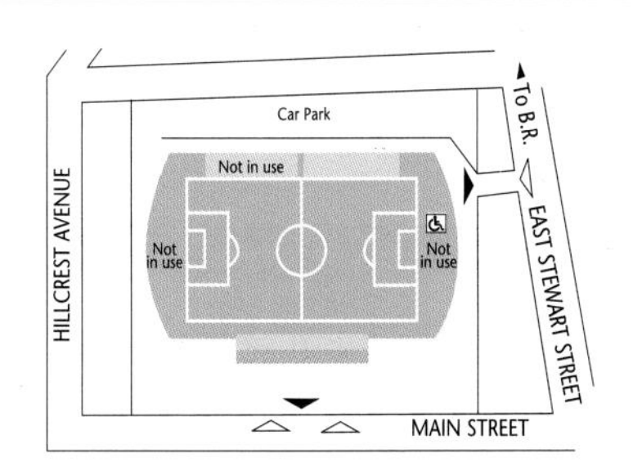

CAPACITY: 2,496; Seated 538, Standing 1,958

PITCH DIMENSIONS: 110 yds x 72 yds

FACILITIES FOR DISABLED SUPPORTERS:
Access from East Stewart Street with toilet facilities and space for wheelchairs, cars etc. Advanced contact with club advised – this area is uncovered.

team playing kits

how to get there

The following routes can be used to reach Cliftonhill Stadium:

BUSES: The ground is conveniently situated on the main Glasgow-Airdrie bus route and there is a stop near the ground. Local buses serving most areas of Coatbridge and Airdrie pass by the stadium every few minutes.

TRAINS: The nearest railway station is Coatdyke on the Glasgow-Airdrie line and the ground is a ten minute walk from there. The frequency of service is 15 minutes.

CARS: Vehicles may park in Hillcrest Avenue, Albion Street and East Stewart Street, which are all adjacent to the ground.

cowdenbeath

Central Park, High Street,
Cowdenbeath, KY4 9QQ

CHAIRMAN
Gordon McDougall

VICE-CHAIRMAN
Albert V. Tait

DIRECTORS
Ian Fraser, Brian Watson,
Dr. Robert Brownlie & Edward Baigan

HON. LIFE MEMBER
Brenda Solomon

GENERAL/COMMERCIAL/ LOTTERY MANAGER
Joe Macnamara

SECRETARY
Thomas Ogilvie

OFFICE ADMINISTRATOR
Kathryn Nellies

MANAGER
Keith Wright

ASSISTANT MANAGER
Mickey Weir

YOUTH TEAM COACHES
David Liddle & Steven McLeish (U19)
Gary McAlpine & Carlo Crolla (U17)
David Stewart, Kevin McCue
& Gary Miller (U16)
Paul Adamson (U14)
Brian Welsh & Andy Galbraith (U13)

WOMEN'S DEVELOPMENT COACH
Graham Thomson

GOALKEEPING COACH
David Westwood

CHIEF SCOUT
David Dair

CLUB DOCTOR
Dr. Robert Brownlie

PHYSIOTHERAPIST
Neil Bryson

FOOTBALL SAFETY OFFICERS' ASSOCIATION REPRESENTATIVE
David Jones (H) (01383) 872074

GROUNDSMAN
Gordon McDougall Jnr.

KIT PERSON
Bert Johnston

MATCHDAY PROGRAMME EDITOR
Andrew Mullen (01383) 611644

TELEPHONES
Ground/Ticket Office/Information
Service (01383) 610166
Sec. Home (01383) 513013
Sec. Bus (01383) 313400
Fax (01383) 512132

E-MAIL & INTERNET ADDRESS
bluebrazil@cowdenbeathfc.com
www.cowdenbeathfc.com

CLUB SHOP
Situated at Stadium. Open 10.00 a.m. – 3.00 p.m. and on Home Match Days

OFFICIAL SUPPORTERS CLUB
Central Park, High Street,
Cowdenbeath, KY4 9QQ

TEAM CAPTAIN
Craig Winter

SHIRT SPONSOR
David Philp – Commercials Ltd

KIT SUPPLIER
Paulas Benara

LIST OF PLAYERS 2003/04

SURNAME	FIRST NAME	MIDDLE NAME	DATE OF BIRTH	PLACE OF BIRTH	DATE OF SIGNING	HEIGHT FT INS	WEIGHT ST LBS	POS. ON PITCH	PREVIOUS CLUB
Bain	Jonathan		28/01/86	Edinburgh	13/05/03	6 0.0	11 0	Def	Wardievale B.C.
Bathgate	Stephen		01/02/87	Kirkcaldy	21/08/03	6 0.0	10 5	Fwd	Raith Rovers Form D U16
Black	Lee		07/04/85	Bellshill	20/06/02	5 11.0	9 10	Fwd	Heart of Midlothian B.C.
Blackadder	Gareth		04/08/85	Dunfermline	27/01/03	6 0.0	11 12	Fwd	Benarty B.C.
Bouglas	Dale		23/01/87	Dunfermline	21/08/03	5 10.0	10 0	Def	Raith Rovers Form D U15
Boyle	Steven	Robert	11/12/80	Edinburgh	06/06/03	5 11.0	11 0	Fwd	Brechin City
Brown	Graeme	Robert	08/11/80	Johannesburg	19/08/97	5 11.0	11 0	Fwd	Broomhall Saints B.C.
Buchanan	Liam		27/03/85	Edinburgh	02/07/02	5 8.0	10 8	Mid	Heart of Midlothian
Campbell	Andrew	Mark	15/03/79	Edinburgh	24/10/01	6 0.0	12 7	Def	Arniston Rangers Juniors
Campbell	Graeme		10/03/87	Kirkcaldy	21/08/03	5 11.0	11 0	Def	Lochgelly
Carlin	Andrew		06/01/81	Glasgow	06/06/03	6 1.0	14 8	Gk	Stenhousemuir
Currie	Paul		30/01/85	Edinburgh	20/06/02	5 10.0	10 0	Mid	Leith Athletic B.C.
Doyle	Darren		24/01/87	Kirkcaldy	21/08/03	6 0.0	11 0	Fwd	Lochgelly Albert Colts
Edgar	Craig		29/05/86	Edinburgh	13/05/03	6 0.0	11 0	Def	Wardievale B.C.
Fallon	John		14/01/82	Bellshill	30/06/03	5 10.0	11 0	Fwd	Stranraer
Fleming	Allan		06/05/84	Dunfermline	26/01/02	6 3.0	11 10	Gk	Musselburgh Windsor Juniors
Ford	Brian		23/09/82	Edinburgh	29/07/03	5 11.0	12 7	Def	Coventry City
Friar	Scott	Michael	04/01/87	Dunfermline	21/08/03	5 11.0	11 0	Def	Cairneyhill
Fusco	Gary	George	01/06/82	Edinburgh	22/07/02	6 1.0	11 5	Mid	Musselburgh Athletic Juniors
Gerrard	Graham		03/09/86	Edinburgh	13/05/03	6 1.0	13 0	Def	Wardievale B.C.
Gilbertson	John		19/12/86	Edinburgh	13/05/03	6 1.0	11 7	Gk	Wardievale B.C.
Gilfillan	Bryan	James	14/09/84	Cardenden	30/06/03	6 0.0	12 2	Def	Inverness Cal. Th.
Gollan	Kevin		17/01/87	Melbourne	21/08/03	5 9.0	9 5	Mid	Crossford U16's
Gordon	Kevin	Mervyn	01/05/77	Tranent	17/06/02	5 8.0	10 4	Fwd	East Stirlingshire
Jahn	Simon		14/11/87	Broxburn	21/08/03	5 9.0	11 0	Fwd	Cairneyhill B.C.
Killin	Grant		16/05/85	Edinburgh	16/08/03	5 9.0	11 2	Fwd	Leith Athletic
MacBride	Ross		28/08/84	Kirkcaldy	28/08/03	5 10.0	10 4	Mid	Crossgates Primrose Juniors
Matheson	Ross		15/11/77	Greenock	30/06/03	5 8.0	10 6	Mid	Raith Rovers
Mauchlen	Iain		11/06/79	Irvine	24/07/01	5 7.0	10 10	Mid/Fwd	Oakley United Juniors
McAlpine	Cameron		02/07/87	Dunfermline	21/08/03	6 1.0	10 0	Def	Raith Rovers Form D U15
McCallum	Ryan		20/12/86	Edinburgh	13/05/03	6 1.0	11 0	Fwd	Fernieside B.C.
McDiarmid	Conan		27/05/85	Edinburgh	30/08/02	6 2.0	12 0	Def	Falkirk
McDonald	Blair		28/01/85	Edinburgh	02/05/02	6 2.0	12 3	Def	Dalkeith B.C.
McEwen	Mark		05/01/86	Edinburgh	13/05/03	6 1.0	11 0	Mid	Wardievale B.C.
McGregor	Darren		07/08/85	Edinburgh	16/08/03	5 11.0	12 0	Def	Leith Athletic
McInally	David		03/03/81	Glasgow	06/06/03	5 7.0	10 4	Def	Arbroath
McKeown	John	Paton	21/04/81	Glasgow	19/07/03	6 4.5	14 0	Def	Dumbarton
Moffat	Adam		07/05/83	Kirkcaldy	12/08/03	5 9.0	11 8	Mid	Raith Rovers
Morris	Ian		28/08/81	Edinburgh	06/06/03	6 1.0	12 2	Mid	Partick Thistle
Mowat	David		17/12/83	Thurso	16/01/03	6 0.0	11 0	Def	Wick Academy
Moyles	Craig		24/02/87	Dunfermline	21/08/03	5 9.0	9 5	Mid	Cairneyhill B.C.
Munro	Daniel		30/04/86	Edinburgh	13/05/03	5 11.0	10 7	Def	Leith Athletic
Myles	Jackie		23/07/85	Edinburgh	20/06/02	5 8.0	10 7	Mid	Edina Colts
Robertson	Kevin		10/09/85	Edinburgh	02/05/02	6 2.0	12 11	Def	Tynecastle Hearts B.C.
Scott	Kevin		11/02/87	Dunfermline	21/08/03	5 10.0	10 0	Def	Cairneyhill B.C.
Shand	Calvin	David	09/11/83	Edinburgh	18/07/03	6 0.0	11 6	Def	Hibernian
Shepherd	Colin		26/03/87	Dunfermline	21/08/03	5 9.0	11 0	Def	Cairneyhill B.C.
Shields	Dene		16/09/82	Edinburgh	28/08/03	6 0.0	12 0	Fwd	Brechin City
Slaven	John		08/10/85	Edinburgh	29/08/03	6 0.0	12 2	Fwd	Carlisle United
Smith	Kevin		14/12/85	Dunfermline	13/05/03	5 10.0	11 0	Gk	East Fife Form D U16
Stewart	Steven		04/12/84	Dundee	29/08/03	5 9.0	11 0	Mid	Dundee
Sweeney	Daniel		03/11/85	Edinburgh	20/06/02	5 9.0	10 7	Def	Edina Hibs
Wilson	Keith	Andrew	31/08/79	Edinburgh	06/07/01	6 3.0	15 0	Def	Coldstream
Winter	Craig	John	30/06/76	Dunfermline	19/07/94	5 9.0	10 0	Mid/Fwd	Raith Rovers

milestones

YEAR OF FORMATION: 1881
MOST CAPPED PLAYER: Jim Paterson
NO. OF CAPS: 3
MOST LEAGUE POINTS IN A SEASON: 60 (Division 2 – Season 1938/39)(2 Points for a Win)
76 (Third Division – Season 2000/01)(3 Points for a Win)
MOST LEAGUE GOALS SCORED BY A PLAYER IN A SEASON: Rab Walls (Season 1938/39)
NO. OF GOALS SCORED: 54
RECORD ATTENDANCE: 25,586 (-v- Rangers – 21.9.1949)
RECORD VICTORY: 12-0 (-v- Johnstone – Scottish Cup, 21.1.1928)
RECORD DEFEAT: 1-11 (-v- Clyde – Division 2, 6.10.1951)

ticket information

SEASON TICKET PRICES

SEATED	ADULT	£130
	(including all cup ties)	
	JUVENILE/OAP	£60

LEAGUE ADMISSION PRICES

SEATED	ADULT	£9
	JUVENILE/OAP	£3.50
STANDING	ADULT	£8
	JUVENILE/OAP	£3

leading goalscorers 1993-2003

Season	Div	No. of Goals	Player
1993-94	S	11	W. Callaghan
1994-95	T	23	M. Yardley
1995-96	T	11	D. Scott
1996-97	T	6	G. Wood
1997-98	T	6	W. Stewart
1998-99	T	7	W. Stewart
1999-00	T	13	M. McDowell
2000-01	T	10	M. McDowell
2001-02	S	17	G. Brown
2002-03	S	10	G. Brown, K. Gordon

the blue brazil's club factfile 2002/03

Date	Venue	Opponents	Att.	Res	O'Connor G.	Miller W.	Campbell Andrew	White D.	Wilson K.	Renwick M.	French H.	Winter C.	Brown G.	Gordon K.	Mauchlen I.	Elliott J.	Gilfillan G.	Dair L.	Munro K.	Dixon J.	Gibb S.	Wright K.	Byle K.	McDonald I.	Risser O.	Obidile E.	Fusco G.	Crabbe G.	Graham M.	Riordan D.	Hilland P.	Buchanan L.	Webster C.	Smith E.	Mowat D.	Bain J.	Myles J.
Aug 3	H	Hamilton Academical	427	1-3	1	2	3	4	5	6	7	8	9	10^1	11	14	15																				
10	A	Stranraer	349	3-2	1	2	3	4^1	5	6	11^1	8	9	10^1	7	14		12																			
17	H	Forfar Athletic	347	1-1	1	2	3	4	5	6	11	8	9^1	10	7	14		12																			
24	H	Raith Rovers	1,678	3-1	1	2	3	4	5	6	11	8	9^1	10^1		12	15	7^1																			
31	A	Airdrie United	1,486	0-0	1	2	3	4	5	6	11	8	9	10		12	15	7																			
Sep 14	A	Brechin City	453	0-0	1	2	3	4	5	6	11	8	9	10			15	7																			
21	H	Stenhousemuir	340	1-0	1	2	3	4	5	6	11	8	9^1	10		12		7																			
28	A	Berwick Rangers	458	1-2	1		3	4	5	6	11	8		10		9		7	2	14^1	15																
Oct 5	H	Dumbarton	363	3-1	1		3	4	5	6		8^1	9^1	12^1	15	11		7	2	10																	
19	H	Stranraer	358	0-1	1	2	3	4	5	6		8	9	11	7	14		12		10																	
26	A	Hamilton Academical	1,052	0-1	1	2	3	4	5	6		8	9	10	11	12		7		14																	
Nov 2	H	Airdrie United	603	0-1	1	2	3	4	5	6		8	9	10	11	12		7				16															
9	A	Raith Rovers	2,428	1-4	1	2	3	4		5			9	10	7	11		8	12		15	16^1	6														
16	H	Brechin City	267	0-1	1	2	3	4	5	6			9	10	7	8		14				16		11													
23	A	Stenhousemuir	377	1-4	1	2	3	4	5	6				10^1	7	9	15						12	11	8	14											
30	A	Dumbarton	754	1-1	1	2	3	4		5		8	9^1	10	14	7							6			11	15										
Dec 14	H	Berwick Rangers	306	1-2	1		3	4	5	2		8	9^1	10	7		14						6			11	15										
28	A	Forfar Athletic	596	1-2	1		3	4	5	2		8	9	10^1		7							6				11	15									
Jan 1	H	Raith Rovers	1,875	1-1			3	4	5	2		8	9^1	10	6	12													1	7	11	16					
18	A	Brechin City	452	7-5			3	4^1	5	2		8	9	10^1	6^1								14						1	7^3	11^1		12				
Feb 8	A	Berwick Rangers	530	2-1			3	4	5	6		8	9^1	10	7	12													1			16^1	11	2	15		
11	A	Airdrie United	1,070	1-1			3	4		6		8	9	10^1	7								14	16					1			15	11	2	5		
25	H	Stenhousemuir	258	3-3			3	4		6		8	9^1	10	7^1	12													1			16	11^1	2	5		
Mar 1	H	Forfar Athletic	323	†2-2			3	5		6		8	9	10	7^1	12								15					1			16	11	2	4		
4	H	Hamilton Academical	281	0-1			12	4	5	6		8	9	10	7	14													1				11	2	3		
8	A	Raith Rovers	1,900	1-2			14	4	5^1	6		8	9	10		7							15						1			16	11	2	3		
11	A	Stranraer	363	4-4			6	4	5	14		8	9^1	10	12	7^2													1				11^1	2	3		
15	H	Airdrie United	585	1-2			3	4	14	12		8	9	10	6	7													1			16^1	11	2	5		
18	H	Dumbarton	184	2-0	1				5	2		8	9	10	6^1	7^1						16		3								11	12		4		
22	A	Stenhousemuir	488	1-1	1				5	6		8	9	10^1	11	7						16		3								14		2	4		
Apr 5	H	Brechin City	274	1-0	1	2	4			6		8	9	10	7^1									3								14	11		5		
12	A	Dumbarton	1,203	1-3	1	2	4	14		6		8	9	10^1	7									3								16	11	15	5		
19	H	Berwick Rangers	256	0-1	1		4		5	2		8	9	10		7						12		3			15						14	11	6		
26	A	Hamilton Academical	1,055	0-2	1	2	4		5	12			9	10		7							14	3			8						11	15	6		
May 3	H	Stranraer	229	0-0	1	2		4	5	8			9	10										3			7						11		6	15	14
10	A	Forfar Athletic	465	1-1	1	2		4	5	8			9	10										3			16					11	14	7	6^1		
TOTAL FULL APPEARANCES					26	19	30	30	28	33	8	30	34	35	22	14		9	2	2			4	10	1	2	3		10	2	2	2	12	11	15		
TOTAL SUB APPEARANCES							2	1	1	3				1	3	14	6	4	1	2	2	6	5	2		1	4	1				10	4	2	1	1	1
TOTAL GOALS SCORED								2	1		1	1	10	10	5	3		1		1		1								3	1	2	2		1		

Small bold figures denote goalscorers. † *denotes opponent's own goal.*

central park

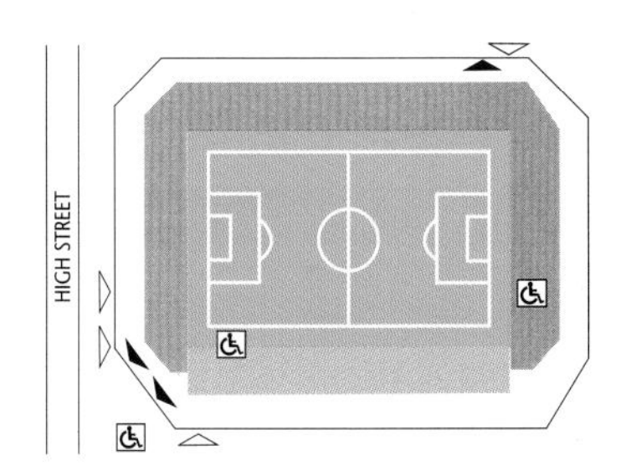

CAPACITY: 4,370; Seated 1,431, Standing 2,939

PITCH DIMENSIONS: 107 yds x 65 yds

FACILITIES FOR DISABLED SUPPORTERS:
Direct access from car park into designated area within ground. Toilet and catering facilities also provided.

team playing kits

how to get there

You can get to Central Park by the following routes:

TRAINS: There is a regular service of trains from Edinburgh and Glasgow (via Edinburgh) which call at Cowdenbeath and the station is only 400 yards from the ground.

BUSES: A limited Edinburgh-Cowdenbeath service stops just outside the ground on matchdays and a frequent service of Dunfermline-Ballingry buses also stop outside the ground, as does the Edinburgh-Glenrothes service.

CARS: Car parking facilities are available in the public car park adjacent to the ground for 190 cars. There are also another 300 spaces at the Stenhouse Street car park, which is 200 yards from the ground.

east stirlingshire

Firs Park, Firs Street,
Falkirk, FK2 7AY

CHAIRMAN
Alan J. Mackin

VICE-CHAIRMAN
Douglas W. Morrison

DIRECTORS
Alexander M. McCabe,
John M. D. Morton
& Alexander S.H. Forsyth

HONORARY PRESIDENT
James Middlemass

CHIEF EXECUTIVE/SECRETARY
Leslie G. Thomson

HEAD COACH
Stephen Morrison

ASSISTANT COACH
Alex Cleland

PHYSIOTHERAPIST
Laura Gillogley

FOOTBALL SAFETY OFFICERS' ASSOCIATION REPRESENTATIVE
Robert Goldie (01324) 634154

GROUNDSMAN/KIT PERSON
James Wilson

MEDIA LIAISON OFFICER
Leslie G. Thomson

TELEPHONES
Ground (01324) 623583
Fax (01324) 637862
Sec. Home (01324) 551099
Sec. Mobile 07739 209648
Manager (at Ground)
(01324) 679796 (evenings only)

E-MAIL & INTERNET ADDRESS
lestshirefc@aol.com
www.east-stirlingshire-fc.co.uk

CLUB SHOP
Situated at ground. Open Mon-Fri
10.00a.m. till 3.00p.m.
(except Wednesday)
and on all home matchdays

CLUB CAPTAIN
Sean McAuley

SHIRT SPONSOR
First Choice:
McFadden's Timber
Second Choice:
Meikle & Co – HR Consultants

KIT SUPPLIER
Pro Star

LIST OF PLAYERS 2003/04

SURNAME	FIRST NAME	MIDDLE NAME	DATE OF BIRTH	PLACE OF BIRTH	DATE OF SIGNING	HEIGHT FT INS	WEIGHT ST LBS	POS. ON PITCH	PREVIOUS CLUB
Baldwin	Christopher	John	31/01/84	Edinburgh	30/05/03	5 9.0	11 0	Def	Salvesen B.C.
Boyle	Gerard		17/04/82	Bellshill	30/07/02	5 8.0	10 2	Fwd	Hamilton Academical
Connolly	Jon	William	03/04/81	Glasgow	08/08/03	6 2.0	14 5	Gk	Cumnock Juniors
Hare	Robert		04/10/70	Glasgow	25/08/03	5 10.0	12 2	Mid	Vale of Clyde Juniors
Kelly	Stuart		01/08/81	Glasgow	31/01/03	5 8.0	10 6	Fwd	Shettleston Juniors
Leishman	Jordan	Nayles	05/04/80	Edinburgh	30/07/02	5 10.0	11 7	Mid	Newtongrange Star Juniors
Livingstone	Scott	Alan	05/04/80	Falkirk	31/08/02	6 0.0	11 2	Mid	Stirling Albion
Mackay	Jamie	Andrew	02/09/81	Glasgow	29/08/02	6 0.0	13 2	Mid	Dumbarton
Maughan	Roderick	Edward	18/12/80	Edinburgh	21/07/01	5 11.0	11 5	Mid	Arbroath
McAuley	Sean		27/02/80	Edinburgh	30/03/01	5 8.0	10 10	Mid	Clyde
McCann	Kevin		17/12/80	Bellshill	15/07/03	6 1.0	12 8	Def	Dumbarton
McCulloch	Gary		15/01/84	Dechmont	30/05/03	5 8.0	9 7	Mid	Livingston
McGhee	Graham		24/09/81	Coatbridge	03/01/01	6 1.0	12 8	Def	Clyde
McLaren	Graeme		08/09/83	Stirling	15/05/02	6 0.0	11 0	Def	Carse Thistle
Morrison	Stephen		15/08/61	St. Andrews	15/07/03	6 0.0	13 10	Def	Dunipace Juniors
Oates	Stephen	John	02/01/84	Falkirk	30/05/03	6 0.0	9 7	Mid	Zeneca Juveniles
Ormiston	David	William	28/11/83	Edinburgh	15/07/03	5 8.0	11 0	Fwd	Gretna
Penman	Craig		09/09/82	Falkirk	27/01/03	5 11.0	12 0	Mid	Everton
Polwart	Douglas		09/03/78	Falkirk	28/07/03	5 8.0	11 0	Mid	Bonnybridge Juniors
Reid	Craig	Andrew	08/09/83	Falkirk	31/01/03	5 11.0	10 13	Def	Bonnybridge Juniors
Rodden	Paul	Andrew	12/08/82	Glasgow	28/07/03	5 6.0	12 3	Fwd	Albion Rovers
Todd	Christopher	James	01/07/82	Stirling	31/01/03	6 1.0	11 6	Gk	Cumbernauld United Juniors
Ure	Derek		20/07/84	Falkirk`	19/02/02	5 9.0	10 0	Fwd	Zeneca Juveniles

milestones

YEAR OF FORMATION: 1881
MOST CAPPED PLAYER: Humphrey Jones
NO. OF CAPS: 5 (for Wales)
MOST LEAGUE POINTS IN A SEASON: 55 (Division 2 – Season 1931/32) (2 Points for a Win)
59 (Third Division – Season 1994/95) (3 Points for a Win)
MOST LEAGUE GOALS SCORED BY A PLAYER IN A SEASON: Malcolm Morrison (Season 1938/39)
NO. OF GOALS SCORED: 36
RECORD ATTENDANCE: 11,500 (-v- Hibernian – 10.2.1969)
RECORD VICTORY: 10-1 (-v- Stenhousemuir – Scottish Cup, 1.9.1888)
RECORD DEFEAT: 1-12 (-v- Dundee United – Division 2, 13.4.1936)

ticket information

	SEASON TICKET PRICES	
SEATED OR STANDING	ADULT	£120
	CONCESSIONS*	£65
	FAMILY TICKET	£150
	LEAGUE ADMISSION PRICES	
SEATED	ADULT	£10
	JUVENILE/OAP	£6
STANDING	ADULT	£8
	CONCESSIONS*	£4

* Concessionary tickets allow OAPs, Juveniles, UB40 holders, Students and people with long term illness to be admitted to ground at the stated concessionary price. Production of DSS Benefit book or similar documentary proof required.

leading goalscorers 1993-2003

Season	Div	No. of Goals	Player
1993-94	S	12	M. McCallum
1994-95	T	16	M. Geraghty
1995-96	T	21	P. Dwyer
1996-97	T	9	G. Inglis
1997-98	T	13	D. Watt
1998-99	T	8	W. McNeill
1999-00	T	9	G. Higgins, S. Laidlaw
2000-01	T	16	S. Hislop
2001-02	T	11	K. Gordon
2002-03	T	5	J. Leishman, D. Ure

the shire's club factfile 2002/03

Date	Venue	Opponents	Att.	Res	Todd C.	Maughan R.	McLaren G.	Bowman G.	McGhee G.	Leishman J.	McAuley Sean	Boyle G.	Ure D.	Carmichael D.	Walker L.	Findlay S.	Struthers W.	Morrison K.	Slythe M.	Drummond J.	Reid C.	Diver D.	Mackay J.	Miller C.	McAuley Scott	Grant D.	Ormiston D.	Fairbairn B.	Livingstone S.	Oates S.	Baldwin C.	Sorbie S.	Penman C.	Clark P.	Allison S.	Lukowiecki M.	Kerr D.	Kelly S.	McCann K.	Campbell M.	McCulloch G.	Skinner J.	Donnelly D.
Aug 3	H	Montrose	287	1-1	1	2	3	4	5	6^{1}	7	8	9	10	12		14	11																									
10	A	East Fife	494	1-4		6	3	4	5	8	7	12	10^{1}	9	15	1	2	11	16																								
17	H	Albion Rovers	321	0-3		2	11		5	6	8		9	10	12	1	7			3	4	14	15																				
24	A	Stirling Albion	434	0-3	1	2	14		5	6	7	10	12				8	11			4			3	9																		
31	H	Morton	748	1-1		2	3		5	6	7	14				1							8			4	9	10	11^{1}														
Sep 14	A	Queen's Park	443	2-0					5	7	8	12^{1}	14			1	2				3		6			4	10^{1}	9	11														
21	H	Gretna	190	0-4					5	7	8	12	14			1	2				3		6			4	10	9	11														
28	H	Elgin City	195	1-2			3		5	7		6	12			1							8		16	4	9^{1}	10	11	2	16												
Oct 5	A	Peterhead	558	0-5	17		3		5	8	7	12	10			1	14						6			4		9	11	2													
19	H	East Fife	315	1-4	1	2	4				7^{1}	16	10				8			3			6			5		9	14		11												
26	A	Montrose	346	2-2		2			5	7	8^{1}	10^{1}	12			1	14			3			6					9	11	4													
Nov 2	A	Morton	1,640	1-4		2	16		5	8^{1}	7	10	14			1				3			6			12		9	11	4													
9	H	Stirling Albion	548	1-1		2	16		5	8	7	10	14^{1}			1				3			6					9	11	4		12											
16	H	Queen's Park	315	0-4		2	16		5	15	8	12	9			1	7			3			4					10		6	11												
23	A	Gretna	221	2-2		2	3		6	11^{1}	10	7	12^{1}			1							8			5		9		4													
30	H	Peterhead	207	1-4		2	3		4	11	7	10	12			1							8			6		9^{1}		5		15											
Dec 17	A	Elgin City	218	1-3	1	2	3		4	11			10^{1}				7						8			6		9	14	5													
28	A	Albion Rovers	326	0-6	1	2	3		5	11	10	7	9				12				6					4			15	14			8										
Jan 1	A	Stirling Albion	593	1-2		2	3			11^{1}	7	12	9			1	8				6								10					4	5								
18	A	Queen's Park	693	4-3	1	2	3			9^{1}	8^{1}	14									4		10											6	5	7	11^{2}						
Feb 8	H	Elgin City	178	2-2		2^{1}	3		6	10	7^{1}	12				1							8										11	4	5			9	14	15			
12	H	Morton	627	0-1		2			3		7		12			1							8											4	5	11		9	6	10			
15	A	Peterhead	584	0-6		2			3	11		15				1							8						16				4	6	5	7		9		10	14		
22	A	East Fife	525	0-3	1	2	3		6	14	7		12																11					4		8		9	5	10	16		
26	H	Gretna	146	1-2	1	2	6			10		14	15										8										7	4	5	11		9		12	3^{1}		
Mar 1	H	Albion Rovers	273	0-4	1	2	3		6	12	7		16										8						15					4	5			9		10	2	11	
8	H	Stirling Albion	302	1-3	1	14	3^{1}		6		7		12										8						11					4	5			9		10	2		16
12	H	Montrose	167	0-3	1	2	3		6	14	7		10										11										8	4	5			9	15	12			
15	A	Morton	2,039	1-2	1	2	3^{1}		8	9	7		12										11											4	5			10	6				
22	A	Gretna	244	1-3	1	2	3		11	16	7		10										8						14					4	5			9^{1}	6	12			
Apr 5	H	Queen's Park	281	0-2	1	2	3		11	12	8	16	10										7											4	5			9	6	15			
12	H	Peterhead	218	1-1	1	2	11		3^{1}	7	8	15																	14				4		5			9	6	10			
19	A	Elgin City	429	0-3	1	2	11		3	7	8	14	12																15				4		5			9	6	10			
26	A	Montrose	235	4-5	1	2	3		6		8	12	10																7^{2}		11		4		5			9^{2}		15	16		
May 3	H	East Fife	511	0-4	1	2	3		6	16	8		10																7		11		4		5			9		14	15		
10	A	Albion Rovers	682	1-3	1	2	3		6		8		10^{1}			21							14						7		11		4					9	5		16		
TOTAL FULL APPEARANCES					19	31	27	2	32	24	32	9	15	3		17	9	3		6	7		24	1	1	10	4	13	14	9	5		10	13	16	5	1	16	8	7	3	1	
TOTAL SUB APPEARANCES					1	1	4			7		16	16		3	1	4		1			1	2		1	1			8	1	1	2							2	7	5		1
TOTAL GOALS SCORED						1	2		1	5	4	2	5														2	1	3								2	3			1		

Small bold figures denote goalscorers. † denotes opponent's own goal.

firs park

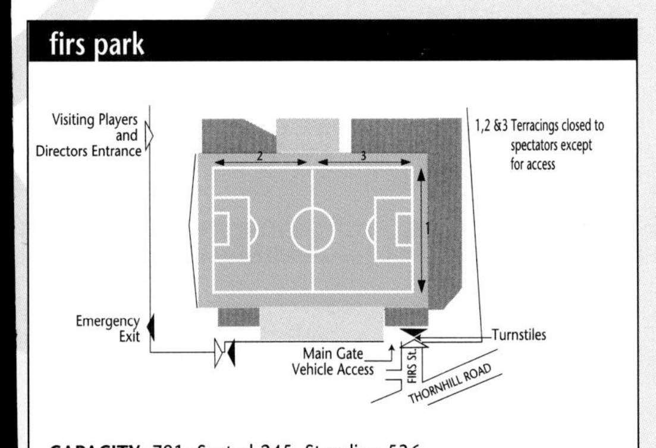

CAPACITY: 781; Seated 245, Standing 536

PITCH DIMENSIONS: 108 yds x 71 yds

FACILITIES FOR DISABLED SUPPORTERS:
By prior arrangement with Secretary.

team playing kits

how to get there

The following routes may be used to reach Firs Park:

TRAINS: Passengers should alight at Grahamston Station and the ground is then five minutes walk.

BUSES: All buses running from the town centre pass close by the ground. The Grangemouth via Burnbank Road and Tamfourhill via Kennard Street services both stop almost outside the ground.

CARS: Car parking is available in the adjacent side streets. There are also spaces available in the car park adjacent to the major stores around the ground.

elgin city

Borough Briggs, Borough Briggs Road, Elgin, IV30 1AP

CHAIRMAN
Denis J. Miller

DIRECTORS
Ronald W. McHardy, John R. Meichan, John A. Milton, William Arif, Norman Green, James Farquhar, Ronald A. Thomson & Roy J. Laing

SECRETARY
John A. Milton

OFFICE ADMINISTRATOR
Audrey Fanning

OFFICE MANAGER/ MATCHDAY PROGRAMME EDITOR
Kevin Cruickshank

MANAGER
David Robertson

ASSISTANT MANAGER
William Furphy

FIRST TEAM COACH
Neil MacLennan

GOALKEEPING COACH
Scott Tait

DIRECTOR OF YOUTH DEVELOPMENT
Harry McFadden

U19 YOUTH COACH
Kenny Black

U15 YOUTH COACHES
Gordon Shanks, Willie McInnes & David Kerr

CLUB DOCTORS
Dr. Alan Rodger, MB, ChB & Dr. Mike Henderson, MB, ChB, MRCGP

FOOTBALL SAFETY OFFICERS' ASSOCIATION REPRESENTATIVE
Steven Hamilton (M)07773 525375

HEAD GROUNDSMAN
Steven Dunn

KIT PERSONS
Ricky Graham & Raymond Miller

STADIUM MAINTENANCE
Bob Cruickshank

COMMERCIAL MANAGER
Michael Teasdale (B)(01343) 551114 (M)07766 148530

TELEPHONES
Ground (01343) 551114
Ground Fax (01343) 547921
Sec. Bus. (01343) 822541
Sec. Home (01343) 546312

E-MAIL
elgincityfc@ukonline.co.uk

CLUB SHOP
Situated at Stadium (01343) 551114
Mon-Fri 9.00a.m.-5.00p.m.
Home Matchdays 10.00a.m.-5.00p.m.

OFFICIAL SUPPORTERS CLUB
Borough Briggs, Borough Briggs Road, Elgin, IV30 1AP
President: Cecil Jack;
Secretary: Mrs. June Jack

ECFC SOCIAL CLUB
Situated within the Main Stand
Tel: (01343) 542710

TEAM CAPTAIN
John Allison

SHIRT SPONSOR
John Fleming – The Merchant

KIT SUPPLIER
ERREA

LIST OF PLAYERS 2003/04

SURNAME	FIRST NAME	MIDDLE NAME	DATE OF BIRTH	PLACE OF BIRTH	DATE OF SIGNING	HEIGHT FT INS	WEIGHT ST LBS	POS. ON PITCH	PREVIOUS CLUB
Allan	Simon	Alexander	15/07/85	Inverness	05/06/03	5 9.0	11 7	Fwd	Elgin City Form S
Allison	John		05/06/70	Dunfermline	17/07/03	5 8.0	11 3	Mid	East Fife
Bone	Alexander	Syme Frew	26/12/71	Stirling	27/05/03	5 9.0	11 7	Fwd	Peterhead
Bremner	Fraser		24/03/85	Elgin	09/07/03	5 11.0	11 7	Mid	Elgin City Form S
Burgess	Graeme	Alistair	25/03/86	Elgin	30/06/03	5 11.0	10 7	Def	Elgin City Form D U16
Campbell	Craig		10/12/83	Dingwall	22/08/03	5 10.0	11 0	Fwd	Ross County
Coulter	Robert	James	25/05/82	Rutherglen	10/07/03	6 3.0	12 7	Def	Stenhousemuir
Davidson	Lee	Ross	25/06/85	Inverness	28/07/03	5 10.0	10 0	Def	Forres Thistle
Gallagher	John		02/06/69	Glasgow	21/01/03	5 9.0	12 0	Def	Queen's Park
Hamilton	Peter	Robert	01/04/85	Glasgow	09/07/03	6 1.0	14 0	Gk	Elgin City Form S
Hind	David	Scott	15/02/82	Inverness	30/03/01	6 1.0	11 7	Def	Inverness Cal. Th.
MacGregor	Michael		30/04/86	Inverness	09/07/03	5 8.0	10 4	Fwd	Elgin City Form D U16
MacGregor	Stuart		30/04/86	Inverness	09/07/03	5 7.0	10 0	Mid	Elgin City Form D U16
Mackay	John	Morrison	16/02/84	Inverness	29/07/03	6 0.0	11 10	Mid	Cowdenbeath
Martin	William	McLean	21/08/81	Glasgow	30/06/03	6 1.0	12 0	Mid/Fwd	Queen's Park
McCormick	Steven	Walter	10/11/75	Bellshill	17/07/03	5 6.0	10 0	Mid/Fwd	Stenhousemuir
McLean	Charles	Crossan	08/11/73	Glasgow	05/06/03	5 10.0	11 7	Fwd	Albion Rovers
McLean	Neil	Peter	30/05/81	Glasgow	17/07/03	5 10.0	12 0	Mid	Forfar Athletic
McMillan	Allister	Scott	08/08/76	Glasgow	31/08/03	6 1.0	13 10	Def	Irvine Meadow Juniors
McMullan	Ryan	James	26/11/81	Bellshill	30/06/03	5 8.0	10 0	Mid/Fwd	Albion Rovers
Moir	Lee	Andrew	12/12/85	Elgin	30/06/03	5 9.0	10 0	Fwd	Elgin City Form S
Murphy	John	Scott	01/12/83	Bellshill	28/07/03	5 8.0	11 7	Mid	Stenhousemuir
Ogboke	Christopher	Koranaki	18/02/82	Aberdeen	08/08/03	6 0.0	12 10	Fwd	Dyce Juniors
Pirie	Martin	James	01/06/72	Aberdeen	26/07/00	6 2.0	13 9	Gk	Peterhead
Robertson	David	Alexander	17/10/68	Aberdeen	29/07/03	5 11.0	13 0	Def	Montrose
Smith	Andrew	Brown	12/03/84	Fochabers	09/08/01	6 3.0	11 0	Def	Elgin City B.C.
Steele	Kevin	James	11/10/81	Dundee	01/08/02	5 11.0	10 7	Fwd	Arbroath
Tait	Scott	MacIntosh	01/02/69	Peterhead	29/08/03	5 10.0	14 0	Gk	Cruden Bay Juniors
Teasdale	Michael	Joseph	28/07/69	Elgin	26/03/02	6 0.0	13 0	Def / Mid	Inverness Cal. Th.
White	James		05/06/80	Glasgow	22/05/03	6 0.0	12 0	Def	Queen's Park

milestones

YEAR OF FORMATION: 1893
MOST CAPPED PLAYER: Douglas Grant (Scotland Amateur Internationalist)
MOST LEAGUE POINTS IN A SEASON: 55 (Highland League - Season 1967/68) (2 Points for a Win)
81 (Highland League - Season 1989/90) (3 Points for a Win)
47 (SFL Third Division - Season 2001/02) (3 Points for a Win)
MOST LEAGUE GOALS SCORED BY A PLAYER IN A SEASON: Ian Gilzean (Season 2001/02)
NO. OF GOALS SCORED: 13
RECORD ATTENDANCE: 12,608 (-v- Arbroath – 17.2.1968)
RECORD VICTORY: 18-1 (-v- Brora Rangers – North of Scotland Cup – 6.2.1960)
RECORD DEFEAT: 1-14 (-v- Heart of Midlothian – Scottish Cup – 4.2.1939)

ticket information

SEASON TICKET PRICES

SEATED

ADULT	£140
JUVENILE /OAP	£80

STANDING

ADULT	£110
JUVENILE /OAP	£50

LEAGUE ADMISSION PRICES

SEATED

ADULT	£9
JUVENILE /OAP	£4

STANDING

ADULT	£7
JUVENILE /OAP	£3

leading goalscorers 1993-2003

Season	Div	No. of Goals	Player
Season 2000-01 was the club's first season in membership of SFL			
2000-01	T	6	Colin Milne, D. Ross
2001-02	T	12	I. Gilzean
2002-03	T	6	K. Steele

the black and whites' club factfile 2002/03

Date	Venue	Opponents	Att.	Res	Pirie M.	MacDonald S.	McBride R.	Hind D.	Mackay D.	Tully C.	Ross D.	Love C.	McMullan R.	Steele K.	Craig D.	Sanderson M.	James R.	Campbell C.	Smith A.	Grant G.	Hosie W.	Teasdale M.	Taylor R.	Bremner F.	Gallagher J.	Rattray S.	Allan S.	Hamilton P.	Tatters G.	MacGregor M.
Aug 3	A	Queen's Park	585	2-1	1	2	3	4	5	6	7	8	9[1]	10[1]	11	14	12													
10	H	Gretna	587	0-2	1	2	3	12	5	6	4	10	9	8	11	15	14	7												
17	A	Stirling Albion	428	1-1	1	2	16	4	5	6	7	8	9	10		11[1]	14		3											
24	H	Peterhead	697	3-0	1	2	16	4	5	6	7[1]	8	9	10		11[1]	14[1]	12	3											
31	A	Montrose	417	0-1	1	2		4	5	6	7	8	9	10		11	14	12	3	15										
Sep 14	H	East Fife	599	1-1	1	2	3	8	5	6	7		9	10	14[1]	11	15	12		4										
21	A	Albion Rovers	303	1-1	1	2	3		5	6	7		9[1]	10	11	4		8		12	14									
28	A	East Stirlingshire	195	2-1	1	2	3		5	6	7[1]	16	9	10[1]	11	4	15	8		12										
Oct 5	H	Morton	895	0-1	1	2	3		5	6	7	4	9	10	12	11		8												
19	A	Gretna	323	0-0	1	2		12	5	6	8	4	9	10	11			7		3		14								
26	H	Queen's Park	567	2-2		2		12	5	6[1]		4[1]	9	10	11	16		7		3		8	1							
Nov 2	H	Montrose	503	0-0	1	2		14	5	6	7	10	9	12	11	16		8		3		4								
9	A	Peterhead	728	2-2	1		3	12	5	6	7	8		10	11[1]	16		9[1]		2		4								
16	A	East Fife	525	0-4	1	14	3	4	5	6	7	8		10	11	16		9		2		12								
23	A	Albion Rovers	253	1-1	1	2	3	4	5	6	7	8	9[1]	10	11					14		12								
30	A	Morton	1,658	0-4	1	2	14	4	3	6	7	8	9	10	11		16			12		5								
Dec 7	H	Peterhead	457	0-4	1		3	4	5	6	7	8	9		11	10	15			2				16						
17	H	East Stirlingshire	218	3-1	1	2	11	4	5	6	7[1]	10	9[1]		14	15[1]	8			12		3								
21	A	Queen's Park	648	2-3	1	2	11	4		6[2]	7	10	9	8	3		12			5				14						
28	H	Stirling Albion	556	0-3	1	5	3	4		6	7	8	9	10	11	14	12			2				15						
Jan 18	H	East Fife	435	0-1	1		8	6				12	9	10		11	7			2		5			3	4	16			
25	A	Montrose	211	0-2	1		8	4	5		7	14	9	10		11	12			2		6			3	15				
Feb 8	A	East Stirlingshire	178	2-2				2	5	6	7[1]	15	9	10		11	8[1]	16				4			3			1		
15	H	Morton	701	0-0				4	5	6	7		9	10		11	8	12				2			3			1		
22	H	Gretna	383	2-2			14	4	5	6	7[1]		9	10[1]		11	8	12				2			3	15		1		
Mar 1	A	Stirling Albion	407	0-4	1		8	4	5	6	7	16	9	10		11	14					2			3	15				
8	A	Peterhead	854	2-3	1		12	4	5	6[1]	7			10[1]		11	9					2			3	8				
15	H	Montrose	377	0-2	1		2	4	5	6			9	10		11	14					3		7		8			16	15
22	H	Albion Rovers	333	0-1				4	5	6			9	10		11	12	8		2				7	3			1		
29	H	Albion Rovers	280	1-2				4	5	6			9	10[1]		11	16	8		2				7	3			1		
Apr 5	A	East Fife	514	0-5	1		12	4	5	6		8	7	10		11	9			2				16	3					
12	A	Morton	1,662	0-2	1			4	5	6		8	9			11				2		10		7	3					16
19	H	East Stirlingshire	429	3-0	1		12	4	5	6		8	9	10		14				2		11[2]		7[1]	3					16
26	H	Queen's Park	444	0-0	1			4	5	6		8	9	10		7				2		11		14	3					16
May 3	A	Gretna	250	1-2	1		2	4	5	6			9[1]	10		11				15		8		7	3					
10	H	Stirling Albion	386	2-2	1		2	4	5	6			9	10[1]		11						8[1]		7	3					
TOTAL FULL APPEARANCES					30	17	19	28	33	34	25	21	33	32	14	23	7	11	3	17		18	1	7	15	3		5		
TOTAL SUB APPEARANCES						1	7	5				5		1	3	9	16	6		7	1	3		5		3	1		1	4
TOTAL GOALS SCORED										4	5	1	5	6	2	3	2	1				3		1						

Small bold figures denote goalscorers. † denotes opponent's own goal.

borough briggs

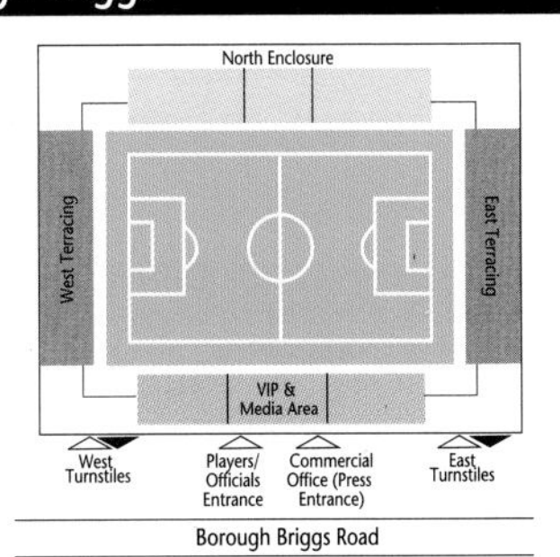

CAPACITY: 4,962; Seated 480, Standing 4,482

PITCH DIMENSIONS: 111 yds x 72 yds

FACILITIES FOR DISABLED SUPPORTERS:
An area is designated in the south east enclosure.

team playing kits

how to get there

Borough Briggs can be reached by the following routes:

TRAINS: – Elgin Railway Station is situated approximately one mile south of the stadium. Regular connections to and from Aberdeen and Inverness.

BUSES: – Elgin Bus Station is situated in the town centre, which is only half a mile from Borough Briggs. Regular connections to and from Aberdeen and Inverness.

CARS: – Elgin is situated on the A96, 38 miles east of Inverness and 67 miles west of Aberdeen. From the south, leave A9 at Aviemore and take the A95 as far as Craigellachie then take A941 to Elgin.

gretna

LIST OF PLAYERS 2003/04

SURNAME	FIRST NAME	MIDDLE NAME	DATE OF BIRTH	PLACE OF BIRTH	DATE OF SIGNING	HEIGHT FT INS	WEIGHT ST LBS	POS. ON PITCH	PREVIOUS CLUB
Allan	James		21/09/79	Glasgow	14/07/03	5 9.0	11 0	Mid	Queen's Park
Armstrong	Kyle	Leslie	01/07/86	Carlisle	02/08/03	6 1.0	12 3	Fwd	Northbank Carlisle
Bain	Jamie	Donald	16/08/86	Edinburgh	02/08/03	5 11.0	10 5	Def	Cowdenbeath
Baldacchino	Ryan		13/01/81	Leicester	22/08/03	5 10.0	10 8	Fwd	Carlisle United
Bell	Martin		21/12/84	Dumfries	27/08/03	5 11.0	11 0	Def	Kello Rovers Juniors
Birch	Mark		05/01/77	Stoke on Trent	21/08/03	5 11.0	13 2	Def	Carlisle United
Bonnar	George		10/09/86	Broxburn	02/08/03	5 10.0	10 2	Mid	Falkirk Form D U16
Cameron	Martin	George	16/06/78	Dunfermline	14/07/03	6 1.0	14 0	Fwd	St. Mirren
Cleeland	Marc		15/12/75	Whitehaven	24/08/02	5 8.0	10 5	Mid	Tarff Rovers
Cohen	Gary	Dane	20/01/84	Leyton	30/07/03	5 10.0	12 3	Fwd	Scarborough
Cosgrove	Stephen		29/12/80	Glasgow	29/08/03	5 9.0	10 7	Mid	Clyde
Cumersky	Ian		09/12/85	Carlisle	01/08/02	5 9.0	9 10	Mid	Carlisle United
Eccles	Mark		16/10/80	Shotley Bridge	22/08/03	6 0.0	11 8	Mid	Tow Law Town
Galloway	Michael	Anthony	13/10/74	Nottingham	01/01/03	5 10.0	12 8	Mid	Carlisle United
Gordon	Wayne		10/07/84	Munster	31/07/02	5 10.0	10 0	Mid	Gretna
Grainger	Daniel	Leslie	28/07/86	Carlisle	19/10/02	6 0.0	12 0	Def	Penrith Juniors
Holdsworth	David	Gary	08/11/68	Walthamstow	24/07/03	6 0.0	13 3	Def	Scarborough
Hore	John	Stephen	18/08/82	Liverpool	02/08/02	6 0.0	12 8	Fwd	Carlisle United
Irons	David	John	18/07/61	Glasgow	31/07/02	5 11.0	11 4	Def	Annan Thistle
Knox	Keith		06/08/64	Stranraer	01/01/03	6 0.0	12 0	Def	Alloa Athletic
Lennon	Daniel	Joseph	06/04/70	Whitburn	18/07/03	5 7.0	10 10	Mid	Partick Thistle
Little	Liam	John	27/07/86	Whangari	02/08/03	6 3.0	12 6	Gk	Picton Rangers
Maddison	Lee	Robert	05/10/72	Bristol	29/08/03	6 2.0	12 11	Def	Carlisle United
Mathieson	David	James	18/01/78	Dumfries	02/08/02	6 0.0	12 10	Gk	Queen of the South
May	Kyle		07/09/82	Carlisle	15/08/02	6 0.0	12 12	Def	Carlisle United
McCaig	James	Francis	01/09/85	Irvine	02/08/03	5 7.0	10 2	Def	Queen of the South
McGuffie	Ryan		22/07/80	Dumfries	05/08/02	6 2.0	12 6	Def/Mid	Newcastle United
McKechnie	Stuart	Andrew	27/10/86	Greenock	02/08/03	5 8.0	11 0	Mid/Fwd	Morton
O'Neill	Paul	Denys	17/06/82	Farnworth	01/08/03	6 2.0	13 0	Def	Macclesfield Town
Patterson	Liam	Collin Allan	16/08/86	Dumfries	02/08/03	6 0.0	11 2	Def	Unattached
Prokas	Richard		22/01/76	Penrith	05/08/03	5 10.0	12 0	Mid	Workington
Robb	Richard		24/01/83	Irvine	11/07/03	6 6.0	13 8	Def	St. Mirren
Skelton	Gavin	Richard	27/03/81	Carlisle	31/07/02	5 10.0	12 10	Def	Gretna
Spence	Colin	William	02/03/84	Irvine	02/08/03	5 9.0	10 5	Mid	Bonnyton Thistle
Summersgill	Craig	William	02/10/85	Hexham	02/08/03	6 2.0	13 4	Gk	Haltwhistle
Wylie	David		04/04/66	Johnstone	31/08/02	6 0.0	13 7	Gk	Gretna

Raydale Park, Dominion Road,
Gretna, DG16 5AP.

PRESIDENT
Brian Fulton

HON. LIFE PRESIDENT
Tom Kerr

CHAIRMAN
Ron MacGregor MA(Hons), FIHM

DIRECTORS
Brooks Mileson, Helen MacGregor,
Paul Grootendorst & Stephen Barker

MANAGING DIRECTOR
Brooks Mileson

NON EXECUTIVE DIRECTOR
Mark Hampson

SECRETARY
Mrs Helen MacGregor MSR, DCR

GENERAL MANAGER
Colin Carter

MANAGER
Rowan Alexander

ASSISTANT MANAGER
Derek Frye

DIRECTOR OF YOUTH FOOTBALL
Leigh Manson

RESERVE COACH
Toby Paterson

U17 COACHES
Neil McKenzie & Dick Wassen

COMMERCIAL DIRECTOR
Steve Barker

CLUB DOCTOR
Dr Kenneth McQueen

PHYSIOTHERAPISTS
Billy Bentley & Gael Moffat

GROUNDSMAN
Paul Barnett

MEDIA LIAISON OFFICER
Ron MacGregor

MATCHDAY PROGRAMME EDITOR
Richard Wharton

TELEPHONES
Ground (01461) 337602
Ground Fax (01461) 338047
Chairman/Secretary's Home & Fax
(01387) 811820

E-MAIL & INTERNET ADDRESS
info@gretnafootballclub.co.uk
www.gretnafootballclub.co.uk

CLUB SHOP
Situated at Ground. (01461) 337602
Open on Home Matchdays
1.00 p.m. to 5.00 p.m.
Contact: Alan Watson (01387) 251550

SUPPORTERS CLUB
Secretary: Richard Wharton
31 Lindisfarne Street, Carlisle CA1 2ND
Tel No. (01228) 547761

TEAM CAPTAIN
Michael Galloway

SHIRT SPONSOR
First Choice: www.warmstrong.co.uk
Second Choice: Kwik-Fit Insurance Services

KIT SUPPLIER
XARA

milestones

YEAR OF FORMATION: 1946
MOST LEAGUE POINTS IN A SEASON: 95 (Northern League (Champions) - Season 1990/91) (3 Points for a Win)
45 (SFL Third Division – Season 2002/03 – 3 Points for a Win)
MOST LEAGUE GOALS SCORED BY A PLAYER IN A SEASON: Dennis "Touchy" Smith (Season 1950/51)
NO. OF GOALS SCORED: 101
RECORD ATTENDANCE: 2,307 (-v- Rochdale – F.A. Cup 1991)
RECORD VICTORY: 20-0 (-v- Silloth – Carlisle & District League 1962)
RECORD DEFEAT: 2-9 (-v- Ashton United – Unibond League Division 1 – 28.10.2000)

ticket information

SEASON TICKET PRICES

SEATED	
ADULT	£135
JUVENILE /OAP	£68
STANDING	
ADULT	£117
JUVENILE /OAP	£59

LEAGUE ADMISSION PRICES

SEATED	
ADULT	£8
JUVENILE /OAP	£4
STANDING	
ADULT	£7
JUVENILE /OAP	£3.50

leading goalscorers 1993-2003

Season 2002-03 was the club's first season in membership of SFL

Season	Div	No. of Goals	Player
2002-03	T	10	M. Dobie

the black and whites club factfile 2002/03

Date	Venue	Opponents	Att.	Res	Mathieson D.	McGuffie R.	Skelton G.	Turner T.	Hewson D.	Henney M.	Skinner S.	Irons D.	Dobie M.	Hore J.	Gordon W.	Alexander R.	May K.	Eeles S.	Smart C.	Cumersky I.	Rooke S.	Thwaites A.	Benjamin A.	McQuilter R.	Cleeland M.	Bell M.	Harding G.	Grainger D.	Barr W.	Milligan S.	Wylie D.	Fairbairn B.	Galloway M.	Knox K.	Thurstan M.	Ormiston D.	Errington R.
Aug 3	H	Morton	1,566	1-1	1	2	3	4	5	6[1]	7	8	9	10	11	14																					
10	A	Elgin City	587	2-0	1	14	3	4	2	6	7[1]	8	9[1]	10			5	11	15	17																	
17	H	Montrose	373	4-1	1	11	3	4	2	6	7	8[1]	9[1]	10[2]			5			17																	
24	H	Albion Rovers	443	2-0	1	11[1]	3	4	2	6	7	8	9	10[1]			5				14																
31	A	Queen's Park	607	0-1	1	11	3	4	2	6	7	8	9	10			5					15	16														
Sep 14	H	Peterhead	357	1-4	1	11		4	2	6	7	8	9	14			5				16	3	10[1]	15													
21	A	East Stirlingshire	190	4-0	1	7	16		11	6[1]	15[1]	8	9	10			4				2	3	14[2]	5													
28	H	Stirling Albion	402	0-2	1	11		15	2	6	14	8	9	17			4				7	3	10	5													
Oct 5	A	East Fife	462	2-3	1		3	4	2	6[1]	7	8	9	10[1]			5					11	16														
19	A	Elgin City	323	0-0	1	16	3	4	2	10	7	8		9			6			14		11	15	5													
26	H	Morton	1,705	2-2	1	2	3	4	6	10		8	14				5[1]	9[1]	16	11					7												
Nov 2	H	Queen's Park	319	2-2	1	2	3	4	7	10		6	14[1]					9[1]		11		15			8	5	17										
9	A	Albion Rovers	332	1-2	1	2[1]		4		10		8	14				5	9		11					7			3	6								
16	A	Peterhead	496	1-1	1	11	3		2	10[1]	7	8	9				5								6	4											
23	H	East Stirlingshire	221	2-2	1	11	3	4	2	10	7[1]	8	9				5			15					6					16							
30	H	East Fife	352	2-3	1	2		4	16	10	7	8	9[1]	14			5		11						6[1]				3								
Dec 7	H	Albion Rovers	289	1-2	1	2		4		10[1]	7	8	9				5	15						6	11					3							
14	A	Stirling Albion	412	1-0	1	2	17	4		11	7	8	9[1]	10			3		15					5	6												
28	A	Montrose	381	2-0	1	2	15		14[1]	6	7	8	9	10[1]			4							5	11				3		12						
Jan 11	A	Queen's Park	934	2-1	1		3	4		11	7	8	9[2]	10			2							5	6							15	14				
18	H	Peterhead	360	1-1	1			4			7	11	9[1]	10			2							5	6								8	3	17		
Feb 8	H	Stirling Albion	292	0-0	1		15	4			7	6	9				2							5	3							10	8	11	16	14	
22	A	Elgin City	383	2-2	1	16	15				7	6	9[1]				3							5	11							10	8[1]	2	4		
26	A	East Stirlingshire	146	2-1	1		15	4			7	11	9[1]											5	3							10	8	2	6	17[1]	
Mar 1	H	Montrose	227	2-2	1	17	3				15	7	9	16										5		6						11[1]	8[1]	2	4	10	
4	A	East Fife	503	1-2	1	7	3					6	9	10[1]			4							5	11								8	2		15	
8	A	Albion Rovers	327	1-1	1	11	3				16	4	9	10[1]										5	6	2							8	7			
15	H	Queen's Park	320	0-1	1	11	3			2		6	9	10						7				5		4						15	8				
22	H	East Stirlingshire	244	3-1	1	6[1]	11		17			5	9	10[1]	7[1]					8						2		3	4			16					
29	H	Morton	601	0-1	1	6	11		7			4		9	10		5									2		3				15	8			14	
Apr 5	A	Peterhead	598	0-1	1	6	11		2			4		9	7		5			15								3				10	8	14			
12	H	East Fife	409	3-3	1	6	11[1]		7			4			10		5[1]									16		3				9	8	2[1]			
19	A	Stirling Albion	376	0-1	1	6	11		7		15	4			10		5			17						16		3				9	8	2			
26	A	Morton	2,422	0-5	1	6	3		11		7	4			10		5			15								16				9	8	2			
May 3	H	Elgin City	250	2-1	1	6	14		5		11[1]	4			9	10[1]									3	16						15	8	2			7
10	A	Montrose	376	1-0		6	11		14		7	5			10											2		3			1	9[1]	8	4			16
TOTAL FULL APPEARANCES					35	27	23	19	20	21	22	36	25	18	9	1	27	4	1	5	2	5	2	15	17	8		7	4	1	1	9	15	12	3	1	1
TOTAL SUB APPEARANCES						4	7	1	4		5		3	4		1		1	3	7	2	2	4	1		3	1	1		1	1	5	1	1	2	4	1
TOTAL GOALS SCORED						3	1		1	5	5	1	10	8	1	1	2	2					3		1							2	2	1		1	

Small bold figures denote goalscorers. † denotes opponent's own goal.

third division

raydale park

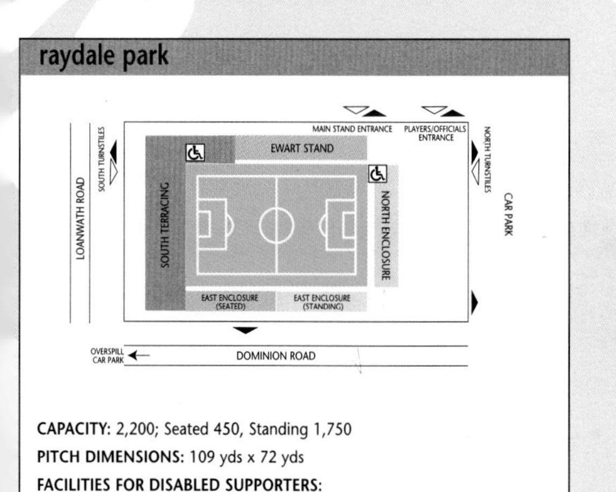

CAPACITY: 2,200; Seated 450, Standing 1,750

PITCH DIMENSIONS: 109 yds x 72 yds

FACILITIES FOR DISABLED SUPPORTERS:
Toilets and ramps in place. Further information available from Secretary.

team playing kits

how to get there

Raydale Park can be reached by the following routes:
BUSES: Buses between Carlisle and Annan and Dumfries serve Gretna.
TRAINS: Gretna Station is on the Glasgow-Carlisle line. Raydale Park is approximately one mile south-west of the station.
CARS: From the North: Leave M74 at sign for Old Blacksmith's Shop Visitor sign (B7076). Go through Springfield into Gretna Green. Turn left and left again. Go through traffic lights into Gretna. Through roundabout take B721 at Crossways Inn. After $\frac{1}{4}$ mile turn left into Dominion Road. Raydale Park is on your right. **From the South:** 8 miles north of Carlisle look for the Old Blacksmith's Shop Visitor Centre sign. Take B7076 to Gretna. In Gretna turn left at Crossways Inn and go on the Annan Road for $\frac{1}{4}$ mile. Turn left into Dominion Road and Raydale Park is on your right. **From the West:** Leave A75 at sign for Gretna (B721). Turn left into Gretna and right into Dominion Road. Raydale Park is on your right.

montrose

Links Park Stadium,
Wellington Street,
Montrose, DD10 8QD

ALL CORRESPONDENCE SHOULD BE ADDRESSED TO:
Secretary, Montrose FC,
16/18 Swan Street, Brechin,
Angus, DD9 6EF

CHAIRMAN
John F. Paton

VICE-CHAIRMAN
Malcolm J. Watters

DIRECTORS
John D. Crawford, David I. Tait,
David G. Skene & Andrew Stephen

HONORARY PRESIDENT
William Johnston, M.B.E., J.P.

SECRETARY/YOUTH CO-ORDINATOR
Malcolm J. Watters

OFFICE ADMINISTRATOR
Andrew Stephen

MANAGER
John Sheran

FIRST TEAM COACH
Henry Hall

COMMERCIAL MANAGER
Mrs Glynis Crawford
(B)(01674) 673200 (H)(01674) 673758

PHYSIOTHERAPIST
Linda Julier

GROUNDSMAN
Ron Marquis

KIT PERSON
Brian Leiper

MATCHDAY PROGRAMME EDITOR
Andrew Stephen
(B) (01356) 626766 (H) (01674) 672314

TELEPHONES
Ground/Commercial (01674) 673200
Sec. Home (01674) 674838
Sec. Bus. (01356) 623408
Ground Fax (01674) 677311

INTERNET ADDRESS
www.montrosefc.co.uk

CLUB SHOP
Situated at Stadium (01674) 674941.
Open 10.30 a.m. – 5.00 p.m. Fri.
and on home matchdays

OFFICIAL SUPPORTERS CLUB
c/o Links Park, Wellington Street,
Montrose, DD10 8QD

TEAM CAPTAIN
Craig Farnan

SHIRT SPONSOR
RGIT Montrose

KIT SUPPLIER
Errea

LIST OF PLAYERS 2003/04

SURNAME	FIRST NAME	MIDDLE NAME	DATE OF BIRTH	PLACE OF BIRTH	DATE OF SIGNING	HEIGHT FT INS	WEIGHT ST LBS	POS. ON PITCH	PREVIOUS CLUB
Black	Roddy		22/02/78	Dundee	29/08/03	5 10.0	12 0	Mid	Brechin City
Brash	Kristofer		01/03/83	Dundee	31/08/03	5 8.0	10 7	Mid	Dundee
Budd	Alan	Douglas	23/02/84	Kirkcaldy	30/08/03	5 10.0	12 0	Mid	Glenrothes Juniors
Butter	James	Ross	14/12/66	Dundee	15/07/03	6 1.0	12 12	Gk	East Fife
Conway	Francis	Joseph	29/12/69	Dundee	30/05/01	6 0.0	12 4	Def	Alloa Athletic
Donachie	Barry	James	21/12/79	Dundee	18/01/03	5 8.0	12 0	Mid	Brechin City
Farnan	Craig		07/04/71	Dundee	15/07/03	5 10.0	12 7	Mid	East Fife
Ferguson	Stuart		09/11/80	Bangour	03/08/00	5 10.0	10 5	Def / Mid	Forfar Athletic
Gibson	Keith		01/05/81	Dundee	24/06/02	6 0.0	9 13	Mid	Dundee
Gilzean	Ian	Roger	10/12/69	Enfield	12/07/02	6 2.0	12 6	Fwd	Elgin City
Hankinson	Michael	Richard	04/07/83	Dundee	31/08/02	6 1.0	11 7	Gk	Tayport Juniors
Henderson	Robbie	Matthew	02/09/81	Perth	30/08/02	5 11.0	10 0	Fwd	Brechin City
Kerrigan	Steven	Paul	29/09/70	Wolverhampton	30/05/01	5 10.0	11 7	Fwd	East Fife
Lannen	Shaun	Francis	19/03/85	Dundee	30/08/02	5 9.0	10 11	Def	Lochee Harp Juniors
McQuillan	John		20/07/70	Stranraer	08/02/02	5 10.0	11 8	Def	Dundee United
Michie	Scott	David	22/08/83	Aberdeen	08/08/03	5 10.0	11 1	Fwd	Aberdeen
Narey	Steven	David	29/09/83	Dundee	30/08/03	5 9.0	10 7	Def	Carnoustie Panmure
Sharp	Graeme		03/05/84	Fraserburgh	31/01/03	5 10.0	10 7	Mid	Banchory St. Ternan Juniors
Simpson	Mark	James	04/11/75	Aberdeen	02/08/03	5 11.0	12 4	Def	Peterhead
Smart	Craig		26/11/78	Kirkcaldy	29/07/03	5 9.0	11 7	Fwd	Hill O' Beath Hawthorn Juniors
Smith	Greig	Robert	26/03/76	Aberdeen	29/07/03	6 0.0	12 6	Def	Peterhead
Stephen	Neil	Andrew	03/07/84	Dundee	14/07/03	6 2.0	12 7	Def	Dundee
Stewart	Michael		26/07/84	Dundee	30/08/02	5 9.0	9 5	Def	Lochee Harp Juniors
Thomson	Graeme	David	23/02/81	Falkirk	22/11/02	5 10.0	10 7	Def	Dundee
Watt	Jamie	Anthony	27/02/78	Aberdeen	15/07/03	5 7.5	11 0	Fwd	Deveronvale
Webster	Kevin	Scott	21/01/83	Dundee	29/03/02	5 9.0	10 0	Mid	Dundee
Wood	Martin		20/08/82	Aberdeen	15/07/03	5 10.0	12 7	Fwd	Ross County

milestones

YEAR OF FORMATION: 1879
MOST CAPPED PLAYER: Sandy Keiller
NO. OF CAPS: 6 (2 whilst with Montrose)
MOST LEAGUE POINTS IN A SEASON: 53 (Division 2 – 1974/75 and Second Division 1984/85) (2 Points for a Win)
67 (Third Division – Season 1994/95) (3 Points for a Win)
RECORD ATTENDANCE: 8,983 (-v- Dundee – 17.3.1973)
RECORD VICTORY: 12-0 (-v- Vale of Leithen – Scottish Cup, 4.1.1975)
RECORD DEFEAT: 0-13 (-v- Aberdeen, 17.3.1951)

ticket information

SEASON TICKET PRICES

SEATED OR STANDING	ADULT	£120
	JUVENILE/OAP	£60
	FAMILY (1 ADULT & 1 JUVENILE)	£140

LEAGUE ADMISSION PRICES

STANDING	ADULT	£8.00
	JUVENILE/OAP	£4.00

leading goalscorers 1993-2003

Season	Div	No. of Goals	Player
1993-94	S	12	D. Grant
1994-95	T	19	C. McGlashan
1995-96	S	16	C. McGlashan
1996-97	T	11	C. McGlashan
1997-98	T	20	C. McGlashan
1998-99	T	7	S. Taylor
1999-00	T	12	S. Taylor
2000-01	T	7	J. Mitchell
2001-02	T	13	S. Laidlaw
2002-03	T	8	S. Kerrigan

the gable endies' club factfile 2002/03

Date	Venue	Opponents	Att.	Res	McGlynn G.	McCheyne G.	Robertson D.	Gibson K.	Conway F.	McQuillan J.	Webster K.	Johnson H.G.	McDonald C.	Webster C.	McKinnon R.	Brand R.	Mitchell J.	Leask M.	Ferguson S.	Sharp G.	Christie G.	Kerrigan S.	Camara M.L.	Henderson R.	Gilzean I.	Craig D.	Campbell J.	Thomson G.	Budd A.	Hankinson M.	Donachie B.	McKechnie G.	Riley P.	Munro K.
Aug 3	A	East Stirlingshire	287	1-1	1	2	3	4	5	6	7	8	9^1	10	11	12	15	14																
10	H	Queen's Park	402	1-0	1	2	3	4	5	6	7^1	8	9	10	11	12	15	14																
17	A	Gretna	373	1-4	1	2	3	4		6	10	8	9	7^1	11	12		16	5	15														
24	A	East Fife	578	0-2	1	2	3		6	4	7	8		10		9			11		5	12	15	16										
31	H	Elgin City	417	1-0	1		3	4^1	6	2	7	8	9	14					11	16	5	15			10									
Sep 14	A	Stirling Albion	439	1-1	1	7	6	4	5	2	14	8	9	11					3			12^1			10	15								
21	H	Morton	543	2-5	1	6	3	4	5	2	12	8		11^1						16		9^1			10	7								
28	H	Peterhead	433	0-3		5		4		6	14	8		12	11	7			3			9			10	2	1							
Oct 5	A	Albion Rovers	380	1-1		6				2	9	8		11	4				3		5	10^1		16	12	7	1							
19	A	Queen's Park	492	1-0		2		4		6	7	8	12	11					3		5	9		10^1	15	14	1							
26	H	East Stirlingshire	346	2-2		2		4		6	7	8^1	12	11	15				3		5	9^1		10	14		1							
Nov 2	A	Elgin City	503	0-0		2		4	5	6	14	8	9	16	11				3			10			12	7	1							
9	H	East Fife	373	0-5				4	5	6	15	8	9		11				3		2	10		16	12	7	1							
16	H	Stirling Albion	364	1-1	1			4		6	7^1	8	9	12	16				3			10		15		2		5	11					
23	A	Morton	1,748	2-4	1			4	2	6	7	8		14	10				3			9		12^2	16			5	11					
30	H	Albion Rovers	271	0-1	1			2	4	6	7	8		15	11				3		5	9		10	12				14					
Dec 14	A	Peterhead	550	2-4	1			2^2	4	6	7	8		14	11	16			3		5	10		9						21				
28	H	Gretna	381	0-2				2	4	6	12	8			11	10			3	7		9		14	15		1	5						
Jan 1	A	East Fife	519	0-2	1			4	6	2	7	8				14			3	15	5	10		11	9				16					
18	A	Stirling Albion	524	1-1	1			4		6		8^1							3		5	15			9				11		2	7	10	12
25	H	Elgin City	211	2-0	1			4	16	6		8	9						3		5	10^1		7^1				15			2		11	
Feb 8	H	Peterhead	442	1-2	1	3		16		6		8^1	10						11		5	9		12				14			2	7	4	
22	H	Queen's Park	315	1-1	1			12	4	6	16	8				15			3		5	10				7					2	9^1	11	
25	H	Morton	343	0-0	1			4		6	7	8				10					5					12		3	16		2	9	11	
Mar 1	A	Gretna	227	2-2	1	5^1		4		6	7	8							15			16		14		10		3			2	9^1	11	
4	A	Albion Rovers	224	0-3	1	12		4		6	7	8				14			3		5	10		15							2	9	11	
8	H	East Fife	455	0-2	1	2		4		6						12			3	15	5	10		14		7		11				9	8	
12	A	East Stirlingshire	167	3-0	1	2		4		6	7		14			12				11	5^2	10^1		9				3			16		8	
15	A	Elgin City	377	†2-0	1	2		4		6	7		14			12				11	5	10		9^1				3			16		8	
22	A	Morton	2,047	0-1	1	2				6	7		12			10			4	11	5			9		14			15		3		8	
Apr 5	H	Stirling Albion	385	0-1	1	2		10		6	7		14						3		5	9		10				15			4		8	
12	H	Albion Rovers	282	1-1	1	5		4	15	6	7		9			12			3			10^1		14				11			2		8	
19	A	Peterhead	709	0-3	1	5		4	15	6	7	16	10			12			3					9				11			2		8	
26	H	East Stirlingshire	235	5-4		10^2		4	12	6	7^1	8							11		5	9^1		15^1				3	14	1	2			
May 3	A	Queen's Park	556	1-1	1			4		6	7	8^1				16			3	15	5	9		10				11			2			
10	H	Gretna	376	0-1	1			4	6		7	8				12			3	16	5	10		9					11		2			
TOTAL FULL APPEARANCES					**28**	**21**	**7**	**31**	**15**	**35**	**25**	**29**	**12**	**9**	**11**	**5**			**29**	**4**	**23**	**25**		**13**	**6**	**9**	**7**	**12**	**4**	**1**	**14**	**7**	**14**	
TOTAL SUB APPEARANCES						**1**		**2**	**4**		**7**	**1**	**6**	**7**	**2**	**14**	**2**	**3**	**1**	**7**		**5**	**1**	**12**	**8**	**4**		**3**	**5**	**1**	**2**			**1**
TOTAL GOALS SCORED						**3**		**3**			**3**	**4**	**1**	**2**							**2**	**8**		**6**								**2**		

Small bold figures denote goalscorers. † denotes opponent's own goal.

links park stadium

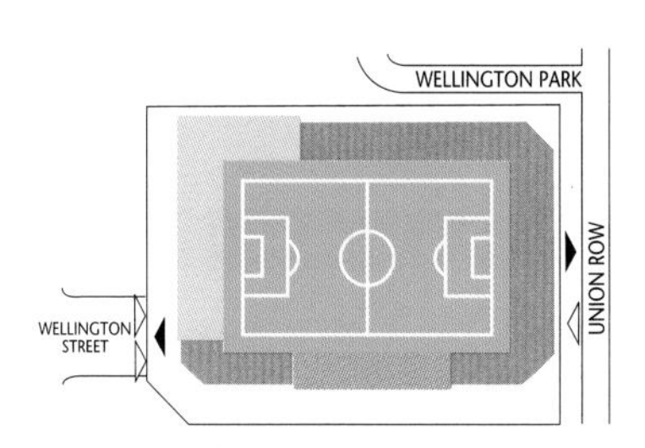

CAPACITY: 3,292; Seated 1,334, Standing 1,958

PITCH DIMENSIONS: 110 yds x 70 yds

FACILITIES FOR DISABLED SUPPORTERS:
Area set aside for wheelchairs and designated area in new stand.

team playing kits

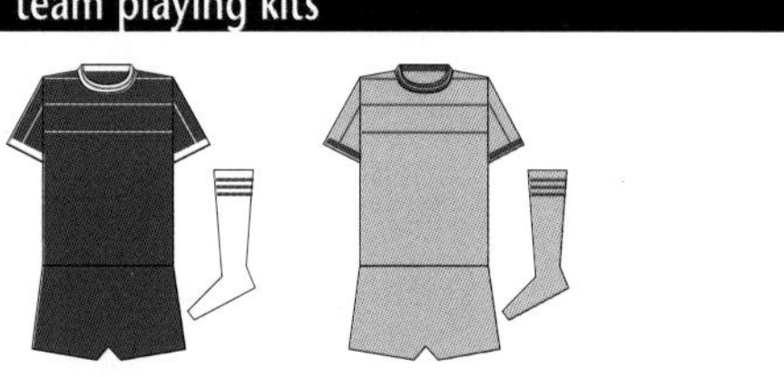

how to get there

Links Park can be reached by the following routes:

TRAINS: Montrose is on the Inter-City 125 route from London to Aberdeen and also on the Glasgow-Aberdeen route. There is a regular service and the station is about 15 minutes walk from the ground.

BUSES: An hourly service of buses from Aberdeen and Dundee stop in the town centre and it is a 15 minute walk from here to the ground.

CARS: Car parking is available in the car park at the ground and there are numerous side streets all round the park which can be used if necessary.

peterhead

Balmoor Stadium, Lord Catto Park, Balmoor Terrace, Peterhead, AB42 1EU

CHAIRMAN
Roger Taylor

VICE-CHAIRMAN
Rodger G. Morrison

DIRECTORS
George Watson & Gerry Gaffney

COMMITTEE
Dave Watson, Arthur Duncan & George Moore

SECRETARY
George Moore

GENERAL MANAGER
Dave Watson

OFFICE ADMINISTRATOR/TREASURER
Shona Aird

MANAGER
Ian Wilson

ASSISTANT MANAGER
Alan Lyons

GOALKEEPING COACH
Kenny Strachan

YOUTH CO-ORDINATOR
Derek Robertson

YOUTH DEVELOPMENT COACHES
Derek Robertson & Brian McCombie

UNDER 19 YOUTH TEAM COACH
Derek Robertson

UNDER 16 YOUTH TEAM COACH
Derek Robertson

CLUB DOCTOR
Dr. Iain Small

PHYSIOTHERAPIST
Sandy Rennie

FOOTBALL SAFETY OFFICERS' ASSOCIATION REPRESENTATIVE
Arthur Duncan (01779) 477201

GROUNDSMAN
Bill Spence

KIT MEN
Allan Park & Robert Duncan

MEDIA LIAISON OFFICERS
Dave Watson (01224) 771100 & George Moore (01224) 820851

MATCHDAY PROGRAMME EDITOR
George Moore

TELEPHONES
Ground (01779) 478256
Sec. Bus. (01224) 820851
Sec. Home (01779) 476870
Fax (01779) 490682

E-MAIL & INTERNET ADDRESS
mooregeo@aol.com
www.peterheadfc.org.uk

OFFICIAL SUPPORTERS CLUB
c/o Balmoor Stadium, Peterhead, AB42 1EU

TEAM CAPTAIN
Robert Raeside

SHIRT SPONSOR
ASCO

KIT SUPPLIER
ProStar

LIST OF PLAYERS 2003/04

SURNAME	FIRST NAME	MIDDLE NAME	DATE OF BIRTH	PLACE OF BIRTH	DATE OF SIGNING	HEIGHT FT INS	WEIGHT ST LBS	POS. ON PITCH	PREVIOUS CLUB
Anderson	Keith	Robert	22/12/85	Aberdeen	27/08/03	5 7.0	9 7	Mid	Fraserburgh
Bain	Clark	Ross	25/10/84	Aberdeen	08/08/03	5 7.0	10 10	Mid	Glentannar Juniors
Bain	Kevin		19/09/72	Kirkcaldy	27/06/02	6 0.0	12 0	Mid	Brechin City
Bavidge	Martin	Mitchell	30/04/80	Aberdeen	24/07/03	6 1.0	13 7	Fwd	Forfar Athletic
Beith	Gavin		07/10/81	Dundee	15/08/03	5 10.0	10 4	Mid	Dundee
Buchanan	Ross	Alexander	20/11/80	Aberdeen	23/08/03	6 2.0	13 10	Gk	Longside Juniors
Duncan	Robert		08/03/83	Peterhead	01/08/03	5 11.0	11 0	Fwd	Aberdeen
Farquhar	John	Graham	31/07/85	Aberdeen	05/08/03	5 11.0	10 7	Gk	Peterhead Form X
Good	Iain	David	09/08/77	Glasgow	24/07/03	6 1.0	12 0	Def	Forfar Athletic
Grant	Roderick	John	16/09/66	Gloucester	31/07/03	6 0.0	13 12	Fwd	Brechin City
Johnston	Martin	Alan	24/06/78	Aberdeen	03/08/00	6 2.0	12 0	Mid/Fwd	Cove Rangers
Keith	Kristofor	John	13/04/85	Peterhead	27/08/03	5 11.0	10 7	Def	Fraserburgh
Kennedy	Adam		04/11/85	Glasgow	31/08/03	5 7.0	9 0	Mid	Form S
Mackay	Stuart	John	03/03/75	Inverness	23/05/01	5 10.0	12 7	Mid	East Fife
Mathers	Paul		17/01/70	Aberdeen	30/05/02	6 0.0	12 7	Gk	Berwick Rangers
McGuinness	Kieran	Joseph	05/05/82	Motherwell	01/08/03	6 0.0	12 5	Def	Dundee
McSkimming	Shaun	Peter	29/05/70	Stranraer	06/08/02	5 11.0	11 7	Mid	Atlanta Silverbacks
Milne	Daniel	Dean	05/01/86	Aberdeen	09/08/03	5 10.0	10 7	Mid	Albion B.C.
Perry	Mark	George	07/02/71	Aberdeen	31/01/03	6 1.0	12 10	Def	Ross County
Petkov	Ivan	Tsvetanov	19/01/85	Sofia	26/03/03	5 9.0	11 9	Fwd	C.S.K.A. Sofia
Raeside	Robert		07/07/72	Petersburg	09/08/02	6 2.0	13 10	Def	Alloa Athletic
Ritchie	Adam		04/03/85	Aberdeen	09/08/03	5 6.0	9 7	Def	Peterhead Form S
Robertson	Colin	David	13/07/85	Aberdeen	09/08/03	5 10.0	10 7	Mid	Unattached
Roddie	Andrew	Robert	04/11/71	Glasgow	22/08/02	5 11.0	11 0	Fwd	Arbroath
Seivwright	James	Collie	14/10/85	Aberdeen	12/08/03	6 1.0	11 0	Def	Peterhead Form S
Shand	Richard		03/05/85	Aberdeen	12/08/03	5 8.0	10 7	Mid	Dundee United
Smith	Daryn	Andrew	09/10/80	Belfast	31/08/03	5 10.0	10 3	Mid	Brechin City
Stewart	Duncan		13/02/84	Aberdeen	01/08/03	5 8.0	11 0	Fwd	Dunfermline Athletic
Stewart	Graeme	John	02/04/82	Aberdeen	11/07/03	6 1.0	12 8	Mid	Inverness Cal. Th.
Stewart	Iain	Angus	23/10/69	Dundee	27/06/02	5 7.0	10 5	Fwd	Inverness Cal. Th.
Tindal	Kevin	Douglas	11/04/71	Arbroath	30/05/02	5 8.0	12 4	Mid	Arbroath
Urquhart	Mark	Mitchell	16/02/85	Fraserburgh	12/08/03	5 10.0	12 0	Def	Peterhead Form S
Watt	Jonathan		26/03/84	Aberdeen	08/08/03	5 11.0	11 0	Def	Huntly

milestones

YEAR OF FORMATION: 1891
MOST LEAGUE POINTS IN A SEASON: 89 (Highland League – Season 1989/90 (3 Points for a Win))
68 (SFL Third Division – Season 2002/03 (3 Points for a Win))
MOST LEAGUE GOALS SCORED BY A PLAYER IN A SEASON: Iain Stewart (Season 2001/02)
NO. OF GOALS SCORED: 23
RECORD ATTENDANCE: 6,310 (-v- Celtic – 1948 at Recreation Park)
2,200 (-v- Aberdeen – 6.7.2002 – at Balmoor Stadium)
RECORD VICTORY: 17-0 (-v- Fort William – Season 1998/99)
RECORD DEFEAT: 0-13 (-v- Aberdeen, Scottish Cup, Season 1923/24)

ticket information

SEASON TICKET PRICES

SEATED

ADULT	£130
ADULT & JUVENILE	£195
OAP	£65

STANDING

ADULT	£110
JUVENILE /OAP	£55

LEAGUE ADMISSION PRICES

SEATED

ADULT	£8
JUVENILE /OAP	£4

STANDING

ADULT	£8
JUVENILE /OAP	£4

leading goalscorers 1993-2003

Season 2000-01 was the club's first season in membership of SFL

Season	Div	No. of Goals	Player
2000-01	T	11	C. Yeats
2001-02	T	19	I. Stewart
2002-03	T	21	I. Stewart

the blue toon's club factfile 2002/03

Date	Venue	Opponents	Att.	Res	Mathers P.	McSkimming S.	Burns G.	Bain K.	Simpson M.	Tindal K.	Cooper C.	Stewart I.	Mackay S.	Johnston M.	Livingstone R.	Robertson K.	Kidd T.	Bissett K.	Raeside R.	Roddie A.	Slater M.	MacDonald C.	Cameron D.	Camara M.L.	Clark S.	McLean D.	Perry M.	Bone A.
Aug 3	H	East Fife	510	0-2	1	2	3	4	5	6	7	8	9	10	11	12	16	14										
10	A	Albion Rovers	430	0-3	1	3	2	4	5	9	7	8	11	10	14	15	16		6									
17	H	Morton	729	4-2	1	3	2	4	5	9		8^{2}	7	10^{1}					6	11^{1}								
24	A	Elgin City	697	0-3	1	3	14	6	5	9	12	8	7	10	11	15					2	4						
31	H	Stirling Albion	500	1-0	1	3	2	6	5	9	7	8^{1}		10		16			4	11			14					
Sep 14	A	Gretna	357	4-1	1	3	2	6	5	7^{1}	12	8	9	10				16	4	11^{2}				15^{1}				
21	H	Queen's Park	597	3-0	1		2	6	5	7	14	8^{3}	9	10					4	11		3	15	12				
28	A	Montrose	433	3-0	1		2	6^{1}	5	7	12	8		10			16		4	11^{1}		3	9	14^{1}				
Oct 5	H	East Stirlingshire	558	5-0	1		2	6	5	7	12	8		10^{3}			16^{1}		4	11^{1}		3	9	15				
19	H	East Stirlingshire	543	2-0	1	15	2	6	5	7^{1}	14	8		10					4	11^{1}		3	9	12				
26	A	East Fife	847	3-3	1	9	2	6	5	7^{1}	12	8^{2}		10					4	11		3	15					
Nov 2	A	Stirling Albion	686	0-1	1	11		6	5	7	2	8	12	10					4			3	9	15				
9	H	Elgin City	728	2-2	1	3		6	5	7	12	8^{1}	9	10^{1}					4	11		2		15				
16	H	Gretna	496	1-1	1	6	2		5	9	15	8	7	10^{1}					4	11		3		16				
23	A	Queen's Park	495	0-2	1	6			5	9	14	8	7	10				16	4	11		3		12	2			
30	A	East Stirlingshire	207	4-1	1	3		6	5	7		8	9	10^{4}					4	11		2		15				
Dec 7	A	Elgin City	457	4-0	1	3		6	5	9		8^{2}	7	10^{1}		15			4	11^{1}		2	12	16				
14	H	Montrose	550	4-2	1			6	5	7		8^{1}	9	10^{2}		16			4	11^{1}		2	12		3			
21	H	East Fife	717	2-2	1	3		6	5	7		8	9	10^{2}					4	11		2	14	15	12			
28	A	Morton	2,640	0-1	1	3		6	5	7		8	9	10		14			4			2	11	15				
Jan 18	A	Gretna	360	1-1	1	3		6	5	4			9	10		12^{1}		15		11		2	7			8		
Feb 8	A	Montrose	442	2-1	1	3		6		7		8		10					4	11		2	9^{1}		16	15	5	14^{1}
15	H	East Stirlingshire	584	6-0	1	3		6		7		8^{3}							4	11		2^{1}	9			14	5	10^{2}
Mar 1	H	Morton	1,086	3-1	1	3		6		7		8^{3}							4	11		2	9				5	10
4	H	Stirling Albion	613	6-0	1	3		6	12	7^{1}						8^{1}			4	11^{1}		2^{1}	10			14^{1}	5	9^{1}
8	H	Elgin City	854	3-2	1	3		6	5	7						8			4	11		2	9			12^{1}		10^{2}
11	A	Albion Rovers	389	0-0	1	3	14	6	5	7									4	11			9	15	2	8		10
15	A	Stirling Albion	564	1-2	1	3	2		5	7			16							11			9	15	6	8^{1}	4	10
22	A	Queen's Park	575	2-1	1	3		6		7		12	15			16			4	11^{2}		2	9			10	5	8
29	H	Queen's Park	589	3-1	1	3	16			7		8^{1}	6^{1}	10^{1}					4	11		2	9	15			5	
Apr 5	H	Gretna	598	1-0	1	3				7		8^{1}	12	10					4	11		2	9				5	6
12	A	East Stirlingshire	218	1-1	1	3				7		8	6			14			4^{1}	11		2	9			12	5	10
19	H	Montrose	709	3-0	1	3				7		8^{1}		6		15			4	11		2^{1}	9			14	5	10^{1}
26	A	East Fife	1,071	2-0	1	3	16	6		7		8							4	11		2	9			15	5	10^{2}
May 3	H	Albion Rovers	1,693	0-0	1	3				7		8	12	6					4	11		2	9				5	10
10	A	Morton	8,497	0-1	1	3		6		7		8		12					4	11		2	9				5	10
TOTAL FULL APPEARANCES					36	31	12	28	24	36	4	30	17	26	2	2			32	31	1	29	21		4	4	13	13
TOTAL SUB APPEARANCES						1	4		1		10	1	5	1	1	11	4	4					6	16	2	7		1
TOTAL GOALS SCORED								1		4		21	1	16		2	1		1	11		3	1	2		3		9

Small bold figures denote goalscorers. † denotes opponent's own goal.

balmoor stadium

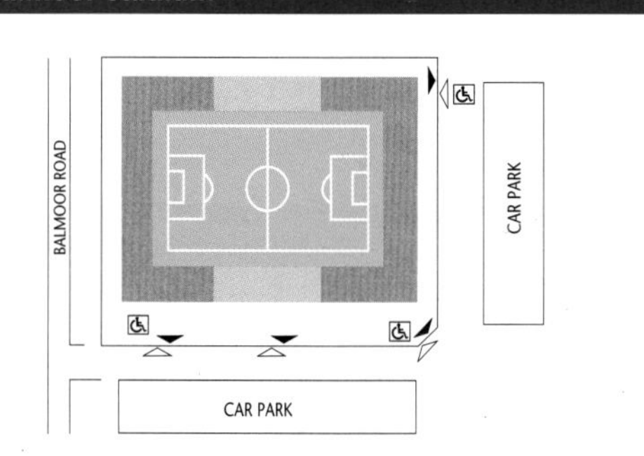

CAPACITY: 3,250; Seated 990, Standing 2,260

PITCH DIMENSIONS: 105 yds x 70 yds

FACILITIES FOR DISABLED SUPPORTERS:
Designated area in new stand.
Lift at main entrance for access to Main Stand.

team playing kits

how to get there

Balmoor Stadium can be reached by the following routes:

TRAINS: The nearest train station is Aberdeen. From Aberdeen you would have to travel by bus to Peterhead. Travel time 1 hour.

BUSES: Buses leave Aberdeen city centre every hour for Peterhead. Travel time 1 hour.

CARS: From Aberdeen city centre: Take A90 to Peterhead, at first roundabout approaching Peterhead take a left at McDonalds to St. Fergus (still on A90). Continue on this road to next roundabout - go straight on to the next T-junction. Take right A980 back into Peterhead - continue on A980 through next roundabout and Balmoor Stadium is about ½ mile past the roundabout on the right hand side.

queen's park

The National Stadium,
Hampden Park, Mount Florida,
Glasgow, G42 9BA

HON. PATRON
The Lord Macfarlane of Bearsden KT

PRESIDENT
David Gordon, B.Acc., A.C.M.A.

COMMITTEE
A. Kenneth C. Harvey, Malcolm D. Mackay, David McNeil, Garry M. Templeman (Treasurer), James M. Hastie LL.B, Dr. Alan S. Hutchison B.Sc., M.B., ChB., F.R.C.P. Glas, F.R.C., P.A.T.H., David B. Stirling, Ross Caven MBA, M.Sc, B.Sc & James Nicholson

SECRETARY
Alistair MacKay

OFFICE ADMINISTRATORS
Mrs. Janice Balmain & Mrs. Susan Kennedy

COACH
Kenneth Brannigan

ASSISTANT COACH
Robert Dickson

COACHING STAFF
Keith MacKenzie, Robert Kelly, Michael Jamieson, Steve Adam, Chic McCarry, Barry McNab, Brian Hamilton, Pat Barkie, Peter McLean, Billy Ogilvie, Alan Simpson & Willie Neil

GOALKEEPING COACH
Ronnie Cant

HEAD OF YOUTH DEVELOPMENT
Ian Cairns

YOUTH DEVELOPMENT COACH
Tommy Wilson

YOUTH TEAM COACHES
U19 – Keith MacKenzie, Robert Kelly & Chic McCarry
U17 – Barry McNab, Michael Jamieson & Brian Hamilton
U16 – Steve Adam & Pat Barkie
U15 – Peter McLean
U14 – Billy Ogilvie
U13 – Willie Neil & Alan Simpson

CLUB DOCTOR
Dr. Alan S. Hutchison

PHYSIOTHERAPISTS
Robert C. Findlay & Andrew Myles

GROUNDSMEN
Stephen Bache & Scott McCreadie

FOOTBALL SAFETY OFFICERS' ASSOCIATION REPRESENTATIVE/ MEDIA LIAISON OFFICER
Alistair MacKay (0141) 632 1275

KIT PERSON
William Neil

COMMERCIAL DIRECTOR
Ross Caven (0141) 632 1275

MATCHDAY PROGRAMME EDITORS
David B. Stirling & Logan Taylor

TELEPHONES
Office (0141) 632 1275
Stadium Operations (0141) 620 4000
Fax (0141) 636 1612

E-MAIL/INTERNET ADDRESS
secretary@queensparkfc.co.uk
www.queensparkfc.co.uk

CLUB SHOP
Home matches only – Hampden Park (Kiosk within BT Scotland Stand). Open 2.15p.m. - 3.00p.m. and 4.45pm - 5.00pm on home match days. Mail Orders may be obtained through the Secretary of the Official Supporters Club.

OFFICIAL SUPPORTERS CLUB
c/o Secretary, Keith McAllister, 58 Brunton Street, Glasgow, G44 3NQ

CLUB CAPTAIN
Danny Ferry

SHIRT SPONSOR
Barr Irn Bru – Original and Best

KIT SUPPLIER
DIADORA

LIST OF PLAYERS 2003/04

SURNAME	FIRST NAME	MIDDLE NAME	DATE OF BIRTH	PLACE OF BIRTH	DATE OF SIGNING	HEIGHT FT INS	WEIGHT ST LBS	POS. ON PITCH	PREVIOUS CLUB
Agostini	Damiano	Pietro	22/11/78	Irvine	13/03/98	6 0.0	12 7	Def	East Fife
Canning	Steven		06/05/83	Glasgow	31/07/01	5 10.0	11 0	Fwd	Queen's Park Form X
Carcary	Derek		11/07/86	Glasgow	28/08/03	5 6.0	10 7	Fwd	Queen's Park Form D U16
Carroll	Frank	Andrew	30/01/81	Glasgow	13/07/99	5 8.0	11 7	Fwd	Benburb Juveniles
Clark	Ross		07/02/83	Rutherglen	31/07/01	5 9.0	11 0	Mid	Queen's Park Form X
Conlin	Ross	John	19/09/84	Glasgow	02/09/03	5 9.0	10 7	Def	Celtic South
Crawford	David		30/06/85	Glasgow	28/08/03	5 10.0	11 7	Gk	Dundee B.C.
Dunning	Allan		02/09/80	Glasgow	21/11/01	6 1.0	12 0	Fwd	Eaglesham Amateurs
Fallon	Steven		08/05/79	Paisley	30/08/02	5 8.5	12 0	Def	Arbroath
Ferry	Daniel		31/01/77	Glasgow	23/06/95	5 7.0	11 4	Mid/Fwd	Queen's Park U18's
Gallagher	Patrick	Joseph	28/12/79	Glasgow	17/07/02	5 9.0	11 0	Fwd	Stranraer
Graham	Alastair	Slowey	11/08/66	Glasgow	29/07/03	6 3.0	14 10	Fwd	Hamilton Academical
Harvey	Paul	Edward	28/08/68	Glasgow	30/08/03	5 9.0	11 7	Mid	Airdrie United
Hendry	Gordon		30/01/85	Greenock	28/08/03	5 9.0	11 0	Def	Queen's Park Form D U16
Hodge	Brian		16/01/85	Glasgow	16/08/02	5 11.0	11 0	Mid	Queen's Park Form D U16
Kettlewell	Stuart		04/06/84	Glasgow	16/08/02	5 11.0	11 0	Mid	Lenzie Youth Club
Livingston	Anthony		15/08/86	Glasgow	28/08/03	5 7.0	11 4	Mid	Queen's Park Form D U15
McAuley	Stephen	Gerard	16/02/83	Bellshill	24/07/03	5 10.0	12 3	Fwd	Airdrie United
McCallum	David	John	07/09/77	Bellshill	31/01/03	5 10.0	10 10	Mid	Partick Thistle
McCue	Brian		24/01/85	Glasgow	18/08/03	6 2.0	13 0	Gk	Dunfermline Athletic
McElhinney	John		11/08/86	Glasgow	28/08/03	5 10.0	11 5	Def	Queen's Park Form D U15
McGinty	Andrew		19/07/84	Glasgow	16/08/02	6 0.0	12 0	Def	Queen's Park Form D U16
McLaughlin	Martyn		16/04/86	Glasgow	28/08/03	5 7.0	11 0	Fwd	Queen's Park Form D U16
Menelaws	David		14/04/78	Chorley	16/07/02	5 8.0	10 0	Fwd	East Stirlingshire
Moffat	Steven	John	03/07/81	Bellshill	22/07/02	6 3.0	13 9	Def	Arbroath
Niven	Ross		24/07/85	East Kilbride	28/08/03	5 9.0	11 0	Def	East Kilbride B.C.
Reilly	Steven	James	29/08/81	Glasgow	22/07/03	6 0.0	12 0	Def	Stirling Albion
Russell	Robert		29/06/86	Glasgow	28/08/03	5 7.0	11 0	Mid	Queen's Park Form D U15
Scrimgour	Derek		29/03/78	Glasgow	31/01/03	6 3.0	14 2	Gk	Dumbarton
Sinclair	Richard		20/05/82	Glasgow	25/05/00	5 10.0	12 0	Def	Queen's Park Form S
Sweeney	Michael		02/03/86	Glasgow	28/08/03	5 9.0	11 2	Def	Queen's Park Form D U16
Thompson	John		10/07/84	Glasgow	16/08/02	5 11.0	11 0	Def/Mid	Queen's Park Form D U16
Weir	John		05/04/85	Glasgow	28/08/03	6 0.0	12 0	Mid	Queen's Park Form D U16
Whelan	Jonathan		10/10/72	Liverpool	30/11/01	6 0.0	12 3	Mid	Berwick Rangers
White	Jordan	Reid	03/12/85	Bellshill	16/08/02	6 1.0	12 7	Mid/Fwd	Queen's Park Form D U16

milestones

YEAR OF FORMATION: 1867
MOST CAPPED PLAYER: Walter Arnott
NO. OF CAPS: 14
MOST LEAGUE POINTS IN A SEASON: 57 (Division 2 – Season 1922/23)(2 Points for a Win)
69 (Third Division – Season 1999/2000)(3 Points for a Win)
MOST LEAGUE GOALS SCORED BY A PLAYER IN A SEASON: William Martin (Season 1937/38)
NO. OF GOALS SCORED: 30
GROUND RECORD ATTENDANCE: 149,547 (Scotland v England – 17.4.1937)
CLUB RECORD ATTENDANCE: 95,772 (-v- Rangers – 18.1.1930)
RECORD VICTORY: 16-0 (-v- St. Peters – Scottish Cup, 29.8.1885)
RECORD DEFEAT: 0-9 (-v- Motherwell – Division 1, 29.4.1930)

ticket information

SEASON TICKET PRICES

BT SCOTLAND STAND	ADULT	£115
	JUVENILE (OVER 12 AND UNDER 16)/OAP	£40
	PARENT & JUVENILE	£125
	FOR EACH ADDITIONAL JUVENILE	£10
	JUVENILE (UNDER 12)	£25

LEAGUE ADMISSION PRICES

BT SCOTLAND STAND	ADULT	£8
	JUVENILE (U16)/OAP	£2
	PARENT & JUVENILE	£9
	JUVENILE/OAP	£1

leading goalscorers 1993-2003

Season	Div	No. of Goals	Player
1993-94	S	18	J. O'Neill
1994-95	T	8	S. McCormick
1995-96	T	6	S. Edgar, K. McGoldrick
1996-97	T	7	D. Ferry
1997-98	T	8	S. Edgar, J. Mercer
1998-99	T	7	S. Edgar
1999-00	T	13	M. Gallagher
2000-01	S	7	M. Gallagher
2001-02	T	5	S. Canning, R. Jackson
2002-03	T	8	J. Gemmell

the spiders' club factfile 2002/03

Date	Venue	Opponents	Att.	Res	Mitchell A.	Ferry D.	Gallagher J.	Moffat S.	Agostini D.	Quinn A.	Lappin G.	Jack S.	Gemmell J.	Canning S.	Allan J.	Fisher C.	Jackson R.	Whelan J.	Lejman K.	Gallagher P.	Martin W.	Taggart C.	Stewart C.	Crozier B.	Sinclair R.	Fallon S.	White James	Dunning A.	Clark R.	Menelaws D.	Kettlewell S.	Cairns M.	McCallum D.	Conlin R.
Aug 3	H	Elgin City	585	1-2	1	2	3	4	5	6	7	8	9	10[1]	11	12	16																	
10	A	Montrose	402	0-1	1	2	3	4	5	6		7	9	10	11			8	16	14	12													
17	H	East Fife	537	0-0	1	2	3	4	5	6		16	9	10	11			8		15	7	14												
24	A	Morton	2,001	0-3	1	2	3	4	5	6		16	9	10	11	15		8			14	7												
31	H	Gretna	607	1-0		2[1]	3	4	5	6			9	14	11	12		8				7	1	10	15									
Sep 14	H	East Stirlingshire	443	0-2		2	11	4	5	6			9	12				8			10	14	1	7	15	3								
21	A	Peterhead	597	0-3		7	3		5	10		15	9	16				8			11	12	1		6	2	4							
28	H	Albion Rovers	506	2-4		7		4[1]		5	2	11[1]			16			8			12	6	1	10		3		9						
Oct 5	A	Stirling Albion	579	0-1		7	3	4	5	6		10	12		11			8		16	9	14	1			2								
19	H	Montrose	492	0-1		2	3	4	5	10		12		7	11			8			9		1			6		14						
26	A	Elgin City	567	2-2		2	3	4[1]	5	10		16		7	11			8[1]			9		1			6		15	14					
Nov 2	A	Gretna	319	2-2		2		4[1]	5	10			9	3	11			8		15[1]			1	16		6		7	14					
9	H	Morton	1,775	1-1		2		4	5	10			9	3[1]	11			8		16			1	15		6		7	14					
16	A	East Stirlingshire	315	4-0		2		4	5	10			9	3	11[2]			8[1]		16			1	15		6		7[1]	14					
23	H	Peterhead	495	2-0		2		5	4	10			9	3	11[1]			8		16	14		1	7		6			12[1]					
30	H	Stirling Albion	657	0-1				4	5	10			9	3	11			8		15	12		1		16	6		7	2					
Dec 7	A	Morton	1,669	1-1				5[1]	4	10			9	3	11			8			7		1		2	6		14						
14	A	Albion Rovers	442	2-0		16	14	4	5	10			9	3	11			8			7[1]		1		2[1]	6			12					
21	H	Elgin City	648	3-2		3	12	4	5				9[3]		11	14		8			7		1		2	6		15	10					
28	A	East Fife	693	1-1		3		4[1]	5		14		9		11			8			7		1		2	6		12	10					
Jan 11	H	Gretna	808	1-2	1	3	11	4	5				9			15		8[1]			7				2	6		14	10	12				
18	H	East Stirlingshire	934	3-4	1	3		4	5		2		9[2]		11[1]			8			7				12	6			10	14	16			
Feb 8	H	Albion Rovers	671	1-1		2			5				9[1]	3	11			8		16					4	6	14		7		15	1	10	
22	A	Montrose	315	1-1		2			5				9	3	11	12		8[1]		16						6	4		15	7		1	10	
Mar 1	H	East Fife	697	1-2		2			5				9		11	16		8		14					3	6	4		7			1	10[1]	
8	H	Morton	1,361	0-1	1	2							9	14	11			8		15					5	6	4		3	12	7		10	
15	A	Gretna	320	1-0		2			5				9		11			8			10				4	6					7	1	3[1]	
19	A	Stirling Albion	465	0-1		2			5				9		11	14				15	10				4	6			8		7	1	3	
22	H	Peterhead	575	1-2		2			5				9		11	14		16			10[1]				4	6	12		8		7	1	3	
29	A	Peterhead	589	1-3		2			5				12[1]	15		11				7	9				4	6			10	16	8	1	3	
Apr 5	A	East Stirlingshire	281	2-0		2			5				9					8		12	15[1]				4	6		16	7	11[1]	10	1	3	
12	H	Stirling Albion	714	3-3		2			5				9[1]					8[1]			15				4[1]	6		3	7	11	10	1		
19	A	Albion Rovers	581	1-2		2			5				9	16				8			15				4	6	12		7	11[1]	10	1	3	
26	A	Elgin City	444	0-0		2			5				9	3				8			10				4	6			7	11		1		
May 3	H	Montrose	556	1-1		2			5				9	7				8		14[1]	12	10			4		16			11		1	3	6
10	A	East Fife	1,996	0-1		8			5				9	15						3	11					6	4	2	7	12	10	1		
TOTAL FULL APPEARANCES					**7**	**33**	**11**	**21**	**34**	**18**	**3**	**4**	**31**	**17**	**25**	**1**		**31**		**2**	**18**	**4**	**16**	**4**	**18**	**30**	**5**	**7**	**16**	**6**	**9**	**13**	**11**	**1**
TOTAL SUB APPEARANCES						**1**	**2**				**1**	**5**	**2**	**7**	**1**	**9**	**1**	**1**	**1**	**15**	**9**	**4**		**3**	**4**		**4**	**7**	**7**	**5**	**2**			
TOTAL GOALS SCORED						**1**		**5**				**1**	**8**	**2**	**4**			**5**		**2**	**3**				**2**			**1**	**1**	**2**			**2**	

Small bold figures denote goalscorers. † denotes opponent's own goal.

the national stadium, hampden park

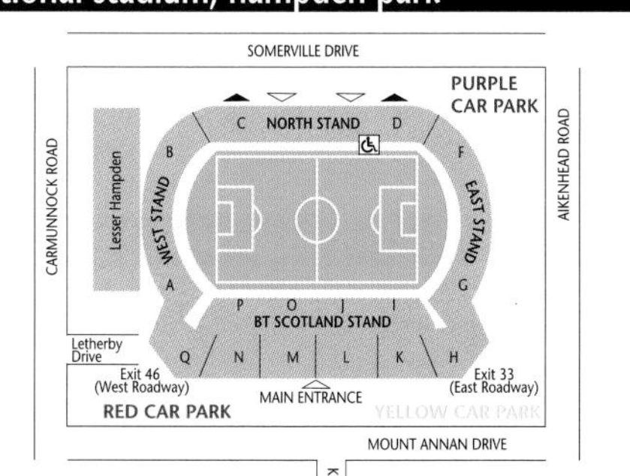

CAPACITY: 52,025 (All Seated)
PITCH DIMENSIONS: 115 yds x 75 yds
FACILITIES FOR DISABLED SUPPORTERS:
Disabled facilities are situated in the BT Scotland Stand as follows:
West Front (44 places & 44 helpers), West Section A (21 places & 21 helpers), Ambulant/Blind (55 places), East Front (44 places & 44 helpers), East Section G (21 places & 21 helpers), Ambulant/Blind (55 places)

team playing kits

how to get there

The following routes may be used to reach The National Stadium, Hampden Park:
TRAINS: There are two stations within five minutes walk of the ground. Mount Florida Station, on the Cathcart Circle, and King's Park Station. A 15 minute service runs from Glasgow Central.
BUSES: Services to approach Mount Florida end of Stadium: From City Centre: 5, 5A, 5B, M5, M14, 31, 37, 66, 66A, 66B, 66C; From Govan Cross; 34; From Drumchapel: 96, 97, Circular Service: 89, 90; G.C.T. Service: 1; Services to approach King's Park end of Stadium; From City Centre: 12, 12A, 74; Circular Service: 89, 90; G.C.T. Service: 19.
CARS: Car and Coach parking facilities are available in the car park in Letherby Drive, which is capable of holding 200 vehicles. Side streets can also be used. Free car parking at all Queen's Park matches.

stirling albion

Forthbank Stadium, Springkerse, Stirling, FK7 7UJ

CHAIRMAN
Peter McKenzie

VICE-CHAIRMAN
Peter Gardiner, C.A.

DIRECTORS
Duncan B. MacGregor & John L. Smith

SECRETARY
Mrs. Marlyn Hallam

COACH
Allan Moore

ASSISTANT COACHES
David Gemmell & Mark McNally

DIRECTOR OF YOUTH DEVELOPMENT
John L. Smith

YOUTH CO-ORDINATOR
Stuart Taylor

U19 YOUTH TEAM COACH
David Gemmell

U15 YOUTH TEAM COACH
Paul Donnelly

U14 YOUTH TEAM COACHES
Mike Kerr & Paul Chalmers

U13 YOUTH TEAM COACHES
Ian McConnell & Tommy Smith

CLUB DOCTOR
Dr. Duncan MacGregor

PHYSIOTHERAPIST
Michael McLaughlan

FOOTBALL SAFETY OFFICERS' ASSOCIATION REPRESENTATIVE
Frank Gordon (01786) 461511

GROUND MAINTENANCE
Greentech, Bandbeath Ind. Est., Throsk

COMMERCIAL MANAGER/ MEDIA LIAISON
Mrs. Marlyn Hallam
Tel (01786) 450399

KIT PERSON
Stuart McColl

MATCHDAY PROGRAMME EDITOR
Allan Grieve (01259) 751152
email: ADGrieve@aol.com

TELEPHONES
Ground/Ticket Office
(01786) 450399
Fax (01786) 448400

INTERNET ADDRESS
www.stirlingalbionfc.co.uk

CLUB SHOP
Situated at Forthbank Stadium. Open Mon. - Fri. and Home Match Days.

OFFICIAL SUPPORTERS CLUB
Stephen Torrance, Secretary, Forthbank Stadium, Springkerse, Stirling, FK7 7UJ

TEAM CAPTAIN
George Rowe

SHIRT SPONSOR
Prudential

KIT SUPPLIER
VIRMA

LIST OF PLAYERS 2003/04

SURNAME	FIRST NAME	MIDDLE NAME	DATE OF BIRTH	PLACE OF BIRTH	DATE OF SIGNING	HEIGHT FT INS	WEIGHT ST LBS	POS. ON PITCH	PREVIOUS CLUB
Anderson	Derek	Christopher	15/05/72	Paisley	18/07/03	6 0.0	13 0	Def	Queen of the South
Berry	Mark	Richard	27/03/85	Bradford	29/08/03	5 8.0	9 0	Def	Stirling Albion Form D U16
Beveridge	Ross		24/08/84	Dunfermline	23/07/01	5 8.5	9 10	Fwd	Rangers
Bonner	Andrew	Patrick	14/06/85	Paisley	26/08/03	6 1.0	13 2	Fwd	Queen's Park
Brown	Craig		13/06/85	Glasgow	26/08/03	5 10.0	10 8	Mid	Queen's Park
Cummings	Darren	David	15/03/85	Falkirk	14/08/02	5 9.0	10 7	Fwd	Stirling Albion Form D U16
Davidson	Ryan		22/09/82	Irvine	08/08/03	5 11.0	11 2	Fwd	Heart of Midlothian
Devine	Stewart		11/04/84	Edinburgh	13/07/00	5 10.0	9 11	Mid	Stirling Albion Youth
Elliot	Barry	Robert	24/10/78	Carlisle	22/07/03	5 10.0	11 7	Fwd	Partick Thistle
Ferguson	Craig	William	03/02/84	Glasgow	22/07/03	6 2.0	13 4	Mid	Maryhill B.C. U'21's
Geddes	Christopher	James	16/04/85	Stirling	22/08/02	5 7.0	10 0	Mid	Stirling Albion Form D U15
Gibson	Andrew	Stewart	02/03/82	Glasgow	15/08/03	5 10.0	10 9	Mid/Fwd	Partick Thistle
Hay	Paul		14/11/80	Glasgow	16/03/01	5 10.0	11 7	Mid	Clyde
Henny	Christopher	Andrew	16/05/85	Stirling	12/08/03	5 10.0	11 6	Gk	Stirling Albion Form D U16
Hogarth	Myles		30/03/75	Falkirk	11/03/03	6 2.5	12 8	Gk	Alloa Athletic
Hutchison	Steven		01/08/85	Stirling	23/07/01	5 11.0	9 7	Fwd	Rangers
Joyce	John		17/09/85	Vale of Leven	14/08/02	5 10.0	11 6	Fwd	Stirling Albion Form D U16
Kelly	Gary	Patrick	01/09/81	Falkirk	25/08/00	5 11.0	11 7	Def	Sauchie Juniors
Lochhead	Christopher		06/05/85	Glasgow	29/08/03	5 8.0	10 0	Mid	Stirling Albion Form D U16
Logan	Edward		03/12/85	Bellshill	22/08/02	5 9.0	10 7	Mid	Stirling Albion Form D U15
McKinnon	Colin	Graham	29/08/69	Glasgow	30/08/02	6 0.0	13 1	Mid	Albion Rovers
McLean	Scott	James	17/06/76	East Kilbride	18/07/03	5 11.5	13 6	Fwd	St. Mirren
McNally	Mark		10/03/71	Motherwell	25/07/02	5 11.0	12 7	Def	Clydebank
Moore	Allan		25/12/64	Glasgow	09/07/02	5 6.0	10 4	Fwd	Queen of the South
Morrison	Scott	John	22/10/81	Glasgow	29/08/03	6 2.0	12 7	Gk	Kilsyth Rangers Juniors
Nugent	Paul	Brian	04/04/83	Alexandria	30/11/01	5 11.0	11 0	Def	Clyde
O'Brien	David		24/01/84	Stirling	20/07/01	5 10.0	9 7	Mid	Denny Amateurs
Reilly	Jamie	Stephen	07/02/85	Perth	29/08/03	5 11.0	11 8	Fwd	Guildtown U18's
Ross	Stuart		14/03/86	Falkirk	29/08/03	6 2.0	11 0	Def	Raith Rovers
Rowe	John	George	23/08/68	Glasgow	25/07/02	6 0.0	13 0	Def	Arbroath
Roycroft	Sean		29/08/85	Stirling	29/08/03	6 0.0	11 0	Fwd	Stirling Albion Form D U16
Scotland	Christopher	James	22/03/85	Stirling	14/08/02	5 11.5	12 0	Def	Stirling Albion Form D U16
Shaw	Kevin	O'Donnell	03/07/86	Falkirk	26/08/03	5 11.0	10 7	Mid	Clyde Form D U16
Smith	Andrew		21/06/83	Craigavon	17/01/03	5 8.0	11 3	Def	Armagh City
Wilson	Douglas	John	27/05/84	Stirling	20/07/01	5 7.0	9 3	Mid	Stirling Albion Form D U16

milestones

YEAR OF FORMATION: 1945
MOST LEAGUE POINTS IN A SEASON: 59 (Division 2 – Season 1964/65)(2 Points for a Win)
81 (Second Division – Season 1995/96)(3 Points for a Win)
MOST LEAGUE GOALS SCORED BY A PLAYER IN A SEASON: Joe Hughes (Season 1969/70)
NO. OF GOALS SCORED: 26
RECORD ATTENDANCE: 26,400 (-v- Celtic – Scottish Cup, 11.3.1959 at Annfield Park)
3,808 (-v- Aberdeen – Scottish Cup, 17.2.1996 at Forthbank Stadium)
RECORD VICTORY: 20-0 (-v- Selkirk – Scottish Cup, 8.12.1984)
RECORD DEFEAT: 0-9 (-v- Dundee United – Division 1, 30.12.1967)

ticket information

SEASON TICKET PRICES

SEATED	ADULT	£140
	JUVENILE/OAP	£85
	YOUNG RED	£60

LEAGUE ADMISSION PRICES

SEATED	ADULT	£8
	JUVENILE	£5
STANDING	ADULT	£7
	JUVENILE/OAP	£4

leading goalscorers 1993-2003

Season	Div	No. of Goals	Player
1993-94	F	13	W. Watters
1994-95	S	15	W. Watters
1995-96	S	25	S. McCormick
1996-97	F	9	A. Bone
1997-98	F	13	A. Bone
1998-99	S	20	A. Bone
1999-00	S	17	A. Graham
2000-01	S	5	C. Feroz, A. Graham
2001-02	T	17	A. Williams
2002-03	T	10	S. Nicholas

the albions' club factfile 2002/03

Date	Venue	Opponents	Att.	Res	Reid C.	Nugent P.	McCole D.	McNally M.	Rowe J.G.	Duncan F.	Moore A.	Hay P.	Munro G.	Nicholas S.	O'Brien D.	Stuart W.	Beveridge R.	Butler D.	Turner I.	Reilly S.	Wilson L.	Davidson H.	Mallan S.	McLellan K.	Dunn R.	McKinnon C.	Wilson D.	Cummings D.	Devine S.	McGeown D.	Morris I.	Crilly M.	Kerrigan S.	Smith A.	Nugent A.	Hogarth M.	Scotland C.
Aug 3	H	Albion Rovers	579	0-1	1	2	3	4	5	6	7	8	9	10	11	15	17	12																			
10	A	Morton	1,757	1-5		2		4	5	3		11	7	10		6	16	14	1	8[1]	9																
17	H	Elgin City	428	1-1		2	3		4	5	12	11	7	10					1	6	16	8	9[1]	15													
24	H	East Stirlingshire	434	3-0		2	3	4	5[1]	11		6	16	7	15				1			8	9[2]		10	14											
31	A	Peterhead	500	0-1		2	3		4	5		11	15	7					1	6		8	9		10	12											
Sep 14	H	Montrose	439	1-1	1	2			5	4	14	11	15	7[1]						6		8	9	12	10	3											
21	A	East Fife	588	1-1	1	2		4	5	6		3	11	10								12	9[1]		7	8											
28	A	Gretna	402	2-0	1	2		4	5	6		3		10[1]	7							12	9		11	8[1]											
Oct 5	H	Queen's Park	579	1-0	1	2		4	5	6	16	3			11					14		12	9		7	8[1]		10									
19	H	Morton	1,089	2-0		2		4	5	6	16	3		10[1]	11[1]				1			12	9		7	8											
26	A	Albion Rovers	489	3-1		2		4	5	12		3		10[1]	11[1]				1			6	9[1]		7	8											
Nov 2	H	Peterhead	686	1-0		2		4	5			3		10	11[1]				1			6	9		7	8											
9	A	East Stirlingshire	548	1-1		2		4	5			3		10[1]	11		14		1			6	9		7	8											
16	A	Montrose	364	†1-1		2		4		5		3			11		10		1	12		6	9	14	7	8			16								
23	H	East Fife	808	0-0		2		4	5		7	3	15	10	11				1			6	9			8											
30	A	Queen's Park	657	1-0		2		4	5			3	10		11		15		1			6	9		7	8[1]	16										
Dec 14	H	Gretna	412	0-1		2		4		5		3	15		11		16		1	12		6	9		10	8	7										
28	A	Elgin City	556	3-0		2		4	5			3		10	11[1]				1	12[1]		8	9		7[1]	6	15	16									
Jan 1	H	East Stirlingshire	593	2-1		2		4	5			3[1]		10	11				1	6			9	12	7[1]	8	14										
18	H	Montrose	524	1-1	1	2		4	5			3	9	10	11								12	14[1]	7	6	15			8							
Feb 8	A	Gretna	292	0-0	1	2		4	5					12	11								9		7	3					6	8	10				
11	A	East Fife	602	1-2	1	2		4	5			8		9	11[1]								12	15	7	3	14				6		10				
26	H	Albion Rovers	466	3-4	1	2		4	5			12		10[1]	11									14	7					6	8[1]		9[1]	3	18		
Mar 1	H	Elgin City	407	4-0		2		4	5	15		3		10[2]	11[1]									12	7	8	16			6	9[1]				1		
4	A	Peterhead	613	0-6		2		4	5	11		3		10	14								12	16	7	6				8	9				1		
8	A	East Stirlingshire	302	3-1		2		4	5[1]			3		10	11								9	14						12	8[1]	6	15[1]	7	1		
11	A	Morton	1,617	2-2		2		4	5			12		10	11								9[1]		7[1]						8	6	14	3		1	
15	H	Peterhead	564	2-1		2			5			4		10[2]	11								9		7		16			14	8	6	12	3		1	
19	H	Queen's Park	465	1-0		2			5			3		10	11[1]								9		7		16				8	6	12	4		1	
22	H	East Fife	866	1-2		2			5	16		3		10	11[1]								9		7	8				15		6	12	4		1	
Apr 5	A	Montrose	385	1-0		2	16	4	5			3			11								10		7			15			12	8[1]	9	6		1	
12	A	Queen's Park	714	3-3		2		4	5			6		12									9		7[1]			16			11[1]	8	10[1]	3		1	
19	H	Gretna	376	1-0		2		4	5			12		10	11										7		16				6	8	9[1]	3		1	
26	A	Albion Rovers	533	1-2		2		4	5			12	15	10	11								14		7						8[1]	6	9	3		1	
May 3	H	Morton	2,039	0-3		2		4	5			3		11						12			9		7		16				8	6	10			1	
10	A	Elgin City	386	2-2		2		4	5[1]			3		11						15			10		16		7				8	6[1]	9			1	12
TOTAL FULL APPEARANCES					9	36	4	30	34	13	2	31	6	29	26	1	1		14	5	1	12	27		30	20	2	1		4	14	12	9	10	3	10	
TOTAL SUB APPEARANCES							1			3	4	4	6	2	2	1	5	2		6	1	4	4	10	1	2	10	3	1	3	1		5		1		1
TOTAL GOALS SCORED									3			1		10	8					2			6	1	4	3						5	2	4			

Small bold figures denote goalscorers. † denotes opponent's own goal.

forthbank stadium

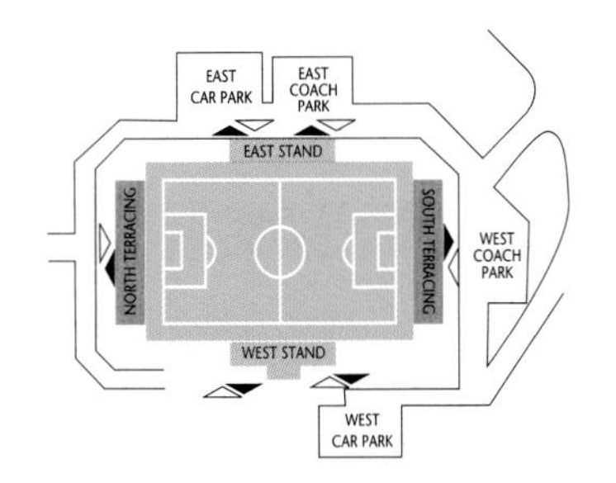

CAPACITY: 3,808, Seated 2,508, Standing 1,300

PITCH DIMENSIONS: 110 yds x 74 yds

FACILITIES FOR DISABLED SUPPORTERS:
Disabled access, toilets and spaces for 36.

team playing kits

how to get there

Forthbank Stadium can be reached by the following routes:

TRAINS: The nearest station is Stirling Railway Station, which is approximately 2 miles from the ground.

BUSES: From Goosecroft Bus Station, Stirling.

CARS: Follow signs for A91 St. Andrews/Alloa. Car Parking is available in the club car park. Home support in West Car Park and visiting support in East Car Park.

stranraer

Stair Park,
London Road,
Stranraer, DG9 8BS

CHAIRMAN
Robert J. Clanachan

VICE-CHAIRMAN
James Bark

COMMITTEE
George F. Compton, James T. Robertson, James Hannah, Alexander McKie, Nigel C. Redhead, Leslie Hannah, R. A. Graham Rodgers, David McMillan, Barry Critchley & Alexander T. Connor

SECRETARY
R. A. Graham Rodgers

MANAGER
Neil Watt

ASSISTANT MANAGER
Stuart Millar

CLUB DOCTORS
Dr. Ronald Spicer, Dr. Niall Balmer & Dr. Paul Carnaghan

FOOTBALL SAFETY OFFICERS' ASSOCIATION REPRESENTATIVE
Alex Connor

GROUNDSMAN
Murray Gibson

COMMERCIAL MANAGER
David McMillan

MATCHDAY PROGRAMME EDITOR
R. A. Graham Rodgers
(01776) 702194

TELEPHONES
Ground (01776) 703271
Fax (01776) 702194
Sec. Home/Ticket Office/ Information Service (01776) 702194

E-MAIL & INTERNET ADDRESS
grodgers_sfc@yahoo.co.uk

CLUB SHOP
Situated at Ground 2.30p.m-3.00pm and half time on Matchdays

OFFICIAL SUPPORTERS CLUB
Situated in North Strand Street, Stranraer. Tel (01776) 704121

TEAM CAPTAIN
Allan Jenkins

SHIRT SPONSOR
Stena Line

KIT SUPPLIER
ICIS

LIST OF PLAYERS 2003/04

SURNAME	FIRST NAME	MIDDLE NAME	DATE OF BIRTH	PLACE OF BIRTH	DATE OF SIGNING	HEIGHT FT INS	WEIGHT ST LBS	POS. ON PITCH	PREVIOUS CLUB
Aitken	Stephen	Smith	25/09/76	Glasgow	10/07/01	5 8.0	11 1	Mid	Morton
Cruickshank	Christopher		25/08/80	Glasgow	25/06/03	5 11.0	12 0	Def	Maryhill Juniors
Cunningham	Daniel		23/08/84	Irvine	13/08/03	6 2.0	11 0	Def	Queen of the South
Essler	Andrew		15/11/76	Glasgow	07/08/03	5 8.0	11 0	Mid	Carvasham
Finlayson	Kevin	Charles	07/12/79	Glasgow	10/07/01	5 10.0	10 11	Fwd	Queen's Park
Graham	David		02/06/83	Stirling	19/06/03	5 9.0	11 0	Fwd	Stenhousemuir
Grant	Allan		01/07/73	Glasgow	24/06/03	5 10.0	11 7	Fwd	Maryhill Juniors
Guy	Graham		15/08/83	Bellshill	25/06/03	6 0.0	11 0	Def	St. Mirren
Henderson	Murray		15/06/80	Lanark	19/06/03	6 3.0	13 0	Def	Balmore Amateurs
Jenkins	Allan	David	07/10/81	Stranraer	03/09/98	6 1.0	13 0	Mid	Ayr Boswell
Kerr	Paul		26/02/78	Ayr	09/07/02	6 1.0	13 6	Fwd	Cumnock Juniors
MacDonald	William	Jamie	10/07/84	Lanark	01/08/03	5 11.5	11 1	Mid	Livingston
Marshall	Stephen		30/04/80	Glasgow	01/08/02	6 0.0	12 8	Mid	Queen's Park
McAllister	Thomas	James	21/02/71	Glasgow	25/06/03	6 0.0	12 0	Mid	Maryhill Juniors
McCaulay	Martin	John	05/06/85	Dumfries	22/07/03	5 10.0	10 0	Gk	Stranraer Athletic
McCondichie	Andrew	Morrison	21/08/77	Glasgow	21/06/03	5 10.5	12 3	Gk	Maryhill Juniors
McPhee	Gary		01/10/79	Glasgow	25/06/03	5 10.0	11 0	Mid	Cumbernauld Juniors
Meechan	Kenneth		16/02/72	Greenock	26/06/03	6 0.0	14 0	Gk	Largs Thistle
Moore	Michael	Jordan	24/03/81	Paisley	01/08/02	6 1.0	11 12	Fwd	Hamilton Academical
Sharp	Lee		22/05/75	Glasgow	01/08/02	5 9.0	12 0	Mid	Ayr United
Swift	Stephen		21/07/80	Glasgow	15/07/03	5 11.0	11 7	Def	Linlithgow Rose Juniors
Turnbull	David		05/09/80	Durban	02/08/03	6 1.0	12 0	Fwd	Maryhill Juniors
Wingate	Derek		26/09/75	Glasgow	10/07/01	6 2.0	13 0	Def	Benburb Juniors
Wright	Fraser		23/12/79	East Kilbride	03/09/98	5 10.0	11 10	Def	St. Mirren B.C.

milestones

YEAR OF FORMATION: 1870
MOST LEAGUE POINTS IN A SEASON: 56 (Second Division – Season 1993/94) (2 Points for a Win)
61 (Second Division – Season 1997/98) (3 Points for a Win)
MOST LEAGUE GOALS SCORED BY A PLAYER IN A SEASON: Derek Frye (Season 1977/78)
NO. OF GOALS SCORED: 27
RECORD ATTENDANCE: 6,500 (-v- Rangers – 24.1.1948)
RECORD VICTORY: 7-0 (-v- Brechin City – Division 2, 6.2.1965)
RECORD DEFEAT: 1-11 (-v- Queen of the South – Scottish Cup, 16.1.1932)

ticket information

	SEASON TICKET PRICES	
SEATED	ADULT	£120
	JUVENILE/OAP	£60
	FAMILY	£40
STANDING	ADULT	£100
	JUVENILE/OAP	£50

	LEAGUE ADMISSION PRICES	
SEATED	ADULT	£10
	JUVENILE/OAP	£5
STANDING	ADULT	£8
	JUVENILE/OAP	£4

leading goalscorers 1993-2003

Season	Div	No. of Goals	Player
1993-94	S	16	T. Sloan
1994-95	F	4	D. Henderson, T. Sloan
1995-96	S	6	A. Grant
1996-97	S	7	P. McIntyre
1997-98	S	11	G. Young
1998-99	S	5	P. Ronald, G. Young
1999-00	S	12	P. Ronald
2000-01	S	13	I. Harty
2001-02	S	16	I. Harty
2002-03	S	12	I. Harty

the blues' club factfile 2002/03

Date	Venue	Opponents	Att.	Res	McCulloch W.	Gaughan K.	Wright F.	Wingate D.	Jenkins A.	Aitken S.	Renicks S.	Marshall S.	Harty I.	Sharp L.	Finlayson K.	Grace A.	Fallon J.	Lurinsky A.	Hodge S.	Moore M.	Hillcoat J.	Kerr P.	Curran H.	Kane A.	Farrell D.	Maclaren R.	Crawford J.	Scott A.
Aug 3	A	Raith Rovers	1,790	1-1	1	2	3	4	5	6	7	8	9	10	11	12	14	16^{1}										
10	H	Cowdenbeath	349	2-3	1	2	3	4	15	6			9	11	7^{1}	8	14	16	5	10^{1}								
17	A	Airdrie United	1,518	1-2		2	3	4	16	8		6		5	7	12	15	11^{1}	10	9	1							
24	A	Stenhousemuir	295	0-2		5	3	4		6	2		14	11	12	8	9	7	15		1	10						
31	H	Brechin City	348	3-1		2	3		4	6			9^{2}	5	7	14			15	10^{1}	1	11	8	12				
Sep 14	A	Berwick Rangers	388	4-3			3	2	5^{1}	6			9^{1}	11^{1}	7			15		8	1	10^{1}			4			
21	H	Dumbarton	455	1-0			3	2	5	6			9	11	7					8	1	10^{1}			4			
28	H	Forfar Athletic	385	2-0			3	2	5	6			9^{1}	11^{1}	7				14	8	1	10			4			
Oct 5	A	Hamilton Academical	1,175	5-1			3	2	8^{1}	6			9^{2}	11^{1}	7^{1}		10		5		1		12	16	4			
19	A	Cowdenbeath	358	1-0			3	2	8	6			9	11	7		14		5^{1}		1	10			4			
26	H	Raith Rovers	608	2-2			3	2	5^{1}	6			9^{1}	11	7		15	8	14		1	10	12		4			
Nov 2	A	Brechin City	426	†1-3		2	3	4	8	6			9	11	7		15		5	10	1			16				
9	H	Stenhousemuir	411	2-1		2	3	4	5	6		15	9	11	7		16		14	8^{2}	1	10						
16	H	Berwick Rangers	412	1-0		2	3	4	5	6			9	11	7				14	10^{1}	1	8	12			16		
23	A	Dumbarton	772	0-3		2	3	4	5	6			9	11	7		14			10	1		8			15		
30	H	Hamilton Academical	397	1-2		2	4	5	8	6			9	3	7		14		11	10^{1}	1		12					
Dec 28	H	Airdrie United	695	2-0		2	3	4	6	7			9^{1}	11					5	8^{1}	1	10	12			15		
Jan 1	A	Stenhousemuir	356	0-1		2	3	4	8	6			9	11			7	16	5		1	10						
18	A	Berwick Rangers	422	0-1		2	6	4	11	8			9	7	15				5	10	1						3	
Feb 1	H	Dumbarton	408	1-2		2	3	4	11	8				14	7				5	9^{1}	1	10	6	15				
8	H	Forfar Athletic	362	3-2			3	2	5^{1}	8			9	15	7^{1}				6	10	1	11^{1}					4	
25	H	Brechin City	371	2-3		2		4	8			7	9	11			16		5	10	1	15^{1}	6				3^{1}	
Mar 1	A	Airdrie United	1,187	3-3		2	3^{1}	4	6	8			9^{1}	15	7				5	11	1	10^{1}						
4	A	Raith Rovers	1,448	0-3		2	3	4	8	6			9	11	7				5	10	1	14	12		16			
11	H	Cowdenbeath	363	4-4		14	3	2	5^{1}	8			9^{2}		7				15	10	1	11		6^{1}	4			16
15	A	Brechin City	488	1-3		2	3	5	8	6			9		7				14	10^{1}	1	15		11	4			
18	A	Hamilton Academical	743	2-1		2	3		8	6		10	9^{1}		7			16	5	11^{1}	1		12	15	4			
30	A	Forfar Athletic	394	1-2			5	2	8	6			9	14	7			16	3	10^{1}	1			11	4			
Apr 1	A	Dumbarton	596	1-1			3	2^{1}	5	8			9	14	7		10			11	1	15		6	4			
5	H	Berwick Rangers	354	0-0	1	2	3	6	5	8			9	11	15					10				14	4			7
8	H	Stenhousemuir	321	0-1	1	2		3	5	6		8	9	11	15					10		16			4			7
12	H	Hamilton Academical	402	0-0	1	2		3	5	6			9	11	8			16		10			12	14	4			7
19	A	Forfar Athletic	391	0-4	1	2		4	5	6		8	9	11	7					10			12	15	3			
26	H	Raith Rovers	617	1-0	1	2	3	4	9	5				11	8^{1}					10			6	15				7
May 3	A	Cowdenbeath	229	0-0	1	2	3	4	5	6				11	9					10		15	8	14				7
10	H	Airdrie United	1,343	1-2	1	2	3	4	5	8			9	11^{1}	7					10			6		12			
TOTAL FULL APPEARANCES					9	26	32	34	33	35	2	6	31	28	29	2	4	3	16	30	27	15	7	4	15		3	5
TOTAL SUB APPEARANCES						1			2			1	1	5	4	3	10	7	8			6	9	10	2	3		1
TOTAL GOALS SCORED							1	1	5				12	4	4			2	1	11		5		1			1	

Small bold figures denote goalscorers. † denotes opponent's own goal.

stair park

LONDON ROAD
ENTRY FOR VISITING SUPPORTERS
NORTH STAND
SOUTH STAND
ENTRY TO SOUTH STAND FOR VISITING SUPPORTERS

CAPACITY: 5,600; Seated 1,830, Standing 3,770

PITCH DIMENSIONS: 110 yds x 70 yds

FACILITIES FOR DISABLED SUPPORTERS:
By prior arrangement with Club Secretary.

team playing kits

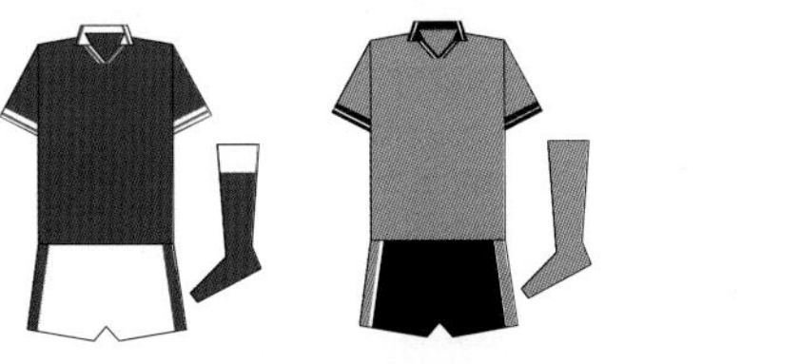

how to get there

Stair Park can be reached by the following routes:

TRAINS: There is a regular service of trains from Ayr and the station is only 1 mile from the ground.

BUSES: Two services pass the park. These are the buses from Glenluce to Portroadie and the Dumfries-Stranraer service.

CARS: Car parking is available in the Public Park at the ground, where there is space for approximately 50 vehicles and also in the side streets around the park. Signs for away supporters will be displayed and parking situated at Stranraer Academy, McMasters Road.

the scottish premier league

ABERDEEN

League Champions:
Division I: 1954/55
Premier Division: 1979/80, 1983/84, 1984/85
League Cup Winners:
1955/56, 1976/77, 1985/86, 1989/90, 1995/96
Scottish Cup Winners: 1947, 1970, 1982, 1983, 1984, 1986, 1990
European Cup Winners' Cup:
1982/83
European Super Cup: 1983
Drybrough Cup Winners:
1970/71, 1980/81

CELTIC

League Champions:
Division I: 1892/93, 1893/94, 1895/96, 1897/98, 1904/05, 1905/06, 1906/07, 1907/08, 1908/09, 1909/10, 1913/14, 1914/15, 1915/16, 1916/17, 1918/19, 1921/22, 1925/26, 1935/36, 1937/38, 1953/54, 1965/66, 1966/67, 1967/68, 1968/69, 1969/70, 1970/71, 1971/72, 1972/73, 1973/74
Premier Division: 1976/77, 1978/79, 1980/81, 1981/82, 1985/86, 1987/88, 1997/98,
SPL: 2000/01, 2001/02
League Cup Winners:
1956/57, 1957/58, 1965/66, 1966/67, 1967/68, 1968/69, 1969/70, 1974/75, 1982/83, 1997/98, 1999/2000, 2000/01
Scottish Cup Winners:
1892, 1899, 1900, 1904, 1907, 1908, 1911, 1912, 1914, 1923, 1925, 1927, 1931, 1933, 1937, 1951, 1954, 1965, 1967, 1969, 1971, 1972, 1974, 1975, 1977, 1980, 1985, 1988, 1989, 1995, 2001
European Cup Winners: 1966/67
Runners-up: 1969/70
UEFA Cup Runners-up: 2002/03
Empire Exhibition Cup Winners: 1938
Coronation Cup Winners: 1953
Drybrough Cup Winners: 1974/75

DUNDEE

League Champions:
Division I: 1961/62
Division II: 1946/47
First Division: 1978/79, 1991/92, 1997/98
League Cup Winners:
1951/52, 1952/53, 1973/74
Scottish Cup Winners: 1910
B&Q Centenary Cup: 1990/91

DUNDEE UNITED

League Champions:
Division II: 1924/25, 1928/29
Premier Division: 1982/83
League Cup Winners:
1979/80, 1980/81
Scottish Cup Winners: 1993/94
UEFA Cup Runners-up: 1986/87

DUNFERMLINE ATHLETIC

League Champions:
Division II: 1925/26
First Division: 1988/89, 1995/96
Second Division: 1985/86
Scottish Cup Winners: 1961, 1968
Scottish Qualifying Cup: 1911/12

HEARTS

League Champions:
Division I: 1894/95, 1896/97, 1957/58, 1959/60
First Division: 1979/80
League Cup Winners: 1954/55, 1958/59, 1959/60, 1962/63
Scottish Cup Winners: 1891, 1896, 1901, 1906, 1956, 1998

HIBERNIAN

League Champions:
Division I: 1902/03, 1947/48, 1950/51, 1951/52
Division II: 1893/94, 1894/95, 1932/33
First Division: 1980/81, 1998/99
League Cup Winners: 1972/73, 1991/92
Scottish Cup Winners: 1887, 1902
Drybrough Cup Winners:
1972/73, 1973/74

KILMARNOCK

League Champions:
Division I: 1964/65
Division II: 1897/98, 1898/99
Scottish Cup Winners:
1920, 1929, 1997
Scottish Qualifying Cup Winners:
1896/97

LIVINGSTON (formerly MEADOWBANK THISTLE)

League Champions:
First Division: 2000/01
Second Division: 1986/87, 1998/99
Third Division: 1995/96

MOTHERWELL

League Champions:
Division I: 1931/32
First Division: 1981/82, 1984/85
Division II: 1953/54, 1968/69
League Cup Winners: 1950/51
Scottish Cup Winners: 1952, 1991

PARTICK THISTLE

League Champions:
First Division: 1975/76, 2001/02
Runners-up: 1991/92 Division II: 1896/97, 1899/1900, 1970/71
Second Division: 2000/01 Runners-up: 1901/02
League Cup Winners: 1971/72
Runners-up: 1953/54, 1956/57, 1958/59
Scottish Cup Winners: 1921 Runners-up: 1930
Glasgow Cup Winners: 1935, 1951, 1952, 1954, 1960, 1981, 1989

RANGERS

League Champions:
Division I: 1890/91 (shared), 1898/99, 1899/1900, 1900/01, 1901/02, 1910/11, 1911/12, 1912/13, 1917/18, 1919/20, 1920/21, 1922/23, 1923/24, 1924/25, 1926/27, 1927/28, 1928/29, 1929/30, 1930/31, 1932/33, 1933/34, 1934/35, 1936/37, 1938/39, 1946/47, 1948/49, 1949/50, 1952/53, 1955/56, 1956/57, 1958/59, 1960/61, 1962/63, 1963/64, 1974/75
Premier Division: 1975/76, 1977/78, 1986/87, 1988/89, 1989/90, 1990/91, 1991/92, 1992/93, 1993/94, 1994/95, 1995/96, 1996/97
SPL: 1998/99, 1999/2000, 2002/03
League Cup Winners:
1946/47, 1948/49, 1960/61, 1961/62, 1963/64, 1964/65, 1970/71, 1975/76, 1977/78, 1978/79, 1981/82, 1983/84, 1984/85, 1986/87, 1987/88, 1988/89, 1990/91, 1992/93, 1993/94, 1996/97, 1998/99, 2001/02, 2002/03
Scottish Cup Winners:
1894, 1897, 1898, 1903, 1928, 1930, 1932, 1934, 1935, 1936, 1948, 1949, 1950, 1953, 1960, 1962, 1963, 1964, 1966, 1973, 1976, 1978, 1979, 1981, 1992, 1993, 1996, 1999, 2000, 2002, 2003
European Cup Winners' Cup:
1971/72
Runners-up: 1960/61, 1966/67
Drybrough Cup Winners:
1979/80

the scottish football league

S·F·L ©

FIRST DIVISION

AYR UNITED
League Champions:
Division II: 1911/12, 1912/13, 1927/28, 1936/37, 1958/59, 1965/66
Second Division: 1987/88, 1996/97

BRECHIN CITY
League Champions:
'C' Division: 1953/54
Second Division: 1982/83, 1989/90
Third Division: 2001/02

CLYDE
League Champions:
Division II: 1904/05, 1951/52, 1956/57, 1961/62, 1972/73,
Second Division: 1977/78, 1981/82, 1992/93, 1999/2000
Scottish Cup Winners:
1939, 1955, 1958

FALKIRK
League Champions:
First Division: 1990/91, 1993/94, 2002/03
Division II: 1935/36, 1969/70, 1974/75
Second Division: 1979/80
Scottish Cup Winners: 1913, 1957
SFL Challenge Cup Winners: 1993/94 (known as B&Q Cup), 1997/98

INVERNESS CALEDONIAN THISTLE
League Champions:
Third Division: 1996/97

QUEEN OF THE SOUTH
League Champions:
Division II: 1950/51
Second Division: 2001/02
Bell's Cup: 2002/03

RAITH ROVERS
League Champions:
First Division: 1992/93, 1994/95
Second Division: 2002/03
Division II: 1907/08, 1909/10 (shared)
1937/38, 1948/49
League Cup Winners: 1994/95

ROSS COUNTY
League Champions:
Third Division: 1998/99

ST. JOHNSTONE
League Champions:
First Division: 1982/83, 1989/90, 1996/97
Division II: 1923/24, 1959/60, 1962/63

ST. MIRREN
League Champions: First Division: 1976/77, 1999/2000
Division II: 1967/68
Scottish Cup Winners:
1926, 1959, 1987
Victory Cup: 1919
Anglo Scottish Cup Winners:
1979/80
Summer Cup: 1943

SECOND DIVISION

AIRDRIE UNITED (formerly CLYDEBANK)
League Champions:
Second Division: 1975/76

ALLOA ATHLETIC
League Champions:
Division II: 1921/22
Third Division: 1997/98
Bell's Challenge Cup Winners:
1999/2000

ARBROATH
League Runners-up: Division II: 1934/35, 1958/59, 1967/68, 1971/72,
Second Division: 2000/01
Third Division: 1997/98

BERWICK RANGERS
League Champions:
Second Division: 1978/79
Runners-up: 1993/94
Third Division Runners-up:
1999/2000

DUMBARTON
League Champions:
Division I: 1890/91 (shared with Rangers), 1891/92
Division II: 1910/11, 1971/72
Second Division: 1991/92
Scottish Cup Winners: 1883

EAST FIFE
League Champions:
Division II: 1947/48
League Cup Winners:
1947/48, 1949/50, 1953/54
Scottish Cup Winners: 1938

FORFAR ATHLETIC
League Champions:
'C' Division: 1948/49
Second Division: 1983/84
Third Division: 1994/95

HAMILTON ACADEMICAL
League Champions:
Division II: 1903/04
First Division: 1985/86, 1987/88
Third Division: 2000/01
B&Q Cup Winners: 1991/92, 1992/93
Scottish Cup Runners-up:
1910/11, 1934/35
Second Division Runners-up:
1952/53, 1964/65, 1996/97
Lanarkshire Cup Winners: 10 Times

MORTON
League Champions:
Division II: 1949/50, 1963/64, 1966/67
First Division: 1977/78, 1983/84, 1986/87
Second Division: 1994/95
Third Division: 2002/03
Scottish Cup Winners: 1922

STENHOUSEMUIR
SFL Challenge Cup Winners: 1995/96

THIRD DIVISION

ALBION ROVERS
League Champions:
Division II: 1933/34
Second Division: 1988/89
Scottish Qualifying Cup: 1913/14

COWDENBEATH
League Champions:
Division II: 1913/14, 1914/15, 1938/39

EAST STIRLINGSHIRE
League Champions:
Division II: 1931/32

ELGIN CITY
Season 2000/01 was the club's first season in membership of S.F.L.:
The club's highest position to date was 6th position in Season 2001/02

GRETNA
Season 2002/03 was the club's first season in membership of S.F.L.:
The club's league position was 6th

MONTROSE
League Champions:
Second Division: 1984/85

PETERHEAD
Season 2000/01 was the club's first season in membership of S.F.L.:
The club's highest league position to date was 4th position in Seasons 2001/02 and 2002/03

QUEEN'S PARK
League Champions:
Division II: 1922/23
'B' Division 1955/56
Second Division: 1980/81
Third Division: 1999/2000
Scottish Cup Winners:
1874, 1875, 1876, 1880, 1881, 1882, 1884, 1886, 1890, 1893
FA Cup: Runners-up: 1884, 1889
FA Charity Shield: 1899 (Shared with Aston Villa)

STIRLING ALBION
League Champions:
Division II: 1952/53, 1957/58, 1960/61, 1964/65,
Second Division: 1976/77, 1990/91, 1995/96

STRANRAER
League Champions:
Second Division: 1993/94, 1997/98
SFL Challenge Cup Winners: 1996/97

s.p.l. and s.f.l. – final tables 2002/2003

BANK OF SCOTLAND PREMIERLEAGUE

	P	W	D	L	F	A	PTS
RANGERS	38	31	4	3	101	28	97
CELTIC	38	31	4	3	98	26	97
HEARTS	38	18	9	11	57	51	63
KILMARNOCK	38	16	9	13	47	56	57
DUNFERMLINE ATHLETIC	38	13	7	18	54	71	46
DUNDEE	38	10	14	14	50	60	44
HIBERNIAN	38	15	6	17	56	64	51
ABERDEEN	38	13	10	15	41	54	49
LIVINGSTON	38	9	8	21	48	62	35
PARTICK THISTLE	38	8	11	19	37	58	35
DUNDEE UNITED	38	7	11	20	35	68	32
MOTHERWELL	38	7	7	24	45	71	28

BELL'S SFL FIRST DIVISION

	P	W	D	L	F	A	PTS
FALKIRK	36	25	6	5	80	32	81
CLYDE	36	21	9	6	66	37	72
ST. JOHNSTONE	36	20	7	9	49	29	67
INVERNESS CAL. THISTLE	36	20	5	11	74	45	65
QUEEN OF THE SOUTH	36	12	12	12	45	48	48
AYR UNITED	36	12	9	15	34	44	45
ST. MIRREN	36	9	10	17	42	71	37
ROSS COUNTY	36	9	8	19	42	46	35
ALLOA ATHLETIC	36	9	8	19	39	72	35
ARBROATH	36	3	6	27	30	77	15

BELL'S SFL SECOND DIVISION

	P	W	D	L	F	A	PTS
RAITH ROVERS	36	16	11	9	53	36	59
BRECHIN CITY	36	16	7	13	63	59	55
AIRDRIE UNITED	36	14	12	10	51	44	54
FORFAR ATHLETIC	36	14	9	13	55	53	51
BERWICK RANGERS	36	13	10	13	43	48	49
DUMBARTON	36	13	9	14	48	47	48
STENHOUSEMUIR	36	12	11	13	49	51	47
HAMILTON ACADEMICAL	36	12	11	13	43	48	47
STRANRAER	36	12	8	16	49	57	44
COWDENBEATH	36	8	12	16	46	57	36

BELL'S SFL THIRD DIVISION

	P	W	D	L	F	A	PTS
MORTON	36	21	9	6	67	33	72
EAST FIFE	36	20	11	5	73	37	71
ALBION ROVERS	36	20	10	6	62	36	70
PETERHEAD	36	20	8	8	76	37	68
STIRLING ALBION	36	15	11	10	50	44	56
GRETNA	36	11	12	13	50	50	45
MONTROSE	36	7	12	17	35	61	33
QUEEN'S PARK	36	7	11	18	39	51	32
ELGIN CITY	36	5	13	18	33	63	28
EAST STIRLINGSHIRE	36	2	7	27	32	105	13

SFL RESERVE LEAGUE EAST

	P	W	D	L	F	A	PTS
BRECHIN CITY	12	8	1	3	27	18	25
FORFAR ATHLETIC	12	7	2	3	25	21	23
RAITH ROVERS	12	5	5	2	26	17	20
ST. JOHNSTONE	12	5	1	6	21	17	16
ARBROATH	12	3	5	4	18	20	14
COWDENBEATH	12	2	6	4	17	29	12
EAST FIFE	12	0	4	8	11	23	4

SFL RESERVE LEAGUE WEST

	P	W	D	L	F	A	PTS
FALKIRK	15	12	2	1	37	14	38
STENHOUSEMUIR	15	8	4	3	29	17	28
HAMILTON ACADEMICAL	15	5	5	5	16	21	20
QUEEN'S PARK	15	4	2	9	18	19	14
ST. MIRREN	15	3	4	8	14	26	13
ALBION ROVERS	15	3	3	9	19	36	12

THE SCOTTISH PREMIER LEAGUE UNDER-21

	P	W	D	L	F	A	PTS
CELTIC	24	16	4	4	76	34	52
RANGERS	24	13	4	7	58	31	43
HEARTS	24	9	10	5	38	29	37
MOTHERWELL	24	11	4	9	45	44	37
HIBERNIAN	24	10	6	8	39	35	36
LIVINGSTON	24	11	2	11	42	48	35
KILMARNOCK	24	8	10	6	41	35	34
PARTICK THISTLE	24	10	3	11	30	47	33
DUNDEE	24	9	5	10	45	58	32
DUNDEE UNITED	24	8	5	11	40	43	29
ABERDEEN	24	6	6	12	46	59	24
ST. JOHNSTONE	24	5	8	11	27	40	23
DUNFERMLINE ATHLETIC	24	5	3	16	40	64	18

SFL UNDER 18 YOUTH DIVISION

	P	W	D	L	F	A	PTS
AYR UNITED	19	16	1	2	68	16	49
ROSS COUNTY	19	15	2	2	51	10	47
QUEEN OF THE SOUTH	19	13	4	2	57	14	43
STIRLING ALBION	19	13	2	4	66	39	41
QUEEN'S PARK	19	11	4	4	36	35	37
COWDENBEATH	19	11	1	7	59	32	34
FALKIRK	19	10	2	7	55	32	32
STENHOUSEMUIR	19	8	6	5	32	27	30
HAMILTON ACADEMICAL	19	8	5	6	47	29	29
EAST FIFE	19	8	5	6	41	29	29
ARBROATH	19	8	3	8	34	30	27
ALLOA ATHLETIC	19	7	4	8	38	40	25
ST. MIRREN	19	6	6	7	38	33	24
ALBION ROVERS	19	6	5	8	32	36	23
MORTON	19	6	5	8	30	41	23
FORFAR ATHLETIC	19	5	2	12	21	49	17
PETERHEAD	19	3	2	14	18	42	11
EAST STIRLINGSHIRE	19	2	4	13	24	60	10
ELGIN CITY	19	2	1	16	17	59	7
BERWICK RANGERS	19	0	0	19	14	125	0

THE SCOTTISH PREMIER LEAGUE UNDER-18 YOUTH DIVISION

	P	W	D	L	F	A	PTS
CELTIC	30	20	4	6	75	36	64
RANGERS	30	18	8	4	57	30	62
KILMARNOCK	30	14	5	11	53	49	47
HEARTS	30	13	7	10	54	39	46
DUNDEE UNITED	30	12	9	9	54	45	45
ABERDEEN	30	12	8	10	49	43	44
HIBERNIAN	30	12	4	14	40	51	40
LIVINGSTON	30	8	10	12	49	56	34
MOTHERWELL	30	9	7	14	42	53	34
DUNDEE	30	8	8	14	47	53	32
DUNFERMLINE ATHLETIC	30	3	2	25	28	93	11

reserve league cup season 2002/2003

FIRST ROUND

21st January, 2003
QUEEN'S PARK 0 **COWDENBEATH 2**
STENHOUSEMUIR 2 **FALKIRK 1**

28th January, 2003
EAST FIFE 1 **ST. MIRREN 0**

10th February, 2003
BRECHIN CITY 3 **RAITH ROVERS 1**

11th February, 2003
ALBION ROVERS 3 **HAMILTON ACADEMICAL 1**

19th February, 2003
ARBROATH 3 **FORFAR ATHLETIC 1**
(AET – 1-1 AFTER 90 MINUTES)
BYES: AYR UNITED & ST. JOHNSTONE

SECOND ROUND

26th February, 2003
EAST FIFE 3 **AYR UNITED 5**

24th March, 2003
COWDENBEATH 1 **ST. JOHNSTONE 2**
(AET – 1-1 AFTER 90 MINUTES)
STENHOUSEMUIR 1 **ARBROATH 0**

1st April, 2003
BRECHIN CITY 2 **ALBION ROVERS 0**

SEMI-FINALS

1st April, 2003
STENHOUSEMUIR 0 **AYR UNITED 1**

29th April, 2003
BRECHIN CITY 1 **ST. JOHNSTONE 2**

FINAL

Wednesday, 7th May, 2003, McDiarmid Park, Perth
ST. JOHNSTONE 2 **AYR UNITED 1**

St. Johnstone: S. Miotto, M. Baxter, E. Malone, C. Johnston, R. Forsyth, M. McCulloch, M. Maher, M. Ferry, S. Noble, E. Panther, C. Strickland
Substitutes not used: N. Gibson, D. Noon, E. Hall, D. Greenhill, R. Gilpin
Ayr United: J. Dodds, W. Lyle, M. Dunlop, S. Chaplain, M. Ferry, P. Lovering, M. McColl, A. McVeigh, S. Kean, A. Black, S. Crawford, (R. Burgess)
Substitutes not used: A. Ferguson, R. Hunter, I. Fulton, D. Johnson
Scorers: St. Johnstone: C. Strickland (2) **Ayr United:** A. McVeigh
Referee: Martin Sproule
Attendance: 308

scottish football association youth cup

SEASON 2002/03

FIRST ROUND

BERWICK RANGERS 2 — PARTICK THISTLE 4
BURNTISLAND SHIPYARD 4 — AIRDRIE UNITED 3
COWDENBEATH 1 — CLYDE 2
DEVERONVALE 4 — LOSSIEMOUTH 3
EDINBURGH CITY 3 — ALLOA ATHLETIC 2
FORFAR ATHLETIC 0 — HEARTS 2
FORT WILLIAM 1 — CLACHNACUDDIN 8
MORTON 7 — BRECHIN CITY 0
HUNTLY 6 — FRASERBURGH 2
KEITH 5 — COVE RANGERS 1
NAIRN COUNTY 1 — BRORA RANGERS 4
NEWTON STEWART 0 — GRETNA 4
ST. CUTHBERT WANDERERS 2 — DALBEATTIE STAR 3
ST. MIRREN 1 — ALBION ROVERS 2
SPARTANS 3 — PRESTON ATHLETIC 0
STENHOUSEMUIR 2 — EAST STIRLINGSHIRE 1
THREAVE ROVERS 2 — QUEEN OF THE SOUTH 4

SECOND ROUND

BRORA RANGERS 0 — PETERHEAD 4
BUCKIE THISTLE 6 — HUNTLY 1
CIVIL SERVICE STROLLERS 2 — BURNTISLAND SHIPYARD 0
CLYDE 3 — STENHOUSEMUIR 1
DALBEATTIE STAR 2 — ANNAN ATHLETIC 0
DEVERONVALE 1 — ROTHES 4
EAST FIFE 1 — MORTON 0
EDINBURGH CITY 3 — ALBION ROVERS 1
GRETNA 1 — QUEEN OF THE SOUTH 0
HEARTS 9 — PARTICK THISTLE 0
KEITH 0 — CLACHNACUDDIN 3
MONTROSE 1 — ST. JOHNSTONE 0
QUEEN'S PARK 11 — SPARTANS 3

THIRD ROUND

CIVIL SERVICE STROLLERS 0 — RANGERS 4
DALBEATTIE STAR 0 — AYR UNITED 5
DUNDEE UNITED 3 — CLYDE 0
DUNFERMLINE ATHLETIC 5 — CLACHNACUDDIN 1
EDINBURGH CITY 0 — ARBROATH 0
(EDINBURGH CITY WON 4-3 ON KICKS FROM THE PENALTY MARK)
FALKIRK 8 — GRETNA 2
HAWICK ROYAL ALBERT 0 — INVERNESS CAL. THISTLE 6
HEARTS 1 — ABERDEEN 4
HIBERNIAN 3 — EAST FIFE 2
KILMARNOCK 1 — HAMILTON ACADEMICAL 0
MONTROSE 2 — CELTIC 8
MOTHERWELL 2 — QUEEN'S PARK 1
PETERHEAD 0 — LIVINGSTON 2
ROSS COUNTY 5 — ELGIN CITY 1
ROTHES 0 — DUNDEE 9
STIRLING ALBION 2 — BUCKIE THISTLE 3

FOURTH ROUND

ABERDEEN 2 — ROSS COUNTY 1
AYR UNITED 3 — EDINBURGH CITY 0
CELTIC 5 — LIVINGSTON 3
DUNFERMLINE ATHLETIC 2 — BUCKIE THISTLE 3
FALKIRK 0 — MOTHERWELL 2
HIBERNIAN 6 — DUNDEE 2
KILMARNOCK 1 — DUNDEE UNITED 2
RANGERS 2 — INVERNESS CAL. THISTLE 2
(INVERNESS CALEDONIAN THISTLE WON 5-4 ON KICKS FROM THE PENALTY MARK)

FIFTH ROUND

ABERDEEN 4 — INVERNESS CAL. THISTLE 1
BUCKIE THISTLE 1 — AYR UNITED 2
DUNDEE UNITED 5 — CELTIC 5
(CELTIC WON 4-3 ON KICKS FROM THE PENALTY MARK)
MOTHERWELL 0 — HIBERNIAN 1

SEMI-FINALS

ABERDEEN 2 — HIBERNIAN 0
CELTIC 3 — AYR UNITED 0

FINAL

Friday, 16th May, 2003 – McDiarmid Park, Perth

ABERDEEN 1 **CELTIC 3**

(AET – 1-1 AFTER 90 MINUTES)

Aberdeen: Hutton, McCulloch, Muirhead, Morrison, Diamond, Jones, (Higgins), Buckley, Souter, Tarditi, (Watson), Foster, McKenzie, (Carella)
Substitutes not used: Kelly, Lombarti

Celtic: Marshall, Irvine, Mulgrew, Lawson, Low, Reid, McGeady, (Ramsey), Beattie, Arbuckle, (Harris), Gardyne, (Pinkowski), Wallace
Substitutes not used: McCormack, McGovern

Scorers: Aberdeen: Foster **Celtic:** Low, Gardyne, Irvine

Referee: Calum Murray

Attendance: 1,946

YOUTH LEAGUE CUP SEASON 2002/03
SECTIONAL RESULTS: SECTION 1

30th March, 2003
ARBROATH 2 **ELGIN CITY 0**

1st April, 2003
MONTROSE 0 **PETERHEAD 2**

6th April, 2003
ARBROATH 2 **MONTROSE 1**
ELGIN CITY 0 **ROSS COUNTY 0**

13th April, 2003
PETERHEAD 1 **ELGIN CITY 0**
ROSS COUNTY 7 **ARBROATH 0**

20th April, 2003
MONTROSE 1 **ROSS COUNTY 2**
PETERHEAD 1 **ARBROATH 2**

27th April, 2003
ROSS COUNTY 4 **PETERHEAD 2**

4th May, 2003
ELGIN CITY 0 **MONTROSE 3**

SECTION 1 – FINAL TABLE

	P	W	D	L	F	A	PTS
ROSS COUNTY	4	3	1	0	13	3	10
ARBROATH	4	3	0	1	6	9	9
PETERHEAD	4	2	0	2	6	6	6
MONTROSE	4	1	0	3	5	6	3
ELGIN CITY	4	0	1	3	0	6	1

SECTION 2

30th March, 2003
QUEEN'S PARK 1 **MORTON 2**
ST. MIRREN 0 **AYR UNITED 0**

6th April, 2003
AYR UNITED 4 **MORTON 1**
QUEEN OF THE SOUTH 3 **QUEEN'S PARK 1**

13th April, 2003
AYR UNITED 1 **QUEEN OF THE SOUTH 0**
MORTON 0 **ST. MIRREN 3**

20th April, 2003
QUEEN OF THE SOUTH 1 **ST. MIRREN 0**

27th April, 2003
ST. MIRREN 2 **QUEEN'S PARK 2**

30th April, 2003
QUEEN'S PARK 0 **AYR UNITED 3**

1st May, 2003
MORTON 1 **QUEEN OF THE SOUTH 2**

SECTION 2 – FINAL TABLE

	P	W	D	L	F	A	PTS
AYR UNITED	4	3	1	0	8	1	10
QUEEN OF THE SOUTH	4	3	0	1	6	3	9
ST. MIRREN	4	1	2	1	5	3	5
MORTON	4	1	0	3	4	10	3
QUEEN'S PARK	4	0	1	3	4	10	1

SECTION 3

31st March, 2003
ALLOA ATHLETIC 8 **EAST STIRLINGSHIRE 0**
FALKIRK 1 **STENHOUSEMUIR 0**

7th April, 2003
ALLOA ATHLETIC 1 **FALKIRK 0**

9th April, 2003
EAST STIRLINGSHIRE 0 **STIRLING ALBION 12**

13th April, 2003
STIRLING ALBION 3 **ALLOA ATHLETIC 2**

27th April, 2003
EAST STIRLINGSHIRE 1 **FALKIRK 6**
STIRLING ALBION 2 **STENHOUSEMUIR 1**

28th April, 2003
STENHOUSEMUIR 2 **ALLOA ATHLETIC 0**

1st May, 2003
STENHOUSEMUIR 3 **EAST STIRLINGSHIRE 1**

4th May, 2003
FALKIRK 2 **STIRLING ALBION 2**

SECTION 3 – FINAL TABLE

	P	W	D	L	F	A	PTS
STIRLING ALBION	4	3	1	0	19	5	10
FALKIRK	4	2	1	1	9	4	7
ALLOA ATHLETIC	4	2	0	2	11	5	6
STENHOUSEMUIR	4	2	0	2	6	4	6
EAST STIRLINGSHIRE	4	0	0	4	2	29	0

SECTION 4

30th March, 2003
ALBION ROVERS 2 **COWDENBEATH 2**

6th April, 2003
ALBION ROVERS 2 **EAST FIFE 1**
COWDENBEATH 0 **HAMILTON ACADEMICAL 1**

13th April, 2003
FORFAR ATHLETIC 1 **COWDENBEATH 2**
HAMILTON ACADEMICAL 1 **ALBION ROVERS 0**

17th April, 2003
EAST FIFE 0 **FORFAR ATHLETIC 2**

20th April, 2003
EAST FIFE 3 **HAMILTON ACADEMICAL 4**
FORFAR ATHLETIC 1 **ALBION ROVERS 0**

27th April, 2003
COWDENBEATH 3 **EAST FIFE 1**
HAMILTON ACADEMICAL 3 **FORFAR ATHLETIC 0**

SECTION 4 – FINAL TABLE

	P	W	D	L	F	A	PTS
HAMILTON ACADEMICAL	4	4	0	0	9	3	12
COWDENBEATH	4	2	1	1	7	5	7
FORFAR ATHLETIC	4	2	0	2	4	5	6
ALBION ROVERS	4	1	1	2	4	5	4
EAST FIFE	4	0	0	4	5	11	0

SEMI-FINAL TIES

5th May, 2003
AYR UNITED 0 **HAMILTON ACADEMICAL 2 (AET)**

7th May, 2003
STIRLING ALBION 0 **ROSS COUNTY 3**

FINAL

Wednesday, 14th May, 2003 – New Douglas Park, Hamilton

HAMILTON ACADEMICAL 1 **ROSS COUNTY 2**

Hamilton Academical: R. Jellema, A. Arbuckle, S. Houston, S. Thomson, C. Smillie, N. Paterson, M. Elfallah, M. Keegans, (R. McGeachie), D. Gribben, (C. Donnelly), C. Dolan, S. Davie, (R. Orr)
Substitutes not used: B. Felvus, M. Wilson

Ross County: K. Miller, K. Dodds, C. Gray, M. Bolochoweckyj, C. Townsley, S. Logan, P. Lynch, D. Wilson, S. Higgins, M. Gardiner, (K. Farrimond), M. Gibson, (C. Kane)
Substitutes not used: J. McAskill, B. Lawrie, T. Wilson

Scorers: Hamilton Academical: N. Paterson
Ross County: M. Gardiner, S. Higgins

Referee: Steven Nicholls

Attendance: 325

leading goalscorers since 1999/2000

1999/2000

Scottish Premier League
25 M. Viduka (Celtic)
19 W. Dodds (10 for Rangers, 9 for Dundee United)
17 J. Albertz (Rangers)
16 R. Wallace (Rangers)
13 W. Falconer (Dundee)
G. McSwegan (Heart of Midlothian)
11 M. Burchill (Celtic)
K. Miller (Hibernian)
J. Spencer (Motherwell)
10 N. Lowndes (St. Johnstone)

First Division
19 M. Yardley (St. Mirren)
16 S. Crawford (Dunfermline Athletic)
B. Lavety (St. Mirren)
15 D. Bingham (Livingston)
14 S. Crabbe (Falkirk)
G. Hurst (Ayr United)
B. McPhee (Livingston)
13 B. Wilson (Inverness Caledonian Thistle)
12 C. Dargo (Raith Rovers)
D. Nicholls (Falkirk)

Second Division
18 B. Carrigan (Clyde)
17 A. Graham (Stirling Albion)
16 C. McGlashan (Arbroath)
15 M. Cameron (Alloa Athletic)
J. McQuade (Stirling Albion)
13 W. Irvine (Alloa Athletic)
S. Mallan (Queen of the South)
G. Shaw (Ross County)
12 P. Ronald (Stranraer)
11 P. Keogh (Clyde)
P. McGrillen (Stirling Albion)

Third Division
16 S. Milne (Forfar Athletic)
14 P. Flannery (Dumbarton)
13 M. Gallagher (Queen's Park)
M. McDowell (Cowdenbeath)
12 G. Brown (Cowdenbeath)
B. Honeyman (11 for Brechin City, 1 for East Fife)
S. Laidlaw (3 Berwick Rangers, 9 for East Stirlingshire)
S. Taylor (Montrose)
11 B. Moffat (East Fife)
9 M. Anthony (Berwick Rangers)
R. Black (Brechin City)
G. Higgins (East Stirlingshire)
B. Robson (Forfar Athletic)

2000/01

Scottish Premier League
35 H. Larsson (Celtic)
17 A. Stavrum (Aberdeen)
14 J. Sara (Dundee)
12 C. Cameron (Heart of Midlothian)
A. Kirk (Heart of Midlothian)
11 T-A. Flo (Rangers)
M-M. Paatelainen (Hibernian)
C. Sutton (Celtic)
10 J. Albertz (Rangers)
S. Elliott (Motherwell)
R. Gillies (St. Mirren)
D. Zitelli (Hibernian)

First Division
24 D. Wyness (Inverness Caledonian Thistle)
18 E. Annand (Ayr United)
17 G. Hurst (Ayr United)
14 D. Bingham (Livingston)
A. Bone (Ross County)
13 P. McGinlay (Ayr United)
B. Wilson (Livingston)
11 G. Hutchison (Falkirk)
P. Sheerin (Inverness Caledonian Thistle)
9 R. Hamilton (Alloa Athletic)
R. Matheson (Morton)

Second Division
18 I. English (Stenhousemuir)
16 S. McLean (Partick Thistle)
P. Weatherson (Queen of the South)
14 M. Hardie (Partick Thistle)
G. Wood (Berwick Rangers)
13 I. Harty (Stranraer)
12 P. Walker (Stranraer)
10 P. Lindau (Partick Thistle)
S. Mallan (Arbroath)
J. O'Neil (Queen of the South)

Third Division
24 D. McFarlane (Hamilton Academical)
22 R. Grant (Brechin City)
17 P. Flannery (Dumbarton)
16 S. Hislop (East Stirlingshire)
12 M. Moore (Hamilton Academical)
11 K. Bain (Brechin City)
G. McKechnie (East Stirlingshire)
C. Yeats (Peterhead)
10 M. McDowell (Cowdenbeath)
9 A. Brown (Dumbarton)
S. Callaghan (Hamilton Academical)

2001/02

Scottish Premier League
29 H. Larsson (Celtic)
19 J. Hartson (Celtic)
17 T.A. Flo (Rangers)
13 R. Winters (Aberdeen)
11 S. Arveladze (Rangers)
J. Sara (Dundee)
10 S. Elliott (Motherwell)
J. McFadden (Motherwell)
G. O'Connor (Hibernian)
9 K. McKenna (Hearts)
B. Wilson (Livingston)

First Division
23 O. Coyle (Airdrieonians)
19 I. Novo (Raith Rovers)
18 D. Wyness (Inverness Caledonian Thistle)
15 P. Ritchie (Inverness Caledonian Thistle)
14 E. Annand (Ayr United)
S. Hislop (Ross County)
12 G. Britton (Partick Thistle)
M. Roberts (Airdrieonians)
11 M. Hardie (Partick Thistle)
P. Keogh (Clyde)
L. Miller (Falkirk)
A. Smith (Raith Rovers)

Second Division
18 J. O'Neil (Queen of the South)
P. Tosh (Forfar Athletic)
17 G. Brown (Cowdenbeath)
16 I. Harty (Stranraer)
15 P. Weatherson (Queen of the South)
14 G. Hutchison (Alloa Athletic)
12 M. Moore (Hamilton Academical)
9 A. Burke (Clydebank)
K. Byers (Forfar Athletic)
G. Wood (Berwick Rangers)
K. Wright (Cowdenbeath)

Third Division
19 I. Stewart (Peterhead)
18 P. Flannery (Dumbarton)
M. Johnston (Peterhead)
17 A. Williams (Stirling Albion)
15 C. Templeman (Brechin City)
13 S. Laidlaw (Montrose)
12 I. Gilzean (Elgin City)
11 K. Gordon (East Stirlingshire)
C. McLean (Albion Rovers)
P. McManus (East Fife)

2002/03

Scottish Premier League
28 H. Larsson (Celtic)
19 S. Crawford (Dunfermline Athletic)
18 J. Hartson (Celtic)
16 A. Burns (Partick Thistle)
R. de Boer (Rangers)
B. Ferguson (Rangers)
15 S. Arveladze (Rangers)
M. De Vries (Hearts)
C. Sutton (Celtic)
13 S. Lovell (Dundee)
J. McFadden (Motherwell)
M. Mols (Rangers)

First Division
20 O. Coyle (Falkirk)
19 D. Wyness (Inverness Caledonian Thistle)
18 P. Ritchie (Inverness Caledonian Thistle)
17 L. Miller (Falkirk)
12 M. Cameron (St. Mirren)
P. Keogh (Clyde)
11 C. Samuel (Falkirk)
10 B. Robson (Inverness Caledonian Thistle)
9 R. Gillies (St. Mirren)
C. Hay (St. Johnstone)
J. O'Neil (Queen of the South)

Second Division
21 C. Templeman (Brechin City)
18 J. Vareille (Airdrie United)
15 M. Bavidge (Forfar Athletic)
13 P. Tosh (Forfar Athletic)
12 A. Burke (Berwick Rangers)
I. Harty (Stranraer)
G. Wood (Berwick Rangers)
11 B. McPhee (Hamilton Academical)
M. Moore (Stranraer)
10 G. Brown (Cowdenbeath)
K. Gordon (Cowdenbeath)
S. McKeown (Airdrie United)

Third Division
23 A. Williams (Morton)
21 I. Stewart (Peterhead)
20 K. Deuchar (East Fife)
16 M. Johnston (Peterhead)
11 J.R. Graham (East Fife)
A. Roddie (Peterhead)
10 M. Dobie (Gretna)
J. Herkes (East Fife)
J. Mercer (Albion Rovers)
S. Nicholas (Stirling Albion)

official list of referees 2003/04

class 1 referees (category 1)
Crawford Allan
Chris Boyle
Iain Brines
Tom Brown
Brian Cassidy
Kenny Clark
Steve Conroy
Hugh Dallas
Stuart Dougal
Jamie Downie
Steven Duff
John Fleming
Alan Freeland
Ian Frickleton
Ian Fyfe
John Gilmour
Colin Hardie
Andrew Hunter
Michael McCurry
Douglas McDonald
Scott MacDonald
Craig MacKay
Eddie Mack
Cammy Melville
Garry Mitchell
Calum Murray
Charlie Richmond
Mike Ritchie
John Rowbotham
Eddie Smith
David Somers
Martin Sproule
Craig Thomson
Kevin Toner
Mike Tumilty
John Underhill
Brian Winter
Willie Young

class 1 referees (category 2)
Jeff Banks
Alan Boyd
Colin Brown
Craig Charleston
Gary Cheyne
Paul Cheyne
William Collum
Mark Doyle
Stephen Finnie
William Gilfillan
Willie Hornby
Anthony Law
John McKendrick
Craig Marshall
Alan Muir
Steven Nicholls
Euan Norris
Stevie O'Reilly
Thomas Robertson
Gary Sweeney

class 1 specialist assistant referees
Graeme Alison
Francis Andrews
James Bee
Neil Brand
Frank Cole
Martin Cryans
Alan Cunningham
Andy Davis
Willie Dishington
David Doig
Martin Doran
George Drummond
Jim Dunne
Wilson Irvine
Robert Johnston
Lawrence Kerrigan
Jim Lyon
Stuart Macaulay
Gordon McBride
Brian McDuffie
Brian McGarry
Gordon Middleton
Ricky Mooney
Tom Murphy
Steve Pullar
Andrew Seymour
Stewart Shearer
Keith Sorbie

class 1 assistant referees
Andrew Aird
Stephen Allan
Ramzan Bashir
Billy Baxter
Stuart Bennett
John Bicknell
Wes Boulstridge
Terry Brunton
Graham Chambers
Derek Clark
Stuart Clingan
Roddy Cobb
Steven Craven
Steven Crichton
Hugh Dalgetty
David Davidson
Ian Elmslie
Andrew Gault
Richard Gough
Kevin Graham
Kevin Grant
Jason Hasson
Gary Hilland
Alan Hogg
Tommy Johnston
Peter Kinney
Gary Kirkwood
Stuart Logan
Paul McDowall
Steve McGeouch
David McIntosh
Gordon MacKay
Cammy McKay
David McKenzie
Steven McLean
James McNeil
Andy McWilliam
Russell Main
Rodney Marshall
Brian Martin
Stephen Martin
Alastair Mather
Ryan Milne
Michael Monaghan
Neil Mooney
Derek Nicholls
Matt Northcroft
Morag Pirie
Pat Rafferty
Eric Robertson
Derek Rose
Charlie Smith
Ricky Smith
Colin Tate
Neil Watters
Willie Weir
Rod Williamson
Ronnie Wright
Chris Young
Craig Young
Ewan Young

scottish league champions since 1890

SEASON	DIVISION ONE	POINTS	DIVISION TWO	POINTS
1890/91	Dumbarton/Rangers	29	(No Competition)	
1891/92	Dumbarton	37	(No Competition)	
1892/93	Celtic	29	(No Competition)	
1893/94	Celtic	29	Hibernian	29
1894/95	Heart of Midlothian	31	Hibernian	30
1895/96	Celtic	30	Abercorn	27
1896/97	Heart of Midlothian	28	Partick Thistle	31
1897/98	Celtic	33	Kilmarnock	29
1898/99	Rangers	36	Kilmarnock	32
1899-1900	Rangers	32	Partick Thistle	29
1900/01	Rangers	35	St. Bernards	25
1901/02	Rangers	28	Port Glasgow	32
1902/03	Hibernian	37	Airdrieonians	35
1903/04	Third Lanark	43	Hamilton Academical	37
1904/05	Celtic (after play-off)	41	Clyde	32
1905/06	Celtic	49	Leith Athletic	34
1906/07	Celtic	55	St. Bernards	32
1907/08	Celtic	55	Raith Rovers	30
1908/09	Celtic	51	Abercorn	31
1909/10	Celtic	54	Leith Athletic	33
1910/11	Rangers	52	Dumbarton	31
1911/12	Rangers	51	Ayr United	35
1912/13	Rangers	53	Ayr United	34
1913/14	Celtic	65	Cowdenbeath	31
1914/15	Celtic	65	Cowdenbeath	37
1915/16	Celtic	67	(No Competition)	
1916/17	Celtic	64	(No Competition)	
1917/18	Rangers	56	(No Competition)	
1918/19	Celtic	58	(No Competition)	
1919/20	Rangers	71	(No Competition)	
1920/21	Rangers	76	(No Competition)	
1921/22	Celtic	67	Alloa	60
1922/23	Rangers	55	Queen's Park	57
1923/24	Rangers	59	St. Johnstone	56
1924/25	Rangers	60	Dundee United	50
1925/26	Celtic	58	Dunfermline Athletic	59
1926/27	Rangers	56	Bo'ness	56
1927/28	Rangers	60	Ayr United	54
1928/29	Rangers	67	Dundee United	51
1929/30	Rangers	60	Leith Athletic*	57
1930/31	Rangers	60	Third Lanark	61
1931/32	Motherwell	66	East Stirlingshire*	55
1932/33	Rangers	62	Hibernian	54
1933/34	Rangers	66	Albion Rovers	45
1934/35	Rangers	55	Third Lanark	52
1935/36	Celtic	66	Falkirk	59
1936/37	Rangers	61	Ayr United	54
1937/38	Celtic	61	Raith Rovers	59
1938/39	Rangers	59	Cowdenbeath	60
Seasons 1939/40 to 1945/46 - (No Competition)				
1946/47	Rangers	46	Dundee	45
1947/48	Hibernian	48	East Fife	53
1948/49	Rangers	46	Raith Rovers*	42
1949/50	Rangers	50	Morton	47
1950/51	Hibernian	48	Queen of the South*	45
1951/52	Hibernian	45	Clyde	44

scottish league champions since 1890

SEASON	DIVISION ONE	POINTS	DIVISION TWO	POINTS
1952/53	Rangers*	43	Stirling Albion	44
1953/54	Celtic	43	Motherwell	45
1954/55	Aberdeen	49	Airdrieonians	46
1955/56	Rangers	52	Queen's Park	54
1956/57	Rangers	55	Clyde	64
1957/58	Heart of Midlothian	62	Stirling Albion	55
1958/59	Rangers	50	Ayr United	60
1959/60	Heart of Midlothian	54	St. Johnstone	53
1960/61	Rangers	51	Stirling Albion	55
1961/62	Dundee	54	Clyde	54
1962/63	Rangers	57	St. Johnstone	55
1963/64	Rangers	55	Morton	67
1964/65	Kilmarnock*	50	Stirling Albion	59
1965/66	Celtic	57	Ayr United	53
1966/67	Celtic	58	Morton	69
1967/68	Celtic	63	St. Mirren	62
1968/69	Celtic	54	Motherwell	64
1969/70	Celtic	57	Falkirk	56
1970/71	Celtic	56	Partick Thistle	56
1971/72	Celtic	60	Dumbarton¥	52
1972/73	Celtic	57	Clyde	56
1973/74	Celtic	53	Airdrieonians	60
1974/75	Rangers	56	Falkirk	54

SEASON	PREMIER DIVISION	POINTS	FIRST DIVISION	POINTS	SECOND DIVISION	POINTS	THIRD DIVISION	POINTS
1975/76	Rangers	54	Partick Thistle	41	Clydebank¥	40		
1976/77	Celtic	55	St. Mirren	62	Stirling Albion	55		
1977/78	Rangers	55	Morton¥	58	Clyde¥	53		
1978/79	Celtic	48	Dundee	55	Berwick Rangers	54		
1979/80	Aberdeen	48	Heart of Midlothian	53	Falkirk	50		
1980/81	Celtic	56	Hibernian	57	Queen's Park	50		
1981/82	Celtic	55	Motherwell	61	Clyde	59		
1982/83	Dundee United	56	St. Johnstone	55	Brechin City	55		
1983/84	Aberdeen	57	Morton	54	Forfar Athletic	63		
1984/85	Aberdeen	59	Motherwell	50	Montrose	53		
1985/86•	Celtic¥	50	Hamilton Academical	56	Dunfermline Athletic	57		
1986/87•	Rangers	69	Morton	57	Meadowbank Thistle	55		
1987/88•	Celtic	72	Hamilton Academical	56	Ayr United	61		
1988/89§	Rangers	56	Dunfermline Athletic	54	Albion Rovers	50		
1989/90§	Rangers	51	St. Johnstone	58	Brechin City	49		
1990/91§	Rangers	55	Falkirk	54	Stirling Albion	54		
1991/92§	Rangers	72	Dundee	58	Dumbarton	52		
1992/93	Rangers	73	Raith Rovers	65	Clyde	54		
1993/94	Rangers	58	Falkirk	66	Stranraer	56		
1994/95†	Rangers	69	Raith Rovers	69	Greenock Morton	64	Forfar Athletic	80
1995/96†	Rangers	87	Dunfermline Athletic	71	Stirling Albion	81	Livingston	72
1996/97†	Rangers	80	St. Johnstone	80	Ayr United	77	Inverness Caledonian Thistle	76
1997/98†	Celtic	74	Dundee	70	Stranraer	61	Alloa Athletic	76
	SCOTTISH PREMIER LEAGUE		**S.F.L. FIRST DIVISION**		**S.F.L. SECOND DIVISION**		**S.F.L. THIRD DIVISION**	
1998/99	Rangers<	77	Hibernian	89	Livingston	77	Ross County	77
1999/2000	Rangers<	90	St. Mirren>	76	Clyde>	65	Queen's Park>	69
2000/01	Celtic<	97	Livingston>	76	Partick Thistle>	75	¥Hamilton Academical>	76
2001/02	Celtic<	103	Partick Thistle>	66	Queen of the South>	67	Brechin City>	73
2002/03¥	Rangers<	97	Falkirk>	81	Raith Rovers>	59	Morton>	72

* *Champions on goal average.* § *Competition known as B&Q League.* † *Competition known as Bell's League Championship.*
¥ *Champions on goal difference.* > *Competition known as Bell's Scottish Football League Championship.*
• *Competition known as Fine Fare League.* < *Competition known as Bank of Scotland Premier League.*

FIRST ROUND

Saturday, 7th September, 2002

BERWICK RANGERS 4 — **ARBROATH 2**
G. Forrest, G. Wood (2), A. Burke — C. Feroz (2)
Berwick Rangers: R. Godfrey, D. Murie, A. Smith, (A. Neill), G. McNicoll, D. Gray, G. Forrest, G. Connelly, M. Neil, G. Wood, A. Burke, (D. Blackley), D. Smith, (J.N. Bennett)
Substitutes not used: G. Connell, H. Smith
Arbroath: G. Gow, R. Currie, G. Henslee, P. Browne, I. Ritchie, G. Bowman, J. McAulay, (J. Cusick), A. Cargill, M. McDowell, (K. Heenan), J. McGlashan, (D. McInally), C. Feroz
Substitutes not used: G. Swankie, T. Woodcock
Referee: David Somers
Attendance: 263

MORTON 2 — **ST. MIRREN 3**
(AET – 2-2 After 90 Minutes)
S. Bannerman, D. Hopkin — M. Cameron, S. Lappin, M. Yardley
Morton: C. Coyle, D. Collins, E. Bottiglieri, D. MacGregor, A. Smith, D. Hopkin, (P. Cannie), J. Uotinen, M. Maisano, A. Williams, J. Maisano, S. Bannerman
Substitutes not used: S. MacDonald, P. Gaughan, C. Riley, R. MacKillop
St. Mirren: K. Robertson, G. Guy, C. Kerr, R. Gillies, G. Denham, (R. Robb), A. Dow, (D. Lowing), H. Murray, M. Cameron, (M. Yardley), B. McGinty, J. Mendes, S. Lappin
Substitutes not used: S. Baltacha, W. Bald
Referee: Eddie Mack
Attendance: 4,276

QUEEN'S PARK 1 — **EAST STIRLINGSHIRE 0**
W. Martin
Queen's Park: C. Stewart, D. Ferry, S. Fallon, S. Moffat, D. Agostini, A. Quinn, C. Fisher, (W. Martin), J. Whelan, J. Gemmell, (R. Jackson), G. Lappin, (S. Canning), J. Allan
Substitutes not used: R. Sinclair, S. Thomson
East Stirlingshire: S. Findlay, R. Maughan, (W. Struthers), G. McLaren, D. Grant, G. McGhee, J. Leishman, (G. Boyle), Sean McAuley, J. Mackay, B. Fairbairn, D. Ormiston, S. Livingstone
Substitutes not used: D. Ure, J. Drummond, Scott McAuley
Referee: Iain Brines
Attendance: 457

ALBION ROVERS 0 — **HAMILTON ACADEMICAL 1**
S. Callaghan
Albion Rovers: S. Shearer, C. Stevenson, (D. Carr), J. McCaig, J. Smith, P. Cormack, T. Lumsden, K. McAllister, (J. Dick), C. Silvestro, J. Bradford, C. McLean, (L. Duncan), J. Mercer
Substitutes not used: J. Coulter, C. Fahey
Hamilton Academical: G. Potter, (I. Macfarlane), Alisdair Graham, J. Sherry, I. Dobbins, S. Sweeney, C. Smillie, M. Bonnar, J. Walker, (M. Keegans), G. Armstrong, (P. McDonald), B. McPhee, S. Callaghan
Substitutes not used: M. Nelson, C. Hillcoat
Referee: George Clyde
Attendance: 420

STRANRAER 6 — **BRECHIN CITY 1**
A. Jenkins, I. Harty (3), M. Moore, L. Sharp — J. Skinner
Stranraer: J. Hillcoat, K. Gaughan, F. Wright, D. Wingate, (D. Farrell), A. Jenkins, S. Aitken, K. Finlayson, M. Moore, I. Harty, P. Kerr, (A. Lurinsky), L. Sharp
Substitutes not used: H. Curran, A. Grace, W. McCulloch
Brechin City: D. Hay, G. Miller, B. Donachie, (P. Riley), J. Smith, H. Cairney, K. Fotheringham, Charles King, (R. Black), J. Skinner, G. Gibson, (R. Grant), C. Jackson, M. Millar
Substitutes not used: P. Campbell, M. Cairns
Referee: Cammy Melville
Attendance: 211

GRETNA 1 — **EAST FIFE 2**
D. Irons — K. Deuchar (2)
Gretna: D. Mathieson, D. Hewson, G. Skelton, (A. Thwaites), T. Turner, K. May, M. Henney, S. Skinner, D. Irons, M. Dobie, J. Hore, (A. Benjamin), R. McGuffie
Substitutes not used: S. Rooke, M. Bell, D. Wylie
East Fife: J. Butter, G. Russell, E. Donaldson, C. Farnan, M. Hall, P. Mortimer, J. Nairn, R. Graham, (J. Allison), G. Gilbert, K. Deuchar, J. Herkes, (J. Ovenstone)
Substitutes not used: C. Lumsden, G. Love, S. Bennett
Referee: John Gilmour
Attendance: 428

AIRDRIE UNITED 1 — **ELGIN CITY 0**
A. Gow
Airdrie United: M. McGeown, P. Armstrong, N. McGowan, A. Stewart, K. Brannigan, S. Vella, (W. McVey), R.L. Gardner, M. Wilson, (P. Harvey), P. Ronald, (A. Gow), S. Docherty, D. McGuire
Substitutes not used: M. Glancy, P. Cherrie
Elgin City: M. Pirie, G. Grant, R. McBride, D. Hind, D. Mackay, C. Tully, D. Ross, K. Steele, (M. Sanderson), R. McMullan, (S. MacDonald), C. Love, D. Craig
Substitutes not used: C. Campbell, R. James, R. Taylor
Referee: Dougie Smith
Attendance: 1,120

QUEEN OF THE SOUTH 2 — **FORFAR ATHLETIC 0**
J. O'Neil (2)
Queen of the South: C. Scott, R. Neilson, J. Crawford, D. Allan, A. Aitken, J. McAlpine, (B. McLaughlin), J.O'Neil, (E. Paton), B. McColligan, (D. Anderson), D. Lyle, P. Shields, P. Weatherson
Substitutes not used: R. Henderson, A. Goram
Forfar Athletic: M. Brown, A. Rattray, S. McCulloch, R. Horn, I. Good, B. Sellars, (W. Stewart), K. Byers, M. Anthony, G. Shaw, (D. Williams), M. Bavidge, D. Henderson
Substitutes not used: P.Lunan, K. Milne, N. Ferrie
Referee: Willie Young
Attendance: 1,155

Tuesday, 10th September, 2002

RAITH ROVERS 2 — **ALLOA ATHLETIC 3**
(AET – 2-2 After 90 Minutes)
M. Prest, B. Carrigan — G. Hutchison, I. Little, R. Hamilton
Raith Rovers: S. Monin, D. Ross, (A. Calderon), P. Hampshire, L. Ellis, S. Dennis, W. Nanou, C. Boylan, (R. Blackadder), F. Rivas, A. Smith, (B. Carrigan), K. Hawley, M. Prest
Substitutes not used: D. Brady, R. Ojeda
Alloa Athletic: J. Evans, C. Valentine, M. Cowan, G. Watson, S. Thomson, A.B. Ferguson, (K. Knox), (A. Seaton), R. Hamilton, W. Macdonald, S. Crabbe, (G. Evans), G. Hutchison, I. Little
Substitutes not used: D. Ferguson, M. Hogarth
Referee: Douglas McDonald
Attendance: 1,261

CLYDE 0 — **ROSS COUNTY 1**
A. Bone
Clyde: B. Halliwell, S. Mensing, J. Potter, B. Smith, (S. Convery), A. Millen, J. Ross, F. Bossy, (D. Hagen), J. Fraser, P. Keogh, C. Nish, S. McConalogue, (L. Hinds)
Substitutes not used: A. McClay, A. Morrison
Ross County: A. Bullock, M. Canning, S. Mackay, (K. Gilbert), M. Perry, B. Irvine, M. McCulloch, S. McGarry, (C. Gethins), M. Wood, (D. Cowie), A. Bone, G. Bayne, H. Robertson
Substitutes not used: S. Webb, L. Fridge
Referee: John Underhill
Attendance: 604

FALKIRK 2 — **PETERHEAD 0**
A. Lawrie, O. Coyle
Falkirk: A. Ferguson, A. Lawrie, J. McQuilken, S. MacKenzie, J. Hughes, K. James, M. Kerr, L. Miller, (I. MacSween), O. Coyle, C. McPherson, S. Tosh, (C. Samuel)
Substitutes not used: S. Rennie, S. Cringean, D. Hill
Peterhead: P. Mathers, G. Burns, (M.L. Camara), S. McSkimming, R. Raeside, (C. MacDonald), M. Simpson, K. Bain, K. Tindal, I. Stewart, D. Cameron, (S. Mackay), M. Johnston, A. Roddie
Substitutes not used: C. Cooper, R. Buchanan
Referee: Steve Conroy
Attendance: 2,157

COWDENBEATH 3 — **MONTROSE 2**
K. Wilson, G. Brown, H. French — D. Robertson, C. McDonald
Cowdenbeath: G. O'Connor, W. Miller, A. Campbell, D. White, K. Wilson, M. Renwick, L. Dair, C. Winter, G. Brown, K. Gordon, (J. Elliott), H. French
Substitutes not used: K. Munro, G. Gilfillan, S. Gibb, M. Graham
Montrose: G. McGlynn, J. McQuillan, S. Ferguson, K. Gibson, F. Conway, D. Robertson, K. Webster, (R. Henderson), I.G. Johnson, C. McDonald, (G. Sharp), I. Gilzean, C. Webster
Substitutes not used: S. Kerrigan, D. Craig, J. Campbell
Referee: Ian Fyfe
Attendance: 173

INVERNESS CALEDONIAN THISTLE 2 **DUMBARTON 0**
D. Wyness, P. Ritchie
Inverness Caledonian Thistle: M. Brown, R. Tokely, (A. Low), S. Golabek, R. Mann, G. Munro, R. McBain, R. Duncan, D. Wyness, R. Hart, (L. Keogh), C. Christie, (P. Ritchie), B. Robson
Substitutes not used: B. Gilfillan, A. Ridgers
Dumbarton: S. Grindlay, M. Dickie, D. Stewart, N. Scally, J. McKeown, N. Collins, M. Crilly, (C. Lynes), C. McEwan, G. McCutcheon, A. Brown, (K. McCann), J. Dillon, (J. Robertson)
Substitutes not used: S. Jack, J. Wight
Referee: Garry Mitchell
Attendance: 667

Wednesday, 11thSeptember, 2002

STIRLING ALBION 3 **STENHOUSEMUIR 3**
R. Dunn, G. Munro, S. Nicholas S. McCormick, B. Crawford, C. Waldie
(AET – 2-2 After 90 Minutes)
Stirling Albion won 4-2 on Kicks from the Penalty Mark
Stirling Albion: C. Reid, P. Nugent, D. McCole, (A. Moore), F. Duncan, J.G. Rowe, H. Davidson, (K. McLellan), P. Hay, S. Reilly, S. Mallan, (G. Munro), R. Dunn, S. Nicholas
Substitutes not used: S. Devine, I. Turner
Stenhousemuir: G. Smith, S. Easton, M. Stone, A. McMillan, J. McKenzie, (S. Murphy), S. Hamilton, C. Waldie, M. Wilson, S. McCormick, (D. Graham), B. Crawford, (M. Harty), J. Stein
Substitutes not used: M. Booth, A. Carlin
Referee: Eric Martindale
Attendance: 478

SECOND ROUND

Tuesday, 24th September, 2002

ROSS COUNTY 3 **HAMILTON ACADEMICAL 0**
M. McCulloch, D. Cowie, Alisdair Graham (o.g.)
Ross County: A. Bullock, M. Canning, H. Robertson, M. Perry, B. Irvine, K. Gilbert, G. Bayne, M. McCulloch, A. Bone, (S. McGarry), S. Ferguson, (D. Cowie), C. Gethins, (M. Wood)
Substitutes not used: C. Campbell, L. Fridge
Hamilton Academical: G. Potter, Alisdair Graham, M. Elfallah, (P. McDonald), I. Dobbins, (J. Walker), S. Sweeney, C. Smillie, M. Bonnar, (G. Armstrong), J. Sherry, Alastair Graham, B. McPhee, S. Callaghan
Substitutes not used: I. McCreadie, R. Jellema
Referee: Ian Fyfe
Attendance: 902

ALLOA ATHLETIC 0 **HIBERNIAN 2**
G. Brebner, G. O'Connor
Alloa Athletic: J. Evans, C. Valentine, A. Seaton, (K. Knox), G. Watson, S. Thomson, M. Cowan, R. Hamilton, D. Ferguson, (W. Macdonald), S. Crabbe, G. Hutchison, (G. Evans), I. Little
Substitutes not used: R. Elliot, M. Hogarth
Hibernian: N. Colgan, P. Fenwick, G. Smith, Y. Zambernardi, J. Matyus, D. Townsley, J. Wiss, G. Brebner, A. Orman, G. O'Connor, (M. Paatelainen), F. Luna, (D. Riordan)
Substitutes not used: K. Nicol, M. Dempsie, T. Caig
Referee: Michael McCurry
Attendance: 1,824

AYR UNITED 0 **FALKIRK 2**
C. Samuel, L. Miller
Ayr United: C. Nelson, W. Lyle, (I. Nicolson), P. Lovering, M. Smyth, M. Campbell, D. Craig, S. Chaplain, N. Murray, (E. Annand), S. Kean, J. Grady, P. Sheerin
Substitutes not used: A. Black, M. Dunlop, J. Dodds
Falkirk: A. Ferguson, C. Samuel, (I. MacSween), J. McQuilken, S. MacKenzie, S. Rennie, K. James, (S. Cringean), M. Kerr, L. Miller, O. Coyle, (J. Henry), C. McPherson, S. Tosh
Substitutes not used: A. Rodgers, D. Hill
Referee: Iain Brines
Attendance: 2,022

BERWICK RANGERS 0 **PARTICK THISTLE 3**
M.J. Buchan, M. Hardie (2)
Berwick Rangers: R. Godfrey, D. Murie, A. Smith, D. Gray, A. Neill, G. Forrest, (G. Connell), G. Connelly, M. Neil, (J.N. Bennett), G. Wood, A. Burke, (M. McCormick), D. Smith
Substitutes not used: D. Blackley, H. Smith
Partick Thistle: K. Arthur, S. Paterson, A. Archibald, S. Craigan, D. Whyte, D. Lilley, J. Mitchell, (R. Waddell), M.J. Buchan, (I. Morris), P. Walker, (J. Charnley), M. Hardie, A. Burns
Substitutes not used: S. McLean, K. Budinauckas
Referee: John Underhill
Attendance: 563

KILMARNOCK 0 **AIRDRIE UNITED 0 (AET)**
Airdrie United won 4-3 on Kicks from the Penalty Mark
Kilmarnock: G. Marshall, G. Hay, C. Innes, J. Fowler, (G. McDonald), B. McLaughlin, S. Fulton, P. Di Giacomo, (S. Murray), A. Mitchell, (A. Mahood), J. Quitongo, K. Boyd, J. Sanjuan
Substitutes not used: S. Dillon, C. Meldrum
Airdrie United: M. McGeown, P. Armstrong, N. McGowan, A. Stewart, K. Brannigan, S. Vella, J. Boyle, (W. Wilson), M. Glancy, (P. Harvey), A. Gow, S. Docherty, J. Vareille, (S. McKeown)
Substitutes not used: D. McGuire, P. Cherrie
Referee: Hugh Dallas
Attendance: 4,150

COWDENBEATH 1 **DUNFERMLINE ATHLETIC 2**
(AET –1-1 After 90 Minutes)
J. Elliott S.M. Thomson, L. Bullen
Cowdenbeath: G. O'Connor, W. Miller, (K. Munro), A. Campbell, D. White, K. Wilson, M. Renwick, L. Dair, (G. Gilfillan), C. Winter, G. Brown, K. Gordon, J. Elliott, (S. Gibb)
Substitutes not used: I. McDonald, M. Graham
Dunfermline Athletic: D. Stillie, C. McGroarty, S.M. Thomson, A. Skerla, S. Wilson, L. Bullen, B. Nicholson, G. Mason, (J. Dair), G. Dempsey, (S. Walker), S. Crawford, (D. Nicholls), S. Kilgannon
Substitutes not used: M. McGarty, M. Ruitenbeek
Referee: Kenny Clark
Attendance: 2,460

DUNDEE UNITED 4 **QUEEN'S PARK 1**
S. Thompson, S. O'Donnell (3) S. Canning
Dundee United: P. Gallacher, D. McCracken, J. Lauchlan, M. Wilson, W. Cummings, J. Paterson, (D. Winters), S. Duff, S. O'Donnell, J. McIntyre, (A. Gunnlaugsson), S. Thompson, D. Lilley, (C. Easton)
Substitutes not used: J. McCunnie, P. Jarvie
Queen's Park: C. Stewart, S. Fallon, J. Gallagher, S. Moffat, D. Agostini, A. Quinn, (J. Whelan), D. Ferry, G. Lappin, W. Martin, (J. Gemmell), C. Taggart, (S. Jack), S. Canning
Substitutes not used: R. Sinclair, S. Thomson
Referee: Willie Young
Attendance: 3,600

EAST FIFE 0 **MOTHERWELL 2**
D. Lehmann, J. McFadden
East Fife: J. Butter, G. Russell, E. Donaldson, P. Mortimer, M. Hall, C. McMillan, G. Love, (J. Ovenstone), C. Farnan, R. Graham, (J. Allison), G. Gilbert, (K. Deuchar), J. Herkes
Substitutes not used: J. Nairn, S. Bennett
Motherwell: S. Woods, M. Corrigan, D. Partridge, S. Hammell, D. Ramsay, (D. Cowan), K. Lasley, S. Ferguson, (I. Russell), S. Leitch, (K. MacDonald), D. Adams, J. McFadden, D. Lehmann
Substitutes not used: F. Dubourdeau, B. Dempsie
Referee: Craig Thomson
Attendance: 970

INVERNESS CALEDONIAN THISTLE 3 **ST. MIRREN 1**
D. Wyness (2), R. Hart M. Cameron
Inverness Caledonian Thistle: M. Brown, R. Tokley, S. Golabek, R. Mann, G. Munro, R. McBain, R. Duncan, D. Wyness, P. Ritchie, R. Hart, B. Robson
Substitutes not used: A. Low, G. Stewart, B. Gilfillan, C. Miller, A. Ridgers
St. Mirren: L. Roy, H. Murray, D. Lowing, (S. Lappin), P. Rudden, R. Robb, (K. Broadfoot), C. Kerr, A. Dow, (J. Dunbar), R. Gillies, M. Cameron, I. Ross, M. Yardley
Substitutes not used: R. Robinson, K. Robertson
Referee: George Clyde
Attendance: 1,194

STRANRAER 1 **ST. JOHNSTONE 3**
(AET – 1-1 After 90 Minutes)
M. McCulloch (o.g.) M. McCulloch, C. Hay (2)
Stranraer: J. Hillcoat, D. Wingate, F. Wright, D. Farrell, (A. Scott), S. Hodge, (J. Fallon), S. Aitken, K. Finlayson, A. Jenkins, I. Harty, P. Kerr, (A. Kane), L. Sharp
Substitutes not used: H. Curran, W. McCulloch
St. Johnstone: K. Cuthbert, J. Robertson, M. McCulloch, S. McCluskey, G. Murray, I. Maxwell, R. McCann, M. Reilly, P. Hartley, R. Stevenson, (K. Parker), C. Russell, (C. Hay)
Substitutes not used: D. Dods, P. Connolly, A. Main
Referee: Charlie Richmond
Attendance: 422

Wednesday, 25th September, 2002

DUNDEE 3 **QUEEN OF THE SOUTH 1**
J. Sara (2), F. Caballero P. Weatherson
Dundee: J. Speroni, D. Mackay, J. Hernandez, T. Hutchinson, L. Wilkie, G. Brady, G. Nemsadze, (G. Beith), G. Rae, S. Lovell, F. Caballero, (S. Milne), J. Sara
Substitutes not used: B. Smith, L. Mair, J. Langfield
Queen of the South: S. Robertson, R. Neilson, R. Henderson, (J. Thomson), B. McColligan, A. Aitken, D. Anderson, B. McLaughlin, (D. Lyle), S. Bowey, P. Weatherson, (E. Paton), P. Shields, J. McAlpine
Substitutes not used: J. O'Neil, J. Crawford
Referee: John Rowbotham
Attendance: 2,190

STIRLING ALBION 2 **HEARTS 3**
S. Mallan, S. Nicholas A. Kirk, J.L. Valois, S. Pressley
Stirling Albion: C. Reid, P. Nugent, P. Hay, M. McNally, J.G. Rowe, F. Duncan, (H. Davidson), R. Dunn, C. McKinnon, S. Mallan, (A. Moore), S. Nicholas, D. O'Brien
Substitutes not used: D. McCole, K. McLellan, I. Turner
Hearts: R. McKenzie, S. Pressley, P. McMullan, A. Maybury, K. McKenna, J.L. Valois, S. Severin, S. Boyack, P. Stamp, (S. Simmons), A. Kirk, (G. Wales), M. De Vries
Substitutes not used: A. Webster, A. McCann, C. Gordon
Referee: Alan Freeland
Attendance: 2,801

THIRD ROUND

Tuesday, 22nd October, 2002

DUNFERMLINE ATHLETIC 2 **FALKIRK 0**
S. Crawford (2)
Dunfermline Athletic: M. Ruitenbeek, A. MacPherson, (J. Dair), S.M. Thomson, C. McGroarty, (S. Walker), S. Wilson, L. Bullen, B. Nicholson, G. Mason, G. Dempsey, (D. Nicholls), S. Crawford, C. Brewster
Substitutes not used: S. Petrie, D. Stillie
Falkirk: A. Ferguson, S. Rennie, J. McQuilken, S. MacKenzie, J. Hughes, K. James, M. Kerr, L. Miller, (C. McPherson), O. Coyle, C. Samuel, S. Tosh, (A. Rodgers)
Substitutes not used: J. Henry, S. Cringean, D. Hill
Referee: Willie Young
Attendance: 6,933

PARTICK THISTLE 1 **DUNDEE 0**
M. Hardie
Partick Thistle: K. Arthur, S. Paterson, A. Archibald, S. Craigan, D. Whyte, D. Lilley, J. Mitchell, M.J. Buchan, (G. Britton), D. Chiarini, M. Hardie, A. Burns
Substitutes not used: J. McKinstry, K. Milne, R. Waddell, K. Budinauckas
Dundee: J. Speroni, D. Mackay, J. Hernandez, Z. Khizanishvili, (B. Smith), L. Wilkie, T. Hutchinson, G. Brady, S. Robb, (I. Novo), M. Robertson, (S. Lovell), S. Milne, J. Sara
Substitutes not used: J. Langfield, L. Mair
Referee: Stuart Dougal
Attendance: 2,652

Wednesday, 23rd October, 2002

CELTIC 4 **INVERNESS CALEDONIAN THISTLE 2**
S. Maloney, J. Hartson (2), A. Thompson P. Ritchie, D. Wyness
Celtic: R. Douglas, T. Boyd, (L. Miller), S. Crainey, D. Balde, (J. Kennedy), A. Thompson, J. Smith, C. Healy, D. Agathe, (R. Wallace), D. Fernandez, S. Maloney, J. Hartson
Substitutes not used: M. Sylla, J. Gould
Inverness Caledonian Thistle: M. Brown, R. Tokely, (L. Keogh), S. Golabek, R. Mann, G. Munro, R. McBain, R. Duncan, D. Wyness, P. Ritchie, (A. Low), R. Hart, B. Robson, (C. Christie)
Substitutes not used: S. McCaffrey, A. Ridgers
Referee: Michael McCurry
Attendance: 32,122

HEARTS 3 **ROSS COUNTY 0**
S. Pressley, S. Simmons, J.L. Valois
Hearts: R. McKenzie, S. Pressley, P. McMullan, A. Maybury, K. McKenna, J.L. Valois, A. Webster, N. Janczyk, (D. McGeown), S. Simmons, (K. Twaddle), G. Wales, (A. Kirk), M. De Vries
Substitutes not used: D. Dunn, C. Gordon
Ross County: A. Bullock, M. Canning, S. Mackay, (D. Cowie), P. Deas, B. Irvine, K. Gilbert, G. Bayne, (C. Gethins), M. McCulloch, S. McGarry, (S. Higgins), S. Hislop, H. Robertson
Substitutes not used: S. Webb, L. Fridge
Referee: John Rowbotham
Attendance: 6,454

Thursday, 24th October, 2002

HIBERNIAN 2 **RANGERS 3**
I. Murray, G. O'Connor D. Townsley (o.g.), C. Caniggia, P. Lovenkrands
Hibernian: N. Colgan, P. Fenwick, A. Orman, (G. Smith), Y. Zambernardi, C. James, I. Murray, J. Wiss, G. Brebner, D. Townsley, (T. McManus), M. Paatelainen, (F. Luna), G. O'Connor
Substitutes not used: T. Caig, S. Brown
Rangers: S. Klos, F. Ricksen, B. Konterman, L. Amoruso, A. Numan, M. Ross, B. Ferguson, M. Arteta, (S. Hughes), R. de Boer, C. Caniggia, P. Lovenkrands
Substitutes not used: M. Mols, K. Muscat, R. Malcolm, A. McGregor
Referee: Hugh Dallas
Attendance: 8,016

Tuesday, 29th October, 2002

AIRDRIE UNITED 1 **DUNDEE UNITED 2**
S. Vella S. Thompson (2)
Airdrie United: M. McGeown, W. Wilson, N. McGowan, (D. Miller), A. Stewart, K. Brannigan, S. Vella, D. McGuire, P. Armstrong, P. Ronald, (M. Glancy), S. Docherty, J. Vareille, (A. Gow)
Substitutes not used: S. McKeown, P. Cherrie
Dundee United: P. Gallacher, D. McCracken, K. McGowne, J. McCunnie, M. Wilson, S. Duff, C. Easton, C. Miller, J. McIntyre, S. Thompson, D. Lilley, (J. Paterson)
Substitutes not used: J. Lauchlan, J. Hamilton, S. O'Donnell, A. Combe
Referee: Douglas McDonald
Attendance: 1,768

ST. JOHNSTONE 0 **LIVINGSTON 0**
Match abandoned after 79 minutes due to fog
St. Johnstone: A. Main, J. Robertson, G. Murray, S. McCluskey, (M. McCulloch), D. Dods, I. Maxwell, C. Hay, M. Reilly, P. Hartley, P. Connolly, K. Parker
Substitutes not used: R. McCann, R. Stevenson, M. Ferry, K. Cuthbert
Livingston: J.S. Broto, P. Brinquin, G. Bollan, O. Rubio, M. Andrews, F. Quino, L. Makel, B. Wilson, E. Dadi, D. Bingham, C. Toure-Maman, (R. Zarate)
Substitutes not used: M. Hart, J.J. Camacho, D. Xausa, D. McEwan
Referee: Kenny Clark
Attendance: 1,806

Tuesday, 5th November, 2002

REPLAYED TIE

ST. JOHNSTONE 0 **LIVINGSTON 1**
E. Dadi
St. Johnstone: A. Main, J. Robertson, G. Murray, R. McCann, D. Dods, I. Maxwell, C. Hay, M. Reilly, (M. Ferry), P. Hartley, P. Connolly, (R. Stevenson), K. Parker
Substitutes not used: M. McCulloch, D. McClune, K. Cuthbert
Livingston: J.S. Broto, P. Brinquin, (D. McNamee), G. Bollan, O. Rubio, M. Andrews, F. Quino, L. Makel, B. Wilson, C. Toure-Maman, D. Xausa, (D. Bingham) E. Dadi, (R. Zarate)
Substitutes not used: B. O'Brien, D. McEwan
Referee: Tom Brown
Attendance: 2,688

Wednesday, 6th November, 2002

ABERDEEN 3 MOTHERWELL 1
L. Mike, E. Deloumeaux, S. Michie D. Adams
Aberdeen: P. Kjaer, P. McGuire, K. Rutkiewicz, R. Anderson, (F. Tiernan), J. McAllister, N. Fabiano, E. Deloumeaux, R. Bisconti, L. Mike, (P. Billio), Derek Young, (Darren Young), S. Michie
Substitutes not used: R. O'Donoghue, D. Preece
Motherwell: S. Woods, M. Corrigan, D. Partridge, S. Hammell, K. Lasley, (D. Ramsay), D. Cowan, S. Pearson, S. Leitch, K. Kemas, (S. Ferguson), D. Adams, D. Lehmann,
Substitutes not used: F. Dubourdeau, K. MacDonald, W. Kinniburgh
Referee: John Rowbotham
Attendance: 6,557

FOURTH ROUND

Wednesday, 6th November, 2002

CELTIC 1 **PARTICK THISTLE 1**
(AET – 1-1 After 90 Minutes)
Celtic won 5-4 on Kicks from the Penalty Mark
P. Lambert A. Burns
Celtic: R. Douglas, U. Laursen, S. Crainey, T. Boyd, J. Smith, N. Lennon, B. Petta, (M. Sylla), P. Lambert, D. Fernandez, (S. Petrov), S. Maloney, J. Hartson
Substitutes not used: S. Lynch, J. Kennedy, J. Gould
Partick Thistle: K. Arthur, S. Paterson, A. Archibald, (K. Milne), S. Craigan, D. Whyte, D. Lilley, D. Chiarini, P. Walker, (J. McKinstry), M. Hardie, G. Britton, (S. McLean), A. Burns
Substitutes not used: R. Waddell, K. Budinauckas
Referee: Willie Young
Attendance: 26,795

Thursday, 7th November, 2002

DUNFERMLINE ATHLETIC 0 **RANGERS 1**
C. Caniggia

Dunfermline Athletic: M. Ruitenbeek, A. MacPherson, (S. Kilgannon), L. Bullen, A. Skerla, S. Wilson, J. Dair, B. Nicholson, G. Mason, (S. Hampshire), G. Dempsey, S. Crawford, C. Brewster
Substitutes not used: A. Karnabeek, S. Walker, D. Stillie
Rangers: S. Klos, F. Ricksen, B. Konterman, R. Malcolm, A. Numan, M. Ross, B. Ferguson, M. Arteta, S. Hughes, (S. Arveladze), M. Mols, (C. Caniggia), P. Lovenkrands
Substitutes not used: K. Muscat, R. Latapy, A. McGregor
Referee: Douglas McDonald
Attendance: 8,415

Tuesday, 12th November, 2002

ABERDEEN 0 **HEARTS 1**
K. McKenna

Aberdeen: P. Kjaer, P. McGuire, K. Rutkiewicz, R. Anderson, J. McAllister, F. Tiernan, E. Deloumeaux, R. Bisconti, (Darren Young), L. Mike, (S. Michie), Derek Young, (B. Thornley), D. Mackie
Substitutes not used: P. Billio, D. Preece
Hearts: R. McKenzie, S. Pressley, P. McMullan, A. Maybury, K. McKenna, A. Webster, S. Severin, N. Janczyk, (N. Macfarlane), P. Stamp, A. Kirk, (A. McCann), G. Wales, (G. Weir)
Substitutes not used: C. Gordon, D. Dunn
Referee: John Underhill
Attendance: 7,576

Wednesday, 13th November, 2002

LIVINGSTON 0 **DUNDEE UNITED 2**
D. Lilley (2)

Livingston: J.S. Broto, D. McNamee, G. Bollan, O. Rubio, M. Andrews, L. Makel, B. Wilson, (R. Zarate), C. Toure-Maman, B. O'Brien, (F. Quino), E. Dadi, D. Bingham, (D. Xausa)
Substitutes not used: M. Hart, D. McEwan
Dundee United: P. Gallacher, D. McCracken, J. Lauchlan, J. McCunnie, M. Wilson, C. Easton, J. Paterson, (A. Smart), C. Miller, J. McIntyre, S. Thompson, (J. Hamilton), D. Lilley, (S. Duff)
Substitutes not used: S. O'Donnell, A. Combe
Referee: Michael McCurry
Attendance: 3,504

Lorenzo Amoruso

SEMI-FINALS

Tuesday, 4th February, 2003
The National Stadium, Hampden Park, Glasgow

HEARTS 0 **RANGERS 1**
R. de Boer

Hearts: T. Moilanen, S. Pressley, S. Mahe, (A. Kirk), A. Maybury, A. Webster, J.L. Valois, S. Severin, N. Macfarlane, P. Stamp, (K. McKenna), G. Wales, M. De Vries
Substitutes not used: A. McCann, S. Boyack, C. Gordon
Rangers: S. Klos, F. Ricksen, C. Moore, L. Amoruso, A. Numan, M. Ross, B. Ferguson, M. Arteta, R. de Boer, M. Mols, (C. Caniggia), N. McCann
Substitutes not used: R. Malcolm, J. Bonnissel, S. Arveladze, A. McGregor
Referee: Michael McCurry
Attendance: 31,609

Thursday, 6th February, 2003
The National Stadium, Hampden Park, Glasgow

CELTIC 3 **DUNDEE UNITED 0**
D. Balde (2), H. Larsson

Celtic: M. Hedman, U. Laursen, J. Valgaeren, D. Balde, J. Smith, (A. Thompson), N. Lennon, D. Agathe, (M. Sylla), P. Lambert, C. Sutton, H. Larsson, J. Hartson, (D. Fernandez)
Substitutes not used: S. Crainey, D. Marshall
Dundee United: A. Combe, D. McCracken, J. Lauchlan, M. Wilson, S. Duff, J. Paterson, (J. McCunnie), C. Easton, C. Miller, (S. O'Donnell), J. McIntyre, W. Dodds, (J. Hamilton), D. Lilley
Substitutes not used: A. Smart, P. Gallacher
Referee: Stuart Dougal
Attendance: 18,856

FINAL

Sunday, 16th March, 2003
The National Stadium, Hampden Park, Glasgow

CELTIC 1 **RANGERS 2**

Celtic: R. Douglas, J. Mjallby, (S. Petrov), J. Valgaeren, D. Balde, A. Thompson, N. Lennon, J. Smith, (M. Sylla), P. Lambert, C. Sutton, (S. Maloney), H. Larsson, J. Hartson
Substitutes not used: J. McNamara, D. Marshall
Rangers: S. Klos, F. Ricksen, C. Moore, L. Amoruso, J. Bonnissel, (M. Ross), B. Ferguson, C. Caniggia, M. Arteta, (B. Konterman), R. de Boer, (S. Arveladze), M. Mols, P. Lovenkrands
Substitutes not used: N. McCann, A. McGregor

Scorers: **Celtic**: H. Larsson **Rangers**: C. Caniggia, P. Lovenkrands

Referee: Kenny Clark
Attendance: 50,034

THE CIS INSURANCE CUP SEASON 2002/03

ROUND BY ROUND GOALS ANALYSIS

	No. of Goals Scored	Ties Played	Average Per Game
First Round	47	14	3.4
Second Round	37	12	3.1
Third Round	25	8	3.1
Fourth Round	6	4	1.5
Semi-Finals	4	2	2
Final	3	1	3

Total No. of Goals Scored: **122**
Total No. of Ties Played **41**
Average Goals per Game: **3**

SEASON 1946/47

5th April, 1947 at Hampden Park; Attendance 82,584; Referee: Mr R. Calder (Rutherglen)

RANGERS 4 — Gillick, Williamson, Duncanson (2)
ABERDEEN 0

SEASON 1947/48

25th October, 1947 at Hampden Park; Attendance 52,781; Referee: Mr P. Craigmyle (Aberdeen)

EAST FIFE 0
FALKIRK 0
After Extra Time

REPLAY

1st November, 1947 at Hampden Park; Attendance 30,664; Referee: Mr. P. Craigmyle (Aberdeen)

EAST FIFE 4 — Duncan (3), Adams
FALKIRK 1 — Aikman

SEASON 1948/49

12th March, 1949 at Hampden Park; Attendance 53,359; Referee: Mr W. G. Livingstone (Glasgow)

RANGERS 2 — Gillick, Paton
RAITH ROVERS 0

SEASON 1949/50

29th October, 1949 at Hampden Park; Attendance 38,897; Referee: Mr W. Webb (Glasgow)

EAST FIFE 3 — Fleming, Duncan, Morris
DUNFERMLINE ATHLETIC 0

SEASON 1950/51

28th October, 1950 at Hampden Park; Attendance 63,074; Referee: Mr J. A. Mowat (Glasgow)

MOTHERWELL 3 — Kelly, Forrest, Watters
HIBERNIAN 0

SEASON 1951/52

27th October, 1951 at Hampden Park; Attendance 91,075; Referee: Mr J. A. Mowat (Glasgow)

DUNDEE 3 — Flavell, Pattillo, Boyd
RANGERS 2 — Findlay, Thornton

SEASON 1952/53

25th October, 1952 at Hampden Park; Attendance 51,830; Referee: Mr J. A. Mowat (Glasgow)

DUNDEE 2 — Flavell (2)
KILMARNOCK 0

SEASON 1953/54

24th October, 1953 at Hampden Park; Attendance 88,529; Referee: Mr J. S. Cox (Rutherglen)

EAST FIFE 3 — Gardiner, Fleming, Christie
PARTICK THISTLE 2 — Walker, McKenzie

SEASON 1954/55

23rd October, 1954 at Hampden Park; Attendance 55,640; Referee: Mr J. A. Mowat (Glasgow)

HEART OF MIDLOTHIAN 4 — Bauld (3), Wardhaugh
MOTHERWELL 2 — Redpath (pen), Bain

SEASON 1955/56

22nd October, 1955 at Hampden Park; Attendance 44,103; Referee: Mr H. Phillips (Wishaw)

ABERDEEN 2 — Mallan (og), Leggat
ST. MIRREN 1 — Holmes

SEASON 1956/57

27th October, 1956 at Hampden Park; Attendance 58,973; Referee: Mr J. A. Mowat (Glasgow)

CELTIC 0
PARTICK THISTLE 0

REPLAY

31st October, 1956 at Hampden Park; Attendance 31,126; Referee: Mr J. A. Mowat (Glasgow)

CELTIC 3 — McPhail (2), Collins
PARTICK THISTLE 0

SEASON 1957/58

19th October, 1957 at Hampden Park; Attendance 82,293; Referee: Mr J. A. Mowat (Glasgow)

CELTIC 7 — Mochan (2), McPhail (3), Wilson, Fernie (pen)
RANGERS 1 — Simpson

SEASON 1958/59

25th October, 1958 at Hampden Park; Attendance 59,960; Referee: Mr R. H. Davidson (Airdrie)

HEART OF MIDLOTHIAN 5 — Murray (2), Bauld (2), Hamilton
PARTICK THISTLE 1 — Smith

SEASON 1959/60

24th October, 1959 at Hampden Park; Attendance 57,974; Referee: Mr R. H. Davidson (Airdrie)

HEART OF MIDLOTHIAN 2 — Hamilton, Young
THIRD LANARK 1 — Gray

SEASON 1960/61

29th October, 1960 at Hampden Park; Attendance 82,063; Referee: Mr T. Wharton (Glasgow)

RANGERS 2 — Brand, Scott
KILMARNOCK 0

SEASON 1961/62

28th October, 1961 at Hampden Park; Attendance 88,635; Referee: Mr R. H. Davidson (Airdrie)

RANGERS 1 — Millar
HEART OF MIDLOTHIAN 1 — Cumming (pen)

REPLAY

18th December, 1961 at Hampden Park; Attendance 47,552; Referee: Mr R. H. Davidson (Airdrie)

RANGERS 3 — Millar, Brand, McMillan
HEART OF MIDLOTHIAN 1 — Davidson

SEASON 1962/63

27th October, 1962 at Hampden Park; Attendance 51,280; Referee: Mr T. Wharton (Glasgow)

HEART OF MIDLOTHIAN 1 — Davidson
KILMARNOCK 0

SEASON 1963/64

26th October, 1963 at Hampden Park; Attendance 105,907; Referee: Mr H. Phillips (Wishaw)

RANGERS 5 — Forrest (4), Willoughby
MORTON 0

SEASON 1964/65

24th October, 1964 at Hampden Park; Attendance 91,000; Referee: Mr H. Phillips (Wishaw)

RANGERS 2 — Forrest (2)
CELTIC 1 — Johnstone

SEASON 1965/66

23rd October, 1965 at Hampden Park; Attendance 107,609; Referee: Mr H. Phillips (Wishaw)

CELTIC 2 — Hughes (2 (2 pen))
RANGERS 1 — Young (o.g.)

SEASON 1966/67

29th October, 1966 at Hampden Park; Attendance 94,532; Referee: Mr T. Wharton (Glasgow)

CELTIC 1 — Lennox
RANGERS 0

SEASON 1967/68

28th October, 1967 at Hampden Park; Attendance 66,660; Referee: Mr R. H. Davidson (Airdrie)

CELTIC 5 – Chalmers (2), Hughes, Wallace, Lennox
DUNDEE 3 – G. McLean (2), J. McLean

SEASON 1968/69

5th April, 1969 at Hampden Park; Attendance 74,000; Referee: Mr W. M. M. Syme (Airdrie)

CELTIC 6 – Lennox (3), Wallace, Auld, Craig
HIBERNIAN 2 – O'Rourke, Stevenson

SEASON 1969/70

25th October, 1969 at Hampden Park; Attendance 73,067; Referee: Mr J. W. Paterson (Bothwell)

CELTIC 1 – Auld
ST. JOHNSTONE 0

SEASON 1970/71

24th October, 1970 at Hampden Park; Attendance 106,263; Referee: Mr T. Wharton (Glasgow)

RANGERS 1 – Johnstone
CELTIC 0

SEASON 1971/72

23rd October, 1971 at Hampden Park; Attendance 62,740; Referee: Mr W. J. Mullan (Dalkeith)

PARTICK THISTLE 4 – Rae, Lawrie, McQuade, Bone
CELTIC 1 – Dalglish

SEASON 1972/73

9th December, 1972 at Hampden Park; Attendance 71,696; Referee: Mr A. MacKenzie (Larbert)

HIBERNIAN 2 – Stanton, O'Rourke
CELTIC 1 – Dalglish

SEASON 1973/74

15th December, 1973 at Hampden Park; Attendance 27,974; Referee: Mr R. H. Davidson (Airdrie)

DUNDEE 1 – Wallace
CELTIC 0

SEASON 1974/75

26th October, 1974 at Hampden Park; Attendance 53,848; Referee: Mr J. R. P. Gordon (Newport on Tay)

CELTIC 6 – Johnstone, Deans (3), Wilson, Murray
HIBERNIAN 3 – Harper (3)

SEASON 1975/76

25th October, 1975 at Hampden Park; Attendance 58,806; Referee: Mr W. Anderson (East Kilbride)

RANGERS 1 – MacDonald
CELTIC 0

SEASON 1976/77

6th November, 1976 at Hampden Park; Attendance 69,268; Referee: Mr J. W. Paterson (Bothwell)

ABERDEEN 2 – Jarvie, Robb
CELTIC 1 – Dalglish (pen.)
After extra-time – 1-1 After 90 Minutes

SEASON 1977/78

18th March, 1978 at Hampden Park; Attendance 60,168; Referee: Mr D. F. T. Syme (Rutherglen)

RANGERS 2 – Cooper, Smith
CELTIC 1 – Edvaldsson
After extra-time – 1-1 After 90 Minutes

SEASON 1978/79

31st March, 1979 at Hampden Park; Attendance 54,000; Referee: Mr I. M. D. Foote (Glasgow)

RANGERS 2 – McMaster (o.g.), Jackson
ABERDEEN 1 – Davidson

SEASON 1979/80 – BELL'S LEAGUE CUP

8th December, 1979 at Hampden Park; Attendance 27,299; Referee: Mr B. R. McGinlay (Balfron)

DUNDEE UNITED 0
ABERDEEN 0
After extra-time

REPLAY

12th December, 1979 at Dens Park; Attendance 28,984; Referee: Mr B. R. McGinlay (Balfron)

DUNDEE UNITED 3 – Pettigrew (2), Sturrock
ABERDEEN 0

SEASON 1980/81 – BELL'S LEAGUE CUP

6th December, 1980 at Dens Park; Attendance 24,466; Referee: Mr R. B. Valentine (Dundee)

DUNDEE UNITED 3 – Dodds, Sturrock (2)
DUNDEE 0

SEASON 1981/82

28th November, 1981 at Hampden Park; Attendance 53,795; Referee: Mr E. H. Pringle (Edinburgh)

RANGERS 2 – Cooper, Redford
DUNDEE UNITED 1 – Milne

SEASON 1982/83

4th December, 1982 at Hampden Park; Attendance 55,372; Referee: Mr K. J. Hope (Clarkston)

CELTIC 2 – Nicholas, MacLeod
RANGERS 1 – Bett

SEASON 1983/84

25th March, 1984 at Hampden Park; Attendance 66,369; Referee: Mr R. B. Valentine (Dundee)

RANGERS 3 – McCoist 3 (1 pen)
CELTIC 2 – McClair, Reid (pen)
After extra-time – 2-2 After 90 Minutes

SEASON 1984/85 – SKOL CUP

28th October, 1984 at Hampden Park; Attendance 44,698; Referee: Mr B. R. McGinlay (Balfron)

RANGERS 1 – Ferguson
DUNDEE UNITED 0

SEASON 1985/86 – SKOL CUP

27th October, 1985 at Hampden Park; Attendance 40,065; Referee: Mr R. B. Valentine (Dundee)

ABERDEEN 3 – Black (2), Stark
HIBERNIAN 0

SEASON 1986/87 – SKOL CUP

26th October, 1986 at Hampden Park; Attendance 74,219; Referee: Mr D. F. T. Syme (Rutherglen)

RANGERS 2 – Durrant, Cooper (pen)
CELTIC 1 – McClair

SEASON 1987/88 – SKOL CUP

25th October, 1987 at Hampden Park; Attendance 71,961; Referee: Mr R. B. Valentine (Dundee)

RANGERS 3 – Cooper, Durrant, Fleck
ABERDEEN 3 – Bett, Falconer, Hewitt
After extra-time – 3-3 After 90 Minutes
Rangers won 5-3 on Kicks from the Penalty Mark

SEASON 1988/89 – SKOL CUP
23rd October, 1988 at Hampden Park; Attendance 72,122; Referee: Mr G. B. Smith (Edinburgh)

RANGERS 3 – **ABERDEEN 2**
McCoist (2), I. Ferguson – Dodds (2)

SEASON 1989/90 – SKOL CUP
22nd October, 1989 at Hampden Park; Attendance 61,190; Referee: Mr G. B. Smith (Edinburgh)

ABERDEEN 2 – **RANGERS 1**
Mason (2) – Walters (pen)
After extra-time – 1-1 after 90 minutes

SEASON 1990/91 – SKOL CUP
28th October, 1990 at Hampden Park; Attendance 62,817; Referee: Mr J. McCluskey (Stewarton)

RANGERS 2 – **CELTIC 1**
Walters, Gough – Elliott
After extra-time – 1-1 After 90 minutes

SEASON 1991/92 – SKOL CUP
27th October, 1991 at Hampden Park; Attendance 40,377; Referee: Mr B. R. McGinlay (Balfron)

HIBERNIAN 2 – **DUNFERMLINE ATHLETIC 0**
McIntyre (pen), Wright

SEASON 1992/93 – SKOL CUP
25th October, 1992 at Hampden Park; Attendance 45,298; Referee: Mr D. D. Hope (Erskine)

RANGERS 2 – **ABERDEEN 1**
McCall, Smith (o.g.) – Shearer
After extra-time – 1-1 after 90 minutes

SEASON 1993/94
24th October, 1993 at Celtic Park; Attendance 47,632; Referee: Mr J. McCluskey (Stewarton)

RANGERS 2 – **HIBERNIAN 1**
Durrant, McCoist – McPherson (o.g.)

SEASON 1994/95 – COCA-COLA CUP
27th November, 1994 at Ibrox Stadium; Attendance 45,384; Referee: Mr J. McCluskey (Stewarton)

RAITH ROVERS 2 – **CELTIC 2**
S. Crawford, G. Dalziel – C. Nicholas, A. Walker
After extra-time – 2-2 after 90 minutes
Raith Rovers won 6-5 on Kicks from the Penalty Mark

SEASON 1995/96 – COCA-COLA CUP
26th November, 1995 at Hampden Park; Attendance 33,099; Referee: Mr L.W. Mottram (Forth)

ABERDEEN 2 – **DUNDEE 0**
D. Shearer, W. Dodds

SEASON 1996/97 – COCA-COLA CUP
24th November, 1996 at Celtic Park; Attendance 48,559; Referee: Mr H. Dallas (Motherwell)

RANGERS 4 – **HEART OF MIDLOTHIAN 3**
P. Gascoigne (2),A. McCoist (2) – D. Weir, S. Fulton, J. Robertson

SEASON 1997/98 – COCA-COLA CUP
30th November, 1997 at Ibrox Stadium; Attendance 49,305; Referee: Mr J. McCluskey (Stewarton)

CELTIC 3 – **DUNDEE UNITED 0**
M. Rieper, H. Larsson, C. Burley

SEASON 1998/99
29th November, 1998 at Celtic Park; Attendance 45,533; Referee: Mr H. Dallas (Motherwell)

RANGERS 2 – **ST. JOHNSTONE 1**
S. Guivarc'h, J. Albertz – N. Dasovic

SEASON 1999/2000 – CIS INSURANCE CUP
19th March, 2000 at The National Stadium, Hampden Park; Attendance 50,073; Referee: Mr K. Clark (Paisley)

CELTIC 2 – **ABERDEEN 0**
V. Riseth, T. Johnson

SEASON 2000/01 – CIS INSURANCE CUP
18th March, 2001 at The National Stadium, Hampden Park; Attendance 48,830; Referee: Mr H. Dallas (Motherwell)

CELTIC 3 – **KILMARNOCK 0**
H. Larsson (3)

SEASON 2001/02 – CIS INSURANCE CUP
17th March, 2002 at The National Stadium, Hampden Park; Attendance 50,076; Referee: Mr H. Dallas (Motherwell)

RANGERS 4 – **AYR UNITED 0**
T.A. Flo, B. Ferguson, C. Caniggia (2)

SEASON 2002/03 – CIS INSURANCE CUP
16th March, 2003 at The National Stadium, Hampden Park; Attendance 50,034; Referee: Mr K. Clark (Paisley)

RANGERS 2 – **CELTIC 1**
C. Caniggia, P. Lovenkrands – H. Larsson

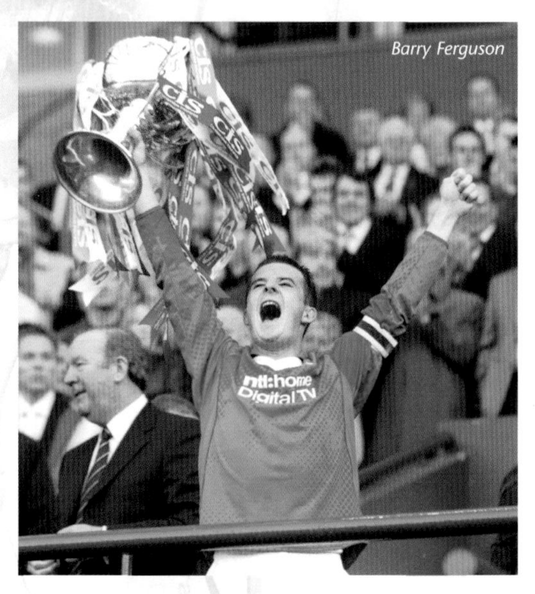

Barry Ferguson

WINNERS AND APPEARANCES IN FINALS

	wins	apps*
RANGERS	23	29
CELTIC	12	25
ABERDEEN	5	12
HEART OF MIDLOTHIAN	4	6
DUNDEE	3	6
EAST FIFE	3	3
DUNDEE UNITED	2	5
HIBERNIAN	2	7
MOTHERWELL	1	2
PARTICK THISTLE	1	4
RAITH ROVERS	1	2
KILMARNOCK	-	4
DUNFERMLINE ATHLETIC	-	2
ST. JOHNSTONE	-	2
AYR UNITED	-	1
FALKIRK	-	1
MORTON	-	1
ST. MIRREN	-	1
THIRD LANARK	-	1

*(Figures do not include replays)

FIRST ROUND

Saturday, 7th December, 2002

STRANRAER 1 — WHITEHILL WELFARE 1
M. Moore — W. Bennett

Stranraer: J. Hillcoat, K. Gaughan, F. Wright, D. Wingate, S. Marshall, (L. Sharp), S. Aitken, K. Finlayson, A. Jenkins, I. Harty, M. Moore, (P. Kerr), A. Scott
Substitutes not used: H. Curran, R. Maclaren, W. McCulloch
Whitehill Welfare: S. Cantley, R. Johnstone, K. Lee, S. Lynes, J. Ewart, C. Martin, D. Cocker, W. Bennett, S. O'Donnell, S. Ronaldson, D. Hope
Substitutes not used: G. Chapman, S. Hunter, S. Price, D. Leslie, D. Walker
Referee: Eddie Mack **Attendance:** 282

PRESTON ATHLETIC 0 — HAMILTON ACADEMICAL 1
B. McPhee

Preston Athletic: G. Lennie, J. Thomson, G. Brown, M. Wojtowycz, C. Scott, C. Nisbett, I. Houston, P. Moffat, (M. Ballantyne Snr.), D. McCall, A. Dixon, M. Ballantyne Jnr.
Substitutes not used: H. Meenan, A. Murray, W. Byrne, S. Trayner
Hamilton Academical: G. Potter, M. Nelson, E. Cunnington, I. Dobbins, S. Sweeney, (M. Elfallah), Alisdair Graham, A. Russell, J. Sherry, Alastair Graham, (M. Keegans), B. McPhee, S. Callaghan
Substitutes not used: R. Jellema, J. Walker, M. Bonnar
Referee: John Fleming **Attendance:** 973

RAITH ROVERS 1 — DUMBARTON 0
R. Blackadder

Raith Rovers: S. Monin, L. Ellis, P. Parkin, D. Brady, S. Dennis, W. Nanou, (S. Miller), R. Blackadder, F. Rivas, A. Smith, (K. Hawley), A. Calderon, P. McManus, (C. Boylan)
Substitutes not used: R. Ojeda, C. Patino
Dumbarton: S. Grindlay, M. Dickie, (D. Stewart), C. Brittain, N. Scally, C. Duffy, N. Collins, J. Robertson, (D. McKelvie), C. McEwan, (S. Bonar), P. Flannery, C. Lynes, J. Dillon
Substitutes not used: J. Wight, J. McKeown
Referee: Calum Murray **Attendance:** 1,639

MONTROSE 2 — BERWICK RANGERS 1
I.G. Johnson, K. Webster — A. Burke

Montrose: G. McGlynn, K. Gibson, S. Ferguson, F. Conway, G. Christie, J. McQuillan, K. Webster, (I. Gilzean), I.G. Johnson, R. Henderson, (C. Webster), S. Kerrigan, (A. Budd), R. McKinnon
Substitutes not used: R. Brand, M. Hankinson
Berwick Rangers:R. Godfrey, D. Murie, A. Smith, E. Forrest, K. Brown, G. Forrest, G. Connelly, (A. Neill), M. Bradley, G. Wood, A. Burke, I. Ferguson, (G. Connell)
Substitutes not used: H. Smith, D. Blackley, C. Avery
Referee: George Clyde **Attendance:** 290

STENHOUSEMUIR 4 — BRECHIN CITY 1
R. Coulter, B. Crawford, D. Graham, D. McFarlane — P. Riley

Stenhousemuir: G. Smith, R. Coulter, G. McKenna, S. Hamilton, S. Easton, M. Booth, C. Waldie, D. Graham, (J. McKenzie), B. Crawford, D. McFarlane, (S. Murphy), J. Stein, (K. Donnelly)
Substitutes not used: A. Carlin, M. Armstrong
Brechin City: M. Cairns, P. Riley, R. Black, J. Smith, H. Cairney, K. Fotheringham, (D. Smith), Charles King, C. Templeman, G. Miller, (G. Gibson), C. Jackson, D. Clark, (Christopher King)
Substitutes not used: G. McDonald, D. Hay
Referee: John Gilmour **Attendance:** 309

EAST STIRLINGSHIRE 1 — THREAVE ROVERS 1
J. Leishman — G. Parker

East Stirlingshire: S. Findlay, R. Maughan, G. McLaren, G. McGhee, D. Grant, S. Oates, Sean McAuley, J. Mackay, B. Fairbairn, G. Boyle, (D. Ure), J. Leishman, (S. Livingstone)
Substitutes not used: W. Struthers, J. Drummond, C. Todd
Threave Rovers: D. Gall, G. Smith, M. Kirkpatrick, J. Wilson, P. McGinley, G. Cochrane, C. Budrys, (D. Armstrong), A. McGinley, M. Adams, G. Parker, M. Baker, (J. Hudson)
Substitutes not used: S. Gault, W. Fitzpatrick, E. Hitchell
Referee: Crawford Allan **Attendance:** 130

SELKIRK 1 — COWDENBEATH 4
D. Kerr — C. Winter, K. Gordon, G. Gilfillan, L. Buchanan

Selkirk: S. Lumsden, A. Biggs, S. Weir, D. Kerr, M. Hume, J. Kayser, I. Potts, P. Edwards, (T. Ross), G. Hastie, D. Whitehead, (S. Linton), A. Kerr, (C. Wilson)
Cowdenbeath: G. O'Connor, M. Renwick, A. Campbell, D. White, K. Wilson, K. Byle, I. Mauchlen, (G. Fusco), C. Winter, G. Gilfillan, (L. Buchanan), K. Gordon, J. Elliott, (G. Crabbe)
Substitutes not used: M. Graham, I. McDonald
Referee: Brian Winter **Attendance:** 405

FORFAR ATHLETIC 3 — HUNTLY 1
M. Bavidge (2), K. Byers — M. De Barros

Forfar Athletic: N. Ferrie, A. Rattray, S. McCulloch, R. Horn, I. Good, P. Lunan, K. Byers, B. Sellars, W. Stewart, M. Bavidge, K. Milne, (D. Henderson)
Substitutes not used: S. Colgan, G. Shaw, M. Anthony, B. McCloy
Huntly: R. Bremner, R. Campbell, D. Henderson, R. Guild, K. Small, E. Copland, (C. Henderson), M. De Barros, G. McGowan, (J.Gillies), M. Stewart, W. Addicoat, (B. Thomson), G. Farmer
Substitutes not used: J. Sturrock, A. Low
Referee: Andrew Hunter **Attendance:** 544

FIRST ROUND REPLAY

Saturday, 14th December, 2002

THREAVE ROVERS 2 — EAST STIRLINGSHIRE 1
G. Smith, M. Adams — G. McLaren

Threave Rovers: D. Gall, G. Smith, M. Kirkpatrick, J. Wilson, P. McGinley, M. Baker, G. Parker, M. Adams, C. Budrys, (J. Hudson), A. McGinley, G. Cochrane
Substitutes not used: W. Fitzpatrick, D. Armstrong, J. Struthers, E. Hitchell
East Stirlingshire: S. Findlay, R. Maughan, G. McLaren, G. McGhee, D. Grant, J. Mackay, Sean McAuley, W. Struthers, (D. Ure), B. Fairbairn, G. Boyle, (D. Diver), J. Leishman
Substitutes not used: C. Todd, S. Livingstone, C. Reid
Referee: Crawford Allan **Attendance:** 391

WHITEHILL WELFARE 2 — STRANRAER 3
W. Bennett, J. Ewart — P. Kerr (2), K. Gaughan

Whitehill Welfare: S. Cantley, R. Archibald, (S. Price), K. Lee, S. Lynes, (S. Hunter), J. Ewart, C. Martin, D. Cocker, W. Bennett, S. O'Donnell, S. Ronaldson, D. Hope
Substitutes not used: G. Chapman, D. Leslie, D. Walker
Stranraer: J. Hillcoat, K. Gaughan, F. Wright, D. Wingate, S. Hodge, (J. Fallon), A. Jenkins, K. Finlayson, S. Aitken, (H. Curran), P. Kerr, (I. Harty), M. Moore, L. Sharp
Substitutes not used: W. McCulloch, S. Marshall
Referee: Eddie Mack **Attendance:** 482

SECOND ROUND

Saturday, 4th January, 2003

QUEEN'S PARK 1 — ALBION ROVERS 1
J. Whelan — I. Diack

Queen's Park: A. Mitchell, R. Sinclair, D. Ferry, S. Moffat, D. Agostini, S. Fallon, W. Martin, J. Whelan, A. Dunning, (D. Menelaws), R. Clark, J. Allan
Substitutes not used: C. Taggart, G. Lappin, S. Kettlewell, C. Lamb
Albion Rovers: S. Shearer, A. Paterson, J. Stirling, J. Smith, J. McCaig, P. Cormack, K. McAllister, (J. Mercer), C. Silvestro, J. Bradford, I. Diack, J. Dick, (C. McLean)
Substitutes not used: M. Weir, L. Duncan, C. Fahey
Referee: Andrew Hunter **Attendance:** 1,117

KEITH 1 — COWDENBEATH 3
D. Nicol — G. Brown, J. Elliott, G. O'Connor

Keith: A. Shearer, B. Morrison, M. Brown, N. Robertson, (D. Calder), K. McKenzie, (K. Gibson), S. King, D. Still, D. Smith, G. Cadger, D. Nicol, (D. Donaldson), A. Reid
Substitutes not used: S. Morrison, I. Pirie
Cowdenbeath: M. Graham, M. Renwick, A. Campbell, D. White, K. Wilson, I. Mauchlen, J. Elliott, C. Winter, G. Brown, K. Gordon, L. Buchanan, (K. Byle)
Substitutes not used: G. O'Connor, G. Fusco, G. Crabbe, G. Gilfillan
Referee: John Fleming **Attendance:** 402

GRETNA 3 **COVE RANGERS 0**
M. Dobie (2), J. Hore
Gretna: D. Mathieson, K. May, G. Skelton, T. Turner, R. McQuilter, M. Cleeland, S. Skinner, D. Irons, (R. McGuffie), M. Dobie, J. Hore, (S. Milligan), M. Henney
Substitutes not used: D. Wylie, D. Hewson, W. Barr
Cove Rangers: M. Coull, C. Summers, (C. Pilichos), D. McGinlay, K. Allan, A. Murphy, C. Yeats, (A. McCraw), G. Clark, (D. Greig), M. Smith, K. Coull, M. Beattie, J. Brown
Substitutes not used: N. Mullen, R. Charles
Referee: Brian Cassidy **Attendance:** 468

Saturday, 11th January, 2003

PETERHEAD 1 **ELGIN CITY 0**
C. Cooper
Peterhead: P. Mathers, C. MacDonald, S. McSkimming, R. Raeside, M. Simpson, K. Bain, (C. Cooper), K. Tindal, I. Stewart, (K. Robertson), S. Mackay, (D. Cameron), M. Johnston, A. Roddie
Substitutes not used: S. Clark, J. Farquhar
Elgin City: M. Pirie, G. Grant, M. Teasdale, D. Hind, D. Mackay, C. Tully, D. Ross, R. McBride, R. McMullan, K. Steele, M. Sanderson, (R. James)
Substitutes not used: G. Tatters, S. Allan, M. McGregor, P. Hamilton
Referee: Brian McGarry **Attendance:** 1,184

Monday, 13th January, 2003

FORFAR ATHLETIC 3 **STENHOUSEMUIR 1**
P. Lunan, P. Tosh, M. Bavidge — S. McCormick
Forfar Athletic: N. Ferrie, A. Rattray, S. McCulloch, R. Horn, I. Good, P. Lunan, W. Stewart, K. Byers, P. Tosh, M. Bavidge, D. Henderson
Substitutes not used: M. Anthony, K. Milne, G. Shaw, B. McCloy, S. Colgan
Stenhousemuir: G. Smith, R. Coulter, G. McKenna, S. Hamilton, S. Easton, (J. McKenzie), M. Booth, C. Waldie, (K. Donnelly), M. Wilson, B. Crawford, (D. Graham), S. McCormick, J. Stein
Substitutes not used: F. Forrest, A. Carlin
Referee: Ian Frickleton **Attendance:** 598

MORTON 4 **DEVERONVALE 3**
J. Uotinen, M. Chisholm (o.g.), D. MacGregor, A. Williams — R. Taylor, B. Dlugonski, P. Gaughan (o.g)
Morton: C. Coyle, D. Collins, E. Bottiglieri, D. MacGregor, P. Gaughan, M. Maisano, (S. Bannerman), S. MacDonald, J. Maisano, A. Williams, W. Hawke, J. Uotinen, (P. Cannie)
Substitutes not used: S. Curran, D. Keenan, D. McGurn
Deveronvale: B. Thompson, S. Dolan, M. Kinghorn, M. Chisholm, (R. Taylor), B. Dlugonski, S. Anderson, D. McAllister, (B. Stephen), L. Stephen, M. McKenzie, I. Murray, N. Montgomery, (R. Brown)
Substitutes not used: P. Urquhart, F. Speirs
Referee: Calum Murray **Attendance:** 1,772

STRANRAER 4 **STIRLING ALBION 1**
D. Wingate, L. Sharp (2), I. Harty — C. McKinnon
Stranraer: J. Hillcoat, K. Gaughan, F. Wright, D. Wingate, S. Hodge, A. Jenkins, L. Sharp, S. Aitken, (H. Curran), I. Harty, P. Kerr, (K. Finlayson), M. Moore
Substitutes not used: S. Marshall, J. Fallon, W. McCulloch
Stirling Albion: C. Reid, P. Nugent, P. Hay, (G. Munro), M. McNally, J.G. Rowe, S. Reilly, (F. Duncan), R. Dunn, C. McKinnon, S. Mallan, S. Nicholas, D. O'Brien
Substitutes not used: G. Kelly, K. McLellan, D. Wilson
Referee: Steve Conroy **Attendance:** 350

RAITH ROVERS 3 **MONTROSE 1**
K. Hawley, A. Smith, B. Carrigan — I. Gilzean
Raith Rovers: R. Ojeda, C. Patino, A. Calderon, (A. Moffat), D. Brady, S. Dennis, W. Nanou, B. Carrigan, (P. McManus), F. Rivas, A. Smith, P. Hampshire, K. Hawley, (M. Prest)
Substitutes not used: L. Ellis, J. Sweeney
Montrose: G. McGlynn, J. McQuillan, G. Thomson, (S. Kerrigan), K. Gibson, G. Christie, F. Conway, K. Webster, (R. Henderson), I.G. Johnson, I. Gilzean, C. Webster, (R. Brand), S. Ferguson
Substitutes not used: G. McCheyne, M. Hankinson
Referee: Steven Duff **Attendance:** 1,515

Tuesday, 14th January, 2003

AIRDRIE UNITED 1 **THREAVE ROVERS 0**
A. Gow
Airdrie United: M. McGeown, W. Wilson, P. Armstrong, A. Stewart, K. Brannigan,(D. McGuire), N. McGowan, A. Gow, R.L. Gardner, (P. Ronald), S. McKeown, S. Docherty, J. Vareille
Substitutes not used: S. Wilson, S. McAuley, P. Cherrie
Threave Rovers: D. Gall, G. Smith, M. Kirkpatrick, J. Wilson, P. McGinley, G. Cochrane, C. Budrys, (D. Armstrong), A. McGinley, G. Parker, M. Adams, M. Baker, (J. Struthers)
Substitutes not used: K. Neilson, E. Hitchell, W. Fitzpatrick
Referee: Craig Thomson **Attendance:** 1,155

Wednesday, 15th January, 2003

HAMILTON ACADEMICAL 1 **EAST FIFE 1**
B. McPhee — K. Deuchar
Hamilton Academical: G. Potter, M. Nelson, E. Cunnington, I. Dobbins, S. Sweeney, Alisdair Graham, (M. Elfallah), M. Bonnar, J. Walker, A. Russell, B. McPhee, S. Callaghan
Substitutes not used: Alastair Graham, N. Paterson, A. Arbuckle, I. Macfarlane
East Fife: J. Butter, G. Russell, E. Donaldson, P. Mortimer, M. Hall, J. Allison, C. McMillan, (C. Farnan), J.R. Graham, K. Deuchar, J. Herkes, G. Gilbert, (G. Love)
Substitutes not used: C. Lumsden, G. Cunningham, C. Martin
Referee: Jamie Downie **Attendance:** 684

SECOND ROUND REPLAYS

Tuesday, 14th January, 2003

ALBION ROVERS 0 **QUEEN'S PARK 2**
J. Allan, W. Martin
Albion Rovers: S. Shearer, A. Paterson, J. Stirling, (C. McLean), J. Smith, (K. McAllister), P. Cormack, (J. Dick), T. Lumsden, J. Mercer, C. Silvestro, J. Bradford, I. Diack, J. McCaig
Substitutes not used: M. Weir, C. Fahey
Queen's Park: A. Mitchell, G. Lappin, D. Ferry, S. Moffat, D. Agostini, S. Fallon, W. Martin, (D. Menelaws), J. Whelan, J. Gemmell, R. Clark, J. Allan, (C. Fisher)
Substitutes not used: C. Taggart, S. Kettlewell, C. Lamb
Referee: Andrew Hunter **Attendance:** 404

Monday, 20th January, 2003

EAST FIFE 2 **HAMILTON ACADEMICAL 2**
(AET – 2-2 After 90 Minutes)
J. Herkes, J.R. Graham — B. McPhee, S. Callaghan
Hamilton Academical won 5-3 on Kicks from the Penalty Mark
East Fife: J. Butter, G. Russell, E. Donaldson, P. Mortimer, M. Hall, J. Allison, C. McMillan, (G. Love), J.R. Graham, (A. Rollo), K. Deuchar, J. Herkes, G. Cunningham, (G. Gilbert)
Substitutes not used: C. Martin, C. Lumsden
Hamilton Academical: G. Potter, M. Nelson, (P. McDonald), E. Cunnington, I. Dobbins, S. Sweeney, Alisdair Graham, (D. Gribben), M. Bonnar, J. Walker, G. Armstrong, (M. Elfallah), B. McPhee, S. Callaghan
Substitutes not used: S. Thomson, I. Macfarlane
Referee: Colin Hardie **Attendance:** 737

THIRD ROUND

Saturday, 25th January, 2003

KILMARNOCK 0 **MOTHERWELL 1**
J. McFadden
Kilmarnock: G. Marshall, G. Shields, C. Innes, S. Dillon, J. Fowler, P. Di Giacomo, (S. Murray), A. Mahood, S. Fulton, A. McLaren, (G. McSwegan), C. Dargo, (B. McLaughlin), K. Boyd
Substitutes not used: C. Meldrum, G. Hay
Motherwell: F. Dubourdeau, M. Corrigan, D. Partridge, S. Hammell, (D. Cowan), W. Kinniburgh, K. Lasley, (S. Fagan), S. Pearson, S. Leitch, D. Adams, J. McFadden, D. Clarkson
Substitutes not used: S. Woods, D. Ramsay, D. Clarke
Referee: John Underhill **Attendance:** 6,882

CELTIC 3 **ST. MIRREN 0**
H. Larsson (2), M. Sylla
Celtic: M. Hedman, J. Mjallby, J. Valgaeren, (S. Crainey), U. Laursen, A. Thompson, (S. Maloney), J. McNamara, M. Sylla, J. Smith, C. Healy, H. Larsson, C. Sutton, (D. Fernandez)
Substitutes not used: J.S. Broto, T. Boyd
St. Mirren: L. Roy, G. Guy, M. Baker, K. Broadfoot, G. Denham, B. McGinty, (D. Lowing), R. Gillies, H. Murray, M. Cameron, (J. Dunbar), J. Mendes, S. Lappin, (R. Robb)
Substitutes not used: K. Robertson, M. Yardley
Referee: Charlie Richmond **Attendance:** 29,703

AIRDRIE UNITED 1 — **ST. JOHNSTONE 1**
D. McGuire — M. Baxter
Airdrie United: M. McGeown, P. Armstrong, W. McVey, A. Stewart, S. Docherty, N. McGowan, M. Wilson, S. McKeown, P. Ronald, J. Vareille, (W. Wilson), D. McGuire, (R.L. Gardner)
Substitutes not used: S. Wilson, M. Glancy, P. Cherrie
St. Johnstone: A. Main, J. Robertson, R. Forsyth, (C. Hay), M. McCulloch, G. Murray, I. Maxwell, P. Connolly, M. Reilly, (D. Dods), P. Hartley, K. Parker, T. Lovenkrands, (M. Baxter)
Substitutes not used: K. Cuthbert, E. Panther
Referee: Mike Ritchie **Attendance:** 2,073

DUNDEE UNITED 2 — **HIBERNIAN 3**
S. O'Donnell, J. Hamilton — G. Brebner (3)
Dundee United: P. Gallacher, J. McCunnie, (J. Hamilton), J. Lauchlan, M. Wilson, D. McCracken, J. Paterson, D. Chiarini, C. Miller, C. Easton, (S. O'Donnell), W. Dodds, J. McIntyre
Substitutes not used: A. Combe, D. Lilley, S. Duff
Hibernian: N. Colgan, P. Fenwick, G. Smith, Y. Zambernardi, A. Orman, I. Murray, J. Wiss, G. Brebner, D. Townsley, (J. O'Neil), M. Paatelainen, T. McManus, (G. O'Connor)
Substitutes not used: I. Westwater, F. Luna, M. Jack
Referee: Tom Brown **Attendance:** 8,986

FORFAR ATHLETIC 2 — **STRANRAER 2**
K. Byers, P. Tosh — P. Kerr, A. Jenkins
Forfar Athletic: N. Ferrie, A. Rattray, S. McCulloch, R. Horn, I. Good, P. Lunan, (D. Williams), K. Milne, (M. Anthony), K. Byers, P. Tosh, M. Bavidge, D. Henderson
Substitutes not used: G. Shaw, B. McCloy, M. Brown
Stranraer: J. Hillcoat, K. Gaughan, F. Wright, D. Wingate, S. Hodge, S. Aitken, K. Finlayson, H. Curran, M. Moore, P. Kerr, A. Jenkins
Substitutes not used: J. Crawford, L. Sharp, A. Kane, A. Lurinsky, W. McCulloch
Referee: Iain Brines **Attendance:** 661

ARBROATH 0 — **RANGERS 3**
B. Ferguson, C. Moore, S. Arveladze
Arbroath: C. Hinchliffe, J. Tait, S. Florence, J. Cusick, (D. Spink), I. Ritchie, R. Currie, P. Brownlie, (G. Swankie), A. Cargill, C. Feroz, J. McGlashan, G. Henslee, (K. Heenan)
Substitutes not used: J. McAulay, T. Woodcock
Rangers: S. Klos, F. Ricksen, C. Moore, L. Amoruso, (R. Malcolm), A. Numan, M. Ross, B. Ferguson, N. McCann, (C. Caniggia), R. de Boer, M. Mols, S. Arveladze, (S. McLean)
Substitutes not used: C. Nerlinger, A. McGregor
Referee: John Rowbotham **Attendance:** 4,153

ROSS COUNTY 1 — **MORTON 2**
D. Winters — A. Williams (2)
Ross County: A. Bullock, M. Perry, H. Robertson, K. Gilbert, B. Irvine, M. McCulloch, (S. Webb), S. Hislop, (S. McGarry), D. Cowie, G. Bayne, K. McLeish, (M. Wood), D. Winters
Substitutes not used: L. Fridge, S. Mackay
Morton: C. Coyle, D. Collins, E. Bottiglieri, D. MacGregor, R. Henderson, M. Maisano, S. MacDonald, J. Maisano, (S. Bannerman), A. Williams, P. Cannie, (J. McAlister), J. Uotinen
Substitutes not used: D. McGurn, P. Gaughan, A. Trouten
Referee: George Clyde **Attendance:** 1,822

PARTICK THISTLE 0 — **DUNDEE 2**
G. Nemsadze, G. Rae
Partick Thistle: K. Arthur, S. Paterson, A. Archibald, S. Craigan, D. Lennon, D. Lilley, J. Mitchell, (P. Walker), M.J. Buchan, (J. McKinstry), M. Hardie, G. Britton, A. Burns
Substitutes not used: K. Budinauckas, A. Gibson, R. Waddell
Dundee: J. Speroni, D. Mackay, Z. Khizanishvili, L. Mair, L. Wilkie, B. Smith, G. Nemsadze, G. Rae, G. Brady, I. Novo, S. Milne
Substitutes not used: J. Langfield, M. Robertson, G. Beith, B. Forbes, S. Robb
Referee: Douglas McDonald **Attendance:** 4,825

LIVINGSTON 1 — **DUNFERMLINE ATHLETIC 1**
G. Bollan — S. Crawford
Livingston: D. McEwan, P. Brinquin, G. Bollan, O. Rubio, M. Andrews, F. Quino, L. Makel, B. O'Brien, (C. Toure-Maman), B. Wilson, (D. Xausa), R. Zarate, (C. McMenamin), D. Bingham
Substitutes not used: A. Creer, G. Bahoken
Dunfermline Athletic: D. Stillie, C. McGroarty, (S. Hampshire), G. Dempsey, A. Skerla, S. Wilson, L. Bullen, B. Nicholson, J. Dair, A. Karnebeek, (S. Kilgannon), S. Crawford, C. Brewster
Substitutes not used: M. Ruitenbeek, S. Walker, M. McGarty
Referee: Alan Freeland **Attendance:** 4,334

INVERNESS CAL THISTLE 2 — **RAITH ROVERS 0**
B. Robson, D. Wyness
Inverness Caledonian Thistle: M. Brown, R. Tokely, S. Golabek, R. Mann, S. McCaffrey, R. McBain, R. Duncan, D. Wyness, P. Ritchie, (C. Christie), R. Hart, B. Robson
Substitutes not used: L. Keogh, G. Stewart, B. Gilfillan, M. Fraser
Raith Rovers: R. Ojeda, C. Patino, (G. Fyfe), L. Ellis, D. Brady, (B. Carrigan), S. Dennis, W. Nanou, (K. Hawley), R. Blackadder, F. Rivas, A. Smith, A. Calderon, P. McManus
Substitutes not used: R. Gonzalez, P. Hampshire
Referee: Dougie Smith **Attendance:** 2,293

GRETNA 1 — **CLYDE 2**
S. Skinner — A. Millen, L. Hinds
Gretna: D. Mathieson, K. Knox, G. Skelton, (J. Hore), T. Turner, R. McQuilter, D. Irons, S. Skinner, M. Galloway, M. Dobie, M. Henney, M. Cleeland, (R. McGuffie)
Substitutes not used: D. Wylie, K. May, D. Hewson
Clyde: B. Halliwell, J. Potter, M. McLaughlin, A. Kernaghan, P. Kane, J. Ross, S. Convery, A. Millen, W. Falconer, (S. McConalogue), S. Cosgrove, L. Hinds, (W. Reid)
Substitutes not used: A. Morrison, P. Doyle, F. Bossy
Referee: Cammy Melville **Attendance:** 973

COWDENBEATH 2 — **ALLOA ATHLETIC 3**
D. Riordan, K. Gordon — S. Crabbe (2), S. Thomson
Cowdenbeath: M. Graham, M. Renwick, A. Campbell, D. White, K. Wilson, I. Mauchlen, D. Riordan, C. Winter, G. Brown, K. Gordon, P. Hilland, (L. Buchanan)
Substitutes not used: K. Byle, G. Fusco, I. McDonald, G. O'Connor
Alloa Athletic: M. Hogarth, C. Valentine, A. Seaton, G. Watson, S. Thomson, M. Christie, R. Walker, D. Ferguson, (M. Cowan), R. Davidson, (S. Crabbe), G. Hutchison, (R. Hamilton), I. Little
Substitutes not used: G. Evans, J. Evans
Referee: Craig Thomson **Attendance:** 529

AYR UNITED 2 — **PETERHEAD 0**
A. Black, J. Grady
Ayr United: C. Nelson, W. Lyle, P. Lovering, (M. Dunlop), A. McManus, M. Campbell, D. Craig, S. Chaplain, (J. Latta), M. Smyth, S. Kean, J. Grady, A. Black
Substitutes not used: M. McColl, A. Ferguson, J. Dodds
Peterhead: P. Mathers, C. MacDonald, S. McSkimming, R. Raeside, M. Simpson, K. Bain, K. Tindal, I. Stewart, D. Cameron, M. Johnston, (K. Robertson), A. Roddie, (D. McLean)
Substitutes not used: K. Bisset, S. Clark, J. Farquhar
Referee: Hugh Dallas **Attendance:** 1,966

QUEEN'S PARK 2 — **HAMILTON ACADEMICAL 2**
J. Gemmell (2) — M. Bonnar, A. Russell
Queen's Park: A. Mitchell, D. Ferry, J. Allan, (D. Menelaws), S. Fallon, D. Agostini, R. Sinclair, R. Clark, P. Gallagher, J. Gemmell, J. Whelan, S. Canning
Substitutes not used: G. Lappin, S. Kettlewell, A. Dunning, S. Thomson
Hamilton Academical: G. Potter, M. Nelson, P. McDonald, (D. Gribben), I. Dobbins, S. Sweeney, Alisdair Graham, M. Bonnar, (Alastair Graham), J. Walker, (M. Elfallah), A. Russell, B. McPhee, S. Callaghan
Substitutes not used: A. Arbuckle, I. Macfarlane
Referee: Stuart Dougal **Attendance:** 1,362

QUEEN OF THE SOUTH 0 — **ABERDEEN 0**
Queen of the South: A. Goram, S. Renicks, D. Anderson, B. McColligan, (S. O'Connor), A. Aitken, J. Thomson, J. O'Neil, S. Bowey, E. Paton, P. Weatherson, B. McLaughlin
Substitutes not used: J. McAlpine, D. Lyle, A. Gray, C. Scott
Aberdeen: D. Preece, P. McGuire, K. Rutkiewicz, R. Anderson, J. McAllister, (R. O'Donoghue), K. McNaughton, (P. Sheerin), S. Tosh, C. Clark, L. D'Jaffo, (L. Mike), Derek Young, D. Mackie
Substitutes not used: P. Kjaer, S. Michie
Referee: Eric Martindale **Attendance:** 5,716

FALKIRK 4 — **HEARTS 0**
C. Samuel (3), O. Coyle
Falkirk: A. Ferguson, J. Henry, S. Rennie, S. MacKenzie, J. Hughes, D. Nicholls, M. Kerr, L. Miller, O. Coyle, C. McPherson, C. Samuel, (I. MacSween)
Substitutes not used: A. Rodgers, P. Creaney, S. Cringean, D. Hill
Hearts: C. Gordon, S. Pressley, S. Mahe, A. Maybury, K. McKenna, J.L. Valois, P. Stamp, S. Boyack, (A. Webster), N. Macfarlane, (S. Severin), G. Weir, (G. Wales), M. De Vries
Substitutes not used: S. Simmons, T. Moilanen
Referee: Willie Young **Attendance:** 7,244

THIRD ROUND REPLAYS

Tuesday, 4th February, 2003

ST. JOHNSTONE 1 — **AIRDRIE UNITED 1**
(AET – 1-1 After 90 Minutes)
P. Connolly — J. Vareille
St. Johnstone won 4-2 on Kicks from the Penalty Mark
St. Johnstone: K. Cuthbert, M. Baxter, (M. Ferry), J. Robertson, M. McCulloch, G. Murray, I. Maxwell, C. Hay, (K. Parker), M. Reilly, P. Hartley, P. Connolly, T. Lovenkrands
Substitutes not used: D. Dods, R. Gilpin, E. Panther
Airdrie United: M. McGeown, P. Armstrong, W. McVey, A. Stewart, (W. Wilson), S. Docherty, N. McGowan, J. Vareille, M. Wilson, P. Ronald, S. McKeown, (R.L. Gardner), D. McGuire, (A. Gow)
Substitutes not used: M. Glancy, P. Cherrie
Referee: Mike Ritchie **Attendance:** 2,105

DUNFERMLINE ATHLETIC 2 — **LIVINGSTON 0**
C. Brewster (2)
Dunfermline Athletic: D. Stillie, L. Bullen, G. Dempsey, A. Skerla, S. Wilson, J. Dair, B. Nicholson, S. Kilgannon, (A. MacPherson), S. Hampshire, S. Crawford, C. Brewster
Substitutes not used: M. Ruitenbeek, A. Karnebeek, C. McGroarty, M. McGarty
Livingston: D. McEwan, P. Brinquin, G. Bahoken, O. Rubio, (C. McMenamin), M. Andrews, F. Quino, C. Toure-Maman, (D. Bingham), B. O'Brien, S. Lovell, R. Zarate, B. Wilson, (J.J. Camacho)
Substitutes not used: A. Creer, W. Snowdon
Referee: Alan Freeland **Attendance:** 3,158

Monday, 10th February, 2003

HAMILTON ACADEMICAL 3 — **QUEEN'S PARK 2**
G. Armstrong, P. McDonald, D. Agostini (o.g.) — J. Gemmell, D. Menelaws
Hamilton Academical: G. Potter, A. Arbuckle, P. McDonald, I. Dobbins, S. Sweeney, Alisdair Graham, M. Bonnar, J. Walker, (A. Russell), G. Armstrong, B. McPhee, S. Callaghan
Substitutes not used: I. Macfarlane, I. McCreadie, M. Elfallah, Alastair Graham
Queen's Park: A. Mitchell, D. Ferry, S. Canning, R. Sinclair, D. Agostini, S. Fallon, R. Clark, (D. Menelaws), J. Whelan, J. Gemmell, P. Gallagher, J. Allan
Substitutes not used: J. Stark, J. White, S. Kettlewell, C. Fisher
Referee: Stuart Dougal **Attendance:** 807

Monday, 17th February, 2003

STRANRAER 1 — **FORFAR ATHLETIC 0**
I. Harty
Stranraer: J. Hillcoat, K. Gaughan, (L. Sharp), S. Hodge, J. Crawford, D. Wingate, F. Wright, K. Finlayson, S. Aitken, I. Harty, M. Moore, P. Kerr, (A. Lurinsky)
Substitutes not used: H. Curran, A. Scott, W. McCulloch
Forfar Athletic: M. Brown, A. Rattray, (M. Cocozza), S. McCulloch, K. Milne, I. Good, (B. McCloy), K. Byers, D. Williams, (C. Hodge), M. Anthony, G. Shaw, M. Bavidge, D. Henderson
Substitutes not used: P. Lunan, N. Ferrie
Referee: Iain Brines **Attendance:** 425

Tuesday, 18th February, 2003

ABERDEEN 4 — **QUEEN OF THE SOUTH 1**
Derek Young, L. D'Jaffo (2), R. Anderson — P. Weatherson
Aberdeen: D. Preece, P. McGuire, (J. McAllister), E. Deloumeaux, (K. Rutkiewicz), R. Anderson, R. O'Donoghue, S. Payne, S. Tosh, (N. Fabiano), C. Clark, P. Sheerin, Derek Young, L. D'Jaffo
Substitutes not used: P. Kjaer, D. Mackie
Queen of the South: C. Scott, S. Renicks, D. Anderson, B. McColligan, A. Aitken, J. Thomson, J. O'Neil, (P. Weatherson), S. Bowey, S. O'Connor, (D. Lyle), E. Paton, (J. McAlpine), B. McLaughlin,
Substitutes not used: J. Campbell, D. Allan
Referee: Garry Mitchell **Attendance:** 6,068

FOURTH ROUND

Saturday, 22nd February, 2003

DUNFERMLINE ATHLETIC 1 — **HIBERNIAN 1**
B. Nicholson — I. Murray
Dunfermline Athletic: D. Stillie, A. MacPherson, (N. Hunt), D. Grondin, (S. Walker), A. Skerla, S. Wilson, J. Dair, B. Nicholson, G. Brannan, G. Mason, S. Crawford, C. Brewster
Substitutes not used: M. Ruitenbeek M. McGarty, G.Dempsey
Hibernian: N. Colgan, P. Fenwick, G. Smith, C. James, M. Doumbe, I. Murray, D. Townsley, (M. Jack), G. Brebner, J. O'Neil, M. Paatelainen, T. McManus, (G. O'Connor)
Substitutes not used: D. Andersson, F. Arpinon, A. Orman
Referee: Stuart Dougal **Attendance:** 6,619

DUNDEE 2 — **ABERDEEN 0**
S. Lovell, I. Novo
Dundee: J. Speroni, D. Mackay, Z. Khizanishvili, L. Mair, L. Wilkie, B. Smith, G. Nemsadze, G. Rae, S. Lovell, (M. Burchill), I. Novo, F. Caballero, (S. Milne)
Substitutes not used: G. Brady, J. Langfield, J. Hernandez
Aberdeen: D. Preece, P. McGuire, E. Deloumeaux, (J. McAllister), R. Anderson, M. Hart, R. O'Donoghue, (N. Fabiano), S. Tosh, C. Clark, (S. Payne), P. Sheerin, Derek Young, L. D'Jaffo
Substitutes not used: D. Mackie, P. Kjaer
Referee: Douglas McDonald **Attendance:** 7,549

CLYDE 0 — **MOTHERWELL 2**
J. McFadden (2)
Clyde: B. Halliwell, (A. Morrison), J. Potter, S. Mensing, A. Kernaghan, P. Kane, J. Ross, D. Hagen, A. Millen, W. Falconer, (S. Convery), S. Cosgrove, S. McConalogue, (P. Shields)
Substitutes not used: J. Fraser, M. McLaughlin
Motherwell: F. Dubourdeau, M. Corrigan, D. Partridge, S. Hammell, T. Vaughan, D. Ramsay, S. Pearson, S. Fagan, (K. Lasley), D. Adams, J. McFadden, (D. Lehmann), S. Craig, (D. Clarkson)
Substitutes not used: S. Woods, D. Cowan
Referee: Kenny Clark **Attendance:** 5,032

MORTON 0 — **STRANRAER 2**
P. Kerr, I. Harty
Morton: C. Coyle, D. Collins, E. Bottiglieri, D. MacGregor, R. Henderson, M. Maisano, S. MacDonald, J. Maisano, (S. Bannerman), A. Williams, W. Hawke, (P. Cannie), J. Uotinen, (J. McAlister)
Substitutes not used: D. McGurn, P. Gaughan
Stranraer: J. Hillcoat, K. Gaughan, F. Wright, D. Wingate, S. Hodge, S. Aitken, K. Finlayson, (L. Sharp), S. Marshall, (J. Crawford), I. Harty, P. Kerr, (A. Lurinsky), A. Jenkins
Substitutes not used: H. Curran, W. McCulloch
Referee: Willie Young **Attendance:** 3,679

ALLOA ATHLETIC 0 — **FALKIRK 2**
O. Coyle, C. Samuel
Alloa Athletic: D. Soutar, R. Walker, A. Seaton, C. Valentine, S. Thomson, M. Christie, R. Hamilton, D. Ferguson, S. Crabbe, (R. Davidson), R. Sloan, (G. Hutchison), I. Little, (G. Evans)
Substitutes not used: G. Watson, M. Hogarth
Falkirk: A. Ferguson, J. Henry, (I. MacSween), J. McQuilken, S. MacKenzie, J. Hughes, D. Nicholls, M. Kerr, L. Miller, O. Coyle, (S. Taylor), C. McPherson, C. Samuel, (A. Rodgers)
Substitutes not used: D. Hill, S. Rennie
Referee: John Underhill **Attendance:** 3,059

INVERNESS CAL THISTLE 6 — **HAMILTON ACADEMICAL 1**
D. Wyness (2), B. Robson (2), P. Ritchie, S. McCaffrey — M. Bonnar
Inverness Caledonian Thistle: M. Brown, R. Tokely, S. Golabek, R. Mann, (G. Munro), S. McCaffrey, R. McBain, R. Duncan, D. Wyness, (L. Keogh), P. Ritchie, C. Christie, B. Robson, (D. Bagan)
Substitutes not used: M. Fraser, G. Stewart
Hamilton Academical: G. Potter, A. Arbuckle, (J. Sherry), P. McDonald, (I. Dobbins), D. Kerr, S. Sweeney, Alisdair Graham, M. Bonnar, J. Walker, G. Armstrong, B. McPhee, (A. Russell), S. Callaghan
Substitutes not used: Alastair Graham, I. Macfarlane
Referee: John Rowbotham **Attendance:** 1,917

AYR UNITED 0 — **RANGERS 1**
R. de Boer
Ayr United: C. Nelson, W. Lyle, P. Lovering, A. McManus, M. Campbell, D. Craig, S. Chaplain, M. Smyth, S. Whalen, (S. Kean), J. Grady, N. Murray
Substitutes not used: J. Latta, J. Dodds, I. Nicolson, M. Dunlop
Rangers: S. Klos, R. Malcolm, (S. Thompson), C. Moore, L. Amoruso, A. Numan, K. Muscat, B. Ferguson, M. Arteta, (S. Hughes), R. de Boer, S. Arveladze, N. McCann, (C. Caniggia)
Substitutes not used: J. Bonnissel, A. McGregor
Referee: Alan Freeland **Attendance:** 9,608

Sunday, 23rd February, 2003

CELTIC 3 — **ST. JOHNSTONE 0**
J. Hartson (2), J. Smith
Celtic: J. S. Broto, (D. Marshall), J. Mjallby, S. Crainey, U. Laursen, M. Sylla, J. Smith, C. Healy, P. Lambert, (S. Maloney), S. Guppy, J. Hartson, D. Fernandez
Substitutes not used: J. McNamara, T. Boyd, S. Petrov
St. Johnstone: K. Cuthbert, M. Baxter, J. Robertson, D. McClune, (C. Hay), D. Dods, I. Maxwell, S. Noble, (E. Panther), K. Parker, P. Hartley, P. Connolly, T. Lovenkrands
Substitutes not used: S. Miotto, R. Forsyth, M. Ferry
Referee: Hugh Dallas **Attendance:** 26,205

FOURTH ROUND REPLAY

Thursday, 6th March, 2003

HIBERNIAN 0 — **DUNFERMLINE ATHLETIC 2**
S. Crawford, S. Wilson

Hibernian: N. Colgan, P. Fenwick, (F. Arpinon), G. Smith, C. James, M. Jack, I. Murray, M. Doumbe, G. Brebner, D. Townsley, (J. O'Neil), G. O'Connor, (M. Paatelainen), T. McManus
Substitutes not used: D. Andersson, A. Orman
Dunfermline Athletic: D. Stillie, A. MacPherson, D. Grondin, (S. Walker), A. Skerla, S.Wilson, M. McGarty, B. Nicholson, G. Brannan, G. Mason, (G. Dempsey), S. Crawford, C. Brewster, (N. Hunt)
Substitutes not used: M. Ruitenbeek, S. Kilgannon
Referee: Hugh Dallas **Attendance:** 5,851

FIFTH ROUND

Saturday, 22nd March, 2003

FALKIRK 1 — **DUNDEE 1**
O. Coyle — I. Novo

Falkirk: A. Ferguson, J. Henry, J. McQuilken, (B. Reid), S. MacKenzie, J. Hughes, D. Nicholls, M. Kerr, L. Miller, O. Coyle, (A. Rodgers), C. McPherson, C. Samuel, (S. Taylor)
Substitutes not used: D. Hill, I. MacSween
Dundee: J. Speroni, D. Mackay, Z. Khizanishvili, J. Hernandez, L. Wilkie, B. Smith, G. Nemsadze, G. Rae, S. Lovell, (S. Milne), I. Novo, (M. Burchill), F. Caballero
Substitutes not used: J. Langfield, L. Mair, G. Brady
Referee: John Rowbotham **Attendance:** 7,403

STRANRAER 0 — **MOTHERWELL 4**
F. Wright (o.g.), J. McFadden, D. Adams, D. Lehmann

Stranraer: J. Hillcoat, K. Gaughan, F. Wright, D. Wingate, D. Farrell, S. Aitken, (H. Curran), K. Finlayson, A. Jenkins, I. Harty, M. Moore, (P. Kerr), S. Hodge, (A. Kane)
Substitutes not used: W. McCulloch, J. Fallon
Motherwell: F. Dubourdeau, M. Corrigan, D. Partridge, (D. Cowan), S. Hammell, T. Vaughan, K. Lasley, S. Pearson, S. Leitch, (S. Fagan), D. Adams, J. McFadden, (D. Clarkson), D. Lehmann
Substitutes not used: S. Woods, S. Craig
Referee: Douglas McDonald **Attendance:** 4,500

Sunday, 23rd March, 2003

DUNFERMLINE ATHLETIC 1 — **RANGERS 1**
D. Grondin — C. Caniggia

Dunfermline Athletic: D. Stillie, A. MacPherson, C. McGroarty, D. Grondin, (S. Kilgannon), S. Wilson, M. McGarty, B. Nicholson, (N. Hunt), G. Brannan, G. Mason, S. Crawford, C. Brewster
Substitutes not used: S. Walker, J. Dair, M. Ruitenbeek
Rangers: S. Klos, F. Ricksen, C. Moore, R. Malcolm, B. Konterman, K. Muscat, B. Ferguson, M. Arteta, R. de Boer, C. Caniggia, N. McCann, (S. Arveladze)
Substitutes not used: A. McGregor, S. Thompson, D. Eggen, M. Ross
Referee: John Underhill **Attendance:** 9,875

INVERNESS CAL THISTLE 1 — **CELTIC 0**
D. Wyness

Inverness Caledonian Thistle: M. Brown, S. McCaffrey, S. Golabek, R. Mann, G. Munro, R. McBain, R. Tokely, D. Wyness, P. Ritchie, (L. Keogh), R. Hart, B. Robson, (C. Christie)
Substitutes not used: M. Fraser, G. Stewart, D. Bagan
Celtic: J.S. Broto, U. Laursen, J. Valgaeren, J. McNamara, N. Lennon, J. Smith, S. Varga, S. Guppy, S. Maloney, (J. Hartson), H. Larsson, D. Fernandez
Substitutes not used: D. Balde, L. Miller, C. Healy, R. Douglas
Referee: Alan Freeland **Attendance:** 6,050

FIFTH ROUND REPLAYS

Wednesday, 9th April, 2003

DUNDEE 4 — **FALKIRK 1**
(AET – 1-1 After 90 Minutes)
F. Caballero, M. Burchill, S. Lovell (2) — S. Taylor

Dundee: J. Speroni, D. Mackay, J. Hernandez, L. Mair, L. Wilkie, B. Smith, G. Nemsadze, G. Rae, (G. Brady), I. Novo, (M. Burchill), F. Caballero, S. Milne, (S. Lovell)
Substitutes not used: J. Langfield, G. Beith
Falkirk: A. Ferguson, J. Henry, J. McQuilken, S. MacKenzie, J. Hughes, (K. Christie), B. Reid, M. Kerr, L. Miller, (A. Rodgers), O. Coyle, (C. Samuel), C. McPherson, S. Taylor
Substitutes not used: D. Hill, I. MacSween
Referee: John Rowbotham **Attendance:** 9,562

RANGERS 3 — **DUNFERMLINE ATHLETIC 0**
P. Lovenkrands, B. Ferguson, M. Arteta

Rangers: S. Klos, F. Ricksen, B. Konterman, L. Amoruso, A. Numan, (N. McCann), R. Malcolm, B. Ferguson, (S. Arveladze), M. Arteta, R. de Boer, (C. Caniggia), M. Mols, P. Lovenkrands
Substitutes not used: A. McGregor, S. Hughes
Dunfermline Athletic: D. Stillie, A. MacPherson, (S. Kilgannon), C. McGroarty, A. Skerla, L. Bullen, G. Mason, B. Nicholson, G. Brannan, (D. Grondin), S. Hampshire, S. Crawford, C. Brewster, (N. Hunt)
Substitutes not used: M. Ruitenbeek, M. McGarty
Referee: John Underhill **Attendance:** 24,752

SEMI-FINALS

Saturday, 19th April, 2003
The National Stadium, Hampden Park, Glasgow

RANGERS 4 — **MOTHERWELL 3**
B. Konterman, M. Mols, L. Amoruso, D. Partridge (o.g.) — S. Craig, J. McFadden, D. Adams

Rangers: S. Klos, F. Ricksen, (S. Hughes), C. Moore, (R. Malcolm), L. Amoruso, A. Numan, B. Konterman, B. Ferguson, K. Muscat, N. McCann, M. Mols, S. Arveladze, (S. Thompson)
Substitutes not used: A. McGregor, S. McLean
Motherwell: F. Dubourdeau, M. Corrigan, D. Partridge, S. Hammell, (D. Cowan), T. Vaughan, S. Craig, (R. Offiong), S. Pearson, S. Leitch, (D. Lehmann), D. Adams, J. McFadden, D. Clarkson
Substitutes not used: S. Woods, K. Lasley
Referee: Michael McCurry **Attendance:** 29,352

Sunday, 20th April, 2003
The National Stadium, Hampden Park, Glasgow

INVERNESS CAL THISTLE 0 — **DUNDEE 1**
G. Nemsadze

Inverness Caledonian Thistle: M. Brown, R. Tokely, S. Golabek, R. Mann, S. McCaffrey, (C. Christie), R. McBain, R. Duncan, (D. Bagan), D. Wyness, P. Ritchie, R. Hart, B. Robson
Substitutes not used: M. Fraser, G. Stewart, L. Keogh
Dundee: J. Speroni, D. Mackay, J. Hernandez, Z. Khizanishvili, L. Wilkie, G. Brady, G. Nemsadze, G. Rae, S. Lovell, (L. Mair), F. Caballero, S. Milne, (I. Novo)
Substitutes not used: J. Langfield, G. Beith, S. Robb
Referee: Douglas McDonald **Attendance:** 14,429

FINAL

Saturday, 31st May, 2003
The National Stadium, Hampden Park, Glasgow

DUNDEE 0 — RANGERS 1

Dundee: J. Speroni, D. Mackay, (S. Milne), J. Hernandez, Z. Khizanishvili, L. Mair, B. Smith, G. Nemsadze, G. Rae, (G. Brady), S. Lovell, F. Caballero, M. Burchill, (I. Novo)
Substitutes not used: J. Langfield, B. Carranza

Rangers: S. Klos, F. Ricksen, C. Moore, L. Amoruso, A. Numan, (K. Muscat), B. Ferguson, S. Arveladze, (S. Thompson), R. Malcolm, R. de Boer, M. Mols, (M. Ross), N. McCannn
Substitutes not used: A. McGregor, S. McLean

Scorer: L. Amoruso

Referee: Kenny Clark
Attendance: 47,136

SEASON 1873/74
21st March, 1874 at First Hampden; Attendance 2,500

QUEEN'S PARK 2 — CLYDESDALE 0
W. McKinnon, Leckie

SEASON 1874/75
10th April, 1875 at First Hampden; Attendance 7,000

QUEEN'S PARK 3 — RENTON 0
A. McKinnon, Highet, W. McKinnon

SEASON 1875/76
11th March, 1876 at Hamilton Crescent; Attendance 10,000

QUEEN'S PARK 1 — THIRD LANARK 1
Highet — Drinnan

REPLAY
18th March, 1876 at Hamilton Crescent; Attendance 6,000

QUEEN'S PARK 2 — THIRD LANARK 0
Highet (2)

SEASON 1876/77
17th March, 1877 at Hamilton Crescent; Attendance 12,000

VALE OF LEVEN 1 — RANGERS 1
Paton — McDougall (o.g.)

REPLAY
7th April, 1877 at Hamilton Crescent; Attendance 15,000

VALE OF LEVEN 1 — RANGERS 1 (AET)
McDougall — Dunlop

SECOND REPLAY
13th April, 1877 at First Hampden; Attendance 8,000

VALE OF LEVEN 3 — RANGERS 2
Watson (o.g.), Baird, Paton — P. Campbell, W. McNeil

SEASON 1877/78
30th March, 1878 at First Hampden; Attendance 5,000

VALE OF LEVEN 1 — THIRD LANARK 0
McDougall

SEASON 1878/79
19th April, 1879 at First Hampden; Attendance 6,000

VALE OF LEVEN 1 — RANGERS 1
Ferguson — Struthers

VALE OF LEVEN WERE AWARDED CUP AFTER RANGERS FAILED TO TURN UP FOR A REPLAY ON 26TH APRIL, 1879.

SEASON 1879/80
21st February, 1880 at First Cathkin; Attendance 7,000

QUEEN'S PARK 3 — THORNLIEBANK 0
Highet (2,) Kerr

SEASON 1880/81
26th March, 1881 at Kinning Park; Attendance 10,000

QUEEN'S PARK 2 — DUMBARTON 1
McNeil, Kay — McAulay

AFTER A PROTEST BY DUMBARTON, A REPLAY WAS ORDERED.

REPLAY
9th April, 1881 at Kinning Park; Attendance 10,000

QUEEN'S PARK 3 — DUMBARTON 1
Smith (2), Kerr — Meikleham

SEASON 1881/82
18th March, 1882 at First Cathkin; Attendance 12,000

QUEEN'S PARK 2 — DUMBARTON 2
Harrower (2) — Brown, Meikleham

REPLAY
1st April, 1882 at First Cathkin; Attendance 15,000

QUEEN'S PARK 4 — DUMBARTON 1
Richmond, Kerr, Harrower, Kay — J. Miller

SEASON 1882/83
31st March, 1883 at First Hampden; Attendance 15,000

DUMBARTON 2 — VALE OF LEVEN 2
Paton, McArthur — Johnstone, McCrae

REPLAY
7th April, 1883 at First Hampden; Attendance 8,000

DUMBARTON 2 — VALE OF LEVEN 1
Anderson, R. Brown — Friel

SEASON 1883/84
23rd February, 1884 at First Cathkin

VALE OF LEVEN — QUEEN'S PARK

VALE OF LEVEN FAILED TO TURN UP FOR THE FINAL WITH QUEEN'S PARK AND IT WAS LATER DECIDED TO AWARD THE CUP TO QUEEN'S PARK.

SEASON 1884/85
21st February, 1885 at Second Hampden; Attendance 2,500

RENTON 0 — VALE OF LEVEN 0

REPLAY
28th February, 1885 at Second Hampden; Attendance 3,500

RENTON 3 — VALE OF LEVEN 1
J. McCall, McIntyre (2) — Gillies

SEASON 1885/86
13th February, 1886 at First Cathkin; Attendance 7,000

QUEEN'S PARK 3 — RENTON 1
Hamilton, Christie, Somerville — Kelso

SEASON 1886/87
12th February, 1887 at Second Hampden; Attendance 10,000

HIBERNIAN 2 — DUMBARTON 1
Smith, Groves — Aitken

SEASON 1887/88
4th February, 1888 at Second Hampden; Attendance 10,000

RENTON 6 — CAMBUSLANG 1
D. Campbell, McCallum, McNee, McCall (2), J. Campbell — H. Gourlay

SEASON 1888/89
2nd February, 1889 at Second Hampden; Attendance 17,000

THIRD LANARK 3 — CELTIC 0
Oswald Jun. (2), Hannah

A REPLAY WAS ORDERED AFTER PROTESTS CONCERNING GROUND CONDITIONS.

REPLAY
9th February, 1889 at Second Hampden; Attendance 16,000

THIRD LANARK 2 — CELTIC 1
Marshall, Oswald Jun. — McCallum

SEASON 1889/90
15th February, 1890 at First Ibrox; Attendance 10,000

QUEEN'S PARK 1 — VALE OF LEVEN 1
Hamilton — McLachlan

REPLAY
22nd February, 1890 at First Ibrox; Attendance 14,000

QUEEN'S PARK 2 — VALE OF LEVEN 1
Hamilton, Stewart — Bruce

SEASON 1890/91
7th February, 1891 at Second Hampden; Attendance 14,000

HEART OF MIDLOTHIAN 1 — DUMBARTON 0
Russell

SEASON 1891/92
12th March, 1892 at First Ibrox; Attendance 40,000

CELTIC 1 — QUEEN'S PARK 0
Campbell

CROWD ENCROACHMENT OCCURRED AT THE ABOVE GAME AND AS A RESULT THE GAME WAS CONSIDERED A FRIENDLY.

REPLAY
9th April, 1892 at First Ibrox; Attendance 20,000

CELTIC 5 — QUEEN'S PARK 1
Campbell (2), McMahon (2), Sillars (o.g.) — Waddell

SEASON 1892/93
25th February, 1893 at First Ibrox; Attendance 20,000

CELTIC 1 — QUEEN'S PARK 0
Towie

A REPLAY WAS ORDERED BECAUSE OF GROUND CONDITIONS AND THE ABOVE GAME WAS CONSIDERED A FRIENDLY.

REPLAY
11th March, 1893 at First Ibrox; Attendance 15,000

QUEEN'S PARK 2 — CELTIC 1
Sellar (2) — Blessington

SEASON 1893/94
17th February, 1894 at Second Hampden; Attendance 15,000

RANGERS 3 — CELTIC 1
H. McCreadie, Barker, McPherson — W. Maley

SEASON 1894/95
20th April, 1895 at First Ibrox; Attendance 13,500

ST. BERNARD'S 2 — RENTON 1
Clelland (2) — Duncan

SEASON 1895/96
14th March, 1896 at Logie Green; Attendance 16,034

HEART OF MIDLOTHIAN 3 — HIBERNIAN 1
Baird, Walker, Michael — O'Neill

SEASON 1896/97
20th March, 1897 at Second Hampden; Attendance 15,000

RANGERS 5 — DUMBARTON 1
Miller (2), Hyslop, McPherson, A. Smith — W. Thomson

SEASON 1897/98
26th March, 1898 at Second Hampden; Attendance 14,000

RANGERS 2 — KILMARNOCK 0
A. Smith, Hamilton

SEASON 1898/99
22nd April, 1899 at Second Hampden; Attendance 25,000

CELTIC 2 — RANGERS 0
McMahon, Hodge

SEASON 1899/1900
14th April, 1900 at Second Hampden; Attendance 25,000

CELTIC 4 — QUEEN'S PARK 3
McMahon, Divers (2), Bell — Christie, W. Stewart, Battles (o.g.)

SEASON 1900/01
6th April, 1901 at Ibrox; Attendance 15,000

HEART OF MIDLOTHIAN 4 — CELTIC 3
Walker, Bell (2), Thomson — McOustra (2), McMahon

SEASON 1901/02
26th April, 1902 at Celtic Park; Attendance 16,000

HIBERNIAN 1 — CELTIC 0
McGeachan

SEASON 1902/03
11th April, 1903 at Celtic Park; Attendance 28,000

RANGERS 1 — **HEART OF MIDLOTHIAN 1**
Stark — Walker

REPLAY
18th April, 1903 at Celtic Park; Attendance 16,000

RANGERS 0 — **HEART OF MIDLOTHIAN 0**

SECOND REPLAY
25th April, 1903 at Celtic Park; Attendance 32,000

RANGERS 2 — **HEART OF MIDLOTHIAN 0**
Mackie, Hamilton

SEASON 1903/04
16th April, 1904 at Hampden Park; Attendance 64,323

CELTIC 3 — **RANGERS 2**
Quinn (3) — Speedie (2)

SEASON 1904/05
8th April, 1905 at Hampden Park; Attendance 55,000

THIRD LANARK 0 — **RANGERS 0**

REPLAY
15th April, 1905 at Hampden Park; Attendance 40,000

THIRD LANARK 3 — **RANGERS 1**
Wilson (2), Johnstone — Smith

SEASON 1905/06
28th April, 1906 at Ibrox; Attendance 30,000

HEART OF MIDLOTHIAN 1 — **THIRD LANARK 0**
G. Wilson

SEASON 1906/07
20th April, 1907 at Hampden Park; Attendance 50,000

CELTIC 3 — **HEART OF MIDLOTHIAN 0**
Orr (Pen), Somers (2)

SEASON 1907/08
18th April, 1908 at Hampden Park; Attendance 55,000

CELTIC 5 — **ST. MIRREN 1**
Bennett (2), Hamilton, Somers, Quinn — Cunningham

SEASON 1908/09
10th April, 1909 at Hampden Park; Attendance 70,000

CELTIC 2 — **RANGERS 2**
Quinn, Munro — Gilchrist, Bennett

REPLAY
17th April, 1909 at Hampden Park; Attendance 60,000

CELTIC 1 — **RANGERS 1**
Quinn — Gordon

CUP WITHHELD AFTER RIOT FOLLOWING REPLAY.

SEASON 1909/10
9th April, 1910 at Ibrox; Attendance 60,000

DUNDEE 2 — **CLYDE 2**
Blair (o.g.), Langlands — Chalmers, Booth

REPLAY
16th April, 1910 at Ibrox; Attendance 20,000

DUNDEE 0 — **CLYDE 0 (A.E.T.)**

SECOND REPLAY
20th April, 1910 at Ibrox; Attendance 24,000

DUNDEE 2 — **CLYDE 1**
Bellamy, Hunter — Chalmers

SEASON 1910/11
8th April, 1911 at Ibrox; Attendance 45,000

CELTIC 0 — **HAMILTON ACADEMICAL 0**

REPLAY
15th April, 1911 at Ibrox; Attendance 25,000

CELTIC 2 — **HAMILTON ACADEMICAL 0**
Quinn, McAteer

SEASON 1911/12
6th April, 1912 at Ibrox; Attendance 45,000

CELTIC 2 — **CLYDE 0**
McMenemy, Gallagher

SEASON 1912/13
12th April, 1913 at Celtic Park; Attendance 45,000

FALKIRK 2 — **RAITH ROVERS 0**
Robertson, T. Logan

SEASON 1913/14
11th April, 1914 at Ibrox; Attendance 55,000

CELTIC 0 — **HIBERNIAN 0**

REPLAY
16th April, 1914 at Ibrox; Attendance 36,000

CELTIC 4 — **HIBERNIAN 1**
McColl (2), Browning (2) — Smith

SEASONS 1914/15 TO 1918/19
NO COMPETITIONS DUE TO FIRST WORLD WAR

SEASON 1919/20
17th April, 1920 at Hampden Park; Attendance 95,000; Referee: Mr W. Bell (Hamilton)

KILMARNOCK 3 — **ALBION ROVERS 2**
Culley, Shortt, J. Smith — Watson, Hillhouse

SEASON 1920/21
16th April, 1921 at Celtic Park; Attendance 28,294; Referee: Mr H. Humphreys (Greenock)

PARTICK THISTLE 1 — **RANGERS 0**
Blair

SEASON 1921/22
15th April, 1922 at Hampden Park; Attendance 75,000 Referee: Mr T. Dougray (Bellshill)

MORTON 1 — **RANGERS 0**
Gourlay

SEASON 1922/23
31th March, 1923 at Hampden Park; Attendance 80,100; Referee: Mr T. Dougray (Bellshill)

CELTIC 1 — **HIBERNIAN 0**
Cassidy

SEASON 1923/24
19th April, 1924 at Ibrox Stadium; Attendance 59,218; Referee: Mr T. Dougray (Bellshill)

AIRDRIEONIANS 2 — **HIBERNIAN 0**
Russell (2)

SEASON 1924/25
11th April, 1925 at Hampden Park; Attendance 75,137; Referee: Mr T. Dougray (Bellshill)

CELTIC 2 — **DUNDEE 1**
Gallacher, McGrory — McLean

SEASON 1925/26
10th April, 1926 at Hampden Park; Attendance 98,620; Referee: Mr P. Craigmyle (Aberdeen)

ST. MIRREN 2 — **CELTIC 0**
McCrae, Howieson

SEASON 1926/27
16th April, 1927 at Hampden Park; Attendance 80,070; Referee: Mr T. Dougray (Bellshill)

CELTIC 3 — **EAST FIFE 1**
Robertson (o.g.), McLean, Connolly — Wood

SEASON 1927/28
14th April, 1928 at Hampden Park; Attendance 118,115; Referee: Mr W. Bell (Motherwell)

RANGERS 4 — **CELTIC 0**
Meiklejohn (pen), Archibald (2), McPhail

SEASON 1928/29
6th April, 1929 at Hampden Park; Attendance 114,708; Referee: Mr T. Dougray (Bellshill)

KILMARNOCK 2 — **RANGERS 0**
Aitken, Williamson

SEASON 1929/30
12th April, 1930 at Hampden Park; Attendance 107,475; Referee: Mr W. Bell (Motherwell)

RANGERS 0 — **PARTICK THISTLE 0**

REPLAY
16th April, 1930 at Hampden Park; Attendance 103,686; Referee: Mr W. Bell (Motherwell)

RANGERS 2 — **PARTICK THISTLE 1**
Marshall, Craig — Torbet

SEASON 1930/31
11th April, 1931 at Hampden Park; Attendance 104,803; Referee: Mr P. Craigmyle (Aberdeen)

CELTIC 2 — **MOTHERWELL 2**
McGrory, Craig (o.g.) — Stevenson, McMenemy

REPLAY
15th April, 1931 at Hampden Park; Attendance 98,579; Referee: Mr P. Craigmyle (Aberdeen)

CELTIC 4 — **MOTHERWELL 2**
R. Thomson (2), McGrory (2) — Murdoch, Stevenson

SEASON 1931/32
16th April, 1932 at Hampden Park; Attendance 111,982; Referee: Mr P. Craigmyle (Aberdeen)

RANGERS 1 — **KILMARNOCK 1**
McPhail — Maxwell

REPLAY
20th April, 1932 at Hampden Park; Attendance 110,695; Referee: Mr P. Craigmyle (Aberdeen)

RANGERS 3 — **KILMARNOCK 0**
Fleming, McPhail, English

SEASON 1932/33
15th April, 1933 at Hampden Park; Attendance 102,339; Referee: Mr T. Dougray (Bellshill)

CELTIC 1 — **MOTHERWELL 0**
McGrory

SEASON 1933/34
21st April, 1934 at Hampden Park; Attendance 113,430; Referee: Mr M. C. Hutton (Glasgow)

RANGERS 5 — **ST. MIRREN 0**
Nicholson (2), McPhail, Main, Smith

SEASON 1934/35
20th April, 1935 at Hampden Park; Attendance 87,286; Referee: Mr H. Watson (Glasgow)

RANGERS 2 — **HAMILTON ACADEMICAL 1**
Smith (2) — Harrison

SEASON 1935/36
18th April 1936 at Hampden Park; Attendance 88,859; Referee: Mr J. M. Martin (Ladybank)

RANGERS 1 — THIRD LANARK 0
McPhail

SEASON 1936/37
24th April, 1937 at Hampden Park; Attendance 147,365; Referee: Mr M. C. Hutton (Glasgow)

CELTIC 2 — ABERDEEN 1
Crum, Buchan — Armstrong

SEASON 1937/38
23rd April, 1938 at Hampden Park; Attendance 80,091; Referee: Mr H. Watson (Glasgow)

EAST FIFE 1 — KILMARNOCK 1
McLeod — McAvoy

REPLAY
27th April, 1938 at Hampden Park; Attendance 92,716; Referee: Mr H. Watson (Glasgow)

EAST FIFE 4 — KILMARNOCK 2
McKerrell (2), McLeod, Miller — Thomson (pen), McGrogan
After extra-time

SEASON 1938/39
22nd April, 1939 at Hampden Park; Attendance 94,799; Referee: Mr W. Webb (Glasgow)

CLYDE 4 — MOTHERWELL 0
Wallace, Martin (2), Noble

SEASONS 1939/40 TO 1945/46
NO COMPETITIONS DUE TO SECOND WORLD WAR

SEASON 1946/47
19th April, 1947 at Hampden Park; Attendance 82,140; Referee: Mr R. Calder (Glasgow)

ABERDEEN 2 — HIBERNIAN 1
Hamilton, Williams — Cuthbertson

SEASON 1947/48
17th April, 1948 at Hampden Park; Attendance 129,176; Referee: Mr J. M. Martin (Blairgowrie)

RANGERS 1 — MORTON 1
Gillick — Whyte
After extra-time

REPLAY
21st April, 1948 at Hampden Park; Attendance 131,975; Referee: Mr J. M. Martin (Blairgowrie)

RANGERS 1 — MORTON 0
Williamson
After extra-time

SEASON 1948/49
23rd April, 1949 at Hampden Park; Attendance 108,435; Referee: Mr R. G. Benzie (Irvine)

RANGERS 4 — CLYDE 1
Young (2 (2 pens)), Williamson, Duncanson — Galletly

SEASON 1949/50
22nd April, 1950 at Hampden Park; Attendance 118,262 Referee: Mr J. A. Mowat (Burnside)

RANGERS 3 — EAST FIFE 0
Findlay, Thornton (2)

SEASON 1950/51
21st April, 1951 at Hampden Park; Attendance 131,943 Referee: Mr J. A. Mowat (Burnside)

CELTIC 1 — MOTHERWELL 0
McPhail

SEASON 1951/52
19th April, 1952 at Hampden Park; Attendance 136,304; Referee: Mr J. A. Mowat (Burnside)

MOTHERWELL 4 — DUNDEE 0
Watson, Redpath, Humphries, Kelly

SEASON 1952/53
25th April, 1953 at Hampden Park; Attendance 129,861; Referee: Mr J. A. Mowat (Burnside)

RANGERS 1 — ABERDEEN 1
Prentice — Yorston

REPLAY
29th April, 1953 at Hampden Park; Attendance 112,619; Referee: Mr J. A. Mowat (Burnside)

RANGERS 1 — ABERDEEN 0
Simpson

SEASON 1953/54
24th April, 1954 at Hampden Park; Attendance 129,926; Referee: Mr C. E. Faultless (Giffnock)

CELTIC 2 — ABERDEEN 1
Young (o.g.), Fallon — Buckley

SEASON 1954/55
23rd April, 1955 at Hampden Park; Attendance 106,111; Referee: Mr C. E. Faultless (Giffnock)

CLYDE 1 — CELTIC 1
Robertson — Walsh

REPLAY
27th April, 1955 at Hampden Park; Attendance 68,735; Referee: Mr C. E. Faultless (Giffnock)

CLYDE 1 — CELTIC 0
Ring

SEASON 1955/56
21st April, 1956 at Hampden Park; Attendance 133,399; Referee: Mr R. H. Davidson (Airdrie)

HEART OF MIDLOTHIAN 3 — CELTIC 1
Crawford (2), Conn — Haughney

SEASON 1956/57
20th April, 1957 at Hampden Park; Attendance 81,057; Referee: Mr J. A. Mowat (Burnside)

FALKIRK 1 — KILMARNOCK 1
Prentice (pen) — Curlett

REPLAY
24th April, 1957 at Hampden Park; Attendance 79,785; Referee: Mr J. A. Mowat (Burnside)

FALKIRK 2 — KILMARNOCK 1
Merchant, Moran — Curlett
After extra-time

SEASON 1957/58
26th April, 1958 at Hampden Park; Attendance 95,123; Referee: Mr J. A. Mowat (Burnside)

CLYDE 1 — HIBERNIAN 0
Coyle

SEASON 1958/59
25th April 1959 at Hampden Park; Attendance 108,951; Referee: Mr J. A. Mowat (Burnside)

ST. MIRREN 3 — ABERDEEN 1
Bryceland, Miller, Baker — Baird

SEASON 1959/60
23rd April, 1960 at Hampden Park; Attendance 108,017; Referee: Mr R. H. Davidson (Airdrie)

RANGERS 2 — KILMARNOCK 0
Millar (2)

SEASON 1960/61
22nd April, 1961 at Hampden Park; Attendance 113,618; Referee: Mr H. Phillips (Wishaw)

DUNFERMLINE ATHLETIC 0 — CELTIC 0

REPLAY
26th April, 1961 at Hampden Park; Attendance 87,866; Referee: Mr H. Phillips (Wishaw)

DUNFERMLINE ATHLETIC 2 — CELTIC 0
Thomson, Dickson

SEASON 1961/62
21st April, 1962 at Hampden Park; Attendance 126,930; Referee: Mr T. Wharton (Clarkston)

RANGERS 2 — ST. MIRREN 0
Brand, Wilson

SEASON 1962/63
4th May, 1963 at Hampden Park; Attendance 129,527; Referee: Mr T. Wharton (Clarkston)

RANGERS 1 — CELTIC 1
Brand — Murdoch

REPLAY
15th May, 1963 at Hampden Park; Attendance 120,263; Referee: Mr T. Wharton (Clarkston)

RANGERS 3 — CELTIC 0
Brand (2), Wilson

SEASON 1963/64
25th April, 1964 at Hampden Park; Attendance 120,982 Referee: Mr H. Phillips (Wishaw)

RANGERS 3 — DUNDEE 1
Millar (2), Brand — Cameron

SEASON 1964/65
24th April, 1965 at Hampden Park; Attendance 108,800; Referee: Mr H. Phillips (Wishaw)

CELTIC 3 — DUNFERMLINE ATHLETIC 2
Auld (2), McNeill — Melrose, McLaughlin

SEASON 1965/66
23rd April, 1966 at Hampden Park; Attendance 126,559; Referee: Mr T. Wharton (Clarkston)

RANGERS 0 — CELTIC 0

REPLAY
27th April, 1966 at Hampden Park; Attendance 96,862; Referee: Mr T. Wharton (Clarkston)

RANGERS 1 — CELTIC 0
Johansen

SEASON 1966/67
29th April, 1967 at Hampden Park; Attendance 127,117; Referee: Mr W. M. M. Syme (Glasgow)

CELTIC 2 — ABERDEEN 0
Wallace (2)

SEASON 1967/68
27th April, 1968 at Hampden Park; Attendance 56,365; Referee: Mr W. Anderson (East Kilbride)

DUNFERMLINE ATH. 3 — HEART OF MIDLOTHIAN 1
Gardner (2), Lister (pen) — Lunn (o.g.)

SEASON 1968/69
26th April, 1969 at Hampden Park; Attendance 132,870; Referee: Mr J. Callaghan (Glasgow)

CELTIC 4 — RANGERS 0
McNeill, Lennox, Connelly, Chalmers

SEASON 1969/70
11th April, 1970 at Hampden Park; Attendance 108,434; Referee: Mr R. H. Davidson (Airdrie)

ABERDEEN 3 — CELTIC 1
Harper (pen), McKay (2) — Lennox

SEASON 1970/71
8th May, 1971 at Hampden Park; Attendance 120,092; Referee: Mr T. Wharton (Glasgow)

CELTIC 1 — RANGERS 1
Lennox — D. Johnstone

REPLAY
12th May, 1971 at Hampden Park; Attendance 103,332; Referee: Mr T. Wharton (Glasgow)

CELTIC 2	RANGERS 1
Macari, Hood (pen)	Callaghan (o.g.)

SEASON 1971/72
6th May, 1972 at Hampden Park; Attendance 106,102; Referee: Mr A. MacKenzie (Larbert)

CELTIC 6	HIBERNIAN 1
McNeill, Deans (3), Macari (2)	Gordon

SEASON 1972/73
5th May, 1973 at Hampden Park; Attendance 122,714; Referee: Mr J. R. P. Gordon (Newport-on-Tay)

RANGERS 3	CELTIC 2
Parlane, Conn, Forsyth	Dalglish, Connelly (pen)

SEASON 1973/74
4th May, 1974 at Hampden Park; Attendance 75,959; Referee: Mr W. S. Black (Glasgow)

CELTIC 3	DUNDEE UNITED 0
Hood, Murray, Deans	

SEASON 1974/75
3rd May, 1975 at Hampden Park; Attendance 75,457; Referee: Mr I. M. D. Foote (Glasgow)

CELTIC 3	AIRDRIEONIANS 1
Wilson (2), McCluskey (pen)	McCann

SEASON 1975/76
1st May 1976 at Hampden Park; Attendance 85,354; Referee: Mr R. H. Davidson (Airdrie)

RANGERS 3	HEART OF MIDLOTHIAN 1
Johnstone (2), MacDonald	Shaw

SEASON 1976/77
7th May, 1977 at Hampden Park; Attendance 54,252; Referee: Mr R. B. Valentine (Dundee)

CELTIC 1	RANGERS 0
Lynch (pen)	

SEASON 1977/78
6th May, 1978 at Hampden Park; Attendance 61,563; Referee: Mr B. R. McGinlay (Glasgow)

RANGERS 2	ABERDEEN 1
MacDonald, Johnstone	Ritchie

SEASON 1978/79
12th May, 1979 at Hampden Park; Attendance 50,610; Referee: Mr B. R. McGinlay (Glasgow)

RANGERS 0	HIBERNIAN 0

REPLAY
16th May, 1979 at Hampden Park; Attendance 33,504; Referee: Mr B. R. McGinlay (Glasgow)

RANGERS 0	HIBERNIAN 0

After extra-time

SECOND REPLAY
28th May, 1979 at Hampden Park; Attendance 30,602; Referee: Mr I. M. D. Foote (Glasgow)

RANGERS 3	HIBERNIAN 2
Johnstone (2), Duncan (o.g.)	Higgins, MacLeod (pen)

After extra-time - 2-2 After 90 Minutes

SEASON 1979/80
10th May, 1980 at Hampden Park; Attendance 70,303; Referee: Mr G. B. Smith (Edinburgh)

CELTIC 1	RANGERS 0
McCluskey	

After extra-time

SEASON 1980/81
9th May, 1981 at Hampden Park; Attendance 53,000; Referee: Mr I. M. D. Foote (Glasgow)

RANGERS 0	DUNDEE UNITED 0

After extra-time

REPLAY
12th May, 1981 at Hampden Park; Attendance 43,099; Referee: Mr I. M. D. Foote (Glasgow)

RANGERS 4	DUNDEE UNITED 1
Cooper, Russell, MacDonald (2)	Dodds

SEASON 1981/82
22nd May, 1982 at Hampden Park; Attendance 53,788; Referee: Mr B. R. McGinlay (Balfron)

ABERDEEN 4	RANGERS 1
McLeish, McGhee, Strachan, Cooper	MacDonald

After extra-time - 1-1 after 90 minutes

SEASON 1982/83
21st May, 1983 at Hampden Park; Attendance 62,979; Referee: Mr D. F. T. Syme (Rutherglen)

ABERDEEN 1	RANGERS 0
Black	

After extra-time

SEASON 1983/84
19th May 1984 at Hampden Park; Attendance 58,900; Referee: Mr R. B. Valentine (Dundee)

ABERDEEN 2	CELTIC 1
Black, McGhee	P. McStay

After extra-time - 1-1 after 90 minutes

SEASON 1984/85
18th May, 1985 at Hampden Park; Attendance 60,346; Referee: Mr B. R. McGinlay (Balfron)

CELTIC 2	DUNDEE UNITED 1
Provan, McGarvey	Beedie

SEASON 1985/86
10th May, 1986 at Hampden Park; Attendance 62,841; Referee: Mr H. Alexander (Irvine)

ABERDEEN 3	HEART OF MIDLOTHIAN 0
Hewitt (2), Stark	

SEASON 1986/87
16th May, 1987 at Hampden Park; Attendance 51,782; Referee: Mr K. J. Hope (Clarkston)

ST. MIRREN 1	DUNDEE UNITED 0
Ferguson	

After extra-time

SEASON 1987/88
14th May, 1988 at Hampden Park; Attendance 74,000; Referee: Mr G. B. Smith (Edinburgh)

CELTIC 2	DUNDEE UNITED 1
McAvennie (2)	Gallacher

SEASON 1988/89
20th May, 1989 at Hampden Park; Attendance 72,069; Referee: Mr R. B. Valentine (Dundee)

CELTIC 1	RANGERS 0
Miller	

SEASON 1989/90
12th May, 1990 at Hampden Park; Attendance 60,493; Referee: Mr G. B. Smith (Edinburgh)

ABERDEEN 0	CELTIC 0

After extra-time. Aberdeen won 9-8 on Kicks from the Penalty Mark

SEASON 1990/91
18th May, 1991 at Hampden Park; Attendance 57,319; Referee: Mr D. F. T. Syme (Rutherglen)

MOTHERWELL 4	DUNDEE UNITED 3
Ferguson, O'Donnell, Angus, Kirk	Bowman, O'Neil, Jackson

After extra-time - 3-3 after 90 minutes

SEASON 1991/92
9th May 1992 at Hampden Park; Attendance 44,045; Referee: Mr D. D. Hope (Erskine)

RANGERS 2	AIRDRIEONIANS 1
Hateley, McCoist	Smith

SEASON 1992/93
29th May, 1993 at Celtic Park; Attendance 50,715; Referee: Mr J. McCluskey (Stewarton)

RANGERS 2	ABERDEEN 1
Murray, Hateley	Richardson

SEASON 1993/94
21st May, 1994 at Hampden Park; Attendance 37,709; Referee: Mr D. D. Hope (Erskine)

DUNDEE UNITED 1	RANGERS 0
Brewster	

SEASON 1994/95
27th May, 1995 at Hampden Park; Attendance 38,672; Referee: Mr L. W. Mottram (Forth)

CELTIC 1	AIRDRIEONIANS 0
Van Hooijdonk	

SEASON 1995/96
18th May, 1996 at Hampden Park; Attendance 37,760; Referee: Mr H. Dallas (Motherwell)

RANGERS 5	HEART OF MIDLOTHIAN 1
Laudrup (2), Durie (3)	Colquhoun

SEASON 1996/97
24th May, 1997 at Ibrox Stadium; Attendance 48,953; Referee: Mr H. Dallas (Motherwell)

KILMARNOCK 1	FALKIRK 0
Wright	

SEASON 1997/98
16th May, 1998 at Celtic Park; Attendance 48,946; Referee: Mr W. Young (Clarkston)

HEART OF MIDLOTHIAN 2	RANGERS 1
Cameron, Adam	McCoist

SEASON 1998/99
29th May, 1999 at The National Stadium, Hampden Park; Attendance 51,746; Referee: Mr H. Dallas (Motherwell)

RANGERS 1	CELTIC 0
Wallace	

SEASON 1999/2000
27th May, 2000 at The National Stadium, Hampden Park; Attendance 50,685; Referee: Mr J. McCluskey

RANGERS 4	ABERDEEN 0
Van Bronckhorst, Vidmar, Dodds, Albertz	

SEASON 2000/01
26th May, 2001 at The National Stadium, Hampden Park; Attendance 51,284; Referee: Mr K. Clark

CELTIC 3	HIBERNIAN 0
McNamara, Larsson (2)	

SEASON 2001/02
4th May, 2002 at The National Stadium, Hampden Park; Attendance 51,138; Referee: Mr H. Dallas

RANGERS 3	CELTIC 2
Lovenkrands (2), Ferguson	Hartson, Balde

SEASON 2002/03
31st May, 2003 at The National Stadium, Hampden Park; Attendance 47,136; Referee: Mr K. Clark

RANGERS 1	DUNDEE 0
Amoruso	

BELL'S — CUP —

FIRST ROUND

Tuesday, 6th August, 2002

ST. JOHNSTONE 3 — **HAMILTON ACADEMICAL 0**
R. Stevenson, R. McCann, P. MacDonald
St. Johnstone: K. Cuthbert, J. Robertson, C. Russell, (M. Maher), S. McCluskey, D. Dods, I. Maxwell, R. McCann, (M. Fotheringham), G. Murray, P. Hartley, R. Stevenson, K. Parker, (P. MacDonald)
Substitutes not used: D. McClune, A. Main
Hamilton Academical: I. Macfarlane, M. Nelson, (C. Smillie), P. McDonald, (N. Paterson), I. Dobbins, S. Sweeney, Alisdair Graham, M. Bonnar, J. Walker, G. Armstrong, Alastair Graham, (I. McCreadie), S. Callaghan
Substitutes not used: D. Grant, G. Potter
Referee: Tom Brown
Attendance: 1,538

MONTROSE 1 — **ALBION ROVERS 0**
I.G. Johnson
Montrose: G. McGlynn, G. McCheyne, D. Robertson, K. Gibson, F. Conway, J. McQuillan, K. Webster, (M. Leask), I.G. Johnson, C. McDonald, C. Webster, (S. Ferguson), R. McKinnon, (R. Brand)
Substitutes not used: J. Mitchell, M. Anderson
Albion Rovers: C. Fahey, A. Paterson, J. Stirling, J. Smith, P. Cormack, T. Lumsden, C. McKinnon, J. Coulter, (I. Diack), C. McLean, (J. Bradford), D. Carr, J. Mercer, (C. Silvestro)
Substitutes not used: G. McCaul, S. Shearer
Referee: Garry Mitchell
Attendance: 320

ARBROATH 0 — **FORFAR ATHLETIC 2**
P. Tosh (2)
Arbroath: C. Hinchcliffe, J. Tait, G. Henslee, R. Currie, (J. McAulay), I. Ritchie, A. Cargill, (D. Spink), K. Heenan, (P. Brownlie), D. McInally, M. McDowell, J. McGlashan, C. Feroz
Substitutes not used: P. Durno, G. Gow
Forfar Athletic: M. Brown, A. Rattray, B. Sellars, B. McCloy, I. Good, K. Byers, (D. Williams), G. Shaw, (W. Stewart), P. Lunan, P. Tosh, (R. Horn), M. Bavidge, D. Henderson
Substitutes not used: K. Milne, N. Ferrie
Referee: John Rowbotham
Attendance: 618

BERWICK RANGERS 1 — **INVERNESS CALEDONIAN THISTLE 0**
J.N. Bennett
Berwick Rangers: N. Inglis, D. Gray, J.N. Bennett, E. Forrest, A. Neill, M. Bradley, G. Forrest, M. Neil, G. Wood, I. Ferguson, (G. Connell), D. Smith, (A. Burke)
Substitutes not used: G. Connelly, D. Murie, R. Godfrey
Inverness Caledonian Thistle: M. Brown, R. Tokely, (A. Low), S. Golabek, R. Mann, S. McCaffrey, G. Munro, R. Duncan, (C. Christie), L. Keogh, P. Ritchie, (D. Wyness), R. Hart, B. Robson
Substitutes not used: B. Gilfillan, A. Ridgers
Referee: John Underhill
Attendance: 338

AIRDRIE UNITED 3 — **RAITH ROVERS 0**
M. Glancy, D. McGuire, S. Docherty
Airdrie United: M. McGeown, J. Boyle, (P. Armstrong), W. McVey, A. Stewart, K. Brannigan, S. Vella, R.L. Gardner, (W. Wilson), M. Wilson, D. McGuire, (P. Ronald), S. Docherty, M. Glancy
Substitute not used: D. Miller
Raith Rovers: R. Ojeda, I. Brown, (J. Mas Farre), L. Ellis, (B. Carrigan), D. Brady, P. Browne, W. Nanou, R. Matheson, F. Rivas, A. Smith, (S. Paliczka), P. Hampshire, M. Prest
Substitutes not used: D. Ross, S. Monin
Referee: Iain Brines
Attendance: 1,649

MORTON 3 — **STIRLING ALBION 2**
W. Hawke, A. Williams (2) — G. Munro, S. Nicholas
Morton: C. Coyle, D. Collins, E. Bottiglieri, D. MacGregor, P. Gaughan, M. Maisano, (S. MacDonald), J. Uotinen, (S. Bannerman), W. Hawke, A. Williams, J. Maisano, C. Reilly
Substitutes not used: P. Cannie, A. Smith, R. McKillop
Stirling Albion: C. Reid, P. Nugent, D. McCole, (R. Beveridge), M. McNally, J.G. Rowe, S. Reilly, (W. Stuart), S. Nicholas, F. Duncan, (D. Butler), S. Mallan, G. Munro, P. Hay
Substitutes not used: A. Moore, I. Turner
Referee: Colin Hardie
Attendance: 1,287

QUEEN'S PARK 2 — **GRETNA 1**
J. Gemmell, S. Canning — M. Dobie
Queen's Park: A. Mitchell, G. Lappin, (D. Ferry), J. Gallagher, S. Moffatt, D. Agostini, A. Quinn, S. Jack, (C. Fisher), J. Whelan, J. Gemmell, S. Canning, J. Allan, (W. Martin)
Substitutes not used: P. Gallagher, S. Thomson
Gretna: D. Mathieson, R. McGuffie, (R. Alexander), G. Skelton, T. Turner, D. Hewson, M. Henney, S. Skinner, D. Irons, M. Dobie, J. Hore, W. Gordon, (C. Smart)
Substitutes not used: V. Parker, S. Rooke, G. Wills
Referee: Ian Frickleton
Attendance: 602

ST. MIRREN 7 — **EAST STIRLINGSHIRE 0**
M. Cameron (4), G. Guy, I. Ross, R. Gillies
St. Mirren: L. Roy, S. Baltacha, A. Dow, J. McGowan, R. Robb, I. Ross, R. Gillies, G. Guy, (S. MacKenzie), B. McGinty, (M. Yardley), M. Cameron, (C. Kerr), S. Lappin
Substitutes not used: P. Rudden, K. Robertson
East Stirlingshire: S. Findlay, C. Dunbar, (W. Struthers), R. Maughan, G. McGhee, G. McLaren, J. Leishman, Sean McAuley, G. Boyle, D. Ure, (L. Walker), D. Carmichael, K. Morrison, (C. Reid)
Substitutes not used: P. McLaughlin, C. Todd
Referee: George Clyde
Attendance: 1,403

COWDENBEATH 0 — **ROSS COUNTY 2 (AET)**
S. Webb, C. Gethins
Cowdenbeath: M. Graham, W. Miller, A. Campbell, D. White, K. Wilson, M. Renwick, I. Mauchlen, (G. Crabbe), C. Winter, G. Brown, (G. Gilfillan), K. Gordon, (J. Elliott), H. French
Substitutes not used: L. Dair, A. Fleming
Ross County: A. Bullock, M. McCulloch, P. Deas, M. Perry, B. Irvine, (G. Bayne), K. Gilbert, S. McGarry, S. Ferguson, A. Bone, (C. Gethins), D. Cowie, S. Mackay, (S. Webb)
Substitutes not used: M. Wood, L. Fridge
Referee: David Somers
Attendance: 193

DUMBARTON 1 — **EAST FIFE 0**
C. Duffy
Dumbarton: S. Grindlay, C. McEwan, D. Stewart, T. Brown, C. Duffy, N. Collins, K. McCann, S. Bonar, (C. Lynes), P. Flannery, (D. McKelvie), A. Brown, J. Dillon
Substitutes not used: J. McKeown, M. Dickie, J. Wight
East Fife: J. Butter, G. Russell, G. Gilbert, C. Farnan, M. Hall, G. Cunningham, C. McMillan, (G. Love), P. Mortimer, R. Graham, (J. Ovenstone), K. Deuchar, (D. Walker), E. Donaldson
Substitutes not used: J. Allison, S. Bennett
Referee: Cammy Melville
Attendance: 452

ELGIN CITY 1 — **BRECHIN CITY 4**
D. Ross — C. Templeman (2), M. Millar, Charles King
Elgin City: M. Pirie, S. MacDonald, R. McBride, D. Ross, D. Mackay, C. Tully, C. Campbell, C. Love, R. McMullan, K. Steele, (R. James), M. Sanderson, (D. Craig)
Substitutes not used: D. Hind, A. Smith, P. Hamilton
Brechin City: M. Cairns, G. Miller, R. Black, (P. Riley), J. Smith, H. Cairney, K. Fotheringham, Charles King, M. Millar, C. Templeman, G. Gibson, (R. Grant), C. Jackson, (P. Campbell)
Substitutes not used: D. Smith, D. Hay
Referee: Alan Freeland
Attendance: 505

STRANRAER 1 — **AYR UNITED 2**
J. Fallon — E. Annand, J. Grady
Stranraer: W. McCulloch, K. Gaughan, F. Wright, D. Wingate, A. Jenkins, (J. Fallon), A. Grace, (A. Lurinsky), S. Renicks, (S. Hodge), S. Aitken, I. Harty, M. Moore, L. Sharp
Substitutes not used: S. Marshall, D. Farrell
Ayr United: C. Nelson, W. Lyle, P. Lovering, I. Nicolson, A. McManus, D. Craig, S. Kean, A. Black, (M. Dunlop), E. Annand, J. Grady, P. Sheerin
Substitutes not used: M. Ferry, A. Ferguson, J. Latta, J. Dodds
Referee: Hugh Dallas
Attendance: 725

PETERHEAD 0 | **QUEEN OF THE SOUTH 2**
J. O'Neil, P. Weatherson
Peterhead: P. Mathers, G. Burns, S. McSkimming, K. Bain, M. Simpson, K. Tindal, C. Cooper, I. Stewart, S. Mackay, K. Robertson, (K. Bisset), R. Livingstone, (T. Kidd)
Substitutes not used M. Slater, K. Rennie, I. Pirie
Queen of the South: C. Scott, A. Gray, D. Anderson, B. McLaughlin, A. Aitken, J. Crawford, J. O'Neil, B. McColligan, D. Lyle, P. Weatherson, (S. O'Connor), J. McAlpine
Substitutes not used: E. Paton, D. Allan, S. Bowey, A. Goram
Referee: Kevin Toner
Attendance: 557

STENHOUSEMUIR 1 | **FALKIRK 1**
(AET – 1-1 After 90 Minutes)
M. Wilson | L. Miller
Falkirk won 3-2 on Kicks from the Penalty Mark
Stenhousemuir: A. Carlin, F. Forrest, (M. Wilson), G. McKenna, S. Hamilton, J. McKenzie, M. Booth, C. Waldie, (K. Donnelly), S. Easton, S. McCormick, (M. Harty), D. McFarlane, J. Stein
Substitutes not used: D. Graham, A. Gillespie
Falkirk: A. Ferguson, A. Lawrie, J. McQuilken, S. Rennie, J. Hughes, K. James, M. Kerr, L. Miller, (A. Rodgers), O. Coyle, C. McPherson, (J. Henry), S. Tosh, (I. MacSween)
Substitutes not used: P. Creaney, D. Hill
Referee: Craig Thomson
Attendance: 1,525

SECOND ROUND

Tuesday, 13th August, 2002

CLYDE 1 | **ST. MIRREN 2**
L. Hinds | S. Baltacha, R. Gillies
Clyde: B. Halliwell, S. Mensing, J. Potter, B. Smith, A. Millen, J. Ross, A. McClay, (S. Convery), J. Fraser, P. Keogh, (A. Kane), L. Hinds, D. Dunn, (S. Cosgrove)
Substitutes not used: F. Bossy, C. Clark
St. Mirren: L. Roy, S. Baltacha, C. Kerr, G. Guy, J. McGowan, A. Dow, R. Gillies, J. Mendes, B. McGinty, M. Cameron, (M. Yardley), I. Ross
Substitutes not used: S. MacKenzie, S. Lappin, P. Rudden, K. Robertson
Referee: Kenny Clark
Attendance: 1,284

BERWICK RANGERS 2 | **AIRDRIE UNITED 0**
A. Burke (2)
Berwick Rangers: R. Godfrey, G. McNicoll, J.N. Bennett, E. Forrest, A. Neill, G. Forrest, G. Connelly, (G. Connell), M. Neil, G. Wood, I. Ferguson, (D. Smith), A. Burke
Substitutes not used: D. Gray, M. Bradley, N. Inglis
Airdrie United: M. McGeown, J. Boyle, W. McVey, (D. Miller), P. Armstrong, K. Brannigan, S. Vella, R.L. Gardner, (W. Wilson), M. Wilson, P. Ronald, S. Docherty, M. Glancy
Substitutes not used: D. McGuire, A. Stewart
Referee: Calum Murray
Attendance: 560

MONTROSE 0 | **FALKIRK 2**
L. Miller, K. James
Montrose: G. McGlynn, G. McCheyne, D. Robertson, K. Gibson, F. Conway, J. McQuillan, K. Webster, (G. Sharp), I.G. Johnson, C. Webster, (M. Leask), R. McKinnon, S. Ferguson
Substitutes not used: R. Brand, G. Christie, M. Anderson
Falkirk: A. Ferguson, A. Lawrie, J. McQuilken, S. Rennie, J. Hughes, K. James, M. Kerr, L. Miller, O. Coyle, (C. Samuel), J. Henry, C. McPherson, (I. MacSween)
Substitutes not used: S. Tosh, S. Cringean, D. Hill
Referee: John Gilmour
Attendance: 805

QUEEN OF THE SOUTH 1 | **MORTON 0**
S. O'Connor
Queen of the South: C. Scott, P. Atkinson, D. Anderson, B. McColligan, A. Aitken, J. Crawford, J. O'Neil, A. Gray, (E. Paton), S. O'Connor, P. Weatherson, (D. Lyle), J. McAlpine, (B. McLaughlin)
Substitutes not used: D. Allan, A. Goram
Morton: C. Coyle, D. Collins, E. Bottiglieri, D. MacGregor, P. Gaughan, A. Smith, J. Uotinen, W. Hawke, (P. Cannie), A. Williams, S. MacDonald, (D. Keenan), C. Reilly
Substitutes not used: S. Curran, D. Carmichael, R. MacKillop
Referee: Eric Martindale
Attendance: 1,982

FORFAR ATHLETIC 2 | **QUEEN'S PARK 2**
(AET – 1-1 After 90 Minutes)
Queen's Park won 6-5 on Kicks from the Penalty Mark
M. Bavidge, P. Tosh | S. Moffat (2)
Forfar Athletic: M. Brown, A. Rattray, S. McCulloch, B. McCloy, I. Good, K. Byers, (N. Ferrie), G. Shaw, (D. Williams), P. Lunan, (W. Stewart), P. Tosh, M. Bavidge, B. Sellars
Substitutes not used: R. Horn, K. Milne
Queen's Park: A. Mitchell, D. Ferry, J. Gallagher, S. Moffat, D. Agostini, A. Quinn, P. Gallagher, (C. Fisher), (R. Sinclair), J. Whelan, J. Gemmell, S. Canning, J. Allan, (W. Martin)
Substitutes not used: D. Magee, S. Thomson
Referee: Brian McGarry
Attendance: 384

DUMBARTON 3 | **AYR UNITED 0**
T. Brown, J. Dillon (2)
Dumbarton: S. Grindlay, C. McEwan, D. Stewart, T. Brown, C. Duffy, N. Collins, M. Crilly, S. Bonar, (M. Dickie), P. Flannery, (D. McKelvie), A. Brown, J. Dillon
Substitutes not used: J. McKeown, K. McCann, J. Wight
Ayr United: C. Nelson, W. Lyle, (J. Latta), P. Lovering, S. Chaplain, A. McManus, (M. Ferry), D. Craig, I. Nicolson, A. Black, E. Annand, (S. Kean), J. Grady, P. Sheerin
Substitutes not used: M. Dunlop, J. Dodds
Referee: Brian Cassidy
Attendance: 983

ALLOA ATHLETIC 0 | **ROSS COUNTY 1**
A.B. Ferguson (o.g.)
Alloa Athletic: J. Evans, C. Valentine, A. Seaton, (J. Fisher), K. Knox, S. Thomson, M. Christie, R. Hamilton, A.B. Ferguson, S. Crabbe, (G. Evans), G. Hutchison, I. Little
Substitutes not used: M. Cowan, H. Curran, M. Hogarth
Ross County: A. Bullock, M. McCulloch, P. Deas, M. Perry, M. Canning, K. Gilbert, S. McGarry, (A. Bone), S. Ferguson, C. Gethins, (S. Mackay), D. Cowie, (C. Campbell), M. Wood
Substitutes not used: S. Webb, L. Fridge
Referee: Willie Young
Attendance: 416

Wednesday, 14th August, 2002

BRECHIN CITY 3 | **ST. JOHNSTONE 2**
R. Grant (2), G. Gibson | G. Murray, P. MacDonald
Brechin City: D. Hay, G. McCulloch, (Charles King), R. Black, (G. Miller), J. Smith, H. Cairney, K. Fotheringham, C. Templeman, C. Jackson, R. Grant, M. Millar, G. Gibson
Substitutes not used: P. Campbell, P. Riley, M. Cairns
St. Johnstone: K. Cuthbert, G. Murray, (M. Ferry), T. Lovenkrands, S. McCluskey, D. Dods, I. Maxwell, M. Maher, (D. McClune), M. Fotheringham, R. Stevenson, C. Russell, (K. Parker), P. MacDonald
Substitutes not used: E. Panther, A. Main
Referee: Ian Fyfe
Attendance: 1,007

THIRD ROUND

Tuesday, 20th August, 2002

ROSS COUNTY 1 | **ST. MIRREN 1**
(AET – 1-1 After 90 Minutes)
St. Mirren won 6-5 on Kicks from the Penalty Mark
C. Gethins | R. Gillies
Ross County: A. Bullock, M. McCulloch, S. Mackay, M. Perry, M. Canning, K. Gilbert, S. McGarry, (G. Bayne), S. Ferguson, A. Bone, (S. Webb), C. Gethins, H. Robertson, (M. Wood)
Substitutes not used: D. Cowie, L. Fridge
St. Mirren: K. Robertson, J. McGowan, C. Kerr, G. Guy, (A. Dow), G. Fellner, S. MacKenzie, R. Gillies, J. Mendes, (S. Lappin), B. McGinty, (M. Yardley), M. Cameron, I. Ross
Substitutes not used: K. Broadfoot, W. Bald
Referee: Douglas McDonald
Attendance: 1,128

QUEEN OF THE SOUTH 2 | **DUMBARTON 0**
J. O'Neil, D. Lyle
Queen of the South: C. Scott, A. Gray, D. Anderson, E. Paton, A. Aitken, J. Crawford, J. O'Neil, B. McColligan, (S. Bowey), D. Lyle, P. Weatherson, (P. Shields), J. McAlpine, (B. McLaughlin)
Substitutes not used: D. Allan, A. Goram
Dumbarton: S. Grindlay, M. Dickie, (C. Lynes), D. Stewart, T. Brown, C. Duffy, N. Collins, M. Crilly, S. Bonar, (C. McEwan), P. Flannery, (D. McKelvie), A. Brown, J. Dillon
Substitutes not used: J. McKeown, J. Wight
Referee: John Underhill
Attendance: 1,722

BRECHIN CITY 1 **FALKIRK 1**
(AET – 1-1 After 90 Minutes)
Brechin City won 5-3 on Kicks from the Penalty Mark
K. Fotheringham C. McPherson
Brechin City: D. Hay, G. Miller, R. Black, (Charles King), J. Smith, H. Cairney, K. Fotheringham, J. Skinner, (G. Gibson), C. Jackson, (P. Riley), R. Grant, C. Templeman, M. Millar
Substitutes not used: P. Campbell, M. Cairns
Falkirk: A. Ferguson, A. Lawrie, (A. Rodgers), J. McQuilken, S. Rennie, J. Hughes, K. James, M. Kerr, (J. Henry), L. Miller, O. Coyle, (C. Samuel), C. McPherson, S. Tosh
Substitutes not used: S. Cringean, D. Hill
Referee: Alan Freeland
Attendance: 844

BERWICK RANGERS 1 **QUEEN'S PARK 2**
D. Murie J. Whelan, J. Allan
Berwick Rangers: R. Godfrey, D. Murie, A. Smith, G. McNicoll, A. Neill, M. Bradley, G. Forrest, G. Connell, (M. Neil), G. Wood, M. McCormick, J.N. Bennett, (A. Burke)
Substitutes not used: E. Forrest, G. Connelly, N. Inglis
Queen's Park: A. Mitchell, D. Ferry, J. White, (R. Sinclair), S. Moffat, D. Agostini, A. Quinn, C. Taggart, (R. Jackson), J. Whelan, W. Martin, (C. Fisher), S. Canning, J. Allan
Substitutes not used: K. Lejman, S. Thomson
Referee: Tom Brown
Attendance: 407

SEMI-FINALS

Tuesday, 27th August, 2002

QUEEN'S PARK 3 **BRECHIN CITY 4**
J. Allan, J. Gemmell, J. Whelan M. Millar, C. Jackson, K. Fotheringham, R. Grant
Queen's Park: A. Mitchell, D. Ferry, J. Gallagher, S. Moffat, D. Agostini, A. Quinn, C. Taggart, (R. Sinclair), J. Whelan, J. Gemmell, S. Canning, (C. Fisher), J. Allan, (W. Martin)
Substitutes not used: P. Gallagher, S. Thomson
Brechin City: D. Hay, G. Miller, R. Black, (Charles King), J. Smith, H. Cairney, K. Fotheringham, J. Skinner, M. Millar, (P. Campbell), R. Grant, G. Gibson, C. Templeman, (C. Jackson)
Substitutes not used: P. Riley, M. Cairns
Referee: Stuart Dougal
Attendance: 1,214

ST. MIRREN 3 **QUEEN OF THE SOUTH 5**
B. McGinty, M. Cameron, G. Fellner P. Shields (2), D. Lyle, S. Bowey, P. Weatherson
St. Mirren: L. Roy, J. McGowan, (S. Baltacha), C. Kerr, H. Murray, G. Fellner, A. Dow, R. Gillies, J. Mendes, B. McGinty, (M. Yardley), M. Cameron, (I. Kristo), I. Ross
Substitutes not used: A. Saleem, K. Robertson
Queen of the South: C. Scott, R. Neilson, P. Atkinson, (D. Anderson), J. McAlpine, A. Aitken, J. Crawford, J. O'Neil, S. Bowey, D. Lyle, (B. McLaughlin), P. Shields, (D. Allan), P. Weatherson
Substitutes not used: B. McColligan, A. Goram
Referee: Michael McCurry
Attendance: 2,528

FINAL

Sunday, 20th October, 2002

Broadwood Stadium, Cumbernauld

BRECHIN CITY 0 **QUEEN OF THE SOUTH 2**
Brechin City: D. Hay, G. McCulloch, R. Black, J. Smith, H. Cairney, K. Fotheringham, Charles King, (D. Clark), P. Riley, (G. Miller), R. Grant, C. Jackson, G. Gibson, (C. Templeman)
Substitutes not used: B. Donachie, M. Cairns
Queen of the South: A. Goram, R. Neilson, D. Anderson, B. McColligan, A. Aitken, J. Thomson, J. O'Neil, S. Bowey, P. Weatherson, (S. O'Connor), D. Lyle, (B. McLaughlin), J. McAlpine
Substitutes not used: P. Atkinson, E. Paton, C. Scott
Scorers: J. O'Neil, D. Lyle
Referee: John Underhill
Attendance: 6,438

ROUND BY ROUND GOALS ANALYSIS

	No. of Goals Scored	Ties Played	Average Per Game
First Round	40	14	2.9
Second Round	21	8	2.6
Third Round	9	4	2.3
Semi-Finals	15	2	7.5
Final	2	1	2
Total No. of Goals Scored			**87**
Total No. of Ties Played			**29**
Average Goals per Game			**3**

league challenge cup final results since 1990/91

(In Season 1990/91 known as The B&Q Centenary Cup; In Seasons 1991/92 to 1994/95 known as The B&Q Cup; In Season 1995/96 to 1997/98 known as the League Challenge Cup; In Seasons 1999/2000 to 2001/02 known as Bell's Challenge Cup; In Season 2002/03 known as Bell's Cup)

SEASON 1990/91
Sunday, 11th November, 1990 at Fir Park, Motherwell;
Attendance 11,506, Referee: K. J. Hope (Clarkston)

AYR UNITED 2	**DUNDEE 3**
(AET - 2-2 After 90 Minutes)	
D. Smyth, I. McAllister	W. Dodds (3)

SEASON 1991/92
Sunday, 8th December, 1991 at Fir Park, Motherwell;
Attendance 9,663, Referee: L.W. Mottram (Forth)

HAMILTON ACADEMICAL 1	**AYR UNITED 0**
C. Harris	

SEASON 1992/93
Sunday, 13th December, 1992 at St. Mirren Park, Paisley;
Attendance 7,391, Referee: J.J. Timmons (Kilwinning)

MORTON 2	**HAMILTON ACADEMICAL 3**
R. Alexander (2)	C. Hillcoat, G. Clark (2)

SEASON 1993/94
Sunday, 12th December, 1993 at Fir Park, Motherwell;
Attendance 13,763, Referee: D.D. Hope (Erskine)

FALKIRK 3	**ST. MIRREN 0**
C. Duffy, J. Hughes, R. Cadette	

SEASON 1994/95
Sunday, 6th November, 1994 at McDiarmid Park, Perth;
Attendance 8,844, Referee: H.F. Williamson (Renfrew)

DUNDEE 2	**AIRDRIEONIANS 3**
(AET - 2-2 After 90 Minutes)	
G. Britton, G. Hay (o.g.)	P. Harvey, J. Boyle, Andrew Smith

SEASON 1995/96
Sunday, 5th November, 1995 at McDiarmid Park, Perth;
Attendance 7,856, Referee: J. Rowbotham (Kirkcaldy)

STENHOUSEMUIR 0	**DUNDEE UNITED 0 (A.E.T.)**

Stenhousemuir won 5-4 on Kicks from the Penalty Mark

SEASON 1996/97
Sunday, 3rd November, 1996 at Broadwood Stadium, Cumbernauld;
Attendance 5,522, Referee: K.W. Clark (Paisley)

STRANRAER 1	**ST. JOHNSTONE 0**
T. Sloan	

SEASON 1997/98
Sunday, 2nd November, 1997 at Fir Park, Motherwell;
Attendance 9,735, Referee: R.T. Tait (East Kilbride)

FALKIRK 1	**QUEEN OF THE SOUTH 0**
D. Hagen	

SEASON 1998/99
No Competition

SEASON 1999/2000
Sunday, 21st November, 1999 at Excelsior Stadium, Airdrie;
Attendance 4,043, Referee: Jim McCluskey

INVERNESS CAL. THISTLE 4	**ALLOA ATHLETIC 4**
(AET – 3-3 after 90 minutes)	
P. Sheerin (3), B. Wilson	G. Clark, M. Cameron (2), M. Wilson

Alloa Athletic won 5-4 on Kicks from the Penalty Mark.

SEASON 2000/01
Sunday, 19th November, 2000 at Broadwood Stadium, Cumbernauld;
Attendance 5,623 Referee: John Rowbotham

LIVINGSTON 2	**AIRDRIEONIANS 2**
(AET–2-2 After 90 Minutes)	
J. Anderson, S. Crabbe	M. Prest, D. McGuire

Airdrieonians won 3-2 on Kicks from the Penalty Mark

SEASON 2001/02
Sunday, 14th October, 2001 at Broadwood Stadium, Cumbernauld;
Attendance 4,548 Referee: Michael McCurry

AIRDRIEONIANS 2	**ALLOA ATHLETIC 1**
O. Coyle, M. Roberts	G. Evans

SEASON 2002/03
Sunday, 20th October, 2002 at Broadwood Stadium, Cumbernauld;
Attendance 6,438 Referee: John Rowbotham

BRECHIN CITY 0	**QUEEN OF THE SOUTH 2**
	J. O'Neil, D. Lyle

Bell's Cup Winners 2002/03 – Queen of the South

player of the year awards

scottish professional footballers' association

1992/93

Premier Division	**Andy Goram** *(Rangers)*
First Division	**Gordon Dalziel** *(Raith Rovers)*
Second Division	**Alexander Ross** *(Brechin City)*
Young Player of the Year	**Eoin Jess** *(Aberdeen)*

1993/94

Premier Division	**Mark Hateley** *(Rangers)*
First Division	**Richard Cadette** *(Falkirk)*
Second Division	**Andrew Thomson** *(Queen of the South)*
Young Player of the Year	**Philip O'Donnell** *(Motherwell)*

1994/95

Premier Division	**Brian Laudrup** *(Rangers)*
First Division	**Stephen Crawford** *(Raith Rovers)*
Second Division	**Derek McInnes** *(Greenock Morton)*
Third Division	**David Bingham** *(Forfar Athletic)*
Young Player of the Year	**Charlie Miller** *(Rangers)*

1995/96

Premier Division	**Paul Gascoigne** *(Rangers)*
First Division	**George O'Boyle** *(St. Johnstone)*
Second Division	**Stephen McCormick** *(Stirling Albion)*
Third Division	**Jason Young** *(Livingston)*
Young Player of the Year	**Jackie McNamara** *(Celtic)*

1996/97

Premier Division	**Paolo Di Canio** *(Celtic)*
First Division	**Roddy Grant** *(St. Johnstone)*
Second Division	**Paul Ritchie** *(Hamilton Academical)*
Third Division	**Iain Stewart** *(Inverness Cal. Thistle)*
Young Player of the Year	**Robbie Winters** *(Dundee United)*

1997/98

Premier Division	**Jackie McNamara** *(Celtic)*
First Division	**James Grady** *(Dundee)*
Second Division	**Paul Lovering** *(Clydebank)*
Third Division	**Willie Irvine** *(Alloa Athletic)*
Young Player of the Year	**Gary Naysmith** *(Heart of Midlothian)*

1998/99

Scottish Premier League	**Henrik Larsson** *(Celtic)*
First Division	**Russell Latapy** *(Hibernian)*
Second Division	**David Bingham** *(Livingston)*
Third Division	**Neil Tarrant** *(Ross County)*
Young Player of the Year	**Barry Ferguson** *(Rangers)*

1999/2000

Scottish Premier League	**Mark Viduka** *(Celtic)*
First Division	**Stevie Crawford** *(Dunfermline Athletic)*
Second Division	**Brian Carrigan** *(Clyde)*
Third Division	**Steven Milne** *(Forfar Athletic)*
Young Player of the Year	**Kenny Miller** *(Hibernian)*

2000/01

Scottish Premier League	**Henrik Larsson** *(Celtic)*
First Division	**David Bingham** *(Livingston)*
Second Division	**Scott McLean** *(Partick Thistle)*
Third Division	**Steve Hislop** *(East Stirlingshire)*
Young Player of the Year	**Stilian Petrov** *(Celtic)*

2001/02

Scottish Premier League	**Lorenzo Amoruso** *(Rangers)*
First Division	**Owen Coyle** *(Airdrieonians)*
Second Division	**John O'Neil** *(Queen of the South)*
Third Division	**Paul McManus** *(East Fife)*
Young Player of the Year	**Kevin McNaughton** *(Aberdeen)*

2002/03

Scottish Premier League	**Barry Ferguson** *(Rangers)*
First Division	**Dennis Wyness** *(Inverness Cal. Thistle)*
Second Division	**Chris Templeman** *(Brechin City)*
Third Division	**Alex Williams** *(Morton)*
Young Player of the Year	**James McFadden** *(Motherwell)*

scottish football writers' association

1965	**Billy McNeill** *(Celtic)*
1966	**John Greig** *(Rangers)*
1967	**Ronnie Simpson** *(Celtic)*
1968	**Gordon Wallace** *(Raith Rovers)*
1969	**Bobby Murdoch** *(Celtic)*
1970	**Pat Stanton** *(Hibernian)*
1971	**Martin Buchan** *(Aberdeen)*
1972	**Dave Smith** *(Rangers)*
1973	**George Connelly** *(Celtic)*
1974	**World Cup Squad**
1975	**Sandy Jardine** *(Rangers)*
1976	**John Greig** *(Rangers)*
1977	**Danny McGrain** *(Celtic)*
1978	**Derek Johnstone** *(Rangers)*
1979	**Andy Ritchie** *(Morton)*
1980	**Gordon Strachan** *(Aberdeen)*
1981	**Alan Rough** *(Partick Thistle)*
1982	**Paul Sturrock** *(Dundee United)*
1983	**Charlie Nicholas** *(Celtic)*
1984	**Willie Miller** *(Aberdeen)*
1985	**Hamish McAlpine** *(Dundee United)*
1986	**Sandy Jardine** *(Heart of Midlothian)*
1987	**Brian McClair** *(Celtic)*
1988	**Paul McStay** *(Celtic)*
1989	**Richard Gough** *(Rangers)*
1990	**Alex McLeish** *(Aberdeen)*
1991	**Maurice Malpas** *(Dundee United)*
1992	**Alistair McCoist** *(Rangers)*
1993	**Andy Goram** *(Rangers)*
1994	**Mark Hateley** *(Rangers)*
1995	**Brian Laudrup** *(Rangers)*
1996	**Paul Gascoigne** *(Rangers)*
1997	**Brian Laudrup** *(Rangers)*
1998	**Craig Burley** *(Celtic)*
1999	**Henrik Larsson** *(Celtic)*
2000	**Barry Ferguson** *(Rangers)*
2001	**Henrik Larsson** *(Celtic)*
2002	**Paul Lambert** *(Celtic)*
2003	**Barry Ferguson** *(Rangers)*

bell's award winners 2002/2003

monthly award winners

AUGUST, 2002
Player — **Kevin Cuthbert** *(St. Johnstone)*
Young Player — **Alex Williams** *(Morton)*
First Division Manager — **Ian McCall** *(Falkirk)*
Second Division Manager — **David Winnie** *(Dumbarton)*
Third Division Manager — **Rowan Alexander** *(Gretna)*
Fan Of The Month — **David Stafford** *(Queen's Park)*

SEPTEMBER, 2002
Player — **Dennis Wyness** *(Inverness Cal. Th.)*
Young Player — **Ryan Blackadder** *(Raith Rovers)*
First Division Manager — **Steve Paterson** *(Inverness Cal. Th.)*
Second Division Manager — **Antonio Calderon** *(Raith Rovers)*
Third Division Manager — **Ian Wilson** *(Peterhead)*
Fan Of The Month — **Donald Smillie** *(Stenhousemuir)*

OCTOBER, 2002
Player — **Dennis Wyness** *(Inverness Cal. Th.)*
Young Player — **David O'Brien** *(Stirling Albion)*
First Division Manager — **Steve Paterson** *(Inverness Cal. Th.)*
Second Division Manager — **Billy McLaren** *(Stranraer)*
Third Division Manager — **Allan Moore** *(Stirling Albion)*
Fan Of The Month — **Willie Frederick** *(Alloa Athletic)*

NOVEMBER, 2002
Player — **Barry Robson** *(Inverness Cal. Th.)*
Young Player — **Alex Williams** *(Morton)*
First Division Manager — **Steve Paterson** *(Inverness Cal. Th.)*
Second Division Manager — **Antonio Calderon** *(Raith Rovers)*
Third Division Manager — **Jim Moffat** *(East Fife)*
Fan Of The Month — **Stuart & Nicki MacNeil** *(Falkirk)*

DECEMBER, 2002
Player — **Tommy Lovenkrands** *(St. Johnstone)*
Young Player — **Scott Shearer** *(Albion Rovers)*
First Division Manager — **Billy Stark** *(St. Johnstone)*
Second Division Manager — **Antonio Calderon** *(Raith Rovers)*
Third Division Manager — **Peter Hetherston** *(Albion Rovers)*
Fan Of The Month — **Jimmy Lawson** *(Albion Rovers)*

JANUARY, 2003
Player — **Collin Samuel** *(Falkirk)*
Young Player — **Mark Kerr** *(Falkirk)*
First Division Manager — **Ian McCall** *(Falkirk)*
Second Division Manager — **Keith Wright** *(Cowdenbeath)*
Third Division Manager — **John McCormack** *(Morton)*
Fan Of The Month — **James Thyne** *(Clyde)*

FEBRUARY, 2003
Player — **Iain Stewart** *(Peterhead)*
Young Player — **Mark Baxter** *(St. Johnstone)*
First Division Manager — **Campbell Money** *(Ayr United)*
Second Division Manager — **Dick Campbell** *(Brechin City)*
Third Division Manager — **Ian Wilson** *(Peterhead)*
Fan Of The Month — **Charles Kavanagh** *(Morton)*

MARCH, 2003
Player — **Paul Hartley** *(St. Johnstone)*
Young Player — **Mark Gilhaney** *(Clyde)*
First Division Manager — **Billy Stark** *(St. Johnstone)*
Second Division Manager — **Sandy Stewart** *(Airdrie United)*
Third Division Manager — **Peter Hetherston** *(Albion Rovers)*
Fan Of The Month — **Keith McAllister** *(Queen's Park)*

APRIL, 2003
Player — **Paul Ritchie** *(Inverness Cal. Th.)*
Young Player — **Alex Williams** *(Morton)*
First Division Manager — **Alan Kernaghan** *(Clyde)*
Second Division Manager — **Sandy Stewart** *(Airdrie United)*
Third Division Manager — **Peter Hetherston** *(Albion Rovers)*
Fan Of The Month — **Jim & Hugh Ferguson** *(Ayr United)*

Young Player of the Year, Lee Miller

season award winners

Player of the Year: **Owen Coyle** *(Falkirk)*
Young Player of the Year: **Lee Miller** *(Falkirk)*
First Division Manager of the Year: **Alan Kernaghan** *(Clyde)*
Second Division Managers of the Year: **Antonio Calderon** *(Raith Rovers)*, **Dick Campbell** *(Brechin City)*
Third Division Manager of the Year: **Ian Wilson** *(Peterhead)*
BELL'S ANGELS: *Stranraer*
BELL'S FAN OF THE YEAR: Keith McAllister *(Queen's Park)*
BELL'S SUPPORTERS PUB OF THE YEAR: *Behind the Wall, Falkirk*

bank of scotland award winners 2002/2003

monthly award winners

AUGUST, 2002
Player — **Mark De Vries** *(Hearts)*
Young Player — **Kris Boyd** *(Kilmarnock)*
Manager — **John Lambie** *(Partick Thistle)*

SEPTEMBER, 2002
Player — **Jean Louis Valois** *(Hearts)*
Young Player — **Mikel Arteta** *(Rangers)*
Manager — **Alex McLeish** *(Rangers)*

OCTOBER, 2002
Player — **Fernando Ricksen** *(Rangers)*
Young Player — **Ian Murray** *(Hibernian)*
Manager — **Bobby Williamson** *(Hibernian)*

NOVEMBER, 2002
Player — **Henrik Larsson** *(Celtic)*
Young Player — **Mark Wilson** *(Dundee United)*
Manager — **Martin O'Neill** *(Celtic)*

DECEMBER, 2002
Player — **John Hartson** *(Celtic)*
Young Player — **Shaun Dillon** *(Kilmarnock)*
Manager — **Jim Jefferies** *(Kilmarnock)*

JANUARY, 2003
Player — **Barry Ferguson** *(Rangers)*
Young Player — **Kris Boyd** *(Kilmarnock)*
Manager — **Jim Duffy** *(Dundee)*

FEBRUARY, 2003
Player — **Lee Wilkie** *(Dundee)*
Young Player — **Shaun Maloney** *(Celtic)*
Manager — **Alex McLeish** *(Rangers)*

MARCH, 2003
Player — **Tom McManus** *(Hibernian)*
Young Player — **Zurab Khizanishvili** *(Dundee)*
Manager — **Jim Duffy** *(Dundee)*

APRIL, 2003
Player — **Bobo Balde** *(Celtic)*
Young Player — **Andy Webster** *(Hearts)*
Manager — **Craig Levein** *(Hearts)*

season award winners

Player of the Year: **Barry Ferguson** *(Rangers)*
Young Player of the Year: **Zurab Khizanishvili** *(Dundee)*
Manager of the Year: **Alex McLeish** *(Rangers)*

EURO 2004 - QUALIFYING COMPETITION AND INTERNATIONAL FRIENDLY MATCHES PLAYED BY SCOTLAND DURING SEASON 2002/03

EURO 2004 - QUALIFYING COMPETITION

Saturday, 7th September, 2002 – Svangaskard Stadium, Toftir

FAROE ISLANDS 2 — **SCOTLAND 2**
Petersen (2) — P. Lambert, B. Ferguson
Faroe Islands: Knudsen, Johannesen, J. Hansen, Thorsteinson, J. Jacobsen, Eittor,(Lakjuni), Benjaminsen, Johnsson, Borg, Petersen, (Flotum), C.Jacobson, (R. Jacobsen)
Substitutes not used: H. Hansen, Joensen, Mikkelsen, S. Jacobsen
Scotland: R. Douglas, M. Ross, (G. Alexander), S. Crainey, C. Dailly, D. Weir, B. Ferguson, P. Dickov, (S. Crawford), S. Dobie, (S. Thompson), K. Kyle, P. Lambert, A. Johnston
Substitutes not used: P. Gallacher, K. McNaughton, L. Wilkie, G. Williams
Referee: Jacek Granat (Poland)
Attendance: 4,000

Paul Lambert is chased by John Petersen

Saturday, 12th October, 2002 – Laugardalsvollur Stadium, Reykjavik

ICELAND 0 — **SCOTLAND 2**
C. Dailly, G. Naysmith
Iceland: Arason, Thorsteinsson, Vidarsson, (Baldvinsson), Gunnarsson, L. Sigurdsson, Runar Kristinsson, Hreidarsson, Ingimarsson, Gudjohnsen, H. Sigurdsson, (H. Helgason), Gudnason, (B. Gudjonsson)
Substitutes not used: B. Kristinsson, Einarsson, Stigsson, J. Gudjonsson
Scotland: R. Douglas, M. Ross, L. Wilkie, S. Pressley, C. Dailly, B. Ferguson, J. McNamara, (C. Davidson), S. Crawford, S. Thompson, (S. Severin), P. Lambert, G. Naysmith, (R. Anderson)
Substitutes not used: P. Gallacher, J. McFadden, S. Gemmill, P. Devlin
Referee: Alain Sars (France)
Attendance: 7,000

Saturday, 29th March, 2003 – Hampden Park, Glasgow

SCOTLAND 2 — **ICELAND 1**
K. Miller, L. Wilkie — Gudjohnsen
Scotland: R. Douglas, G. Alexander, L. Wilkie, C. Dailly, S. Pressley, B. Ferguson, S. Crawford, P. Lambert, K. Miller, (J. McNamara), D. Hutchison, (P. Devlin), G. Naysmith
Substitutes not used: P. Gallacher, C. Cameron, S. Gemmill, R. Malcolm, A. Gray
Iceland: Arason, Thorsteinsson, Vidarsson, (I. Sigurdsson), L. Sigurdsson, Gunnarsson, R. Kristinsson, Bergsson, Ingimarsson, E. Gudjohnsen, J. Gudjonsson, Gretarsson
Substitutes not used: B. Kristinsson, Marteinsson, T. Gudjonsson, Einarsson, Baldvinsson
Referee: Rene H.J. Temmink (Holland)
Attendance: 37,938

Kenny Miller

Wednesday, 2nd April, 2003 – S. Darius & S. Girenas Sport C., Kaunas

LITHUANIA 1 — **SCOTLAND 0**
Razanauskas
Lithuania: Stauce, Semberas, Dedura, Barasa, Petrenko, (Maciulevicius), Zvirgzdauskas, Morinas, Mikalajunas, (Buitkus), Jankauskas, (Formenko), Razanauskas, Gleveckas
Substitutes not used: Karcemarskas, Papeckys, Poderis, Dziaukstas
Scotland: P. Gallacher, G. Alexander, L. Wilkie, C. Dailly, S. Pressley, J. McNamara, (A. Gray), S. Crawford, (P. Devlin), P. Lambert, K. Miller, D. Hutchison, (C. Cameron), G. Naysmith
Substitutes not used: R. Malcolm, S. Gemmill, M. Ross, K. Arthur
Referee: Fritz Stuchlik (Austria)
Attendance: 6,400

Saturday, 7th June, 2003 – Hampden Park, Glasgow

SCOTLAND 1 — **GERMANY 1**
K. Miller — Bobic
Scotland: R. Douglas, M. Ross, (J. McNamara), G. Naysmith, C. Dailly, S. Pressley, A. Webster, P. Devlin, (G. Rae), P. Lambert, K. Miller, (S. Thompson), S. Crawford, C. Cameron
Substitutes not used: N. Alexander, G. Alexander, A. Gray, L. Wilkie
Germany: Kahn, Friedrich, Rau, (Freier), Worns, Ramelow, Frings, Bobic, Schneider, (Kehl), Klose, (Neuville), Ballack, Jeremies
Substitutes not used: Rost, Rehmer, Hinkel, Kuranyi
Referee: Domenico Messina (Italy)
Attendance: 48,047

GROUP TABLE

	P	W	D	L	F	A	PTS
GERMANY	5	3	2	0	8	3	11
ICELAND	5	3	0	2	9	5	9
SCOTLAND	5	2	2	1	7	5	8
LITHUANIA	6	2	1	3	4	9	7
FAROE ISLANDS	5	0	1	4	4	10	1

FULL INTERNATIONAL FRIENDLY MATCHES

Wednesday, 21st August, 2002 – Hampden Park, Glasgow

SCOTLAND 0 — **DENMARK 1**
Sand
Scotland: R. Douglas, M. Ross, G. Naysmith, (A. Johnston), D. Weir, (S. Severin), C. Dailly, B. Ferguson, K. McNaughton, (S. Crainey), R. Stockdale, (G. Alexander), K. Kyle, P. Lambert, (D. McInnes), S. Thompson, (S. Dobie)
Substitutes not used: N. Sullivan, L. Wilkie, G. Williams, P. Gallacher
Denmark: Sorensen, Bogelund, (Gronkjaer), Henriksen, (Lustu), Laursen, (Wieghorst), N. Jensen, Poulsen, Gravesen, (C. Jensen), Lovenkrands, (Silberbauer), Tomasson, Rommedahl, (Michaelsen), Sand
Substitute not used: S. Jensen
Referee: Leslie Irvine (Northern Ireland)
Attendance: 28,766

Barry Ferguson and Thomas Gravesen

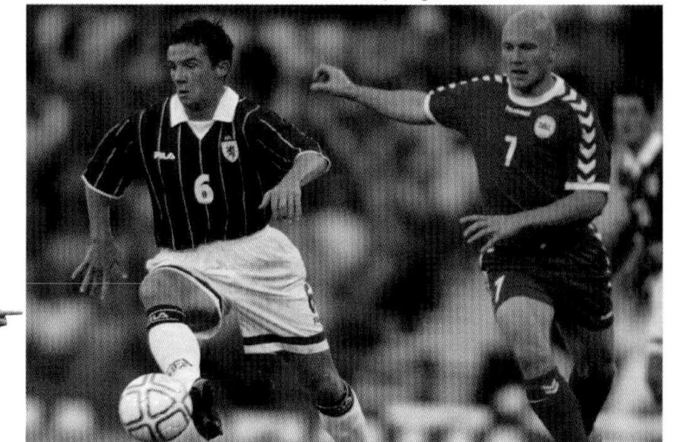

Tuesday, 15th October, 2002 – Easter Road Stadium, Edinburgh

SCOTLAND 3 — **CANADA 1**
S. Crawford (2), S. Thompson — de Rosario
Scotland: P. Gallacher, M. Ross, (C. Davidson), L. Wilkie, (I. Murray), S. Pressley, C. Dailly, R. Anderson, G. Alexander, S. Crawford, (K. Kyle), S. Thompson, (J. McFadden), S. Gemmill, (S. Severin), P. Devlin
Substitutes not used: N. Alexander, G. Caldwell, G. Williams

Canada: Hirschfeld, Fenwick, Hastings, McKenna, Pozniak, Imhof, (Xausa), Stalteri, Nsaliwa, Radzinski, de Rosario, de Guzman
Substitutes not used: Nash, Hutchinson, Onstad
Referee: Luc Huyghe (Belgium)
Attendance: 16,207

Wednesday, 20th November, 2002 – Estadio Primeiro de Maio, Braga

PORTUGAL 2 — **SCOTLAND 0**
Pauleta (2)
Portugal: Quim, (Nelson), Couto, Rui Jorge, (Ribeiro), Meira, Rocha, Figo, (Ferreira), Rui Costa, (Mendes), Conceicao, Simao, (Neca), Tiago, (Assis) Pauleta, (Nuno Gomes)
Substitutes not used: Silva, Sergio
Scotland: R. Douglas, R. Anderson, (D. McInnes), M. Ross, (P. Devlin), S. Pressley, C. Dailly, L. Wilkie, (S. Severin), G. Alexander, S. Crawford, S. Dobie, (K. Kyle), P. Lambert, (G. Williams), G. Naysmith
Substitutes not used: P. Gallacher, S. Caldwell, N. Alexander
Referee: Vierol Anghelieni (Romania)
Attendance: 8,000

Wednesday, 12th February, 2003 – Hampden Park, Glasgow

SCOTLAND 0 — **REPUBLIC OF IRELAND 2**
Kilbane, Morrison
Scotland: N. Sullivan, (P. Gallacher), R. Anderson, G. Naysmith, S. Caldwell, C. Dailly, B. Ferguson, (C. Cameron), G. Alexander, S. Crawford, (S. Thompson), D. Hutchison, (P. Devlin), P. Lambert, (S. Gemmill), N. McCann, (J. Smith)
Substitutes not used: K. Miller, S. Dobie, K. Kyle, J. McNamara, N. Alexander, R. Malcolm
Republic of Ireland: Kiely, (Colgan), Carr, Harte, O'Shea, (Dunne), Breen, (O'Brien), Holland, Reid, (Carsley), Kinsella, (Healy), Doherty, (Connolly), Morrison, Kilbane
Substitutes not used: Maybury, McPhail, Barrett
Referee: Eric Braamhaar (Holland)
Attendance: 33,337

Wednesday, 30th April, 2003 – Hampden Park, Glasgow

SCOTLAND 0 — **AUSTRIA 2**
Kirchler, Haas
Scotland: P. Gallacher, L. Wilkie, A. Webster, C. Dailly, (S. Gemmill), S. Pressley, C. Burley, (C. Cameron), P. Devlin, (J. Smith), D. Hutchison, (K. Miller), S. Thompson, (S. Crawford), J. McFadden, G. Naysmith
Substitutes not used: N. Alexander, G. Alexander, R. Malcolm, M. Ross, K. Arthur
Austria: Mandl, Scharner, Ehmann, Stranzl, Dospel, Aufhauser, Schopp, Flogel, (Hieblinger), Haas, (Brunmayr), Wagner, Kirchler, (Herzog)
Substitutes not used: Payer, Pogatetz, Wallner, Holler
Referee: Nicolai Vollquartz (Denmark)
Attendance: 12,189

Tuesday, 27th May, 2003 – Tynecastle Stadium, Edinburgh

SCOTLAND 1 — **NEW ZEALAND 1**
S. Crawford — Nelsen
Scotland: R. Douglas, M. Ross, (G. Alexander), G. Naysmith, A. Webster, S. Pressley, C. Dailly, P. Devlin, J. McNamara, (B. Kerr), K. Kyle, (A. Gray), S. Crawford, J. McFadden
Substitutes not used: N. Alexander, S. Caldwell, G. Caldwell, I. Murray, K. Arthur
New Zealand: Utting, (Batty), Mulligan, (Oughton), Zoricich, (Smith), Lines, (Bouckenooghe), Burton, Jackson, (De Gregorio), Nelsen, Coveny, Elliott, Davis, Hickey
Substitutes not used: Hay, Paston
Referee: Martin Ingvarsson (Sweden)
Attendance: 10,016

James McFadden shoots against New Zealand

FUTURE INTERNATIONAL FRIENDLY MATCHES

Tuesday, 17th December, 2002 – Bruchweg Stadium, Mainz

GERMANY "B" 3 — **SCOTLAND FUTURE 3**
Kuranyi, Meier, Voigt — K. Kyle, S. Hughes, R. Malcolm
Germany: Jentsch, Hinkel, (Kringe), Voigt, Preuss, Franz, Schindzielorz, Bierofka, Ernst, Daun, Kuranyi, (Meier), Frommer, (Meyer)
Substitutes not used: Borel, Borowski
Scotland: P. Gallacher, S. Caldwell, R. Malcolm, G. Caldwell, S. Crainey, (P. Canero), G. Rae, (J. Kennedy), B. Nicholson, (S. Hughes), I. Murray, S. Glass, (S. Murray), K. Miller, (K. Harper), K. Kyle
Substitutes not used: G. Alexander, J.P. McGovern, K. Arthur
Referee: L. Duhamel (France)
Attendance: 5,200

25th February, 2003 – Ataturk Stadium, Antalya

TURKEY "B" 1 — **SCOTLAND FUTURE 1**
Ceyhun — A. Gray
Turkey: Gokhan, Gunes, Orhan, Erdinc, Erman, Hakan, Karadeniz, Veysel, Necati, (Mustafa), Ozgur, Ceyhun
Substitutes not used: Bora, Timucin, Ahmet, Fazli, Bekiroglu, Seyhan
Scotland: P. Gallacher, R. Stockdale, (P. Canero), A. Webster, R. Malcolm, G. Caldwell, G. Williams, A. Gray, B. Nicholson, K. Kyle, (D. Noble), D. Hutchison, K. Harper, (J. McAllister)
Substitutes not used: D. Stillie, C. Doig, S. Wilson, W. Cummings, K. Arthur
Referee: Peter Sippel (Germany)
Attendance: 2,000

Tuesday, 20th May, 2003 – Firhill Stadium, Glasgow

SCOTLAND FUTURE 2 — **NORTHERN IRELAND "B" 1**
D. Hutchison, K. Kyle — Jones
Scotland: P. Gallacher, (K. Arthur), G. Alexander, G. Naysmith, C. Dailly, S. Caldwell, (D. Fletcher), G. Caldwell, P. Devlin, B. Kerr, K. Kyle, (S. Lynch), D. Hutchison, (A. Gray), J. McFadden, (M. Ross)
Substitutes not used: D. Noble, D. Soutar
Northern Ireland: Evans, (Morris), Duff, Grant, McCann, Craigan, (Holmes), McAuley, (Hamilton), Griffin, Jones, (Hamill), Doherty, Kirk, Smith, Elliott, (Carlisle)
Referee: Michael McCurry (Scotland)
Attendance: 1,502

EUROPEAN "UNDER-21" CHAMPIONSHIP

Friday 11th October, 2002 – Kaplakrikavollur, Hafnarfjordur

ICELAND 0 — **SCOTLAND 2**
K. Kyle, S. Lynch
Iceland: Johannsson, Skulason, Gudmundsson, Arnarson, (Thorvaldsson), Bjornsson, Sigurdsson, Steinsson, Danielsson, (Hjalmsson), Sigurdsson, Kristjansson, Bjornsson, (Thorsteinsson)
Substitutes not used: Jonsson, Mete
Scotland: D. Soutar, G. Caldwell, I. Murray, J. Kennedy, C. Doig, B. Kerr, S. Duff, G. Williams, K. Kyle, S. Hughes, (D. Fletcher), T. McManus, (S. Lynch)
Substitutes not used: C. Gordon, J. McCunnie, S. Simmons, S. Hammell, S. McLean
Referee: Sten Kaldma (Estonia)
Attendance: 1,000

Friday 28th March, 2003 – Broadwood Stadium, Cumbernauld

SCOTLAND 1 — **ICELAND 0**
S. Maloney
Scotland: D. Soutar, G. Caldwell, I. Murray, J. Kennedy, A. Webster, B. Kerr, P. Canero, G. Williams, K. Kyle, M. Stewart, (S. Hughes), J. McFadden, (S. Maloney)
Substitutes not used: A. McGregor, C. Doig, S. Pearson, T. McManus, S. Lynch
Iceland: Johannsson, Arnarson, Eiriksson, Mete, Gudmundsson, Steinsson, Johannsson, (Sigurdsson), Danielsson, Bjornsson, Thorvaldsson, Thorsteinsson, (Snorrason)
Substitutes not used: Halldorsson, Kristjansson, Elisabetarson
Referee: Kostadin Kostadinov (Bulgaria)
Attendance: 3,162

Tuesday, 1st April, 2003 – Zalgiris Stadium, Vilinius

LITHUANIA 2 — **SCOTLAND 1**
Kucys, Cesnauskis — K. Kyle
Lithuania: Karcemarskas, Paulauskas, Petreikis, Klimavicius, Mikuckis, Savenas, Tamasauskas, Kucyz, (Miceika), Stankevicius, (Radzinevivius), Mizigurskis, (Kalonas), Cesnauskis
Substitutes not used: Rapalis, Majus, Kavaliauskas, Mikoliunas

Scotland: D. Soutar, G. Caldwell, I. Murray, J. Kennedy, A. Webster, B. Kerr, P. Canero, (S. Lynch), G. Williams, K. Kyle, M. Stewart, J. McFadden, (S. Maloney)
Substitutes not used: A. McGregor, D. McCracken, S. Hammell, T. McManus, S. Hughes
Referee: Jari Maisonlahti (Finland)
Attendance: 2,000

Friday, 6th June, 2003 – Rugby Park, Kilmarnock

SCOTLAND 2 — GERMANY 2
S. Lynch, G. Caldwell — Lauth, Balitsch

Scotland: D. Soutar, G. Caldwell, I. Murray, J. Kennedy, S. Crainey, B. Kerr, P. Canero, S. Pearson, K. Kyle, D. Fletcher, (P. Gallagher), S. Lynch, (T. McManus)
Substitutes not used: C. Gordon, D. McCracken, N. Montgomery, S. Hammell, S. Duff
Germany: Starke, Preuss, Madlung, Tiffert, Lapaczinski, Gemiti, Feulner, (Schlicke), Balitsch, Auer, (Kringe) Hitzlsperger, (Azaouagh), Lauth
Substitutes not used: Haas, Franz, Burkhart
Referee: Luis Medina Cantalejo (Spain)
Attendance: 5,052

Gary Caldwell (centre) celebrates his goal

GROUP TABLE

	P	W	D	L	F	A	PTS
LITHUANIA	5	3	0	2	8	7	9
GERMANY	3	2	1	0	7	3	7
SCOTLAND	4	2	1	1	6	4	7
ICELAND	4	0	0	4	1	8	0

UNDER-21 INTERNATIONAL FRIENDLY MATCHES

Tuesday, 20th August, 2002 – East End Park, Dunfermline

SCOTLAND 1 — DENMARK 1
P. Canero — Bechmann

Scotland: D. Soutar, (A. McGregor), J. McCunnie, I. Murray, A. Dowie, C. Doig, B. Kerr, P. Canero, S. Hughes, (S. McLean), G. O'Connor, M. Stewart, (T. McManus), S. Maloney, (J. McFadden)
Substitutes not used: J. Kennedy, D. McCracken, S. Duff, D. Fletcher, S. Lynch
Denmark: Andersen, Hansen, Andreasen, Bischoff, (Krause), Kristiansen, Wurtz, Traore, (Kamper), Frederiksen, (Pedersen), Sorensen, Hakansson, (Jensen), Bechmann
Substitute not used: Serensen
Referee: David Malcolm (Northern Ireland)
Attendance: 2,914

Wednesday, 4th September, 2002 – New Douglas Park, Hamilton

SCOTLAND 2 — ISRAEL 1
S. Maloney, J. Kennedy — Barda

Scotland: A. McGregor, (C. Gordon), J. McCunnie, (J. Kennedy), S. Hammell, A. Dowie, (G. Caldwell), C. Doig, B. Kerr, S. Duff, S. Pearson, (B. O'Brien), J. McFadden, (S. Lynch), M. Stewart, S. Maloney
Substitutes not used: S. McLean, T. McManus, D. Soutar

Shaun Maloney (11) scores with a header for the Under-21s

Israel: Sekel, Moosa, Siam, (Nagar), Mishaeloff, Cohen, Gazal, Ohayon, (Israelevich), Luzon, (Biton), Degu, (Azu), Barda, Golan, (Mashiach)
Substitutes not used: Nir, Attia
Referee: John Feighery (Republic of Ireland)
Attendance: 3,021

Friday, 6th September, 2002 – St. Mirren Park, Paisley

SCOTLAND 1 — NORTHERN IRELAND 1
Clyde (o.g.) — McEvilly

Scotland: D. Soutar, (D. McEwan), J. McCunnie, S. Hammell, J. Kennedy, C. Doig, B. Kerr, P. Canero, (S. Duff), S. Pearson, (S. Lynch), J. McFadden, (S. McLean), M. Stewart, S. Maloney, (T. McManus)
Substitutes not used: A. Dowie, B. O'Brien, A. McGregor
Northern Ireland: Morris, Baird, Capaldi, Clyde, Simms, Melaugh, Close, (McCann), Toner, McEvilly, (McFlynn), Browne, (Braniff), Morrison, (McCourt)
Substitutes not used: Hunter, Herron, Haveron
Referee: Egill Mar Markusson (Iceland)
Attendance: 2,351

Monday, 14th October, 2002 – Palmerston Park, Dumfries

SCOTLAND 2 — GHANA 0
G. Caldwell, B. Kerr

Scotland: C. Gordon, (D. McEwan), G. Caldwell, S. Hammell, J. Kennedy, C. Doig, B. Kerr, S. Duff, (A. McParland), I. Murray, (S. Simmons), J. McFadden, (S. McLean), S. Hughes, (B. O'Brien), T. McManus, (S. Lynch)
Ghana: Agyepong, Lukman, (Rasheed), Thompson, Ocansey, Quartey, Mantey, (Agyemang), Peprah, Habib, Coleman, Chibsah, Muntari
Substitutes not used: Egyir, Gariba, Amponsah
Referee: Eric Blareau (Belgium)
Attendance: 3,119

Tuesday, 19th November, 2002 – Stade Edmond Machtens, Molenbeek

BELGIUM 2 — SCOTLAND 0
Chatelle, Snelders

Belgium: Mardulier, (Bourdon), Vanbeuren, (De Decker), Tucari, Deschacht, van Damme, (Ingrao), Mundingayi, (Swerts), Chatelle, (Vangeffelen), Geraerts, Huysegems, (Snelders), de Beule, (Dinbala-Mawongo), Blondel
Scotland: D. Soutar, (A. McGregor), C. Doig, (S. Hammell), G. Caldwell, J. Kennedy, S. Crainey, S. Hughes, (S. Pearson), I. Murray, B. Kerr, S. Duff, (P. Canero), S. Maloney, (S. McLean), S. Lynch, (K. Boyd)
Substitute not used: A. Dowie
Referee: Frederick Mercie (Belgium)
Attendance: 643

Scotland v Republic of Ireland (under-21) – Simon Lynch scores

Tuesday, 11th February, 2003 – Rugby Park, Kilmarnock

SCOTLAND 2 — REPUBLIC OF IRELAND 0
S. Maloney, S. Lynch

Scotland: D. Soutar, (A. McGregor), G. Caldwell, S. Hammell, J. Kennedy, C. Doig, (S. Crainey), B. Kerr, P. Canero, (S. Duff), S. Pearson, (S. Hughes), K. Kyle, (S. Lynch), G. Williams, (M. Stewart), S. Maloney, (J. McFadden)
Substitutes not used: A. Dowie, D. Mackie, L. Miller, C. Gordon
Republic of Ireland: Stack, Brennan, Tierney, (R. Byrne), C. Byrne, Goodwin, Thompson, (Hunt), Butler, Reid, (Thornton), Barrett, (Daly), Dempsey, (Lester), Hoolahan, (Melligan)
Substitute not used: Murphy
Referee: Ben Haverkort (Holland)
Attendance: 2,987

Tuesday, 29th April, 2003 – Dens Park Stadium, Dundee

SCOTLAND 1 — **AUSTRIA 0**

S. Lynch

Scotland: D. Soutar, (A. McGregor), G. Caldwell, S. Pearson, J. Kennedy, S. Crainey, B. Kerr, P. Canero, (S. Duff), S. Hughes, (D. Noble), T. McManus, (S. Lynch), M. Stewart, (N. Montgomery), S. Maloney

Substitutes not used: S. Dillon, C. Gordon

Austria: H. Berger, Ibertsberger, Pircher, M. Berger, (Pauschenwein), Horvath, (Saumel), Ziervogel, Parapatits, (Kuhrer), Kulovits, Linz, (Lasnik), Kienast, (D. Berger), Sturm

Substitutes not used: Gspurning, Kampel

Referee: Emil Laursen (Denmark)

Attendance: 2,085

UEFA UNDER-19 CHAMPIONSHIP
First Qualifying Round
Qualifying Group 10 – Tournament in Slovenia

Monday, 21st October, 2002 – Ljudski vrt, Maribor

SLOVENIA 1 — **SCOTLAND 2**

Bozic — C. Beattie (2)

Slovenia: Handanovic, Brecko, Hadzic, Berko, Jesenicnik, (Urbanc), Kelhar, Bozic, (Semler), Sehic, Dedic, Dare, (Komljenovic), Robnik

Substitutes not used: Dario, Pevec, Sikur, Stevanovic

Scotland: K. Renton, M. Wilson, S. Morrison, W. Kinniburgh, C. McLeod, C. Beattie, (S. Whittaker), P. Lawson, G. Weir, R. Foy, (A. Barrowman), T. Brighton, G. Law

Substitutes not used: C. Samson, P. Sweeney, R. Harding, K. Thomson, S. Fagan

Referee: Athanassios Briakos (Greece)

Wednesday, 23rd October, 2002 – Sportni Park, Beltinci

SCOTLAND 1 — **YUGOSLAVIA 4**

G. Weir — Jankovic, Milovanovic, Mrda, Basta

Scotland: K. Renton, M. Wilson, S. Morrison, W. Kinniburgh, C. McLeod, C. Beattie, P. Lawson, (P. Sweeney), G. Weir, T. Brighton, (K. Thomson), G. Law, (R. Harding), S. Whittaker

Substitutes not used: C. Samson, R. Foy, S. Fagan, A. Barrowman

Yugoslavia: Kahriman, Andjelkovic, Tosic, Lazarevic, Gegic, Milovanovic, Krasic, Basta, Mrda, (Purovic), Jankovic, (Rahdjelovic), Perovic, (Stanic)

Substitutes not used: Dimovski, Dronov

Referee: Martin Hansson (Sweden)

Friday, 25th October, 2002 – Lesoplast, Krizevci

ICELAND 1 — **SCOTLAND 2**

Sigurjonsson — C. Beattie (2)

Iceland: Davidson, Gudmundsson, Elisabetarson, Valdimarsson, (Gislason),Vidarsson, Gardarsson, Palmason, Helgason, Sigurjonsson, (Gudmundsson), Magnusson, Thorvardarson, (Hauksson)

Substitutes not used: Kristjanson, Hallfredsson, Josepsson

Scotland: C. Samson, M. Wilson, S. Morrison, W. Kinniburgh, C. McLeod, C. Beattie, P. Lawson, G. Weir, R. Foy, (A. Barrowman), T. Brighton, (K. Thomson), G. Law, (P. Sweeney)

Substitutes not used: K. Renton, R. Harding, S. Whittaker, S. Fagan

Referee: Vitaliy Godulyan (Ukraine)

GROUP TABLE

	P	W	D	L	F	A	PTS
SLOVENIA	3	2	0	1	7	4	6
YUGOSLAVIA	3	2	0	1	8	6	6
SCOTLAND	3	2	0	1	5	6	6
ICELAND	3	0	0	3	3	7	0

SCOTLAND UNDER-19 FRIENDLY MATCHES

Wednesday, 25th September, 2002 – Strathclyde Homes Stadium, Dumbarton

SCOTLAND 2 — **SWITZERLAND 1**

C. Beattie (2) — Vonlanthen

Scotland: K. Renton, R. Harding, (A. Barrowman), S. Morrison, W. Kinniburgh, C. McLeod, P. Sweeney, (S. Fagan), S. Whittaker, (G. Law), P. Lawson, C. Beattie, R. Foy, T. Brighton, (K. Thomson)

Referee: Charlie Richmond (Scotland)

Attendance: 250

Scotland v Iceland (under-19) Ross McLeod and Gunnar Orn Jonsson

Tuesday, 22nd April, 2003 – Forthbank Stadium, Stirling

SCOTLAND 1 — **ICELAND 2**

J. Winter — Finnbogason, Bjornsson

Scotland: A. Reid, R. McLeod, (D. Campbell), S. Low, P. Quinn, S. Smith, G. Irvine, J. Winter, R. Wallace, M. Baxter, K. Wright, (M. Woods), A. Ferguson, (R. Foster)

Referee: Craig Thomson (Scotland)

Attendance: 350

Thursday, 24th April, 2003 – Recreation Park, Alloa

SCOTLAND 3 — **ICELAND 3**

D. Campbell, R. Wallace, P. Quinn — Thorarinsson, Johnson, Finnbogason

Scotland: J. Hutchison, S. Low, G. Irvine, (R. McLeod), J. Winter, S. Tarditi, M. Woods, R. Wallace, (A. Ferguson), F. Coyle, S. Watt, (P. Quinn), D. Campbell, (S. Anderson), R. Foster, (S. Brown)

Referee: Iain Brines (Scotland)

Attendance: 275

UNDER-18 INTERNATIONAL FRIENDLY MATCHES

Tuesday, 12th November, 2002 – Hasetal Stadium, Herzlake

GERMANY 1 — **SCOTLAND 0**

Glasner

Scotland: A. Reid, F. Coyle, R. McLeod, S. Low, S. Watt, C. Adams, (D. Pinkowski), G. Irvine, J. Winter, D. Clarkson, (A. Ferguson), R. Wilkie, R. Wallace

Referee: Mike Otte (Germany)

Attendance: 5,500

Thursday, 14th November, 2002 – August Wenzel Stadium, Barsinghausen

GERMANY 2 — **SCOTLAND 0**

Podolski, Sahr

Scotland: A. Reid, (A. Brown), F. Coyle, (G. Irvine), S. Low, (S. Watt), C. Adams, (D. Pinkowski), J. Winter, D. Clarkson, R. Wilkie, (J. Doyle), R. Wallace, J. McNulty, (R. McLeod), B. McLean, (A. Ferguson), P. Quinn

Referee: Babak Rafati (Germany)

Attendance: 1,500

UEFA UNDER-17 CHAMPIONSHIP
First Qualifying Round
Qualifying Group 11 - Tournament in Azerbaijan

Thursday, 3rd October, 2002 – Mehti Huseynzade, Sumgayit

SCOTLAND 3 — **UKRAINE 2**

R. Davidson, K. McKinlay (2) — Yaroshenko (2)

Scotland: E. McLean, S. Campbell, S. McDaid, D. Campbell, C. Reid, C. Mulgrew, S. Anderson, (A. Dick), R. Davidson, M. Woods, K. McKinlay, (M. Lombardi), G. Watson

Substitutes not used: C. Reidford, M. Pelosi, M. Gardyne, G. Port, R. Quinn

Ukraine: Kopyl, Chygrynskiy, Kachan, Yatsenko, (Milko), Khalyavka, Yaroshenko, Komar, (Korolkov), Makoviychuk, Krawtchenko, Yermak, Kruglyak, (Karpenko)

Substitutes not used: Lenko, Antonyuk, Patula, Kocherov

Referee: Gerald Lehner (Austria)

Saturday, 5th October, 2002 – Shafa, Baku

SCOTLAND 2 — **AZERBAIJAN 1**
C. Reid, M. Woods — Akhmad

Scotland: E. McLean, S. McDaid, S. Campbell, C. Reid, C. Mulgrew, (R. Quinn), D. Campbell, R. Davidson, M. Woods, K. McKinlay, (M. Gardyne), M. Pelosi, G. Port, (A. Dick)
Substitutes not used: C. Reidford, S. Anderson, G. Watson, M. Lombardi
Azerbaijan: Arhayev, Gasimov, Yusifov, Nurmagamed, Abdullayev, (Abbasov), Valiyev, Akhmad, Rajabov, Gashimov, (Elshad), Abdul, (Vugar), Akim
Substitutes not used: Iikin, Elmar, Aliyev, Nadizov
Referee: Johny ver Eecke (Belgium)

Monday, 7th October, 2002 – Mehti Huseynzade, Sumgayit

TURKEY 3 — **SCOTLAND 1**
R. Davidson (o.g.), Ozturk (2) — D. Campbell

Turkey: Topaloglu, Akyuz, Sam, Aydin, Yasar, (Donmez), Ozturk, Bayraktar, Ozkan, Kahraman, Oruc, (Guzeldal), Kaya
Substitutes not used: Yaranli, Arat, Gursoy, Ucar
Scotland: C. Reidford, A. Dick, (M. Pelosi), S. McDaid, S. Campbell, C. Reid, D. Campbell, S. Anderson, R. Davidson, M. Woods, M. Gardyne, (C. Mulgrew), R. Quinn, (M. Lombardi)
Substitutes not used: E. McLean, K. McKinlay, G. Port, G. Watson
Referee: Gerald Lehner (Austria)

GROUP TABLE

	P	W	D	L	F	A	PTS
SCOTLAND	3	2	0	1	6	6	6
AZERBAIJAN	3	1	1	1	5	5	4
TURKEY	3	1	1	1	5	4	4
UKRAINE	3	0	2	1	7	8	2

Second Qualifying Round
Qualifying Group 6 - Tournament in England

Wednesday, 12th March, 2003 – Haig Avenue, Southport

SLOVAKIA 0 — **SCOTLAND 0**

Slovakia: Kosicky, Pekarik, Mackovcin, Lintner, Janek, (Sebik), Izvolt, (Levicky), Bernat, Bartos, Gajdos, Piroska, Halaska
Substitutes not used: Hrdlicka, Lisivka, Novysedlak, Hagara, Kubanka
Scotland: E. McLean, G. Watson, S. McDaid, S. Campbell, C. Reid, C. Mulgrew, D. Campbell, S. Anderson, (R. Quinn), R. Davidson, (M. Gardyne), M. Woods, R. McCormack, (K. McKinlay)
Substitutes not used: D. Johnson, C. Sives, A. Dick, J. Reilly
Referee: Asif Kenan (Israel)

Friday, 14th March, 2003 – Deva Stadium, Chester

CZECH REPUBLIC 0 — **SCOTLAND 3**
K. McKinlay, D.Campbell, R. Davidson

Czech Republic: Svenger, Parys, Ciganek, Sedlacek, Blazek, Fiala, Malcharek, Tomasak, Hanzlik, (Lisicky), Vorisek, Honka, (Zachoval)
Substitutes not used: Kraus, Kral, Filip, Svec
Scotland: E. McLean, G. Watson, S. McDaid, S. Campbell, C. Reid, C. Mulgrew, D. Campbell, (J. Reilly), M. Gardyne, K. McKinlay, M. Woods, R. McCormack, (R. Davidson)
Substitutes not used: D. Johnson, S. Anderson, R. Quinn, C. Sives, A. Dick
Referee: Nebojsa Rabrenovic (Serbia & Montenegro)

Sunday, 16th March, 2003 – Prenton Park, Birkenhead

ENGLAND 2 — **SCOTLAND 0**
Noble, Lennon

England: Heaton, Ifil, Noble, Taylor, Crainie, Doyle, Moore, Leadbitter, Holmes, (Lennon), Taylor, Jarvis, (Morrison)
Substitutes not used: Martin, Giddings, O'Hara, McMahon, Forte
Scotland: E. McLean, G. Watson, S. McDaid, S. Campbell, C. Reid, C. Mulgrew, D. Campbell, R. Davidson, M. Woods, M. Gardyne, K. McKinlay, (R. McCormack)
Substitutes not used: D. Johnson, S. Anderson, R. Quinn, C. Sives, A. Dick, J. Reilly
Referee: Nebojsa Rabrenovic (Serbia & Montenegro)

PLEASE NOTE: It was subsequently discovered that Michael Gardyne was not eligible to play for Scotland in the final match against England because of two previous cautions. The match was therefore recorded by UEFA as a statutory 3-0 win for England.

GROUP TABLE

	P	W	D	L	F	A	PTS
ENGLAND	3	3	0	0	9	0	9
SCOTLAND	3	1	1	1	3	2	4
CZECH REPUBLIC	3	1	0	2	3	5	3
SLOVAKIA	3	0	1	2	0	8	1

Viseu International Under-17 Tournament in Portugal

Wednesday, 9th April, 2003 – Estadio Municipal, Mangualde

PORTUGAL 4 — **SCOTLAND 2**
Dias, Freitas, Veloso, Curto — R. McCormack, R. Davidson

Scotland: E. McLean, G. Watson, S. McDaid, S. Campbell, C. Reid, C. Mulgrew, M. Gardyne, (D. Gribben), S. Anderson, (M. Pelosi), R. Davidson, M. Woods, R. McCormack, (R. Quinn)
Referee: Muhittin Bosat (Turkey)

Thursday, 10th April, 2003 – Estadio Municipal, Penalva do Castelo

TURKEY 1 — **SCOTLAND 0**
Ozturk

Scotland: E. McLean, S. McDaid, S. Campbell, C. Reid, R. Davidson, M. Woods, R. McCormack, R. Quinn, (C. Mulgrew), M. Pelosi, A. Dick, (G. Watson), J. Reilly, (M. Gardyne)
Referee: Kris Hermans (Belgium)

Saturday, 12th April, 2003 – Estadio Municipal, Santa Comba Dao

SCOTLAND 2 — **BELGIUM 1**
M. Gardyne, R. Davidson — van Geel

Scotland: C. Reidford, G. Watson, S. McDaid, S. Campbell, C. Reid, C. Mulgrew, M. Gardyne, S. Anderson, (R. Quinn), R. Davidson, M. Woods, D. Gribben
Referee: Antonio Costa (Portugal)

UNDER-17 INTERNATIONAL FRIENDLY MATCHES

Monday, 13th January, 2003 – Ta 'Qali Training Grounds, Valletta

MALTA 0 — **SCOTLAND 5**
M. Gardyne, S. Anderson, R. McCormack, D. Campbell, D. Gribben

Scotland: C. Reidford, G. Watson, (A. Dick), S. Campbell, C. Reid, (C. Sives), M. Pelosi, D. Campbell, (M. McGlinchey), S. Anderson, (J. Reilly), C. Mulgrew, (R. Quinn), M. Gardyne, R. Davidson, R. McCormack, (D. Gribben)
Referee: Marco Borg (Malta)

Wednesday, 15th January, 2003 – Ta 'Qali Training Grounds, Valletta

MALTA 2 — **SCOTLAND 3**
Schembri, G. Watson (o.g.) — D. Campbell, R. McCormack, R.Davidson

Scotland: D. Johnson, A. Dick, (G. Watson), S. Campbell, C. Reid, M. Pelosi, (C. Sives), M. Gardyne, (D. Campbell), S. Anderson, (J. Reilly), R. Quinn, C. Mulgrew, R. Davidson, (M. Lombardi), R. McCormack, (K. Macaulay)
Referee: Adrian Casha (Malta)

Monday, 10th February, 2003 – Belle Vue, Rhyl

WALES 0 — **SCOTLAND 1**
R. Davidson

Scotland: C. Reidford, M. Crainie, M. Pelosi, S. Campbell, (C. Sives), D. Campbell, S. Anderson, (J. Reilly), R. Davidson, R. McCormack, G. Watson, K. McKinlay, (R. Quinn), G. Port
Referee: Andrew Woodthorpe (England)

Wednesday, 12th February, 2003 – Meurig Park, Bethesda

WALES 4 — **SCOTLAND 0**
Kift, Stone, Evans, Fleetwood

Scotland: D. Johnson, M. Crainie, M. Pelosi, D. Campbell, (D. Gribben), R. Davidson, K. McKinlay, (R. McCormack), G. Port, (S. Anderson), R. Quinn, (G. Watson), A. Dick, (C. Reid), J. Reilly, C. Sives, (S. Campbell)
Referee: S.L. Evans (Wales)

UEFA CHAMPIONS LEAGUE

Third Qualifying Round - First Leg

Wednesday, 14th August, 2002, Celtic Park, Glasgow

CELTIC 3 — **BASEL 1**
Larsson, Sutton, Sylla — Gimenez

Celtic: Douglas, Sylla, Valgaeren, Balde, Larsson, Sutton, Lambert, (McNamara), Petta, (Guppy), Lennon, Petrov, Mjallby
Substitutes not used: Hedman, Hartson, Fernandez, Maloney, Crainey
Basel: Zuberbuhler, Zwyssig, (Quennoz), Esposito, Hakin Yakin, Barberis, Gimenez, Murat Yakin, Duruz, Cantaluppi, Ergic, (Varela), Rossi, (Turn)
Substitutes not used: Rapo, Koumantarakis, Degen, Atouba
Referee: Manuel Enrique Mejuto Gonzalez (Spain)
Attendance: 58,520

Third Qualifying Round - Second Leg

Wednesday, 28th August, 2002, Saint Jakob Park, Basel

BASEL 2 — **CELTIC 0**
Gimenez, Murat Yakin

Basel: Zuberbuhler, Quennoz, Varela, (Degen), Hakan Yakin, Barberis, Gimenez, (Koumantarakis), Murat Yakin, Duruz, Cantaluppi, Ergic, Rossi, (Turn)
Substitutes not used: Rapo, Savic, Streller, Atouba
Celtic: Douglas, Sylla, (Hartson), Valgaeren, Balde, Larsson, Sutton, Lambert, (Agathe), Laursen, (Guppy), Lennon, Petrov, Mjallby
Substitutes not used: McNamara, Hedman, Fernandez, Crainey
Referee: Anders Friske (Sweden)
Attendance: 30,000
(Aggregate 3-3) (Basel won on Away Goals Rule)

UEFA CUP

Qualifying Round - First Leg

Tuesday, 13th August, 2002, Rheinpark, Vaduz

VADUZ 1 — **LIVINGSTON 1**
Burgmeier — Rubio

Vaduz: Peiser, Martin Stocklasa, Brugnoli, Slekys, Obhafuoso, Perez, (Gerster), Burgmeier, (Beck), Zarn, Telser, Niederhauser, Merenda, (Polverino)
Substitutes not used: Silva, Walz, Buchel, Michael Stocklasa
Livingston: Broto, Brinquin, Bollan, Rubio, Wilson, (Hart), Camacho Barnola, (Bingham), Zarate, Quinovert, Makel, Bahoken, Dadi, (Xausa)
Substitutes not used: McEwan, Fullarton, Brittain, Toure-Maman
Referee: Sinisa Zrnic (Bosnia Herzegovina)
Attendance: 1,322

Thursday 15th August, 2002, Pittodrie Stadium, Aberdeen

ABERDEEN 1 — **NISTRU 0**
Mackie

Aberdeen: Kjaer, McNaughton, Anderson, McGuire, Bisconti, Darren Young, Derek Young, Mackie, Clark, (McAllister), Deloumeaux, D'Jaffo, (Mike)
Substitutes not used: Preece, Tiernan, O'Donoghue, Michie, Payne
Nistru: Dinov, Lupasco, (Matiura), Lascenkov, Kovalkov, Pidhayetskyy, Bursuc, Popescu, (Kopystyanskyy), Pogreban, Groshev, Blajco, (Yanchuc), Mincev
Substitutes not used: Bunea, Starovyk, Malitskyy
Referee: Tonny Kolbech Poulsen (Denmark)
Attendance: 9,894

Qualifying Round - Second Leg

Thursday, 29th August, 2002, West Lothian Courier Stadium, Livingston

LIVINGSTON 0 — **VADUZ 0**

Livingston: Broto, Brinquin, Bahoken, Andrews, Rubio, Toure-Maman, (Makel), Lovell, Quinovert, Bingham, (Dadi), Zarate, Camacho Barnola, (Wilson)
Substitutes not used: McEwan, Xausa, Dorado, Bollan
Vaduz: Peiser, Niederhauser, Obhafuoso, (Polverino), Martin Stocklasa, Brugnoli, Slekys, Merenda, (Buchel), Perez, Burgmeier, (Beck), Zarn, Telser
Substitutes not used: Silva, Walz, Michael Stocklasa, Ritter
Referee: Ivan Novak (Croatia)
Attendance: 7,219
(Aggregate 1-1)
(Livingston won on Away Goals Rule)

Republican, Kishinev

NISTRU 0 — **ABERDEEN 0**

Nistru: Dinov, Lupasco, Lascenkov, Kovalkov, Pidhayetskyy, Bursuc, Popescu, (Matiura), Kopystyanskyy, (Malitskyy), Groshev, Yanchuc, Blajco, (Pogreban)
Substitutes not used: Mura, Tcaciuc, Starovyk, Mincev
Aberdeen: Kjaer, Deloumeaux, McAllister, Anderson, McGuire, Derek Young, Darren Young, McNaughton, Tiernan, (Mackie), Bisconti, (Clark), D'Jaffo
Substitutes not used: Preece, Mike, O'Donoghue, Michie, Payne
Referee: Mustafa Culcu (Turkey)
Attendance: 6,000
(Aberdeen won 1-0 on Aggregate)

First Round - First Leg

Tuesday, 17th September, 2002, Pittodrie Stadium, Aberdeen

ABERDEEN 0 — **HERTHA 0**

Aberdeen: Kjaer, McNaughton, McAllister, (Fabiano), Anderson, McGuire, Bisconti, Darren Young, Derek Young, (Mike), Mackie, (Michie), Deloumeaux, D'Jaffo
Substitutes not used: Preece, Clark, Payne, Billio
Hertha: Kiraly, Friedrich, Sverrisson, Goor, Luizao, Marcelinho, Dardai, Neuendorf, (Mladenov), Hartmann, Tretschok, (Marx), Madlung
Substitutes not used: Fiedler, Karwan, Pinto, Rafael, Maas
Referee: Victor Jose Esquinas Torres (Spain)
Attendance: 10,180

Strahov Stadium, Prague

VIKTORIA ZIZKOV 2 — **RANGERS 0**
Pikl, Straceny

Viktoria Zizkov: Kucera, Buryan, Mlejnsky, Klimpl, Janousek, (Kruty), Smarda, Sabou, Scasny, Pikl, Straceny, (Licka), Chihuri, (Sebesta)
Substitutues not used: Vacek, Mikulik, Dirnbach, Chvatal
Rangers: Klos, Ricksen, Moore, (Konterman), Ferguson, Caniggia, (Latapy), Malcolm, de Boer, (Mols), Muscat, Ross, Arveladze, Lovenkrands
Substitutes not used: McGregor, Dodds, Gibson, Dowie
Referee: Julian Rodriguez Santiago (Spain)
Attendance: 3,427

Thursday, 19th September, 2002, Celtic Park, Glasgow

CELTIC 8 — **SUDUVA 1**
Larsson (3), Petrov, Sutton, Lambert, Hartson, Valgaeren — Radzinevicius

Celtic: Douglas, Sylla, Valgaeren, Balde, Larsson, (Hartson), Sutton, Lambert, Laursen, (Crainey), Lennon, (Fernandez), Petrov, Guppy
Substitutes not used: Gould, McNamara, Thompson, Agathe
Suduva: Padimanskas, Sendzikas, Suliaskas, Grigas, Devetinas, Kunevicius, Adomaitus, (Krapavicius), Zitinskas, (Stankevicius), Sidlauskas, (Maciulis), Slavickas, Radzinevicius
Substitutes not used: Balnys, Klevinskaus, Rukavicius, Larcenka
Referee: Miroslav Liba (Czech Republic)
Attendance: 36,824

Arnold Schwarzenegger Stadium, Graz

STURM 5 — **LIVINGSTON 2**
Wetl, Szabics, Dag, Mujiri (2) — Zarate, Lovell

Sturm: Hoffman, Neukirchner, Mahlich, Strafner, Brzeczek, (Korsos), Golemac, Wetl, Masudi, (Kienzl), Mujiri, Szabics, (Heldt), Dag
Substitutes not used: Weber, Krammer, Rauter, Amoah
Livingston: Broto, Brinquin, Bollan, Rubio, Andrews, Lovell, Quinovert, Bahoken,(Toure-Maman), Camacho Barnola, (Bingham), Zarate, Wilson, (Dadi)
Substitutes not used: McEwan, Dorado
Referee: Sergey Shebek (Ukraine)
Attendance: 2,785

First Round - Second Leg

Tuesday, 1st October, 2002, Olympiastadion, Berlin

HERTHA 1 **ABERDEEN 0**
Preetz
Hertha: Kiraly, Friedrich, van Burik, Goor, Luizao, (Preetz), Marcelinho, Pinto, Neuendorf, Hartmann, Marx, (Dardai), Rehmer, (Lapaczinski)
Substitutes not used: Fiedler, Tretschok, Maas, Madlung
Aberdeen: Kjaer, McAllister, Anderson, McGuire, Bisconti, (Billio), Darren Young, Derek Young, (Fabiano), Mackie, Rutkiewicz, Delomeaux, D'Jaffo, (Mike)
Substitutes not used: Preece, Clark, Michie, Payne
Referee: Grzegorz Gilewski (Poland)
Attendance: 30,770
(Hertha won 1-0 on Aggregate)

Thursday, 3rd October, 2002, West Lothian Courier Stadium, Livingston

LIVINGSTON 4 **STURM 3**
Wilson (2), Xausa, Andrews Szabics (2), Mujiri
Livingston: Broto, McNamee, Bollan, Rubio, Andrews, Quinovert, (Toure-Maman), Hart, O'Brien, (Camacho Barnola), Wilson, Xausa, (Zarate), Bingham
Substitutes not used: McEwan, Whalen, Brittain, Bahoken
Sturm: Hoffman, Neukirchner, Mahlich, Strafner, Brzeczek, (Bosnar), Golemac, Wetl, Masudi, (Heldt), Szabics, Mujiri, (Korsos), Dag
Substitutes not used: Weber, Pregelj, Kienzl, Amoah
Referee: Roy Helge Olsen (Norway)
Attendance: 5,020
(Sturm won 8-6 on Aggregate)

Ibrox Stadium, Glasgow

RANGERS 3 **VIKTORIA ZIZKOV 1**
de Boer (2), Arveladze Licka
Rangers: Klos, Ricksen, Moore, Amoruso, Numan, Ferguson, Arteta, Konterman, (Muscat), Lovenkrands, (McCann), Arveladze, de Boer, (Caniggia)
Substitutes not used: McGregor, Dodds, Muscat, Latapy, Ross
Viktoria Zizkov: Kucera, Buryan, Mlejnsky, Klimpl, Janousek, (Kruty), Smarda, Sabou, Scasny, Pikl, Straceny, (Dirnbach), Chihuri, (Licka)
Substitutes not used: Vacek, Novotny, Mikulik, Chvatal
Referee: Athanassios Briakos (Greece)
Attendance: 47,646
(Aggregate 3-3)
(Viktoria Zizkov won on Away Goals Rule)

S. Darius & S. Girenas Sport C, Kaunas

SUDUVA 0 **CELTIC 2**
Fernandez, Thompson
Suduva: Padimanskas, Sendzikas, (Krapavicius), Devetinas, Kunevicius, Grigas, Adomaitus, (Maciulis), Suliaskas, (Sidlauskas), Zitinskas, Larcenka, Slavickas, Radzinevicius
Substitutes not used: Balnys, Stankevicius, Rukavicius, Klevinskas
Celtic: Gould, McNamara, (Miller), Thompson, Hartson, Fernandez, Petta, (Lynch), Agathe, Healy, Maloney, Crainey, Kennedy, (Smith)
Substitutes not used: Douglas, Sylla, Balde, Laursen
Referee: Ferenc Bede (Hungary)
Attendance: 1,200
(Celtic won 10-1 on Aggregate)

Second Round - First Leg

Thursday, 31st October, 2002, Celtic Park, Glasgow

CELTIC 1 **BLACKBURN ROVERS 0**
Larsson
Celtic: Douglas, Valgaeren, Balde, Larsson, Thompson, Sutton, Lambert, (Hartson), Laursen, Agathe, (Sylla), Lennon, Petrov
Substitutes not used: Gould, Fernandez, Maloney, Guppy, Crainey
Blackburn Rovers: Friedel, Neill, Short, Kerimoglu, Flitcroft, Duff, (Dunn), Johansson,Yorke, Thompson, Taylor, Ostenstad, (Cole)
Substitutes not used: Jansen, Grabbi, Kelly, Gillespie, Douglas
Referee: Hermann Albrecht (Germany)
Attendance: 59,553

Second Round - Second Leg

Thursday, 14th November, 2002, Ewood Park, Blackburn

BLACKBURN 0 **CELTIC 2**
Larsson, Sutton
Blackburn Rovers: Friedel, Neill, Kerimoglu, Short, Dunn, Cole, Duff, Johansson, Curtis, (Gillespie), Yorke, (Jansen), Thompson
Substitutes not used: Kelly, Todd, Grabbi, Ostenstad, Douglas
Celtic: Douglas, Valgaeren, Balde, Larsson, Sutton, Hartson, (Lambert), Laursen, Agathe, (Sylla), Lennon, Petrov, (Thompson), Guppy
Substitutes not used: Gould, Fernandez, Maloney, Crainey
Referee: Cosimo Bolognino (Italy)
Attendance: 29,698
(Celtic won 3-0 on Aggregate)

Third Round - First Leg

Thursday, 28th November, 2002, Celtic Park, Glasgow

CELTIC 1 **CELTA VIGO 0**
Larsson
Celtic: Douglas, Valgaeren, Balde, Larsson, Sutton, Hartson, Laursen, Agathe, (Sylla), Lennon, Petrov, Guppy, (Thompson)
Substitutes not used: Gould, McNamara, Fernandez, Lambert, Maloney
Celta Vigo: Pinto, Silvinho, Berizzo, Mostovoi, Lopez, (McCarthy), Juanfran, Ignacio, Pardinas, Fernandez, Luccin, Catanha, (Edu)
Substitutes not used: Cavallero, Caceres, Giovanella, Coudet, Castro
Referee: Claude Colombo (France)
Attendance: 53,726

Third Round - Second Leg

Thursday, 12th December, 2002, Balaidos, Vigo

CELTA VIGO 2 **CELTIC 1**
Jesuli, McCarthy Hartson
Celta Vigo: Pinto, Caceres, Berizzo, (Castro), Lopez, Juanfran, Ignacio, Pardinas, (Vagner), Edu, Jesuli, Luccin, McCarthy
Substitutes not used: Cavallero, Silvinho, Giovanella, Coira, Coudet
Celtic: Douglas, Valgaeren, Balde, Larsson, Thompson, Sutton, Hartson, (McNamara), Laursen, Agathe, Lennon, (Lambert), Petrov
Substitutes not used: Gould, Sylla, Fernandez, Maloney, Guppy
Referee: Claus Bo Larsen (Denmark)
Attendance: 19,000
(Aggregate 2-2) (Celtic won on Away Goals Rule)

Fourth Round - First Leg

Thursday, 20th February, 2003, Celtic Park, Glasgow

CELTIC 3 **STUGGART 1**
Lambert, Maloney, Petrov Kuranyi
Celtic: Douglas, McNamara, Valgaeren, Balde, (Laursen), Thompson, (Smith), Sutton, Lambert, Agathe, Lennon, Petrov, Maloney
Substitutes not used: Marshall, Sylla, Fernandez, Healy, Guppy
Stuggart: Hildebrand, Hinkel, Bordon, Meira, Meissner, (Rundio), Balakov, Gerber, Amanatidis, (Dangelmayr), Gleb, (Carnell), Soldo, Kuranyi
Substitutes not used: Ernst, Tiffert, Seitz, Ganea
Referee: Pierluigi Collina (Italy)
Attendance: 59,000

Fourth Round – Second Leg

Thursday, 27th February, 2003, Gottlieb-Daimler, Stuttgart

STUTTGART 3 **CELTIC 2**
Tiffert, Gleb, Mutzel Thompson, Sutton
Stuttgart: Hildebrand, Hinkel, Wenzel, Balakov, Amanatidis, Gerber, (Seitz), Tiffert, (Mutzel), Gleb, Soldo, Kuranyi, Dangelmayr, (Ganea)
Substitutes not used: Ernst, Schneider, Luz, Rundio
Celtic: Douglas, Valgaeren, Balde, Thompson, Sutton, (McNamara), Hartson, Lambert, (Maloney), Laursen, Agathe, Lennon, Petrov
Substitutes not used: Marshall, Sylla, Guppy, Mjallby, Crainey
Referee: Jan W. Wegereef (Holland)
Attendance: 50,600
(Celtic won 5-4 on Aggregate)

Larsson gets the only goal in the first game against Blackburn

Quarter Finals – First Leg

Thursday, 13th March, 2003, Celtic Park, Glasgow

CELTIC 1	LIVERPOOL 1
Larsson	Heskey

Celtic: Douglas, Mjallby, Valgaeren, Balde, Smith, Lennon, Petrov, Thompson, (Guppy), Sutton, Larsson, (Lambert), Hartson
Substitutes not used: Marshall, Sylla, McNamara, Maloney, Crainey
Liverpool: Dudek, Carragher, Hyypia, Traore, Riise, Murphy, Hamann, Gerrard, Heskey, Diouf, (Biscan), Owen
Substitutes not used: Arphexad, Baros, Smicer, Diao, Cheyrou, Mellor
Referee: Terje Hauge (Norway)
Attendance: 59,759

Quarter Finals – Second Leg

Thursday, 20th March, 2003, Anfield, Liverpool

LIVERPOOL 0	CELTIC 2
	Thompson, Hartson

Liverpool: Dudek, Hyypia, Smicer, (Baros), Heskey, Owen, Murphy, Hamann, Gerrard, Riise, Carragher, Traore
Substitutes not used: Arphexad, Berger, Diao, Biscan, Cheyrou, Mellor
Celtic: Douglas, Sylla, (Smith), Valgaeren, Balde, Larsson, Thompson, Hartson, Lambert, (McNamara), Lennon, Petrov, Mjallby
Substitutes not used: Marshall, Laursen, Maloney, Guppy, Crainey
Referee: Markus Merk (Germany)
Attendance: 44,238
(Celtic won 3-1 on Aggregate)

Semi-Finals – First Leg

Thursday, 10th April, 2003, Celtic Park, Glasgow

CELTIC 1	BOAVISTA 1
Larsson	Valgaeren (o.g.)

Celtic: Douglas, Valgaeren, Balde, Larsson, Thompson, Hartson, Lambert, Agathe, (Sylla), Lennon, Petrov, (Fernandez), Mjallby
Substitutes not used: Marshall, McNamara, Maloney, Smith, Crainey
Boavista: Ricardo, Avalos, Turra, Eder, Erivan, Duda, Martelinho, Loja, Claudio, (Cafu), (Bosingwa), Pedrosa, (Oscar), Anunciacao
Substitutes not used: William, Silva, Jocivalter, Yuri
Referee: Frank De Bleeckere (Belgium)
Attendance: 60,000

Semi-Finals – Second Leg

Thursday, 24th April, 2003, Do Bessa, Porto

BOAVISTA 0	CELTIC 1
	Larsson

Boavista: Ricardo, Avalos, Eder, Erivan, (Jocivalter), Duda, Silva, (Claudio), Martelinho, Santos, Loja, Pedrosa, (Yuri), Anunciacao
Substitutes not used: William, Oscar, Bosingwa, Goulart
Celtic: Douglas, Valgaeren, (Smith), Balde, Larsson, Thompson, Hartson, Lambert, (Sutton), Agathe, Lennon, Petrov, Mjallby
Substitutes not used: Marshall, Sylla, McNamara, Laursen, Maloney
Referee: Valentin Ivanov (Russia)
Attendance: 11,000
(Celtic won 2-1 on Aggregate)

FINAL

Wednesday, 21st May, 2003, Olimpico Stadium, Seville

CELTIC 2	PORTO 3 (AET – 2-2 After 90 Minutes)
Larsson (2)	Derlei (2), Alenichev

Celtic: Douglas, Valgaeren, (Laursen), Balde, Mjallby, Agathe, Lennon, Lambert, (McNamara), Petrov, (Maloney), Thompson, Sutton, Larsson
Substitutes not used: Hedman, Sylla, Fernandez, Smith
Porto: Baia, Paulo Ferreira, Jorge Costa, (Emanuel), Carvalho, Valente, Costinha, (Ricardo Costa), Alenichev, Deco, Maniche, Capucho, (Marco Ferreira), Derlei
Substitutes not used: Simoes, Peixoto, Clayton, Tiago
Referee: Lubos Michel (Slovakia)
Attendance: 52,972

Derlei ends Celtic's dream by scoring the winner in extra time

scottish programme awards

SCOTTISH PROGRAMME OF THE YEAR AWARDS 2002/03

SCOTTISH PREMIER LEAGUE

02/03	(01/02)	CLUB
1.	(1)	Aberdeen
2.	(2)	Dunfermline Athletic
3=.	(3)	Hearts
3=.	(2 (FD))	Partick Thistle
5.	(5)	Dundee
6.	(4)	Dundee United
7.	(10)	Celtic
8.	(6)	Kilmarnock
9.	(11)	Livingston
10.	(9)	Rangers
11.	(7)	Hibernian
12.	(12)	Motherwell

SFL FIRST DIVISION

02/03	(01/02)	CLUB
1.	(1)	Clyde
2.	(3)	Falkirk
3.	(8 (SPL))	St. Johnstone
4.	(4)	St. Mirren
5.	(5)	Ayr United
6.	(3 (SD))	Queen of the South
7.	(6)	Inverness Cal Thistle
8.	(7)	Ross County
9.	(4 (SD))	Alloa Athletic
10.	(9)	Arbroath

SFL SECOND DIVISION

02/03	(01/02)	CLUB
1.	(4 (TD))	Brechin City
2.	(2)	Stenhousemuir
3.	(5)	Forfar Athletic
4.	(6 (TD))	Dumbarton
5.	(10 (*))	Airdrie United
6.	(8 (FD))	Raith Rovers
7.	(6)	Berwick Rangers
8.	(7)	Cowdenbeath
9.	(8)	Stranraer
10.	(1)	Hamilton Academical

(– formerly known as Clydebank)*

SFL THIRD DIVISION

02/03	(01/02)	CLUB
1.	(2)	Queen's Park
2.	(1)	Montrose
3.	(9 (SD))	Morton
4.	(3)	Stirling Albion
5.	(5)	Albion Rovers
6.	(8)	East Fife
7.	(10)	Peterhead
8.	(7)	Elgin City
9.	(-)	Gretna
10.	(9)	East Stirlingshire

SCOTTISH PROGRAMMES OF THE YEAR – PREVIOUS WINNERS

1973/74	Ayr United
1974/75	Hamilton Academical
1975/76	Heart of Midlothian
1976/77	Motherwell
1977/78	Hamilton Academical
1978/79	Hamilton Academical
1979/80	Berwick Rangers
1980/81	Aberdeen
1981/82	Hamilton Academical
1982/83	Dundee
1983/84	Dundee United
1984/85	Aberdeen
1985/86	Celtic
1986/87	Rangers
1987/88	Rangers
1988/89	Rangers
1989/90	Aberdeen
1990/91	Celtic
1991/92	Aberdeen
1992/93	Rangers
1993/94	Rangers
1994/95	Rangers
1995/96	Clyde
1996/97	Clyde
1997/98	Clyde
1998/99	Clyde
1999/2000	Clyde
2000/01	Clyde
2001/02	Clyde
2002/03	Clyde

PREMIER LEAGUE PROGRAMME OF THE YEAR

(as above, except for ...)

1974/75 (old Div.One)	Motherwell
1975/76	Heart of Midlothian
1976/77	Motherwell
1977/78	Rangers
1978/79	Morton
1979/80	Morton
1995/96	Kilmarnock
1996/97	Dundee United
1997/98	Dundee United
1998/99	Dundee United
1999/2000	Dundee United
2000/01	Dunfermline Athletic
2001/02	Aberdeen
2002/03	Aberdeen

FIRST DIVISION PROGRAMME OF THE YEAR

1975/76	Hamilton Academical
1976/77	Hamilton Academical
1977/78	Hamilton Academical
1978/79	Hamilton Academical
1979/80	Berwick Rangers
1980/81	Hamilton Academical
1981/82	Hamilton Academical
1982/83	Queen's Park
1983/84	Hamilton Academical
1984/85	Clyde
1985/86	Clyde
1986/87	Clyde
1987/88	Hamilton Academical & Clydebank
1988/89	Dunfermline Athletic
1989/90	Airdrieonians
1990/91	Dundee
1991/92	Partick Thistle
1992/93	Kilmarnock
1993/94	Dunfermline Athletic
1994/95	Dunfermline Athletic
1995/96	Dundee United
1996/97	Partick Thistle
1997/98	St. Mirren
1998/99	Hibernian
1999/2000	Dunfermline Athletic
2000/01	Clyde
2001/02	Clyde
2002/03	Clyde

SECOND DIVISION PROGRAMME OF THE YEAR

1973/74	Hamilton Academical
1974/75	Hamilton Academical
1975/76	Berwick Rangers
1976/77	Albion Rovers
1977/78	Meadowbank Thistle
1978/79	Berwick Rangers
1979/80	Albion Rovers
1980/81	Clyde
1981/82	Clyde
1982/83	Stirling Albion
1983/84	Stirling Albion
1984/85	Stirling Abion
1985/86	Stirling Albion
1986/87	Raith Rovers
1987/88	Stirling Albion
1988/89	Stirling Albion
1989/90	Kilmarnock
1990/91	Stirling Albion
1991/92	Clyde
1992/93	Clyde
1993/94	Forfar Athletic
1994/95	Clyde
1995/96	Clyde
1996/97	Clyde
1997/98	Clyde
1998/99	Clyde
1999/2000	Clyde
2000/01	Partick Thistle
2001/02	Hamilton Academical
2002/03	Brechin City

THIRD DIVISION PROGRAMME OF THE YEAR

1994/95	Forfar Athletic
1995/96	Livingston
1996/97	Inverness Cal. Thistle
1997/98	Montrose
1998/99	Queen's Park
1999/2000	Queen's Park
2000/01	Montrose
2001/02	Montrose
2002/03	Queen's Park

Information supplied by John Litster (Editor of "Programme Monthly & Football Collectable" Magazine)
Tel no: (01592) 268718
website: www.pmfc.co.uk

Saturday 9th August 2003

FIRST DIVISION
Clyde v. Ayr United
Falkirk v. Inverness Cal. Th.
Raith Rovers v. St. Mirren
Ross County v. Brechin City
St. Johnstone v. Queen of the South

SECOND DIVISION
Alloa Athletic v. Dumbarton
Arbroath v. Berwick Rangers
East Fife v. Stenhousemuir
Hamilton Academical v. Forfar Athletic
Morton v. Airdrie United

THIRD DIVISION
Albion Rovers v. Stranraer
Elgin City v. East Stirlingshire
Gretna v. Queen's Park
Montrose v. Peterhead
Stirling Albion v. Cowdenbeath

Saturday 16th August 2003

FIRST DIVISION
Ayr United v. Falkirk
Brechin City v. Raith Rovers
Inverness Cal. Th. v. Clyde
Queen of the South v. Ross County
St. Mirren v. St. Johnstone

SECOND DIVISION
Airdrie United v. Alloa Athletic
Berwick Rangers v. Hamilton Academical
Dumbarton v. Arbroath
Forfar Athletic v. East Fife
Stenhousemuir v. Morton

THIRD DIVISION
Cowdenbeath v. Albion Rovers
East Stirlingshire v. Montrose
Peterhead v. Gretna
Queen's Park v. Elgin City
Stranraer v. Stirling Albion

Saturday 23rd August 2003

FIRST DIVISION
Clyde v. Brechin City
Falkirk v. Queen of the South
Raith Rovers v. Ayr United
Ross County v. St. Mirren
St. Johnstone v. Inverness Cal. Th.

SECOND DIVISION
Alloa Athletic v. Stenhousemuir
Arbroath v. Forfar Athletic
East Fife v. Berwick Rangers
Hamilton Academical v. Airdrie United
Morton v. Dumbarton

THIRD DIVISION
Albion Rovers v. Queen's Park
Elgin City v. Peterhead
Gretna v. Stranraer
Montrose v. Cowdenbeath
Stirling Albion v. East Stirlingshire

Saturday 30th August 2003

FIRST DIVISION
Ayr United v. Queen of the South
Raith Rovers v. Falkirk
Ross County v. Inverness Cal. Th.
St. Johnstone v. Brechin City
St. Mirren v. Clyde

SECOND DIVISION
Airdrie United v. Dumbarton
Arbroath v. Hamilton Academical
Berwick Rangers v. Alloa Athletic
Morton v. East Fife
Stenhousemuir v. Forfar Athletic

THIRD DIVISION
East Stirlingshire v. Cowdenbeath
Gretna v. Albion Rovers
Montrose v. Elgin City
Peterhead v. Stranraer
Queen's Park v. Stirling Albion

Saturday 6th September 2003

THIRD DIVISION
Albion Rovers v. Elgin City

Saturday 13th September 2003

FIRST DIVISION
Brechin City v. St. Mirren
Clyde v. St. Johnstone
Falkirk v. Ross County
Inverness Cal. Th. v. Ayr United
Queen of the South v. Raith Rovers

SECOND DIVISION
Alloa Athletic v. Arbroath
Dumbarton v. Berwick Rangers
East Fife v. Airdrie United
Forfar Athletic v. Morton
Hamilton Academical v. Stenhousemuir

THIRD DIVISION
Albion Rovers v. Montrose
Cowdenbeath v. Queen's Park
Elgin City v. Gretna
Stirling Albion v. Peterhead
Stranraer v. East Stirlingshire

Saturday 20th September 2003

FIRST DIVISION
Brechin City v. Inverness Cal. Th.
Clyde v. Falkirk
Ross County v. Ayr United
St. Johnstone v. Raith Rovers
St. Mirren v. Queen of the South

SECOND DIVISION
Airdrie United v. Arbroath
East Fife v. Alloa Athletic
Forfar Athletic v. Dumbarton
Morton v. Hamilton Academical
Stenhousemuir v. Berwick Rangers

THIRD DIVISION
Cowdenbeath v. Gretna
Peterhead v. East Stirlingshire
Queen's Park v. Montrose
Stirling Albion v. Albion Rovers
Stranraer v. Elgin City

Saturday 27th September 2003

FIRST DIVISION
Ayr United v. Brechin City
Falkirk v. St. Johnstone
Inverness Cal. Th. v. St. Mirren
Queen of the South v. Clyde
Raith Rovers v. Ross County

SECOND DIVISION
Alloa Athletic v. Forfar Athletic
Arbroath v. Morton
Berwick Rangers v. Airdrie United
Dumbarton v. Stenhousemuir
Hamilton Academical v. East Fife

THIRD DIVISION
Albion Rovers v. Peterhead
East Stirlingshire v. Queen's Park
Elgin City v. Cowdenbeath
Gretna v. Stirling Albion
Montrose v. Stranraer

Saturday 4th October 2003

FIRST DIVISION
Brechin City v. Queen of the South
Clyde v. Ross County
Inverness Cal. Th. v. Raith Rovers
St. Johnstone v. Ayr United
St. Mirren v. Falkirk

SECOND DIVISION
East Fife v. Dumbarton
Forfar Athletic v. Airdrie United
Hamilton Academical v. Alloa Athletic
Morton v. Berwick Rangers
Stenhousemuir v. Arbroath

THIRD DIVISION
Albion Rovers v. East Stirlingshire
Cowdenbeath v. Stranraer
Gretna v. Montrose
Queen's Park v. Peterhead
Stirling Albion v. Elgin City

Saturday 18th October 2003

FIRST DIVISION
Ayr United v. St. Mirren
Falkirk v. Brechin City
Queen of the South v. Inverness Cal. Th.
Raith Rovers v. Clyde
Ross County v. St. Johnstone

SECOND DIVISION
Airdrie United v. Stenhousemuir
Alloa Athletic v. Morton
Arbroath v. East Fife
Berwick Rangers v. Forfar Athletic
Dumbarton v. Hamilton Academical

THIRD DIVISION
East Stirlingshire v. Gretna
Elgin City v. Albion Rovers
Montrose v. Stirling Albion
Peterhead v. Cowdenbeath
Stranraer v. Queen's Park

Saturday 25th October 2003

FIRST DIVISION
Clyde v. Inverness Cal. Th.
Falkirk v. Ayr United
Raith Rovers v. Brechin City
Ross County v. Queen of the South
St. Johnstone v. St. Mirren

SECOND DIVISION
Alloa Athletic v. Airdrie United
Arbroath v. Dumbarton
East Fife v. Forfar Athletic
Hamilton Academical v. Berwick Rangers
Morton v. Stenhousemuir

THIRD DIVISION
Albion Rovers v. Cowdenbeath
Elgin City v. Queen's Park
Gretna v. Peterhead
Montrose v. East Stirlingshire
Stirling Albion v. Stranraer

Saturday 1st November 2003

FIRST DIVISION
Ayr United v. Clyde
Brechin City v. Ross County
Inverness Cal. Th. v. Falkirk
Queen of the South v. St. Johnstone
St. Mirren v. Raith Rovers

SECOND DIVISION
Airdrie United v. Morton
Berwick Rangers v. Arbroath
Dumbarton v. Alloa Athletic
Forfar Athletic v. Hamilton Academical
Stenhousemuir v. East Fife

THIRD DIVISION
Cowdenbeath v. Stirling Albion
East Stirlingshire v. Elgin City
Peterhead v. Montrose
Queen's Park v. Gretna
Stranraer v. Albion Rovers

Saturday 8th November 2003

FIRST DIVISION
Ayr United v. Inverness Cal. Th.
Raith Rovers v. Queen of the South
Ross County v. Falkirk
St. Johnstone v. Clyde
St. Mirren v. Brechin City

SECOND DIVISION
Airdrie United v. East Fife
Arbroath v. Alloa Athletic
Berwick Rangers v. Dumbarton
Morton v. Forfar Athletic
Stenhousemuir v. Hamilton Academical

THIRD DIVISION
East Stirlingshire v. Stranraer
Gretna v. Elgin City
Montrose v. Albion Rovers
Peterhead v. Stirling Albion
Queen's Park v. Cowdenbeath

Saturday 15th November 2003

FIRST DIVISION
Brechin City v. St. Johnstone
Clyde v. St. Mirren
Falkirk v. Raith Rovers
Inverness Cal. Th. v. Ross County
Queen of the South v. Ayr United

SECOND DIVISION
Alloa Athletic v. Berwick Rangers
Dumbarton v. Airdrie United
East Fife v. Morton
Forfar Athletic v. Stenhousemuir
Hamilton Academical v. Arbroath
THIRD DIVISION
Albion Rovers v. Gretna
Cowdenbeath v. East Stirlingshire
Elgin City v. Montrose
Stirling Albion v. Queen's Park
Stranraer v. Peterhead

Saturday 22nd November 2003
FIRST DIVISION
Brechin City v. Ayr United
Clyde v. Queen of the South
Ross County v. Raith Rovers
St. Johnstone v. Falkirk
St. Mirren v. Inverness Cal. Th.

Saturday 29th November 2003
FIRST DIVISION
Ayr United v. Ross County
Falkirk v. Clyde
Inverness Cal. Th. v. Brechin City
Queen of the South v. St. Mirren
Raith Rovers v. St. Johnstone
SECOND DIVISION
Alloa Athletic v. East Fife
Arbroath v. Airdrie United
Berwick Rangers v. Stenhousemuir
Dumbarton v. Forfar Athletic
Hamilton Academical v. Morton
THIRD DIVISION
Albion Rovers v. Stirling Albion
East Stirlingshire v. Peterhead
Elgin City v. Stranraer
Gretna v. Cowdenbeath
Montrose v. Queen's Park

Saturday 6th December 2003
FIRST DIVISION
Brechin City v. Falkirk
Clyde v. Raith Rovers
Inverness Cal. Th. v. Queen of the South
St. Johnstone v. Ross County
St. Mirren v. Ayr United
SECOND DIVISION
Airdrie United v. Berwick Rangers
East Fife v. Hamilton Academical
Forfar Athletic v. Alloa Athletic
Morton v. Arbroath
Stenhousemuir v. Dumbarton
THIRD DIVISION
Cowdenbeath v. Elgin City
Peterhead v. Albion Rovers
Queen's Park v. East Stirlingshire
Stirling Albion v. Gretna
Stranraer v. Montrose

Saturday 13th December 2003
FIRST DIVISION
Ayr United v. St. Johnstone
Falkirk v. St. Mirren
Queen of the South v. Brechin City
Raith Rovers v. Inverness Cal. Th.
Ross County v. Clyde
SECOND DIVISION
Airdrie United v. Forfar Athletic
Alloa Athletic v. Hamilton Academical
Arbroath v. Stenhousemuir
Berwick Rangers v. Morton
Dumbarton v. East Fife
THIRD DIVISION
East Stirlingshire v. Albion Rovers
Elgin City v. Stirling Albion
Montrose v. Gretna
Peterhead v. Queen's Park
Stranraer v. Cowdenbeath

Saturday 20th December 2003
FIRST DIVISION
Clyde v. Ayr United
Falkirk v. Inverness Cal. Th.
Raith Rovers v. St. Mirren
Ross County v. Brechin City
St. Johnstone v. Queen of the South

Saturday 27th December 2003
FIRST DIVISION
Ayr United v. Raith Rovers
Brechin City v. Clyde
Inverness Cal. Th. v. St. Johnstone
Queen of the South v. Falkirk
St. Mirren v. Ross County
SECOND DIVISION
East Fife v. Arbroath
Forfar Athletic v. Berwick Rangers
Hamilton Academical v. Dumbarton
Morton v. Alloa Athletic
Stenhousemuir v. Airdrie United
THIRD DIVISION
Cowdenbeath v. Peterhead
Gretna v. East Stirlingshire
Queen's Park v. Stranraer
Stirling Albion v. Montrose

Saturday 3rd January 2004
FIRST DIVISION
Ayr United v. Queen of the South
Raith Rovers v. Falkirk
Ross County v. Inverness Cal. Th.
St. Johnstone v. Brechin City
St. Mirren v. Clyde
SECOND DIVISION
Airdrie United v. Hamilton Academical
Berwick Rangers v. East Fife
Dumbarton v. Morton
Forfar Athletic v. Arbroath
Stenhousemuir v. Alloa Athletic
THIRD DIVISION
Cowdenbeath v. Montrose
East Stirlingshire v. Stirling Albion
Peterhead v. Elgin City
Queen's Park v. Albion Rovers
Stranraer v. Gretna

Saturday 17th January 2004
FIRST DIVISION
Brechin City v. St. Mirren
Clyde v. St. Johnstone
Falkirk v. Ross County
Inverness Cal. Th. v. Ayr United
Queen of the South v. Raith Rovers
SECOND DIVISION
Alloa Athletic v. Dumbarton
Arbroath v. Berwick Rangers
East Fife v. Stenhousemuir
Hamilton Academical v. Forfar Athletic
Morton v. Airdrie United
THIRD DIVISION
Albion Rovers v. Stranraer
Elgin City v. East Stirlingshire
Gretna v. Queen's Park
Montrose v. Peterhead
Stirling Albion v. Cowdenbeath

Saturday 24th January 2004
FIRST DIVISION
Brechin City v. Inverness Cal. Th.
Clyde v. Falkirk
Ross County v. Ayr United
St. Johnstone v. Raith Rovers
St. Mirren v. Queen of the South
SECOND DIVISION
Airdrie United v. Arbroath
East Fife v. Alloa Athletic
Forfar Athletic v. Dumbarton
Morton v. Hamilton Academical
Stenhousemuir v. Berwick Rangers
THIRD DIVISION
Cowdenbeath v. Gretna
Peterhead v. East Stirlingshire
Queen's Park v. Montrose
Stirling Albion v. Albion Rovers
Stranraer v. Elgin City

Saturday 31st January 2004
FIRST DIVISION
Ayr United v. Brechin City
Falkirk v. St. Johnstone
Inverness Cal. Th. v. St. Mirren
Queen of the South v. Clyde
Raith Rovers v. Ross County
SECOND DIVISION
Alloa Athletic v. Forfar Athletic
Arbroath v. Morton
Berwick Rangers v. Airdrie United
Dumbarton v. Stenhousemuir
Hamilton Academical v. East Fife
THIRD DIVISION
Albion Rovers v. Peterhead
East Stirlingshire v. Queen's Park
Elgin City v. Cowdenbeath
Gretna v. Stirling Albion
Montrose v. Stranraer

Saturday 7th February 2004
SECOND DIVISION
Alloa Athletic v. Arbroath
Dumbarton v. Berwick Rangers
East Fife v. Airdrie United
Forfar Athletic v. Morton
Hamilton Academical v. Stenhousemuir
THIRD DIVISION
Albion Rovers v. Montrose
Cowdenbeath v. Queen's Park
Elgin City v. Gretna
Stirling Albion v. Peterhead
Stranraer v. East Stirlingshire

Saturday 14th February 2004
FIRST DIVISION
Brechin City v. Queen of the South
Clyde v. Ross County
Inverness Cal. Th. v. Raith Rovers
St. Johnstone v. Ayr United
St. Mirren v. Falkirk
SECOND DIVISION
Airdrie United v. Dumbarton
Arbroath v. Hamilton Academical
Berwick Rangers v. Alloa Athletic
Morton v. East Fife
Stenhousemuir v. Forfar Athletic
THIRD DIVISION
East Stirlingshire v. Cowdenbeath
Gretna v. Albion Rovers
Montrose v. Elgin City
Peterhead v. Stranraer
Queen's Park v. Stirling Albion

Saturday 21st February 2004
FIRST DIVISION
Ayr United v. St. Mirren
Falkirk v. Brechin City
Queen of the South v. Inverness Cal. Th.
Raith Rovers v. Clyde
Ross County v. St. Johnstone
SECOND DIVISION
Airdrie United v. Stenhousemuir
Alloa Athletic v. Morton
Arbroath v. East Fife
Berwick Rangers v. Forfar Athletic
Dumbarton v. Hamilton Academical
THIRD DIVISION
East Stirlingshire v. Gretna
Elgin City v. Albion Rovers
Montrose v. Stirling Albion
Peterhead v. Cowdenbeath
Stranraer v. Queen's Park

Saturday 28th February 2004

FIRST DIVISION
Ayr United v. Falkirk
Brechin City v. Raith Rovers
Inverness Cal. Th. v. Clyde
Queen of the South v. Ross County
St. Mirren v. St. Johnstone

SECOND DIVISION
East Fife v. Dumbarton
Forfar Athletic v. Airdrie United
Hamilton Academical v. Alloa Athletic
Morton v. Berwick Rangers
Stenhousemuir v. Arbroath

THIRD DIVISION
Albion Rovers v. East Stirlingshire
Cowdenbeath v. Stranraer
Gretna v. Montrose
Queen's Park v. Peterhead
Stirling Albion v. Elgin City

Saturday 6th March 2004

SECOND DIVISION
Airdrie United v. Alloa Athletic
Berwick Rangers v. Hamilton Academical
Dumbarton v. Arbroath
Forfar Athletic v. East Fife
Stenhousemuir v. Morton

THIRD DIVISION
Cowdenbeath v. Albion Rovers
East Stirlingshire v. Montrose
Peterhead v. Gretna
Queen's Park v. Elgin City
Stranraer v. Stirling Albion

Saturday 13th March 2004

FIRST DIVISION
Clyde v. Brechin City
Falkirk v. Queen of the South
Raith Rovers v. Ayr United
Ross County v. St. Mirren
St. Johnstone v. Inverness Cal. Th.

SECOND DIVISION
Alloa Athletic v. Stenhousemuir
Arbroath v. Forfar Athletic
East Fife v. Berwick Rangers
Hamilton Academical v. Airdrie United
Morton v. Dumbarton

THIRD DIVISION
Albion Rovers v. Queen's Park
Elgin City v. Peterhead
Gretna v. Stranraer
Montrose v. Cowdenbeath
Stirling Albion v. East Stirlingshire

Saturday 20th March 2004

FIRST DIVISION
Ayr United v. Inverness Cal. Th.
Raith Rovers v. Queen of the South
Ross County v. Falkirk
St. Johnstone v. Clyde
St. Mirren v. Brechin City

SECOND DIVISION
Airdrie United v. East Fife
Arbroath v. Alloa Athletic
Berwick Rangers v. Dumbarton
Morton v. Forfar Athletic
Stenhousemuir v. Hamilton Academical

THIRD DIVISION
East Stirlingshire v. Stranraer
Gretna v. Elgin City
Montrose v. Albion Rovers
Peterhead v. Stirling Albion
Queen's Park v. Cowdenbeath

Saturday 27th March 2004

FIRST DIVISION
Brechin City v. St. Johnstone
Clyde v. St. Mirren
Falkirk v. Raith Rovers
Inverness Cal. Th. v. Ross County
Queen of the South v. Ayr United

SECOND DIVISION
Alloa Athletic v. Berwick Rangers
Dumbarton v. Airdrie United
East Fife v. Morton
Forfar Athletic v. Stenhousemuir
Hamilton Academical v. Arbroath

THIRD DIVISION
Albion Rovers v. Gretna
Cowdenbeath v. East Stirlingshire
Elgin City v. Montrose
Stirling Albion v. Queen's Park
Stranraer v. Peterhead

Saturday 3rd April 2004

FIRST DIVISION
Brechin City v. Ayr United
Clyde v. Queen of the South
Ross County v. Raith Rovers
St. Johnstone v. Falkirk
St. Mirren v. Inverness Cal. Th.

SECOND DIVISION
Airdrie United v. Berwick Rangers
East Fife v. Hamilton Academical
Forfar Athletic v. Alloa Athletic
Morton v. Arbroath
Stenhousemuir v. Dumbarton

THIRD DIVISION
Cowdenbeath v. Elgin City
Peterhead v. Albion Rovers
Queen's Park v. East Stirlingshire
Stirling Albion v. Gretna
Stranraer v. Montrose

Saturday 10th April 2004

FIRST DIVISION
Ayr United v. Ross County
Falkirk v. Clyde
Inverness Cal. Th. v. Brechin City
Queen of the South v. St. Mirren
Raith Rovers v. St. Johnstone

SECOND DIVISION
Alloa Athletic v. East Fife
Arbroath v. Airdrie United
Berwick Rangers v. Stenhousemuir
Dumbarton v. Forfar Athletic
Hamilton Academical v. Morton

THIRD DIVISION
Albion Rovers v. Stirling Albion
East Stirlingshire v. Peterhead
Elgin City v. Stranraer
Gretna v. Cowdenbeath
Montrose v. Queen's Park

Saturday 17th April 2004

FIRST DIVISION
Brechin City v. Falkirk
Clyde v. Raith Rovers
Inverness Cal. Th. v. Queen of the South
St. Johnstone v. Ross County
St. Mirren v. Ayr United

SECOND DIVISION
East Fife v. Arbroath
Forfar Athletic v. Berwick Rangers
Hamilton Academical v. Dumbarton
Morton v. Alloa Athletic
Stenhousemuir v. Airdrie United

THIRD DIVISION
Albion Rovers v. Elgin City
Cowdenbeath v. Peterhead
Gretna v. East Stirlingshire
Queen's Park v. Stranraer
Stirling Albion v. Montrose

Saturday 24th April 2004

FIRST DIVISION
Ayr United v. St. Johnstone
Falkirk v. St. Mirren
Queen of the South v. Brechin City
Raith Rovers v. Inverness Cal. Th.
Ross County v. Clyde

SECOND DIVISION
Airdrie United v. Forfar Athletic
Alloa Athletic v. Hamilton Academical
Arbroath v. Stenhousemuir
Berwick Rangers v. Morton
Dumbarton v. East Fife

THIRD DIVISION
East Stirlingshire v. Albion Rovers
Elgin City v. Stirling Albion
Montrose v. Gretna
Peterhead v. Queen's Park
Stranraer v. Cowdenbeath

Saturday 1st May 2004

FIRST DIVISION
Ayr United v. Clyde
Brechin City v. Ross County
Inverness Cal. Th. v. Falkirk
Queen of the South v. St. Johnstone
St. Mirren v. Raith Rovers

SECOND DIVISION
Airdrie United v. Hamilton Academical
Berwick Rangers v. East Fife
Dumbarton v. Morton
Forfar Athletic v. Arbroath
Stenhousemuir v. Alloa Athletic

THIRD DIVISION
Cowdenbeath v. Montrose
East Stirlingshire v. Stirling Albion
Peterhead v. Elgin City
Queen's Park v. Albion Rovers
Stranraer v. Gretna

Saturday 8th May 2004

FIRST DIVISION
Clyde v. Inverness Cal. Th.
Falkirk v. Ayr United
Raith Rovers v. Brechin City
Ross County v. Queen of the South
St. Johnstone v. St. Mirren

SECOND DIVISION
Alloa Athletic v. Airdrie United
Arbroath v. Dumbarton
East Fife v. Forfar Athletic
Hamilton Academical v. Berwick Rangers
Morton v. Stenhousemuir

THIRD DIVISION
Albion Rovers v. Cowdenbeath
Elgin City v. Queen's Park
Gretna v. Peterhead
Montrose v. East Stirlingshire
Stirling Albion v. Stranraer

Saturday 15th May 2004

FIRST DIVISION
Ayr United v. Raith Rovers
Brechin City v. Clyde
Inverness Cal. Th. v. St. Johnstone
Queen of the South v. Falkirk
St. Mirren v. Ross County

SECOND DIVISION
Airdrie United v. Morton
Berwick Rangers v. Arbroath
Dumbarton v. Alloa Athletic
Forfar Athletic v. Hamilton Academical
Stenhousemuir v. East Fife

THIRD DIVISION
Cowdenbeath v. Stirling Albion
East Stirlingshire v. Elgin City
Peterhead v. Montrose
Queen's Park v. Gretna
Stranraer v. Albion Rovers

Saturday 9th August 2003
Dundee United v Hibernian
Dunfermline Athletic v Celtic
Hearts v Aberdeen
Motherwell v Dundee
Partick Thistle v Livingston
Rangers v Kilmarnock

Saturday 16th August 2003
Aberdeen v Rangers
Celtic v Dundee United
Kilmarnock v Partick Thistle
Livingston v Motherwell

Sunday 17th August 2003
Dundee v Dunfermline Athletic
Hibernian v Hearts

Saturday 23rd August 2003
Aberdeen v Dunfermline Athletic
Dundee v Livingston
Hearts v Dundee United
Motherwell v Kilmarnock
Partick Thistle v Celtic
Rangers v Hibernian

Saturday 30th August 2003
Celtic v Livingston
Hibernian v Aberdeen
Motherwell v Partick Thistle

Sunday 31st August 2003
Dundee United v Rangers
Hearts v Dunfermline Athletic
Kilmarnock v Dundee

Saturday 13th September 2003
Aberdeen v Partick Thistle
Dundee v Celtic
Hibernian v Motherwell
Kilmarnock v Hearts
Livingston v Dundee United
Rangers v Dunfermline Athletic

Saturday 20th September 2003
Celtic v Motherwell
Dundee v Aberdeen
Dunfermline Athletic v Hibernian
Hearts v Rangers
Livingston v Kilmarnock
Partick Thistle v Dundee United

Saturday 27th September 2003
Aberdeen v Livingston
Dundee United v Kilmarnock
Dunfermline Athletic v Partick Thistle
Hibernian v Celtic
Motherwell v Hearts
Rangers v Dundee

Saturday 4th October 2003
Dundee United v Motherwell
Hearts v Dundee
Kilmarnock v Aberdeen
Livingston v Dunfermline Athletic
Partick Thistle v Hibernian
Rangers v Celtic

Saturday 18th October 2003
Aberdeen v Dundee United
Celtic v Hearts
Dundee v Partick Thistle
Dunfermline Athletic v Kilmarnock
Hibernian v Livingston
Motherwell v Rangers

Saturday 25th October 2003
Celtic v Aberdeen
Dundee United v Dundee
Hibernian v Kilmarnock
Livingston v Rangers
Motherwell v Dunfermline Athletic
Partick Thistle v Hearts

Saturday 1st November 2003
Aberdeen v Motherwell
Dundee v Hibernian
Dunfermline Athletic v Dundee United
Hearts v Livingston
Kilmarnock v Celtic
Rangers v Partick Thistle

Saturday 8th November 2003
Aberdeen v Hearts
Celtic v Dunfermline Athletic
Dundee v Motherwell
Hibernian v Dundee United
Kilmarnock v Rangers
Livingston v Partick Thistle

Saturday 22nd November 2003
Dundee United v Celtic
Dunfermline Athletic v Dundee
Hearts v Hibernian
Motherwell v Livingston
Partick Thistle v Kilmarnock
Rangers v Aberdeen

Saturday 29th November 2003
Celtic v Partick Thistle
Dundee United v Hearts
Dunfermline Athletic v Aberdeen
Hibernian v Rangers
Kilmarnock v Motherwell
Livingston v Dundee

Saturday 6th December 2003
Aberdeen v Hibernian
Dundee v Kilmarnock
Dunfermline Athletic v Hearts
Livingston v Celtic
Partick Thistle v Motherwell
Rangers v Dundee United

Saturday 13th December 2003
Celtic v Dundee
Dundee United v Livingston
Dunfermline Athletic v Rangers
Hearts v Kilmarnock
Motherwell v Hibernian
Partick Thistle v Aberdeen

Saturday 20th December 2003
Aberdeen v Dundee
Dundee United v Partick Thistle
Hibernian v Dunfermline Athletic
Kilmarnock v Livingston
Motherwell v Celtic
Rangers v Hearts

Saturday 27th December 2003
Celtic v Hibernian
Dundee v Rangers
Hearts v Motherwell
Kilmarnock v Dundee United
Livingston v Aberdeen
Partick Thistle v Dunfermline Athletic

Saturday 3rd January 2004
Aberdeen v Kilmarnock
Celtic v Rangers
Dundee v Hearts
Dunfermline Athletic v Livingston
Hibernian v Partick Thistle
Motherwell v Dundee United

Saturday 17th January 2004
Dundee United v Aberdeen
Hearts v Celtic
Kilmarnock v Dunfermline Athletic
Livingston v Hibernian
Partick Thistle v Dundee
Rangers v Motherwell

Saturday 24th January 2004
Aberdeen v Celtic
Dundee v Dundee United
Dunfermline Athletic v Motherwell
Hearts v Partick Thistle
Kilmarnock v Hibernian
Rangers v Livingston

Saturday 31st January 2004
Celtic v Kilmarnock
Dundee United v Dunfermline Athletic
Hibernian v Dundee
Livingston v Hearts
Motherwell v Aberdeen
Partick Thistle v Rangers

Tuesday 10th February 2004
Partick Thistle v Livingston

Wednesday 11th February 2004
Dundee United v Hibernian
Dunfermline Athletic v Celtic
Hearts v Aberdeen
Motherwell v Dundee
Rangers v Kilmarnock

Saturday 14th February 2004
Aberdeen v Rangers
Celtic v Dundee United
Dundee v Dunfermline Athletic
Hibernian v Hearts
Kilmarnock v Partick Thistle
Livingston v Motherwell

Saturday 21st February 2004
Aberdeen v Dunfermline Athletic
Dundee v Livingston
Hearts v Dundee United
Motherwell v Kilmarnock
Partick Thistle v Celtic
Rangers v Hibernian

Saturday 28th February 2004
Celtic v Livingston
Dundee United v Rangers
Dunfermline Athletic v Hearts
Hibernian v Aberdeen
Kilmarnock v Dundee
Motherwell v Partick Thistle

Saturday 6th March 2004
Aberdeen v Partick Thistle
Dundee v Celtic
Hibernian v Motherwell
Kilmarnock v Hearts
Livingston v Dundee United
Rangers v Dunfermline Athletic

Saturday 13th March 2004
Celtic v Motherwell
Dundee v Aberdeen
Dunfermline Athletic v Hibernian
Hearts v Rangers
Livingston v Kilmarnock
Partick Thistle v Dundee United

Saturday 20th March 2004
Aberdeen v Livingston
Dundee United v Kilmarnock
Dunfermline Athletic v Partick Thistle
Hibernian v Celtic
Motherwell v Hearts
Rangers v Dundee

Saturday 27th March 2004
Dundee United v Motherwell
Hearts v Dundee
Kilmarnock v Aberdeen
Livingston v Dunfermline Athletic
Partick Thistle v Hibernian
Rangers v Celtic

Saturday 3rd April 2004
Aberdeen v Dundee United
Celtic v Hearts
Dundee v Partick Thistle
Dunfermline Athletic v Kilmarnock
Hibernian v Livingston
Motherwell v Rangers

Saturday 10th April 2004
Celtic v Aberdeen
Dundee United v Dundee
Hibernian v Kilmarnock
Livingston v Rangers
Motherwell v Dunfermline Athletic
Partick Thistle v Hearts

Saturday 17th April 2004
Aberdeen v Motherwell
Dundee v Hibernian
Dunfermline Athletic v Dundee United
Hearts v Livingston
Kilmarnock v Celtic
Rangers v Partick Thistle

the cis insurance cup draw season 2003/04

1st Round

East Fife	-v-	Airdrie United
Arbroath	-v-	Raith Rovers
Inverness Caledonian Thistle	-v-	Queen's Park
Ayr United	-v-	Dumbarton
East Stirlingshire	-v-	Ross County
Elgin City	-v-	Brechin City
Gretna	-v-	Peterhead
St. Mirren	-v-	St. Johnstone
Hamilton Academical	-v-	Albion Rovers
Montrose	-v-	Stirling Albion
Cowdenbeath	-v-	Alloa Athletic
Stenhousemuir	-v-	Queen of the South
Forfar Athletic	-v-	Berwick Rangers

Above Ties to be played on Tuesday, 2nd September, 2003

Morton -v- Stranraer

Above Tie to be played on Wednesday 3rd September, 2003

2nd Round

.... -v- ....
.... -v- ....
.... -v- ....
.... -v- ....
.... -v- ....
.... -v- ....
.... -v- ....
.... -v- ....
.... -v- ....
.... -v- ....
.... -v- ....
.... -v- ....

Ties to be played on Tuesday, 23rd or Wednesday, 24th September, 2003

3rd Round

.... -v- ....
.... -v- ....
.... -v- ....
.... -v- ....
.... -v- ....
.... -v- ....
.... -v- ....
.... -v- ....

Ties to be played on Tuesday, 28th or Wednesday, 29th October, 2003

4th Round

.... -v- ....
.... -v- ....
.... -v- ....
.... -v- ....

Ties to be played on Tuesday, 2nd or Wednesday, 3rd December, 2003

Semi–Finals

.... -v- ....
.... -v- ....

Ties to be played on Tuesday, 3rd and Thursday 5th February, 2004

THE CIS INSURANCE CUP FINAL

.... -v- ....

To be played on Sunday, 14th March, 2004

In the event of a draw after normal time in all rounds, extra time of 30 minutes (i.e. 15 minutes each way) will take place and thereafter, if necessary, Kicks from the Penalty Mark in accordance with the Rules laid down by The International Football Association Board will be taken.

the bell's cup draw season 2003/04

1st Round

St. Mirren	-v-	Queen's Park
Albion Rovers	-v-	East Fife
Cowdenbeath	-v-	Ross County
Hamilton Academical	-v-	St. Johnstone
Airdrie United	-v-	Montrose
Morton	-v-	Arbroath
Brechin City	-v-	Falkirk
Stenhousemuir	-v-	Peterhead
Ayr United	-v-	Stirling Albion
Stranraer	-v-	Queen of the South
Gretna	-v-	Inverness Caledonian Thistle
Alloa Athletic	-v-	Clyde
East Stirlingshire	-v-	Raith Rovers
Forfar Athletic	-v-	Elgin City

Byes: Dumbarton and Berwick Rangers

Above ties to be played on Saturday, 2nd August, 2003

2nd Round

.... -v- ....
.... -v- ....
.... -v- ....
.... -v- ....
.... -v- ....
.... -v- ....
.... -v- ....
.... -v- ....

Ties to be played on Tuesday, 12th or Wednesday, 13th August, 2003

3rd Round

.... -v- ....
.... -v- ....
.... -v- ....
.... -v- ....

Ties to be played on Tuesday, 26th or Wednesday, 27th August, 2003

Semi-Finals

.... -v- ....
.... -v- ....

Ties to be played on Tuesday, 16th or Wednesday, 17th September, 2003

THE BELL'S CUP FINAL

.... -v- ....

To be played on Sunday, 26th October, 2003

In the event of a draw after normal time in all rounds, extra time of 30 minutes (i.e. 15 minutes each way) will take place and thereafter, if necessary, Kicks from the Penalty Mark in accordance with the Rules laid down by The International Football Association Board will be taken.

the scottish premier league

ABERDEEN
STEVE PATERSON
Player: Manchester United, Sheffield United, Hong Kong Rangers, Sydney Olympic, Yorniuri Tokyo
Manager: Inverness Caledonian Thistle, Aberdeen

CELTIC
MARTIN O'NEILL
Player: Distillery, Derry City, Nottingham Forest, Norwich City, Manchester City, Norwich City, Notts County, Northern Ireland
Manager: Wycombe Wanderers, Leicester City, Celtic

DUNDEE
JIM DUFFY
Player: Celtic, Greenock Morton, Dundee, Partick Thistle, Dundee
Manager: Falkirk, Dundee, Hibernian, Dundee

DUNDEE UNITED
IAN McCALL
Player: Queen's Park, Dunfermline Athletic, Rangers, Bradford City, Dunfermline Athletic, Dundee,Falkirk, Hamilton Academical, Happy Valley (Hong Kong), Hamilton Academical, Partick Thistle, Clydebank
Manager: Clydebank, Morton, Airdrieonians, Falkirk, Dundee United

DUNFERMLINE ATHLETIC
JAMES CALDERWOOD
Player: Birmingham City, Cambridge United (loan), Sparta Rotterdam, Willem II, Roda JC, SC Heracles
Manager: Rietvogels, FC Zwolle, SC Cambuur, Leeuwarden, Willem II, NEC Nijmegan, Dunfermline Athletic

HEARTS
CRAIG LEVEIN
Player: Cowdenbeath, Heart of Midlothian, Scotland
Manager: Cowdenbeath, Heart of Midlothian

HIBERNIAN
BOBBY WILLIAMSON
Player: Clydebank, Rangers, West Bromwich Albion, Rotherham United, Kilmarnock
Manager: Kilmarnock, Hibernian

KILMARNOCK
JIM JEFFERIES
Player: Heart of Midlothian, Berwick Rangers
Manager: Berwick Rangers, Falkirk, Heart of Midlothian, Bradford City, Kilmarnock

LIVINGSTON
MARCIO MAXIMO BARCELLOS
Player: Americano (RJ) U14, AABB, Batatouo U17 & U20, Federal University & Brazil University Selection
Head Coach: Ara'Cautuba (RJ), Americano (RJ), Barradatijuca (RJ), Rio de Janeiro Selection, Brazil (U17, U20 & Olympic Team), Qatar, Al Ahli (Saudi Arabia), Cayman Islands, Livingston

MOTHERWELL
TERRY BUTCHER
Player: Ipswich Town, Rangers, Coventry City, Sunderland, Clydebank, England
Manager: Coventry City, Sunderland, Motherwell

PARTICK THISTLE
GERRY COLLINS
Player: Albion Rovers, Ayr United, Hamilton Academical, Partick Thistle, Hamilton Academical, Partick Thistle
Manager: Partick Thistle

RANGERS
ALEX McLEISH
Player: Aberdeen, Motherwell, Scotland
Manager: Motherwell, Hibernian, Rangers

the scottish football league

FIRST DIVISION

AYR UNITED
CAMPBELL MONEY
Player: St. Mirren, Stranraer
Manager: Stranraer, Ayr United

BRECHIN CITY
DICK CAMPBELL
Player: Brechin City, East Stirlingshire
Manager: Dunfermline Athletic, Brechin City

CLYDE
ALAN KERNAGHAN
Player: Middlesbrough, Charlton Athletic, Manchester City, Bolton Wanderers, Bradford City, St. Johnstone, Brechin City, Clyde, Republic of Ireland
Manager: Clyde

FALKIRK
JOHN HUGHES
Player: Berwick Rangers, Swansea City, Falkirk, Celtic, Hibernian, Ayr United, Falkirk
Coach: Falkirk

INVERNESS CALEDONIAN THISTLE
JOHN ROBERTSON
Player: Heart of Midlothian, Newcastle United, Heart of Midlothian, Dundee (loan), Livingston
Manager: Inverness Caledonian Thistle

QUEEN OF THE SOUTH
JOHN CONNOLLY
Player: St. Johnstone, Everton, Birmingham City, Newcastle United, Hibernian, Scotland
Manager: Queen of the South

RAITH ROVERS
ANTONIO CALDERON
Player: Cadiz, Real Mallorca, Rayo Ravanello de Madrid, Unio Esportiva Lleida, Airdrieonians, Kilmarnock, Raith Rovers
Manager: Raith Rovers

ROSS COUNTY
ALEX SMITH
Player: Stirling Albion, East Stirlingshire, Albion Rovers, Stenhousemuir
Manager: Stenhousemuir, Stirling Albion, St. Mirren, Aberdeen, Clyde, Dundee United, Ross County

ST. JOHNSTONE
BILLY STARK
Player: St. Mirren, Aberdeen, Celtic, Kilmarnock, Hamilton Academical, Kilmarnock, Celtic
Manager: Morton, St. Johnstone

ST. MIRREN
JOHN COUGHLIN
Player: Meadowbank Thistle, Berwick Rangers
Manager: St. Mirren

SECOND DIVISION

AIRDRIE UNITED
SANDY STEWART
Player: Heart of Midlothian, Kilmarnock, Airdrieonians, Partick Thistle, Airdrieonians, Airdrie United
Manager: Airdrie United

ALLOA ATHLETIC
TERRY CHRISTIE
Player: Dundee, Raith Rovers, Stirling Albion
Manager: Meadowbank Thistle, Stenhousemuir, Alloa Athletic

ARBROATH
JOHN BROWNLIE
Player: Hibernian, Newcastle United, Middlesbrough, Hartlepool United, Berwick Rangers, Scotland
Manager: Cowdenbeath, East Stirlingshire, Arbroath

BERWICK RANGERS
PAUL SMITH
Player: Dundee, Dundee United, Raith Rovers, Motherwell, Dunfermline Athletic, Falkirk, Dunfermline Athletic, Heart of Midlothian, Ayr United, Berwick Rangers
Manager: Berwick Rangers

DUMBARTON
BRIAN FAIRLEY
Player: Hibernian, Cowdenbeath
Manager: Stenhousemuir, Dumbarton

EAST FIFE
JIM MOFFAT
Player: Montrose, Hamilton Academical, Dunfermline Athletic, Forfar Athletic, Montrose (loan), East Fife (loan), Brechin City, East Fife (loan), East Fife, Montrose, Forfar Athletic, Cowdenbeath, East Stirlingshire, Albion Rovers, Cowdenbeath, Forfar Athletic, Stirling Albion, East Fife
Manager: East Fife

FORFAR ATHLETIC
RAYMOND STEWART
Player: Dundee United, West Ham United, St. Johnstone, Stirling Albion, Scotland
Manager: Livingston, Stirling Albion, Forfar Athletic

HAMILTON ACADEMICAL
ALLAN MAITLAND
Player: Did Not Play at Senior Level.
Manager: Clyde, Hamilton Academical

MORTON
JOHN McCORMACK
Player: Clydebank, St. Mirren, Dundee, Airdrieonians, Partick Thistle
Manager: Dundee, Queen's Park (Coach), Morton

STENHOUSEMUIR
JOHN McVEIGH
Player: Airdrieonians, Clyde, Hamilton Academical, Kilmarnock, Falkirk
Manager: Partick Thistle, Raith Rovers, Albion Rovers, Stenhousemuir

THIRD DIVISION

ALBION ROVERS
PETER HETHERSTON
Player: Falkirk, Sheffield United, Watford, Falkirk, Raith Rovers, Aberdeen, Airdrieonians, Partick Thistle
Manager: Raith Rovers, Albion Rovers

COWDENBEATH
KEITH WRIGHT
Player: Raith Rovers, Dundee, Hibernian, Raith Rovers, Morton, Stenhousemuir, Cowdenbeath, Scotland
Manager: Cowdenbeath

EAST STIRLINGSHIRE
STEPHEN MORRISON
Player: Aberdeen, Dunfermline Athletic, Hamilton Academical, Dumbarton, Clyde, Alloa Athletic, Larne, Alloa Athletic, Clydebank, Dumbarton (loan), Clydebank
Manager: East Stirlingshire

ELGIN CITY
DAVID ROBERTSON
Player: Aberdeen, Rangers, Leeds United, Montrose, Scotland
Manager: Elgin City

GRETNA
ROWAN ALEXANDER
Player: Queen of the South, St. Mirren, Brentford, Greenock Morton, Queen of the South, Gretna
Manager: Queen of the South, Gretna

MONTROSE
JOHN SHERAN
Player: Montrose
Manager: Montrose

PETERHEAD
Ian Wilson
Player: Aberdeen, Dundee, Leicester City, Everton, Derby County, Wigan Athletic, Bury, Besiktas, Scotland
Manager: Peterhead

QUEEN'S PARK
KENNY BRANNIGAN
Player: Queen's Park, Sheffield Wednesday, Stockport County (loan), Doncaster Rovers (loan), St. Mirren, Kilmarnock, Falkirk, East Stirlingshire, Stranraer, Stenhousemuir, Clydebank, Partick Thistle, Clydebank, Berwick Rangers, Stirling Albion, Airdrie United
Coach: Queen's Park

STIRLING ALBION
ALLAN MOORE
Player: Dumbarton, Heart of Midlothian, St. Johnstone, Dunfermline Athletic, Livingston, Airdrieonians, Partick Thistle, Morton, Queen of the South, Stirling Albion
Manager: Stirling Albion

STRANRAER
NEIL WATT
Player: Celtic, Forfar Athletic, East Stirlingshire, Stirling Albion, Stranraer, Clyde
Manager: Stranraer

INFORMATION COMPILED BY JIM JEFFREY

FIFA:
General Secretary: Dr. Urs Linsi
Hitzigweg 11, P.O. Box 85, 8030 Zurich, Switzerland.
Tel: 00 411 384 9595 **Fax:** 00 411 384 9696
Website: www.fifa.com

UEFA:
Chief Executive: Gerhard Aigner (until 31.12.2003),
Lars-Christer Olsson (from 01.01.2004)
Route de Genève 46, CH-1260, Nyon 2, Switzerland.
Tel: 00 41 22 994 4444 **Fax:** 00 41 22 994 4488
Website: www.uefa.com

LEAGUES IN THE INTERNATIONAL FOOTBALL LEAGUE BOARD

THE SCOTTISH FOOTBALL LEAGUE:
Secretary: Peter Donald, Hampden Park, Glasgow, G42 9EB.
Tel: 0141 620 4160 **Fax:** 0141 620 4161
e-mail: info@scottishfootballleague.com
Website: www.scottishfootballleague.com

THE SCOTTISH PREMIER LEAGUE:
Secretary: Iain Blair, Hampden Park, Glasgow, G42 9DE.
Tel: 0141 620 4140 **Fax:** 0141 620 4141
e-mail: iainblair@scotprem.com
Website: www.scotprem.com

THE F.A. PREMIER LEAGUE:
Secretary: Mike Foster, 11 Connaught Place, London, W2 2ET.
Tel: 0207 298 1600 **Fax:** 0207 298 1601
e-mail: general@fapl.co.uk
Website: www.premierleague.com

THE FOOTBALL LEAGUE:
Director of Operations: Andy Williamson
Edward VII Quay, Navigation Way, Preston, PR2 2YF.
Tel: 0870 442 0 1888 **Fax:** 0870 442 1188
e-mail: fl@football-league.co.uk
Website: www.football-league.co.uk

THE IRISH FOOTBALL LEAGUE:
Secretary: Harry Wallace, 96 University Street, Belfast,BT7 1HE.
Tel: 02890 242888 **Fax:** 02890 330773
e-mail: irishleague@talk21.com
Website: www.irish-league.co.uk

NATIONAL ASSOCIATIONS WITHIN THE UNITED KINGDOM

THE SCOTTISH FOOTBALL ASSOCIATION:
Chief Executive: David Taylor, The National Stadium, Hampden Park,
Glasgow, G42 9AY.
Tel: 0141 616 6000 **Fax:** 0141 616 6001
e-mail: info@scottishfa.co.uk
Website: www.scottishfa.co.uk

THE FOOTBALL ASSOCIATION:
Chief Executive: Mark Palios, 25 Soho Square, London, W1D 4FA.
Tel: 0207 745 4545 **Fax:** 0207 745 7151
e-mail: info@the-fa.com
Website: www.the-fa.org

THE IRISH FOOTBALL ASSOCIATION:
Secretary: David I. Bowen, 20 Windsor Avenue, Belfast, BT9 6EG.
Tel: 02890 669458 **Fax:** 02890 667620
e-mail: enquiries@irishfa.com
Website: www.irishfa.com

THE FOOTBALL ASSOCIATION OF WALES:
Secretary: David G. Collins, 3 Westgate Street, Cardiff, CF10 1DP.
Tel: 02920 372325 **Fax:** 02920 343961
e-mail: dcollins@faw.co.uk
Website: www.faw.org.uk

OTHER LEAGUES IN SCOTLAND

THE HIGHLAND FOOTBALL LEAGUE:
Secretary: John H. Grant, 35 Hamilton Drive, Elgin, IV30 4NN.
Tel/Fax: 01343 544995
e-mail: hfleague@globalnet.co.uk
Website: www.highlandfootballleague.com

THE EAST OF SCOTLAND LEAGUE:
Secretary: John M. Greenhorn, 2 Babberton Mains Court,
Edinburgh, EH14 3ER.
Tel: (House) 0131 442 1402, (Business) 0131 453 4411 Ext. 145
Fax: 0131 442 1402
e-mail: john.greenhorn@tesco.net
Website: www.eastofscotlandfa.org

THE SOUTH OF SCOTLAND LEAGUE:
Secretary: Richard Shaw M.B.E., 8 Kirkland Road, Heathhall,
Dumfries, DG1 3RN.
Tel: (House) 01387 261736 (Business) 01387 254853
Fax: 01387 254853
e-mail: richardshaw@M-B-E.freeserve.co.uk

AFFILIATED NATIONAL ASSOCIATIONS OF THE SCOTTISH FOOTBALL ASSOCIATION

THE SCOTTISH JUNIOR FOOTBALL ASSOCIATION:
Secretary: Tom Johnston, Hampden Park, Glasgow, G42 9DD.
Tel: 0141 620 4560 **Fax:** 0141 620 4561
e-mail: scottishjuniorfa@scottish-football.com
Website: www.scottish-juniors.co.uk

THE SCOTTISH AMATEUR FOOTBALL ASSOCIATION:
Secretary: Hugh Knapp, Hampden Park, Glasgow, G42 9DB.
Tel: 0141 620 4550 **Fax:** 0141 620 4551
e-mail: hughknapp@scottishamateurfa.co.uk
Website: www.scottishamateurfa.co.uk

THE SCOTTISH YOUTH FOOTBALL ASSOCIATION:
Secretary: David Little, Hampden Park, Glasgow, G42 9BF.
Tel: 0141 620 4590 **Fax:** 0141 620 4591
e-mail: info@scottishyouthfa.co.uk
Website: www.scottishyouthfa.co.uk

THE SCOTTISH WELFARE FOOTBALL ASSOCIATION:
Secretary: Donald McNair, 14 Yair Drive, Glasgow, G52 2JX.
Tel: 0141 883 5008 **Fax:** 01324 813527

THE SCOTTISH SCHOOLS FOOTBALL ASSOCIATION:
Secretary: John C. Watson, Hampden Park, Glasgow, G42 9AZ.
Tel: 0141 620 4570 **Fax:** 0141 620 4571
e-mail: jcwatson@lineone.net

SCOTTISH WOMEN'S FOOTBALL:
Executive Administrator: Mrs. Maureen McGonigle,
Hampden Park, Glasgow, G42 9DF.
Tel: 0141 620 4580/4582 **Fax:** 0141 620 4581
e-mail: maureen@scottishwomensfootball.com
Website: www.scottishwomensfootball.com

PLAYER'S UNION

THE SCOTTISH PROFESSIONAL FOOTBALLERS ASSOCIATION:
Secretary: Tony Higgins, Fountain House, 1/3 Woodside Crescent,
Charing Cross, Glasgow, G3 7UJ.
Tel: 0141 332 8641 **Fax:** 0141 332 4491
e-mail: SPFA@gmb.org.uk
Website: www.spfa.org.uk

the highland football league directory of clubs

BRORA RANGERS F.C.

Secretary: Kevin MacKay
Club Address: Dudgeon Park, Dudgeon Drive, Brora, KW9 6QN.
Ground Tel/Fax: 01408 621231
Sec Bus: 01408 623005/623018
Sec Home/Fax: 01408 621114
E-Mail: kevin.a.mackay@diageo.com
Year of Formation: 1879
Capacity: Total: 4,000, 250 Seated, 3,750 Standing
Pitch Dimensions: 112 yds x 70 yds
Playing Kits: **1st Choice**
Shirt: Red with White Collar
Shorts: Red
Stockings: Red and White
2nd Choice
Shirt: White with Red Collar
Shorts: White
Stockings: White

BUCKIE THISTLE F.C.

Secretary: Andrew Smith
Manager: Kevin Will
Club Address: Victoria Park, Midmar Street, Buckie, AB56 1BJ.
Ground Tel No: 01542 836468 (Matchdays Only)
Sec Bus: 01542 832101
Sec Bus Fax: 01542 832182
Sec Home: 01569 731558
Sec Mobile: 07751 417052
Website: www.buckiethistle.com
E-Mail: smithag67@aol.com
Year of Formation: 1889
Capacity: Total: 5,400, 400 Seated, 5,000 Standing
Pitch Dimensions: 109 yds x 73 yds
Playing Kits: **1st Choice**
Shirt: Green & White Hoops
Shorts: White
Stockings: White
2nd Choice
Shirt: White
Shorts: Green
Stockings: White

CLACHNACUDDIN F.C. (1990) LTD.

Secretary: Martin Mitchell
Manager: Robert Williamson
Club Address: Grant Street Park, Wyvis Place, Inverness, IV3 6DR.
Ground Tel No: 01463 238825
Sec Home: 01463 230638
Sec Mobile: 07836 241970
Fax No: 01463 718261
E-Mail: mrtnmitchell@aol.com
Year of Formation: 1886
Capacity: Total: 3,000, 154 Seated, 2,846 Standing
Pitch Dimensions: 108 yds x 70 yds
Playing Kits: **1st Choice**
Shirt: White
Shorts: Black
Stockings: White
2nd Choice
Shirt: Yellow
Shorts: Yellow
Stockings: Yellow

COVE RANGERS F.C.

Secretary: Duncan Little
Manager: Kevin Walker
Club Address: Allan Park, Loirston Road, Cove, Aberdeen, AB12 3NR.
Ground Tel No: 01224 890433
Sec Bus: 01224 854990
Sec Home: 01224 896282
Fax No: 01224 895199
E-Mail: duncanl@coverangersfc.freeserve.co.uk
Year of Formation: 1922
Capacity: Total: 2,300, 200 Seated, 2,100 Standing
Pitch Dimensions: 104 yds x 65 yds
Playing Kits: **1st Choice**
Shirt: Blue & White
Shorts: Blue & White
Stockings: White & Blue
2nd Choice
Shirt: Yellow & Blue
Shorts: Blue & Yellow
Stockings: Yellow & Blue

DEVERONVALE F.C.

Secretary: Stewart McPherson
Manager: Gregg Carrol
Club Address: Princess Royal Park, 56 Eirlie Gardens, Banff, AB45 1HB.
Ground Tel No: 01261 818303
Sec Mobile: 07813 733617
Fax No: 01261 833646
Website: www.deveronvale.co.uk
E-Mail: princessroyal@lineone.net
Year of Formation: 1938
Capacity: Total: 2,600, 300 Seated, 2,300 Standing
Pitch Dimensions: 109 yds x 78 yds
Playing Kits: **1st Choice**
Shirt: Red with White Trim
Shorts: White
Stockings: Black with Red Tops
2nd Choice
Shirt: Sky Blue with White Trim
Shorts: White
Stockings: Sky Blue

FORRES MECHANICS F.C.

Secretary: David Macdonald
Manager: Alan Scott
Club Address: Mosset Park, Lea Road, Forres, Moray, IV36 0AU.
Ground Tel/Fax No: 01309 675096
Sec Home: 01343 544294
Sec Mobile: 07779 782799
Sec Business: 01309 694012
E-Mail: d_w_macdonald@hotmail.com
Year of Formation: 1884
Capacity: Total: 6,540, 540 Seated, 6,000 Standing
Pitch Dimensions: 106 yds x 69 yds
Playing Kits: **1st Choice**
Shirt: Chocolate and Gold Stripes
Shorts: Gold
Stockings: Gold
2nd Choice
Shirt: White
Shorts: White
Stockings: White

FORT WILLIAM F.C.

Secretary: James Campbell
Manager: Danny Conlon
Club Address: Claggan Park, Fort William
Sec Home/Fax: 01397 772298
Website: www.fortwilliamfc.org.uk
E-Mail: mike@lochaberplumbing.co.uk
Year of Formation: 1984
Capacity: Total: 4,600 , 400 Seated, 4,200 Standing
Pitch Dimensions: 102 yds x 80 yds
Playing Kits: **1st Choice**
Shirt: Gold
Shorts: Black
Stockings: Gold
2nd Choice
Shirt: Black with Blue Sleeves
Shorts: Blue
Stockings: Black

FRASERBURGH F.C.

Secretary: Finlay M. Noble
Manager: Charles Duncan
Club Address: Bellslea Park, Seaforth Street, Fraserburgh, AB43 9BD.
Ground Tel No: 01346 518444
Fax No: 01346 516414
Sec Bus/Mobile: 07747 003806
Sec Home: 01346 513474
Website: www.fraserburghfc.net
E-Mail: finlay@fraserburghfc.net
Year of Formation: 1910
Capacity: Total: 4,500, 480 Seated, 4,020 Standing
Pitch Dimensions: 106 yds x 66 yds
Kits: **1st Choice**
Shirt: Black and White Stripes
Shorts: Black
Stockings: Red
2nd Choice
Shirt: Blue Tartan
Shorts: Blue
Stockings: White

HUNTLY F.C.

Secretary: Peter Morrison
Manager: Billy Anderson
Club Address: Christie Park, East Park Street, Huntly, AB54 8JE.
Ground Tel/Fax No: 01466 793548
Sec Bus: 01466 793286
Sec Home: 01466 793269
Sec Mobile: 07957 283127
Website: www.huntlyfc.co.uk
E-Mail: petermorrison@rm-engineering.co.uk
Year of Formation: 1928
Capacity: Total: 4,500, 270 Seated, 4,230 Standing
Pitch Dimensions: 105 yds x 72 yds
Playing Kits: **1st Choice**
Shirt: Black & Gold
Shorts: Black
Stockings: Black with Gold Trim
2nd Choice
Shirt: White
Shorts: White
Stockings: White

INVERURIE LOCO WORKS F.C.

Secretary: Gordon Park
Manager: John Gardiner
Club Address: Harlaw Park, Harlaw Road, Inverurie, AB51 4SG.
Ground Tel No: 01467 622168
Sec Bus: 01467 624500
Sec Home: 01467 621347
Sec Mobile: 07816 604434
Website: www.eteamz.com/inverurielocoworks
E-Mail: gordon@parkfamily.free-online.co.uk
Year of Formation: 1903
Capacity: Total: 1,925, 125 Seated, 1,800 Standing
Pitch Dimensions: 103 yds x 71 yds
Playing Kits: **1st Choice**
Shirt: Black & Red Vertical Stripes
Shorts: Black
Stockings: Red
2nd Choice
Shirt: White & Black Vertical Stripes
Shorts: White
Stockings: White with Black Trim

KEITH F.C.

Secretary: David Ross
Manager: Martin Allan
Club Address: Kynoch Park, Balloch Road, Keith, AB55 5EN.
Ground Tel No: 01542 882629
Sec Bus/Fax: 01542 882629
Sec Home: 01542 887492
Sec Mobile: 07766 705862
Website: www.keith-fc.co.uk
E-Mail: keithfootballclub@hotmail.com
Year of Formation: 1919
Capacity: Total: 4,500, 450 Seated, 4,050 Standing
Pitch Dimensions: 110 yds x 75 yds
Playing Kits: **1st Choice**
Shirt: Maroon/Sky Blue Facings
Shorts: Maroon/Sky Blue
Stockings: Maroon
2nd Choice
Shirt: White with Dark Blue Trim
Shorts: Dark Blue
Stockings: White

LOSSIEMOUTH F.C.

Secretary: Alan McIntosh
Manager: Graham Tatters
Club Address: Grant Park, Kellas Avenue, Lossiemouth, IV31 6JG.
Ground Tel No: 01343 813717
Sec Home: 01343 813328
Sec Bus/Mobile: 07890 749053
Fax No: 01343 815440
E-Mail: alanlfcsec@aol.com
Year of Formation: 1945
Capacity: Total: 3,500, 250 Seated, 3,250 Standing
Pitch Dimensions: 110 yds x 60 yds
Playing Kits: **1st Choice**
Shirt: Red
Shorts: Red
Stockings: Red
2nd Choice
Shirt: Yellow with Blue Trim
Shorts: Blue with Yellow Trim
Stockings: Blue with Yellow Trim

NAIRN COUNTY F.C.

Secretary: John McNeill
Manager: Ronald Sharp
Club Address: Station Park, Balblair Road, Nairn, IV12 5LT.
Ground Tel No: 01667 454298
Sec Bus: 01463 792424
Sec Home/Fax: 01667 462510
E-Mail: jhnmcneill@aol.com
Year of Formation: 1914
Capacity: Total: 3,800, 250 Seated, 3,550 Standing
Pitch Dimensions: 110 yds x 62 yds
Playing Kits: **1st Choice**
Shirt: Yellow with Navy Blue Trim
Shorts: Navy Blue
Stockings: Navy Blue
2nd Choice
Shirt: Red with White Trim
Shorts: White
Stockings: White

ROTHES F.C.

Secretary: Neil McKenzie
Manager: Graham McBeath
Club Address: Mackessack Park, Station Street, Rothes, Aberlour
Ground Tel No: 01340 831972
Sec Mobile: 07802 773695
Sec Home: 01340 831344
E-Mail: neil.r.mckenzie@btinternet.com
Year of Formation: 1938
Capacity: Total: 2,650, 160 Seated, 2,490 Standing
Pitch Dimensions: 108 yds x 74 yds
Playing Kits: **1st Choice**
Shirt: Tangerine with Black Trim
Shorts: Black
Stockings: Tangerine with Three Black Hoops
2nd Choice
Shirt: Black with Tangerine Trim
Shorts: Tangerine
Stockings: Black with Three Tangerine Hoops

WICK ACADEMY F.C.

Secretary: Andrew Carter
Manager: Alistair Budge
Club Address: Harmsworth Park, South Road, Wick, KW1 5NH.
Ground Tel/Fax No: 01955 602446
Sec Bus: 01847 802277
Sec Home: 01955 604275
Sec Mobile: 07776 175132
Website: www.wickacademy-fc.co.uk
E-Mail: andyscotland1024@aol.com
Year of Formation: 1893
Capacity: Total: 2,000, 433 Seated, 1,567 Standing
Pitch Dimensions: 106 yds x 76 yds
Playing Kits: **1st Choice**
Shirt: Black and White Stripes
Shorts: Black
Stockings: Black with White Tops
2nd Choice
Shirt: White with Red/Maroon Trim
Shorts: Red
Stockings: Maroon with White Tops

THE SCOT-ADS HIGHLAND LEAGUE FINAL TABLE – SEASON 2002/03

	P	W	D	L	F	A	Pts
Deveronvale	28	21	6	1	90	24	69
Keith	28	17	1	10	66	35	52
Buckie Thistle	28	15	6	7	63	36	51
Cove Rangers	28	14	7	7	70	46	49
Nairn County	28	13	7	8	67	47	46
Fraserburgh	28	14	4	10	61	45	46
Clachnacuddin	28	13	4	11	46	50	43
Huntly	28	12	5	11	53	42	41
Inverurie Locos	28	11	7	10	50	50	40
Lossiemouth	28	12	4	12	41	53	40
Forres Mechanics	28	12	2	14	59	62	38
Rothes	28	8	5	15	26	50	29
Wick Academy	28	8	2	18	33	68	26
Brora Rangers	28	3	6	19	30	77	15
Fort William	28	2	4	22	20	90	10

the east of scotland football league directory of clubs

ANNAN ATHLETIC F.C.

Secretary: Alan T. Irving
Manager: Bill Sim
Club Address: Galabank, North Street, Annan, Dumfries & Galloway.
Ground Tel No: 01461 204108
Sec Bus: 01461 207218
Sec Home/ Fax No: 01461 203702
Website: www.annanathletic.2fs.com
E-Mail: ibroxx@aol.com
Year of Formation: 1942
Capacity: Total: 2,000 (All Standing)
Pitch Dimensions: 110 yds x 65 yds
Playing Kits:
1st Choice:
Shirt: Black and Gold Vertical Stripes
Shorts: Black
Stockings: Black with Gold Hoops
2nd Choice:
Shirt: Blue
Shorts: Blue
Stockings: Blue with White Hoops

CIVIL SERVICE STROLLERS F.C.

Secretary: Edward S. Turnbull
Manager: Alex Fyvie
Club Address: Civil Service Sports Ground, Marine Drive, Edinburgh.
Ground Tel No: 0131 332 1175 (Matchdays Only)
Sec Bus: 0131 314 4220
Sec Home: 0131 539 0171
Sec Mobile: 07765 220117
Fax No: 0131 314 4344
Website: www.strollers.org.uk
E-Mail: eddie.turnbull@gro-scotland.gov.uk
Year of Formation: 1908
Capacity: Total: 500 (All Standing)
Pitch Dimensions: 110 yds x 75 yds
Playing Kits:
1st Choice:
Shirt: White
Shorts: Black/Blue
Stockings: Red
2nd Choice:
Shirt: Red
Shorts: Black/Blue
Stockings: Red

COLDSTREAM F.C.

Secretary: Mrs. Morag Evans
Manager: Brian Lough
Club Address: Home Park, Coldstream, Berwickshire.
Ground Tel/Fax No: 01890 883085
Sec Home: 01890 883352
E-Mail: coldstreamfc@icscotland.net
Year of Formation: 1895
Capacity: Total: 1,500 (All Standing)
Pitch Dimensions: 100 yds x 60 yds
Playing Kits:
1st Choice:
Shirt: Royal Blue with Black Trim
Shorts: Black
Stockings: Royal Blue
2nd Choice:
Shirt: Red
Shorts: Red
Stockings: Red

CRAIGROYSTON F.C.

Secretary: Jim Sivewright
Manager: Alan Whyte
Club Address: St. Mark's Park, Warriston, Edinburgh.
Sec Bus: 0131 346 5753
Sec Home: 0131 228 1803
Year of Formation: 1976
Capacity: Total: 1,000, All Standing
Pitch Dimensions: 106 yds x 76 yds
Playing Kits:
1st Choice:
Shirt: Yellow
Shorts: Blue
Stockings: Yellow
2nd Choice:
Shirt: Royal Blue
Shorts: White
Stockings: Royal Blue

DALBEATTIE STAR F.C.

Secretary: Robert Geddes
Manager: Brian Aitchison
Club Address: Islecroft Stadium, Dalbeattie.
Ground Tel No: 01556 611151
Sec Bus/Home: 01556 610563
Sec Mobile: 07860 549444
Fax No: 01556 611747
E-Mail: bob@solwaypressservices.freeserve.co.uk
Year of Formation: 1905 (approx)
Capacity: Total: 4,000 (All Standing)
Pitch Dimensions: 110 yds x 70 yds
Playing Kits:
1st Choice:
Shirt: Red and Black Stripes
Shorts: Black
Stockings: Red
2nd Choice:
Shirt: Sky Blue and Maroon
Shorts: Maroon
Stockings: Maroon

EASTHOUSES LILY F.C.

Secretary: Robert Paul
Manager: David McQueenie
Club Address: Mayfield Park, Newbattle, Easthouses.
Sec Home: 0131 663 9768
Year of Formation: 1969
Capacity: Total: 1,000 (All Standing)
Pitch Dimensions: 110 yds x 67 yds
Playing Kits:
1st Choice:
Shirt: Red
Shorts: Black
Stockings: Red
2nd Choice:
Shirt: Blue/Black
Shorts: Blue
Stockings: Blue/Black

EDINBURGH ATHLETIC F.C.

Secretary: Stewart Thomas
Manager: Eugene Taylor
Club Address: Civil Service Sports Ground, Marine Drive, Edinburgh.
Ground Tel No: 0131 332 1175
Sec Home: 0131 339 1769
Website: www.edinburghathletic.com
Year of Formation: 1968
Capacity: Total: 500 (All Standing)
Pitch Dimensions: 100 yds x 60 yds
Playing Kits:
1st Choice:
Shirt: Navy Blue
Shorts: Navy Blue
Stockings: Navy Blue
2nd Choice:
Shirt: Green
Shorts: Black
Stockings: Black

EDINBURGH CITY F.C.

Secretary: Grant Coffin
Manager: Tom Steven
Club Address: Meadowbank Stadium, London Road, Edinburgh, EH7 6AE.
Ground Tel No: 0131 661 5351
Sec Bus: 07740 443944
Sec Home: 0131 332 5506
Website: www.edinburghcityfc.com
E-Mail: webmaster@edinburghcityfc.com
Year of Formation: 1928
Capacity: Total: 13,841 (All Seated)
Pitch Dimensions: 105 yds x 72 yds
Playing Kits:
1st Choice:
Shirt: White
Shorts: Black
Stockings: Black
2nd Choice:
Shirt: Yellow
Shorts: Black
Stockings: Yellow

EDINBURGH UNIVERSITY ASSOCIATION F.C.

Secretary: Jeremy King
Manager: Douglas Samuel
Club Address: East Peffermill Playing Fields, Peffermill Road, Edinburgh.
Sec Bus: 07769 706076
Fax No: 0131 650 2371
Website: www.eusu.ed.ac.uk/clubs/euafc
E-Mail: euafc@ed.ac.uk
Year of Formation: 1878
Capacity: Total: 1,012; 12 Seated, 1,000 Standing
Pitch Dimensions: 115 yds x 66 yds
Playing Kits: **1st Choice:**
Shirt: Green/Navy Blue Sleeves
Shorts: Navy Blue
Stockings: Navy Blue
2nd Choice:
Shirt: White with Claret Sleeves
Shorts: Claret
Stockings: Claret
3rd Choice:
Shirt: Black/White
Shorts: Black
Stockings: Black

EYEMOUTH UNITED F.C.

Secretary: Ian Thomson
Manager: Alec Flockhart
Club Address: Warner Park, Johns Road, Eyemouth
Sec Home: 01890 751301
Year of Formation: 1949
Capacity: Total: 1,000 (All Standing)
Pitch Dimensions: 102 yds x 65 yds
Playing Kits: **1st Choice:**
Shirt: Maroon
Shorts: Maroon
Stockings: Maroon
2nd Choice:
Shirt: White
Shorts: Sky Blue
Stockings: Sky Blue

GALA FAIRYDEAN F.C.

Secretary: John Clayton
Manager: John Clark
Club Address: Netherdale, Galashiels.
Ground Tel No: 01896 753554
Sec Home/Bus: 01896 753797
Sec Mobile: 07768 616397
Fax: 01896 754412
Website: www.galafairydean.com
E-Mail: john.clayton@sepa.org.uk
Year of Formation: 1907
Capacity: Total: 5,500, 495 Seated, 5,005 Standing
Pitch Dimensions: 110 yds x 72 yds
Playing Kits: **1st Choice:**
Shirt: White/Black band down Arms & Sides
Shorts: Black
Stockings: Black with White Top
2nd Choice:
Shirt: Sky Blue/Navy Blue band down Arms & Sides
Shorts: Navy Blue
Stockings: Sky Blue/Navy Blue Stripe

HAWICK ROYAL ALBERT F.C.

Secretary: Douglas J. Purves
Manager: Graham Halfpenny
Club Address: Albert Park, Mansfield Road, Hawick.
Ground Tel No: 01450 374231
Sec Bus: 0131 537 9241
Sec Home: 01450 371261
E-Mail: prvsjason@aol.com
Year of Formation: 1947
Capacity: Total: 2,000, 500 Seated, 1,500 Standing
Pitch Dimensions: 100 yds x 68 yds
Playing Kits: **1st Choice:**
Shirt: Royal Blue with White and Red Stripe
Shorts: Royal Blue
Stockings: Royal Blue
2nd Choice:
Shirt: Red and Black
Shorts: Black
Stockings: Black and Red Stripe

HERIOT-WATT UNIVERSITY F.C.

Secretary: Jamie Lynch
Manager: Jim Glover
Club Address: Heriot-Watt University Riccarton Campus, Riccarton, Edinburgh.
Ground Tel No: 0131 451 3000
Sec Home: 07940 255857
Website: www.hwufc.org.uk
E-Mail: alimath01@yahoo.co.uk
Year of Formation: 1945
Capacity: Total: 1,000 (All Standing)
Pitch Dimensions: 115 yds x 75 yds
Playing Kits: **1st Choice:**
Shirt: Yellow, Blue trim
Shorts: Blue
Stockings: Yellow
2nd Choice:
Shirt: Blue
Shorts: Blue
Stockings: Blue

KELSO UNITED F.C.

Secretary: Andrew Torrance
Manager: Peter McNulty
Club Address: Woodside Park, Kelso.
Ground Tel No: 01573 223780
Sec Home: 01573 420432
Year of Formation: 1924
Capacity: Total: 1,000 (All Standing)
Pitch Dimensions: 107 yds x 67 yds
Playing Kits: **1st Choice:**
Shirt: Black and White Stripes
Shorts: Black
Stockings: Black & White
2nd Choice:
Shirt: Red
Shorts: Navy Blue
Stockings: Red

LOTHIAN THISTLE F.C.

Secretary: Tom Allison
Manager: George Bowmaker
Club Address: Saughton Enclosure, Edinburgh.
Ground Tel No: 0131 444 0422 (Matchdays Only)
Sec Bus: 0131 333 1976
Sec Home: 0131 336 1751
Website: www.lothianthistlefc.co.uk
E-Mail: secretary@lothianthistlefc.co.uk
Year of Formation: 1969
Capacity: Total: 1,000 (All Standing)
Pitch Dimensions: 108 yds x 74 yds
Playing Kits: **1st Choice:**
Shirt: White/Black Trim
Shorts: White/Black Trim
Stockings: White/Black Trim
2nd Choice:
Shirt: Maroon/Sky Sleeve
Shorts: White/Maroon
Stockings: White

ORMISTON F.C.

Secretary: John M. Greenhorn
Manager: Murray Cheyne
Club Address: Recreation Park, Ormiston.
Sec Bus: 0131 453 4411
Sec Home: 0131 538 0289
Sec Mobile: 07740 680904
E-Mail: john.greenhorn@tesco.net
Year of Formation: 1884
Capacity: Total: 1,000 (All Standing)
Pitch Dimensions: 108 yds x 68 yds
Playing Kits: **1st Choice:**
Shirt: Maroon
Shorts: Maroon
Stockings: Maroon
2nd Choice:
Shirt: White/Sky Blue Trim
Shorts: Sky Blue
Stockings: White

PEEBLES ROVERS F.C.

Secretary: Gareth Smith
Manager: David Rodger
Club Address: Whitestone Park, Peebles.
Sec Home: 01721 723532
Website: www.memberstripod.com/peeblesrovers
E-Mail: vandgsmith@hotmail.com
Year of Formation: 1893
Capacity: Total: 1,000, 200 Seated, 800 Standing
Pitch Dimensions: 110 yds x 75 yds
Playing Kits: **1st Choice:**
Shirt: Red/White
Shorts: Red
Stockings: Red
2nd Choice:
Shirt: Yellow/Black Stripe
Shorts: Black
Stockings: Yellow/Black Hoops

PRESTON ATHLETIC F.C.

Secretary: Dr Andrew Waddell
Manager: Stephen Myatt
Club Address: Pennypitt Park, Rope Walk, Prestonpans, East Lothian.
Ground Tel No: 01875 815221
Sec Bus: 0131 664 7838
Sec Home: 0131 664 3135
Sec Mobile: 07720 894947
Website: www.prestonathletic.com
E-Mail: preston.athletic@virgin.net
Year of Formation: 1945
Capacity: Total: 4,000, 313 Seated, 3,687 Standing
Pitch Dimensions: 110 yds x 70 yds
Playing Kits:
1st Choice:
Shirt: Blue
Shorts: White
Stockings: Blue
2nd Choice:
Shirt: Red/Black facings
Shorts: Black
Stockings; White/Black tops

SELKIRK F.C.

Secretary: Miss Lesley Hamilton
Manager: Fraser Lothian
Club Address: Yarrow Park, Selkirk.
Sec Bus: 01750 23912
Sec Home: 01750 725392
Sec Mobile: 07796 307990
Fax: 01750 23912
Year of Formation: 1880
Capacity: Total: 1,000 (All Standing)
Pitch Dimensions: 108 yds x 70 yds
Playing Kits:
1st Choice:
Shirt: Blue and White Stripe
Shorts: Blue
Stockings: Blue
2nd Choice:
Shirt: White
Shorts: Blue
Stockings: Red

SPARTANS F.C.

Secretary: James Murray
Co-Managers: Sam Lynch & Mike Lawson
Club Address: City Park, Ferry Road, Edinburgh.
Sec Bus/Fax: 0131 667 9923
Sec Home: 0131 668 2188
Sec Mobile: 07710 723563
Website: www.spartansfc.com
E-Mail: Jim.Murray@ICScotland.net
Year of Formation: 1951
Capacity: Total: 3,000 (All Standing)
Pitch Dimensions: 110 yds x 65 yds
Playing Kits:
1st Choice:
Shirt: White
Shorts: Red
Stockings: White
2nd Choice:
Shirt: Blue
Shorts: Blue
Stockings: Blue

THREAVE ROVERS F.C.

Secretary: Ian Bendall
Manager: Paul McGinley
Club Address: Meadow Park, Castle Douglas, Dumfries & Galloway.
Ground Tel No: 01556 504536
Sec Home Tel/Fax: 01556 650310
Sec Bus: 01556 503713
Website: www.threaveroversfc.co.uk
E-Mail: ianbendall@msn.com
Year of Formation: 1953
Capacity: Total: 5,000 (All Standing)
Pitch Dimensions: 110 yds x 74 yds
Playing Kits:
1st Choice:
Shirt: Black and White
Shorts: Black
Stockings: Black
2nd Choice:
Shirt: Red
Shorts: Red
Stockings: Red

TOLLCROSS UNITED F.C.

Secretary: Alistair Wilkie
Manager: Ronnie Dignan
Club Address: Fernieside Recreation Park, Fernieside Avenue, Edinburgh.
Sec Bus: 0131 467 5555
Sec Home: 0131 622 1148
Year of Formation: 1971
Capacity: Total: 1,000 (All Standing)
Pitch Dimensions: 115 yds x 72 yds
Playing Kits:
1st Choice:
Shirt: Red with White Sleeves
Shorts: White
Stockings: White
2nd Choice:
Shirt: White
Shorts: Black
Stockings: White

VALE OF LEITHEN F.C.

Secretary: Alex Currie
Co Managers: Jackie Diamond & Stuart Robertson
Club Address: Victoria Park, Innerleithen.
Sec Home: 01896 830708
Sec Mobile: 07952 809694
E-Mail: vale@leithen.freeserve.co.uk
Year of Formation: 1891
Capacity: Total: 1,500 (All Standing)
Pitch Dimensions: 100 yds x 75 yds
Playing Kits:
1st Choice:
Shirt: White with Navy Blue Band
Shorts: Navy Blue
Stockings: Navy Blue
2nd Choice:
Shirt: Red
Shorts: Red
Stockings: Red

WHITEHILL WELFARE F.C.

Secretary: Peter McGauley
Manager: David Smith
Club Address: Ferguson Park, Carnethie Street, Rosewell, Midlothian.
Ground Tel No: 0131 440 0115
Sec Home: 0131 440 3417
Website: www.whitehillwelfare.com
Year of Formation: 1953
Capacity: Total: 4,000 (All Standing)
Pitch Dimensions: 110 yds x 66 yds
Playing Kits:
1st Choice:
Shirt: Claret Body with Sky Blue Sleeves
Shorts: White
Stockings: White
2nd Choice:
Shirt: Sky Blue
Shorts: Claret
Stockings: Sky Blue

EAST OF SCOTLAND LEAGUE

FINAL TABLES – SEASON 2002/03

PREMIER DIVISION

	P	W	D	L	F	A	Pts
Whitehill Welfare	22	14	6	2	55	18	48
Annan Athletic	22	14	2	6	59	32	44
Spartans	22	13	4	5	71	38	43
Gala Fairydean	22	12	5	5	55	42	41
Threave Rovers	22	11	4	7	51	37	37
Craigroyston	22	10	3	9	47	49	33
Lothian Thistle	22	8	5	9	32	42	29
Edinburgh City	22	8	4	10	36	40	28
Preston Athletic	22	8	3	11	37	46	27
Vale of Leithen	22	5	4	13	39	57	19
Coldstream	22	5	4	13	36	65	19
Peebles Rovers	22	1	2	19	23	75	5

FIRST DIVISION

	P	W	D	L	F	A	Pts
Edinburgh University	22	17	0	5	56	27	51
Civil Service Strollers	22	13	3	6	52	26	42
Dalbeattie Star	22	11	7	4	53	32	40
Kelso United	22	11	5	6	48	33	38
Edinburgh Athletic	22	10	7	5	37	23	37
Heriot-Watt University	22	10	5	7	46	42	35
Ormiston	22	7	5	10	27	33	26
Selkirk	22	7	5	10	44	52	26
Hawick Royal Albert	22	6	7	9	36	40	25
Easthouses Lily	22	5	7	10	32	44	22
Tollcross United	22	4	5	13	28	46	17
Eyemouth United	22	1	4	17	22	83	7

the south of scotland football league directory of clubs

ABBEY VALE F.C.

Secretary: David Morton
Manager: James Neil
Club Address: Maryfield Park, New Abbey
Fax No: 01387 256004
Sec Bus: 07762 230648
Sec Home: 01387 256004
Year of Formation: 1974
Playing Kits: **1st Choice**
Shirt: Black and Gold
Shorts: Black
Stockings: Yellow
2nd Choice
Shirt: Red
Shorts: Black
Stockings: Black

ANNAN ATHLETIC F.C.

Secretary: Alan T. Irving
Manager: Bill Sim
Club Address: Galabank, North Street, Annan, Dumfries & Galloway.
Ground Tel No: 01461 204108
Sec Bus: 01461 207218
Sec Home/Fax: 01461 203702
Website: www.annanathletic.2fs.com
E-Mail: ibroxx@aol.com
Year of Formation: 1942
Capacity: 2,000 (All Standing)
Pitch Dimensions: 110 yds x 65 yds
Playing Kits: **1st Choice**
Shirt: Black and Gold Vertical Stripes
Shorts: Black
Stockings: Black with Gold Hoops
2nd Choice
Shirt: Blue
Shorts: Blue
Stockings: Blue with White Hoops

CREETOWN F.C.

Secretary: Andrew Ward
Manager: James McCrossan
Club Address: Castlecary Park, Creetown.
Sec Home: 01671 820251
Year of Formation: 1894
Pitch Dimensions: 110 yds x 66 yds
Playing Kits: **1st Choice**
Shirt: Yellow & Black
Shorts: Yellow & Black
Stockings: Yellow & Black Hoops
2nd Choice
Shirt: Burgundy & White
Shorts: Burgundy
Stockings: Burgundy

CRICHTON F.C.

Secretary: Kenny Cameron
Assistant Secretary: Jane Brown
Manager: Phil Johnstone
Club Address: Crichton Park, Dumfries
Sec Home: 01387 265930
Sec Bus: 01387 258462
Asst. Sec Home: 01387 255658
E-Mail: kenny-ac.cameron@gbr.dupont.com
Year of Formation: 1970 (As Blackwood Dynamos)
Capacity: Total: 2,500 (Standing)
Pitch Dimensions: 106 yds x 67 yds
Playing Kits: **1st Choice**
Shirt: Blue & White
Shorts: Blue
Stockings: Blue
2nd Choice
Shirt: Red & White
Shorts: Black
Stockings: Red

DALBEATTIE STAR F.C.

Secretary: Robert Geddes
Manager: Brian Aitchison
Club Address: Islecroft Stadium, Dalbeattie.
Ground Tel: 01556 611151
Sec Bus/Home: 01556 610563
Sec Mobile: 07860 549444
Fax No: 01556 611747
E-Mail: bob@solwaypressservices.freeserve.co.uk
Year of Formation: 1905 (approx)
Capacity: Total: 4,000 (All Standing)
Pitch Dimensions: 110 yds x 70 yds
Playing Kits: **1st Choice**
Shirt: Red and Black Stripes
Shorts: Black
Stockings: Red
2nd Choice
Shirt: Sky Blue and Maroon
Shorts: Maroon
Stockings: Maroon

DUMFRIES F.C.

Secretary: Tommy Parker
Manager: Colin Lennox
Club Address: Norfolk Park, Dumfries.
Sec Home: 01387 263285
Sec Bus: 07710 679794
Website: www.dumfriesfc.co.uk
E-Mail: tparker3659@aol.com
Year of Formation: 2000
Capacity: Total: 500 (Standing)
Pitch Dimensions: 105 yds x 63 yds
Playing Kits: **1st Choice**
Shirt: Yellow & Navy Blue
Shorts: Navy Blue
Stockings: Navy Blue
2nd Choice
Shirt: Navy Blue &Yellow
Shorts: Navy Blue
Stockings: Navy Blue

GIRVAN F.C.

Secretary: Ronnie Hutcheson
Manager: Stewart Maxwell
Club Address: Hamilton Park, Girvan.
Sec Bus: 01465 713581
Sec Home: 01465 714780
Sec Mobile: 07761 867717
E-Mail: ronnie.hutcheson@virgin.net
Year of Formation: 1947
Capacity: Total: 700 (Approx), 200 Seated, 500 Standing
Pitch Dimensions: 104.5 yds x 70 yds
Playing Kits: **1st Choice**
Shirt: Azure Blue with Black Vertical Stripes
Shorts: Black with White Trim
Stockings: Black with White Trim
2nd Choice
Shirt: Purple Body and Black Sleeves
Shorts: Black
Stockings: Purple

MID ANNANDALE F.C.

Secretary: George Trudt
Manager: Sean Ross
Club Address: King Edward Park, Lockerbie
Sec Home: 01576 202757
Sec Mobile: 07710 087783
Year of Formation: 1958
Pitch Dimensions: 116 yds x 66 yds
Playing Kit: **1st Choice:**
Shirt: Yellow with Black Trimming
Shorts: Black with Two White Side Panels
Stockings: Yellow with Two Black Hoops on Tops
2nd Choice:
Shirt: Blue with Yellow Trimming
Shorts: Blue with Yellow Side Panels
Stockings: Blue

NEWTON STEWART F.C.

Secretary: John R. McNaught
Manager: Alan Groves
Club Address: Blairmount Park, Newton Stewart
Sec Bus/Home: 01671 403066
E-Mail: mc.holm.hol@talk21.com
Playing Kits: **1st Choice**
Shirt: Black and White Vertical Stripes
Shorts: Black
Stockings: Black
2nd Choice
Shirt: Silver and Grey Vertical Stripes
Shorts: Black
Stockings: Black

NITHSDALE WANDERERS F.C.

Secretary: Sam MacFarlane
Sec Home: 01659 50546
Treasurer: William Watson
Treasurer's Home: 01659 58312
Club Address: Lorimer Park, Sanquhar
Coaches: Sam MacFarlane, Iain Mitchell, George Bain
Playing Kits: **1st Choice**
Shirt: Blue and White
Shorts: Blue
Stockings: Blue
2nd Choice
Shirt: Black and White
Shorts: White
Stockings: White

QUEEN OF THE SOUTH F.C.

Secretary: Richard Shaw M.B.E.
Manager: Gordon Hyslop
Club Address: Palmerston Park, Terregles Street, Dumfries, DG2 9BA
Ground Tel/Fax No: 01387 254853
Website: www.qosfc.co.uk
E-Mail: mail@qosfc.co.uk
Year of Formation: 1919
Capacity: Total: 6,412, 3,509 Seated, 2,903 Standing
Pitch Dimensions: 112 yds x 73 yds
Playing Kits: **1st Choice**
Shirt: Royal Blue with White Sleeves and White V Neck Collar
Shorts: White
Stockings: Royal Blue
2nd Choice
Shirt: Canary Yellow with Royal Blue Sleeves and Royal Blue V Neck Collar
Shorts: Royal Blue
Stockings: Canary Yellow

ST. CUTHBERT WANDERERS F.C.

Secretary: Brian Mellon
Manager: Jim Thompson
Club Address: St. Mary's Park, Kirkcudbright.
Sec Bus/Home/Fax: 01557 500233
Sec Mobile: 07703 875812
Year of Formation: 1879
Pitch Dimensions: 100 yds x 56 yds
Playing Kits: **1st Choice**
Shirt: Blue with White Hoops
Shorts: Blue
Stockings: White
2nd Choice
Shirt: Red and Black Hoops
Shorts: Black
Stockings: Black with Red Hoops

STRANRAER F.C.

Secretary: R.A. Graham Rodgers
Manager: Barney Duffy
Club Address: Stair Park, London Road, Stranraer, DG9 8BS
Ground Tel: 01776 703271
Sec Home/Fax: 01776 702194
E-Mail: grodgers_sfc@yahoo.co.uk
Year of Formation: 1870
Capacity: Total: 5,600, 1,830 Seated, 3,770 Standing
Pitch Dimensions: 110 yds x 70 yds
Playing Kit: **1st Choice**
Shirt: Royal Blue. White Collar with Royal Blue Stripe and Insert, White Cuffs with Royal Blue Stripe
Shorts: White with Royal Blue Side Panel
Stockings: Royal Blue with White Tops
2nd Choice
Shirt: Fluorescent Orange. Black Collar with White Stripe and Orange Insert
Shorts: Black with Fluorescent Orange Side Panel Trimmed with White Piping
Stockings: Fluorescent Orange

STRANRAER ATHLETIC F.C.

Secretary: Ian McWhirter
Manager: Sandy Sutherland
Club Address: Stranraer Academy, Stranraer
Sec Home: 01776 702783
Playing Kit: Shirt: Blue and White
Shorts: Blue and White
Stockings: Blue and White

THREAVE ROVERS F.C.

Secretary: Ian Bendall
Manager: Paul McGinley
Club Address: Meadow Park, Castle Douglas, Dumfries & Galloway.
Ground Tel No: 01556 504536
Sec Home Tel/Fax: 01556 650310
Sec Bus: 01556 503713
Website: www.threaveroversfc.co.uk
E-Mail: ianbendall@msn.com
Year of Formation: 1953
Capacity: Total: 5,000 (All Standing)
Pitch Dimensions: 110 yds x 74 yds
Playing Kits: **1st Choice**
Shirt: Black and White
Shorts: Black
Stockings: Black
2nd Choice
Shirt: Red
Shorts: Red
Stockings: Red

WIGTOWN AND BLADNOCH F.C.

Secretary: Arlene Broll
Manager: Robert Boyd
Club Address: Trammondford Park, Wigtown.
Ground Tel/Fax: 01988 402322
Sec Home: 01988 700677
Sec. Mobile: 07766 658999
Year of Formation: 1880
Capacity: Total: 1,500 (All Standing)
Pitch Dimensions: 110 yds x 74 yds
Playing Kits: **1st Choice**
Shirt: Red with White Trim
Shorts: Red/Pinstripe White
Stockings: Red/Pinstripe White
2nd Choice
Shirt: Blue and Yellow Trim
Shorts: Blue and Yellow Trim
Stockings: Blue and Yellow Trim

SOUTH OF SCOTLAND LEAGUE FINAL TABLE – SEASON 2002/03

	P	W	D	L	F	A	Pts
Stranraer Athletic	28	22	2	4	93	43	68
Tarff Rovers	28	18	3	7	68	43	57
Gretna	28	16	5	7	85	50	53
Girvan	28	15	6	7	81	43	51
St. Cuthbert Wanderers	28	14	8	6	66	48	50
Abbey Vale	28	15	3	10	76	57	48
Crichton	28	13	4	11	63	70	43
Dumfries	28	12	6	10	82	67	42
Nithsdale Wanderers	28	11	4	13	74	87	37
Wigtown & Bladnoch	28	9	5	14	56	66	32
Creetown	28	7	7	14	59	67	28
*Threave Rovers	28	10	1	17	48	74	28
Annan Athletic	28	8	2	18	54	79	26
*Dalbeattie Star	28	5	4	19	31	76	13
*Newton Stewart	28	4	2	22	35	101	8

* Threave Rovers had 3 Points Deducted
* Dalbeattie Star had 6 Points Deducted
* Newton Stewart had 6 Points Deducted